W9-ASW-865

THE OXFORD HANDBOOK OF

# HUMAN
# RESOURCE
# MANAGEMENT

# THE OXFORD HANDBOOK OF

# HUMAN

# RESOURCE

# MANAGEMENT

*Edited by*
PETER BOXALL,
JOHN PURCELL,
*and*
PATRICK WRIGHT

OXFORD
UNIVERSITY PRESS

# OXFORD

UNIVERSITY PRESS

Great Clarendon Street, Oxford OX2 6DP

Oxford University Press is a department of the University of Oxford.
It furthers the University's objective of excellence in research, scholarship,
and education by publishing worldwide in

Oxford  New York

Auckland  Cape Town  Dar es Salaam  Hong Kong  Karachi
Kuala Lumpur  Madrid  Melbourne  Mexico City  Nairobi
New Delhi  Shanghai  Taipei  Toronto

With offices in

Argentina  Austria  Brazil  Chile  Czech Republic  France  Greece
Guatemala  Hungary  Italy  Japan  Poland  Portugal  Singapore
South Korea  Switzerland  Thailand  Turkey  Ukraine  Vietnam

Oxford is a registered trade mark of Oxford University Press
in the UK and in certain other countries

Published in the United States
by Oxford University Press Inc., New York

© Oxford University Press 2007

The moral rights of the authors have been asserted
Database right Oxford University Press (maker)

First published 2007

All rights reserved. No part of this publication may be reproduced,
stored in a retrieval system, or transmitted, in any form or by any means,
without the prior permission in writing of Oxford University Press,
or as expressly permitted by law, or under terms agreed with the appropriate
reprographics rights organization. Enquiries concerning reproduction
outside the scope of the above should be sent to the Rights Department,
Oxford University Press, at the address above

You must not circulate this book in any other binding or cover
and you must impose the same condition on any acquirer

British Library Cataloguing in Publication Data

Data available

Library of Congress Cataloging in Publication Data

Data available

Typeset by SPI Publisher Services, Pondicherry, India
Printed in Great Britain
on acid-free paper by
Biddles Ltd., King's Lynn, Norfolk

ISBN 978–0–19–928251–7

1 3 5 7 9 10 8 6 4 2

# Contents

## II. CORE PROCESSES AND FUNCTIONS

## III. PATTERNS AND DYNAMICS

## IV.   MEASUREMENT AND OUTCOMES

# List of Figures

# List of Tables

# LIST OF CONTRIBUTORS

**Mathew R. Allen** is a doctoral candidate in human resource management at Cornell University where his research is concerned with the relationship between HR practices and firm performance among small businesses.

**Stephen Bach** is Reader in Employment Relations and Management at King's College, University of London. His research interests include public sector restructuring and public sector unionism and his publications include *Employment Relations and the Health Service: The Management of Reforms* (Routledge).

**Rosemary Batt** is Professor of Women and Work at the New York State School of Industrial and Labor Relations, Cornell University. Her research ranges across high-performance work systems, unions, international and comparative workplace studies, technology, and work and family issues, and her publications include *The New American Workplace: Transforming Work Systems in the U.S.* (ILR Press, Cornell) with Eileen Appelbaum.

**Paul Boselie** is an Assistant Professor in Human Resources Studies in the Faculty of Social and Behavioural Sciences at Tilburg University. His research traverses human resource management, institutionalism, strategic management, and industrial relations.

**Peter Boxall** is Professor in Human Resource Management at the University of Auckland where he has served as Head of the Department of Management and Employment Relations and as an Associate Dean. His research is concerned with the links between HRM and strategic management and with the changing nature of work and employment systems and he is the co-author of *Strategy and Human Resource Management* (Palgrave Macmillan) with John Purcell.

**Bill Cooke** is a Visiting Professor in the School of Labor and Industrial Relations at Michigan State University. His research concerns multinational companies and foreign and global human resource/collective bargaining strategies, the integration of technology and HRM strategies, work team systems, and union–management cooperation, and he is editor of *Multinational Companies and Global Human Resource Strategies* (Greenwood Publishing).

**John Cordery** is Professor of Organizational and Labour Studies in the School of Economics and Commerce at the University of Western Australia where he has served as Head of Department. His research focuses on new technology and work design, team-based work organization and organizational trust.

**Helen De Cieri** is Professor of Human Resource Management and Director of the Australian Centre for Research in Employment and Work (ACREW) at Monash University. Her research is concerned with strategic human resource management, global HRM, and HRM in multinational networks, and she is co-author of *Human Resource Management in Australia* (McGraw-Hill) with Robin Kramar.

**Rick Delbridge** is Professor of Organizational Analysis at Cardiff Business School and Senior Fellow of the Advanced Institute of Management Research. His research areas include work organization, workplace and inter-organizational relations, and the management of innovation, and he is the author of *Life on the Line in Contemporary Manufacturing* (Oxford University Press).

**John E. Delery** is Professor of Management in the Sam Walton College of Business at the University of Arkansas. His research is concerned with the strategic management of human resources, the structure of human resource management systems, personnel selection, and the selection interview.

**Barry Gerhart** is Bruce R. Ellig Distinguished Chair in Pay and Organizational Effectiveness at the School of Business, University of Wisconsin-Madison. His research spans compensation, HR strategy, incentives, and staffing, and his books include *Compensation: Theory, Evidence, and Strategic Implications* (Sage) with Sara Rynes.

**Damian Grimshaw** is Professor in Employment Studies and Director of the European Work and Employment Research Centre (EWERC) at the University of Manchester. His research covers several areas of employment policy and practice and his publications include *The Organisation of Employment: An International Perspective* (Palgrave Macmillan) with Jill Rubery.

**David E. Guest** is Professor of Organizational Psychology and Human Resource Management at King's College, University of London. His research examines the relationship between human resource management, corporate performance, and employee well-being as well as including studies of psychological contracting and the future of the career.

**James P. Guthrie** is the William and Judy Docking Professor of Human Resource Management in the School of Business at the University of Kansas. His current research interests include the impact of HR systems on firm performance and alternative reward systems.

**Bill Harley** is Associate Professor in the Department of Management at the University of Melbourne and Associate Dean (International) in the Faculty of Economics and Commerce. His research interests range across HRM and industrial relations and his publications include *Democracy and Participation at Work* (Palgrave Macmillan), edited with Jeff Hyman and Paul Thompson.

**Bruce E. Kaufman** is Professor of Economics and Senior Associate of the W. T. Beebe Institute of Personnel and Employment Relations at Georgia State University. His research interests span labor markets, industrial relations, and human resource management, and his books include *The Global Evolution of Industrial Relations* (ILO).

**Sven Kepes** is a doctoral candidate in management at the Sam Walton College of Business, University of Arkansas, where he is researching in the areas of strategic HRM, compensation, and employee turnover.

**Ian Kessler** is Reader in Employment Relations at Said Business School, Oxford University, and a Fellow of Templeton College. His research interests include reward strategies, employee communications, and the psychological contract.

**Brian Kim** is a doctoral candidate in psychology at Michigan State University where he is conducting research on selection instruments and processes.

**Nicholas Kinnie** is Reader in Human Resource Management in the School of Management at the University of Bath. His research concerns the links between HRM and organizational performance, the role of people management practices in professional service firms, and HRM in customer response centers, and he is the co-author of *Understanding the People and Performance Link: Unlocking the Black Box* (CIPD) with John Purcell, Sue Hutchinson, Bruce Rayton, and Juani Swart.

**Thomas Kochan** is the George Maverick Bunker Professor of Management at MIT's Sloan School of Management and Co-Director of the MIT Workplace Center and the Institute for Work and Employment Research. His research covers a variety of topics in industrial relations and human resource management and his recent books include *Restoring the American Dream: A Working Families' Agenda for America* (MIT Press).

**Ellen Ernst Kossek** is a Professor of Human Resource Management and Organizational Behavior at Michigan State University's Graduate School of Labor and Industrial Relations. Her interests span human resource management, organizational support of work/life integration, and diversity, and her books include *Work and Life Integration* (Lawrence Erlbaum Associates) with Susan Lambert.

**Gary Latham** is Secretary of State Professor of Organizational Behaviour in the Rotman School of Management at the University of Toronto. His research traverses goal-setting, employee motivation, performance appraisal, training, organizational justice, and organizational citizenship in the workplace.

**David Lepak** is Professor of Human Resource Management in the School of Management and Labor Relations at Rutgers University. He is interested in the strategic management of human capital, in different modes of employment, and in the links between HRM and performance.

**Heather MacDonald** is a doctoral candidate in psychology at the University of Waterloo where she is conducting research on leadership, work motivation, and performance appraisal.

**Mick Marchington** is Professor of Human Resource Management at the University of Manchester where he has also served as Dean of Management Studies. His research traverses worker participation and voice and the changing nature of work, and his most recent book is *Fragmenting Work: Blurring Organizational Boundaries and Disordering Hierarchies* (Oxford University Press), co-edited with Damian Grimshaw, Jill Rubery and Hugh Willmott.

**Lilian M. de Menezes** is a senior lecturer in the Cass Business School, City University, London. Her research focuses on forecasting, human resource management, and measurement in the social sciences.

**Marc Orlitzky** is an Associate Professor in the School of Business at the University of Redlands in California. His research includes studies of corporate social-financial performance, corporate social responsibility and business ethics, and strategic HRM.

**Jaap Paauwe** is Professor in Human Resource Studies in the Faculty of Social and Behavioural Sciences at Tilburg University. His research ranges across HRM and industrial relations and his publications include *HRM and Performance: Achieving Long-Term Viability* (Oxford University Press).

**Sharon K. Parker** is Professor of Occupational Psychology at the Institute of Work Psychology, University of Sheffield, and the Institute's Director. Her research interests include work design, employee learning and development, organizational change, and workplace health, and her publications include *Job and Work Design: Organizing Work to Promote Well-Being and Effectiveness* (Sage) with Toby Wall.

**Shaun Pichler** is a doctoral candidate at the School of Labor and Industrial Relations at Michigan State University with research interests in EEO and the management of diversity.

**John Purcell** is Professor of Human Resource Management at the University of Bath where he is Head of Research in the School of Management and where he leads the Work and Employment Research Centre (WERC). His research interests span the impact of people management on organizational performance, HRM in multi-divisional firms, employee relations' styles, and changing forms of work and employment, and his books include *Strategy and Human Resource Management* (Palgrave Macmillan) with Peter Boxall.

**Jill Rubery** is Professor of Comparative Employment Systems and head of the People, Management, and Organization Division of Manchester Business School and founder and Co-Director of the European Work and Employment Research Centre (EWERC) at the University of Manchester. Her research is concerned with the ways in which work and employment systems vary across organizations and societies and her publications include *The Organisation of Employment: An International Perspective* (Palgrave Macmillan) with Damian Grimshaw.

**Neal Schmitt** is Professor and Chairperson of the Department of Psychology at Michigan State University. He researches in the areas of personnel testing and selection, job placement, and performance appraisal and his books include *Organizational Staffing* (Lawrence Erlbaum & Associates) with Robert Ployhart and Benjamin Schneider.

**Scott A. Snell** is Professor of Human Resource Studies and Director of Executive Education in the School of Industrial and Labor Relations at Cornell University. His research focuses on the development and deployment of intellectual capital as a foundation of an organization's core competencies and he is the author of *Managing Human Resources* (Southwestern Publishing) with G. W. Bohlander.

**Lorne M. Sulsky** is Professor of Management and Organizational Behavior at Wilfred Laurier University. His research traverses performance management, training, and work stress, and he is the co-author with Dr Carlla Smith of *Work Stress* (Wadsworth Publishing).

**Juani Swart** is a Senior Lecturer and Director of MBA programmes in the School of Management at the University of Bath. Her research interests include knowledge management, intellectual capital, and knowledge workers, and she is the co-author of *Understanding the People and Performance Link: Unlocking the Black Box* (CIPD) with John Purcell, Nicholas Kinnie, Sue Hutchinson, and Bruce Rayton.

**Paul Thompson** is Professor and Head of the Department of Human Resource Management at the University of Strathclyde. His research traverses the labor process, organization theory, and workplace misbehavior and conflict, and he is the co-editor of the recent *Oxford Handbook on Work and Organization* (Oxford University Press) with Stephen Ackroyd, Rosemary Batt, and Pamela Tolbert.

**Tony Watson** is Professor of Organizational Behaviour at Nottingham University Business School where he is head of the OB/HRM division. His research is concerned with organizations, managerial work, strategy-making, entrepreneurship, HRM, and industrial sociology, and his books include *Organising and Managing Work* (Prentice Hall).

**Jonathan Winterton** is Professor of Human Resource Development and Director of Research and International at Toulouse Business School. His research interests span management development, vocational education and training, social dialog, industrial relations, and employee turnover. His publications include *Developing Managerial Competence* (Routledge) with Ruth Winterton.

**Stephen Wood** is Professor and Deputy Director of the Institute of Work Psychology at the University of Sheffield. His recent research has concerned high-involvement management, employee voice, idea-capturing schemes, portfolio working, and the social challenges of nanotechnology. He is editor (with Howard Gospel) of *Representing Workers: Trade Union Recognition and Membership in Britain* (Routledge).

**Patrick Wright** is Professor of Human Resource Studies and Director of the Cornell Center for Advanced Human Resource Studies in the School of Industrial and Labor Relations, Cornell University. His research interests span the relationship between HR practices and firm performance, the creation of a strategic HR function, and HR's role in corporate governance, and he is the co-author of *Fundamentals of Human Resource Management* (McGraw Hill) with Raymond Noe, John Hollenbeck, and Barry Gerhart.

# CHAPTER 1

# HUMAN RESOURCE MANAGEMENT
## SCOPE, ANALYSIS, AND SIGNIFICANCE

PETER BOXALL

JOHN PURCELL

PATRICK WRIGHT

HUMAN resource management (HRM), the management of work and people towards desired ends, is a fundamental activity in any organization in which human beings are employed. It is not something whose existence needs to be elaborately justified: HRM is an inevitable consequence of starting and growing an organization. While there are a myriad of variations in the ideologies, styles, and managerial resources engaged, HRM happens in some form or other. It is one thing to question the *relative* performance of particular models of HRM in particular contexts or their contribution to enhanced organizational performance *relative* to other organizational investments, such as new production technologies, advertising campaigns, and property acquisitions. These are important lines of analysis. It is quite another thing, however, to question the necessity of the HRM process itself, as if organizations could somehow survive or grow without making a reasonable attempt at organizing work and managing people (Boxall and Steeneveld 1999). To wish HRM away is to wish away all but the very smallest of firms.

With such an important remit, there need to be regular reviews of the state of formal knowledge in the field of HRM. Edited from the vantage point of the middle of the first decade of the twenty-first century, this Handbook reveals a management discipline which is no longer *arriviste*. Debates that exercised us in the 1980s and 1990s, concerned with the advent of the HRM terminology, with how it might be different from its predecessor, personnel management, or with how it might threaten trade unions and industrial relations, have given way to 'more substantive issues: the impact of HRM on organizational performance and employees' experience of work' (Legge 2005: 221). These earlier debates retain a salient role in our understanding of the subject, but the literature is no longer preoccupied with them.

In the last ten years, the connections between HRM and the study of strategic management have deepened and links with organizational theory/behavior have grown. The literature on HRM outside the Anglo-American world has burst over the levee, reminding us constantly of the different socio-political contexts in which HRM is embedded. A process of maturing has been taking place which we affirm in this Handbook. Looking outwards, the discipline is more aware of different environments, and is the better for it. Looking inwards, it is more concerned with interactions, with cause–effect chains, with how management initiatives enlist employee support, or fail to do so, and is the better for it. There are major challenges for theory and methodology but we wish to cement these trajectories: they mean that HRM is poised to assume a greater role in the theory of organizational effectiveness. In this introductory chapter, we outline what we see as the scope of the subject, identify key characteristics of what we call 'analytical HRM', underline the significance of the discipline, and provide a guide to the chapters that follow.

# 1.1 THE SCOPE OF HRM: THREE MAJOR SUBFIELDS

Judging by the literature, HRM refuses to be any one thing. Not only does the field cover a vast array of styles but there are three major subdomains of knowledge, each bursting its banks.

Micro HRM ('MHRM') covers the subfunctions of HR policy and practice (Mahoney and Deckop 1986). These can be further grouped into two main categories. The largest group of subfunctions is concerned with managing individuals and small groups, including such areas as recruitment, selection, induction, training and development, performance management, and remuneration. These topics each cover a vast array of practices, underpinned by an extensive body of research, much of it informed by personnel or industrial-organizational psychology and, to some extent, by personnel and institutional economics. A smaller group of subfunctions concerned with work organization and employee voice systems (including management–union relations) is less driven by psychological concepts and is more associated with industrial sociology and industrial relations.

The depth of research in the HR subfunctions has grown enormously over the years and some areas, such as Human Resource Development, can legitimately claim to be fields in their own right. Regular reviews testify to this depth while pointing out the way in which MHRM research often remains 'silo based' and, thus, poorly connected to the wider set of HR practices and to broader workplace problems (e.g. Wright and Boswell 2002). On the other hand, each of these subfunctional domains represents recurring organizational processes which carry major costs and simultaneously offer opportunities to improve performance. The conventionally designed first course in HRM in any country is a survey course which attempts to summarize MHRM research across the major subfunctional domains and, in the better-designed programs, relate it to local laws, customs, organizations, and markets. A vast range of textbooks published by the largest international publishers serve this need.

Strategic HRM ('SHRM') is concerned with systemic questions and issues of serious consequence—with how the pieces just described might fit together, with how they might connect to the broader context and to other organizational activities, and with the ends they might serve. SHRM focuses on the overall HR strategies adopted by business units and companies and tries to measure their impacts on performance (e.g. Dyer 1984; Delery and Doty 1996). Much of the 'big push' in the recognition of the field of HRM came from landmark works in the 1980s which sought to take a strategic perspective, arguing that general managers, and not simply HR specialists, should be deeply concerned with HRM and alert to its competitive possibilities (e.g. Beer et al. 1984). The area now has major texts reviewing a research domain in which HRM bridges out to theory and research in strategic management as well as industrial relations and organizational behavior (e.g. Boxall and Purcell 2003; Paauwe 2004). The links with strategic management are well known, particularly through the two fields' mutual interest in the resource-based view of the firm and in processes of strategic decision-making (e.g. Boxall 1996; Wright et al. 2003). The links with industrial relations are also very important, currently shown in the shared interest in the notion of 'high-performance work systems,' while the connections with organizational behavior are evidenced in mutual interest in such notions as psychological contracting and social exchange (e.g. Wright and Boswell 2002; Purcell et al. 2003).

A third major domain is International HRM ('IHRM'). Less engaged with the theoretical bridges that are important in strategic HRM, IHRM concerns itself with HRM in companies operating across national boundaries (e.g. Brewster and Harris

1999; Evans et al. 2002; Dowling and Welch 2004). This connects strongly to issues of importance in the fields of international business, including the internationalization process. International HRM is an amalgam of the micro and the macro with a strong tradition of work on how HR subfunctions, such as selection and remuneration, might be adapted to international assignments. When, however, the field examines the ways in which the overall HR strategies of organizations might grapple with the different socio-political contexts of different countries (as, for example, in several chapters of Harzing and Van Ruysseveldt's (2004) edited collection), it takes on more strategic features.

We have, then, three major subdomains, summarized here under the acronyms MHRM, SHRM, and IHRM. Researchers have pursued questions in all sorts of specialized niches in these three domains, some publishing for decades on one minor aspect of a field (the age-old academic strategy of looking for new angles in a small corner of a perpendicular field). For much of the time, the three subdomains seem to have been developing in parallel. While this has added to the volume of publication, over-specialization brings problems and much can be done to enhance learning about theory and/or methodology from one domain to another (Wright and Boswell 2002). We think there are some important characteristics of an analytical approach to HRM that are critical for the intellectual life of all three domains.

# 1.2 ANALYTICAL HRM: THREE KEY CHARACTERISTICS

We use the notion of 'analytical HRM' to emphasize that the fundamental mission of the academic management discipline of HRM is not to propagate perceptions of 'best practice' in 'excellent companies' but, first of all, to identify and explain what happens in practice. Analytical HRM privileges explanation over prescription. The primary task of analytical HRM is to build theory and gather empirical data in order to account for the way management actually behaves in organizing work and managing people across different jobs, workplaces, companies, industries, and societies.

We are not simply making an academic point here. Education founded on an analytical conception of HRM should help practitioners to understand relevant theory and develop analytical skills which can be applied in their specific situation and that do not leave them flat-footed when they move to a new environment. The weaknesses of a de-contextualized propagation of 'best practices' were classically exposed by Legge (1978) in her critique of the personnel management literature. She pointed out how personnel management textbooks commonly failed to recognize differences in the goals of managers and workers and the way in which favorite prescriptions worked well in some contexts but not in others. This argument has been reinforced by similar critiques in the HRM literature (e.g. Marchington and Grugulis 2000), by major reviews of the relationships between contextual variables and HR practices (e.g. Jackson and Schuler 1995), and by studies of the embeddedness of HRM systems (e.g. Gooderham et al. 1999). The growth of the field of IHRM has strongly emphasized the way in which models of HRM vary across cultures and reflect the impact of different employment laws and societal institutions (e.g. Brewster 1999; Paauwe and Boselie 2003). To quote the technical language of methodology, 'moderators' are important in our understanding of models of HRM: some things work well under some conditions and not under others. The challenge, of course, is very much to move on from a general genuflection to the importance of context to models which incorporate the most vital contingencies (Purcell 1999).

A key implication, however, is that analytical HRM is deeply sceptical about claims of universal applicability for particular HR practices or clusters of practices, such as the lists offered in the works of the US writer Jeffery Pfeffer (e.g. 1994, 1998). This does not rule out the search for general principles in the management of work and people—far from it—but it does caution strongly against prescription at the level of specific HR practices (Becker and Gerhart 1996; Youndt et al. 1996; Boxall and Purcell 2003).

A deep respect for context also implies that we make an attempt to understand the goals of HRM within the wider context of the goals and politics of firms. Like personnel management before it, MHRM has a tendency to begin with surveys or case studies of favourite practices, such as 360-degree appraisal, which never raise the question of what the overarching HRM principles might be or how they might situate within management's general goals for the organization. This stems, to some extent, from the influence of psychology in MHRM, which does not offer a theory of business. One of the benefits of the strategic and international schools of HRM, both more concerned with the economic and social motives of firms, is that they have opened an analysis of strategic HR goals and their relationship to wider organizational goals (e.g. Evans 1986; Wright and Snell 1998; Boxall and Purcell 2003). The key message from this work is that the general motives of HRM are multiple, subject to paradox or 'strategic tension,' and negotiated through political and not simply 'rational' processes. This helps us to guard against two erroneous extremes. One extreme is held by those who think that HRM only exists to serve the profit-oriented 'bottom line,' and who continually seek to justify HR policies in these terms. This misunderstands the plurality of organizational effectiveness. While HRM does need to support commercial outcomes (often called the 'business case'), it also exists to serve organizational needs for social legitimacy (e.g. Lees 1997; Gooderham et al. 1999). The other extreme is held by those who seem to imagine that managers are waiting with bated breath to implement their most recent conception of 'best practice.' This pole seriously underestimates the way businesses are affected by the economics of production in their chosen sector, creating a natural scepticism among managers about claims that some new technique will inevitably improve their business.

Building on the way in which analytical HRM seeks to locate HRM in its wider contexts, a key trend in analysis is the construction of models of *how* HRM might work, models that lay out the cause–effect chains, intervening variables, or 'mediators' involved. There are two drivers of this trend in analysis. One stems from the debate in SHRM concerning the need to show how human resources contribute to business viability and might lay a basis for sustained competitive advantage. To make the resource-based view of the firm truly useful, we need to show how HRM helps create valuable capabilities and helps erect barriers to imitation (Mueller 1996; Boxall and Purcell 2003; Wright et al. 2003). A second key driver stems from the realization that to work well, HR policies must be effectively enacted by line managers and must positively enhance employee attitudes and encourage productive behaviors (e.g. Guest 1999, 2002; Wright and Boswell 2002; Purcell 1999; Purcell et al. 2003). This means that notions such as organizational culture and constructs associated with psychological contracting and social exchange, which have been important in the companion discipline of organizational behavior (OB), are now being integrated into models of the process of HRM. We have embarked on a long-overdue process of investigating the way in which HR policies and practices affect job satisfaction, trust-in-management, attitudinal commitment, discretionary job behavior, behavioral commitment, and beyond.

This extremely important analytical development has quite a job to do. On the one hand, it means that HRM must become better integrated with theory in organizational behavior and with other accounts of how HRM works, such as those in industrial relations (IR) and labor economics. It also means that HRM research must become more sophisticated methodologically. Not only are there are issues around the way HRM researchers measure the presence (or otherwise) of HR practices and systems (Gerhart et al. 2000), but recent reviews of the quality of the evidence for the performance impacts of particular models of HRM find it seriously wanting (Wall and Wood 2005; Wright et al. 2005). These reviews show that a huge proportion of the studies measuring both HR practices of some kind and firm performance have found associations all right—but between the former and *past* performance, thus leaving us poorly placed to assert that causality runs from the selected HR practices to performance. This stems from the preponderance of cross-sectional studies, which actually pick up *historical* financial data while asking about *current* HR practices, and the existence of very few genuinely longitudinal studies.

This brings us to our final point about analytical HRM: it is concerned with assessing outcomes. This is obvious in terms of the way in which SHRM has generated a slew of studies on the HRM–performance link; however, in the light of what we have just said about the mediating role of employee attitudes and behavior, it is not simply about outcomes sought by shareholders or by their imperfect agents, managers. HRM research is taking on board the question of mutuality (e.g. Guest 1999, 2002; Peel and Boxall 2005); it is examining the extent to which employer and worker outcomes are mutually satisfying and, thus, more sustainable in our societies over the long run. It is, therefore, becoming less true to say that HRM is dominated by fascination with management initiatives, as was very much true of the literature of the 1980s. HRM is moving on, as Legge (2005) argues. It is becoming more interactional, a process that will inevitably challenge other disciplines offering a narrative about how employees experience work and which will better equip HRM research to speak to the public policy debate.

In our view, then, analytical HRM has three important characteristics. First, it is concerned with the 'what' and 'why' of HRM, with understanding what management tries to do with work and people in different contexts and with explaining why. Second, it is interested in the 'how' of HRM, in the chain of processes that make models of HRM work well (or poorly), thus building much stronger links to companion disciplines such as strategic management and organizational behavior. Third, it is interested in questions of 'for whom and how well,' with assessing the outcomes of HRM, taking account of both employee and managerial interests, and laying a basis for theories of wider social consequence.

# 1.3 ON THE OFFENSIVE: THE SIGNIFICANCE OF HRM

The emphasis we place on understanding HRM as the management of work and people in organizations (MWP—an acronym we quite like) and the analytical approach we take to this means that the boundaries between HRM, industrial/employment relations, organizational behavior/theory, economics, sociology, psychology, and labor law (and more) are, at the least, porous. As a management discipline, HRM draws insights, models, and theories from cognate disciplines and applies them to real world settings. It is characteristic of such disciplines that they beg, steal, and borrow from more basic disciplines to build up a credible body of theory, and make no apology for it.

The conception of HRM that we advance here is not a narrow subject area. The narrowness of perceiving HRM as solely what HR departments do (where they exist) or of perceiving HRM as only about one style of people management are enemies of the subject's relevance and intellectual vigor. So, too, are the excesses of academic specialization. The differentiation of management theory has gone too far, aided and abetted by the 'chapterization' of management theory that occurs in such organizations as the US Academy of Management, and the shortening of academic vision that can occur through processes such as the UK's research assessment exercise. We live in a time when the perverse aspects of these institutional academic practices need to be challenged and the 'scholarship of integration' (Boyer 1997) needs to be fostered. An integration across the 'people disciplines' taught in business schools—HRM, organizational behavior, and industrial/employment relations—is particularly important, as is a reaching out to operations management, a subject presently preoccupied with technical programming and barely aware of the issues associated with managing work and people that actually fall into the lap of operations managers. The same could be said for marketing. In the service–profit chain (Heskett et al. 1997), where the employee–customer interface is central, understanding the worker dimension is poorly developed. HRM has much to offer here.

Our aim, then, is to foster a more integrated conception of HRM with much better connections to the way production is organized in firms and the way workers experience the whole management process and culture of the organization. We see HRM as the management discipline best placed to assert the importance of work and employment systems in company performance and the role of such systems, embedded as they are in sectoral and societal resources and institutional regimes, to national economic performance and well-being. In taking this view, we oppose the way writers in general or strategic management continue to downplay the importance of work organization and people management (Boxall and Purcell 2003). To be sure, resource-based theory has reawakened the human side of strategy and, on a practical level, support for the importance of HRM has come from Kaplan and Norton's (1996, 2001) 'balanced scorecard,' which starts from the premiss that it is *executed* strategy that counts in firm performance. HRM is central to developing the skills and attitudes which drive good execution. This in itself is enormously important but, more than this, the contribution of HRM is dynamic: it either helps to foster the kind of culture in which clever strategies are conceived and reworked over time or, if handled badly, it hinders the dynamic capability of the firm. In our assessment, more work is needed to reframe general or strategic management so that it assigns appropriate value to work and employment systems and the organizational and sectoral-societal contexts which nurture or neglect them.

## 1.4 THE HANDBOOK OF HUMAN RESOURCE MANAGEMENT: DESIGN AND CONTRIBUTIONS

We designed the Oxford Handbook of Human Resource Management to place emphasis on the analytical approach we have just outlined. In the first part, contributors lay down their theoretical foundations and review major conceptual frameworks. This begins with Bruce Kaufman's review of the history of HRM (Chapter 2), tracing key intellectual and professional developments over the last 100 years. US developments naturally play a central role in the chapter but Kaufman also draws in research on Britain, Germany, France, Japan, and other parts of the world. In Chapter 3, Peter Boxall asks the question: what are employers seeking through engaging in HRM and how do their goals for HRM relate to their broader business goals? The chapter emphasizes the ways in which employers try to adapt effectively to their specific economic and socio-political context, arguing that the critical goals of HRM are plural and inevitably imply the management of strategic tensions.

This then leads to chapters which cover the relationship between HRM and three major academic disciplines: economics, strategic management, and organization theory. Damian Grimshaw and Jill Rubery examine the connections with economics in Chapter 4. Finding the mainstream premises underpinning 'personnel economics' wanting in terms of their understanding of workplace behavior, they examine more fruitful influences stemming from heterodox schools of economics. This leads them to argue that the comparative study of employment institutions is vital in locating firm-oriented analysis in HRM within the 'interlocking web' of national institutions. In Chapter 5, Mathew Allen and Patrick Wright investigate the important links that have developed between HRM and strategic management theory. This includes reviewing the application to HRM of the resource-based view (RBV) of the firm and notions of fitting HRM to context. They highlight key unanswered questions and call for an expanded understanding of the role of strategic HRM. In Chapter 6, Tony Watson explains the need to ground HRM theory in a theory of organization and considers four strands of organization theory of particular relevance: the functionalist/systems and contingency strand, the Weberian strand, the Marxian strand, and the post-structuralist and discursive strand. He shows how these traditions have, to some extent, been applied to analysis in HRM and indicates how they could be more fully applied to enhance our understanding of patterns of HRM in the workplace.

The following two chapters focus on particular theoretical perspectives, drawn from organizational behavior and industrial relations, that assist us to interpret how the processes of HRM affect workers. In Chapter 7, David Guest engages with the OB notion of psychological contracting, which accords a central role to mutuality questions, to how employees perceive and respond to employer promises. Reviewing research on worker well-being, he argues that greater use of high-commitment HR practices, involving greater making and keeping of promises by the employer, enhances the psychological contract and brings benefits to both parties. This positive interpretation is juxtaposed with Chapter 8 in which Paul Thompson and Bill Harley contrast what they perceive as the fundamental premisses of HRM with the premisses of labor process theory (LPT), an area of

IR theory which offers an analysis of the dynamics of employer–employee conflict. Starting from assumptions about a 'structured antagonism' (Edwards 1990) in the capitalist employment relation, LPT generates a different set of conclusions about the extent to which current workplace trends in employee control, work organization, and skill demands have enhanced mutuality. In Chapter 7, the glass of worker well-being is at least half-full, while in Chapter 8 it is clearly half-empty. In juxtaposing these chapters, we invite readers to decide which account they find more compelling. Finally in the first section, Jaap Paauwe and Paul Boselie use institutional theory to explain in Chapter 9 how HRM is embedded, and evolves, in different social contexts, producing, for example, very different patterns in 'Rhineland' countries such as the Netherlands and Germany from those found in the Anglo-American world. They emphasize the need for firms to find a 'strategic balance' between economic and justice/legitimacy objectives and, like Rubery and Grimshaw, emphasize the value of comparative analysis in building an understanding of the forces that shape HRM. Thus, the first part of the book reviews theory which helps us to understand the management of work and employment but does so in a way that pays due respect to different theoretical and ideological premises and to the diverse histories and contexts of HRM.

While the first part of the Handbook reflects much that stems from SHRM and IHRM, the second part of the Handbook acknowledges the ongoing importance of MHRM and seeks to properly acknowledge both the individual and collectively oriented dimensions. The core processes and functions of HRM reviewed here start with Chapter 10 on work organization in which Sharon Parker and John Cordery adopt a systems approach to outline the characteristics and outcomes for firms and workers of three archetypal work configurations: mechanistic, motivational, and concertive work systems. Their analysis emphasizes the ways in which relationships among a range of contingent factors affect the adoption of different work systems and their chances of success. In Chapter 11, David Lepak and Scott Snell consider employment subsystems, recognizing the problems in defining a core workforce and subsequent tensions in managing different types of HRM for different segments, whether internally or through outsourcing/offshoring. They note how HRM used to be about managing jobs but, as the knowledge economy grows, it is increasingly about managing people. Here questions of knowledge-sharing become more important, placing yet further tensions on variegated employment subsystems.

In Chapter 12, Mick Marchington reviews employee voice systems, analyzing direct modes of voice and the extent to which voice practices are embedded. On this basis, he builds a model of the major societal, organizational, and workplace factors that either promote or impede employee voice, enabling us to understand why some voice systems are more prevalent in some contexts than in others. In Chapter 13, Ellen Kossek and Shaun Pichler interrogate EEO and the management of diversity. While they note that these concepts are socially constructed, they argue, drawing on US experience and perspectives, that we should subscribe to some 'best practices' in this field and that the challenge for employers is to move beyond legal compliance to create more inclusive workplaces. In Chapter 14, Marc Orlitzky takes us into one of the less well-developed areas—recruitment strategy. The research we have on how organizations recruit implies that hiring practices vary based on labor market conditions, on what other firms are doing, and on industry factors such as capital intensity. In contrast to the previous chapter, Orlitzky's review reveals very little evidence for 'best practice takeaways' in the research on recruitment strategy and underlines the need for theoretical and methodological development. The much more heavily tilled field of selection decision-making is reviewed by Neal Schmitt and Brian Kim in Chapter 15. Beginning with an outline of the variety and validity of selection methods, they devote the bulk of their chapter to some key developments that are adding complexity, controversy, and challenge to the selection process: for example, they review theory and research on how firms might select individuals who perform in a team-based and more dynamic sense, examine the debate around selection practices and minority representation in organizations, and consider how organizations might predict (and minimize) deviance and counterproductivity.

In Chapter 16, Jonathan Winterton covers the enormous terrain of training, development, and competence. He offers a deeply contextualized account of trends in these areas, showing the extent to which national vocational education and training systems vary, and how something like the notion of competence, developed in the USA, is taken up and applied in different ways in countries like Germany, France, and the UK. James Guthrie reviews remuneration in Chapter 17, covering research on pay levels, pay structure, and pay forms and drawing on both economic and psychological approaches. Rather like Marc Orlitzky, he shows the 'deep-seated disagreement as to what constitutes "best practice" in compensation management.' Gary Latham, Lorne Sulsky, and Heather MacDonald tackle performance management in Chapter 18. They review theory on the meaning of performance, on the efficacy of appraisal instruments, and on the value of appraiser training. While much of this is about 'best practice' questions, they underline the ways in which appraisal practices are affected by the belief systems and cognitive biases of managers and are located in the political context of the firm.

In Part II, then, the authors follow a classical set of dividers in MHRM. Each of the chapters illustrates the enormous depth that can be found in the literature on the subfunctions of HRM. While some authors in this section of the book argue that there are some universally better practices in the subfunction on which they have focused (which tend to be those in which techniques at the individual level have been the subject of a long tradition of psychological studies), the overall tenor of the section underlines the diversity of HR practice in different contexts and our need to understand how it emerges. Rather than focusing on static notions of 'best practice,' most authors point to the need for us to understand the principles underpinning why and how HR practices vary across different occupational, company, industry, and societal contexts.

The engagement with context is taken further in Part III, where we offer a different shuffling of the pack suggested by concerns in SHRM and IHRM. The idea is to look at how the subfunctional processes of HRM might be blended in different ways, examining HRM challenges in different economic sectors and in firms operating across national borders. This begins with Chapter 19, in which Sven Kepes and John Delery analyze the important notion of 'internal fit' or the question of internal integration in HRM. They outline a comprehensive theoretical framework and examine research on synergistic effects—including 'powerful connections' and 'deadly combinations.' While pointing to areas where we need more research, they argue that there is, indeed, evidence for the importance of synergies. Choices in SHRM and the internal fit of MHRM are strongly influenced by the firm's sector and the dominant work processes within it. The next four chapters look at manufacturing, the service sector, knowledge workers, and the public sector. Rick Delbridge (Chapter 20) focuses on the way in which HRM in high-cost manufacturing countries has evolved towards 'lean manufacturing' and 'high-performance work systems,' examining the impacts on worker interests and considering alternatives to the lean model. Much of the early research in HRM was undertaken in manufacturing yet, as Delbridge shows, many controversies remain unresolved. The service sector is now so large and diverse, and such an important part of modern economies, that no one analysis is sufficient. Rosemary Batt examines HRM and the service encounter in Chapter 21, showing how services management calls for careful integration of marketing, operations and human resource functions. She outlines the implications for HRM of different service strategies and, in particular, explores the tensions between operational management, which emphasizes efficiency and cost reduction, and marketing, where satisfying the customer is the dominant consideration. These create conflicting pressures for HRM. Juani Swart focuses on the growing number of workers who trade on their knowledge and work in knowledge-intensive firms. The dilemmas in managing them are explored in Chapter 22. These types of workers, whose work is central to the firm, are likely to have distinctive, and multiple, identities and aspirations, which may not match those desired by their employer. Getting the most effective HRM in place is no easy matter. In Chapter 23, Stephen Bach and Ian Kessler review HRM in the public sector, analyzing the distinctive features of the state as an employer. They consider the way in which the 'new public management' of the 1990s, and subsequent developments that incorporate some learning about its strengths and weaknesses, have challenged the nature of HRM, but also show that institutional patterns of behavior are embedded and hard to change. Together, these four chapters show how sectoral and occupational analysis has tremendous value. They show the limitation of taking the individual firm as the unit of analysis and offer much deeper understanding both of context and of different forms of management relevant to particular market characteristics. Future research could usefully be focused much more on sectors or occupations rather than just the atomized organization.

In the last two chapters in the section, the focus is on large, complex firms operating internationally. In Chapter 24, Bill Cooke develops an analytical framework which helps us understand how multinational firms think about the economics of global HR strategy. He reviews evidence that shows that multinational firms typically invest less in countries with lower average education levels and higher average costs and less in countries in which they perceive IR systems as driving up the unit costs of production, either directly or indirectly through greater restrictions on management prerogative. Helen De Cieri looks at how transnational firms are dealing with the reality of cultural diversity in Chapter 25. Her chapter underlines the fact that there are diverse views about the value and management of cultural diversity and highlights the challenges HR managers face in managing pressures for global integration and local adaptation in transnational firms. Together, these two chapters help us to analyze the ways in which the HR activities of multinational firms affect, and are affected by, different economies and societies around the world.

Part IV is concerned with the outcomes of HRM. In Chapter 26, John Purcell and Nick Kinnie review the research on links between HRM and performance. They examine problems associated with methodology, with how we define performance and HRM, and with the theory linking them. They then develop a model that postulates a number of key mediating elements, including line manager and employee responses, which can be used to guide HRM–performance studies, both qualitative and quantitative. The methodological issues are scrutinized in Chapter 27 by Barry Gerhart, drawing heavily on how statistical procedures have been improved in the much more established fields of Psychology and Economics. This chapter is not for the numerically challenged but is essential reading for anyone skeptical about the claims made in some well-cited studies, and wanting to design more rigorous quantitative studies of the relationship between HRM and performance.

The last two chapters are concerned with mutuality of outcomes. We agreed with these authors that they could adopt approaches which are somewhat different from the general chapter brief adopted for the other chapters in the book. In Chapter 28, Stephen Wood and Lilian de Menezes examine the relationships among family-friendly management, EEO, and high-involvement management. Looking to see if an underlying orientation underpins these three forms of management, they report their analysis of British data on the associations among these forms of management and their relationships with performance. In Chapter 29, Tom Kochan applies the criterion of social legitimacy to the work of HR specialists in the USA, arguing that the quest for senior management approval has gone too far, has ignored the fraying American 'social contract,' and calling for a major re-evaluation of the values and professional identity that inform specialist HR roles. These last two chapters help to reinforce the point that an analytical approach to HRM can be used to guide critique of the patterns that HRM assumes in particular societies and whether these need reform by the state, by firms, and by professional bodies.

In sum, the Handbook is designed to enable readers to form an overview of the major theoretical perspectives that help to illuminate the broad practice of HRM and to read contextually sensitive reviews of the classical subfunctions of MHRM. But it also offers examinations of the more holistic contexts and dynamic questions about patterns and outcomes that are the stuff of SHRM and IHRM. There are, naturally, omissions but we trust the Handbook offers a comprehensive overview of contemporary HRM and provides important guideposts for its future development in theory, research, and curriculum. Most HRM textbooks are parochial, but rarely recognize this single country, and often single topic, limitation. This is not just a limitation of content and relevance but one of 'seeing' and 'conceptualizing.' We three editors, from New Zealand, Britain, and the USA, have become increasingly aware of our own mental maps in working with each other, and in particular working with the authors of the chapters. We have often challenged each other, and them, to think beyond traditional boundaries of the topic even where they are subject specialists of high renown. The authors have nearly always responded with enthusiasm, making significant alterations to second or third drafts. We thank them most warmly for that. We hope this collection of original essays reflects this learning process. It means that the chapters are not potted summaries of all we know about a topic in HRM but challenge what we know, or what we thought we knew, and set signposts for further exploration.

## REFERENCES

BECKER, B., and GERHART, B. (1996). 'The Impact of Human Resource Management on Organizational Performance: Progress and Practice.' *Academy of Management Journal*, 39: 779–801.

BEER, M., SPECTOR, B., LAWRENCE, P., QUINN MILLS, D., and WALTON, R. (1984). *Managing Human Assets*. New York: Free Press.

BOXALL, P. (1996). 'The Strategic HRM Debate and the Resource-Based View of the Firm.' *Human Resource Management Journal*, 6/3: 59–75.

—— and Purcell, J. (2003). *Strategy and Human Resource Management*. New York: Palgrave Macmillan.

—— and Steeneveld, M. (1999). 'Human Resource Strategy and Competitive Advantage: A Longitudinal Study of Engineering Consultancies.' *Journal of Management Studies*, 36/4: 443–63.

BOYER, E. (1997). *Scholarship Reconsidered: Priorities of the Professoriate*. San Francisco: Jossey-Bass.

BREWSTER, C. (1999). 'Different Paradigms in Strategic HRM: Questions Raised by Comparative Research.' In P. Wright, L. Dyer, J. Boudreau, and G. Milkovich (eds.), *Research in Personnel and Human Resource Management*, Supplement 4: *Strategic Human Resources Management in the Twenty-First Century*. Stamford, Conn.: JAI Press.

—— and Harris, H. (eds.) (1999). *International Human Resource Management: Comtemporary Issues in Europe*. London: Routledge.

DELERY, J., and DOTY, D. (1996). 'Modes of Theorizing in Strategic Human Resource Management: Tests of Universalistic, Contingency, and Configurational Performance Predictions.' *Academy of Management Journal*, 39/4: 802–35.

DOWLING, P. J., and WELCH, D. E. (2004). *International Human Resource Management: Managing People in a Multinational Context*. London: Thomson.

DYER, L. (1984). 'Studying Human Resource Strategy.' *Industrial Relations*, 23/2: 156–69.

EDWARDS, P. (1990). 'Understanding Conflict in the Labour Process: The Logic and Autonomy of Struggle.' In D. Knights and H. Willmott (eds.), *Labour Process Theory*. London: Macmillan.

EVANS, P. (1986). 'The Strategic Outcomes of Human Resource Management.' *Human Resource Management*, 25/1: 149–67.

—— PUCIK, V., and BARSOUX, J.-L. (2002). *The Global Challenge: Frameworks for International Human Resource Management*. New York: McGraw-Hill.

GERHART, B., WRIGHT, P. M., McMAHAN, G. C., and SNELL, S. A. (2000). 'Measurement Error in Research on Human Resources and Firm Performance: How Much Error is There and How Does it Influence Effect Size Estimates?' *Personnel Psychology*, 53: 803–34.

GOODERHAM, P., NORDHAUG, O., and RINGDAL, K. (1999). 'Institutional and Rational Determinants of Organizational Practices: Human Resource Management in European Firms.' *Administrative Science Quarterly*, 44: 507–31.

GUEST, D. E. (1999). 'Human Resource Management: The Workers' Verdict.' *Human Resource Management Journal*, 9/3: 5–25.

—— (2002). 'Human Resource Management, Corporate Performance and Employee Well-Being: Building the Worker into HRM.' *Journal of Industrial Relations*, 44/3: 335–58.

HARZING, A.-W., and VAN RUYSSEVELDT, J. (eds.) (2004). *International Human Resource Management*. London: Sage.

HESKETT, J. L., SASSER, W. E., and SCHLESINGER, L. A. (1997). *The Service Profit Chain: How Leading Companies Link Profit and Growth to Loyalty, Satisfaction and Value*. New York: Free Press.

JACKSON, S., and SCHULER, R. (1995). 'Understanding Human Resource Management in the Context of Organizations and their Environments.' *Annual Review of Psychology*, 46: 237–64.

KAPLAN, R., and NORTON, D. (1996). *The Balanced Scorecard: Translating Strategy into Action*. Boston: Harvard Business School Press.

—— —— (2001). *The Strategy-Focused Organization*. Boston: Harvard Business School Press.

LEES, S. (1997). 'HRM and the Legitimacy Market.' *International Journal of Human Resource Management*, 8/3: 226–43.

LEGGE, K. (1978). *Power, Innovation, and Problem-Solving in Personnel Management*. London: McGraw-Hill.

—— (2005). 'Human Resource Management.' In S. Ackroyd, R. Batt, P. Thompson, and P. Tolbert (eds.), *Oxford University Press Handbook of Work and Organization*. Oxford: Oxford University Press.

MAHONEY, T., and DECKOP, J. (1986). 'Evolution of Concept and Practice in Personnel Administration/Human Resource Management (PA/HRM).' *Journal of Management*, 12: 223–41.

MARCHINGTON, M., and GRUGULIS, I. (2000). ' "Best practice" Human Resource Management: Perfect Opportunity or Dangerous Illusion?' *International Journal of Human Resource Management*, 11/6: 1104–24.

MUELLER, F. (1996). 'Human Resources as Strategic Assets: An Evolutionary Resource-Based Theory.' *Journal of Management Studies*, 33/6: 757–85.

PAAUWE, J. (2004). *HRM and Performance: Achieving Long-Term Viability*. Oxford: Oxford University Press.

—— and BOSELIE, P. (2003). 'Challenging "Strategic HRM" and the Relevance of the Institutional Setting.' *Human Resource Management Journal*, 13/3: 56–70.

PEEL, S., and BOXALL, P. (2005). 'When is Contracting Preferable to Employment? An Exploration of Management *and* Worker Perspectives.' *Journal of Management Studies*, 42/8: 1675–97.

PFEFFER, J. (1994). *Competitive Advantage through People*. Boston: Harvard Business School Press.

—— (1998). *The Human Equation: Building Profits by Putting People First*. Boston: Harvard Business School Press.

PURCELL, J. (1999). 'The Search for "Best Practice" and "Best Fit": Chimera or Cul-de-Sac?' *Human Resource Management Journal*, 9/3: 26–41.

—— KINNIE, N., HUTCHINSON, S., RAYTON, B., and SWART, J. (2003). *Understanding the People and Performance Link: Unlocking the Black Box*. London: CIPD.

WALL, T. D., and WOOD, S. (2005). 'The Romance of Human Resource Management and Business Performance, and the Case for Big Science.' *Human Relations*, 58/4: 429–62.

WRIGHT, P., and. BOSWELL, W. (2002). 'Desegregating HRM: A Review and Synthesis of Micro and Macro Human Resource Management Research.' *Journal of Management*, 28/3: 247–76.

—— and SNELL, S. (1998). 'Toward a Unifying Framework for Exploring Fit and Flexibility in Strategic Human Resource Management.' *Academy of Management Review*, 23/4: 756–72.

—— DUNFORD, B., and SNELL, S. (2003). 'Human Resources and the Resource Based View of the Firm.' *Journal of Management*, 27: 701–21.

—— GARDNER, T., MOYNIHAN, L., and ALLEN, M. (2005). 'The Relationship between HR Practices and Firm Performance: Examining Causal Order.' *Personnel Psychology*, 58: 409–46.

YOUNDT, M., SNELL, S., DEAN, J., and LEPAK, D. (1996). 'Human Resource Management, Manufacturing Strategy, and Firm Performance.' *Academy of Management Journal*, 39/4: 836–66.

# PART I

# FOUNDATIONS AND FRAMEWORKS

CHAPTER 2

# THE DEVELOPMENT OF HRM IN HISTORICAL AND INTERNATIONAL PERSPECTIVE

## BRUCE E. KAUFMAN

## 2.1 INTRODUCTION

THE human resource function in the business enterprise has its origins in the rise of modern industry in the late nineteenth century. In this chapter, I provide a survey of its historical development both as a functional area of management practice and as an area of research and teaching in universities. Although, for reasons to be described, the bulk of attention is on the United States, I endeavor to put the subject in an international context. Also provided is an account of the field's progress, shortcomings, and controversies.

## 2.2 THE ORIGINS AND EARLY
## DEVELOPMENT OF HRM

Viewed as a generic activity involving the management of other people's labor in production, human resource management (HRM) goes back to the dawn of human history. The first visible roots of the HRM function as practiced today in modern business organizations appeared in the late nineteenth century more or less contemporaneously in England, France, Germany, and the United States. Japan experienced a broadly similar development a decade or so later.

The generic practice of HRM does not require a formal human resource department or any specialized personnel staff. This was the arrangement practiced in most late nineteenth- to early twentieth-century enterprises, even in large-size factories and mills employing several thousand people. The HRM functions of hiring, training, compensation, and discipline/termination were performed in alternative ways. Considerable reliance was placed on the labor market, for example, to set pay rates and provide motivation for hard work (through the threat of termination and unemployment), while other HRM functions were done by the owner or plant manager or were delegated to foremen and inside contractors. Interestingly, this arrangement is still the norm today in many small firms. In their national survey conducted in the mid-1990s, for example, Freeman and Rogers (1999: 96) found that 30 percent of the American workers were employed in firms that had no formal HRM department.

The modern HRM department grew out of two earlier developments. The first was the emergence of industrial welfare work. Starting in the 1890s, a number of companies started to provide a variety of workplace and family amenities for their employees, such as lunch rooms, medical care, recreational programs, libraries, company magazines, and company-provided housing (Eilbirt 1959; Gospel 1992; Spencer 1984). Frequently, a new staff position was created to administer these activities, called a 'welfare secretary,' and women or social workers were often appointed. The impetus behind welfare work was an amalgam of good business, humanitarian concern for employees, and religious principle. German companies were pioneers in welfare work in the nineteenth century, but employers in all the industrializing countries participated.

The second antecedent was the creation of some type of separate employment office. These offices, often staffed by one or several lower-level clerks and supervisors, were created to centralize and standardize certain employment-related functions, such as hiring, payroll, and record-keeping. The introduction of civil service laws in several countries also led to the creation of employment departments in various levels of government. A stand-alone employment office reportedly existed in large European companies as far back as the 1890s. Farnham (1921) reports, for example, that the German steel company Krupp had a long-established Personnelbüro to handle staff administration, while the French steel firm Le Creusot had a similar Bureau de Personnel Ouvrier. The earliest employment department in America is reported to have been established at the B. F. Goodrich Co. in 1906 (Eilbirt 1959). The movement to create a separate employment department in American firms started to coalesce in 1912 with the formation of the Boston Employment Managers Association. Quickly the term 'employment management' became the accepted descriptor for this new management function and in 1916 it had spread widely enough to support the creation of a nationwide Employment Managers Association.

The rise of the employment management function is tightly linked with another seminal development—the emergence of the doctrine and practice of scientific management (SM). The first professional/scientific writings on business organization and management appeared in the early 1880s in the United States, authored primarily by engineers. The engineers sought to use principles of science to increase the efficiency of business production systems. Inevitably they were led to consider the 'people' side of production, including methods of employee selection, job assignment, supervision, work pace, and compensation. This new approach found its most influential and strategic formulation in the writings of Frederick Taylor, particularly his book *Principles of Scientific Management* (1911). In America, employers' interest in applying SM to labor management was substantially heightened by two new and much publicized empirical findings reported in the early to mid-1910s. The first was the huge cost of employee turnover (often in excess of 100 percent annually); the second was the cost savings from the recently inaugurated industrial safety movement (Jacoby 1985).

The First World War had a great impact on the development of the HRM function throughout the industrial world (Eilbirt 1959; Kaufman 2004a). The major combatants sought to harness their economies to maximum war production, greatly stimulating the pressures to rationalize management and achieve higher productivity. Governments in several countries sponsored research on industrial fatigue and instituted screening tests for new recruits into the armed forces (Baritz 1960; Niven 1967). Likewise, war production led to an economic boom and dramatically higher employee turnover rates, escalating wage pressures, and problems with discipline and work effort. Finally, labor unrest, strikes, and union organizing greatly mounted—factors that, with the Bolshevik Revolution in Russia in 1917, caused widespread concern that the 'Labor Problem' was on the verge of boiling over into revolution in other countries. Out of this fear was born, in turn, a new movement for *industrial democracy* (Lichtenstein and Harris 1993). In response, companies expanded welfare activities, created new employment departments, and in hundreds of cases established shop committees and employee representation plans.

In the American context, two new terms for labor management quickly emerged. The first of these was *personnel management* (or personnel administration). By the end of the war many American firms took the two functions of welfare work and employment management and combined them into a new department called personnel management. At the time, this was framed as bringing under one roof both the 'employment' and 'service' parts of the HRM function. Some European firms also used the 'personnel' term, but particularly in Britain the most common descriptor through the 1920s remained 'welfare work.' Illustratively, the first professional employment association in Britain was the Association of Welfare Workers, established in 1913, and it did not change its name to Institute of Labor Management until 1931 (Niven 1967). The 'personnel' term, in turn, did not become widely accepted until after the Second World War (Chartered Institute of Personnel and Development 2005). In continental Europe, a number of firms established employee 'social' departments, again emphasizing the welfare side of personnel management.

The second new term was *industrial relations* (occasionally also called 'employment relations'). The industrial relations term came into widespread usage in the USA and Canada in 1919–20, not coincidentally at the same time as corporate worries about labor unrest and government regulation were at a peak. The term was not, however, widely adopted in other countries until after the Second World War and then typically with a narrower (union management) meaning.

In early usage, the subject domain of industrial relations was the entire employer–employee relationship (Kaufman 2004a). In the corporate world, it was conceived as representing a more broad-based and strategic ('management policy') approach to labor management, including the subject of workforce governance. Industrial relations thus subsumed the narrower employment function of personnel management, just as personnel management subsumed employment management and welfare work. In this vein, Kennedy (1919: 358) states, 'employment management is, and always must be, a subordinate function to the task of preparing and administering a genuine labor policy, which is properly the field of industrial relations.'

During the sharp recession of 1920–1 many companies disbanded their newly formed personnel departments, partly as a cost-saving measure and partly because employee turnover and the threat of unions dissipated. The setback was temporary, however, and over the rest of the 1920s the personnel/industrial relations movement gradually regrouped and resumed growth. Jacoby (1985) provides these suggestive data: in 1915 perhaps 3–5 percent of workers employed in medium–large firms (over 250 employees) had a personnel/IR department; by 1920 this figure had increased to 25 percent and to 34 percent by 1929. By 1929 over one-half of firms with over 5,000 employees had a formalized HRM function. In the vanguard of the movement were leading corporate giants in the 1920s Welfare Capitalist movement, such as AT&T, Standard Oil, Dupont, and General Electric, and small- to medium-size firms run by progressive owner/entrepreneurs, such as Dennison Manufacturing and Plimpton Press. These firms abandoned the pre-war 'market' model of HRM, in which labor was traded and used more or less like any other commodity, and moved to what labor economist John Commons (1919) described as a combination of a 'machine' (scientific management), 'good will' (high commitment), and 'industrial citizenship' (democratic governance) model. Also noteworthy, Commons (1919: 129) used the term 'human resource' to connote the idea that investment in human skills and education makes labor more productive and counseled employers to take a strategic approach to labor, observing that '[employee] goodwill is a competitive advantage' (1919: 74).

If there were two themes that pervaded the 1920s HRM literature, it was that labor must be looked at as a distinctly *human factor* and that the central purpose of HRM is to foster *cooperation* and *unity of interest* between the firm and workers (Kaufman 2003*a*). To achieve these goals, the leading practitioners of Welfare Capitalism created extensive internal labor markets (ILMs), complete with what Leiserson (1929) called the 'crown jewel' of the Welfare Capitalist movement—the employee representation plan. These plans were early forerunners of modern forms of participative management and employee involvement (Taras 2003; Kaufman 2000*a*). Many of the specific employment practices in these companies were tactical in nature and administered by lower-level personnel staff. The overall design and mission of these new HRM programs, however, was done at the highest executive level with clear-cut strategic goals in mind. Indeed, the need to take a strategic approach to HRM was widely cited in the 1920s. For example, in the first article in the *Harvard Business Review* on the new practice of HRM, titled 'Industrial Relations Management,' the author (Hotchkiss 1923: 440) tells readers, 'When, however, we pass from tactics to the question of major strategy, industrial relations management is essentially functional rather than departmental. ... [It] deals with a subject matter which pervades all departments. ... [and] must to succeed exercise an integrating, not a segregating, force on the business as a whole.'

Not only did the practice of HRM take root and start to develop in major companies in the USA in the 1920s; so too did a supporting infrastructure of journals, associations, consulting firms, and university teaching and research programs. After the Industrial Relations Association of America folded, a new association called the National Personnel Association was founded. It later became the American Management Association. Also founded in 1922 was the Personnel Research Federation which promoted academic and industrial research and published it in the *Journal of Personnel Research*. In 1926 industrialist John D. Rockefeller, Jr. donated funds to start the nation's first large-scale (non-profit) HRM consulting/research organization, Industrial Relations Counselors, Inc. (Kaufman 2003*b*). In the academic world, the first personnel textbook appeared in 1920, *Personnel Administration* by Tead and Metcalf, and was shortly followed by several others. In 1920 the University of Wisconsin was the first to offer an area of study in industrial relations (comprised of coursework in personnel management, labor legislation, industrial (workforce) government, and unemployment) and in 1922 Rockefeller donated funds to Princeton University to establish an Industrial Relations Section, the first academic unit in an American university dedicated to research on HRM practices in industry. During the 1920s a number of business schools also introduced courses on personnel management. Institutional labor economists were the largest contingent of researchers and teachers on labor management, but a small cadre of academics from industrial psychology and commerce were also active in the field (Kaufman 2000*b*).

The development of HRM in other countries during the 1920s was slower, more piecemeal, and less strategic. Industrialization, for example, was less advanced or on a smaller scale in a number of countries. Australia is a case in point. In the mid-1920s there were perhaps six full-time welfare workers in the entire country (Hinder 1925) and only during the Second World War production boom did labor management departments start to appear (Wright 1991). Even in countries with large-scale industry, HRM lagged behind. One person estimated that the development of labor management in Britain in the early 1920s was five years behind America (Fryer 1924). Also illustrative is the remark of Mary Fleddérus, a Dutch welfare manager (quoted in *Journal of Personnel Research*, 1/1: 175) who stated in 1922, 'Broadly speaking, welfare work in Holland seems to me, as in other countries, to have arrived at a transition state. I have the impression that it chiefly looks to America for the lines on which it will go on working.' In a similar vein, Englishman Harold Butler (1927: 107) observed, 'The American literature on the subject [industrial relations] probably exceeds that of the rest of the world put together.'

To be sure, there were advances in HRM research and practice outside America in the 1920s. German academics and industrial researchers, for example, pioneered a new field called *Arbeitswissenschaft* (science of work) which explored subjects such as ergonomics, fatigue, and job satisfaction (Campbell 1989). Next to the USA, Germany was also the most active site for work in the new fields of industrial psychology (called 'psychotechniks') and industrial sociology. In Britain, little work was pushed forward on labor management or industrial psychology and sociology in universities during the 1920s, in part due to the tepid interest of the British in scientific management principles (Guillén 1994). Burns (1967: 198) notes, for example, that British academics had an 'ideological bias against business and against internal studies of business undertakings.' Some vocational training and applied research in labor management was sponsored, however, by the government, the Institute of Welfare Work, and technical schools. Limiting the development of HRM in not only Britain but all of Europe was, in addition, the fact that these countries were more advanced than the USA with regard to labor legislation, social insurance programs, and trade unionism, all of which reduced the opportunity and incentive for European employers to take a more individualized and strategic approach to labor management (Rodgers 1998; Kaufman 2004*a*).

Perhaps the country outside the USA that saw the most significant advance in HRM practice during the 1920s was Japan. Japan was an early and enthusiastic adopter of Taylor's credo of scientific management and, more so than in England, France, and Germany, Japanese employers strove to implement it (Merkle 1980; Tsutsui 1998). In the 1920s a number of individual employers and government-sponsored business groups from Japan visited the USA specifically to observe American industrial practices and they took back and adopted (with modifications) a number of elements of the Welfare Capitalism project. An association of academics, business managers, and government officials, called the Kyochokai (Society for Harmonious Cooperation), was formed to promote improved industrial relations practices, and the first labor management consultants appeared (Gordon 1985; Kinzley 1991). Japanese firms began to develop ILMs, created personnel/IR departments, and started numerous HRM practices such as recruiting programs, hiring tests, incentive wage plans, job evaluation programs, and shop committees (Dore 1973; Hazama 1997; Jacoby 1991). These practices were also fostered by the American corporations that had branch plants in Japan.

A notable event in the history of HRM is the world's first international conference devoted to the subject. Held in Flushing, the Netherlands, in 1925, it was titled International Industrial Welfare (Personnel) Congress. The conference lasted seven days and featured first-hand reports on the status of the welfare/personnel movement in twenty-two countries. The conference organizers chose to call it a congress on 'welfare work,' since this title was the most common in Britain and British colonial territories (India, South Africa, etc.), but put the word 'personnel' in parentheses in recognition of the shift in nomenclature in the United States. The conference proceedings explained that the term 'welfare work' was used in a broad sense to include personnel management activities, but nonetheless its use gave emphasis to what was described as the 'paternal and social side' (p. 45). It goes on to say that the term 'personnel' as used in the USA stresses that the function is 'recognized as part of the Management' and that personnel is not just a staff function but includes 'anyone who supervises employees, from the assistant foreman to the president' (p. 46). Several years later the association abandoned both the welfare and personnel terms and adopted the name 'International Industrial Relations Association' (Kaufman 2004a).

## 2.3 THE MIDDLE PERIOD: 1930–1965

From its birth in the mid-1910s to the late 1920s, the new management function of HRM made considerable progress and was quite favorably viewed by academic observers in the United States. Illustratively, labor economist and mediator William Leiserson (1929: 164) concluded, 'when the contributions of personnel management are recapitulated in some such fashion as we have attempted, the result is bound to be an impressive sum.' Stated another labor scholar (Slichter 1929: 432), 'modern personnel methods are one of the most ambitious social experiments of the age.'

Over the next ten years, however, the prestige and influence of HRM, and particularly the strategic 'goodwill' version associated with the Welfare Capitalist movement, took a dramatic nose-dive. The Great Depression began in late 1929 and the economy went into a downward spiral until in early 1933 gross domestic product had fallen 30 percent and one-quarter of the workforce was unemployed. The economies of other countries followed suit and, indeed, Great Britain had started the descent earlier.

Companies had no choice but to retrench and look for deep cost savings. The term 'rationalization' became an oft-used phrase on both sides of the Atlantic. Thus, smaller, less profitable, or less progressive companies first began to cut wages, make lay-offs, and disband their personnel programs. Then the pressures of competition and imminent bankruptcy forced the others to fall in line, leading even the vanguard of Welfare Capitalist companies to start liquidating labor (Cohen 1990). Doing so of course meant losing their costly investment in employee goodwill, but without profits they could not afford a progressive HRM program and mass unemployment solved the turnover and selection problems and provided a highly effective alternative method for inducing hard work and compliant behavior. Surveying the wreckage created by the Depression, Leiserson (1933: 114) observed, 'depression has undone fifteen years or so of good personnel work.' Presciently, he also noted, 'labor is going to look to legislation and not to personnel management for a solution of the unemployment problem.'

Public policy in the United States made a dramatic U-turn in order to solve the economic debacle. The Roosevelt administration launched the New Deal in mid-1933 and attempted to stimulate purchasing power by raising wages and household income through minimum wage laws, social insurance programs (unemployment and old age insurance), mass unionism, and public works spending. Government intrusion into employment relations thus noticeably increased. Most worrisome to business, the New Deal encouraged workers to join unions and they did so by the millions. In the space of five years, union density almost doubled in the United States and the bulk of the mass production industries were unionized. Suddenly, unilateral employer determination of wages, conditions, and employment procedures through HRM was replaced by joint determination through collective bargaining. To help ensure that collective bargaining displaced the Welfare Capitalist non-union HRM model, the employer-created representation plans were legally banned (Kaufman 2000a). The extent of change was even greater in some other countries, such as Germany and Japan. Fascist governments came to power, banished opposition political parties and trade unions, extended a tight grip of state control over industry, and mobilized their economies for war.

These events had both positive and negative repercussions on the HRM function (Jacoby 2003). On the positive side, the rapid spread of collective bargaining actually worked to the advantage of HRM in several ways. For example, in an effort to avoid unionization many companies quickly established or strengthened their personnel programs. Also, once the companies were unionized they needed to add personnel and labor relations staff to conduct collective negotiations with the union and administer the contracts. And, finally, unions pushed for wage standardization, job classification systems, formal grievance systems, and written employment rules, all of which required personnel/labor relations staff to develop and administer. The new government labor and social insurance laws had much the same effect.

But there were also several distinctly negative effects. The early part of the 1930s effectively eviscerated many corporate labor programs and left others badly weakened. The HRM function had also lost a great deal of professional prestige, worker confidence, and public approval. Now HRM appeared to many people as a largely empty promise, a set of techniques to manipulate workers, and a covert tool for union avoidance. Most damaging, however, was HRM's loss of power and influence at the strategic level. While the tactical and administrative parts of HRM may have experienced net growth in the latter part of the 1930s, the new collective bargaining model had little place for the strategic component built on the unitarist/mutual-gain (and paternalist) vision of Welfare Capitalism. Collective bargaining was now widely seen as the preferred method to govern and administer employment, unions were the new source of innovation and strategic change, and cooperation and goal alignment were replaced by conflict of interest, power balancing and adversarial negotiations (Kochan et al. 1986). Indicative of this new viewpoint is the dramatic turn-around of opinion of Leiserson. By the late 1930s he has abandoned the non-union HRM model and declares: 'Popular judgment now favors collective bargaining ... The organization of labor and collective bargaining [are] necessary and inevitable' (1938: 40, 43).

The events and pressures associated with the Second World War amplified and extended these disparate trends in HRM in the United States. In most of Europe and Asia, HRM had gone into arrested development in the 1930s and then largely disappeared amidst the economic devastation of the Second World War. Illustratively, the International Industrial Relations Association continued to hold conferences in Europe in the 1930s but the topics shifted from plant-level personnel work to world economic planning, and then, with the outbreak of war in 1939, the association disbanded (Kaufman 2004a).

During the war both collective bargaining and government regulation of employment expanded and solidified in the United States, thus further limiting HRM's independent room for maneuver. But there were also a number of positive developments. The hiring boom set off by the war created a need for recruitment and selection specialists, while concerns with holding down turnover grew apace.

Likewise, the mushroom growth in new war-related production plants and hiring of inexperienced workers created a huge need for training programs and staff. In order to comply with government wage control programs and prevent strikes, companies also had to implement new job evaluation procedures and systematize and formalize their compensation procedures. And, finally, employee benefit programs proliferated during the war since benefits fell outside the government's wage control program. The net result was a considerable expansion of personnel programs and departments. Data provided by Jacoby (1985), for example, show that only 39 percent of companies in 1929 with 1,000–5,000 employees had a personnel department, while in 1935–6 this ratio rose to 62 percent and then to 73 percent in 1946–8.

The United States emerged from the Second World War as the undisputed world economic leader. Much of Europe and Asia lay in ruins. Over the next fifteen years American industry enjoyed a golden age, Germany and Japan picked up the pieces and started on a sustained industrial recovery, Great Britain slowly advanced in absolute terms but declined in relative terms, and many nations in South America, Asia, and Africa started to join the industrial world.

In a number of respects the two decades after the Second World War period saw further advance in American HRM. Nonetheless, the field entered the 1960s with a pervading sense of low status and marginal importance.

In the 1920s many large-sized firms still did not have any organized HRM function; by the mid-1950s nearly every medium–large-size company had one. Furthermore, these departments were adding staff, taking on new duties, and growing in importance. American firms grew in size during this period, partly as plant size expanded to take advantage of economies of scale and partly due to mergers, acquisitions, and the rise of the conglomerate corporation. As Jacoby (2003) notes, the 1950s was the era of the 'organization man,' symbolized by the rise of mega-corporations, such as General Motors, IBM, and Sears Roebuck, and the swelling ranks of middle management and white-collar technicians and staff. With increasing corporate size came a need for more systematized and centralized personnel practices.

Application of industrial psychology, industrial sociology, and 'human relations' to employment problems also emerged in the 1940s as a hot topic and created new opportunities for HRM (Wren 2005). The human relations movement grew out of the pioneering Hawthorne experiments at the Western Electric Company, led by Elton Mayo. Whereas most of the focus of industrial psychologists in the 1920s had been on narrow 'technique' applications, such as employee selection tests and the relationship between work hours and fatigue, in the 1940s the focus among behavioral scientists shifted to more overtly psycho-social topics, such as the relationship between morale and work effort, interpersonal dynamics in small work groups, and the role of non-financial incentives. These topics had many potential applications to HRM and spurred the founding of a new applied research journal, *Personnel Psychology*. According to Brown and Myers (1956: 89) coming out of human relations research was 'a pervasive belief in the existence of a positive correlation between the degree of "morale," "job satisfaction," or "loyalty," on the one hand, and the productive efficiency of the enterprise on the other hand.' These were the key variables that personnel management in the 1950s was enlisted to promote.

The 1950s also saw the high water mark in union density and collective bargaining. The most popular title for the corporate HRM function in large companies, particularly in the union sector, was 'industrial relations.' The industrial relations department was typically divided, in turn, into the labor relations (collective bargaining) section and personnel (employment) section (Heneman and Turnbull 1952: p. iii).The idea that industrial relations should be practiced in a strategic manner, first articulated in the 1920s, was not lost on writers in the 1950s. Economist E. Wight Bakke, for example, wrote on this theme in an article aptly titled 'From Tactics to Strategy in Industrial Relations' (1948), while the practitioner-oriented *Personnel Handbook* (Mee 1951: 3, emphasis in original) counsels readers on the first page, 'the detailed work of employee testing, of job evaluation, or other day-to-day personnel operations is of little value *unless these activities are welded together in a carefully planned, well-integrated, efficient, and effective program* to help achieve the objectives of the business.' But given the importance of union–management relations at the time, the strategic focus in HRM was most often oriented toward unions and collective bargaining (Kochan and Cappelli 1984).

However, as union density began to recede in the late 1950s and collective bargaining became routinized, resources and programs began to move back toward the personnel part of the HRM function (Jacoby 1985). In non-union companies, the HRM function was sometimes called personnel and sometimes industrial relations, but the primary focus at the strategic level was union prevention and maintaining a stable, motivated workforce. Personnel departments in the top tier of progressive non-union corporations tended to be influential players, given that these companies developed highly structured internal labor markets and gave great emphasis to maintaining employee morale and job satisfaction (Foulkes 1980; Jacoby 1997). At the large bulk of American companies, however, the personnel department typically had little contact with strategic business and employment policy and instead focused on tactical administration of various personnel activities. Often the personnel function was regarded as one of the lowest rungs in the management hierarchy and a place for low-level administrators and clerks. For example, Peter Drucker (1954: 275) characterized personnel as 'partly a file clerk's job, partly a housekeeping job, partly a social worker's job and partly "fire-fighting" to head off union trouble or to settle it.' Twenty years later, Foulkes (1975: 74) noted that only 150 of the Harvard Business School's 39,000 graduates were employed in a personnel position. He explained this anomaly by noting, 'Many of them [the graduates] feel the personnel field is "low status" and "bad news".'

A similar pattern developed in Japan after the Second World War. Japan developed a 'dual' industrial sector with giant national and multinational firms in the primary sector and small- to medium-size subcontractor and supplier firms in the secondary sector. Primary sector firms developed a distinctive employment system with highly developed and formalized ILMs featuring lifetime employment, seniority wages, extensive job rotation, and enterprise unions (Shirai 1983). Powerful personnel departments were created to administer these ILMs. According to Hirano (1969), these Japanese personnel departments had more authority and range of responsibilities than the personnel departments of the leading American companies in Japan. In the secondary sector, on the other hand, personnel programs in Japanese firms were far more informal and less developed. In the 1980s the Japanese economy experienced a 'productivity miracle' and many foreign observers concluded that a large part of the explanation resided with the ability of the Japanese HRM system to foster loyalty, cooperation, and hard work. Books and articles on Japanese management practices proliferated and now it was the Americans and Europeans who were trekking to Japan for plant tours and management seminars. Largely lost from sight, however, was the fact that many of the pillars of the Japanese management model were imported from America, including not only the scientific management and total quality management principles of Taylor and Edwards Deming but also the unitarist 'goodwill' employment model pioneered by leading American writers and practitioners of industrial relations in the 1920s (Kaufman 2004a; Wren 2005).

In Europe, by way of contrast, HRM only slowly recovered and developed from the disasters of the Second World War, even as European industry rebounded. F. T. Malm (1960) wrote a survey of personnel management in Europe. He observed that 'personnel administration does not have the professional status in Europe it enjoys in the United States, except for the United Kingdom' (1960: 77). With respect to Europe, he provided this overview (1960: 72):

Many European enterprises do not appear to think in terms of an integrated personnel and industrial relations program. In some countries, the social welfare approach to employee relations problems has received special attention. In others, the 'personnel department' turns out to be the 'lohnbüro' or payroll office having no concern with basic personnel problems. In still another, the 'personnel officer' saw his function as that of a records manager. ... In the United States, modern consideration of personnel staff departments emphasizes the variety of functional roles: advisory, service, coordinative, and analytical (or 'control'). European personnel departments are often limited to the 'service' concept, and have too low status and recognition to permit effective participation in problem-solving and policy-formulation.

Malm went on to observe that (1960: 79), 'The most serious and basic of the problems affecting European personnel administration are those in executive development and management education ... The problem in much of Europe is the lack of a professional approach to management.' He also noted, however, that a more

American approach to HRM was slowly taking hold in Europe due to the substantial transfer of management methods to Europe initiated under the Marshall Plan and then carried forward through the 1950s sponsored by American foundations and the American government. Many American business people and academics traveled to Europe as members of productivity mission teams and for sponsored consulting and teaching, while numerous Europeans came to the USA for professional management training at universities and companies.

Shifting attention to the status of HRM in universities, a distinctly mixed picture emerges. Outside of the USA, HRM received little attention in either research or teaching, most particularly with respect to the personnel management part of the subject. Malm notes, for example, that 'Relatively little material on "personnel management" is included in the curricula of universities in Europe, or even in technical institutes or graduate schools of business and economics' (1960: 78). One reason for this situation is that in many European countries, such as Germany, the employment relationship was (and still is) heavily regulated by labor law, making legal education more important than management education for personnel directors. A partial exception to this situation existed in Great Britain. Universities gave very modest attention to personnel management per se, but significant vocational training was provided by technical schools and professional groups, such as the Institute of Personnel Management (Chartered Institute of Personnel and Development 2005). Also, relative to other European countries universities in Britain provided greater teaching and research in human relations and industrial relations (and, correspondingly, relatively little in labor law, reflecting the light degree of legal regulation of employment in Britain). Industrial relations, however, was typically defined narrowly in Britain to include only labor–management (union) relations, although starting in the mid-1960s the subject of management began to garner more attention (Gospel 1992; Kaufman 2004a).

The 1945–65 period in the USA was a boom time for HRM broadly defined, but a relatively stagnant time for personnel management per se. Into the 1950s the term 'industrial relations' continued to be defined broadly in America to include all aspects of employment, including personnel. Prior to the Second World War only a handful of universities had formal programs in industrial relations; after the war several dozen new industrial relations centers and institutes were established (Kaufman 2004a). The impetus for these new programs came foremost from the dramatic spread of unionism and the pressing problems of collective bargaining, dispute resolution, and contract administration. But also important was the swelling interest in industrial human relations and its applications to management and organization design. These new industrial relations programs greatly expanded teaching and research in the HRM area and drew thousands of students to the subject. The programs were multidisciplinary, had a social science orientation, and sometimes were housed in business schools but more often were established as free-standing units in the university (in order to ensure impartiality between labor and management). According to a curriculum survey (Estey 1960), the four core courses in these industrial relations programs were: labor economics, collective bargaining, personnel management (and human relations), and labor law. It is fair to say, however, that the emphasis was on labor–management relations.

The personnel management side of the field was not held in high regard during this time period and did not attract many students. A foundation-sponsored assessment of American business education in the late 1950s reached this scathing conclusion: 'next to the course in production, perhaps more educational sins have been committed in the name of personnel management than in any other required course in the business curriculum' (Gordon and Howell 1959: 189). Also indicative is this remembrance of a former student at the Institute of Labor and Industrial Relations at Illinois (Weber 1987: 15): 'When I studied at Illinois in 1950–1951, there were a few students at the institute who were taking personnel; they were déclassé by definition. I would approach these fellows and quizzically ask why they were going into personnel. ... They always gave one of two answers which were descriptive of the field: (1) "I did it in the Army," or (2) "I like people." '

# 2.4 THE DEVELOPMENT AND INTERNATIONALIZATION OF CONTEMPORARY HRM

In the post-Second World War period HRM in the USA experienced a low point in its fortunes during the 1960s. Then the field slowly revived and expanded and by the early to mid-1990s was at a new high in energy, activities, and reputation. Yet, as century's end neared there were also signs of continued problems and perhaps some slippage in HRM in both industry and academe. Beginning in the early 1980s, the modern version of HRM also quickly spread beyond North America and was transplanted to Europe, Asia, and other parts of the world. The subject is now taught at universities in all parts of the globe and the term 'human resource management,' either in English or translated into the national language (e.g. Gestión de Recursos Humanos in Spanish), is increasingly the name companies everywhere use to label their people management function.

The 'doldrums' experienced by HRM in the 1960s had several sources. I focus on the academic end. As previously described, HRM was through the 1950s subsumed as part of industrial relations. After 1960, however, the two fields gradually drifted apart with IR more narrowly focused on unions and labor–management relations and HRM on the functional parts of employee management. Accompanying the divorce of IR and HRM was a divorce between labor economists and scholars from management and the behavioral sciences.

Up to the 1950s in the USA, economics was regarded as the foundation discipline of business education, per the statement of Craig (1923: 36) that 'Business has always been recognized as a branch of the subject of economics.' Thus, personnel management was widely regarded as 'applied labor economics' and through the 1950s many of the most recognized authorities on personnel, and authors of leading personnel texts, were labor economists (broadly defined) and industrial relations specialists (Kaufman 2000*b*, 2002). These economists, such as Heneman, Myers, Strauss, and Yoder, were affiliated with industrial relations and tended to emphasize the macro ('external'), governance, and strategic dimensions of HRM, typically with an emphasis on labor markets and labor relations. But by the late 1950s these people were either retiring from academe or moving away from HRM to other topics, while the new generation of neoclassical labor economists had little interest in management.

As the economists exited, the HRM field became increasingly the preserve of scholars from management and the behavioral sciences. Naturally, their interests in employment had a more organizational ('internal') and psychological orientation and were centered on subjects such as organizational design and control, leadership styles, effective management principles, and the psychological and social aspects of human interactions in the workplace. In the 1950s this group of researchers, such as Arensberg, Argyris, McGregor, and Whyte, was most often affiliated with the human relations movement, not HRM per se. In the early 1960s human relations was absorbed in the new field of organizational behavior (OB), and its offshoot organizational development (OD), and most of the leading behavioral scientists in management and business schools became active in it (Wren 2005). The net result was that the HRM field in the 1960s—largely perceived at this point as personnel management—was left in a rather marginalized position. On one side, the economists and IR scholars drifted away, while on the other the behavioral scientists and management scholars gave their time and attention to the new field of OB. Both groups looked down on PM as a largely a theoretic subject dealing with a collection of largely disconnected administrative procedures and employment tools (Mahoney and Deckop 1986). Tangible evidence in support of this verdict is provided in the volume *Classics in Personnel Management* (Patten 1979). The articles in it illustrate the intellectual dominance of OB, the absence of economists, and the depressingly low-level administrative nature of PM.

From this low point the field of HRM embarked on a slow but cumulatively significant upward movement in intellectual substance, vigor, and participation in the academic world. To a large degree, the status of HRM in the practical world of industry mirrored this trajectory.

The term 'human resource management' first appeared in the textbook literature in the mid-1960s in the USA (Strauss 2001). The inspiration for the term appears to come from a published lecture given several years earlier by economist E. Wight Bakke entitled 'The Human Resources Function' (1958), although as noted the phrase 'human resources' has an earlier origin. It is worthwhile to quote Bakke's conception of the human resources function for it bears on later debates about the meaning of the term. He states (1958: 5–6, emphasis in original), 'The general type of activity in any function of management ... is to use resources effectively for an organizational objective ... The function which is related to the understanding, maintenance, development, effective employment, and integration of the potential in the resource 'people' I shall call simply *the human resources function*.' He also states (1958: 4, emphasis in original), 'The first thing that we ought to be clear on is that there is nothing new about the managerial function of dealing with people. ... Like other sub-functions of management ... it has been *carved out of* the *general* managerial function, not *put into* it.'

For the next fifteen to twenty years the terms personnel management and human resource management largely coexisted and were often used interchangeably, albeit with some sentiment that HRM reflected a more up-to-date terminology and conception of the people management function. But then, starting in the early 1980s, two separate lines of thought developed. The first followed tradition and argued that HRM and PM were largely different labels for the same subject. But according to a second line of thought, the HRM term represented a new model and philosophy of people management that was fundamentally different from the traditional approach of PM and IR.

An early and influential expression of this position was by Harvard management professor Michael Beer and colleagues in the book *Managing Human Assets* (1984) and by Beer and co-author Bert Spector in an article entitled 'Human Resource Management: The Integration of Industrial Relations and Organizational Development.' In the book and article they describe what is called 'a new HRM paradigm.' In their article they list fourteen characteristics that distinguish the traditional employment management model, which they identify as 'industrial relations' (including personnel), from the new paradigm they label 'human resource management.' For example, they claim IR/PM are reactive, piecemeal, part of a command and control employment system, mediators of conflicting interests, and take a short-term perspective; HRM on the other hand is proactive, integrative, part of an employee commitment and participation system, creator of a unity of interest, and takes a long-term perspective. They summarize the new HRM paradigm as reflecting (1984: 292) 'the emerging view that people are an asset and not a cost' and 'an HR function fully aware of and involved in all strategic and business decisions' (1984: 293).

Where did this second conception of HRM come from? Two intellectual developments were key.

The first, as suggested by the title of Beer and Spector's article, is the melding of theories and insights from OB/OD into traditional IR/PM. This process began in the 1960s, per the comment of Dunnette and Bass (1963) that 'many of the leading schools of business and industrial administration have shifted from the descriptive study of current personnel practices to the application of principles of the social sciences to the analysis of organizational problems. ... The behavioral sciences are making rapid strides and are moving to a central position in the study of industrial behavior.' A decade later Martin echoed this observation, stating (1975: 150), 'Personnel administration and management as taught in collegiate schools of business changed drastically during the 1960s. This change stemmed in large part from two 1959 foundation-sponsored studies of business schools, which argued persuasively that business school curricula should incorporate more of the behavioral sciences.' Martin found that the five most cited academic authors in the practitioner personnel literature were all behavioral scientists associated with OB/OD: Herzberg, McGregor, Porter, Maslow, and Argyris.

The common denominator in the writings of these OB/OD scholars is that organizations can gain higher productivity and performance by designing work and practicing management in ways that take into account that employees are people with psychological and social needs and aspirations, rather than the traditional model that (allegedly) follows economic theory and treats employees as akin to an inert factor input and the self-interested 'economic man.' This duality is captured, for example, in McGregor's (1960) 'theory X and theory Y' management system (command and control versus consensual and participative) and Walton's (1985) influential article 'From Control to Commitment in the Workplace.' The bedrock idea is that by treating employees as organizational assets rather than disposable commodities, structuring work to make it more interesting and self-controlled, and creating mutual-gain forms of compensation the employment model is transformed from an inflexible, high-conflict, and low-productivity system (the traditional pluralist IR model) to a flexible, low-conflict, and high-productivity unitarist HRM system. This new organizational/management model became widely known by various labels, such as 'high-commitment' workplace and 'high-performance work system' (HPWS), and the new HRM paradigm that emerged in the 1980s was the 'people management' component. As such, HRM was clearly positioned as different from traditional IR/PM and also as a superior performer, as extolled in books such as *In Search of Excellence* (Peters and Waterman 1982), *The Ultimate Advantage: Creating the High-Involvement Organization* (Lawler 1992), and *Competitive Advantage through People* (Pfeffer 1994). The influence of OB became so strong that in many universities HRM gravitated toward a course in 'applied organizational behavior.'

The second key event that heavily influenced and shaped the new HRM paradigm was the development and popularization of the strategic management concept (Boxall and Purcell 2000). Strategic management—earlier called strategic planning and earlier still management policy, originated out of work by Michael Porter, H. Igor Ansoff, and others (Wren 2005). It was soon imported into personnel/HRM.

In one of the earliest contributions, for example, Devanna et al. (1982: 11) say of the traditional personnel function, 'The recent popularity of human resources management is causing major problems for traditional personnel departments. For years they have been explaining their mediocre status by bewailing their lack of support and attention from the CEO.' They then go on to outline a new approach, saying: 'Whether the human resources component survives as a valuable and essential contribution to effective management will largely depend on the degree to which it is integrated as a vital part of the planning system in organizations. In large part, the management of human resources must become an indispensable consideration in both strategy formulation and strategy implementation.'

The next two decades witnessed a veritable explosion of writing and research on strategic aspects of HRM, leading in short order to the creation of an entirely new subfield called 'strategic human resource management' (SHRM). As with the term HRM, some authors define SHRM as a generic practice/approach, while others give it a more particularized meaning. Wright and McMahan (1992: 298), for example, state that SHRM is: '[t]he pattern of planned human resource deployments and activities intended to enable an organization to achieve its goals.' This conceptualization is generic since it encompasses all types of organizations and systems of people management and requires only that the HRM deployments be chosen in a forward-looking, integrated fashion in order to achieve the organization's goals. It also suggests HRM and PM are largely equivalent (since by logical inference if SHRM is strategic then HRM is largely tactical, like PM). Other authors, however, define SHRM more narrowly so it is effectively coterminous with the employment model in the HPWS. In this spirit, McMahan et al. (1998: 197) state, 'Today, what we call strategic human resource management may well be "second generation" employee involvement with a relationship to firm strategy and performance.' This conceptualization of SHRM is both narrower and more prescriptive—narrower since it seems to limit the room for strategic choice to some permutation of the HPWS and more prescriptive since it suggests that a strategic approach to HRM should incorporate employee involvement and other HPWS practices.

Regardless of definitional disputes, what can be unambiguously stated is that the development of the SHRM concept led to a substantial resurgence of academic interest in the HRM function and strengthening of both the theory and practice of people management. In the area of theory, for example, SHRM provided intellectual support for the idea that a firm's employees and HRM system can potentially provide a long-run source of competitive advantage (Boxall 1996; Wright et al. 2001)—a contention that appeared to receive empirical support in studies that found a positive link between advanced HRM practices and firm performance (e.g. Huselid 1995; Becker and Gerhart 1996).

HRM in all guises was also promoted by several developments outside academe. One example is the large-scale growth of government regulation of employment in the post-1960s period, including legislation regulating discrimination and equal opportunity, pensions, treatment of disabled employees, and family medical leave. Companies typically assigned compliance and administration of these new laws to the personnel/HRM department, thus leading to new staff positions and responsibilities.

Also important was the ongoing decline of the union sector. Companies gained new opportunity to switch from defensive union avoidance and a pluralist collective bargaining approach of employment management to a more proactive, unitarist, and high-performance approach. Many companies, to signal this shift, relabeled their personnel and industrial relations departments as human resources departments. Likewise, in the USA, the field's major professional group, the American Society of Personnel Administrators (ASPA), changed its name in 1989 to Society for Human Resource Management (SHRM).

A final factor that had a large impact was the tremendous economic success enjoyed by Japanese industry in the 1970s–1980s and the widespread conviction that a key ingredient was the Japanese HRM model built on high performance practices, such as participative management, extensive investment in employees, and a mutual gain philosophy (Thurow 1992).

By the early to mid-1990s the practice and study of HRM had clearly experienced a rejuvenation. This trend was clearly evident in universities. Student enrollment in HRM courses was booming, business schools were hiring dozens of new HRM professors, membership and participation in the HR Division of the Academy of Management steadily rose, the leading management scholarly journals (e.g. *Academy of Management Journal*) were featuring far more HRM-related articles, and new HRM field journals were born (e.g. *Human Resource Management Review*) or renamed and strengthened (e.g. *Human Resource Management*). Adding to the sense of resurgence was the palpable decline of the once-dominant industrial relations field and its rival approach emphasizing a social science, multidisciplinary curriculum.

Amidst this upbeat mood arose two other developments in the 1990s that threatened the comfortable status quo and brought into light some long-standing deficiencies and vulnerabilities that all the hoopla about SHRM and HPWS had temporarily masked.

The first of these developments was the return of economists and industrial relationists to the HRM field. In the late 1980s a new subfield of labor economics emerged, called the economics of personnel, and quickly grew in terms of participants and publishing activity. Using the tools of neoclassical microeconomics, these economists, led by Edward Lazear, developed a wide array of sophisticated models to explain a plethora of personnel practices, such as different forms of compensation, mandatory retirement rules, and screening models of employee selection (Lazear 1999; Gunderson 2001). Other economists, coming from an institutional and industrial relations perspective, have developed insightful models that explain the choice of employment systems across firms (Begin 1991; Marsden 1999) and the 'make versus buy' choice with respect to producing HRM services in-house or purchasing these services from an external provider (Kaufman 2004b). On one hand, the return of economists to the HRM field was a 'plus' for it substantially added to and strengthened the theoretical and empirical work in the area, particularly with regard to the macro (external) dimension. But also brought to light were unmet opportunities and potential vulnerabilities. Evidence reveals, for example, that the economics and management/behavioral science wings of the field were often like the proverbial ships passing in the night, either unaware of or uninterested in the other and thus forfeiting intellectual gains from trade (Mitchell 2001; Kaufman 2004b). Also, a good deal of the management literature, particularly at the textbook level, continued to be heavily descriptive and prescriptive and thus vulnerable to encroachment by economists.

A second development also introduced a discordant note into the otherwise bright picture. Even as the academic and practitioner literatures were brimming with books and articles extolling the new HRM paradigm, evidence was also accumulating that while individual HPWS practices were widely diffusing, relatively few firms had adopted the full package (Freeman and Rogers 1999; Osterman 2000). Further, many companies continued to practice HRM in a fairly traditional manner not much distinguishable from PM and IR. Indeed, while some companies were moving toward the human capital/mutual-gains HRM model, many others moved in the opposite direction. For them, 'high performance' was gained by repeated downsizings, re-engineering programs, and corporate restructurings, accompanied by large lay-offs, the end of employment security, the dismantling of ILMs, the externalization of employment to temporary workers and contracted employees, and the roll-back or elimination of many benefit programs (Cappelli 1999; Purcell and Purcell 1999). Accompanying this movement were, in many cases, major reductions in the size and influence of corporate HRM departments and the externalization of HRM services to call centers, temp firms, consultants, and independent contractors (Jacoby 2003).

This scenario of events led to a degree of intellectual schizophrenia in HRM. For example, if HRM is built on the idea that employees are assets then what type of labor management system is being used at all the companies practicing down-sizings and lay-offs? PM? IR? Likewise, if HRM is synonymous with a HPWS employment model, then are companies such Wal-Mart and McDonald's using non-HRM? Most writers sidestepped these thorny conceptual issues, or focused only on paradigmatic 'best practice' cases.

Also evident in the 1990s was a certain sense of desperation and prescriptive boosterism in academic and practitioner writings on HRM. Part of the outpouring of research on SHRM was a thinly veiled attempt to defend and enhance the organizational survival of HRM in universities and companies (Kaufman 2004b). Prescription also became wrapped up with a somewhat apocalyptic vision that

HRM faced a stark choice of 'transform or die.' A number of articles, for example, appeared with titles such as 'Repositioning the Human Resource Management Function: Transformation or Demise?' (Schuler 1990). Also illustrative is the article by David Ulrich in the *Harvard Business Review* (1998). He states (1998: 124), 'Should we do away with HR? ... there is good reason for HR's beleaguered reputation. It is often ineffective, incompetent, and costly; in a phrase, it is value sapping. Indeed if HR were to remain configured as it is today in many companies, I would have to answer the question above with a resounding "yes—abolish the thing!"' Ulrich's statement suggests that despite all the much ballyhooed emphasis on HRM as a strategic business partner, in many companies the function (apparently) remains not much different from the low-level, administrative version so often criticized in the past. One could also easily read this statement and reach the mistaken conclusion that the function/practice of HRM is equivalent to the staff and activities of the HRM department. The two, however, are quite distinct (if overlapping), as recognized by writers from the earliest days of the field.

Before ending I want to briefly discuss the movement of modern HRM outside North America. To give this topic the coverage it deserves, however, would require another chapter.

Through the 1960s and 1970s the subject and practice of personnel management had a secure if small and relatively low-status position in business firms and universities outside of North America. In Britain and Australia, for example, personnel courses were offered in universities as part of a commerce program and a small number of personnel texts were available. The subject, however, suffered from both an overall neglect of management as an academic discipline and the dominant position of industrial relations and collective bargaining (Wood 1983; Bacon 2003; Kelly 2003). But the situation markedly changed in the 1980s and early 1990s, not only in these countries but many others, and opened the door for contemporary HRM to enter. Relevant factors include: growing national interest in new management methods to stimulate productivity, industrial performance, and competitive advantage in the world economy; the swing in public opinion and national economic policy—epitomized by the coming to power of the Thatcher government in the UK—away from labor collectivism and toward a neo-liberal policy of open markets and individualized employment relations; the widespread perception that American management methods were 'best practice' and thus to be imported and emulated; the beginning of American-style professional business schools; and a new research program on management by a small set of industrial relations scholars. At this time the Japanese were also opening up new plants in Britain and elsewhere with their own version of HRM and this further heightened interest in the subject.

Although personnel slowly gave way to HRM in America over a twenty-year period beginning in the mid-1960s, the switch-over was more sudden and controversial in a number of other countries. I focus on Britain and Australia. In Britain the term 'HRM' started to appear in the mid-1980s (e.g. Hendry and Pettigrew 1986; Guest 1987) in journal articles. A particularly influential early book was John Storey's edited volume *New Perspectives on Human Resource Management* (1989). As recounted by Kelly (2003), the topic of HRM entered academic discourse in Australia in a significant way only in the late 1980s. She cites several influential papers, such as Boxall and Dowling (1990). Common to both countries was an initial period of hot debate and deep skepticism about this new import from America. Kelly states, for example, that the response of many Australian academics was (p. 152) 'dismay, doubt, and deep concern. Scholars rejected the foundations of HRM, the suggestions to integrate their field with HRM, and even notions that the emergent field of study should be taken seriously. Debate followed debate.' A number of British authors wrote highly critical assessments of HRM, suggesting it was little more than 'rhetoric,' 'ritualism,' and 'religious fervor' (Strauss 2001).

Why did HRM engender such a sharp and divided reaction? In part it was because HRM threatened the well-established industrial relations group and in part because HRM was seen as a stalking horse for union avoidance and Thatcherist neo-liberalism (Guest 1987; Purcell 1995). But also crucial to the debate was the ambiguous and to some degree contradictory definition and model of HRM that had come over from America. Was HRM a generic concept covering all forms of labor management, another name for personnel management, or a new 'human asset' model of labor management? The Americans tended to say, either pragmatically or uncritically depending on one's viewpoint, that HRM was all three and 'let's get on with it.' Nor were American HRM scholars interested in a deeper probe of the new paradigm's underlying normative and ideological principles. What went largely unquestioned in America, however, did not go unquestioned by scholars in Britain and elsewhere. A minority view was that HRM was largely a repackaged version of PM and thus not anything to get excited about. But many British and Australian writers opted for the view that HRM was indeed a substantively different model built on unitarism, individualism, high commitment, and strategic alignment (e.g. Guest 1987; Storey 1995). Given this, several strands of critical commentary and outright rejection emerged. One criticism, for example, was that HRM is inherently flawed because it mixes positive/descriptive with normative/prescriptive (Legge 1989); a second was that HRM is practiced in only a distinct minority of workplaces and may thus be of small practical significance outside the USA (Sisson 1993); a third was that HRM focuses only on corporate goals and ignores employees' interests (Mabey et al. 1998); and a fourth was that HRM did not seem to deliver the advertised positive performance effects (Hope-Hailey et. al. 1997).

From the early 1990s onward, the dust started to settle and HRM became more firmly established and less controversial in Britain and Australia. The boundaries and content of HRM remain unsettled to the present time, but a growing body of thought holds that for HRM to be a useful intellectual construct across counties it must be defined in a broad, generic, and value-free way. Representative is the statement by Boxall and Purcell (2003: 1) that HRM represents 'all those activities associated with the management of the employment relationship.' Illustrative of HRM's rising fortunes, Britain is home to two well-recognized scholarly journals, *Human Resource Management Journal* and *International Journal of Human Resource Management*, a number of British universities have established departments and chairs of HRM, numerous HRM textbooks are available, and most universities offer HRM courses.

In the 1990s HRM also spread rapidly to continental Europe, Asia, Latin America, and Africa. As was true in the British case, in each of these regions the concept of HRM and the mode of teaching and research reflects differences in university systems and economic and political environments (Lawrence 1992). Also arising out of the globalization of HRM is a new subfield of research on international and comparative HRM. Numerous articles and books have appeared in recent years, for example, on the practice and structure of HRM in Europe (e.g. Brewster 1995), comparative differences in the HRM systems and practices in American, British, German, and Japanese companies (e.g. French 1995), and strategic HRM from an international perspective (e.g. Schuler et al. 2002).

## 2.5 CONCLUSION

The practice and academic study of HRM has made huge progress over the last century. At the turn of the twentieth century the concept of human resource management had not yet been invented, its practice in industry was highly informal and often grossly inefficient and inequitable, and no organized research or teaching on HRM existed. At the beginning of the twenty-first century, the situation is transformed. Not only has the idea of HRM spread across the world, it is now recognized and practiced as a fundamental part of business, is the subject of a voluminous academic and practitioner research literature, and has greatly promoted efficient enterprise and more equitable and harmonious employee relations. This is surely quite a positive record.

But the evolution of HRM is not without problem areas and shortcomings. Some of these remain today. Compared to some other areas of business management, such as finance, marketing, and accounting, HRM has often ranked lower in strategic importance, corporate investment, and professional status. Likewise, while some companies 'walk the talk', view employees as organizational assets, and make HRM a strategic driver of competitive advantage, many others have either significantly scaled back their investment in employees and HRM or continue to practice people management in a largely tactical, administrative, and cost-focused manner. With regard to academic research, this last issue highlights the fact that at any point in time a wide frequency distribution of firms exists ranked by their breadth and depth of HRM practices. This frequency distribution also varies in systematic ways among countries, depending on their respective histories, business institutions, legal environments, and cultures. A considerable portion of recent academic research on HRM has been focused on the top tier of companies in a small number of countries, leading to an unbalanced and overly ethnocentric and normative (prescriptive) account. But the evidence provided in this review also suggests that the progress of research in these areas is surely in the right direction.

## REFERENCES

BACON, N. (2003). 'Human Resource Management and Industrial Relations.' In P. Ackers and A. Wilkinson (eds.), *Understanding Work and Employment: IndustrialRelations in Transition*. London: Oxford University Press.

BAKKE, E. W. (1948). *From Tactics to Strategy in Industrial Relations*. New Haven: Labor-Management Center, Yale University.

—— (1958). *The Human Resources Function*. New Haven: Labor-Management Center, Yale University.

BARITZ, L. (1960). *The Servants of Power: A History of the Use of Social Sciences in American Industry*. Middletown, Conn.: Wesleyan University Press.

BECKER, B., and GERHART, B. (1996). 'The Impact of Human Resource Management on Organizational Performance: Progress and Prospects.' *Academy of Management Journal*, 39/4: 779–801.

BEER, M., and SPECTOR, B. (1984). 'Human Resources Management: The Integration of Industrial Relations and Organizational Development.' In K. Rowland and G. Ferris (eds.), *Research in Personnel and Human Resources Management*, vol. ii. Greenwich, Conn.: JAI Press.

—— —— LAWRENCE, P., MILLS, D. Q., and WALTON, R. (1984). *Managing Human Assets*. New York: The Free Press.

BEGIN, J. (1991). *Strategic Employment Policy: An Organizational Systems Perspective*. Englewood Cliffs, NJ: Prentice-Hall.

BOXALL, P. (1996). 'The Strategic HRM Debate and the Resource-Based View of the Firm.' *Human Resource Management Journal*, 6/3: 59–75.

—— and DOWLING, P. (1990). 'Human Resource Management, Employee Relations and the Industrial Relations Tradition in Australia and New Zealand.' In G. Griffin (ed.), *Current Research in Industrial Relations*. Melbourne: Proceedings of the 5th AIRAANZ Conference, Melbourne University.

—— and PURCELL, J. (2000). 'Strategic Human Resource Management: Where Have We Come From and Where Are We Going?' *International Journal of Management Reviews*, 2/2: 183–203.

—— —— (2003). *Strategy and Human Resource Management*. London: Palgrave Macmillan.

BREWSTER, C. (1995). 'Towards a European Model of HRM.' *Journal of International Business Studies*, 26/1: 1–21.

BROWN, V. D., and MYERS, C. (1956). 'The Changing Industrial Relations Philosophy of American Management.' In *Proceedings of the Ninth Annual Meeting of the Industrial Relations Research Association*. Madison: Industrial Relations Research Association.

BURNS, T. (1967). 'The Sociology of Industry.' In A. Welford et al. (eds.), *Society: Problems and Methods of Study*. London: Routledge.

BUTLER, H. (1927). *Industrial Relations in the United States*. Series A, No. 27. Geneva: International Labor Organization.

CAMPBELL, J. (1989). *Joy in Work, German Work*. Princeton: Princeton University Press.

CAPPELLI, P. (1999). *Change at Work*. New York: Oxford University Press.

Chartered Institute of Personnel and Development (2005). *The History of the CIPD*. www.cipd.co.uk/about/history.htm.

COHEN, L. (1990). *Making a New Deal: Industrial Workers in Chicago, 1919–1939*. New York: Columbia University Press.

COMMONS, J. (1919). *Industrial Goodwill*. New York: McGraw-Hill.

COWDRICK, E. (1924). 'The Expanding Field of Industrial Relations.' *American Management Review*, December: 3–5.

CRAIG, D. (1923). 'Book Review: Management: A Study of Industrial Organization.' *Journal of Personnel Research*, 2/1: 36–7.

DEVANNA, M., FONBRUN, C., TICHY, N., and WARREN, L. (1982). 'Strategic Planning and Human Resource Management.' *Human Resource Management*, 21/Spring: 11–16.

DORE, R. (1973). *British Factory—Japanese Factory: The Origins of National Diversity in Industrial Relations*. Berkeley and Los Angeles: University of California Press.

DRUCKER, P. (1954). *The Practice of Management*. New York: Harper.

DUNNETTE, M., and BASS, B. (1963). 'Behavioral Scientists and Personnel Management.' *Industrial Relations*, 3/May: 115–30.

EILBIRT, H. (1959). 'The Development of Personnel Management in the United States.' *Business History Review*, 33/5: 345–64.

ESTEY, M. (1960). 'Unity and Diversity in Industrial Relations Education: The Report of the IRRA Survey.' In *Proceedings of the Thirteenth Annual Meeting*. Madison: Industrial Relations Research Association.

FARNHAM, D. (1921). *America vs. Europe in Industry*. New York: Ronald Press.

FOULKES, F. (1975). 'The Expanding Role of the Personnel Function.' *Harvard Business Review*, 53/2: 71–84.

—— (1980). *Personnel Policies at Large Nonunion Companies*. Englewood Cliffs, NJ: Prentice Hall.

FREEMAN, R., and ROGERS, J. (1999). *What Workers Want*. Ithaca, NY: Cornell University Press.

FRENCH, J. L. (1995). 'Japanese and German Human Resource Practices: Convergence of West with East?' In S. Prasad (ed.), *Advances in International Comparative Management*, vol. x. Greenwich, Conn.: JAI Press.

FRYER, D. (1924). 'Psychology and Industry in France and Great Britain.' *Journal of Personnel Research*, 2/10: 396–402.

GORDON, A. (1985). *The Evolution of Labor Relations in Japan: Heavy Industry, 1853–1955*. Cambridge, Mass.: Harvard University Press.

GORDON, R., and HOWELL, J. (1959). *Higher Education for Business*. New York: Columbia University Press.

GOSPEL, H. (1992). *Markets, Firms, and the Management of Labour in Modern Britain*. Cambridge: Cambridge University Press.

GUEST, D. (1987). 'Human Resource Management and Industrial Relations.' *Journal of Management Studies*, 24/5: 503–21.

GUILLÉN, M. (1994). *Models of Management: Work, Authority, and Organization in Comparative Perspective*. Chicago: University of Chicago Press.

GUNDERSON, M. (2001). 'Economics of Personnel and Human Resource Management.' *Human Resource Management Review*, 11/4: 431–53.

HARTMANN, H. (1959). *Authority and Organization in German Management*. Princeton: Princeton University Press.

HAZAMA, H. (1997). *The History of Labour Management in Japan*. London: Macmillan.

HENDRY, C., and PETTIGREW, A. (1986). 'The Practice of Strategic Human Resource Management.' *Personnel Review*, 15: 3–8.

HENEMAN, H., and TURNBULL, J. (1952). *Personnel Administration and Labor Relations: A Book of Readings*. New York: Prentice-Hall.

HINDER, E. (1925). 'Australia and New Zealand.' In *Report of the Proceedings of the International Industrial Welfare (Personnel) Congress*. Flushing: International Industrial Welfare (Personnel) Congress.

HIRANO, R. (1969). 'Personnel Management in Foreign Corporations.' In R. Ballon (ed.), *The Japanese Employee*. Tokyo: Sophia University.

HOPE-HAILEY, V., GRATTON, L., McGOVERN, P., and TRUSS, C. (1997). 'A Chameleon Function: HRM in the 90s.' *Human Resource Management Journal*, 7/3: 5–18.

HOTCHKISS, W. (1923). 'Industrial Relations Management.' *Harvard Business Review*, 1/July: 438–50.

HUSELID, M. (1995). 'The Impact of Human Resource Management Practices on Turnover, Productivity, and Corporate Financial Performance.' *Academy of Management Journal*, 38/3: 635–72.

International Industrial Welfare (Personnel) Congress (1925). *Report of the Proceedings of the International Industrial Welfare (Personnel) Congress*. Flushing: International Industrial Welfare (Personnel) Congress.

JACOBY, S. (1985). *Employing Bureaucracy: Managers, Unions, and the Transformation of Work in American Industry, 1900–1945*. New York: Columbia University Press.

—— (1991). 'Pacific Ties: Industrial Relations and Employment Systems in Japan and the United States since 1900.' In N. Lichtenstein and H. Harris (eds.), *Industrial Democracy in America: The Ambiguous Promise*. New York: Cambridge University Press.

—— (1997). *Modern Manors: Welfare Capitalism since the New Deal*. Princeton: Princeton University Press.

—— (2003). 'A Century of Human Resource Management.' In B. Kaufman, R. Beaumont, and R. Helfgott (eds.), *Industrial Relations to Human Resources and Beyond: The Evolving Process of Employee Relations Management*. Armonk, NY: M. E. Sharpe.

KAUFMAN, B. (2000*a*). 'The Case for the Company Union.' *Labor History*, 41/3: 321–50.

—— (2000*b*). 'Personnel/Human Resource Management: Its Roots as Applied Economics.' In R. Backhouse and J. Biddle (eds.), *Toward a History of Applied Economics*. Durham, NC: Duke University Press.

—— (2001). 'The Theory and Practice of Strategic HRM and Participative Management: Antecedents in Early Industrial Relations.' *Human Resource Management Review*, 11/4: 505–34.

—— (2002). 'The Role of Economics and Industrial Relations in the Development of the Field of Personnel/Human Resource Management.' *Management Decisions*, 40/1: 962–79.

—— (2003a). 'The Quest for Cooperation and Unity of Interest in Industry.' In B. Kaufman, R. Beaumont, and R. Helfgott (eds.), *Industrial Relations to Human Resources and Beyond: The Evolving Process of Employee Relations Management*. Armonk, NY: M. E. Sharpe.

—— (2003b). 'Industrial Relations Counselors, Inc.: Its History and Significance.' In B. Kaufman, R. Beaumont, and R. Helfgott (eds.), *Industrial Relations to Human Resources and Beyond: The Evolving Process of Employee Relations Management*. Armonk, NY: M. E. Sharpe.

—— (2004a). *The Global Evolution of Industrial Relations: Events, Ideas and the IIRA*. Geneva: International Labor Organization.

—— (2004b). 'Toward an Integrative Theory of Human Resource Management.' In B. Kaufman (ed.), *Theoretical Perspectives on Work and the Employment Relationship*. Champaign, Ill.: Industrial Relations Research Association.

KELLY, D. (2003). 'A Shock to the System? The Impact of HRM on Academic IR in Australia in Comparison with USA and UK, 1980–95.' *Asia Pacific Journal of Human Resources*, 41/2: 149–71.

KENNEDY, D. (1919). 'Employment Management and Industrial Relations.' *Industrial Management*, 58/5: 353–8.

KINZLEY, W. (1991). *Industrial Harmony in Japan: Invention of a Tradition*. London: Routledge.

KOCHAN, T., and CAPPELLI, P. (1984). 'The Transformation of the Industrial Relations and Personnel Function.' In P. Osterman (ed.), *Internal Labor Markets*. Cambridge, Mass.: MIT Press.

—— KATZ, H., and McKERSIE, R. (1986). *The Transformation of American Industrial Relations*. New York: Basic Books.

LAWLER, E. (1992). *The Ultimate Advantage: Creating the High-Involvement Organization*. San Francisco: Jossey-Bass.

LAWRENCE, P. (1992). 'Management Development in Europe: A Study in Cultural Contrasts.' *Human Resource Management Journal*, 3/Autumn: 11–23.

LAZEAR, E. (1999). 'Personnel Economics: Past Lessons and Future Directions.' *Journal of Labor Economics*, 17/2: 199–236.

LEGGE, K. (1989). 'Human Resource Management: A Critical Assessment.' In J. Storey (ed.), *New Perspectives on Human Resource Management*. London: Routledge.

LEISERSON, W. (1929). 'Contributions of Personnel Management to Improved Labor Relations.' In *Wertheim Lectures on Industrial Relations*. Cambridge, Mass.: Harvard University Press.

—— (1933). 'Personnel Problems Raised by the Current Crisis.' *Management Review*, 22/April: 114.

—— (1938). *Right and Wrong in Labor Relations*. Berkeley and Los Angeles: University of California Press.

LICHTENSTEIN, N., and HARRIS, H. (1993). *Industrial Democracy in America: The Ambiguous Promise*. New York: Oxford University Press.

MABEY, C., SKINNER, D., and CLARK, T. (1998). *Experiencing Human Resource Management.* London: Sage.

MACDUFFIE, J. (1995). 'Human Resource Bundles and Manufacturing Performance: Organizational Logic and Flexible Productions Systems in the World Auto Industry.' *Industrial and Labor Relations Review*, 48/2: 197–221.

McGREGOR, D. (1960). *The Human Side of Enterprise.* New York: McGraw-Hill.

McMAHAN, G., BELL, M., and VIRICK, M. (1998). 'Strategic Human Resource Management: Employee Involvement, Diversity, and International Issues.' *Human Resource Management Review*, 8/3: 193–214.

MAHONEY, T., and DECKOP, J. (1986). 'Evolution of Concept and Practice in Personnel Administration/Human Resource Management (PA/HRM).' *Journal of Management*, 12: 223–41.

MALM, F. (1960). 'The Development of Personnel Administration in Western Europe.' *California Management Review*, 3/Fall: 69–83.

MARSDEN, D. (1999). *A Theory of Employment Systems.* London: Oxford University Press.

MARTIN, J. (1975). 'The Influence of the Behavioral Sciences on Management Literature.' *Personnel Journal*, 54/March: 150–3.

MEE, J. (1951). *Personnel Handbook.* New York: Ronald Press.

MERKLE, J. (1980). *Management and Ideology: The Legacy of the International Scientific Management Movement.* Berkeley and Los Angeles: University of California Press.

MITCHELL, D. (2001). 'IR Journal and Conference Literature from the 1960s to the 1990s: What Can HR Learn from it? Where is it Headed?' *Human Resource Management Review*, 11/4: 375–94.

NIVEN, M. (1967). *Personnel Management 1913–63: The Growth of Personnel Management and the Development of the Institute.* London: Institute of Personnel Management.

NOLAN, M. (1994). *Visions of Modernity: American Business and the Modernization of Germany.* New York: Oxford University Press.

OSTERMAN, P. (2000). 'Work Reorganization in an Era of Restructuring: Trends in Diffusion and Effects on Employee Welfare.' *Industrial and Labor Relations Review*, 53/January: 179–96.

PATTEN, T., Jr. (1979). *Classics of Personnel Management.* Oak Park, Ill.: Moore.

PETERS, T., and WATERMAN, R. (1982). *In Search of Excellence: Lessons from America's Best-Run Companies.* New York: Harper & Row.

PFEFFER, J. (1994). *Competitive Advantage through People: Unleashing the Power of the Workforce.* Cambridge, Mass.: Harvard University Press.

PURCELL, J. (1995). 'Ideology and the End of Institutional Industrial Relations.' In C. Crouch and F. Traxler (eds.), *Organized Industrial Relations in Europe: What Future?* Aldershot: Avebury.

—— and PURCELL, K. (1999). 'Insourcing, Outsourcing and the Growth of Contingent Labour as Evidence of Flexible Employment Strategies.' *Bulletin of Comparative Labour*, 35: 151–62.

—— and SISSON, K. (1983). 'Strategies and Practice in the Management of Industrial Relations.' In G. Bain (ed.), *Industrial Relations in Britain.* Oxford: Basil Blackwell.

RODGERS, D. (1998). *Atlantic Crossings: Social Politics in a Progressive Era.* Cambridge, Mass.: Harvard University Press.

SCHULER, R. (1990). 'Repositioning the Human Resource Function: Transformation or Demise?' *Academy of Management Executive*, 4/3: 49–59.

—— BUDHWAR, P., and FLORKOWSKI, G. (2002). 'International Human Resource Management: Review and Critique.' *International Journal of Management Reviews*, 4/March: 41–70.

SHIRAI, T. (1983). *Contemporary Industrial Relations in Japan.* Madison: University of Wisconsin Press.

SISSON, K. (1993). 'In Search of HRM.' *British Journal of Industrial Relations*, 31/June: 200–10.

SLICHTER, S. (1929). 'The Current Labor Policies of American Industries.' *Quarterly Journal of Economics*, 43/May: 393–435.

SPENCER, E. (1984). *Management and Labor in Imperial Germany.* New Brunswick, NJ: Rutgers University Press.

STOREY, J. (1989). *New Perspectives on Human Resource Management.* London: Routledge.

—— (1995). *Human Resource Management: A Critical Text.* London: Routledge.

STRAUSS, G. (2001). 'HRM in the United States: Correcting Some British Impressions.' *International Journal of Human Resource Management*, 12/September: 873–97.

TARAS, D. (2003). 'Voice in the North American Workplace: From Employee Representation to Employee Involvement.' In B. Kaufman, R. Beaumont, and R. Helfgott (eds.), *Industrial Relations to Human Resources and Beyond: The Evolving Process of Employee Relations Management.* Armonk, NY: M. E. Sharpe.

TEAD, O., and METCALF, H. (1920). *Personnel Administration: Its Principles and Practice.* New York: McGraw-Hill.

THUROW, L. (1992). *Head to Head: The Coming Economic Battle among Japan, Europe, and America.* New York: Morrow.

TSUTSUI, W. (1998). *Manufacturing Ideology: Scientific Management in Twentieth Century Japan.* Princeton: Princeton University Press.

ULRICH, D. (1998). 'A New Mandate for Human Resources.' *Harvard Business Review*, 76/1: 124–34.

WALTON, R. (1985). 'From Control to Commitment in the Workplace.' *Harvard Business Review*, 63/2: 76–84.

WEBER, A. (1987). 'Industrial Relations and Higher Education.' In D. Mitchell (ed.), *The Future of Industrial Relations.* Los Angeles: UCLA Institute of Industrial Relations.

WOOD, S. (1983). 'The Study of Management in British Industrial Relations.' *British Journal of Industrial Relations*, 13/2: 51–61.

WREN, D. (2005). *History of Management Thought*, 5th edn. New York: Wiley.

WRIGHT, C. (1991). 'The Origins of Australian Personnel Management: Developments in Employment, Selection and Training Procedures in Manufacturing Industry, 1940–1960.' Sydney: ACIRRT Working Paper No. 8, University of Sydney.

WRIGHT, P., and McMAHAN, G. (1992). 'Theoretical Perspectives for Human Resource Management.' *Journal of Management*, 18/2: 295–320.

—— DUNFORD, B., and SNELL, S. (2001). 'Human Resources and the Resource Based View of the Firm.' *Journal of Management*, 27/6: 701–21.

# CHAPTER 3

## THE GOALS
## OF HRM

### PETER BOXALL

## 3.1 INTRODUCTION

HUMAN resource management covers a vast array of activities and shows a huge range of variations across occupations, organizational levels, business units, firms, industries, and societies. This confusing detail and profound diversity naturally begs a fundamental question: what are employers seeking through engaging in HRM and how do their goals for HRM relate to their broader business goals? The question that drives this chapter is not about the reasons for individual HR policies and practices, important though they may be, but about the underpinning objectives of employers. In terms of the 'level of analysis' involved, the focus is on goals that characterize whole employing units: that is, firms or, where these are diversified and devolved in labor management, business units, or establishments within them. This unit of analysis should not, however, be seen as implying that firms are somehow isolated islands. The chapter will lay emphasis on the fact that employer goals are inevitably affected by the sectoral and societal contexts within which firms operate.

The task is a difficult one: at this level of analysis, research shows that the goals of HRM are often implicit (Gratton et al. 1999; Purcell and Ahlstrand 1994). Only the largest firms tend to have formal or explicit goal statements for their overall HR strategy. Even when they do, we need to be careful in taking them at face value. In HRM, aspirational rhetoric may mask a more opportunistic and pragmatic reality

(Legge 2005; Marchington and Grugulis 2000). Broad policies are always open to the interpretations of managers, both general and specialist, and sometimes their active subversion. Furthermore, particular patterns of HRM are laid down or 'sedimented' (cf. Giddens 1979) at certain critical moments in an organization's history (Poole 1986) and managers find themselves working within these traditions without necessarily being able to explain how all the pieces got here. Goals may not be seriously analyzed unless some kind of crisis emerges in the firm's growth or performance that forces reconsideration and restructuring (e.g. Colling 1995; Snape et al. 1993). Our task, then, is better understood as trying to infer the general intentions of labor management, recognizing that we are studying a complex, collective process, built up historically in firms and inevitably subject to a degree of interpretation, politicking, and inconsistent practice.

This chapter examines a range of frameworks, theories, and research contributions that throw some light on the goals of HRM. As a business school discipline, much of the literature in HRM is normative, designed to support management education and thus setting out an argument about what managers *should* do or, more modestly, offering an analytical framework to assist practitioners to shape their own policy prescriptions. Fortunately, it also contains studies that test the predictions of theoretical models and thus provide a descriptive picture of what employers *actually* do. The chapter reviews both normative and empirical contributions within the HRM canon but its prime objective is to outline what we know about the goals of HRM in practice and what needs further research.

The chapter treats HRM as a broad, generic term equivalent to 'labor management' (Boxall and Purcell 2003; Gospel 1992). This definition needs to be contrasted with two others. First, it differs from the school of thought that sees HRM as a high-commitment model of labor management (e.g. Guest 1987; Storey 1995), one in which employers invest heavily in employees to secure high motivation and low labor turnover. Such models exist but employer styles are actually much more diverse (e.g. Katz 2005; Marchington and Parker 1990; Purcell and Ahlstrand 1994; Rubery and Grimshaw 2003) and the goal of this chapter is to understand why. Second, the definition used here differs from the school that sees HRM as an anti-union employer strategy, as a form of union substitution, or as attack on the collective institutions of industrial relations (e.g. Barbash 1987). Given the fact that the rise of HRM has correlated with a major decline in private-sector union density in Anglo-American countries, this reading is understandable, but it is again too restrictive, as we shall see.

While the literature referenced in this chapter is mainly drawn from HRM, use is also made of key sources in the industrial relations and labor economics literatures which contain some important theory and studies on the goals of employers. Although ideological perspectives and scholarly methods vary across these disciplines, one thing unites the various works cited: they share an assumption that firms do not employ people for 'the sheer hell of it.' They assume an underpinning rationale to employment, envisaging it as a costly and purposeful human activity, serving some kind of desired end. Whether, of course, all parties are enamored of the same ends is another matter.

## 3.2 GOAL FRAMEWORKS IN HRM

As was widely noted in the late 1980s and early 1990s (e.g. Boxall 1992; Poole 1990), the Harvard framework (Beer et al. 1984) provided one of the first major statements in the HRM canon on the issue of employer goals (Fig. 3.1). In this framework, managers in firms are encouraged to set their own priorities in HRM based on the interplay of stakeholder interests and situational factors. HR outcomes, in turn, are seen as having longer-term impacts on organizational effectiveness and on societal

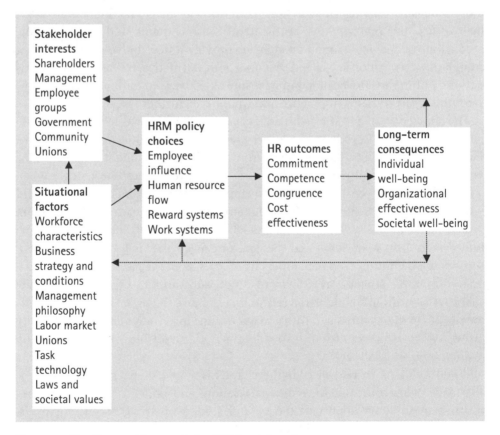

**Fig. 3.1. The Harvard 'map of the HRM territory'**

*Source:* Beer et al. 1984.

and individual well-being. As the emphasis on stakeholders and contextual factors implies, the model was offered more as an analytical framework and teaching device than as a theory (Beer et al. 1984: 17).

In terms of our understanding of overarching HRM goals, the most important chapter in the Harvard text was the last one in which the authors sought to integrate the huge range of HR choices that might be adopted by considering the differences between 'bureaucratic', 'market', and 'clan' models of HRM, a set of categories that draws on the work of Ouchi (1980). The fundamental goals of HRM are seen to differ across these styles or models. The bureaucratic model is seen as concerned with 'control and efficiency,' using traditional authority and such staples of personnel management as job descriptions and job evaluation to provide order and equity (Beer et al. 1984: 179). This HRM approach is regarded as relevant to markets with stable technology and employment levels. The market HRM approach, on the other hand, aims to treat employees more like subcontractors, fostering short-term exchanges and performance-related pay systems. This is seen as relevant to fast-changing environments such as high-fashion merchandising, advertising, and professional sports (ibid.: 180). Finally, clan HRM systems are seen as building more diffuse kinship links, fostering shared values, teamwork, and strong commitment in organizations seeking 'long-term adaptability' (ibid.: 181). This is seen as relevant to firms pursuing quality and innovation. Combining aspects of two or even three models is seen as useful when facing complex environments (ibid.: 184).

While the links between HRM goals and the firm's business strategy and environment are only very briefly sketched in the book, the main message is that HRM goals can, and should, vary based on contextual factors and that firms should aim to develop a relatively consistent style. Beer et al. (1984: 178, 184) argue that 'HRM policies need to fit with business strategy' and with 'situational constraints' while also envisaging a role for management values (ibid.: 190–1). Most of this is not well developed but the goal of fit with broader business strategy and context, followed by internal consistency in HR choices, was argued to be the essential purpose of HRM.

The Harvard framework was followed by a range of similar models (e.g. Baron and Kreps 1999; Dyer and Holder 1988). In Dyer and Holder's (1988) framework, management's goals in HRM are analyzed across the dimensions of contribution (what kind of employee behaviour is expected?), composition (what headcount, staffing ratio, and skill mix?), competence (what general level of ability is desired?), and commitment (what level of employee attachment and identification?). Like Beer et al. (1984), Dyer and Holder (1988: 10) advocate 'consistency between HR goals ... and the underlying business strategy and relevant environmental conditions' (with the latter, like the Harvard framework, including influences such as labor law, unions, labor markets, technology, and management values). In Baron and Kreps's (1999) framework, managers are advised to consider the impact of 'five forces' on HR policy choices: the external environment (social, political, legal, and economic), the workforce, the organization's culture, its strategy, and the technology of production and organization of work. This advice is not offered in a simple, deterministic fashion: managers still have choices (such as where to locate plants in manufacturing) but once some choices are made, certain environmental consequences do follow (e.g. if you locate in the USA rather than Honduras, US laws, culture, and workforce characteristics inevitably come into play). The goal of achieving internal consistency in whatever model of HRM is adopted (often called 'internal' or 'horizontal' fit) is then strongly emphasized by Baron and Kreps (1999).

In a similar fashion to Beer et al. (1984), Dyer and Holder (1988) also identify three broad styles of labor management but go further than the Harvard authors by providing more detail on how their three types of HR strategy—'inducement,' 'investment,' and 'involvement'—are linked to environmental conditions. Inducement, seen as having its roots in Scientific Management, aims for reliable, cost-efficient employee behavior (ibid.: 18–24). This is deemed suitable for firms operating in very competitive markets with simple, slowly evolving technologies. Environmental conditions are seen as 'largely benign, although militant unions are not unheard of' (ibid.: 22). The investment strategy, with its roots in Welfare Capitalism and Human Relations movements, pursues high employee competence and commitment in a generously staffed organization. These goals stem from paternalistic founders and are seen as consistent with a business strategy of competing through differentiation rather than price in rapidly changing technological environments (ibid.: 24–7). Unions are rare in these environments. Finally, the involvement strategy, owing something to the Human Relations movement but also to more contemporary emphases on participative management, aims for very high employee commitment, competence, and creativity. Self and team management loom large in this model. Firms pursuing involvement fall mainly into two types: those in highly competitive markets (like inducers) and those pursuing innovation or agility. Some firms may be pursuing the model not for any product market reasons but as a response to 'today's highly educated and narcissistic labor force' (ibid.: 28). The model is not seen as antithetical to unions but clearly requires a high level of union–management cooperation in a unionized environment (ibid.: 30).

Like the Harvard authors, if not more emphatically, Dyer and Holder (1988) and Baron and Kreps (1999) argue for a contingent understanding of HR strategy or the necessity of molding HRM goals and means to the firm's particular context. Dyer and Holder (1988: 31) conclude that 'the inescapable conclusion is that what is best, depends.' Baron and Kreps (1999: 33) assert that 'in HRM, there is no one size that fits every situation' and when considering the high-commitment model of HRM argue that it should not be adopted unless the benefits outweigh the costs (ibid.: ch. 9). None of these frameworks is inherently anti-union or takes the view that HRM is restricted to one style. The message in terms of the goals of HRM is one of fit or adaptation.

# 3.3  GOAL THEORIES AND RESEARCH IN HRM

In terms of theoretical development, there are, however, problems with the broad frameworks just described. It is hard to form testable propositions when it is argued that HRM goals depend somehow on so many variables (Guest 1997; Purcell 1999). The objective of fitting HRM to key features of the organization's external and internal environment rapidly became a key theme in the HRM literature but theoretical models of what this meant became more parsimonious.

In one of the earliest sources, Baird and Meshoulam (1988) argued that HR activities, like structure and systems, should fit the organization's stage of development, implying informal, more flexible styles of HRM among start-up firms and more formal, professionalized styles as firms become more mature. Theoretically, however, most models of 'best fit' in HRM did not follow Baird and Meshoulam's (1988) emphasis on adapting to organizational size and stage of development but argued that the key goal was to achieve fit with the firm's competitive strategy. While there are other models of what is variously called 'external' or 'vertical' fit in HRM, Schuler and Jackson (1987) used Porter's typology of generic competitive strategies (cost leadership versus differentiation, either on a broad or niche basis) to create what became the most influential model. Their model is normative: it argues that HR practices ought to be designed to mutually reinforce the firm's choice of competitive strategy and, if so, business performance will improve. If, for example, management chooses a competitive strategy of differentiation through product innovation, this would call for high levels of creative, risk-oriented, and cooperative behavior. On the other hand, if management wants to pursue cost leadership, the model suggests designing jobs which are fairly repetitive, training workers as little as is practical, cutting staff numbers to the minimum, and rewarding high output and predictable behavior.

Although competitive posture can be complex, there are now several studies which can be cited as offering some support for the argument that firms try to relate a variety of HR practices to their competitive strategies (e.g. Delery and Doty 1996; Guthrie et al. 2002; Jackson et al. 1989; Sanz-Valle et al. 1999; Youndt et al. 1996). In a study of 200 Spanish firms, for example, Sanz-Valle et al. (1999) find that those with an innovation or a quality strategy do indeed provide more training and greater opportunities for employee participation than those pursuing cost leadership, as Schuler and Jackson's (1987) model predicts. They also find that innovators pay better wages than those focusing on cost, again as the model predicts. However, the fit between HR strategy and competitive strategy is not overwhelming. These mixed results are typical for this kind of study. They suggest that current competitive strategy is indeed playing some role in shaping goals in HRM but that HRM goals are complex and various factors exert influence over time.

This means that single-factor explanations of HRM goals (such as, 'employers simply seek to manage people in a way consistent with their competitive strategy') are likely to be misleading. Without reverting to excessively complicated frameworks, what other factors are needed? In manufacturing, surveys and case studies indicate that the impact of competitive strategy on HR strategy is affected by the dominant technology used in the sector and the firm (Boxall 1999; Purcell 1999; Snell and Dean 1992; Youndt et al. 1996). In labor-intensive, low-technology manufacturing, labor costs are typically in competition and firms commonly seek to employ labor at least cost, as Schuler and Jackson (1987) predict (Table 3.1, first row). Where these pressures are intense, firms are often observed shifting their production facilities to low-cost countries or 'offshoring' workforces (Boxall and

**Table 3.1  Predicting HR strategy: two different scenarios despite the same type of competitive strategy**

| Firm's choice of competitive strategy | Nature of productive technology in the sector | Worker actions and impacts of state regulation | Implications for HR strategy |
|---|---|---|---|
| Cost leadership | Low technology, often highly labour-intensive operations and large scale | Where workforces are strongly unionized, this often strengthens the drive to locate operations in low-wage countries. Among lightly unionized workforces, employment regulation sets the lower bound of wages and conditions. | HR strategy is dominated by the need to survive in an environment where labor costs are in competition. Prediction: firms seek out low-wage sites where output is high and quality is acceptable. Firms will pay the going rate in the local labor market but avoid paying premium conditions or over-investing in training. |
| Cost leadership | High technology or highly capital intensive; often low staff numbers but key specialist skills very important to operations | If organized into unions, workers may extract more of a wage premium but this is not likely to affect the economics of the firm unless work practices are inefficient or unduly inflexible. Regulation by the state is not likely to have much relevance because wages and conditions are high in the sector. | HR strategy is based on developing and motivating workers to maximize the benefits of the technology (which will help to achieve the cost leadership strategy). Prediction: high-wage, high-skill models of labor management are cost effective. Investments in creating 'high-performance work systems' are likely to be justified. |

*Source*: Adapted from Boxall and Purcell 2003: 59.

Purcell 2003). On the other hand, when a firm has expensive investments in advanced technology, which requires highly skilled and careful handling, managers are likely to adopt high-commitment HR models for core workers, *even if* their competitive goal is to achieve the lowest unit costs in the industry (Godard 1991; Steedman and Wagner 1989) (Table 3.1, second row). In effect, where there are high 'interaction risks' between specialized capital assets (in which the firm has major 'sunk costs') and the behavior of workers, managers are likely to adopt employment models that foster greater expertise and buy greater loyalty and care. As a result, two firms which notionally have the same competitive strategy (in this case, lowest unit costs) may move in different directions in HR strategy once the influence of technology factors and cost dynamics in their sector is considered.

There is potential for a similar kind of interaction in services where the appropriate question concerns how management chooses to handle the balance between tangibles and intangibles in the service offer (Lashley 1998; Lloyd 2005). Haynes and Fryer (2000) illustrate this in their study of five-star hotels in Auckland. The hotels all have excellent facilities, without which they cannot be five star hotels, but this neutralizes tangibles as a form of competitive advantage and makes competition through intangible elements (service quality) the main way in which managers of the hotels can try to outperform others in their market segment. Performance is improved through better investment in human resources: through better systems for employee appraisal, development, and two-way communication, which improve service quality and customer loyalty. On the other hand, it needn't operate this way in services. In Lloyd's (2005) study of British fitness centers, managers in the more highly priced fitness centers typically decided not to compete through the quality of employee skills and, thus, the ability of their employees to advise customers intelligently on appropriate fitness regimes. Tolerating high rates of labor turnover, managers opted to compete through the quality of their facilities (more luxurious and spacious premises with a greater range of fitness devices and free grooming products) and not through people. Thus, in this case, a premium service offer did not translate into high investment in human resources. While high service prices are often associated with high-commitment models of HRM, as we will note later in this chapter, managers in service firms may opt instead to compete through the tangible elements of the service offer. As in manufacturing, then, we must be careful with deductions directly from competitive strategy to HR strategy or with models that suggest the former is the only key influence on the latter.

Besides the impact of technology or tangibles, reviews of 'best fit' models in HRM have noted how employer goals vary with the characteristics of employees and the state of labor markets (e.g. Boxall 1992, 1996; Lees 1997). Large firms often adopt one set of goals for managing their management cadres (particularly senior managers) and another set for the rest of the workforce (e.g. Pinfield and Berner 1994; Purcell 1987). In terms of managers, models of HRM typically involve much greater investments—either in building the clanlike, long-term loyalty that

Beer et al. (1984) describe or, alternatively, in offering their short-term, 'market' model with large bonuses for reaching key targets or a severance package for failing to do so. Within large firms, there may also be major variations among non-managerial workforce groups that reflect different union contracts, different labor market pressures and differences in the degree to which the type of labor is critical to production (e.g. Godard 1991; Osterman 1987). When labor markets are tight or workers control critical know-how, managers tend to respond with more generous employment offers and more motivating conditions.

Furthermore, as noted in Table 3.1, state regulation has an impact on the process of adaptation to context that takes place in a firm's HRM. Labor laws and labor market institutions vary from country to country, as do cultural norms. There are fundamental differences, for example, between US employment systems and those that prevail in the 'Rhineland countries' of Germany, France, and the Netherlands where 'social partnership' models accord a strong role to trade unions and works councils (Paauwe and Boselie 2003; this Handbook, Ch. 9). This argument can be linked to the observation that capital markets and the governance systems of firms vary across 'varieties of capitalism' (Hall and Soskice 2001). Anglo-American stock markets are seen as according high priority to shareholder returns and encouraging shorter time horizons in management thinking, implying more flexible employment regimes and less investment in human resource development than is typically found in countries like Germany and Japan with more patient capital providers (e.g. Gospel and Pendleton 2003).

At a minimum, then, we observe employers adapting their goals to a context in which their own competitive choices, the technologies or service tangibles they adopt, the characteristics of their employees, the state of labor markets, and the societal regulations and national cultures they encounter are all playing a significant, interactive role. On top of this, the personal values, internal politics, and cognitive limitations of management inevitably exert some influence. Adaptation to economic realities is clearly a fundamental driver of employer behavior, but so too is adaptation to the socio-political climate of work, both inside and outside the firm.

# 3.4 THE GOALS OF HRM: A SYNTHESIS

The purpose of this section is to draw on the frameworks and research insights we have discussed to present a synthesis of what we presently understand about the fundamental goals of employers. As suggested immediately above, it helps if we analyze the goals of HRM in terms of two broad categories: economic and socio-political objectives.

## 3.4.1 The Economic Objectives of HRM

The job for firms in what economists call the 'short run' is to secure their economic viability in the industry or industries in which they have chosen to compete. In order to support economic viability, firms are naturally concerned with labor productivity, with the problem of how to establish a cost-effective system of labor management (Boxall and Purcell 2003; Geare 1977; Godard 2001; Osterman 1987). Cost effectiveness can be understood as the need for every firm to stabilize a production system that enables it to compete in its chosen market (Rubery 1994; Rubery and Grimshaw 2003). The economics of production systems, involving what is possible with certain types of technology and work organization, varies very significantly across industries (Batt and Doellgast 2005). In other words, there are a limited number of viable ways of producing products or services (sometimes called 'dominant designs') in each industry segment and the firm's HR strategy needs to support them or the firm will fail. The process of forming a pattern of HRM that will underpin business viability takes place at founding and during the early growth of successful firms (Boxall and Purcell 2003). Founding leaders play a key role in this process: they either establish the basic HR strategy needed for viability or the firm fails. This allows for their personal values and philosophies to have an impact (as, for example, in firms such as the John Lewis Partnership in the UK and Hewlett Packard in the USA) but only in a way that supports the need to be economically viable or does not undermine it.

The fundamental need to adapt HR strategy to the economics of production introduces major variation into HRM. Very expensive, high-skill models of labor management, incorporating rigorous selection, high pay, and extensive internal development, are unusual among firms in those services, such as fast food, gas stations, and supermarkets, which are characterized by intense, margin-based competition (Boxall 2003). In such circumstances, firms typically adopt a low-commitment model of labor management, offering adequate rather than excellent service standards because customers are more price than quality sensitive. On the other hand, as Godard and Delaney (2000) argue, costly, high-commitment HR practices are more often found where the production system is capital intensive or where high technology is involved. In these conditions, the absolute level of labor cost may be quite low but workers have a major effect on how well the technology is utilized. It is thus economically 'efficient' to remunerate and train them very well, making better use of their skills, and ensuring their motivation is kept high. In fact, high-commitment models of HRM of this kind are now frequently a 'table stake' in certain types of advanced manufacturing and in many knowledge-intensive professional service industries in the high-wage countries (Boxall and Purcell 2003). Firms either adopt these systems or they won't survive in the business.

Identifying cost effectiveness as the most basic economic driver in HRM helps to explain why employers do not, however, adopt high-commitment models of HRM across the board. To do so would ignore the impact of industry differences in productive technologies and customer attitudes on which models of HRM are economically sustainable. The emphasis on cost within cost effectiveness also helps to indicate that 'strategic tensions' between employer and employee are inevitable in any model of HRM, no matter how superficially appealing it is (Evans 1986; Boxall 1999; Evans and Genadry 1999). Boxall and Purcell (2003) argue that coping with the twin tensions of labor scarcity and labor motivation within the economic resources of the firm poses serious dilemmas for most, if not all, firms. Many small firms fail because they cannot afford the labor they need or they survive but remain fragile, tenuous organizations with high labor turnover and ongoing recruitment problems (Hendry et al. 1995; Hornsby and Kuratko 2003; Marchington et al. 2003; Rubery 1994; Storey 1985). Furthermore, assuming an adequate labor supply, questions of employee motivation, once workers are hired, are so central to the problem of cost effectiveness that they have often been argued to be the primary problem itself. Research in industrial relations, including the labor process literature (this Handbook, Ch. 8), typically grounds its understanding of management's goals in an analysis of the employment relationship as an open-ended, indeterminate contract. In this view, the winning of workforce cooperation is seen as an 'inherently fragile' process and 'continuing preoccupation' for management (Keenoy 1992: 93). Another way of saying this is that management is concerned with a critical, ongoing problem of employee motivation because the impact of HRM is inevitably mediated through line-manager and employee responses and interactions (e.g. Bartel 2004; Coyle-Shapiro and Kessler 2000; Guest and Peccei 2001; Purcell et al. 2003).

The picture is further complicated by the reality of change in the environments of firms. Labor productivity or cost effectiveness is aimed for in a *given* context. In other words, given a particular market and a certain type of technology (among other things), it is about making the firm's labor resources productive at competitive cost. The thrust is naturally towards *stabilizing* production regimes and the work and employment systems that are central to them, enhancing predictability and certainty in the management process (Osterman 1987; Rubery 1994). However, some element of flexibility must be embedded in the firm's approach to HRM if it is to survive given the fact that industries, including their viable production systems and costs structures, evolve. Theoretical reviews in labor economics and industrial relations in the 1980s (Osterman 1987; Streeck 1987) underlined the need to bring capacity to change or 'organizational flexibility' more firmly into our understanding of employer goals and the same kind of concern has permeated the HRM literature (e.g. Evans 1986; Wright and Snell 1998).

As with cost effectiveness, the flexibility dimension inevitably implies the need to manage strategic tensions, including trade-offs with the interests of workers. Even high-commitment firms will periodically need lay-offs: employer commitment to employees is always conditional (Hyman 1987). Boxall and Purcell (2003) distinguish between 'short-run responsiveness'—in which firms build a capacity to make marginal adjustments to staffing levels or labor costs when conditions change—and 'long-run agility' (Dyer and Shafer 1999), a much more powerful ability to learn in an environment that can change radically. At a minimum, organizations need some degree of short-run responsiveness and this form of flexibility must now be considered an employer goal alongside cost effectiveness. While some firms aspire to long-run agility, organizational ecologists such as Carroll and Hannan (1995), who study patterns of firm birth, growth, and decline in industries, observe that this is very hard to achieve because core features of organizations are hard to change once laid down in the early stages of establishment and growth. In other words, there is a strategic tension between stabilizing a cost-effective work and employment system and creating the capacity for radical change.

This discussion has outlined employer goals in relation to the viability problem of the firm. A key question in the literature concerns the conditions under which firms can, and do, pursue 'sustained competitive advantage' through HRM (e.g. Boxall and Steeneveld 1999; Mueller 1996; Wright et al. 1994; this Handbook, Chapter 5). In thinking about this question, it is helpful to distinguish between labor cost advantages and labor differentiation advantages and to consider the extent to which either form of advantage can be sustained. There is abundant evidence that firms engaged in basic manufacturing industries such as clothing and footwear have relocated plants to low-wage countries to take advantage of lower labor costs (Boxall and Purcell 2003: 100–2). This, however, might simply be a viability strategy, not one that brings *sustained* advantage: the firms that do it first enjoy some temporary advantages but then these are competed away as others follow suit. Differentiation in labor quality, through better-quality human capital and smarter organizational processes (Boxall 1996), is much more what people have in mind when they think of sustained human resource advantage. When do firms embrace this goal? Boxall (2003) reviews existing studies on service sector HR strategy, including Batt's (2000) study of call centers and Hunter's (2000) study of rest homes, and develops a framework and set of propositions which argues that firms rarely adopt this goal when they are locked into the cost-based competition that occurs in mass services (Table 3.2). In mass services, customers are price sensitive and will typically take part in self-service if the price is right. However, the goal of HR advantage is envisaged as a possibility in more differentiated service markets ('Type 2' and 'Type 3') where a group of more affluent customers will pay a premium for better service. In these conditions, firms may pursue a goal of sustained HR advantage through differentiating the quality of what people do. This does not necessarily mean that they will do so: management may not see the value or may choose to compete in other ways (Boxall 2003: 16–17). As noted above, Lloyd's (2005) study of UK fitness centers demonstrates that firms at the high end of the market may simply seek to compete through better-quality facilities and not employee skills (the tangibles rather than the intangibles). On the other hand, a study by Skaggs and Youndt (2004) on a sample of 234 US service firms provides

Table 3.2  Market characteristics, competitive dynamics, and HR strategy in
         services

| Service market type | Knowledge content of service | Typical work design | Competitive dynamics in the sector | Predictions for HR strategy in firms |
|---|---|---|---|---|
| Type One: Mass service markets (e.g. gas stations, fast food, supermarkets) | Low: key managers or franchisees have critical knowledge but general labor uses limited, mostly generic know-how | Low discretion; may be highly 'Taylorized' in international franchises or major chains; otherwise unrationalized, low-skill work | Cost-based competition except to the extent limited by unions and state regulation; substitution of labor for technology and self-service; some branding strategies possible | Firms typically fit HR strategy to their cost-driven competitive strategies through paying only the market-clearing wage and complying minimally with labor laws; very limited prospects for 'HR advantage' except where premium brands can be created and sustained |
| Type Two: A mix of mass markets and higher value-added segments (e.g. elder care, hotels, call centers) | Low to moderate knowledge levels; mix of skill levels needed in the workforce | Traditionally low to moderate discretion but potential for job enrichment and HPWSs | A mix of cost and quality-based competition; greater profit opportunities for firms that identify higher value-added segments | In mass markets, HR strategies are Type One but possibilities exist for 'HR advantage' in higher value-added segments; potential problems with imitability and appropriability |
| Type Three: Very significantly, if not totally, differentiated markets (e.g. high-level professional services) | High knowledge intensity | High discretion; the natural home of HPWSs | Expertise and quality-based competition but with some anchors on relative pricing; some services may be routinized and migrate back to Type Two competition | Extensive opportunities for 'HR advantage' in expertise-driven niches; potential problems with imitability and appropriability; use of lower-cost HR strategies where expertise is routinized |

*Source*: Boxall 2003.

some of the best evidence available at this point. It shows that firms that match high-quality human capital to a strategy of high-service customization outperform those that do not. This implies that for the time being, at least, these firms are enjoying competitive advantage through HRM.

## 3.4.2 The Socio-Political Objectives of HRM

As intimated earlier in the discussion of the process of adaptation in HRM, the goals of HRM are best understood as plural (Evans 1986). There is no such thing as a single 'bottom line' in HRM: viability has more than an economic meaning. Employers are concerned with some degree of social legitimacy *while simultaneously* pursuing labor productivity (Boxall and Purcell 2003). If firms want to be seen as legitimate and have ready access to society's resources, then their employment practices must be seen to comply with labor laws and strongly held social norms (Lees 1997). The need for social legitimacy means that variation in HRM based on responses to different national institutional environments is strong (Gooderham et al. 1999). This is emphasized in all the broad analytical frameworks in HRM. Without denying that some multinationals wield considerable power (Rubery and Grimshaw 2003), individual firms rarely have opportunities to influence social standards and generally take the established ethical framework in relation to labor management as a given. Doing so helps to secure good order within the workplace and institutional support outside it.

In this connection, it is useful to make a comment about the oft-advocated objective of 'internal fit.' Because social legitimacy is a necessary goal (for all firms that wish to avoid social sanctions, legal, moral, and economic), the notion of 'internal fit' must be treated with some caution (Boxall and Purcell 2003: 56–8, 243–5). It is clearly impossible to make *all* HR policies reflective of a chosen competitive or economic mission. Some of a firm's employment policies are there simply to ensure compliance with labor laws and social conventions and have no necessary connection to its competitive strategies. Here, then, is another strategic tension associated with the goals of HRM: if firms cannot afford to meet baseline regulatory requirements in a particular country, they cannot do legitimate business there.

As with economic motives, it is useful to subject socio-political motives to dynamic analysis. This suggests a fourth fundamental motive concerned with enhancing, if not maximizing, managerial autonomy. In a classic study of management ideology, Reinhard Bendix (1956: p. xxiii) argued that 'ideologies of management are attempts by leaders of enterprises to justify the privilege of voluntary action and association for themselves, while imposing upon all subordinates the duty of obedience and of service to the best of their ability.' Gospel (1973) refers to management as having a less openly acknowledged 'security objective' alongside its profit (cost effectiveness) motive, a goal to maximize its control over an uncertain environment including threats to its power from work groups and trade unions. In situations where the problem of employee motivation escalates to levels where employment relations become unstable and managerial authority is threatened, securing the power to govern becomes the pressing management objective. Even where such dramatic threats are rare, the natural tendency of management is to act, over time, to enhance its room to manoeuver. We see this in the way multinational firms tend to favor investment in countries with less demanding labor market regulations (e.g. Cooke 2001; this Handbook, Ch. 24). We also see it at industry and societal levels, in the tendency of employer federations to lobby, over time, for greater freedom to manage and to resist new employment regulations seen to be diminishing management prerogative.

As with the tension between short-run productivity and long-run flexibility, there is a tension between the need to secure social legitimacy and the desire to enhance managerial autonomy. Sufficient levels of managerial autonomy are needed if management is going to tackle the problems of building productive and flexible enterprises in sensible ways that win support from investors and the community at large. Rational management needs space for action. However, excessive degrees of management autonomy come at the expense of worker rights and can escalate income dispersion, making society more fragile and less cohesive. Similarly, as is widely noted, management control of key information can be used to enhance management rewards to the detriment of both shareholders and workers.

By way of summary, Fig. 3.2 depicts the major motives that this chapter argues underpin management's HR activities. The arrows indicate the presence of strategic tensions: there are tensions between economic and socio-political objectives as well as within each of these goal domains. Space constraints limit any discussion of patterns that arise across these four motives but the framework opens up important lines of analysis. For example, one can readily identify firms in which management is seeking to maximize autonomy and productivity (for example, through locating all production in low-cost and loosely regulated countries). This is likely, however, to come at the cost of some forms of agility and is likely, in time, to be met with legitimacy challenges.

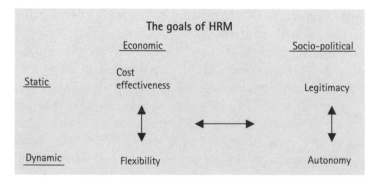

Fig. 3.2. The goals of HRM: a synthesis

## 3.5 CONCLUSIONS

Management's motives in HRM are both economic and social-political. Issues of cost effectiveness, organizational flexibility, social legitimacy, and managerial autonomy are all involved. At the most basic level, the mission of HRM is to support the viability of the firm through stabilizing a cost-effective *and* socially legitimate system of labor management. This is a critical task in the founding and early growth stages of firms, just like the need to establish satisfactory marketing and financial systems. If management cannot achieve this balance, the firm will fail because an adequate set of human resources—a capable group of people with sufficient motivation to work together productively and economically—is a necessary condition of business survival. And if an element of flexibility is not built into its HRM regime, the firm will fail at some subsequent point even if its initial model of HRM is cost effective and legitimate.

As this makes clear, any serious analysis of the goals of HRM throws the spotlight on the management of 'strategic tensions.' Among the most important of these are the tensions between employer control and employee motivation, between short-run productivity and long-run adaptability, between corporate survival and employee security, and between managerial autonomy and social legitimacy. The management of these dilemmas is so important that it is useful to understand the goals of HRM as fundamentally about the management of strategic tensions.

We need to advance our understanding of the goals of HRM in respect of both viability and sustained advantage. Progress has been made in a variety of ways, including multivariate analysis of survey data to identify key associations and effects, and in-depth case studies. Both approaches should be encouraged but, in the study of HRM goals, it is clear that we need greater methodological emphasis on dynamics, as has long been advocated (e.g. Dyer 1984). In other words, we need to study goals at major transition or crisis points such as founding, growth spurts, and restructuring (Purcell 1999) when we have a chance to uncover how particular models of HRM get there and how they link to broader economic and socio-political considerations. Longitudinal studies of 'strategic groups' of firms, competing in the same market segment, looking at what makes them similar and what differentiates them in HRM, would be especially helpful.

## REFERENCES

BAIRD, L., and MESHOULAM, I. (1988). 'Managing Two Fits of Strategic Human Resource Management.' *Academy of Management Review*, 13/1: 116–28.

BARBASH, J. (1987). 'Like Nature, Industrial Relations Abhors a Vacuum: The Case of the Union-Free Strategy.' *Relations industrielles*, 42: 168–79.

BARON, R., and KREPS, D. (1999). *Strategic Human Resources: Frameworks for General Managers.* New York: Wiley.

BARTEL, A. (2004). 'Human Resource Management and Organizational Performance: Evidence from Retail Banking.' *Industrial and Labor Relations Review,* 57/2: 181–203.

BATT, R. (2000). 'Strategic Segmentation in Front-Line Services: Matching Customers, Employees and Human Resource Systems.' *International Journal of Human Resource Management,* 11/3: 540–61.

—— and DOELLGAST, V. (2005). 'Groups, Teams, and the Division of Labor.' In S. Ackroyd, R. Batt, P. Thompson, and P. Tolbert (eds.), *Oxford University Press Handbook of Work and Organization.* Oxford: Oxford University Press.

BEER, M., SPECTOR, B., LAWRENCE, P., QUINN MILLS, D., and WALTON, R. (1984). *Managing Human Assets.* New York: Free Press.

BENDIX, R. (1956). *Work and Authority in Industry.* Berkeley and Los Angeles: UCLA Press.

BOXALL, P. (1992). 'Strategic Human Resource Management: Beginnings of a New Theoretical Sophistication?' *Human Resource Management Journal,* 2/3: 60–79.

—— (1996). 'The Strategic HRM Debate and the Resource-Based View of the Firm.' *Human Resource Management Journal,* 6/3: 59–75.

—— (1999). 'Human Resource Strategy and Industry-Based Competition: A Conceptual Framework and Agenda for Theoretical Development.' In P. Wright, L. Dyer, J. Boudreau, and G. Milkovich (eds.), *Research in Personnel and Human Resource Management,* Supplement 4: *Strategic Human Resources Management in the Twenty-First Century.* Stamford, Conn.: JAI Press.

—— (2003). 'HR Strategy and Competitive Advantage in the Service Sector.' *Human Resource Management Journal,* 13/3: 5–20.

—— and PURCELL, J. (2003). *Strategy and Human Resource Management.* New York: Palgrave Macmillan.

—— and STEENEVELD, M. (1999). 'Human Resource Strategy and Competitive Advantage: A Longitudinal Study of Engineering Consultancies.' *Journal of Management Studies,* 36/4: 443–63.

CARROLL, G. R., and HANNAN, M. T. (eds.) (1995). *Organizations in Industry: Strategy, Structure and Selection.* New York: Oxford University Press.

COLLING, T. (1995). 'Experiencing Turbulence: Competition, Strategic Choice and the Management of Human Resources in British Airways.' *Human Resource Management Journal,* 5/5: 18–32.

COOKE, W. N. (2001). 'The Effects of Labor Costs and Workplace Constraints on Foreign Direct Investment among Highly Industrialised Countries.' *International Journal of Human Resource Management,* 12/5: 697–716.

COYLE-SHAPIRO, J., and KESSLER, I. (2000). 'Consequences of the Psychological Contract for the Employment Relationship.' *Journal of Management Studies,* 35/4: 439–56.

DELERY, J., and DOTY, D. (1996). 'Modes of Theorizing in Strategic Human Resource Management: Tests of Universalistic, Contingency, and Configurational Performance Predictions.' *Academy of Management Journal,* 39/4: 802–35.

DYER, L. (1984). 'Studying Human Resource Strategy.' *Industrial Relations,* 23/2: 156–69.

—— and HOLDER, G. (1988). 'A Strategic Perspective of Human Resource Management.' In L. Dyer (ed.), *Human Resource Management: Evolving Roles & Responsibilities.* Washington: BNA.

—— and SHAFER, R. (1999). 'Creating Organizational Agility: Implications for Strategic Human Resource Management.' In P. Wright, L. Dyer, J. Boudreau, and G. Milkovich (eds.), *Research in Personnel and Human Resource Management*, Supplement 4: *Strategic Human Resources Management in the Twenty-First Century*. Stamford, Conn.: JAI Press.

EVANS, P. (1986). 'The Strategic Outcomes of Human Resource Management.' *Human Resource Management*, 25/1: 149–67.

—— and GENADRY, N. (1999). 'A Duality-Based Perspective for Strategic Human Resource Management.' In P. Wright, L. Dyer, J. Boudreau, and G. Milkovich (eds.), *Research in Personnel and Human Resources Management*, Supplement 4: *Strategic Human Resources Management in the Twenty-First Century*. Stamford, Conn.: JAI Press.

GEARE, A. J. (1977). 'The Field of Study of Industrial Relations.' *Journal of Industrial Relations*, 19/3: 274–85.

GIDDENS, A. (1979). *Central Problems in Social Theory*. London: Macmillan.

GITTLEMAN, M., HORRIGAN, M., and JOYCE, M. (1998). '"Flexible" Workplace Practices: Evidence from a Nationally Representative Survey.' *Industrial and Labor Relations Review*, 52/1: 99–115.

GODARD, J. (1991). 'The Progessive HRM Paradigm: A Theoretical and Empirical Re-examination.' *Relations industrielles*, 46/2: 378–400.

—— (2001) 'Beyond the High-Performance Paradigm? An Analysis of Variation in Canadian Managerial Perceptions of Reform Programme Effectiveness.' *British Journal of Industrial Relations*, 39/1: 25–52.

—— and DELANEY, J. (2000) 'Reflections on the "High Performance" Paradigm's Implications for Industrial Relations as a Field.' *Industrial and Labor Relations Review*, 53/3: 482–502.

GOODERHAM, P., NORDHAUG, O., and RINGDAL, K. (1999). 'Institutional and Rational Determinants of Organizational Practices: Human Resource Management in European Firms.' *Administrative Science Quarterly*, 44: 507–31.

GOSPEL, H. (1973). 'An Approach to a Theory of the Firm in Industrial Relations.' *British Journal of Industrial Relations*, 11/2: 211–28.

—— (1992). *Markets, Firms, and the Management of Labour in Modern Britain*. Cambridge: Cambridge University Press.

—— and PENDLETON, A. (2003). 'Finance, Corporate Governance and the Management of Labour: A Conceptual and Comparative Analysis.' *British Journal of Industrial Relations*, 42/3: 557–82.

GRATTON, L., HOPE-HAILEY, V., STILES, P., and TRUSS, C. (1999). *Strategic Human Resource Management: Corporate Rhetoric and Human Reality*. Oxford: Oxford University Press.

GUEST, D. (1987). 'Human Resource Management and Industrial Relations.' *Journal of Management Studies*, 24/5: 503–21.

—— (1997). 'Human Resource Management and Performance: A Review and Research Agenda.' *International Journal of Human Resource Management*, 8: 263–76.

—— and PECCEI, R. (2001). 'Partnership at Work: Mutuality and the Balance of Advantage.' *British Journal of Industrial Relations*, 39/2: 207–36.

GUTHRIE, J., SPELL, C., and NYAMORI, R. (2002). 'Correlates and Consequences of High Involvement Work Practices: The Role of Competitive Strategy.' *International Journal of Human Resource Management*, 13/1: 183–97.

HALL, P., and SOSKICE, D. (2001). 'An Introduction to Varieties of Capitalism.' in P. Hall and D. Soskice (eds.), *Varieties of Capitalism: The Institutional Foundations of Comparative Advantage*. Oxford: Oxford University Press.

HAYNES, P., and FRYER, G. (2000) 'Human Resources, Service Quality and Performance: A Case Study.' *International Journal of Contemporary Hospitality Management*, 12/4: 240–8.

HENDRY, C., ARTHUR, M., and JONES, A. (1995). *Strategy through People.* London: Routledge.

HORNSBY, J., and KURATKO, D. (2003). 'Human Resource Management in US Small Businesses: A Replication and Extension.' *Journal of Developmental Entrepreneurship,* 8/1: 73–92.

HUNTER, L. (2000). 'What Determines Job Quality in Nursing Homes?' *Industrial and Labor Relations Review,* 53/3: 463–81.

HYMAN, R. (1987). 'Strategy or Structure? Capital, Labour and Control.' *Work, Employment & Society,* 1/1: 25–55.

JACKSON, S., SCHULER, R., and RIVERO, J. (1989). 'Organizational Characteristics as Predictors of Personnel Practices.' *Personnel Psychology,* 42/4: 727–86.

KATZ, H. (2005). 'Industrial Relations and Work.' In S. Ackroyd, R. Batt, P. Thompson, and P. Tolbert (eds.), *Oxford Handbook of Work and Organization.* Oxford: Oxford University Press.

KEENOY, T. (1992). 'Constructing Control.' In J. Hartley and G. Stephenson (eds.), *Employment Relations: The Psychology of Influence and Control at Work.* Oxford: Blackwell.

LASHLEY, C. (1998). 'Matching the Management of Human Resources to Service Operations.' *International Journal of Contemporary Hospitality Management,* 10/1: 24–33.

LEES, S. (1997). 'HRM and the Legitimacy Market.' *International Journal of Human Resource Management,* 8/3: 226–43.

LEGGE, K. (2005). *Human Resource Management: Rhetorics and Realities.* Basingstoke: Palgrave Macmillan.

LLOYD, C. (2005). 'Competitive Strategy and Skills: Working out the Fit in the Fitness Industry.' *Human Resource Management Journal,* 15/2: 15–34.

MARCHINGTON, M., and GRUGULIS, I. (2000). '"Best Practice" Human Resource Management: Perfect Opportunity or Dangerous Illusion?' *International Journal of Human Resource Management,* 11/6: 1104–24.

—— and PARKER, P. (1990). *Changing Patterns of Employee Relations.* London: Harvester Wheatsheaf.

—— CARROLL, M., and BOXALL, P. (2003). 'Labour Scarcity and the Survival of Small Firms: A Resource-Based View of the Road Haulage Industry.' *Human Resource Management Journal,* 13/4: 3–22.

MUELLER, F. (1996). 'Human Resources as Strategic Assets: An Evolutionary Resource-Based Theory.' *Journal of Management Studies,* 33/6: 757–85.

OSTERMAN, P. (1987). 'Choice of Employment Systems in Internal Labor Markets.' *Industrial Relations,* 26/1: 46–67.

OUCHI, W. (1980). 'Markets, Bureaucracies and Clans.' *Administrative Science Quarterly,* 25: 129–41.

PAAUWE, J., and BOSELIE, P. (2003). 'Challenging "Strategic HRM" and the Relevance of the Institutional Setting.' *Human Resource Management Journal,* 13/3: 56–70.

PINFIELD, L., and BERNER, M. (1994) 'Employment Systems: Toward a Coherent Conceptualisation of Internal Labour Markets.' *Research in Personnel and Human Resources Management,* 12: 41–78.

POOLE, M. (1986). *Industrial Relations: Origins and Patterns of National Diversity.* London: Routledge.

—— 1990. 'Editorial: Human Resource Management in an International Perspective.' *International Journal of Human Resource Management,* 1/1: 1–15.

PURCELL, J. (1987). 'Mapping Management Styles in Employee Relations.' *Journal of Management Studies,* 24/5: 533–48.

—— (1999). 'The Search for "Best Practice" and "Best Fit:" Chimera or Cul-De-Sac?' *Human Resource Management Journal*, 9/3: 26–41.

—— and AHLSTRAND, B. (1994). *Human Resource Management in the Multidivisional Company.* Oxford: Oxford University Press.

—— KINNIE, N., HUTCHINSON, S., RAYTON, B., and SWART, J. (2003). *Understanding the People and Performance Link: Unlocking the Black Box.* London: CIPD.

RUBERY, J. (1994). 'Internal and External Labour Markets: Towards an Integrated Analysis.' In J. Rubery and F. Wilkinson (eds.), *Employer Strategy and the Labour Market.* Oxford: Oxford University Press.

—— and GRIMSHAW, D. (2003). *The Organization of Employment.* New York: Palgrave Macmillan.

SANZ-VALLE, R., SABATER-SANCHEZ, R., and ARAGON-SANCHEZ, A. (1999). 'Human Resource Management and Business Strategy Links: An Empirical Study.' *International Journal of Human Resource Management*, 10/4: 655–71.

SCHULER, R., and JACKSON, S. (1987). 'Linking Competitive Strategies and Human Resource Management Practices.' *Academy of Management Executive*, 1/3: 207–19.

SKAGGS, B., and YOUNDT, M. (2004). 'Strategic Positioning, Human Capital, and Performance in Service Organizations: A Customer Interaction Approach.' *Strategic Management Journal*, 25: 85–99.

SNAPE, E., REDMAN, T., and WILKINSON, A. 1993. 'Human Resource Management in Building Societies: Making the Transformation?' *Human Resource Management Journal*, 3/3: 44–61.

SNELL, S., and DEAN, J. (1992). 'Integrated Manufacturing and Human Resources Management: A Human Capital Perspective.' *Academy of Management Journal*, 35/3: 467–504.

STEEDMAN, H., and WAGNER, K. (1989). 'Productivity, Machinery and Skills: Clothing Manufacture in Britain and Germany.' *National Institute Economic Review*, May: 40–57.

STOREY, D. J. (1985). 'The Problems Facing New Firms.' *Journal of Management Studies*, 22/3: 327–45.

STOREY, J. (1995). *Human Resource Management: A Critical Text.* London: Routledge.

STREECK, W. (1987). 'The Uncertainties of Management in the Management of Uncertainty: Employers, Labour Relations and Industrial Adjustment in the 1980s.' *Work, Employment & Society*, 1/3: 281–308.

WRIGHT, P., and SNELL, S. (1998). 'Toward a Unifying Framework for Exploring Fit and Flexibility in Strategic Human Resource Management.' *Academy of Management Review*, 23/4: 756–72.

—— McMAHAN, G., and McWILLIAMS, A. (1994). 'Human Resources and Sustained Competitive Advantage: A Resource-Based Perspective'. *International Journal of Human Resource Management*, 5/2: 301–26.

—— DUNFORD, B., and SNELL, S. (2003). 'Human Resources and the Resource Based View of the Firm.' *Journal of Management*, 27: 701–21.

YOUNDT, M., SNELL, S., DEAN, J., and LEPAK, D. (1996). 'Human Resource Management, Manufacturing Strategy, and Firm Performance.' *Academy of Management Journal*, 39/4: 836–66.

CHAPTER 4

.....................................................................................................................

# ECONOMICS AND HRM

.....................................................................................................................

## DAMIAN GRIMSHAW

## JILL RUBERY

## 4.1 INTRODUCTION

.....................................................................................................................

THERE is another class of questions which have been brought to the forefront by recent theoretical work. One of these concerns the objectives of firms, the reasons for their existence and the manner of their decision taking. Each of these questions will require modes of analysis quite different from those which have dominated this century ... When we ask why firms exist we think of transaction costs and of increasing returns. Neither is well understood and both, except for trivial cases, resist incorporation in traditional modes of analysis ... As to a firm's organisation, we know that 'the entrepreneur' will not do and the understanding will require not only organisation, information and team theory but almost surely social psychology and an account of historical development.

(Hahn 1991: 49–50)

One of the leading protagonists of neoclassical economic theory, Frank Hahn, in setting out his stall as to where economic theory and economics theorizing needs to develop over the next century, prioritizes the theory of the firm as the subject matter and the development of interdisciplinary and historical perspectives as the methodological challenge. Human resource management (HRM) is a core part of the theory of the firm; it is concerned primarily with how organizations manage the workforce, once decisions relating to the existence of the firm and the boundaries of the firm have effectively been taken. Traditionally, economics has had little to say about the management of organizations. The association of economics with an individualized methodology and with the operation of the market, without due attention to the institutions that structure and shape the market, make it a discipline peculiarly unsuited to the study of organizations and their workforces. As Herbert Simon (1979) remarked, the key characteristic of the modern economy is the amount of coordination, activity, and transactions taking place *within* organizations; even in deregulated societies, there is still a tendency to form long-term employment relationships, with most job changes occurring early on in careers. Moreover, although a decision to 'buy'—that is to outsource—is treated as a market transaction, in most cases the result is a contract between organizations and not with individual self-employed sole traders. These subcontract organizations still have to 'manage' their own workforces, so that the internal organization of labor is much more dominant than the market versus hierarchy analysis implies.[1]

In order for economics to have much to say about HRM it is essential, as Hahn implies, to identify a role for organizations and indeed for actors within organizations. Most of the theoretical work on the importance of firm strategy is found outside the core mainstream, associated more with heterodox economists researching innovation and varieties of capitalism. It is here that one finds various models or approaches to economics that have resonances with the HRM literature; in particular the work of Penrose (1995) on the growth of the firm and March and Simon (1958) in developing notions of bounded rationality and the internal management of labor.[2] The resource-based view of the firm that underpins much of HRM is based on a methodology that is quite distinct from mainstream economics. The focus is on the internal development of the organization—on its path dependency that determines its access to unique resources—rather than on the organization's predictable and rational responses to external market forces. For Penrose, 'It is the heterogeneity, and not the homogeneity, of the productive services available or potentially available from its resources that gives each firm its unique character. Not only can the personnel of a firm render a heterogeneous variety of unique services, but also the material resources of the firm can be used in different ways' (1995: 75).

---

[1]  At a macro level, the market versus hierarchy analysis is used to explain the existence of firms but at an organization level, decisions to source products or processes from the market are treated as if they were simple market contracts with sole traders, unless the notion of hybrid forms or relational contracting is introduced.

[2]  There are also important antecedents of the study of HRM in the institutionalist economics traditions associated with Commons and others, as reviewed by Kaufman (2004: 335–6). However, this more open approach to economic analysis gave way to the hegemonic neoclassical theory of the firm.

The economics profession's preference for methodological individualism[3] inhibits its contribution to the understanding of collective actions within institutional or organizational structures. Problems such as principal–agent differences, application of game theory, and modelling decision-making in households may have been the stuff of recent economic debate and advances, but for those working within other disciplines that explicitly focus on group dynamics, internal politics and power relations, and complex motivation theory (rather than simple profit or utility maximization models), such developments may appear at best to be well overdue and at worst to be trivial and partial. Furthermore, the dominant focus of mainstream economics is on issues of static allocation of resources. As Hahn (1991) further points out, economic theory has not been able effectively to incorporate 'learning'—let alone innovation—into its theoretical frameworks. There is a need to return to more evolutionary approaches to the theory of the firm where differences in the management and development of resources, including human resources, may impact upon the likelihood of being and remaining among the survivors.

A methodological difference between HRM and economics is the use of normative language, the focus on what should be rather than simply on what is happening (Kaufman 2004). This can be partly explained by the greater interest in the management literature in how organizations not only become but also remain competitive. The embedding of knowledge and capacities for innovation in the workforce provides scope for arguing that HRM policies should be designed not just to meet current needs but also to ensure future competitive success (Wright and Snell 1998). Purcell argues for the development of a strategic approach where the overriding motivation in shaping HRM policies is to ensure the achievement of 'organisational flexibility and longevity' (Purcell 1999: 8). This requires not only adaptation to, but also management of, the external environment of the firm. Mainstream economics is peculiarly unsuited to the development of what Purcell terms 'transition management'. Managers need to do more than respond to current or predicted price incentives: creating a high-performing environment, characterized by the capacity to incorporate new knowledge, may be a means of anticipating obsolescence rather then waiting until the market provides appropriate signals.

These differences in HRM methodology allow new questions to be asked outside of the core of economic analysis. However, the analytical separation from economics also results in much of the specialist HR literature failing seriously to address issues of markets and costs (exceptions include Boxall and Purcell 2003; Baron and Kreps 1999). The strategic HR literature's focus on labour as an asset obscures its continuing role as a cost. While the rhetoric succeeds in highlighting the positive and

---

[3] Methodological individualism was first articulated by Hobbes and asserts that explanations for social phenomena must be presented wholly in terms of facts about individuals.

productive elements of the employment relationship, it deflects attention from the most interesting aspect of employment—that employers want labor to be 'both dependable and disposable' (Hyman 1987: 43). As a consequence, even the secure and protected employment for the core labor force is not guaranteed, but is contingent, *inter alia*, upon markets and cost conditions inside and outside the organization.

An analogous problem is found in the resource-based theory of the firm where the value of the firm's resources is treated as independent of the structuring of the external market, a position challenged by Priem and Butler (2001), Porter (1990), and others on the grounds that changes in markets can both undermine and even create the value. Barney (1991) acknowledges the potential for 'creative destruction' of value through Schumpeterian-type changes to competitive conditions, but Boxall and Purcell (2003) also advise against taking too literally the notion that the resources which provide the sustained competitive advantage of the firm must be inimitable and non-substitutable. Distinctive characteristics may grant an organization competitive advantage for a while but eventually other organizations will imitate and catch up, such that the distinctive characteristic becomes an industry standard—or an enabling rather than a distinctive capability (ibid.: 82). In the next stage, new distinctive characteristics will be developed, endowing either the same organization or new organizations with competitive advantage. In short, the focus in HRM on the organization as the unit of analysis is both a strength and a weakness: it reveals the important issue of path dependency but a more fully integrated analysis of the interplay between the internal environment and resources and the external environment in which the organisation operates is still lacking.

The embedding of HRM in the market, political, institutional, and social environment should provide insights into why HR strategies vary in form and outcome over time and space. At a minimum, the degree of tightness in the labor market could shed light on variations in retention and recruitment strategies and outcomes. But, as Kaufman (2004) points out, such external 'economic' conditions tend to be ignored in the HRM literature. Even less attention is paid to the institutional environment within which the organization is functioning. The outcome is a neglect not only of the changing dynamics of the market environment, but also of the more deeply rooted institutional structures associated with the varieties of capitalism literature. Theories of best practice management of work may make little sense if there are systematic variations both in governance and in the operation of markets to which these practices should and indeed do adjust.

The chapter is organized in three parts. In the first, we consider the development of personnel economics and argue that there are shortcomings that reflect the one-sided integration of economics into HRM. The second considers a selection of studies that provide a more integrated attempt to span the economics and HRM boundaries. In the third, we turn to the neglect of variations in national institutions and business systems in the analyses of HRM policies within organizations.

## 4.2 ONE-SIDED INTEGRATION: THE CASE
## OF PERSONNEL ECONOMICS

For the HRM scholar, economics provides several potentially interesting points of departure. It has a long-standing theory of how markets allocate labor between firms and how wage levels derive from prices set through product market competition, on the one hand, and the price at which workers are willing to sell their labor, given the opportunity cost of working, on the other. It has a theory for how risk aversion and incentives shape investment in human capital; a theory of the firm, which purports to define the conditions under which allocation of labor by command is more efficient than its allocation through market exchange; and a theory of international trade, from which can be derived explanations of the international division of labor. And it has a tradition of theorizing growth, beginning with Adam Smith, which has sought to understand how factor inputs (land, labor, and capital) contribute to a country's economic growth and productivity.

Compared to the disciplinary weight of economics, with its roots in classical political economy of the eighteenth and nineteenth centuries, HRM falls into the category of small fry. It was established in the USA as an academic discipline during the early 1980s (see this Handbook, Chapter 2) and is still searching for a theoretical framework (single or multiple) to lend rigor to a fast-growing body of empirical research. However, while HRM scholars have largely developed their approach separate to the discipline of economics, since the early 1980s economists have turned their eyes to problems addressed within HRM. Our argument here is that this largely one-sided integration has not been fruitful since (*a*) many of the analytical tools from the economists' bag of tricks are inappropriate for understanding the management of labor and (*b*) with some notable exceptions, the effort has been led by mainstream economists, rather than heterodox economists, thus establishing a too narrow view of how economics might be applied to HRM.

The one-sided integration has been inspired by a perceived need to toughen up the analytical approach to HRM. The new field of 'personnel economics' purports to remove the 'fuzziness' from HRM discussions, as one of its founders, Edward Lazear, claims:

Until recently, there has been no systematic discipline on which to base human resources decisions. Personnel matters were always regarded as too soft and too human to be dealt with rigorously. ... There is nothing more frustrating to a professional, or a student for that matter, then hearing a question answered, 'it all depends,' or, 'one cannot generalise about emotions.' If one cannot generalise or provide answers that can be proven right or wrong, then the field is vacuous and, unsurprisingly, of little value to practitioners. Fortunately, things have changed during the past two decades. Personnel is now a science that provides detailed unambiguous answers to the issues that trouble managers today. (Lazear 1998: 1)

The approach applies notions from economics, such as incentives, opportunity costs, and diminishing returns, to HRM issues such as recruitment and selection, payment systems, training, lay-offs, job ladders, teamworking, and outsourcing. Diffusion of new ideas about agency and contracts among economists were perhaps a catalyst for the founding of this new field (Lazear 2000). As the above quote suggests, the claims are ambitious and include providing answers to questions such as, 'when is it optimal to lay off workers?,' 'what ratio of benefits to wages maximizes the interests of both workers and firms?,' 'how much authority ought a worker be given?,' and 'what monetary incentives produce high levels of teamwork?' Also, a measure of its success is its backwards integration into conventional labor economics textbooks (e.g. Bosworth et al. 1996: chs. 18–21).

The application of incentives is illustrated by the worker effort/productivity problem. Drawing on the principal–agent paradigm, first elaborated to analyze the incentives for managers to act in the shareholders' interests (Jensen and Meckling 1976), personnel economics defines the employer as the principal and the worker as agent. The root of the problem is the conflicting, self-interested objectives of principal and agent; the principal aims to maximize returns to labor costs and the agent wishes to maximize utility, where wage is a good and effort a bad. As in HRM, personnel economics recognizes that effort is rarely observable. Conditions of uncertainty and imperfect information (modeled variously as asymmetric information or as symmetric ignorance) make the contract incomplete, generating risks for both parties. Incentive theory, in this context, aims to devise contracts that maximize worker effort at the least cost to the firm. Several prescriptions for HRM policy follow. For example, a firm may use expensive systems of screening where effort is hard to determine to identify employees whose individual output is less than their cost (if the scale of losses associated with less productive workers warrants the practice). Or, a firm may use output-based pay, which both induces workers who are inefficient to quit (because pay is low) and provides direct incentives to productive workers to produce more. Another option presented is to widen the spread of the internal wage structure, creating higher effort levels due to the so-called tournament model, which states that the higher the spread the more a given worker exerts effort to obtain promotion to the higher-paid position. Finally, where effort is difficult to observe (or to define), and screening is prohibitively costly, steep seniority wage profiles can be designed that create higher incentives for workers not to shirk, particularly if combined with relatively large penalties for substandard worker performance.

Certain assumptions underpin this application of incentive theory. First, the worker and the employer are rational, self-interested, maximizing agents. Second, equilibrium conditions prevail. And thirdly, constrained maximizing behavior by workers and firms generates efficiency (Lazear 2000). Given these assumptions, HRM scholars drawn from the softer social sciences may be forgiven for suspecting economists to have a profoundly unsophisticated approach to human motivation.

Amartya Sen, arguably the most influential current non-mainstream thinker in economics, has attributed this to the increasing dominance of the 'engineering' approach in economics, namely the focus on logistic issues based on a given set of simple human motives, and the associated decline of the ethics-related view of social achievement ('how should one live?') (Sen 1988). While Smith, Mill, and Marx embraced both ethical and engineering issues in their writings, twentieth-century economics increasingly eschewed ethical, or normative, considerations in a collective effort to advance a 'positive economics'. But the historical disjuncture from moral philosophy has weakened the usefulness of economics. In particular, the simplified assumption of self-interested maximizing behavior is problematic (Hirschman 1970; Simon 1979). It is not clear, as Sen argues (1988: 15–22), why it is assumed all behavior other than self-interested maximizing behaviour is irrational.

Developments in game theory offer a potentially more interesting approach but these have not yet found their way into mainstream approaches to personnel economics. For example, behavioral game theory assumes a 'social utility' function, where individuals care about what other players get as well as themselves. Experimental tests of a range of games find evidence that players do care about the social allocation of rewards (Camerer 1997), providing several possible linkages with HRM issues concerning employee consultation and negotiation: players cooperate because of expectations founded on the reciprocal nature of social values; and players are more willing to accept unfair offers when generated by a chance device (Blount 1995).

HRM scholars may be less inclined than mainstream economists to assume incentives have to be devised to correct workers' 'natural' impulse to shirk. This 'neo-Hobbesian' approach (Bowles 1985) has drawn strong criticism from organizational theorists:

In the economists' view, people are assumed to be lazy, dishonest, and at odds with the goals of managers. Although each of these assumptions may be valid in a specific situation, or for a particular individual (for instance, when managing economists themselves), none is likely to be right in most settings with normal human beings. (O'Reilly and Pfeffer 2000, cited in Lazear 2000)

The reply from economists would be that such assumptions are only applied at the margin—that up to a certain level workers are happy to exert effort for a given wage, but beyond this level effort becomes a bad and incentive measures are required. Similarly, monitoring mechanisms are only needed for a specific part of worker behavior that is at odds with management interests (Lazear 2000). However, the narrow view of human behavior, coupled with simplifying assumptions of perfect implementation of policies, directs attention away from many of the more interesting consequences of incentive-led HRM policies.[4] For example,

---

[4] There are instances within the personnel economics approach where more of the complexity of the world of work is acknowledged. For example, Lazear (1998) notes that output-based pay shifts the

studies of output-based pay have highlighted several problems: where performance is difficult to specify, notions of acceptable behavior may be targeted instead; subjectivity in the appraisal process may lead to favoritism and bias; emphasis on easily quantifiable outputs may lead to a decline in quality; emphasis on material incentives may conflict with other norms of job satisfaction or work ethos; and payments may be skewed because of their link with overall firm performance (Grimshaw 2000; Marsden and Richardson 1994; Rubery 1995). Such studies suggest those HRM policies that do focus on problems at 'the margin' can do severe damage by alienating the many workers for whom rational behavior does not solely involve self-interested maximization.

While incentive theory is at the heart of the personnel economics approach, other tricks from the economists' toolbox are also routinely applied to HRM issues. For example, the Cobb–Douglas production function (where firm output depends on a quantifiable matrix of inputs, including capital and labor) is applied to calculate, using information on wage rates and productivity levels, the optimum mix of high-skill and low-skill workers such that, in equilibrium, the ratios of respective salaries and outputs deliver the maximum output (Lazear 1998). The modeling can be adapted for differences in work organization, including situations where each worker's output is independent of others, as well as situations where there is interdependency—with the output of skilled workers shaping that of unskilled workers, or vice versa—or where worker output is contingent upon the level and quality of capital. One problem is the assumption that data on the output effects of teamworking and worker–capital complementarities can be easily collected. Moreover, the skill mix is taken to determine output, holding all other factors constant. But many studies in HRM, from the Hawthorne experiments to the recent studies of high-commitment work systems (HCWSs), indicate that HRM policies themselves may have an impact on output (Huselid 1995; MacDuffie 1995). This is consistent with economists' notion of 'efficiency wages' where the wage paid influences output through promoting effort. Cross-national comparative studies also highlight the role of institutions such as training systems in shaping skill mix, systems of work organization, and utilization of technology, all of which interact to impact upon output levels (Steedman and Wagner 1989; Mason 2000).

Another applied economists' trick is the use of transaction costs to prescribe when a firm ought to outsource or internalize a business activity. For Lazear, the outsourcing decision depends upon a balancing of data on a subcontractor firm's

risk of changing business conditions to the worker, despite the fact that firms are better able to bear risk (since they can diversify risk by pooling across projects or spreading investments across financial markets). And this risk is especially difficult for low-wage workers for whom variations in income impact upon their ability to pay for basic needs (food, housing, clothing). But, it is argued, the personnel economist must balance this against the fact that effort is typically easier to observe among those with less complex tasks, making output-based pay an efficient choice (Lazear 1998: 119–20).

cost per unit output compared to the firm's cost per unit output, adjusting for the opportunity cost of altering workforce size (1998: 346–50). Coase (1937) argued, however, that the costs of using the market price mechanism to organize production often remain hidden. Such costs include those of finding out market information (e.g. the wage and output data pulled from the air in examples provided in personnel economics textbooks) and those of establishing repeated market exchanges (e.g. the costs of managing, negotiating, and respecifying contracts). Again, qualitative evidence from HRM studies reveals the range of costs associated with outsourcing, but some, such as those related to worker morale and commitment (e.g. George 2003; Logan et al. 2004), do not lend themselves to inclusion in neat models. A deeper problem is that the practice of comparing internal and external firm data on cost per unit output presumes it is possible and desirable to assess firm performance using narrow market-based yardsticks. Studies rooted in a 'dynamic capabilities' approach (Teece 2002) argue instead that the use of market benchmarks and incentives in determining the strategy of the firm may have the unintended consequence of reducing the value attached to those firm-specific activities which cannot be organized using markets, especially learning and cooperative activity. As Teece argues, 'the properties of [firm] organization cannot be replicated by a portfolio of business units amalgamated just through formal contracts, as many distinct elements of internal organization simply cannot be replicated in the market' (2002: 158).

# 4.3 TOWARDS MORE INTEGRATED APPROACHES

While the integration of economics reasoning into human resource management or vice versa has been limited, we can find several examples of serious efforts to integrate the two approaches from both directions. Rather than attempt a comprehensive review, we pick out two sets of examples: first, explanations of the choice of HR practices; and second, internal labor market theory.

## 4.3.1 Selection of HR Practices

The selection of HR practices presupposes a prior choice between market and hierarchy, or make and buy. Kaufman (2004) argues for a more rigorous economic analysis both of the make and buy decision and of the precise choice of HR policies, on the grounds that HR policies carry costs that must be covered by improvements in output at the margin. These practices may have direct and indirect impacts on productivity or output—direct by, for example, improving the selection and thus the quality of labor, indirect by changing worker morale and thereby effort levels. A standard economic framework (the Cobb–Douglas production function, see above), whereby additional units of an HR practice are adopted provided the marginal revenue exceeds the marginal cost, is then used to explain why not all organizations are interested in developing high-commitment systems and to move beyond the assertion of the existence of synergies between the different elements of the HR package in the HPWS literature into an empirically testable hypothesis. This approach serves to introduce a healthy note of scepticism as to the efficacy of universal HR best practice bundles, but the framework assumes that the costs and benefits of HR practices are known and calculable. Nor is it able to deal with the issues of long-term and strategic flexibility (Wright and Snell 1998; Purcell 1999) which may require the building in of a capability to respond to future needs.

A second example of an integrated approach to choice of HR strategy is the HR architecture model provided by two HR theorists, Lepak and Snell (1999), who 'draw on the resource-based view of the firm, human capital theory, and transaction cost economics to develop a HR architecture of four different employment modes: internal development, acquisition, contracting and alliance' (1999: 31). Two variables explain the choice of HR practice—the value of skill and the specificity (or uniqueness) of skill. The market versus hierarchy interface between HRM and economics is expanded into a richer, more multilayered approach that distinguishes usefully between the value and the specificity of skill and between relational and transactional contracting.

Following the personnel economics and HRM traditions, the focus is on describing practices within the organization and not on the interactions between HR policy and the operation of the labor market. For example, in deciding between making or buying skilled labor (internal development or acquisition), the institutional arrangements that produce a supply of ready skilled labor are not considered. As economists have demonstrated (Marsden 1986), an effectively functioning occupational labor market (where a ready supply of skilled labor can transfer between organizations) requires that there is an institutionalization of systems of training, skill-based job titles, and occupational structures. Differences in make/buy decisions between organizations, sectors, and countries may therefore depend more on the availability of ready trained labor than on the importance of the uniqueness of skill. Another problem with the HR architecture approach is its focus on the value of skill and not on the interactions between different job categories. According to Boxall (1998), the strategic HRM literature has focused on the contribution HR makes to strategic goals rather than operational efficiency. In Lepak and Snell (1999), external contracting is proposed where human capital 'is generic and of limited strategic value' and can therefore be 'treated essentially as a commodity' (ibid.: 39). The reliance on labor for operational efficiency, with all its reputational effects, is ignored. While low-skilled labor may or may not be readily replaced—dependent on the state of the external labor market—there is a constant need on a daily basis to ensure that incumbent staff are motivated and working in the interests of the client organization and cooperating in many cases with other parts of the production chain. These requirements often go beyond the compliance with rules and regulations specified by Lepak and Snell (Marchington et al. 2005). There is thus a danger that by incorporating mainstream economic reasoning into the HR area, the insights into the complexity of managing human resources that derive from the traditions of industrial relations or personnel management may be discarded.

These problems are perhaps more successfully avoided in Baron and Krep's (1999) textbook on strategic HRM, a collaboration between an economist and an HR specialist. Baron and Kreps accept a high level of indeterminacy in HR outcomes as 'the employment transaction will be incomplete a priori to be filled in as contingencies arise; and when the filling in takes place subsequently, the discipline of the market will be dulled' (ibid.: 81). They move beyond the notion of economic rationality and self-interest as the only issue motivating behavior and assert:

that the management of human resources is complex because the basic element is the behaviour of people, whose perceptions and expectations are coloured by their perceptual abilities and by their social experiences, and whose objectives mix (to varying degrees) pure self-interest, comparisons with others, and social obligation. Moreover, because the issues involved are so important to individuals, society has an enormous stake in the outcome, and society will express its interests in the outcome thorough social and legal constraints on organisations and their relationship with employees. (Baron and Kreps 1999: 8)

This more complex approach is evidenced in their identification of six factors associated with outsourcing, including the strategic nature of the task and the degree of specific human capital required, cited by Lepak and Snell, but adding the degree of interdependency with the core tasks, the need for staff to internalize the firm's welfare, the open-endedness of the task requirement, and the social distance between the internal workforce and the type of workers who are to be outsourced. Thus, this list is expanded to include complexities in production organization, the scope for even low-skilled workers to disrupt or damage production systems if they do not 'internalize the firm's welfare', and the role of social or labor market segmentation in promoting outsourcing and fragmentation of production systems. The consequence of this broader interdisciplinary approach is, from an economics perspective, a loss of theoretical elegance and explanatory power. But the force of this criticism depends upon whether the purpose, or indeed likely outcome, of social science is to explain complex behavior and social organization by one unified theory.

## 4.3.2 Internal Labor Markets and Dual Labor Market Theory

Without internalized labor and continuous employment contracts, there would be little substance to the subject of HRM. The existence of internalized labor and the development of internalized rules for the management of labor has been explained within mainstream economics through the transaction costs or new institutional economics literature, associated with the work of Williamson (1975) from the 1970s onwards. The use of open-ended and incomplete contracts is explained by the costs of spot contracting, while the presence of firm-specific skills provides the rationale for operating internalized labor markets designed to provide incentives to labor with firm-specific skills to remain with the organization and cooperate in its objectives.

Doeringer and Piore's (1971) famous institutional analysis of internal labor markets was not only published effectively contemporaneously with transaction costs explanations of similar phenomena but the two approaches also shared some conceptual similarities, with the identification of firm specific skills as a core rationale for the emergence of structured internal labor markets in both accounts of hierarchy. However, in objectives and in methodologies the accounts diverge. Doeringer and Piore's motivation for the book was to escape from 'reliance upon market imperfections or non market institutions to explain deviations from the results predicted by conventional economic theory' (1971: 1). Instead they started the analysis with the core institutional structures that shape the operation of the labor market—firms' internal labor markets—and asserted administrative rules to be not only present, but also relatively rigid, leading to quantity rather than price adjustments. Job evaluation and custom and practice took precedence over market information in shaping internal wage structures. This analysis thus rejects the notion that institutions and customs in the labor market are dependent upon their continued compatibility with market needs.

The novelty of their work was in the linkage of the emergence of internal labor markets with the processes that create social exclusion and disadvantage. Failure to gain entry to internal labor markets resulted in long-term and often increasing inequalities as those in the primary market gained access to training and advancement and those in the secondary sector were regarded increasingly as inappropriate recruits for the primary market, even at times of labor shortage. Thus Doeringer and Piore did what few HR theorists have done and considered the implications of organizational HR strategies for the overall functioning of the labor market. They also broke ranks with mainstream economic theory by pointing to the possibility of economic or market-based structures contributing to labor market segmentation and disadvantage. Most economics accounts attribute any segmentation or disadvantage to pre-market factors. To some extent, the Doeringer and Piore model stands unsatisfactorily between the pure transaction costs accounts of the development of internal labor markets and more fully developed social and historical accounts (Jacoby 1984; Rubery 1978; Wilkinson 1981) of the processes by which labor markets have come to be structured or 'balkanised' (Kerr 1954). Two main critiques have been made: first, they overemphasized the importance of firm-specific skills as the main explanatory factor and failed sufficiently to consider the development and utilization of worker bargaining power; second, they presented a general theoretical approach, but in practice this reflected the institutional characteristics of the US labor market. However, as we discuss below, Doeringer and Piore are not alone in the HR field in failing to consider different societal approaches to the management of human resources.

# 4.4 THE LESSONS OF COMPARATIVE ANALYSIS: UNDERSTANDING HOW NATIONAL INSTITUTIONS SHAPE FIRM BEHAVIOR

In this final section, we argue there are lessons to learn for HRM from comparative studies by scholars who have adapted economists' analytical techniques to understand how country differences in institutions impact upon HRM practices. We focus on two approaches, Marsden's (1999) micro-founded theory of employment systems and the 'varieties of capitalism' field of studies associated with Hall and Soskice (2001).

These two approaches share several principles of theory and method. Both use a deductive approach to establish possible varieties of employment practices and thus argue for the testing of an exhaustive typology of diverse systems. Both explore the mutual interplay between firm-level practices and strategic decision-making, but extend this to include the interplay between firm strategies and practices and national-level institutions as operationalized through social actors. And both explore the effects of multiple, mutually reinforcing institutions, with the argument that it is the particular societal bundle of institutions that matters rather than an easily quantifiable institutional measure to be examined in abstract. Finally, both are based upon what economists refer to as micro-foundations—a rational choice incentive theory of behavior that is responsive to institutionalized rules of the game (both approaches deploy game-theoretic terminology), which reduce uncertainty and facilitate coordination of productive activity. For many, this theoretical foundation is a strength as it demonstrates the importance of institutions without reliance on 'non-economic' reasoning. For others, however, the insights of the theories are limited by the adoption of a narrow conception of the motivations for human behavior.

Marsden's work straddles the HRM–economics divide as is evident in his research on incentive-based payment systems (e.g. Marsden and French 1998) and on vocational training (e.g. Marsden and Ryan 1990). His 1986 book—*The End of Economic Man*—further establishes his credentials as a non-mainstream economist. As such, his application of microeconomic principles and concepts such as transaction costs is unorthodox and owes more to the work of Herbert Simon than to Coase or Williamson. Moreover, Marsden's analytical framework is enriched by a historical perspective gleaned from industrial relations research. Nevertheless, the questions he poses follow the mainstream focus on opportunism—e.g. Is it possible to specify a viable form of transaction that gives sufficient protection to worker and employer against possible opportunism by the other? Moreover, Marsden's method fits neatly within the economics discipline since it is deductive, not inductive as is much of the HRM literature.

Marsden establishes a typology of four national varieties of work organization based on employment rules derived from alternative options for satisfying two contractual constraints: (*a*) to align job demands with worker competences (firms can emphasize complementarities either among production tasks or among worker skills); and (*b*) to design an easily enforceable and transparent system of task assignment (firms can choose a task-centered approach or a function/ procedure approach) (1999: ch. 2). The four identified types of transaction rules for the employment relationship are said to be 'constitutive,' 'in the sense that without them there would be no lasting agreement between employers and workers to cooperate in this way' (ibid.: 61). Moreover, applying economic reasoning from game theory models (which fits neatly as an application of methodological individualism reasoning), Marsden seeks to show how each rule can emerge in a world of uncoordinated, decentralized decision-making with repeated interactions between workers and employers and is then diffused throughout the major sectors of an economy. Importantly, he does not rule out the supportive role of labor market institutions in this process (especially through the state, unions and employers—ibid.: 107–9), but warns against the use of labor market institutions to impose a particular rule as this may conflict with norms at a workplace level (ibid.: 83–4). Marsden also shows how transaction rules have a mutually supporting relationship with institutional features of labor markets—a production approach to task allocation fits with patterns of employment mobility associated with internal labor markets, and a training approach similarly fits with occupational labor markets. The argument incorporates a relatively detailed, historical account of labor market institutions, including, for example, the role of the tripartite system of dual apprenticeship in Germany in propping up its 'qualification rule' approach to employment organization, the problems of declining coordination among British employers for preserving a 'tools of the trade' approach, and the importance of inter-firm support for job classification systems in France.

The analysis illuminates how firm-level HR practices interact with, and are reinforced by, societal institutions as evidenced through the roles of social actors. Also, unlike many comparative studies of HRM, it seeks to test an interesting set of theoretical principles, extending our knowledge of the functioning of the open-ended employment relationship to a cross-national setting. However, by accepting a rational choice framework, where worker and employer exercise free choice, Marsden has very little to say about situations where a worker is not free to reject a situation where the risk of employer opportunism is high. Very little is offered to explain patterns of labor market inequality, the undervaluation of women's work, or the poor conditions associated with secondary labor markets.[5] There may be an opportunity, therefore, for adapting Marsden's theoretical framework to incorporate notions of power imbalance between worker and employer, although this would then clearly depart from the equilibrium notions at the core of his work.

Like Marsden, Hall and Soskice's varieties of capitalism approach begins with a consideration of the incentive structures of the firm and the employment relationship (mainly following Milgrom and Roberts 1992). They identify two ideal types of institutional arrangements, in which firms resolve coordination problems in alternative ways—termed liberal and coordinated market economies. But where Marsden emphasizes institutions as providing a supporting role to the strategic decisions of firms, for Hall and Soskice institutions act as an interlocking system of collective rules and networks ('socialising agencies'): in their words, 'In any national economy, firms will gravitate toward the mode of coordination for which there is institutional support' (2001: 9) and, similarly, 'institutions offer firms a particular set of opportunities; and companies can be expected to gravitate toward strategies that take advantage of these opportunities' (ibid.: 15). As such, their approach is radically different from the field of HRM, where firm strategy is typically viewed as relatively unconstrained by national institutions. In particular, as Culpepper has noted, the varieties of capitalism approach can make 'grim reading' for public policy makers since it implies that where certain preferred firm strategies are not compatible with a given institutional framework, it is better to stick with alternative strategies that are compatible, 'even if that means abandoning goals that could improve both the competitiveness of firms and the wages of workers' (2001: 275).

But by granting stronger agency to institutions, the varieties of capitalism approach can illuminate firm strategy with regard to HRM. For example, with respect to training decisions, the varieties of capitalism approach argues that firms

---

[5] Marsden does recognize this limitation and points to the work of economists in specifying the way employers in low-wage labor markets act with a degree of monopsony in setting wage rates and, perhaps more importantly, opting to run with high levels of vacancies, thus generating higher workloads for employees (1999: 231–2).

will only collaborate effectively in vocational training schemes if institutions (operationalized through the state, employer associations, and unions) can provide the necessary coordinating functions of information circulation, deliberation (where collective discussions among social actors are encouraged), monitoring, and sanctioning. In their absence, whatever its intentions and objectives, an individual firm will not commit to large investments in transferable worker skills for fear of poaching by firms that do not make such investments, and workers will not participate unless they have a credible assurance that new skills will be appropriately remunerated. Moreover, because this approach stresses institutional complementarities—where a given type of coordination in one institutional sphere is complemented by coordination rules in other spheres (Aoki 1994; see, also, Amable 2003)—the analysis can be extended to include the character of corporate governance (especially regarding the types of finance of the firm, the exercise of control, and the objectives of finance providers), the legal conditions for employment protection, and the institutions of industrial relations (especially the content and coverage of collective bargaining and the roles of works councils, unions, and employer associations). The approach thus presents a considerable challenge to the field of HRM to recast the firm through the lens of how an interlocking web of institutions enables or constrains particular strategic choices. Prescriptions for firms to implement an HCWS bundle of HRM policies would be contingent upon whether or not this fits with the character of a country's corporate governance system (can firms access capital with terms independent of short-term fluctuations in profitability?), the system of vocational training (can employees be certain of highly reputable, certified training?), and the industrial relations system (can social actors discourage poaching through monitoring and sanctioning devices?).

The approach has nevertheless been criticized for an overly functionalist and static view of a country's interlocking set of institutions—a weakness that to a great extent reflects the incorporation of mainstream economists' notions of rational choice and equilibrium into the analysis. With a focus on 'rules of the game,' country institutions are presented as establishing equilibrium 'solutions' to coordination problems. Such an approach contrasts with that of historical institutionalists where the focus is on the shifting balances of power and resources and on how the multiple institutional processes at various levels interact in ways that often do not fit together in a coherent whole, creating opportunities for actors to trigger changes (Pierson and Skocpol 2002). Also, while a country systems approach is useful for highlighting broad country differences, it glosses over important differences within countries, especially concerning the extent to which the major institutional framework covers the diversity of forms of employment relationships and all groups of workers across labor market segments.

## 4.5 CONCLUSION

In this chapter we have explored the suitability of an economics framework for the study of HRM, considered the value of selected approaches that go some way towards integrating the two worlds of economics and HRM, and argued for the need to incorporate some of the rich empirical and theoretical insights derived from comparative institutional analysis of employment organization. The starting position of the mainstream economist is a set of assumptions that derive from methodological individualism, which do not immediately marry with the concerns of HRM and its focus on organizations and workforces. However, economists have a capacity to adapt and develop their methodology to move into fresh areas of research, and their entry into the world of HRM is no exception. With advances in ideas about incentive theory, several economists have presented new ideas about the workings of the firm, recasting it as 'an incentive system', drawing on a fast-growing literature on principal–agent problems of coordination and game theory (Alchian and Demsetz 1972; Holmstrom 1982; Holmstrom and Milgrom 1994). Such ideas form the bedrock of studies in the field of personnel economics, but while they may add a rich analytical flavor in addressing HRM issues, this field has developed through a one-sided integration and it is the field of HRM proper where the complex realities of the employment relationship are better recognized.

Various scholars have sought to develop a more integrated approach, but it is the studies by those starting from a non-mainstream economics background that appear most convincing. The lesson is that while economics is dominated by a so-called mainstream approach, it is large enough to be home to an important minority of economists who are sensitive to the limits of conventional analytical tools, and it is perhaps within the non-mainstream camp where future integration of HRM with economists' analytical techniques ought to begin.

We ended our chapter with a review of the contributions of the comparative study of employment organization to the understanding of HRM. It is through a comparative perspective that the importance of institutions becomes clear, not simply in shaping some fuzzy context to the workings of organizations, but in generating 'institutional signals' (to adapt the economists' terminology) to which firm strategy gravitates. Moreover, a focus on coordination problems enables these approaches to consider both the micro and macro consequences of alternative HRM practices; as we have argued in this chapter, the field of HRM has not adequately incorporated issues of national policy and national goals into an analysis of the organization. Within the field of HRM, an embracing of a comparative approach could take these types of analysis further. For example, it might consider how and under what institutional conditions varieties of HRM practices are possible. What are the potential disjunctures among national institutions and the spaces made available for progressive (or destructive) HRM practices? And how and in what ways do institutions shape the power relations between social actors in the redefining of HRM and working conditions?

# REFERENCES

ALCHIAN, A., and DEMSETZ, H. (1972). 'Production, Information Costs, and Economic Organisation.' *American Economic Review*, 62/5: 777–95.

AMABLE, B. (2003). *The Diversity of Modern Capitalism*. Oxford: Oxford University Press.

AOKI, M. (1994). 'The Contingent Governance of Teams: Analysis of Institutional Complementarity.' *International Economic Review*, 35/3: 657–76.

BARNEY, J. B. (1991). 'Firm Resources and Sustained Comparative Advantage.' *Journal of Management*, 17/ 1: 99–120.

BARON, J N , and KREPS, D. M. (1999) *Strategic Human Resources: Frameworks for General Managers*. New York: John Wiley and Sons.

BLOUNT, S. (1995). 'When Social Outcomes aren't Fair: The Effect of Causal Attributions on Preferences.' *Organisational Behaviour and Human Decision Processes*, 63/2: 131–44.

BOSWORTH, D., DAWKINS, P., and STROMBACK, T. (1996). *The Economics of the Labour Market*. Harlow: Addison Wesley Longman Ltd.

BOWLES, S. (1985). 'The Production Process in a Competitive Economy: Walrasian, Marxian and Neo-Hobbesian Models.' *American Economic Review*, 75/1: 16–36.

BOXALL, P. (1998). 'Achieving Competitive Advantage through Human Resource Strategy: Towards a Theory of Industry Dynamics.' *Human Resource Management Review*, 8/3: 265–88.

—— and PURCELL, J. (2003). *Strategy and Human Resource Management*. Basingstoke: Palgrave.

CAMERER, C. F. (1997). 'Progress in Behavioural Game Theory.' *Journal of Economic Perspectives*, 11/4: 167–088.

COASE, R. (1937). 'The Nature of the Firm.' *Economica*, November: 386–405.

CULPEPPER, P. D. (2001). 'Employers, Public Policy and the Politics of Decentralised Cooperation in Germany and France.' In Hall and Soskice (2001).

DOERINGER, P. B., and PIORE, M. J. (1971). *Internal Labour Markets and Manpower Analysis*. Lexington, Mass.: Heath.

GEORGE, E. (2003). 'External Solutions and Internal Problems: The Effects of Employment Externalisation on Internal Workers' Attitudes.' *Organization Science*, 14/4: 386–402.

GRIMSHAW, D. (2000). 'The Problem with Pay Flexibility: Changing Pay Practices in the UK Health Sector.' *International Journal of Human Resource Management*, 11/5: 943–66.

HAHN, F. (1991). 'The Next Hundred Years.' *Economic Journal*, 101/404/January: 47–50.

HALL, P., and SOSKICE, D. (eds.) (2001). *Varieties of Capitalism: The Institutional Foundations of Comparative Advantage*. Oxford: Oxford University Press.

HIRSCHMAN, A. O. (1970). *Exit, Voice and Loyalty*. Cambridge, Mass.: Harvard University Press.

HOLMSTROM, B. (1982). 'Moral Hazard in Teams.' *Bell Journal of Economics*, 13/2: 324–40.

HOLMSTROM, B., and MILGROM, P. (1994). 'The Firm as an Incentive System.' *American Economic Review*, 84/4: 972–91.

HUSELID, M. A. (1995). 'The Impact of Human Resource Management Practices on Turnover, Productivity, and Corporate Financial Performance.' *Academy of Management Journal*, 38/3: 635–72.

HYMAN, R. (1987). 'Strategy or Structure? Capital, Labour and Control.' *Work, Employment and Society*, 1/1: 25–55.

JACOBY, S. M. (1984). 'The Development of Internal Labour Markets in American Manufacturing firms.' In P. Osterman (ed.), *Internal Labour Markets*. Cambridge, Mass.: MIT Press.

JENSEN, M. C., and MECKLING, W. H. (1976). 'Theory of the Firm: Managerial Behavior, Agency Costs, and Capital Structure.' *Journal of Financial Economics*, 3/4: 305–60.

KAUFMAN, B. E. (2004). 'Toward an Integrative Theory of Human Resource Management.' In B. E. Kaufman (ed.), *Theoretical Perspectives on Work and the Employment Relationship*. Ithaca, NY: Cornell University Press.

KERR, C. (1954). 'The Balkanisation of Labor Markets.' In E. W. Bakke (ed.), *Labor Mobility and Economic Opportunity*. Cambridge, Mass.: MIT Press.

LAZEAR, E. (1998). *Personnel Economics for Managers*. New York: John Wiley and Sons.

—— (2000). 'The Future of Personnel Economics.' *Economic Journal*, 110/467: F611–39.

LEPAK, D., and SNELL, S. (1999). 'The Human Resource Architecture: Towards a Theory of Human Capital Allocation and Development.' *Academy of Management Review*, 24/1: 31–48.

LOGAN, M. S., FAUGHT, K., and GANSTER, D. C. (2004). 'Outsourcing a Satisfied and Committed Workforce: A Trucking Industry Case Study.' *International Journal of HRM*, 15/1: 147–62.

MACDUFFIE, J. P. (1995). 'Human Resource Bundles and Manufacturing Performance: Organizational Logic and Flexible Production Systems in the World Auto Industry.' *Industrial and Labor Relations Review*, 48: 197–221.

MARCH, J., and SIMON, H. (1958). *Organizations*. New York: Wiley.

MARCHINGTON, M., GRIMSHAW, D., RUBERY, J., and WILLMOTT, H. (eds.) (2005). *Fragmenting Work: Blurring Organisational Boundaries and Disordering Hierarchies*. Oxford: Oxford University Press.

MARSDEN, D. (1986). *The End of Economic Man? Custom and Competition in Labour Markets*. Brighton, Wheatsheaf Books.

—— (1999). *A Theory of Employment Systems: Micro-foundations of Societal Diversity*. Oxford: Oxford University Press.

—— and FRENCH, S. (1998). *What a Performance: Performance-Related Pay in the Public Services*. London: Centre for Economic Performance Special Report, London School of Economics.

—— and RICHARDSON, R. (1994). 'Performing for Pay? The Effects of "Merit Pay" on Motivation in a Public Service.' *British Journal of Industrial Relations*, 32/2: 243–62.

—— and RYAN, P. (1990). 'Institutional Aspects of Youth Employment and Training Policy in Britain.' *British Journal of Industrial Relations*, 28/3: 351–70.

MASON, G. (2000). 'Production Supervisors in Britain, Germany and the United States: Back from the Dead Again?' *Work, Employment and Society*, 14/4: 625–45.

MILGROM, P., and ROBERTS, J. (1992). *Economics, Organization and Management*. Englewood Cliffs, NJ: Prentice-Hall.

O'REILLY, C. A., and PFEFFER, J. (2000). *Hidden Value: How Great Companies Achieve Extraordinary Results with Extraordinary People*. Boston: Harvard Business School Press.

PENROSE, E. (1995). *The Theory of the Growth of the Firm*, 3rd edn. Oxford: Oxford University Press.

PIERSON, P., and SKOCPOL, T. (2002). 'Historical Institutionalism in Contemporary Political Science.' In I. Katznelson and H. Milner (eds.), *Political Science: The State of the Discipline*. New York: Norton.

PORTER, M. (1990). *The Competitive Advantage of Nations*. New York: Free Press.

PRIEM, R., and BUTLER, J. (2001). 'Is the Resource-Based "View" a Useful Perspective for Strategic Management Research?' *Academy of Management Review*, 26/1: 22–40.

PURCELL, J. (1999). 'The Search for "Best Practice" and "Best Fit": Chimera or Cul-de-sac?' *Human Resource Management Journal*, 9/3: 26–41.

RUBERY, J. (1978). 'Structured Labour Markets, Worker Organisation and Low Pay.' *Cambridge Journal of Economics*, 2/1: 17–36.

—— (1995). 'Performance-Related Pay and the Prospects for Gender Pay Equity.' *Journal of Management Studies*, 32/5: 637–54.

SEN, A. (1988). *On Ethics and Economics* Oxford: Basil Blackwell.

SIMON, H. (1979). *Models of Thought*. New Haven: Yale University Press.

STEEDMAN, H., and WAGNER, K. (1989). 'Productivity, Machinery and Skills: Clothing Manufacture in Britain and Germany.' *National Institute Economic Review*, May: 40–57.

TEECE, D. J. (2002). 'Dynamic Capabilities.' In W. Lazonick (ed.), *The Handbook of Economics*. London: Thomson.

WILKINSON, F. (1981). *The Dynamics of Labour Market Segmentation*. London: Academic Press.

WILLIAMSON, O. (1975). *Markets and Hierarchies*. New York: Free Press.

WRIGHT, P., and BREWSTER, C. (2003). 'Learning from Diversity: HRM is not Lycra.' *International Journal of Human Resource Management*, 14/8: 1299–307.

—— and SNELL, S. (1998). 'Toward a Unifying Framework for Exploring Fit and Flexibility in Strategic Human Resource Management.' *Academy of Management Review*, 23/4: 756–72.

CHAPTER 5

# STRATEGIC MANAGEMENT AND HRM

MATHEW R. ALLEN

PATRICK WRIGHT

## 5.1 INTRODUCTION

IT has been said that the most important assets of any business walk out the door at the end of each day. Indeed, people and the management of people are increasingly seen as key elements of competitive advantage (Boxall and Purcell 2003; Pfeffer 1998; Gratton et al. 2000). Spurred on by increasing competition, fast-paced technological change, globalization, and other factors, businesses are seeking to understand how one of the last truly competitive resources, their human resources, can be managed for competitive advantage.

This idea that the human resources of a firm can play a strategic role in the success of an organization has led to the formation of a field of research often referred to as strategic human resource management (SHRM). This relatively young field represents an intersection of the strategic management and human resource management (HRM) literatures (Boxall 1998; Boxall and Purcell 2000). Wright and McMahan (1992) defined strategic human resource management as 'the pattern of planned human resource deployments and activities intended to enable the firm to achieve its goals' (1992: 298).

The purpose of this chapter is to discuss this intersection between Strategic Management and HRM, what we know, and future directions for SHRM research. We will begin by briefly discussing the concept of strategy and the popularization of the resource-based view (RBV) of the firm. Next we will address its role in creating the link between HRM and Strategic Management including key questions that the RBV has raised in relation to SHRM. We will then examine the current state of affairs in SHRM; the progress made, and key questions and concerns occupying the attention of SHRM researchers. Finally, we will conclude with our views on future directions for SHRM research.

# 5.2 STRATEGY AND THE RESOURCE-BASED VIEW OF THE FIRM

The field of strategy focuses on how firms can position themselves to compete, and its popularity began increasing exponentially in the mid-1980s with two books. First, Peters and Waterman's (1982) *In Search of Excellence* provided a practitioner-oriented analysis of excellent companies and the common threads that united them. However, Porter's (1980) *Competitive Strategy* presented a more academically based analysis of strategy, but in a way that practitioners/executives quickly gravitated toward. This Industrial/Organization Economics-based analysis primarily focused on industry characteristics, in particular the five forces of barriers to entry, power of buyers, power of suppliers, substitutes, and competitive rivalry as the determinants of industry profitability. While this analysis did propose four generic strategies (cost, differentiation, focus, and 'stuck in the middle'), the bulk of the analysis focused on external factors that determined company profitability. This framework seemed to dominate strategic management thinking of the early 1980s.

However, with the advent of the resource-based view of the firm (Barney 1991; Wernerfelt 1984), strategic management research moved to a more internal focus. Rather than simply developing competitive strategies to address the environment, the resource-based view suggested that firms should look inward to their resources, both physical and intellectual, for sources of competitive advantage. Though others had addressed the concept of the RBV previously, Barney (1991) specifically explicated how firm resources contribute to the sustained competitive advantage of the firm. He suggested that resources that are valuable, rare, inimitable, and non-substitutable will lead to competitive advantage.

Value in this context is defined as resources either exploiting opportunities or neutralizing threats to the organization and rarity is defined as being a resource that is not currently available to a large number of the organization's current or future competitors (Barney 1991). Inimitability refers to the fact it is difficult for other firms to copy or otherwise reproduce the resources for their own use. Finally, non-substitutability means that other resources cannot be used by competitors in order to replicate the benefit (Barney 1991). When all four of these conditions are met, it is said that the firm or organization possess resources which can potentially lead to a sustained competitive advantage over time.

The resource-based view has become almost the assumed paradigm within strategic management research (Barney and Wright 2001). It has been the basic theoretical foundation from which much of the current strategic management research regarding knowledge-based views of the firm (Grant 1996), human capital (Hitt et al. 2001), and dynamic capabilities (Teece et al. 1997) are derived. In fact, Priem and Butler (2001*a*) mapped RBV studies against eighteen strategy research topics, demonstrating the breadth of its diffusion within the strategic management domain. More importantly from the standpoint of this chapter, the resource-based view has become the guiding paradigm on which virtually all strategic HRM research is based (Wright et al. 2001).

In spite of the wide acceptance of the RBV, it is not without criticism. Priem and Butler (2001*a*, 2001*b*) have leveled the most cogent critique to date suggesting that the RBV does not truly constitute a theory. Their argument focuses primarily on two basic issues. First, they suggest that the RBV is basically tautological in its definition of key constructs. They note that Barney's statement that 'if a firm's valuable resources are absolutely unique among a set of competing and potentially competing firms, those resources will generate at least a competitive advantage (Barney 2001: 102)' essentially requires definitional dependence. In other words, without definitional dependence (i.e. 'valuable resources') the diametrical statement—that unique firms possess competitive advantages—does not logically follow.

Their second major criticism of the RBV as a 'theory' focuses on the inability to test it (Priem and Butler 2001*b*). They note the necessity condition of 'falsifiability' for a theory. In other words, in order for a set of stated relationships to constitute a theory, the relationships must be able to be measured and tested in a way that allows for the theory to be found to be false. This relates directly to the tautology criticism, but brings the debate into the empirical realm.

In spite of these criticisms, even the critics agree that the impact of the RBV on strategic management research has been significant and that the effort to focus on the internal aspects of the organization in explaining competitive advantage has been a useful one (Priem and Butler 2001*b*). While the debate might continue as to the theoretical implications of the RBV for strategic management research, it is clear that it has made a significant contribution to Strategic Management and, more specifically, SHRM research (Wright et al. 2001).

# 5.3 A Brief History of Strategic HRM

Wright and McMahan's (1992) definition of strategic human resource management illustrates that the major focus of the field should be on aligning HR with firm strategies. Jim Walker's (1980) classic book *Human Resource Planning* was one of the first to directly suggest considering a firm's business strategy when developing a human resource plan. Devanna et al.'s (1981) article 'Human Resources Management: A Strategic Perspective' added to the foundation. These attempts tended to take an existing strategy typology (e.g. Miles et al.'s (1978) prospectors, analysts, and defenders) and delineate the kinds of HRM practices that should be associated with each strategy. These attempts to tie HRM to strategy have been referred to as 'vertical alignment' (Wright and McMahan 1992).

Beer et al. (1984) introduced an alternative to the individual HR subfunction framework for HR strategy. They argued that viewing HRM as separate HR subfunctions was a product of the historical development of HRM and current views of HR departments. They proposed a more generalist approach to viewing HRM with the focus on the entire HR system rather than single HR practices. This led to a focus on how the different HR subfunctions could be aligned and work together to accomplish the goals of HRM and a more macro view of HRM as whole rather than individual functions. This alignment of HR functions with each other is often referred to as 'horizontal alignment' (see this Handbook, Chapter 19).

The combination of both vertical and horizontal alignment was a significant step in explaining how HRM could contribute to the accomplishment of strategic goals. However, given the external focus of the strategic management literature at that time, HR was seen to play only a secondary role in the accomplishment of strategy with an emphasis on the role that HRM played in strategy implementation, but not strategy formulation. Lengnick-Hall and Lengnick-Hall (1988) stated, 'strategic human resource management models emphasize implementation over strategy formulation. Human resources are considered means, not part of generating or selecting strategic objectives. Rarely are human resources seen as a strategic capacity from which competitive choices should be derived' (1988: 456). A shift in strategic management thinking would be required to change that perception and open the door for further development of the SHRM literature.

The diffusion of the resource-based view into the Strategic HRM literature spurred this paradigmatic shift in the view of the link between strategy and HRM. Because the resource-based view proposes that firm competitive advantage comes from the internal resources that it possesses (Wernerfelt 1984; Barney 1991), the RBV provided a legitimate foundation upon which HRM researchers could argue that people and the human resources of a firm could in fact contribute to firm-level performance and influence strategy formulation.

This resulted in a number of efforts to conceptually or theoretically tie strategic HRM to the resource-based view. For instance, Wright et al. (1994) suggested that while HR practices might be easily imitated, the human capital pool of an organization might constitute a source of sustainable competitive advantage. Lado and Wilson (1994) argued that HR practices combined into an overall HR system can be valuable, unique, and difficult to imitate, thus constituting a resource meeting the conditions necessary for sustained competitive advantage. Boxall (1996, 1998) proposed a distinction between human resource advantage (advantage stemming from a superior human capital pool) and organizational process advantage (advantage stemming from superior processes for managing human capital).

The resource-based view also provided the theoretical rationale for empirical studies of how HR practices might impact firm success. One of the early empirical studies of this relationship was carried out by Arthur (1994). Using a sample of steel mini-mills, he found that a specific set of HR practices was significantly related to firm performance in the form of lower scrap rates and lower turnover. Huselid (1995), in his landmark study, demonstrated that the use of a set of thirteen HRM practices representing a 'high-performance work system' was significantly and positively related to lower turnover, and higher profits, sales, and market value for the firms studied. In a similar study, MacDuffie (1995), using data from automobile manufacturing plants, demon- strated that different bundles of HR practices led to higher performance, furthering the argument that the integrated HR system, rather than individual HR practices, leads to higher performance. Delery and Doty (1996) similarly demonstrated the impact of HR practices on firm performance among a sample of banks.

This vein of research quickly expanded in the USA (e.g. Batt 1999; Huselid et al. 1997; Youndt et al. 1996), the UK (e.g. Brewster 1999; Guest 2001; Guest et al. 2003; Tyson 1997), elsewhere in Europe (e.g. d'Arcimoles 1997; Lahteenmaki et al. 1998; Rodriguez and Ventura 2003), and Asia (e.g. Bae and Lawler 2000; Lee and Chee 1996; Lee and Miller 1999), as well as in multinational corporations operating in multiple international environments (Brewster et al. 2005).

In sum, the RBV, with its focus on the internal resources possessed by a firm, has given the field a theoretical understanding of why human resources systems might lead to sustainable competitive advantage and provided the spark to generate empirical research in this vein (Guest 2001; Paauwe and Boselie 2005; Wright et al. 2005).

# 5.4 KEY QUESTIONS RAISED BY THE APPLICATION OF RBV TO SHRM

In spite of the significant amount of research demonstrating a link between HRM practices and firm performance, there are several key questions regarding the RBV and its implications for SHRM research that remain unanswered. First, there is some question as to whether current research on HRM and performance is truly testing the RBV. Second, there is still a general lack of understanding around the concept of fit, and its role in the link between strategy and HRM. Third, there are still unanswered questions regarding HRM and whether or not HRM defined as systems of HR practices truly constitutes a resource under the conditions outlined by Barney (1991) and, specifically, whether those resources are truly sustainable over time. Finally, there are several measurement and methodological issues that, while not within the direct scope of this chapter, are worth mentioning as they are pertinent to our discussion of this intersection between Strategic Management and HRM research.

## 5.4.1 Testing of the RBV within SHRM

While the SHRM research just discussed has used the RBV as a basis for the assertion that HRM contributes to performance, it has not actually tested the theory that was presented in Barney's (1991) article (Wright et al. 2001). Most of this research has taken a similar view on how HR practices can lead to firm performance. The model generally argues that HRM in the form of HR practices directly impacts the employees either by increasing human capital or motivation or both. This in turn will have an impact on operational outcomes such as quality, customer service, turnover, or other operational-level outcomes. These operational outcomes will in turn impact firm-level outcomes such as financial performance in the form of revenues, profits or other firm-level measures of performance (Dyer 1984).

In a similar vein, Wright et al. (2001) point out that there are three important components of HRM that constitute a resource for the firm which are influenced by the HR practices or HR system. First, there is the human capital pool comprised of the stock of employee knowledge, skills, motivation, and behaviors. HR practices can help build the knowledge and skill base as well as elicit relevant behavior.

Second, there is the flow of human capital through the firm. This reflects the movement of people (with their individual knowledge, skills, and abilities) as well as knowledge itself. HR practices can certainly influence the movement of people. However, more importantly, the types of reward systems, culture, and other aspects of HRM influence the extent to which employees are willing to create, share, and apply knowledge internally.

Third, the dynamic processes through which organizations change and/or renew themselves constitute the third area illustrating the link between HRM and the resource-based view of the firm. HR practices are the primary levers through which the firm can change the pool of human capital as well as attempt to change the employee behaviors that lead to organizational success.

There appears to be a general consensus among SHRM researchers around the general model of the HR to performance relationship and the role of HR practices, the human capital pool, and employee motivation and behaviors as discussed by Dyer (1984) and others. The implications of this for RBV and SHRM research is that while separate components of the full HRM to performance model have been tested such as HR practices (Huselid 1995; MacDuffie 1995) and human capital (Richard 2001; Wright et al. 1995), a full test of the causal model through which HRM impacts performance has not (Wright et al. 2005; Wright et al. 2001; Boxall 1998). Current research has established an empirical relationship between HR practices and firm performance, but more remains to be done. By testing the full model, including the additional components of the human capital pool and employee relationships and behaviors, a more complete test of the underlying assumptions of the RBV could be established, thus adding credibility to the theoretical model of the relationship between HRM and performance.

## 5.4.2 Fit and the Resource-based View of the Firm

In the Priem and Butler (2001a) critique of the RBV, one of the points brought up as a theoretical weakness of the RBV is lack of definition around the boundaries or contexts in which it will hold. They point out that 'relative to other strategy theories ... little effort to establish the appropriate contexts for the RBV has been apparent' (2001a: 32). The notion of context has been an important issue in the study of SHRM (Delery and Doty 1996; Boxall and Purcell 2000). Most often referred to as contingencies (or the idea of fit), contextual arguments center on the idea that the role that HRM plays in firm performance is contingent on some other variable. We break our discussion of fit into the role of human capital and HR practices.

### 5.4.2.1 *Human Capital and Fit*

The most often cited perspective for explaining contingency relationships in SHRM is the behavioral perspective (Jackson et al. 1989) which posits that different firm strategies (other contingencies could be inserted as well) require different kinds of behaviors from employees. Consequently, the success of these strategies is dependent at least in part on the ability of the firm to elicit these behaviors from its employees (Cappelli and Singh 1992; Wright and Snell 1998).

Going back to the distinction between human capital skills and employee behavior, Wright and Snell (1998) noted that skills and abilities tend to be necessary but not sufficient conditions for employee behavior. Consequently, any fit to firm strategy must first consider the kinds of employee behavior (e.g. experimentation and discovery) required to successfully execute the strategy (e.g. focused on offering innovative products), and the kinds of skills necessary to exhibit those behaviors (e.g. scientific knowledge). Obviously, the workforce at Nordstrom's (an upscale retailer) is quite different from the workforce at Wal-Mart (a discount retailer). Thus, the resource-based application to SHRM requires focusing on a fit between the skills and behaviors of employees that are best suited to the firm's strategy (Wright et al. 1995).

While this idea of fit focuses on across-firm variance in the workforce, Lepak and Snell (1999) developed a framework that simultaneously addresses variation across firms and variations in HR systems within firms (see this Handbook, Chapter 11). Their model of 'human resource architecture' posits that the skills of individuals or jobs within a firm can be placed along two dimensions: value (to the firm's strategy) and uniqueness. Their framework demonstrates how different jobs within firms may need to be managed differently, but it also helps to explain differences across firms. For instance, within Wal-Mart, those in charge of logistics have extremely valuable and unique skills, much more so than the average sales associate. On the other hand, at Nordstrom's, because customer service is important, sales associate skills are more critical to the strategy than those of the logistics employees.

### 5.4.2.2  HR Practices and Fit

The theoretical assumption that the skills and behaviors of employees must fit the strategic needs of the firm in order for the workforce to be a source of competitive advantage leads to the exploration of how HR practices might also need to achieve some form of fit. With regard to vertical fit, as noted previously, business strategies require different skills and behaviors from employees. Because HR practices are generally the levers through which the firm manages these different skills and behaviors, one would expect to see different practices associated with different strategies. For instance, one would expect that firms focused on low cost might not pay the same level of wages and benefits as firms focused on innovation or customer service.

Horizontal fit refers to a fit between HR practices to ensure that the individual HR practices are set up in such a way that they support each other (Boxall and Purcell 2003; Baird and Meshoulam 1988; Delery 1998). An example of this would be a selection process that focuses on finding team players and a compensation system that focuses on team-based rewards. Theoretically, the rationale for horizontal fit suggests that (*a*) complementary bundles of HR practices can be redundantly reinforcing the development of certain skills and behaviors resulting in a higher likelihood that they will occur and (*b*) conflicting practices can send mixed signals to employees regarding necessary skills and behaviors that reduce the probability that they will be exhibited (Becker and Huselid 1998). There appears to be some agreement in the literature that both types of fit are necessary for optimal impact of HRM on performance (Baird and Meshoulam 1988; Delery 1998; Delery and Doty 1996; Boxall and Purcell 2003), but not necessarily empirical support for these types of fit (see this Handbook, Chapter 27; Wright and Sherman 1999).

### 5.4.2.3 *Potential Pitfalls of Fit*

The idea of fit, whether it be vertical or horizontal, raises two important questions for SHRM researchers. The first question focuses on empirical support for the idea of fit. Second, even if fit has positive consequences in the short term, does fitting HRM practices with strategy or other contingent variables universally lead to positive results? That is, are there negative implications of fit?

As previously discussed, numerous researchers have argued for fitting HRM to contingent variables. However, the efficacy of fit has not received much empirical support (Paauwe 2004; Wright and Sherman 1999). Huselid's (1995) landmark study sought to test the fit hypothesis using a variety of conceptualizations of fit, yet found little support. Similarly, Delery and Doty (1996) only found limited support across a number of fit tests. The lack of empirical support may largely be due to focusing only on a fit between generic HRM practices and strategy, rather than the outcomes, or products (Wright 1998), of the HRM practices (skills, behaviors, etc.). Thus, it seems that it may be too early to draw any definite conclusions about the validity of the fit hypothesis.

However, while fit between HRM practices and various contingency variables might enhance the ability of HRM to contribute to firm performance, there is also the possibility that a tight fit between HRM and strategy may inhibit the ability of the firm to remain flexible enough to adapt to changing circumstances. Firms are increasingly required to adapt to environments that are constantly changing, both within and outside the firm. A tight fit may appear to be desirable but during times of transition and/or change a lack of fit might make adaptation and change more efficient (Lengnick-Hall and Lengnick-Hall 1988). Wright and Snell (1998) developed a framework in which HRM contributes to fit and flexibility simultaneously without conflict between the two, but this framework has yet to be tested and the question remains as to when and where fit might be more or less appropriate.

The second question raised by contextual issues surrounding SHRM and the idea of fit is related to the efficacy of fit. Regardless of whether or not fit can have a positive effect on organizational outcomes, there is still some question as to whether or not true fit with key contingencies is feasible. Large organizations operate in complex environments, often across multiple products, industries, and geographies. This complexity leads to questions regarding the ability of the firm to fit HRM practices to all of these diverse and complex circumstances (Boxall and Purcell 2003).

In addition, Boxall and Purcell (2003) argue that there are competing ideals within a business that require trade-offs in fit. They describe fit as 'a process that involves some tension among competing objectives in management and inevitably implies tensions among competing interests' (2003: 188). A simple example of these tensions can be seen in attempting to fit a strategy of commitment to employees with a hostile or extremely competitive operating environment. A firm with a strategic commitment to the well-being of employees operating in an economic downturn or time of increased competition may be forced to make choices between commitment to employees and a need for restructuring, lay-offs, or other non-friendly actions toward employees in order to stay solvent. In these situations, compromises will have to be made on either the fit with the strategy or the fit with the environment or both, raising the question again as to whether or not a true fit with contingencies is feasible.

These questions regarding the ability to achieve fit and the desirability of achieving fit do not diminish the importance of understanding contextual issues in SHRM research. Understanding the contextual issues surrounding HRM and its impact on performance remains critical. In spite of the interest in the role of contextual issues and fit in SHRM, findings in support of contingency relationships have been mixed (Wright and Sherman 1999). Much of this criticism could be due to ineffective methods used in the measurement of HRM or the contingency and performance variables studied or that the correct contingencies have not yet been studied (Becker and Gerhart 1996; Rogers and Wright 1998; Wright and Sherman 1999). In addition, Boxall and Purcell (2000) have argued that more complex and comprehensive models of contingency relationships are needed in order to understand the impact of context on the HRM to performance relationship. Regardless of the reasoning, it is clear that the impact of context on this important relationship is not yet completely understood and more research is needed to understand the role of context, as well as questions surrounding models of fit in SHRM research.

## 5.4.3 HRM Practices and Sustainable Competitive Advantage

Another issue that has been raised by the RBV and its application to SHRM research is the sustainability of HRM as a competitive advantage. Whether one focuses on bundles of HR practices as an HR system, the human capital pool, or employee relationships and behaviors, there remains the question as to whether HRM as a resource meets the inimitability and non-substitutability conditions that are required in the RBV for sustained competitive advantage (Barney 1991).

According to Barney (1991), there are three general reasons why firm resources would be difficult to imitate: the resources are created and formed under unique historical conditions, the resources are causally ambiguous, or the resources are socially complex.

Labeled as path dependency by Becker and Gerhart (1996), the unique historical conditions under which HRM is formed in individual firms may make its under-standing and replication extremely difficult, if not impossible. HR systems are developed over time and the complex history involved in their development makes them difficult to replicate. The development and implementation of a single HR practice such as a variable pay system takes place over time including time to solicit management input and buy-in, work out discrepancies, and align the practice with current strategies as well as firm culture and needs. The end result is a practice that reflects the philosophies and culture of the firm and its management, created to solve the specific needs of the company. Compound that single HR practice with a whole system of practices each with its own history and evolution specific to a particular firm, its philosophies, and current situation and you have an HR system that cannot be bought or easily replicated without a significant investment of both time and financial resources.

Causal ambiguity implies that the exact manner in which human resource management contributes to the competitive advantage of the firm is either un-known or sufficiently ambiguous so as to be difficult or impossible to imitate. According to Becker and Gerhart (1996), the ability to replicate a successful HR system would require an understanding of how all of the elements of this complex system interact and in turn impact the performance of an organization. Given the previous discussion of the basic HRM to performance model and the manner in which it is expected that HRM contributes to firm performance, it is difficult to imagine how the intricate interplay among various HR practices, human capital and employee behaviors, employee outcomes, operational outcomes and firm-level outcomes, could be understood by a competitor in a meaningful way.

Finally, Barney (1991) points out that competitors will find it difficult to replicate a competitive advantage based on complex social phenomena. Given the nature of HRM and its direct relation to employees, almost every aspect of the HR system, the human capital, and especially the employee behavior and relationships has a social component. The way in which HR practices are communicated and implemented among different departments and parts of the organization is influenced by the various social relationships involved; top management to general managers, general managers to department heads or managers, and those managers to employees as well as interactions between departments and employees. The complexity of the social relationships in the case of HRM makes it difficult for competitors to imitate it.

Finally, for a resource to constitute a source of sustainable competitive advantage it must be non-substitutable. This implies that competitors should not be able to use a different set of resources in order to achieve similar results (Barney 1991). This concept has not yet been tested, but could provide for interesting research in the area of contextual factors and SHRM.

If, in fact, it is found that a particular set of HR practices is positively related to performance in a given context, then a follow-on question to that which would get at the substitutability question might be whether or not there is another set of HR practices for which the results are similar. This could lead to discussions about strategic configurations of HR practices rather than universal high-performance work systems that have dominated past research (Delery and Doty 1996). Regardless of whether there is one or many ways to achieve similar results in different contextual situations, the testing of these possibilities would lead to an increased understanding of the relationship between the RBV and SHRM research and the sustainability of HRM as a strategic resource.

### 5.4.4 Measurement and Methodological Issues

In addition to key questions surrounding the RBV and SHRM research, there are also several measurement and methodological issues which have hindered our ability to better understand the relationship between strategy and HRM. Measurement issues relating to the HRM, competitive advantage and key control variables have made the comparison of results across studies and interpretation of findings difficult (Rogers and Wright 1998; Dyer and Reeves 1995). In addition, there are questions around the appropriate level of analysis within the firm at which to test these relationships as well as issues related to the mixing of variables measured at different levels of analysis (Rogers and Wright 1998; Becker and Gerhart 1996). Finally, as was pointed out, the majority of research to date has focused on the relationship between HR systems and firm-level performance and, while the findings indicate a positive relationship, there is insufficient evidence at this point to be able to infer that the relationship is causal (Wright et al. 2005). A full discussion of these issues is beyond the scope of this chapter and a more thorough discussion may be found in other chapters in this text (see particularly Chapters 26 and 27), but it is important to note in discussing key questions in SHRM that they exist and need to be addressed or at least considered in future research.

## 5.5 FUTURE DIRECTIONS

Research on SHRM management over the past decade has made significant progress in developing our understanding of the role that HRM plays in firm performance. The field now has a significant foundation upon which to build future research. In our opinion, future research should focus on both answering key questions that remain in understanding the relationship between HRM and performance and expanding or broadening what is considered SHRM. Such extension would encompass both other resources and other theories currently studied in strategic management research.

### 5.5.1 Key Unanswered Questions

The previous portion of the chapter pointed out several key questions that have been raised as a result of the application of the RBV to SHRM research that are not yet answered. First, research that directly tests the concepts outlined in the RBV has not been done (Priem and Butler 2001*a*). Thus future research should focus on testing the concepts of the RBV by testing the full model through which HRM leads to competitive advantage or firm performance. Do HR practices impact the human capital pool and the relationships and behaviors of the employees and do those outcomes in turn impact both operational and firm-level performance? Answering these questions by testing the full causal model would be a significant contribution to our understanding of the strategic nature of HRM. In essence, this reflects the 'black box process' that Priem and Butler (2001*a*) argued must be addressed by RBV theorists and researchers.

Second, future research should focus on understanding the contextual questions surrounding the HRM to performance relationship. Mixed results in past contextual research are not reason enough to abandon the question all together. It is highly likely that HRM matters more or less in certain situations or under certain conditions. Efforts should be made to continue to test established models of HRM in new and unique situations. In addition, more thorough tests of moderating variables in the HRM to performance relationship should be tested. Given the complexity involved in the measurement and testing of these relationships and the mixed results of past research in this area it is likely that researchers will need to seek out contexts with reduced complexity such as departments within large organizations or small businesses where reduced complexity will provide more meaningful measures of potential moderating variables and more meaningful tests of the moderating relationships can be performed.

Another step that needs to be taken in understanding the role of context in the HRM to performance relationship is to move away from universal-type models of HRM such as high-performance work systems and high-involvement work systems and develop and test different configurations of HR practices that might apply to specific situations. In doing this, researchers will be able to better understand the specific bundles or HR practices that are applicable or fit with different types of organizations or situations, thus making a significant contribution to our understanding of the types of HRM that will matter in a given situation.

## 5.5.2  Expanding the Role of SHRM

Future research in SHRM should focus on conceptually expanding what is considered to be the role of SHRM. Historically, SHRM has been viewed as the interface between HRM and strategic management (Boxall 1996) with the focus of much research being on understanding how the HRM function (namely HRM practices) can be strategically aligned so as to contribute directly to competitive advantage. This implies a concern with how HR practices can contribute to strategy implementation without addressing the larger question of how HRM can contribute or play a role in strategy formulation (Lengnick-Hall and Lengnick-Hall 1988).

Wright et al. (2001) argued that it is the human capital (the knowledge skills and abilities of the human resources) as well as the relationships and motivation of the employees that leads to competitive advantage. The purpose of HR practices is to develop or acquire this human capital and influence the relationships and behaviors of the employees so that they can contribute to the strategic goals of the firm. Future research should examine human capital and the social interactions and motivations of the human element within a firm (Snell et al. 2001), not only as independent variables but also as mediating and dependent variables. A focus in this area will bring the field more in line with contemporary views in strategic management. Research in this area will also help us to get beyond questions regarding how HR practices can facilitate the strategic goals of a firm and begin to understand how organizations can understand the resources found in their human element and use that understanding to influence or even drive their decisions about their strategic direction. For instance, IBM's strong HR processes/competencies led it into the business of offering outsourced HR services. This was an internal resource that was extended into a new product line, and illustrates how an understanding of such resources can influence strategic direction.

Along these same lines, another way to break away from this notion of HRM as a facilitator of the strategic direction of the firm is by focusing on some of the resources currently salient to strategic management researchers. In their review of the RBV and SHRM relationship, Wright et al. (2001) argue that the RBV created a link between HRM and strategic management research and that as a result of this link the two fields were converging. Because of this convergence, the potential impact of SHRM research on mainstream strategy issues is tremendous. Increasingly, strategy researchers are focusing on knowledge and knowledge-based resources (Argote et al. 2000; Grant 1996), human capital (Hitt et al. 2001), social capital (Inkpen and Tsang 2005; McFadyen and Cannella 2004), capabilities (Dutta et al. 2005), and dynamic capabilities (Teece et al. 1997), as critical resources that lead to organizational success. While HRM practices strongly influence these resources, the SHRM literature seems almost devoid of empirical attention to them. Only recently have researchers begun to explore these issues (Kinnie et al.

2005; Thompson and Heron 2005). Additional research in these areas would provide tremendous synergy between HRM and strategy.

In addition, alternative theories such as 'learning organizations' (Fiol and Lyles 1985; Fisher and White 2000), real options theory (McGrath 1997; Trigeorgis 1996), and institutional theory (Meyer and Rowan 1977) can be combined with SHRM research to enhance our understanding of the strategic nature of HRM. For instance, Bhattacharya and Wright (2005) showed how real options theory can be applied to understanding flexibility in SHRM. In addition, Paauwe and Boselie (Chapter 9) provide a detailed analysis of how institutional theory can better inform SHRM research. The use of these in addressing questions in SHRM research will provide new lenses through which researchers are able to view the HRM to performance relationship, potentially providing new insights and ideas that will further our understanding of SHRM.

# 5.6 Conclusion

While the field of strategic HRM is relatively young, significant progress has been made at a rapid pace. Researchers have provided great theoretical and empirical advancements in a period of just over twenty-five years. Much of this progress is the result of the RBV and its emphasis on the internal resources of the firm as a source of sustainable competitive advantage. The RBV and its application to SHRM research created an important link between strategic management and HRM research. Its application has been followed by a significant amount of research using the RBV as a basis for assertions about the strategic nature of HRM.

However, the link between HRM and strategic management can be strengthened by breaking away from the focus on HR practices. Other key resources currently being researched in strategic management have the potential to be directly influenced by HRM, but their coverage by SHRM researchers has been minimal, leaving a tremendous opportunity for future research in this area. In addition to this, new theories relevant to strategic management have yet to be combined with SHRM research, leaving potential for additional contributions to our understanding of the intersection between strategic management and HRM.

## References

Argote, L., Ingram, P., Levine, J. M., and Moreland, R. L. (2000). 'Knowledge Transfer in Organizations: Learning from the Experience of Others.' *Organizational Behavior & Human Decision Processes*, 82/1: 1–8.

ARTHUR, J. B. (1994). 'Effects of Human Resource Systems on Manufacturing Performance and Turnover.' *Academy of Management Journal*, 37/3: 670–87.

BAE, J., and LAWLER, J. J. (2000). 'Organizational and HRM Strategies in Korea: Impact on Firm Performance in an Emerging Economy.' *Academy of Management Journal*, 43/3: 502–17.

BAIRD, L., and MESHOULAM, I. (1988). 'Managing Two Fits of Strategic Human Resource Management.' *Academy of Management Review*, 13/1: 116–28.

BARNEY, J. (1991). 'Firm Resources and Sustained Competitive Advantage.' *Journal of Management*, 17/1: 99–120.

—— and WRIGHT, P. (1998). 'On Becoming a Strategic Partner: Examming the Role of Human Resources in Gaining Competitive Advantage.' *Human Resource Management Journal*, 37/1: 31–46.

—— (2001). 'Is the Resource-Based "View" a Useful Perspective for Strategic Management Research? Yes.' *Academy of Management Review*, 26/1: 41.

BATT, R. (1999). 'Work Organization, Technology, and Performance in Customer Service and Sales.' *Industrial & Labor Relations Review*, 52/4: 539–64.

BECKER, B., and GERHART, B. (1996). 'The Impact of Human Resource Management on Organizational Performance: Progress and Prospects.' *Academy of Management Journal*, 39/4: 779–801.

—— and HUSELID, M. A. (1998). 'High Performance Work Systems and Firm Performance: A Synthesis of Research and Managerial Applications.' *Research in Personnel and Human Resources Management*, 16:53–101.

BEER, M., SPECTOR, M., LAWRENCE, P. R., MILLS, D. Q., and WALTON, R. E. (1984). *Managing Human Assets*. New York: Free Press.

BHATTACHARYA, M., and WRIGHT, P. (2005). 'Managing Human Assets in an Uncertain World: Applying Real Options Theory to HRM.' *International Journal of Human Resource Management* 16: 929–48.

BOXALL, P. (1996). 'The Strategic HRM Debate and the Resource-Based View of the Firm.' *Human Resource Management Journal*, 6: 59–75.

—— (1998). 'Achieving Competitive Advantage through Human Resource Strategy: Towards a Theory of Industry Dynamics.' *Human Resource Management Review*, 8/3: 265–88.

—— and PURCELL, J. (2000). 'Strategic Human Resource Management: Where have we Come from and Where should we be Going?' *International Journal of Management Reviews*, 2/2: 183–203.

—— —— (2003). *Strategy and Human Resource Management*. New York: Palgrave Macmillan.

BREWSTER, C. (1999). 'Different Paradigms in Strategic HRM: Questions Raised by Comparative Research.' In P. Wright, L. Dyer, J. Boudreau, and G. Milkovich (eds.), *Research in Personnel and Human Resource Management: Strategic HRM in the 21st Century*, Supplement 4. Greenwich, Conn.: JAI Press.

—— SPARROW, P., and HARRIS, H. (2005). 'Towards a New Model of Globalizing HRM.' *International Journal of Human Resource Management*, 16: 953–74.

CAPELLI, P., and SINGH, H. (1992). 'Integrating Strategic Human Resources and Strategic Management.' In D. Lewin, O. S. Mitchell, and P. D. Sherer (eds.), *Research Frontiers in Industrial Relations and Human Resources*. Madison: IRRA.

COLLINS, C. J., and CLARK, K. D. (2003). 'Strategic Human Resource Practices, Top Management Team Social Networks, and Firm Performance: The Role of Human

Resource Practices in Creating Organizational Competitive Advantage.' *Academy of Management Journal*, 46/6: 740–51.

D'ARCIMOLES, C. (1997). 'Human Resource Policies and Company Performance: A Quantitative Approach Using Longitudinal Data.' *Organization Studies (Walter De Gruyter GmbH & Co.KG.)*, 18/5: 857–74.

DELERY, J. E. (1998). 'Issues of Fit in Strategic Human Resource Management: Implications for Research.' *Human Resource Management Review*, 8/3: 289–309.

—— and DOTY, D. H. (1996). 'Modes of Theorizing in Strategic Human Resource Management: Tests of Universalistic, Contingency, and Configurational Performance Predictions.' *Academy of Management Journal*, 39/4: 802–35.

DEVANNA, M. A., FOMBRUN, C., and TICHY, N. (1981). 'Human Resources Management: A Strategic Perspective.' *Organizational Dynamics*, 9/3: 51–67.

DUTTA, S., NARASIMHAN, O., and RAJIV, S. (2005). 'Conceptualizing and Measuring Capabilities: Methodology and Empirical Application.' *Strategic Management Journal*, 26/3: 277–85.

DYER, L. (1984). 'Studying Human Resource Strategy.' *Industrial Relations*, 23/2: 156–69.

—— and REEVES, T. (1995). 'Human Resource Strategies and Firm Performance: What do we Know and Where do we Need to Go?' *International Journal of Human Resource Management*, 6/3: 656–70.

FIOL, C. M., and LYLES, M. A. (1985). 'Organizational Learning.' *Academy of Management Review*, 10/4: 803–13.

FISHER, S. R., and WHITE, M. A. (2000). 'Downsizing in a Learning Organization: Are There Hidden Costs?' *Academy of Management Review*, 25/1: 244–51.

GRANT, R. M. 1. (1996). 'Toward a Knowledge-Based Theory of the Firm.' *Strategic Management Journal*, 17: 109–22.

GRATTON, L., HAILEY, V. H., and TRUSS, C. (2000). *Strategic Human Resource Management*. New York: Oxford University Press.

GUEST, D. E. (2001). 'Human Resource Management: When Research Confronts Theory.' *International Journal of Human Resource Management*, 12/7: 1092–106.

—— MICHIE, J., CONWAY, N., and SHEEHAN, M. (2003). 'Human Resource Management and Corporate Performance in the UK.' *British Journal of Industrial Relations*, 41/2: 291–314.

HITT, M., BIERMAN, L., SHIMIZU, K. and KOCHAR, R. (2001). 'Direct and Moderating Effects of Human Capital on the Strategy and Performance in Professional Service Firms: A Resource-Based Perspective.' *Academy of Management Journal*, 44: 13–28.

—— IRELAND, R. D., and HOSKISSON, R. E. (2005). *Strategic Management Competitiveness and Globalization*, 6th edn. Mason, Oh.: Thompson South-Western.

HUSELID, M. A. (1995). 'The Impact of Human Resource Management Practices on Turnover, Productivity, and Corporate Financial Performance.' *Academy of Management Journal*, 635–72.

—— JACKSON, S. E., and SCHULER, R. S. (1997). 'Technical and Strategic Human Resources Management Effectiveness as Determinants of Firm Performance.' *Academy of Management Journal*, 40/1: 171–88.

INKPEN, A. C., and TSANG, E. W. K. (2005). 'Social Capital, Networks, and Knowledge Transfer.' *Academy of Management Review*, 30/1: 146–65.

JACKSON, S. E., SCHULER, R. S., and CARLOS RIVERO, J. (1989). 'Organizational Characteristics as Predictors of Personnel Practices.' *Personnel Psychology*, 42/4: 727–86.

KINNIE, N., SWART, J., and PURCELL, J. (2005). 'Influences on the Choice of HR Systems: The Network Organization Perspective.' *International Journal of Human Resource Management*, 16: 949–70.

KOGUT, B., and ZANDER, U. (1992). 'Knowledge of the Firm, Combinative Capabilities, and the Replication of Technology.' *Organization Science: A Journal of the Institute of Management Sciences*, 3/3: 383–97.

LADO, A. A., and WILSON, M. C. (1994). 'Human Resource Systems and Sustained Competitive Advantage: A Competency-Based Perspective.' *Academy of Management Review*, 19/4: 699–727.

LAHTEENMÄKI, S., STOREY, J., and VANHALA, S. (1998). 'HRM and Company Performance: The Use of Measurement and the Influence of Economic Cycles.' *Human Resource Management Journal*, 8/2: 51–65.

LEE, J. and MILLER, D. (1999). 'People Matter: Commitment to Employees, Strategy and Performance in Korean Firms.' *Strategic Management Journal*, 20/6: 579–93.

LEE, M. B., and CHEE, Y. (1996). 'Business Strategy, Participative Human Resource Management and Organizational Performance: The Case of South Korea.' *Asia Pacific Journal of Human Resources*, 34: 77–94.

LENGNICK-HALL, C. A., and LENGNICK-HALL, M. L. (1988). 'Strategic Human Resources Management: A Review of the Literature and a Proposed Typology.' *Academy of Management Review*, 13/3: 454–70.

LEPAK, D. P., and Snell, S. A. (1999). 'The Human Resource Architecture: Toward a Theory of Human Capital Allocation and Development.' *Academy of Managemen Review*, 24: 31–48.

MacDUFFIE, J. P. (1995). 'Human Resource Bundles and Manufacturing Performance: Organizational Logic and Flexible Production Systems in the World Auto Industry.' *Industrial & Labor Relations Review*, 197–221.

McFADYEN, M. A., and CANNELLA Jr., A. A. (2004). 'Social Capital and Knowledge Creation: Diminishing Returns of the Number and Strength of Exchange Relationships.' *academy of Management Journal*, 47/5: 735–46.

McGRATH, R. G. (1997). 'A Real Options Logic for Initiating Technology Positioning Investments.' *Academy of Management Review*, 22/4: 974–96.

MAHONEY, J., and PANDIAN, J. (1992). 'Resource-Based View within the Conversation of Strategic Management.' *Strategic Management Journal*, 13: 363–80.

MEYER, J., and ROWAN, E. (1977). 'Institutionalize Organizations: Formal Structure as Myth and Ceremony.' *American Journal of Sociology*, 83: 340–63.

MILES, R. E., SNOW, C. C., and MEYER, A. D. (1978). 'Organizational Strategy, Structure, and Process.' *Academy of Management Review*, 3/3: 546–62.

PAAUWE, J. (2004). *HRM and Performance: Achieving Long Term Viability.* Oxford: Oxford University Press.

—— and BOSELIE, P. (2003). 'Challenging "Strategic HRM" and the Relevance of the Institutional Setting.' *Human Resource Management Journal*, 13/3: 56–70.

—— —— BOSELIE, P. (2005). 'Best Practices...in Spite of Performance: Just a Matter of Imitation?' *International Journal of Human Resource Management*, 16/6: 987–1003.

PETERS, T. J., and WATERMAN, R. (1982). *In Search of Excellence.* New York: Harper and Row.

PFEFFER, J. (1998). *The Human Equation: Building Profits by Putting People First.* Boston: Harvard Business School Press.

PORTER, M. E. (1980). *Competitive Strategy.* New York: New York Free Press.

PORTER, M. E. (1985). *Competitive Advantage*. New York: New York Free Press.

PRIEM, R., and BUTLER, J. (2001*a*). 'Is the Resource-Based "View" a Useful Perspective for Strategic Management Research?' *Academy of Management Review*, 26: 22–41.

—— —— (2001*b*). 'Tautology in the Resource-Based View and the Implications of Externally Determined Resource Value: Further Comments.' *Academy of Management Review*, 26: 57–67.

RICHARD, O. (2001). 'Racial Diversity, Business Strategy, and Firm Performance: A Resource-Based View.' *Academy of Management Journal*, 43: 164–77.

RODRÍGUEZ, J. M., and VENTURA, J. (2003). 'Human Resource Management Systems and Organizational Performance: An Analysis of the Spanish Manufacturing Industry.' *International Journal of Human Resource Management*, 14/7: 1206–26.

ROGERS, E. W., and WRIGHT, P. M. (1998). 'Measuring Organizational Performance in Strategic Human Resource Management: Problems, Prospects, and Performance Information Markets.' *Human Resource Management Review*, 8/3: 311–31.

SCHULER, R. S., and JACKSON, S. E. (1987). 'Linking Competitive Strategies with Human Resource Management Practices.' *Academy of Management Executive*, 1/3: 207–19.

SNELL, S. A., SHADUR, M. A., and WRIGHT, P. M. (2001). 'Human Resources Strategy: The Era of our Ways.' In *Blackwell Handbook of Strategic Management*. Oxford: Blackwell.

TEECE, D. J., PISANO, G., and SHUEN, A. (1997). 'Dynamic Capabilities and Strategic Management.' *Strategic Management Journal*, 18/7: 509–33.

THOMPSON, M., and HERON, P. (2005). 'Management Capability and High Performance Work Organization.' *International Journal of Human Resource Management*, 16: 1029–48.

TRIGEORGIS, L. (1996). *Real Options: Managerial Flexibility and Strategy in Resource Allocation*. Cambridge, Mass.: MIT Press.

TRUSS, C., and GRATTON, L. (1994). 'Strategic Human Resource Management: A Conceptual Approach.' *International Journal of Human Resource Management*, 5/3: 663–86.

TYSON, S. (1997). 'Human Resource Strategy: A Process for Managing the Contribution of HRM to Organizational Performance.' *International Journal of Human Resource Management*, 8/3: 277–90.

WALKER, J. (1980). *Human Resource Planning*. New York: McGraw-Hill.

WAN, D., ONG, C. H., and KOK, V. (2002). 'Strategic Human Resource Management and Organizational Performance in Singapore.' *Compensation & Benefits Review*, 34/4: 33–42.

WERNERFELT, B. (1984). 'A Resource-Based View of the Firm.' *Strategic Management Journal*, 5/2: 171–80.

WRIGHT, P. (1998). 'Strategy-HR Fit: Does it Really Matter?' *Human Resource Planning*, 21/4: 56–7.

—— and GARDNER, T. M. (2003). 'Theoretical and Empirical Challenges in Studying the HR Practice–Firm Performance Relationship.' In D. Holman, T. D. Wall, C. Clegg, P. Sparrow, and A. Howard (eds.), *The New Workplace: People Technology, and Organisation*. Bnghton: Wiley.

—— McMAHAN, G. C. (1992). 'Theoretical Perspectives for Strategic Human Resource Management.' *Journal of Management*, 18/2: 295–320.

—— SHERMAN, S. (1999). 'Failing to Find Fit in Strategic Human Resource Management: Theoretical and Empirical Problems.' In P. Wright, L. Dyer, J. Boudreau, and G. Milkovich (eds.), *Research in Personnel and Human Resource Management*, Supplement 4. Greenwich, Conn.: JAI Press.

—— and SNELL, S. A. (1991). 'Toward an Integrative View of Strategic Human Resource Management.' *Human Resource Management Review*, 1/3: 203–25.

—— (1998). 'Toward a Unifying Framework for Exploring Fit and Flexibility in Strategic Human Resource Management.' *Academy of Management Review*, 23/4: 756–72.

—— McMAHAN, G. C., and McWILLIAMS, A. (1994). 'Human Resources and Sustained Competitive Advantage: A Resource-Based Perspective.' *International Journal of Human Resource Management*, 5/2: 301–26.

—— —— and SMART, D. L. (1995). 'Matches between Human Resources and Strategy among NCAA Basketball Teams.' *Academy of Management Journal*, 38/4: 1052–74.

—— DUNFORD, B. B., and SNELL, S. A. (2001). 'Human Resources and the Resource-Based View of the Firm.' *Journal of Management*, 27/6: 701–21.

—— GARDNER, T. M., MOYNIHAN, L. M., and ALLEN, M. R. (2005). 'The Relationship between HR Practices and Firm Performance: Examining Causal Order.' *Personnel Psychology*, 58/2: 409–46.

YOUNDT, M. A., SNELL, S. A., DEAN, J. W., Jr, and LEPAK, D. P. (1996). 'Human Resource Management, Manufacturing Strategy, and Firm Performance.' *Academy of Management Journal*, 39/4: 836–66.

.....................................................................................................................

# ORGANIZATION THEORY AND HRM

## TONY WATSON

## 6.1 INTRODUCTION

.....................................................................................................................

HUMAN Resource Management is an activity that occurs in work organizations across the industrialized world. HRM is also an academic 'subject' that is taught and researched, primarily in higher education in those same industrialized societies. However, this latter 'HRM' is not an academic activity which has a clear body of theoretical ideas of its own. There is almost no literature on the 'the theory of HRM.' This is not to say, however, that theories are absent from academic HRM. Use is made of theoretical concepts from areas such as psychology, sociology, employee relations, economics, and strategic management. And, to some degree, use is made of ideas from organization theory. The purpose of the present chapter is to identify the contributions that have been made by ideas from organization theory to our understanding of the organizational activity of human resource management—and its earlier 'personnel management' manifestation. Attention will also be given to ways in which greater use might be made of organization theory in the analysis of HRM activities and processes in the future.

HRM processes are organizational processes. They occur within all work organizations and they cannot be understood separately from the way in which we understand organizations themselves. The same can be argued about management more broadly. In effect, any 'theory of management,' like any 'theory of HRM,' has to be grounded in a 'theory of organization.' Managerial work generally and human resourcing work specifically is 'organizing work.' And it occurs in formally structured enterprises which utilize human labor. These work organizations constitute the topic of organization theory.

# 6.2 ORGANIZATIONS AND ORGANIZATION THEORY

Organization theory can be characterized as *an intellectual activity which utilizes methodological and conceptual resources from social science disciplines such as sociology, social psychology, and anthropology in order to provide explanations of how things happen in the sphere of authoritatively co-coordinated human enterprises.* The wording 'authoritatively coordinated human enterprises' is a more sociologically sophisticated way of referring to work organizations. It recognizes that the social arrangements under consideration—companies, schools, churches, armies, public administrations, and so on—are all characterized by their use of bureaucratic ways of coordinating task-based activities. And Max Weber's classic characterization of bureaucracy emphasized the centrality of 'authority' (legitimized power) in these organizing processes (Weber 1978). Bureaucracy, in the seminal Weberian formulation, involves the control and coordination of work tasks through a hierarchy of appropriately qualified office holders, whose authority derives from their expertise and who rationally devise a system of rules and procedures that are calculated to provide the most appropriate means of achieving specified ends. This characterization comes from Weber's 'ideal type' of bureaucracy (a construct of what a bureaucracy would look like if it existed in a pure form—*not* a description of what an bureaucracy ideally *should* be). Managers in work organizations are 'appropriately qualified office holders' in this sense. An HR manager is thus appointed, in principle, on the grounds of their experience and qualifications as the best person available to do the HR tasks specified in a formal organizational 'job description.' Their 'right' or their authority to appoint people, instruct staff, or make workers redundant derives from their technical HR expertise and its linking, through their formal role in the managerial hierarchy, to specific organizational tasks.

Whilst recognizing the necessity of organization theory's attending to the formal aspects of organizational life, we must remember that the formal or 'official' aspects are always in interplay with the informal or unofficial within the 'negotiated order' of every organization (Strauss et al. 1963; Strauss 1978; Day and Day 1997; Watson 2001a). And we must also remember that organizations are 'sites of situated social action' which are influenced not only by 'explicitly organized and formal disciplinary knowledges' such as marketing, production, or HRM but also by 'practices embedded in the broad social fabric, such as gender, ethnic and other culturally defined social relations' (Clegg and Hardy 1999: 4). The fact, for example, that HR managers occupy a different class position from those occupied by many of the workers with whom they deal inevitably influences manager–worker interactions. And it has been observed that gender factors can significantly color the interactions between HR and other managers (Miller and Coghill 1964; Watson 1977; Gooch and Ledwith 1996).

## 6.3 THE EMERGENCE OF ORGANIZATION THEORY

Although bureaucracy has existed for a long time, the prevalence of bureaucratized organizations across both public administrative and industrial spheres has been a more recent phenomenon, coming about over the last two centuries of human history. Over this period, various writers made contributions which might be seen as attempts to theorize these organizational developments, most notably Adam Smith (1776), Charles Babbage (1832), Andrew Ure (1835), Karl Marx (1867), Frederick W. Taylor (1911), Max Weber (1922), Elton Mayo (1933), Chester Barnard (1938), and F. J Roethlisberger and W. J Dickson (1939). Although these writers cannot all be directly identified with a growing social scientific way of thinking and writing about organizations they are all people who have been taken up as sources of ideas or as inspirations by social scientists over the last half-century or so—the period in which the recognized academic subject of organization theory has existed (sometimes as 'organization studies,' sometimes as 'organization science'). But there were other very significant and previously neglected strands of organizational thinking that went into the subject which emerged as organization theory in the USA in the middle of the twentieth century. These were produced by the mechanical engineers who moved beyond an interest in solving technological problems to an interest in solving organizational dilemmas (Jacques 1996; Shenhav 1994, 1995, 1999; Shenhav and Weitz 2000). At first sight, we might not expect these engineers to have a great deal of relevance to what we these days call HR issues. But as we shall see later (pp. 113–14) this is anything but the case.

For present purposes, we simply need to note that engineers had a significant influence on the 'new' subject of organization theory. Their contributions fit into one of the two themes which Starbuck identifies as 'motivating' the birth of organization theory: the theme of finding ways in which 'organizations can operate more effectively' (Starbuck 2003: 171–4). This theme can be identified with the 'opportunities' that organizations were perceived to be offering mankind. The second theme, however, was one identified with perceived 'threats' presented by bureaucratic organization. This was the theme of 'bureaucracy and its defects' (Starbuck 2003: 162). A key role in bringing these two themes into a single organization theory was played by Selznick (1948) who, influenced by various managerial writers like Chester Barnard, 'departed from the sociological focus on "bureaucracy" and framed his discussions in more general language about "organizations" and "formal organizations"' (Starbuck 2003: 170). And, says Starbuck, by the 1960s organization theory had 'arrived'—but with that arrival and the subsequent 'expansion and affluence' of the subject (coming about with the massive expansion of degree programs in business) there has been significant fragmentation (2003: 174). This is a matter with which we must now come to terms. Organization theory is anything but a unified subject and, in examining its relevance to and connection with HRM, we have deal with the fact that, in effect, there is more than one organization theory that HRM has or to which HRM might relate

# 6.4 VARIETIES OF ORGANIZATION THEORY

Anyone wishing to turn to organization theory as a resource for the analysis of activities like HRM faces the difficulty that there is no single coherent OT framework readily available to them. Instead they find themselves presented with a variety of theoretical perspectives. One recent overview of organization theories covers over thirty of these (Vibert 2004) whilst another assembles the variety of approaches into three main perspectives: the modern, the symbolic, and the postmodern (Hatch 2006). And things have perhaps been made even more daunting by the arguments among organization theorists themselves about the extent to which the main *paradigms* (the clusters of assumptions about the world and about scientific knowledge adopted by different theorists) allegedly underlying these various approaches are compatible with each other. Some argue, for example, that the different theoretical, methodological, and political orientations of the various sets of theorists are fundamentally incompatible with each other. Thus, it is argued that any given researcher needs to locate themselves within one particular *paradigm*—a functionalist, an interpretative, a radical humanist, or a radical structuralist paradigm, say (Burrell and Morgan 1979; Jackson and Carter 2000). An alternative approach is to switch back and forth between these various paradigms to find insights pertinent to the area being analyzed. Hassard (1993) has demonstrated the advantages of this strategy for organizations generally and

Kamoche (2000) for HRM—analyzing recruitment and training within the functionalist paradigm before looking at HRM generally within the terms, first, of a radical paradigm and, second, an interpretative paradigm. Other writers, however, argue for the development of a single frame of reference for studying organizations (Pfeffer 1993; Donaldson 2001).

The organization theory paradigm debate continues in the organization theory literature (Burrell 2002; Keleman and Hassard 2003). Tsoukas and Knudsen try to cut through all of this, however, by observing that when it comes to investigating 'particular topics, in particular sites,' organizational researchers do not so much 'apply' or 'follow' paradigms as 'explore' what is available to them and, 'having to cope coherently with all the puzzles and tensions stemming from the complexity of the phenomena they investigate, they extend, synthesize, and/or invent concepts (cf. Rorty 1991: 93–110)' (Tsoukas and Knudsen 2003: 13). This corresponds to a strategy of *pragmatic pluralism* (Watson 1997) which similarly follows the basic principle of Philosophical Pragmatism (Putnam 1995; Mounce 1997; Rorty 1982) in which knowledge is assessed in terms of how effectively it informs the projects of the human beings who make use of it, as opposed to judging it in terms of how closely it 'mirrors' or represents objectively existing realities (Rorty 1980). The pragmatic pluralist investigator, in producing an analysis of a particular aspect of social life, such as HRM, or of a particular set of social events or circumstances, draws upon elements from various disciplines or perspectives to produce an analytical framework which can stand as the conceptual foundation for that particular investigation. Concepts are selected on the criterion of relevance to the issues arising in the investigation. The framework which emerges must, nevertheless, have its own ontological, epistemological, and methodological integrity. It cannot, for example, jump from an ontological assumption at one stage of the analysis that organizations are pluralistic patterns of interaction involving varying goals of a multiplicity of organizational actors to an assumption, at another stage of the analysis, that organizations are entities possessing 'organizational goals' of their own (Watson 2006).

# 6.5 FOUR STRANDS OF ORGANIZATION THEORY RELEVANT TO HRM

Having established how we might bring together for purposes such as analyzing HRM practices ideas from different 'approaches' within organization theory, we need briefly to map out some examples from this variety of perspectives and note briefly how they have played a part in the emergence of HRM so far. To do this, it is helpful to identify several 'strands' of thinking. This mapping, it must be stressed, is produced, once again, in the spirit of Philosophical Pragmatist thinking. It has been devised in order to help the traveler proceed on their journey, as opposed to producing a totally 'correct' or accurate representation of the nature of the ground over which that journey is to occur.

## 6.5.1 The Functionalist/Systems and Contingency Strand

In this strand of thinking, organizations are viewed as systems: as social entities which function as self-regulating bodies which exchange energy and matter with their environment in order to survive. They ingest 'inputs' which they convert into 'outputs.' The approach has some of its roots deep in historical social thought and, at a level nearer the surface of the soil in which it grew, in the 'structural functional' style of sociological thinking which set out to explain various social institutions and aspects of social institutions in terms of the functions that they fulfill for the overall social 'whole' (or 'system') of which they are a part (Abrahamson 2001; Colomy 1990). Thus, to take a very simple example, one would explain the high rewards paid to senior managers, relative to the wages paid to ordinary workers, by arguing that the organizational system in which these people are employed, in order to continue in existence, *needs* the expertise that can only be obtained if those relatively higher incomes are provided. Relative differences of class or organizational power are not considered and neither are the deliberate efforts of managers to give themselves a relative material advantage in the organizations which they run. In spite of the danger of removing human initiative or agency from explanations of what happens in organizations, systems analyses have the advantage of making us constantly aware that organizations are more than the sums of the parts from which they are made: they are patterns of relations which need constantly to be adapted to allow the organization to continue in existence. It also stresses that what happens in one part of an organization (in one 'subsystem') tends to have implications for what happens in other parts or 'subsystems.'

Systems approaches to organizations have roots other than those in social thought and social science. They have also been influenced by biological thinking and by 'general systems thinking,' a cross-disciplinary scientific way of thinking about a whole range of different phenomena (Boulding 1956; Von Bertalanffy 1972; Emery 1969). But systems thinking in the organizational sphere has also been significantly influenced by the contributions made by engineers (above p. 110). The outcome of this is that a powerful metaphor in management thought, which has been of immense attractiveness to managers, has been that of the organization as a system, as a big social machine which takes in raw material, knowledge, and human effort and outputs various goods and services, with this whole apparatus being designed and controlled by the expert 'human engineer' managers who are appointed to fulfill the organization's 'goals' (Watson 2006). Such a conception inevitably has a powerful attraction for people trying both to explain and give legitimacy to the personnel management or HR 'function' in an organization: its role is portrayed as one of dealing with the human 'input' to the organizational system, not just recruiting the labor that the system needs but also administering and developing it so that it most effectively plays its role in producing the system's outputs. Personnel matters played a central part in the work of the engineering 'systematizers' who were, in effect, the proto-organization theorists who did so much to shape both organization theory and management practices in the twentieth century. These people, Shenhav tells us, applied mechanical engineering methods, not just to the administrative restructuring of firms and their accounting procedures but also to the determination of wages and the selection criteria in employment (2003: 187). Among the magazines that helped disseminate this systems ideology was the periodical *Personnel* and, as Shenhav notes, 'many of the subsequent scholars of organizations were readers and writers for these magazines' and the articles, often collected in book form, provided 'the seedbed from which discourse on rational organizations grew' (2003: 191).

The discourse on rational organization and personnel management that emerged and is most clearly made manifest in the textbooks used across the English-speaking world was not just rooted in a systems view of organizations, it was also normative and prescriptive, as Legge's (1978) analysis of those texts shows. In reaction to this tendency, Legge took a significant step forward by arguing for a non-prescriptive organization theory approach to personnel management. The prescriptive approach, she argued, led to confusions about organizational goals and personnel objectives which, in turn, led to further confusions 'about the nature of the personnel function itself' (1978: 16). Also, the 'prescriptive intention of these books' succumbed to 'stilted generalizations that neglect both the complexities and dynamism of real organizations' (1978: 16). This move is significant because it marks the point—alongside the present author's sociological study of the personnel occupation (Watson 1977 and below, p. 117)—where personnel/HR matters began to be studied in a social scientific style where the priority is given to analysis, explanation, and understanding of employment management phenomena as opposed to seeking 'best practices' that managers might adopt. Legge's research focused on the tensions and ambiguities with which personnel managers have to deal and she pointed to contingency theory as a resource which personnel managers, acting as applied social scientists within their own organizations, might use to overcome some of these tensions and conflicts. The contingency theory version of systems thinking (Donaldson 2001) is concerned with how the contingent circumstances of organizations (their size, technology, business environment, and so on) 'influence the organization's internal structures and processes' (Legge 1978: 97). The 'contingency insight,' as we might call it, has been brought forward into a non-functionalist style of analysis (i.e. one in which contingencies are given no 'determining' role) by Child (1972, 1997), who links contingent circumstances to strategic managerial *choices*, an insight that can valuably inform how we understand the ways in which different HR strategies are chosen in different circumstances (Watson 2004, 2005).

In the 1980s, the employment management aspects of organizations began to be examined in a new way, one which saw a relabeling of the activity as HRM rather than as personnel management or personnel administration. The factors behind this and the key characteristics of the 'new' HRM are discussed in Chapter 2. The renewal of scholarly interest in employment management processes and practices might have been a point at which organization theory resources were turned to. But this did not happen. And HRM has continued to 'follow a different lead' theoretically (Morgan 2000: 860). Why was this the case? On the one hand, there was the fact that organization theory had moved firmly away from its earlier managerial origins, with its re-engagement with the more critical version of Weberian sociology that was now available (below pp. 116 17), the revisiting of Marxian labor process thinking (below pp. 117–19) and the growing 'interpretativist' interest in human agency, language, and meanings which followed from the broad sociological rejection of functionalist theorizing (this clearly signaled by Silverman 1970; see also Reed 1996). This meant that organization theory was moving quickly away from its earlier systems-thinking base. But, on the other hand, systems ideas were too valuable to the HRM project for them to be abandoned in the way organization theory had largely done. Systems thinking had what might almost be seen as a natural affinity with the new HRM. 'HRM' thinking therefore tended to follow its own direction. This was one more consistent with the earlier, more managerially engaged, systems-based, organization theory. As Jacques observes, the three themes of the new thinking—'comprehensive as opposed to patchwork direction of the human function in organizations; linking operational HR issues to the firm's strategy and structure; learning to regard expenditures on labor and worker-embodied knowledge as an investment rather than an expense'—represented a clear continuity with earlier managerially oriented American social science (1995: 202). The message of the new HRM, to put it at its simplest, was 'integrate, integrate, integrate' and, theoretically, this tends to mean in the social sciences 'systems, systems, systems.' What Greenwood calls a 'mainstream HRM' thus takes a 'systems maintenance or functionalist approach, viewing HRM as a mechanism for the attainment of organizational goals' (2002: 262).

The main theoretical thrust within HRM research and writing is clearly in the area of the relationship between HRM practice and corporate strategies (Tichy et al. 1982; Schuler et al. 2001). This work is covered in Chapters 3, 5, 26, and 27. There is a considerable input here from economics, a discipline which, as Guest notes, is very much 'theory-led,' and therefore has the potential to help overcome the general theoretical inadequacies of HRM (2001: 1093). But a systems emphasis plays a significant role in this work (Sanchez-Runde 2001) and systems ideas are advocated, beyond this, as a means to better integrated management performance (Broedling 1999), as a means for analyzing different national models of HRM (Hendry 2003), and as a means for linking HRM to general management (Ghorpade 2004).

## 6.5.2 The Weberian Strand

As has already been implied, Max Weber is a key figure, if not *the* key figure, in organization theory. It has often been commented that much of the six-or-so decades of the history of organization theory has been a debate with Weber's ideas on bureaucracy. But the 'Weberian' ideas that were brought into early organization theory in mid-twentieth-century America were a particular version of those ideas that were selected and 'framed' in a way that resonated with the dominant managerial interests of the time in overcoming the problems inherent in bureaucracy and finding ways of improving the effectiveness of organizations. In this early organization theory writing, scholars such as Blau (1955), Gouldner (1954), and Thompson (1967) 'assumed that Weber equated rationality with efficiency' (Shenhav 2003: 196), with the effect that 'bureaucracy was reified and was used as an ahistorical framework for effective functioning implying a per-formative intent in his scheme' (Shenhav 2003: 197). This strand of thinking in organization theory, which we might cheekily label the 'counterfeit-Weberian' strand, has to be contrasted with a much more sociological, critical, and theoret-ically sophisticated version of Weber's contribution to the field which scholars subsequently found themselves able to make in the light of newer translations and readings of his work (Albrow 1970; Beetham 1996; Eldridge 1971; Kalberg 2005; Ray and Reed 1994; Ritzer and Goodman 2003: ch. 4; Turner 1996).

The newer appreciation of Weber's work recognizes that his key contribution is to locate bureaucratized organizations in their historical and political context and to acknowledge that, alongside whatever significant advantages they offer human beings, they also present problems for human freedom and expression. The contemporary, non-managerialist, Weberian strand of thinking in organization theory, then, is one that recognizes that organizations are sites of rivalries, conflicts of interest, and power in which a 'paradox of consequence' typically comes into play: a tendency for the means chosen to achieve ends in the social world to undermine or defeat those ends. A simple example of this, in practice, might be the well-known tendency for performance indicators or metrics (often introduced by HR managers to monitor certain organizational behaviors with a view to encouraging people to perform better) to set minimum standards of performance in practice, thus actually discouraging improved performances ('We have fulfilled our quota of job upgradings for this month, why should we do any more?').

The means chosen to achieve a certain end has become an end it itself—thus undermining the achieving of the purpose for which it was designed.

The present author's study of the personnel management occupation (Watson 1977) set the work of personnel managers firmly in this context of handling conflicts and contradictions in social life, at the societal, organizational, and departmental level. The personnel occupation was shown to have come about, not because of the 'system needs' which required it (which would be a functionalist analysis) but—following Weber's focus upon the interaction of ideas and interests in processes of social change (Bendix 1966)—because particular historical actors came forward and created an occupation to handle some of the unintended consequences of processes of rationalization. Personnel management is thus shown to be both an outcome of the rationalization process of social life and employment and a reactor to it—in the sense that it takes on many of the tensions, conflicts, contradictions, and ambiguities that come about in the modern bureaucratized enterprise.

New institutionalism is a development of broadly Weberian thinking. It is increasingly being applied to HRM (Purcell 1999), in part to counter an over-emphasis on economic rationality of the 'resource-based view' of the firm which plays a key role in economic/strategic management analyses (Boxall 1996). The new institutionalism follows Weber in putting alongside economic rationality factors (*zweckrationalität*), normative or value-based (*wertrationalität*) factors. It puts particular emphasis on the various pressures on organizations to become similar to each other. Paauwe and Boselie (2003 and this Handbook, Chapter 9), for example, suggest ways in which the three institutional mechanisms influencing organizational decision-making identified in DiMaggio and Powell's (1983) seminal article can be related to HRM. Coercive mechanisms include trade unions and government legislation; mimetic mechanisms include the imitating of the strategies of competitors and the various management fads and fashions; normative mechanisms include such things as occupational HR training and links through HR managers' professional bodies (Paauwe and Boselie 2003: 60). And Boxall and Purcell point to the pursuit of 'social legitimacy' (one of the 'three key goals for HRM', 2003: 33; cf. Lees 1997) as a significant factor pressing organizations to become similar to each other.

## 6.5.3 The Marxian Strand

The notion of unintended consequences of deliberate human actions that plays a key role in the Weberian strand of thinking also arises in Marxian thinking in the notion of the contradictions within capitalism. Modern institutions of employment, of which 'HRM' is a part, are central to the capitalist mode of production. But these institutions are part and parcel of a class system, given that they are based on a logic in which a capital-owning class, through a managed 'labor process,' extracts surplus value from members of an employee class. And within this set of relations lie the seeds of the capitalist political economy's eventual destruction. The people working for a wage or salary eventually come to realize that they share the objective position of being exploited. They reject the ideologies that misled them into accepting their situation and they abandon a 'falsely conscious' appreciation of their place in society. They consequently 'rise up' and throw off their oppressors. This may seem so unlikely to any observer of the contemporary scene that they are tempted to dismiss out of hand such a way of looking at organizational structures and class processes. However, the underlying insight may still be valid: just because contradictions do not seem likely to lead to capitalist failure in any foreseeable future, it does not mean that the underlying fault lines are not there and do not need to be taken account of in any realistic organization theory. And as Desai (2002) has pointed out, there are characteristics in the dominant forms that capitalism is coming to take in the twenty-first century that are far from inconsistent with the long-term analysis in Marx's writing.

Marxian thinking has perhaps had its greatest impact on organization theory in the analysis of trends in the shaping of labor processes in modern organizations (Grugulis et al. 2000–1; Spencer 2000; see also Chapter 8 below). This analysis of trends in the design, control, and monitoring of work activities by managers (acting as agents of the capital-owning class to extract surplus value from the labor activity of employees) was stimulated by Braverman's (1974) argument that the logic of capitalist employment relations has led to a general trend towards the deskilling, routinizing, and mechanizing of jobs across the employment spectrum. In his influential book, he wrote of the role of people like personnel managers as 'the maintenance crew for the human machinery:' 'personnel departments and academics have busied themselves with the selection, training, manipulation, pacification and adjustment of "manpower" to suit the work processes' (1974: 87). Subsequent thinking, however, whilst working within the same radical tradition as Braverman, has recognized that capitalist interests are better served by upgrading work in some circumstances and by downgrading it in others (Friedmann 1977; Edwards 1979). This insight can be incorporated into broader critical thinking about HRM by considering ways in which HR strategists will tend to lean towards 'low commitment, direct control, human resourcing practices *when employee constituencies are perceived as creating low strategic uncertainty*' and towards 'high commitment, indirect control, human resourcing practices *when employee constituencies are perceived as creating high strategic uncertainty*' (Watson 2004: 458).

Marxist thinking has perhaps not had as significant a direct impact on theorizing about HRM as it has had on academic industrial relations (Hyman 1989). But its indirect influence is there in all those approaches which pay attention to the indeterminacy of employment relationships and to the structural conflicts of interest which pervade them (e.g. Boxall 1992; Coff 1997; Evans and Genadry 1999; Purcell and Ahlstrand 1994). Marxist thinking also informs the 'currently popular distinction between the rhetoric and reality of HRM in contemporary debates' which 'essentially replays an identical relationship between ideological practice and the truth' to that seen in Marxist discourse (Barratt 2003: 1071). Legge illustrates this Marxian tendency when she analyzes HRM rhetoric, for example, as 'masking the intensification and commodification of labor' (1995: 325). Although it was recast in Weberian terms as an example of the paradox of consequences, there was an echo of Marx in the Watson (1977) account of the societal role of personnel management as one caught up in managing some of the 'contradictions of capitalism.'

## 6.5.4 The Post-Structuralist and Discursive Strand

The post-structuralist element of social thought, closely connected to 'postmodern' thinking, treats human and social reality as if it were a text—a set of signs which are not tied into any kind of pre-existing reality. The implication of this is that there is no basic truth outside language and that there is no reality separate from the ways in which we write and talk about the world. Thus, as Westwood and Linstead put it with regard to organizations, 'Organization has no autonomous, stable or structural status outside the text that constitutes it' (2001: 4). This means, Reed observes, that any 'quest for universal, scientific generalizations or principles of organization and management, that has played a dominant role in organization theory's historical and intellectual development, is firmly rejected in favor of a much more relativist and political conception of knowledge production and diffusion' (2005: 1623). The post-structuralist theorist who has had the greatest impact on organization theory has been Foucault, and central to the parts of his work that have been taken up by writers on work and organization has been his emphasis on 'decentring the human subject.' This entails rejecting any concept of an autonomous thinking and feeling human subject with an essential and unique personality or 'self.' The human being's notion of 'who and what they are' is shaped by the discourses which surround them. These discourses exert power over people by creating the categories into which they are fitted: 'the homosexual,' 'the criminal,' the 'mentally ill,' for example (Foucault 1980). Such categories not only define for people 'who they are' but lay down the ways in which people are to be treated by others.

The relevance of these insights to issues of human resourcing is fairly obvious. Discourses are society's statements of 'truth and knowledge' and, as McKinlay and Starkey (1998) put it, these are the means whereby 'society manages itself.' There is a potential, then, for theorizing HRM in these terms: as a set of statements of truth and knowledge through which people's subjectivities are managed in modern societies. This has been taken up by Townley who analyzes HRM as a 'discourse and technology of power that aims to resolve the gap inherent in the contract of employment between the capacity to work and its exercise and, thereby, organize workers into a collective, productive power or force' (1994: 138). Findlay and Newton (1998) focus on appraisal practices to demonstrate the insights that Foucauldian thinking has to offer and Barratt (2003) puts forward a spirited defense of Foucauldian perspectives on HRM and HRM-related issues in response to its critics. Legge (1995) looks at the discourse of HRM in a similar manner and has also utilized post-structuralist ideas of deconstruction (Derrida 1978) to enable readers of HRM to 'take apart the texts and stories of the advocates of human resource management' to bring out their paradoxes, contradictions, and absences (2001: 53).

Discourse analysis, it should be noted, is not only used by organization theorists following a post-structuralist line of argument (see Alvesson and Karreman 2000; Grant et al. 1998, 2004). Watson (2001b) used a concept of discourse to identify two rival ways in which human resourcing issues were understood and acted upon in a large business organization and Francis and Sinclair have applied it to cases of 'HRM-based change' (2003).

# 6.6 CONCLUSIONS: THEORIZING HRM WITH RESOURCES FROM ORGANIZATION THEORY

It was suggested earlier that the way forward in the relationship between organization theory and HRM might be one in which pragmatic pluralist principles are followed. This would mean that, within an ontologically and epistemologically consistent framework, concepts are drawn from the various theoretical traditions or 'strands' to deepen our understanding of HRM practices. Table 6.1 summarizes the above analysis of the various strands of organization theory which have had an impact on HRM. And, in its right-hand column, the table identifies some of the ideas that can be brought together from the four strands to analyze HRM practices and events.

The theoretical resources set out in the right-hand column of Table 6.1 do not constitute a complete 'theory of HRM.' What is provided here is nevertheless inevitably informed by the broader theorizing of personnel and HR institutions developed by the present author. That theorizing has occurred in the context of attempting to make sense of and explain events observed in detailed case-study research on the shaping of HR strategies in 'real life' (as opposed to textbook idealizations) practices of employing organizations. The analysis of strategic changes in a case study business (Watson 2004, 2005) attempts to go beyond what is typically produced in the mainstream HRM literature and handles—and relates to each other—both the 'micro' and the 'macro' aspects of HRM processes.

## Table 6.1 The contributions of four strands of organization theory to HRM

| | Role of proto-OT in the emergence of personnel practices | Role of OT in the social scientific study of personnel management | Role of OT in academic HRM | The potential role of OT in the future analysis of HRM: contributions from four OT strands which might be utilized within a 'pragmatic pluralist' framework |
| --- | --- | --- | --- | --- |
| *Functionalist/ systems strand* | Mechanical engineers and the 'systematizing' of employment practices | Contingency theory identified as an expert resource which personnel managers might use to deal with the ambiguities and tensions inherent in their roles (Legge 1978) | Preference for a systems (and often prescriptive) style of thinking which OT had largely abandoned; greater influence of strategic management and economics in more formal theorizing than OT | Acceptance of the notion of the organization as a recognizable pattern of actions and commitments but without retaining a conception of the organization as an entity with goals or purposes of its own; contingent circumstances understood as matters interpreted by managers and taken into account in strategic choices |
| *Weberian strand* | | Personnel management seen as both a manifestation of societal rationalization processes and a handler of its unintended consequences in the sphere of employment; interaction of human 'interests and ideas' in context of rival priorities among personnel and other managers (Watson 1977) | Emerging attention to the institutional pressures towards organizational 'isomorphism' which make HR practices more similar across different employing organizations and disseminate HRM thinking generally (Paauwe and Boselie 2003; Boxall and Purcell 2003) | HRM experts understood as employed by owning/dominant interests to work within a bureaucratic logic of authority based on expertise; the division of labor within that bureaucracy leading to (unintended) tensions and rivalries between HR and other managers who, at the same time as working to bring about the continuation of the enterprise, act to further their personal and career interests—all of this occurring in the context of (*a*) the ambiguities, conflicts, and uncertainties inherent in work organizations and |

(continued)

**Table 6.1  (continued)**

| | Role of proto-OT in the emergence of personnel practices | Role of OT in the social scientific study of personnel management | Role of OT in academic HRM | The potential role of OT in the future analysis of HRM: contributions from four OT strands which might be utilized within a 'pragmatic pluralist' framework |
|---|---|---|---|---|
| | | | | employment relationships and (b) the continuous danger of chosen means coming to subvert the ends which they were designed to fulfill |
| *Marxian strand* | | Marxist industrial relations (Hyman 1989) | Conflict management seen as a vital part of HRM; labor process analysis; ideology unmasking in 'critical HRM' (Legge 1995) | HRM activities set in the context of the reproduction of patterns of advantage and disadvantage, globally as well as nationally |
| *Post-structuralist and discursive strand* | | | Post-structuralist 'critical HRM' (Townley 1994) | HRM discourse understood as shaping working assumptions of HR actors and providing sense-making resources for their use in sense-making and initiatives |

Attention is paid to the detailed roles played by specific organizational actors with their particular personal values, career interests, and organizational situations. But these issues in the case study business are analytically located within and related to a global political economy and a broader societal culture in which matters like class, gender, and occupation are shown to play an important part. Similarly, the theorizing pays attention to the interplay between material interests and structures of domination, on the one hand, and matters of language and discursive practice on the other. And, further, the theorizing is sensitive to the interplay between constraining/enabling circumstances and contingencies, on the one hand, and managerial and personal choices on the other.

The style of organizational theorizing advocated here is a critical and a social scientific one. This fits with the general trend whereby organization theory has broken free from its earlier managerialist anchor and its concern with making organizations more competitive or effective. HRM writers, it would seem, have been reluctant to sever these ropes (Watson 2004). Hence, it can be argued that there needs to be more utilizing of critical social science thinking generally and non-managerialist organization theory specifically in the study of HRM. But in no way whatsoever is this to argue for HRM research and writing which lacks relevance for people with a practical involvement in HRM. Nobody at all is helped by analyses that confuse the 'is' and the 'ought' of HR practices. In the final analysis, good theory tells us about 'how things work in the world.' And if organization theory can help us produce 'good theories' about how HRM processes 'work' in practice then it will be of equal relevance and value to everyone involved with HRM. It will equally inform the thinking and the actions of people who want to develop HRM skills, people who want to challenge HRM institutions, and people who simply want to reflect in a detached and scholarly manner upon HRM institutions and practices.

# REFERENCES

ABRAHAMSON, M. (2001). 'Functional, Conflict and Neofunctional Theories.' In G. Ritzer and B. Smart (eds.), *Handbook of Social Theory*. London: Sage.

ALBROW, M. (1970). *Bureaucracy*. London: Macmillan.

ALVESSON, M., and KARREMAN, D. (2000). 'Varieties of Discourse: On the Study of Organization through Discourse Analysis.' *Human Relations*, 53/9: 1125–49.

BABBAGE, C. (1832). *On the Economy of Machinery and Manufacture*. London: Charles Knight.

BARNARD, C. I. (1938). *The Functions of the Executive*. Cambridge, Mass.: Harvard University Press.

BARRATT, E. (2003). 'Foucault, HRM and the Ethos of the Critical Management Scholar.' *Journal of Management Studies*, 40/5: 1069–87.

BEETHAM, D. (1996). *Bureaucracy*. Buckingham: Open University Press.

BENDIX, R. (1966). *Max Weber: An Intellectual Portrait*. London: Methuen.

BLAU, P. M. (1955). *The Dynamics of Bureaucracy*. Chicago: University of Chicago Press.

BOULDING, K. E. (1956). 'General Systems Theory: The Skeleton of Science.' *Management Science*, 2: 197–208.

BOXALL, P. (1992). 'Strategic Human Resource Management: Beginnings of a New Theoretical Sophistication?' *Human Resource Management Journal*, 2: 60–79.

—— (1996). 'The Strategic Human Resource Debate and the Resource-Based View of the Firm.' *Human Resource Management Journal*, 6/3: 59–75.

—— and Purcell, J. (2003). *Strategy and Human Resource Management*. Basingstoke: Palgrave Macmillan.

BRAVERMAN, H. (1974). *Labor and Monopoly Capital*. New York: Monthly Review Press.

BROEDLING, L. A. (1999). 'Applying a Systems Approach to Human Resource Management.' *Human Resource Management*, 38/3: 269–78.

BURRELL, G. (2002). 'Organizational Paradigms.' In A. Sorge (ed.), *Organization*. London: Thomson Learning.

—— and MORGAN, G. (1979). *Sociological Paradigms and Sociological Analysis*. London: Heinemann.

CHILD, J. (1972). 'Organizational Structure, Environment and Performance.' *Sociology*, 6/1: 2–22.

—— (1997). 'Strategic Choice in the Analysis of Action, Structure, Organizations and Environment: Retrospect and Prospect.' *Organization Studies*, 18/1: 43–76.

CLEGG, S. R., and HARDY, C. (1999). 'Introduction.' In C. Clegg and C. Hardy (eds.), *Studying Organizations: Theory and Method*. London: Sage.

COFF, R. (1997). 'Human Assets and Management Dilemmas: Coping with Hazards on the Road to Resource-Based Theory.' *Academy of Management Review*, 22: 374–402.

COLOMY, P. (ed.) (1990). *Functionalist Sociology*. Brookfield, Vt.: Elgar.

DAY, R. A., and DAY, J. (1997). 'A Review of the Current State of Negotiated Order Theory: An Appreciation and Critique.' *Sociological Quarterly*, 18:126–42.

DERRIDA, J. (1978). *Writing and Difference*. London: Routledge.

DESAI, M. (2002). *Marx's Revenge*. London: Verso.

DiMAGGIO, P., and Powell, W. (1983). 'The Iron Cage Revisited: Institutional Isomorphism and Collective Rationality in Organizational Fields.' *American Sociological Review*, 48/2: 147–60.

DONALDSON, L. (2001). *The Contingency Theory of Organizations*. London: Sage.

EDWARDS, R. (1979). *Contested Terrain*. London: Heinemann.

ELDRIDGE, J. E. T. (1971). 'Weber's Approach to the Study of Industrial Workers.' In A. Sahay (ed.), *Max Weber and Modern Sociology*. London: Routledge and Kegan Paul.

EMERY, F. E. (ed.) (1969). *Systems Thinking*. Harmondsworth: Penguin.

EVANS, P., and GENADRY, N. (1999). 'A Duality-Based Perspective for Strategic Human Resource Management.' in P. Wright, L. Dyer, J. Boudreau, and G. Milkovich (eds.), *Research in Personnel and Human Resources Management*. Stamford, Conn.: JAI Press.

FINDLAY, P., and NEWTON, T. (1998). 'Reframing Foucault: The Case of Performance Appraisal.' In A. McKinlay and K. Starkey (eds.), *Foucault, Management and Organization Theory*. London: Sage.

FOUCAULT, M. (1980). Power/*Knowledge: Selected Interviews and Other Writings*. Brighton: Harvester.

FRANCIS, H., and SINCLAIR, J. (2003). 'A Processual Analysis of HRM-Based Change.' *Organization*, 10/4: 687–707.

FRIEDMAN, A. L. (1977). *Industry and Labor*. London: Macmillan.

GHORPADE, J. (2004). 'Management and the Human Resource Function: A Model Based on Social Systems Theory.' *International Journal of Human Resources Development and Management*, 4/3: 235–51.

GOOCH, L., and LEDWITH, S. (1996). 'Women in Personnel Management.' In S. Ledwith and F. Colgan (eds.), *Women in Organizations*. Basingstoke: Macmillan.

GOULDNER, A. W. (1954). *Patterns of Industrial Bureaucracy*. Glencoe, Ill.: Free Press.

GRANT, D., KEENOY, T., and OSWICK, C. (eds.) (1998). *Discourse and Organization*. London: Sage.

—— HARDY, C., OSWICK, C., and PUTNAM, L. (2004) *The Sage Handbook of Organizational Discourse*. London: Sage.

GREENWOOD, M. R. (2002). 'Ethics and HRM: A Review and Conceptual Analysis.' *Journal of Business Ethics*, 36/3: 261–78.

GRUGULIS, I., WILLMOTT, H., and KNIGHTS, D. (2000–1). *The Labor Process Debate: International Studies of Management and Organization*, 30/4.

GUEST, D. E. (2001). 'Human Resource Management: When Theory Confronts Research.' *International Journal of Human Resource Management*, 12/7: 1092–106.

HASSARD, J. (1993). *Sociology and Organization Theory: Positivism, Paradigms and Postmodernity*. London: Sage.

HATCH, M.-J. with CUNLIFFE, A. (2006). *Organization Theory: Modern, Symbolic and Postmodern Perspectives*, 2nd edn. Oxford: Oxford University Press.

HENDRY, C. (2003). 'Applying Employment Systems Theory to the Analysis of National Models of HRM.' *International Journal of Human Resource Management*, 14/8: 1430–42.

HYMAN, R. (1989). *The Political Economy of Industrial Relations*. London: Macmillan.

JACKSON, N., and CARTER, P. (2000). *Rethinking Organizational Behaviour*. Harlow: FT Prentice-Hall.

JACQUES, R. (1995). *Manufacturing the Employee: Management Knowledge from the 19th to the 21st Centuries*. London: Sage.

KALBERG, S. (ed.) (2005). *Max Weber: Readings and Commentary on Modernity*. Oxford: Blackwell.

KAMOCHE, K. (2000). *Sociological Paradigms and Human Resources: An African Context*. Aldershot: Ashgate.

KELEMAN, M., and HASSARD, J. (2003). 'Paradigm Plurality: Exploring Past Present and Future Trends.' In R. Westwood and S. Clegg (eds.), *Debating Organization: Point-Counterpoint in Organization Studies*. Oxford: Blackwell.

LEES, S. (1997). 'HRM and the Legitimacy Market.' *International Journal of Human Resource Management*, 8: 226–43.

LEGGE, K. (1978). *Power, Innovation and Problem Solving in Personnel Management*. London: McGraw Hill.

—— (1995). *Human Resource Management: Rhetorics and Realities*. Basingstoke: Macmillan.

—— (2001). 'Deconstruction Analysis and Management.' In M. Poole and M. Warner (eds.), *The IEBM Handbook of Human Resource Management*. London: Thomson Learning.

McKINLAY, A., and STARKEY, K. (eds.) (1998). *Foucault, Management and Organization Theory: From Panopticon to Technologies of Self*. London: Sage.

MARX, K. (1867). *Das Capital: Kritik der politischen Oekonomie*. Hamburg: Meissner.

MAYO, E. (1933). *The Human Problems of an Industrial Civilisation*. New York: Macmillan.

MILLER, F. B., and COGHILL, M. A. (1964). 'Sex and the Personnel Manager.' *Industrial and Labor Relations Review*, 18/1: 32–44.

MORGAN, P. (2000). 'Paradigms Lost and Paradigms Regained? Recent Developments and New Directions for HRM/OB in the UK and USA.' *International Journal of Human Resource Management*, 11/4: 853–66.

MOUNCE, H. O. (1997). *The Two Pragmatisms*. London: Routledge.

PAAUWE, J., and BOSELIE, P. (2003). 'Challenging "Strategic HRM" and the Relevance of the Institutional Setting.' *Human Resource Management Journal*, 13/3: 56–70.

PFEFFER, J. (1993). 'Barriers to the Advance of Organizational Science: Paradigm Development as a Dependent Variable.' *Academy of Management Review*, 18: 599–620.

PURCELL, J. (1999). 'Best Practice and Best Fit: Chimera or Cul de Sac?' *Human Resource Management Journal*, 93: 26–41.

—— and Ahlstrand, B. (1994). *Human Resource Management in the Multidivisional Company.* Oxford: Oxford University Press.

PUTNAM, H. (1995). *Pragmatism.* Oxford: Blackwell.

RAY, L. J., and REED, M. (eds.) (1994). *Organizing Modernity: New Weberian Perspectives on Work.* London: Routledge.

REED, M. (1996). 'Organization Theorizing: A Historically Contested Terrain.' In S. R. Clegg, C. Hardy, and W. Nord (eds.), *Handbook of Organization Studies.* London: Sage.

—— (2005). 'Reflections on the "Realist Turn" in Organization and Management Studies.' *Journal of Management Studies*, 42: 1621–44.

RITZER, G., and GOODMAN, D. J (2003). *Sociological Theory.* New York: McGraw Hill.

ROETHLISBERGER, F. J., and DICKSON, W. J. (1939). *Management and the Worker.* Cambridge, Mass.: Harvard University Press.

RORTY, R. (1980). *Philosophy and the Mirror of Nature.* Oxford: Blackwell.

—— (1982). *Consequences of Pragmatism.* Brighton: Harvester.

—— (1991). *Objectivity, Relativism and Truth.* Cambridge: Cambridge University Press.

SANCHEZ-RUNDE, C. (2001). 'Strategic Human Resource Management and the New Employment Relationship: A Research Review and Agenda.' In J. Gual and J. E. Ricart (eds.), *Strategy, Organization and the Changing Nature of Work.* Cheltenham: Elgar.

SCHULER, R. S., JACKSON, S. E., and STOREY, J. (2001). 'HRM and its Link with Strategic Management.' In J. Storey (ed.), *Human Resource Management: A Critical Text*, 2nd edn. London: Thomson Learning.

SELZNICK, P. (1948). 'Foundations of the Theory of Organization.' *American Sociological Review*, 13: 25–35.

SHENHAV, Y. (1994). 'Manufacturing Uncertainty or Uncertainty in Manufacturing: Managerial Discourse and the Rhetoric of Organizational Theory.' *Science in Context*, 7: 275–305.

—— (1995). 'From "Chaos" to Systems: The Engineering Foundations of Organization Theory 1877–1932.' *Administrative Science Quarterly*, 40: 557–85.

—— (1999). *Manufacturing Rationality: The Engineering Foundations of the Managerial Revolution.* Oxford: Oxford University Press.

—— (2003). 'The Historical and Epistemological Foundations of Organization Theory: Fusing Sociological Theory with Engineering Discourse.' In H. Tsoukas and C. Knudsen (eds.), *The Oxford Handbook of Organization Theory.* Oxford: Oxford University Press.

—— and WEITZ, E. (2000). 'The Roots of Uncertainty in Organization Theory: A Historical Constructivist Analysis.' *Organization*, 7: 373–85.

SILVERMAN, D. (1970). *The Theory of Organizations.* London: Heinemann.

SMITH, A. (1974). *The Wealth of Nations.* Harmondsworth: Penguin (1st pub. 1776).

SPENCER, D. A. (2000). 'Braverman and the Contribution of Labor Process Analysis to the Critique of Capitalist Production: Twenty-Five Years on.' *Work, Employment and Society*, 14: 223–43.

STARBUCK, W. H. (2003). 'The Origins of Organization Theory.' In H. Tsoukas and C. Knudsen (eds.), *The Oxford Handbook of Organization Theory.* Oxford: Oxford University Press.

STRAUSS, A. (1978). *Negotiations.* New York: Wiley.

—— Schatzman, L., Erlich, D., Bucher, R., and Sabsin, M. (1963). 'The Hospital and its Negotiated Order.' In E. Friedson (ed.), *The Hospital in Modern Society*. New York: Macmillan.

Taylor, F. W. (1911). *The Principles of Scientific Management*. New York: Harper.

Thompson, J. D. (1967). *Organizations in Action*. New York: McGraw-Hill.

Tichy, N. M., Fombrun, C. J. and Devanna, M. A. (1982). 'Strategic Human Resource Management.' *Sloan Management Review*, 23/2: 47–61.

Townley, B. (1994). *Reframing Human Resource Management*. London: Sage.

Tsoukas, H., and Knudsen, C. (2003). 'Introduction.' In H. Tsoukas and C. Knudsen (eds.), *The Oxford Handbook of Organization Theory*. Oxford: Oxford University Press.

Turner, B. S. (1996). *For Max Weber: Essays in the Sociology of Fate*. London: Sage.

Ure, A. (1835). *The Philosophy of Manufactures*. London: Charles Knight.

Vibert, C. (2004). *Theories of Macro-Organizational Behavior*. Armonk, NY: M. E. Sharpe.

Von Bertalanffy, L. (1972). 'The History and Status of General Systems Theory.' *Academy of Management Journal*, 15: 407–26.

Watson, T. J. (1977). *The Personnel Managers*. London: Routledge.

—— (1997). 'Theorising Managerial Work: A Pragmatic Pluralist Approach to Interdisciplinary Research.' *British Journal of Management*, 8: 3 8.

—— (2001a). 'Negotiated Orders, in Organizations.' In N. J. Smelser and P. B. Baltes (eds.), *International Encyclopedia of the Social and Behaviour Sciences*. Amsterdam: Elsevier.

—— (2001b). *In Search of Management*, rev. edn. London: Thomson.

—— (2004). 'Human Resource Management and Critical Social Science Analysis.' *Journal of Management Studies*, 41/3: 447–67.

—— (2005). 'Organizations, Strategies and Human Resourcing.' In J. Leopold, L. Harris, and T. J. Watson (eds.), *The Strategic Management of Human Resources*. London: FT Prentice Hall.

—— (2006). *Organizing and Managing Work*, 2nd edn. Harlow: FT Prentice-Hall.

Weber, M. (1922). *Wirtschaft und Gesellschaft*. Tübingen: Paul Siebeck.

—— (1978). *Economy and Society*. Berkeley and Los Angeles: University of California Press.

Weick, K. E. (1979). *The Social Psychology of Organizing*. Reading, Mass.: Addison-Wesley.

Westwood, R., and Linstead, S. (2001) 'Language/Organization: Introduction.' In R. Westwood and S. Linstead, *The Language of Organization*. London: Sage.

CHAPTER 7

......................................................................

# HRM AND THE WORKER

## TOWARDS A NEW PSYCHOLOGICAL CONTRACT?

......................................................................

DAVID E. GUEST

## 7.1 INTRODUCTION

......................................................................

For managers who accept the argument that effective management of human resources provides a distinctive basis for competitive advantage (Barney and Wright 1998), the case for taking human resource management seriously is compelling. But terms sometimes associated with advocacy of strategic human resource management such as a 'full utilization of the workforce' or 'exploiting your assets' do not bode well for the workers who constitute those human resources. So what's in it for the workers? Does human resource management (HRM) offer them a positive deal or is it, as Keenoy (1990) once suggested, 'a wolf in sheep's clothing?' This chapter will explore HRM from a worker's perspective. It will build on an analytic framework proposed by Wright and Boswell (2002) and utilize the concept of the psychological contract to consider how HRM helps to shape workers' attitudes and behavior and in particular their satisfaction and well-being.

Some of the language of strategic HRM has provided ammunition for critics who might see it as little more than a different system of management control designed to enmesh the worker more deeply in the organization while offering little in return. This means that we must first consider what we mean by HRM and how it relates to the long-standing issue of managerial control. This is important because it helps to provide a context for some of the debates on the role of HRM and in particular some of the more critical writing about HRM as a potential form of exploitation of workers. The analysis of the shifting basis for control can also be linked to debates about a 'new deal' that have helped to stimulate interest in the psychological contract.

## 7.2 HRM, Managerial Control, and the New Psychological Contract

In highlighting the role of HRM as a potential source of competitive advantage, Barney was pointing to an opportunity but not providing a solution, since he did not advocate a form of HRM most likely to provide competitive advantage. His background in strategic management meant that he leant towards a contingency approach whereby HRM should be designed to fit with the wider strategic thrust of the organization. However, this still leaves open the question of whether it is possible to identify dominant approaches to HRM that might be adopted in specific contexts. Writers from Miles and Snow (1984) to Boxall and Purcell (2003) have tried to provide answers.

Not everyone agreed that a contingency approach was appropriate. Walton (1985), an early and influential voice in the debates on HRM, argued that we needed to move from what he termed 'control' to 'commitment' as the basis for managing the workforce. Walton's essential case was that the traditional model of tight managerial control over the workforce was no longer effective, largely because it was based on the wrong set of assumptions about the nature of contemporary work and the contemporary workforce and therefore about how best to manage it. Furthermore, he argued that there were efficiencies in a high-commitment model since it meant that workers exercised self-control, obviating the need for external control over behavior and performance, and research on organizational commitment (e.g. Meyer and Allen 1997) reveals a consistent association with lower labor turnover. Therefore, there are likely to be gains for the organization through improved performance and improved retention and gains for the workforce through greater autonomy, control, and intrinsic job satisfaction. More controversially, Walton implied that the commitment model was likely to be more effective in all contexts. He was therefore an early advocate of a universalist model of HRM.

High-commitment management, as a distinctive approach to HRM, challenged the traditional basis for management control by suggesting that what was required was a move from external control through management systems, technology, and supervision to self-control by workers or teams of workers who, because of their commitment to the organization, would exercise responsible autonomy and control in the interests of the organization. Another way of describing it is to suggest that the way in which managers and professionals have traditionally been managed, based on assumptions about their motivation and commitment, should be extended throughout the workforce. To many managers, this might appear to be a high risk.

The contrast between control and commitment has been used to describe different approaches to HRM. The distinction has also been described as top-down versus bottom-up management (Appelbaum and Batt 1994), a 'low road' and a 'high road' approach (Milkman 1997), and 'hard' versus 'soft' HRM (Storey 1992).

Influenced partly by the vogue for process re-engineering and partly by research in organizational psychology and labor economics, another approach to HRM is often manifested through an emphasis on performance management. The effective adoption of best HR practices remains as the heart of this approach; but it differs from the high-commitment model in the important respect that management retains much of its control. The focus is on the adoption of practices designed to maximize high performance by ensuring high levels of competence and motivation. The relevant HR practices, which have their roots in goal-setting theory (Locke and Latham 1990) and, to a lesser extent, expectancy theory (Lawler 1971), offer an approach to fully utilizing employees. If the focus remains exclusively on high performance, it displays little concern for worker well-being.

This short analysis reveals two 'ideal type' approaches to HRM that address the issue of control of workers in rather different ways. The 'high-commitment' model appears to cede control to employees by emphasizing self-control alongside but also as a means of generating high commitment. The 'performance management' model allows managers to retain control and uses HR practices as a means of directing workers' efforts more effectively. The former emphasizes intrinsic control and intrinsic rewards; the latter emphasizes external control and extrinsic rewards.

Attempts have been made to integrate elements of these two contrasting approaches. At a strategic level, this might be achieved through the concept of flexibility. In the UK, the initial idea of the flexible firm was based on a distinction between a core group of key workers and a peripheral group who were less central to the success of the organization (Atkinson 1984). The implication was that most key workers could be managed using a high-commitment model while peripheral workers required tighter performance management. Indeed, this second group could either be managed differently or possibly offered different kinds of contract or subcontracted to other firms.

A somewhat different perspective on flexibility has been presented by Lepak and Snell (1999) who argue that it is appropriate to recognize different categories of worker and to develop distinctive HR practices to reflect these differences. In their model, they outline four categories based on the value and uniqueness of human capital. Where both are high, they suggest that a high-commitment approach to HRM will be most appropriate; where both are low, a more contractual relationship with a narrower focus on performance will be more effective. The core of the flexibility argument is that the approach to HRM should be determined by strategically identified characteristics of the workforce. It implies that HRM is likely to be differentiated across organizations but also within organizations and therefore, potentially, to affect different categories of worker in different ways.

A second attempt to reconcile these contrasting approaches to HRM and control of the workforce is offered by advocates of what has come to be described as 'high performance' or 'high involvement' (Batt 2002) work systems. Building on expectancy theory, Becker et al. (1997) and Guest (1997) suggested that high performance depends on adopting HR practices that lead to workers having high ability/ competence, high motivation, and an opportunity to contribute through jobs that provide the discretion, autonomy, and control to use the knowledge and skills and to exercise motivation. A key feature of this approach is that it places employees at the centre of HRM. Furthermore, with its elements of internal and external control and intrinsic and extrinsic incentives, it perhaps offers a pragmatic approach to high performance. Nevertheless, its focus is on performance, and despite taking account of issues such as trust and job security, it has little explicit to say about workers' satisfaction and well-being. The key challenge for HRM within the framework being adopted here, which places the worker at the centre of the agenda, is to identify the circumstances under which HR policy and practice can result in both high performance and high levels of employee satisfaction and well-being.

While the differing approaches to HRM and management control imply rather different views about workers and may appear to show different degrees of concern about workers' well-being, they are all invariably presented essentially as routes to better performance. Walton implies that, like it or not, in the contemporary workplace there is no choice but to manage with the commitment rather than the compliance of the workforce. Yet this is still an argument about organizational performance rather than worker well-being and leaves open questions about the association between organizational performance and worker well-being.

Although there has been a continuing, albeit often low-key dimension in the debate on the relationship between HRM and performance about the need to take more seriously the role of employees, in practice, most of the research on HRM and performance has neglected what has been termed the 'black box' or the process whereby HRM affects performance. However, it is generally acknowledged that it must be partly through its impact on the attitudes and behavior of the workforce.

There is therefore a strong case for exploring the impact of HRM on employees or, to put it another way, how employees react to HRM. There is an even stronger case for incorporating this into the study of any link between HRM and performance to test for any full or partial mediation effect of employee attitudes and behavior. These issues are explored in some detail elsewhere in the book and we will therefore not pursue them further here. Instead we will focus more directly on outcomes of primary concern to employees. These include intrinsic and extrinsic rewards, job satisfaction, well-being, and the wider issues of work–life balance, health, and life satisfaction. The framework of the psychological contract, which is introduced in the next section, implies that a positive deal may result in benefits for both the employer and the employees; in other words, while the focus is on employee-centered outcomes, they may be linked to employer-relevant outcomes as well.

Before moving on, it is important to clarify two central terms used in the remainder of this chapter. First, a distinction has been drawn between approaches to HRM. As other chapters highlight, there is no clear consensus in research and writing about either the conceptual or operational definition of HRM. Reference will be made to studies that address 'high-involvement,' 'high-commitment' and 'high-performance work systems.' As implied above, these overlap considerably. Irrespective of the term used, the focus will be on their association with employee attitudes, behavior, and well-being.

The second term that is extensively used in this chapter is 'worker well-being.' This goes beyond job satisfaction to cover the mental and physical health of workers. Therefore, while it includes job satisfaction, it also covers work-related stress and in the context of current debates, and insofar as there is spillover, can also be extended to include work–life balance and satisfaction with life as a whole. These are issues of central concern to many workers but of more marginal interest to organizations. They have not been a typical focus of studies of the impact of HRM.

## 7.3 THE ROLE OF THE PSYCHOLOGICAL CONTRACT

The aim of achieving both organizational and individual goals—of gaining both high performance and high employee satisfaction—implies some form of exchange, a deal in which both sides can win. It is in this context that the psychological contract may help to provide some insights. There have been three main reasons for the growth of interest in the psychological contract as a potentially useful analytic framework. The first is the belief that the core of the deal is changing

(Rousseau 1995; Herriot and Pemberton 1995). The second is that organizational change is now so pervasive that sooner or later any deal is in trouble, creating scope for breach and violation (Morrison and Robinson 1997), and making the retention of employee commitment, even with the best of HR practices, more difficult to achieve. The third is the argument that the nature of deal-making is changing from general deals to more idiosyncratic deals, putting more pressure on local management to make and manage them (Rousseau 2001).

Before exploring these issues in more detail, we need to define the psychological contract. There are various definitions but the one that we will use defines the psychological contract as 'the perceptions of both parties to the employment relationship, organization and individual, of the reciprocal promises and obligations implied in that relationship' (Herriot and Pemberton 1997; Guest and Conway 2002b). These promises and obligations can range from those that are clear and explicit and close to components of the formal employment contract, such as more pay in exchange for better performance; to others that are more informal and implicit such as a boss–subordinate agreement about flexible working hours to accommodate domestic circumstances. While both parties should be aware of the exchange, there is scope, particularly in the more informal deals, for misunderstanding and disagreement. It has been suggested elsewhere (Guest 2004) that to fully understand the potential consequences of the psychological contract, it is important additionally to take into account issues of fairness and trust. This is because the 'deal' may have been agreed by a worker but may be judged partly in the context of the deals made with others. Also, it is possible that promises are being met at present but a continuing contribution is likely to be based partly on an assessment of whether the other party to the deal can be trusted to continue to deliver in the future.

The argument about the changing nature of the psychological contract is sometimes presented in terms of an old and a new deal (Herriot and Pemberton 1995). In the context of managerial and professional workers, this can be described as a shift from an upwardly mobile long-term career with the same organization in return for loyalty and good performance, to provision of challenging work and development opportunities in exchange for high performance. The distinctive changes concern a reduced focus on loyalty and commitment in return for security, with greater emphasis instead on notions of employability (Bridges 1995) and boundaryless careers (Arthur and Rousseau 1996). For non-managerial workers, the change is away from the old idea of a fair day's work for a fair day's pay towards a greater emphasis on pay related to contribution and an expectation of flexibility that can fly in the face of traditional approaches to defining roles and rewards based on job analysis and job evaluation. All this implies a more challenging environment for workers at all levels.

These changes have been defined within the psychological contract literature along a number of dimensions of which the best known is the distinction between transactional and relational contracts. Transactional contracts are those that are clearly defined, time bound, and easy to monitor. Relational contracts are more implicit and informal and less easy to tie down and monitor. Some of the literature, focusing on change in psychological contracts, and mindful of the claimed growth in numerical flexibility reflected in portfolio workers and boundaryless careers, has suggested a move towards transactional contracts. A contrasting literature, focusing more on functional flexibility, has suggested a move to relational contracts. An example of this would be a blurring of what constitutes organizational citizenship behavior and a concern that extra-role activities such as staying late at work as a matter of course, and reflecting a long hours culture, becomes an informal norm. The transactional–relational distinction was initially brought to the analysis of psychological contracts by Rousseau, who found support for it in some of her early empirical work (Rousseau 1990). However, Coyle-Shapiro and Kessler (2000) found three factors and Hui et al. (2004) also found three, adding a 'balanced' factor to the first two. Furthermore, the boundary between transactional and relational elements is, in some cases, far from clear. There is therefore some doubt about the validity of the distinction, doubt about the direction of any change, and, more fundamentally, doubt about whether it makes sense to consider a move in one direction or another. If two or three relatively independent dimensions are identified, then it should be possible to be simultaneously high or low on each or all of them.

Nevertheless, the argument about the changing nature of the psychological contract poses distinctive challenges for the human resource function. First, it is important to have policies and practices that can keep up with a rapidly changing context and also tap in to changing employee expectations. In recent years, the growing interest in work–life balance provides a good example of this. Second, it is probably wise to expect that some people are going to believe that their psychological contract has been breached. Indeed, Conway and Briner (2002a) found that psychological contracts are breached on an almost daily basis. However, they also indicate that if breach of the psychological contract is an everyday occurrence, then it may not be too serious. Morrison and Robinson (1997) have drawn a distinction between breach and violation. The step up to violation occurs when there is an emotional reaction and the worker feels affronted and upset by the experience. The challenge for the HR profession is to ensure that this rarely happens since it is invariably associated with negative outcomes for both individual and employer (Conway and Briner 2005).

A related challenge for the HR function is a shift from general to idiosyncratic contracts. General deals are relatively easy to monitor and manage from the centre. The case made by Rousseau (2001, 2003) is that the growth in flexibility, concerns for work–life balance, and the reducing size of many workplaces means that key elements of the psychological contract are negotiated at the local level between the employee and her line manager. The kind of social exchange that has long been recognized in the context of leader—member exchange (LMX) theory

(Yukl 2005) will become more pervasive. As a result, they may be out of the control of the HR department, which needs to ensure that line managers fully understand their obligations as agents of the organization in making informal arrangements with employees.

One way in which this might be achieved has been suggested by Bowen and Ostroff (2004). They argue that to understand how HRM has an impact, we need to look not only at the system of practices but also at supporting processes. They highlight in particular the role of organizational climate as a powerful mediating variable, a view supported in the research of Gelade and Ivery (2003). More specifically, they acknowledge, in line with the conventional analysis of the psychological contract, that on the basis of their experiences, individuals will perceive psychological climates; they argue that the key is to turn these into collective climates and thereby enhance the strength of the HR system. Social exchange theory has been used extensively within organizational behavior to explain how this might be achieved, notably through the concepts of perceived organizational support (Eisenberger et al. 1986). By providing a degree of consistency in supporting a strong organizational climate, these additional elements of the environment should provide an important complement to the system of human resource practices.

Wright and Boswell (2002: 261) argue that the psychological contract is important for the analysis of the relationship between HRM and workers because 'psychological contracts and related perceptions are perhaps best viewed as linking mechanisms between HR practices and individual attitudes and behavior.' This view is reinforced by Rousseau (Rousseau 1995; Rousseau and Greller 1994) who suggests that experience of HR practices helps to shape workers' perceptions of the exchange relationship. In other words, the psychological contract provides an important linking mechanism that can help to explain how HRM might influence employee attitudes and behavior and, if the further link can be demonstrated, organizational performance. One advantage of utilizing the psychological contract, also noted by Wright and Boswell, is that it focuses on workers' perceptions of HR practices. The emphasis therefore shifts from the organizational level and managers' statements about practices to the individual level and accounts of how workers experience HRM (Mabey et al. 1998).

# 7.4 HRM, the Psychological Contract, and Worker Well-Being

Conway and Briner (2005) suggest there are three ways in which the psychological contract might affect behavior. Each in turn can be related to human resource practices. First, psychological contracts, more particularly the promises and commitments made by the organization and its agents, provide a goal structure that can help to motivate and direct behavior. Second, psychological contracts might operate through a system of social exchange, based on what Gouldner (1960) termed the norm of reciprocity. Third, they may operate through a form of equity theory, reflected in a balanced psychological contract. Where there is a balance between the promises and obligations of employer and employee, it would be predicted that the outcomes will be more positive than when there is imbalance. Conway and Briner note that the evidence relating to each of these explanations about how the psychological contract influences outcomes is relatively limited. However, there is an extensive literature in support of the positive impact of goal-setting (Locke and Latham 1990). There is rather more psychological contract research relating to social exchange. The results are somewhat mixed but generally support the view that a positive offer, manifested in promises from the employer, will be reciprocated by more promises on the part of the employee as well as commitment and motivation to meet the promises and obligations (Conway and Coyle-Shapiro 2004). The one key study that addresses issues of equity or balance (Shore and Barksdale 1998), albeit conducted within an explicitly social exchange framework, does show that where there is a balance, whether it is based on high or low levels of reciprocal promises and commitments, then the outcomes for employees are more positive.

The promises and obligations that form the core of the psychological contract are likely to be shaped by a variety of factors, including the organization's human resource practices. These will be communicated initially though the information provided during the recruitment and selection process, including, in some cases, more or less realistic job previews. They will be reinforced and perhaps modified through further processes of socialization (de Vos et al. 2003), social information-processing (Salancik and Pfeffer 1978), and various forms of communication (Guest and Conway 2002b). Guest and Conway explored the ways in which organizations sought to communicate the psychological contract and which processes were rated most effective by HR managers. They found three broad types of communication, covering communication around the process of recruitment, communication from the top of the organization, including mission statements and broad general promises, and local communication that was more job and person related. Perhaps not surprisingly, communication and promises associated with local communication of the psychological contract were rated most effective and those coming from the top of the organization were least effective in managing the psychological contract and the employment relationship.

We noted earlier that the impact of HR practices and the way in which the organization seeks to communicate the deal are likely to be at least partly a function of the characteristics of the workers who form part of the exchange. Conway and Briner (2005) review the evidence about individual characteristics that might help to shape the deal and perceptions of it. They report Coyle-Shapiro and Neumann's (2004) research concerning different ideologies of exchange which suggests that these are relatively stable personality characteristics. They found variations between those they labeled 'entitleds' who generally expect to receive more than they give in exchange, 'equity sensitives' who are concerned to achieve a balance, and 'benevolents' with a creditor ideology who are happy to give more than they receive. These different orientations to the exchange are likely to shape perceptions of the deal and reactions to it. Raja et al. (2004) found that differences in personality characteristics such as neuroticism affected preferences for relational and transactional contracts. These individual differences may strengthen the case for promoting idiosyncratic deals. They also support the need for a consistent context, which, as Bowen and Ostroff (2004) suggest, might be reinforced by a supportive climate, providing a strong HR system and encouraging a positive exchange between employee and employer. HR practices applied at the organization or establishment level thus set a framework but the 'deal' will often be elaborated at the local level between the line manager and each of her staff.

Despite the assumption of Rousseau (1995) that HRM will help to shape the psychological contract, there is little published evidence that explicitly considers either this or any subsequent link to employee attitudes, behavior, and well-being. One exception is a series of surveys in the UK by Guest and Conway. Guest and Conway's (2002b) study of 1,306 employers found that more promises are likely to be made and more are likely to be kept by the organization where more 'high-involvement' HR practices are in place. Surveys of UK workers report similar findings (see, for example, Guest and Conway 2002a, 2004a). Workers reporting that they experience more HR practices also report that more promises are made by the organization and that they are more likely to be kept. These results from both employers and employees suggest that the presence of HR practices may help to make the promises more visible and explicit or, in the language of the psychological contract, more transactional. Transactional psychological contracts may be easier to monitor and attract stronger obligations on the part of management to keep them. In summary, greater numbers of HR practices are associated with a more extensive psychological contract and with a greater likelihood that the promises and obligations will be met.

The next step is therefore to determine the consequences of meeting the promises and obligations in the psychological contract. This has been the major focus of research on the psychological contract, although most attention has been paid to the consequences of non-fulfillment or breach of the psychological contract. Studies (e.g. Conway and Briner 2002a; Robinson 1995; Robinson and Rousseau 1994; Turnley and Feldman 1999) have confirmed that breach of the psychological contract is commonplace and that when it escalates to violation (Robinson and Morrison 2000) it has more serious negative consequences. It has consistently been associated with reduced commitment to the organization, lower job satisfaction, reduced organizational citizenship behavior, and an increased turn-over intention and actual staff turnover (see Conway and Briner 2005 for a review). It is important to bear in mind that if breach is associated with negative outcomes, then fulfillment of promises, which, as we have seen, is associated with greater numbers of HR practices, leads to positive outcomes (see, for example, Turnley et al. 2003).

While these outcomes are of interest from a worker's perspective, with the exception of job satisfaction, they are likely to be of more concern to the organization. Very few studies have actually considered outcomes associated with workers' well-being. In their review of all the published studies concerned with breach and violation of the psychological contract, Conway and Briner (2005) could find only two concerned with well-being, both by themselves (Conway and Briner 2002*a*, 2002*b*). These found that violation of the psychological contract was associated with poorer moods and feelings of reduced well-being. However, there is relevant data in the surveys by Guest and Conway (2002*a*, 2004*a*) using the analytic framework set out in Fig. 7.1. Based each year on a sample of 1,000 workers broadly representative of the UK working population with respect to age, gender, and occupational status, a core set of questions covered experience of human resource practices, the psychological contract, and outcomes such as satisfaction, stress at work, and aspects of well-being, life satisfaction, and work–life balance.

After controlling for other factors, greater experience of human resource practices is associated with a greater number of reported promises and a higher level of reported fulfillment of promises in the psychological contract. There is a direct

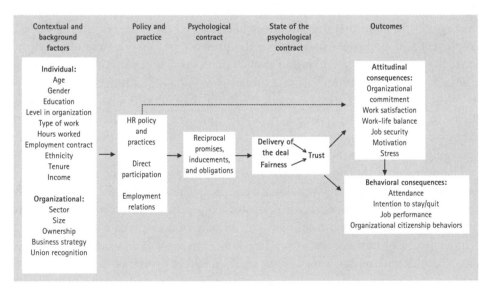

**Fig. 7.1. A framework for the analysis of the psychological contract**

association between HRM and the range of attitudinal outcomes including work satisfaction, life satisfaction, and satisfaction with work–life balance but this association is either fully or partially mediated by the measure of the state of the psychological contract. There is a small positive association between greater experience of HR practices and stress. However, there is a strong negative association between a positive state of the psychological contract and stress and evidence that the state of the psychological contract moderates the relationship between HRM and stress. With respect to other aspects of well-being, a positive state of the psychological contract is associated with fewer reports of harmful experiences at work and with a much lower likelihood that the demands of work will be perceived as harmful. On a more positive note, those reporting a positive state of the psychological contract are also likely to report that they find their work more exciting. The 2004 survey explored the concept of a 'healthy workplace' as defined by the UK Health and Safety Executive (Cousins et al. 2004) following concern about the rapid growth in long-term absence due to non-physical ill health. The survey found a strong association between greater experience of HR practices and worker reports of a 'healthier workplace.' Both a 'healthier workplace' and a more positive state of the psychological contract were associated with much lower levels of work-related stress.

While this section has focused on the role of the psychological contract, it is important to note that there have been other studies linking HRM and employee attitudes. There is evidence from both the USA (see, for example, Appelbaum et al. 2000; Batt 2002) and from the UK (Guest 2002; Patterson et al. 1997) linking more extensive experience of HR practices and greater satisfaction, motivation, and commitment.

In summary, what these studies reveal is that, based on employee reports of their experiences of 'high-involvement' HR practices, an approach recommended by Gerhart et al. (2000) to ensure that data is collected on actual practices, there is an association between greater current experience of these practices and a range of outcomes associated with employee well-being. Specifically, they are associated with higher levels of work and life satisfaction and better work–life balance. They are also associated with greater job security and a better quality of workplace. All of these outcomes are partially or fully mediated by the measure of the state of the psychological contract which includes as its central component a measure of fulfillment of promises by the organization. This measure is also strongly associated with lower levels of stress at work and serves to moderate the small positive association between HRM and stress at work. These surveys also show a positive association between both greater experience of HR practices and a positive state of the psychological contract and a range of organizationally relevant outcomes such as greater commitment, motivation, and intention to stay. Since there is also evidence, elsewhere in the book, that greater use of HR practices is associated with positive organizational outcomes and some evidence that these are mediated by employee attitudes and behavior, there is support for a provisional conclusion that through greater use of 'high-commitment' HRM, everyone wins. It would seem that we are getting closer to finding the conditions under which it is possible to have high performance and high worker well-being.


# 7.5 WORKER WELL-BEING OR WORKER EXPLOITATION?

The evidence presented above consistently reveals a positive association between the greater use of high-commitment HRM and various indicators of workers' well-being. It also confirms that the psychological contract acts as a mediator between HRM and employee attitudes. Despite this, there have been critical voices raised against HRM, partly because of its potentially negative consequences for workers.

A major concern is that HRM is likely to be associated with the intensification of work. One of the aims of HRM is to raise performance; the issue is how this is raised. There is empirical evidence that in the UK work has become more intensive (Green 2001) with longer hours for some workers but also more time spent in productive activity, leaving less space in the working day for recovery or reflection. However, since there is also evidence that there has at the same time been only a relatively modest implementation of HR practices (Cully et al. 1999), it is difficult to support a claim that intensification can be attributed to HRM. Insofar as there is any substance to the claim, it might be attributable to the greater focus on performance management which falls within the 'hard' or 'low-road' version of HRM, designed to direct worker effort to increasing performance.

One of the indications of externally imposed demands is higher work-related stress (Karasek and Theorell 1990). Appelbaum et al. (2000) found that workers reported less stress in US organizations with high-performance work practices. In contrast, the study by Ramsay et al. (2000) using the UK WERS data found an association between their measure of HRM and higher reported stress among workers. This finding must be viewed with some caution since their measure of HRM does not conform to any standard model. However, it does suggest there may be some substance in the claims that HRM might have negative consequences. The two studies by Guest and Conway (2002a, 2004a) found a modest but significant association between greater experience of HRM and work-related stress. However, in both surveys, the association was moderated by the state of the psychological contract. In other words, HRM is only associated with stress where management fails to meet its promises and obligations.

The second major concern expressed by critics of HRM is that it promotes a unitarist system which reduces workers' collective voice. Evidence from the UK Workplace Employee Relations Survey (Guest and Conway 2004*b*) and from the annual surveys of the psychological contract (Guest and Conway 1999) shows that trade union membership and trade union recognition is associated with lower levels of satisfaction with work, after controlling for a range of individual and organizational factors. Guest and Conway (1999) compared the impact of union membership and a set of high-commitment HR practices on work satisfaction and other outcomes and found that the positive impact on outcomes such as satisfaction was derived from the HR practices rather than the union presence. The most positive workers were those reporting high levels of HR practices and no union membership while the most negative workers were those with low levels of HR practices and trade union membership rather than those without both. This suggests that a union presence may provide voice but often this voice will not be associated with work satisfaction.

Despite the absence in these surveys of any association between a union presence and positive worker satisfaction and well-being, there is evidence from other sources that a mutual-gains (Kochan and Osterman 1995) or partnership model (Guest and Peccei 2001) may benefit both the organization and its employees. Where there is an established trade union presence and a climate of cooperation, this may be an appropriate means of promoting the link between HRM and worker satisfaction and well-being while also providing the kind of safeguards that are sometimes necessary to ensure that individual managers do not seek to bypass the spirit of trust that partnership can help to promote. If the psychological contract operates at the individual level, then the mutual-gains or partnership model offers a more collective equivalent. In terms of Bowen and Ostroff's (2004) analysis, it helps to promote the strength of the HR system. To date, there are few reported cases of the effective implementation of this kind of working arrangement.

The third broad criticism of HRM is that it is a form of deceit, promising one thing and delivering another, using subtle approaches to incorporate workers into an organizational way of thinking and in effect brainwashing them to become 'willing slaves' (Scott 1994). This concern has been voiced in the UK by Legge (1995, 2000) and Keenoy (1990) and has been addressed in some detail elsewhere (Guest 1999). Essentially, it boils down to the issue of whether we take workers' accounts of their experiences seriously. The case for taking workers' accounts seriously is compelling; and as the workforce becomes increasingly well educated and well informed, it becomes even stronger. The available accounts generally do not support the view that they feel deceived or exploited by HRM.

In summary, there is some evidence that HRM, in whatever form, increases the demands of the job, either by providing greater autonomy or through externally shaped controls, and can be associated with slightly higher stress. However, there are powerful mediating and moderating factors, including the psychological contract, suggesting that this need not be a major concern. There is no evidence that a trade union presence serves to alleviate stress or improve worker well-being more generally. Nevertheless, where a union is well established, a case can be made for pursuing a mutual-gains model that might serve to protect and enhance worker well-being, reinforcing the positive impact of HRM.

# 7.6 SUMMARY AND CONCLUSION

This chapter has explored human resource management from the perspective of the worker. We have been concerned primarily with the non-managerial workers, but, as noted above, it is important to recognize that the workforce is increasingly well qualified and the proportion of what can be described as 'knowledge workers' is growing. This affects the balance of workers' orientations and priorities in work and life outside work. It also gives more credence to the view of HRM as a process of extending policies and practices directed to managerial and professional workers to the rest of the workforce.

The chapter has given some emphasis to the question of management control and the implication of how the challenge to control is resolved through the approach to HRM that is adopted. This matters because the 'hard,' top-down perspective is more management centered and management controlled while the 'soft' bottom-up approach is more likely to result in the high-involvement HR practices that take some account of workers' concerns and place employee attitudes and behavior closer to the heart of the policy framework.

The psychological contract has been used to help to explain how HRM has an impact on employee attitudes and behavior. Building on social exchange theory, it is suggested that when the employer offers promises and makes commitments, these will be reciprocated by the employee. The evidence presented confirms that greater use of HR practices is associated with a greater number of promises in the psychological contract, a greater level of fulfillment of these, and better levels of perceived fairness of the deal and trust in management. Fairness and trust are strongly implicated in the traditional employment relationship and these findings, reinforced by ratings of the state of employer–employee relations, confirm that a positive state of the psychological contract is associated with better employment relations as well as a whole range of additional positive outcomes. This suggests that even in the absence of a trade union and traditional pluralist industrial relations, policies and practices designed to ensure a fair exchange within the psychological contract can promote effective employment relations. This helps to counter some of the concerns about exploitation in the absence of a union presence.

There is still a case to be made and a battle to be won to promote greater adoption of the high-commitment/high-performance work system approach to HRM. In those organizations that do adopt it, the benefits to the organization and, in this context, more particularly to the workers are apparent. It is likely to lead to a more secure and better quality of working life, a better work–life balance, and greater overall life satisfaction. These are outcomes that are well worth pursuing.

# REFERENCES

APPELBAUM, E., and BATT, R. (1994). *The New American Workplace*. Ithaca, NY: Cornell University Press.

—— BAILEY, T., BERG. P., and KALLEBERG, A. (2000). *Manufacturing* Advantage: Ithaca, NY: Cornell University Press.

ARTHUR, M., and ROUSSEAU, D. (1996). *The Boundaryless Career*. Oxford: Oxford University Press.

ATKINSON, J. (1984). 'Manpower Strategies for Flexible Organizations.' *Personnel Management*, August: 28–31.

BARNEY, J., and WRIGHT, P. (1998). 'On Becoming a Strategic Partner: The Role of Human Resources in Gaining Competitive Advantage.' *Human Resource Management*, 37: 31–46.

BATT, R. (2002). 'Managing Customer Services: Human Resource Practices, Quit Rates, and Sales Growth.' *Academy of Management Journal*, 45: 587–98.

BECKER, B., HUSELID, M., PICKUS, P., and SPRATT, M. (1997). 'HR as a Source of Shareholder Value: Research and Recommendations.' *Human Resource Management*, 36: 39–47.

BOWEN, D., and OSTROFF, C. (2004). 'Understanding HRM–Firm Performance Linkages: The Role of the "Strength" of the HRM System.' *Academy of Management Review*, 29: 203–21.

BOXALL, P., and PURCELL, J. (2003). *Strategy and Human Resource Management*. Basingstoke: Palgrave Macmillan.

BRIDGES, W. (1995). *Job Shift: How to Prosper in a Workplace without Jobs*. London: Nicholas Brearley.

CONWAY, N., and BRINER, R. (2002a). 'A Daily Diary Study of Affective Responses to Psychological Contract Breach and Exceeded Promises.' *Journal of Organizational Behavior*, 23: 287–302.

—— —— (2002b). 'Full-Time Versus Part-Time Employees: Understanding the Links between Work Status, Psychological Contract and Attitudes.' *Journal of Vocational Behavior*, 61: 279–301.

—— —— (2005). *Understanding Psychological Contracts at Work*. Oxford: Oxford University Press.

—— and COYLE-SHAPIRO, J. (2004). 'The Employment Relationship through the Lens of Social Exchange.' In J. Coyle-Shapiro, L. Shore, M. S. Taylor, and L. Tetrick (eds.), *The Employment Relationship: Examining Psychological and Contextual Perspectives*. Oxford: Oxford University Press.

COUSINS, R., MACKAY, C., CLARKE, S., KELLY, C., KELLY, P., and McHAIG, R. (2004). ' "Management Standards" and Work-Related Stress in the UK: Practical Development.' *Work and Stress*, 18: 113–36.

COYLE-SHAPIRO, J., and KESSLER, I. (2000). 'Consequences of the Psychological Contract for the Employment Relationship: A Large-Scale Survey.' *Journal of Management Studies*, 37: 903–30.

—— and NEUMANN, J. (2004). 'Individual Dispositions and the Psychological Contract: The Moderating Effects of Exchange and Creditor Ideologies.' *Journal of Vocational Behavior*, 64: 150–64.

CULLY, M., WOODLAND, S., O'REILLY, A., and DIX, S. (1999). *Britain at Work*. London: Routledge.

DE VOS, A., BUYENS, D., and SCHALK, R. (2003). 'Psychological Contract Development during Organizational Socialization: Adaptation to Reality and the Role of Reciprocity.' *Journal of Organizational Behavior*, 24: 537–58.

EISENBERGER, R., HUNTINGDON, R., HUTCHISON, S., and SOWA, D. (1986). 'Perceived Organizational Support.' *Journal of Applied Psychology*, 71: 500–7.

GELADE, G., and IVERY, M. (2003). 'The Impact of Human Resource Management and Work Climate on Organizational Performance.' *Personnel Psychology*, 56: 383–404.

GERHART, B., WRIGHT, P., MAMAHAN, G., and SNELL, S. (2000). 'Measurement Error in Research on Human Resources and Firm Performance: How Much Error is there and How does it Influence Size Effect Estimates?' *Personnel Psychology*, 53: 805–34.

GOULDNER, A. (1960). 'The Norm of Reciprocity: A Preliminary Statement.' *American Sociological Review*, 25: 161–78.

GREEN, F. (2001). 'It's been a Hard Day's Night: The Concentration and Intensification of Work in Late Twentieth Century Britain.' *British Journal of Industrial Relations*, 39: 53–80.

GUEST, D. (1997). 'Human Resource Management and Performance: A Review and Research Agenda.' *International Journal of Human Resource Management*, 8: 263–76.

—— (1999). 'Human Resource Management: The Workers' Verdict.' *Human Resource Management Journal*, 9/3: 5–25.

—— (2002). 'Human Resource Management, Corporate Performance and Employee Well-Being: Building the Worker into HRM.' *Journal of Industrial Relations*, 44: 335–58.

—— (2004). 'The Psychology of the Employment Relationship: An Analysis Based on the Psychological Contract.' *Applied Psychology: An International Review*, 53: 541–55.

—— and Conway, N. (1999). 'Peering into the Black Hole: The Downside of the New Employment Relations in the UK.' *British Journal of Industrial Relations*, 37: 367–89.

—— —— (2002a). *Pressure at Work and the Psychological Contract*. London: CIPD.

—— —— (2002b). 'Communicating the Psychological Contract: An Employer Perspective.' *Human Resource Management Journal*, 12: 22–39.

—— —— (2004a). *Employee Well-Being and the Psychological Contract*. London: CIPD.

—— —— (2004b). 'Exploring the Paradox of Unionised Worker Dissatisfaction.' *Industrial Relations Journal*, 35: 102–21.

—— and PECCEI, R. (2001). 'Partnership at Work: Mutuality and the Balance of Advantage.' *British Journal of Industrial Relations*, 39: 207–36.

HERRIOT, P., and PEMBERTON, C. (1995). *New Deals: The Revolution in Managerial Careers*. Chichester: Wiley.

—— —— (1997). 'Facilitating New Deals.' *Human Resource Management Journal*, 7: 45–56.

HUI, C., LEE, C., and ROUSSEAU, D. (2004). 'Psychological Contracts in China: Investigating Instrumentality and Generalisability.' *Journal of Applied Psychology*, 89: 311–21.

KARASEK, R., and THEORELL, T. (1990). *Healthy Work*. New York: Basic Books.

KEENOY, T., (1990). 'HRM: A Case of the Wolf in Sheep's Clothing?' *Personnel Review*, 19/2: 3–9.

KOCHAN, T., and OSTERMAN, P. (1995). *The Mutual Gains Enterprise*. Cambridge, Mass.: Harvard University Press.

LAWLER, E. (1971). *Pay and Organizational Effectiveness*. New York: McGraw-Hill.

LEGGE, K. (1995). *Human Resource Management: Rhetorics and Realities*. London: Macmillan.

—— (2000). 'Silver Bullet or Spent Round? Assessing the Meaning of the "High Commitment/Performance" Relationship.' In J. Storey (ed.), *Human Resource Management: A Critical Text*, 2nd ed. London: Thomson Learning.

LEPAK, D., and SNELL, S. (1999). 'The Human Resource Architecture: Toward a Theory of Human Capital Allocation.' *Academy of Management Review*, 24: 31–48.

LOCKE, E., and LATHAM, G. (1990). *A Theory of Goal-Setting and Task Performance*. Englewood Cliffs, NJ: Prentice-Hall.

MABEY, C., SKINNER, D., and CLARK, T. (eds.) (1998). *Experiencing Human Resource Management*. London: Sage.

MEYER, J., and ALLEN, N. (1997). *Commitment in the Workplace*. London: Sage.

MILES, R., and SNOW, C. (1984). 'Designing Strategic Human Resource Systems.' *Organizational Dynamics*, 12/2: 36–52.

MILKMAN, R. (1997). *Farewell to the Factory: Auto Workers in the Twentieth Century*. Berkeley and Los Angeles: University of California Press.

MORRISON, E., and ROBINSON, S. (1997). 'When Employees Feel Betrayed: A Model of how Psychological Contract Violation Develops.' *Academy of Management Review*, 22: 226–56.

PATTERSON, M., WEST, M., LAWTHOM, R., and NICKELL, S. (1997). *Impact of People Management Practices on Business Performance*. London: IPD.

RAJA, U., JOHNS, G., and NTALIANIS, F. (2004). 'The Impact of Personality on Psychological Contracts.' *Academy of Management Journal*, 47: 350–67.

RAMSAY, H., SCHOLARIOS, D., and HARLEY, B. (2000). 'Employees and High Performance Work Systems: Testing Inside the Black Box.' *British Journal of Industrial Relations*, 38: 501–31.

ROBINSON, S. (1995). 'Violations of Psychological Contracts: Impact on Employee Attitudes.' In L. Tetrick and J. Barling (eds.), *Changing Employment Relations: Behavioral and Social Perspectives*. Washington: American Psychological Association.

—— and MORRISON, E. (2000). 'The Development of Psychological Contract Breach and Violation: A Longitudinal Study.' *Journal of Organizational Behavior*, 21: 525–46.

—— and ROUSSEAU, D. (1994). 'Violating the Psychological Contract: Not the Exception but the Norm.' *Journal of Organizational Behavior*, 15: 245–59.

ROUSSEAU, D. (1990). 'New Hire Perceptions of their Own and their Employer's Obligations: A Study of Psychological Contracts.' *Journal of Organizational Behavior*, 11: 389–400.

—— (1995). *Psychological Contracts in Organizations*. Thousand Oaks, Calif.: Sage.

—— (2001). 'The Idiosyncratic Deal: Flexibility Versus Fairness.' *Organizational Dynamics*, 29: 260–73.

—— (2003). 'Under the Table Deals: Preferential, Authorised or Idiosyncratic?' In A. O'LEARY-KELLY and R. GRIFFIN (eds.), *The Darkside of Organizational Life*. San Francisco: Jossey-Bass.

—— and GRELLER, M. (1994). 'Human Resource Practices: Administrative Contract Makers.' *Human Resource Management*, 33: 385–401.

SALANCIK, G., and PFEFFER, J. (1978). 'A Social Information Processing Approach to Job Attitude and Task Design.' *Administrative Science Quarterly*, 23: 224–53.

SCOTT, A. (1994). *Willing Slaves? British Workers under Human Resource Management.* Cambridge: Cambridge University Press.

SHORE, L., and BARKSDALE, K. (1998). 'Examining Degree of Balance and Level of Obligation in the Employment Relationship: A Social Exchange Approach.' *Journal of Organizational Behavior*, 19: 731–45.

STOREY, J. (1992). *Developments in the Management of Human Resources.* Oxford: Blackwell.

TURNLEY, W., and FELDMAN, D. (1999). 'The Impact of Psychological Contract Violations on Exit, Voice, Loyalty and Neglect.' *Human Relations*, 52: 895–922.

—— BOLINO, M., LESTER, S., and BLOODGOOD, J. (2003). 'The Impact of Psychological Contract Fulfilment on the Performance of In-Role and Organizational Citizenship Behavior.' *Journal of Management*, 29: 187–206.

WALTON, R. (1985). 'From Control to Commitment.' *Harvard Business Review*, 63: 77–84.

WRIGHT, P., and BOSWELL, W. (2002). 'Desegregating HRM: A Review and Synthesis of Micro and Macro Human Resource Management Research.' *Journal of Management*, 28: 247–76.

YUKL, G. (2005). *Leadership in Organizations*, 6th edn. Englewood Cliffs, NJ: Prentice-Hall.

# CHAPTER 8

# HRM AND THE WORKER
## LABOR PROCESS PERSPECTIVES

PAUL THOMPSON

BILL HARLEY

## 8.1 INTRODUCTION

OUR starting point for this discussion is that HRM and LPT, as bodies of theory and research, have some fundamental commonalities of purpose. That is, both are concerned with the dynamics and regulation of work and employment relations. Rather than target a straw man or pop management versions of HRM, we aim to focus on the growing body of work which utilizes empirical and theoretical analyses to develop an informed understanding of key issues such as what HRM means in terms of concrete practices, their drivers, and implications for workers, managers, and organizations. As will become clear in the course of the chapter, we take issue with a number of the key claims made by scholars of HRM, but we nonetheless recognize that there is a growing body of work which deserves serious consideration if we are to continue to develop and refine our understanding of the regulation of work and employment.

One problem with such engagement is that HRM is not a homogeneous body of scholarship. The most obvious distinction is between those who see HRM itself as a distinctive approach to managing the employment relationship based on a high-skill, high-commitment workforce and a central role for human capital in firm strategy (Guest 1987; Storey 1985); and those who take a more contingent perspective and seek to identify 'what HR practices are profit-rational in which contexts' (Boxall and Purcell 2003: 10). To the extent that the first group is more likely to make distinctive, contrastable claims, our engagement is more with them than the second. However, the difference is not as substantial as it may appear. For the latter group, HRM is not merely a territory (e.g. work, employment, and industrial relations) to write about. Its prime purpose is still normative—to derive general, though context-dependent rules that guide and enhance the quality of labor management in the firm. So, Boxall and Purcell (2003) utilize a framework in which the critical HR goals of cost effectiveness (through labor productivity), organizational flexibility, and social legitimacy create multiple bottom lines whose tensions can and must be managed by successful firms. There is, in our view, sufficient commonality to refer to 'core propositions.'

## 8.2 CORE PROPOSITIONS OF HRM

We argue that there are at least three core claims to which most scholars of HRM subscribe. The first is that major changes in the nature of the environment in which organizations operate have placed pressure on organizations to be more strategic in their management of employees. This is the familiar view that most organizations are now operating in increasingly global, competitive, and volatile markets in which they must be flexible and able to develop unique products and services which are not easily imitable. Whilst some sector differentiation is made, according to most of the HRM literature it is through employees that such competitiveness can best be developed, because employees possess the kinds of skills that allow flexibility and which are difficult to imitate.

Second, largely as a result of changes mapped out above, there has been a shift away from management practices that involve the attempt to control employees towards those which seek to win employee commitment and generate motivation. The essence of this argument is that Taylorist labor management practices, with their emphasis on squeezing effort from employees, simply do not work in an environment where organizations must harness the skills and creativity of their workforces.

The third, and closely related, claim is that in the context of these changes and *contra* the arguments of radical or conflict theories of the employment relationship, both workers and managers can increasingly be beneficiaries of the new approaches to work and employment. This is because in an environment where employee skills and commitment are central to organizational success, it is precisely by giving employees more that organizations will gain more. HRM is based explicitly or implicitly on a pluralist perspective of competing, but containable interests among stakeholders. Successful strategies therefore rely on the 'principle of aligning employer and employee interests' (Boxall and Purcell 2003: 245).

## 8.3 LABOR PROCESS THEORY: CORE PROPOSITIONS

What equivalent observations can be made with respect to the key claims of LPT? Since the publication of Braverman's (1974) *Labor and Monopoly Capital*, considerable conceptual and geographic diversity means that, like HRM, LPT does not speak with one voice. Nevertheless, we would argue that there is a core theory— indeed from the *Labor Process Theory* volume onwards (Knights and Willmott 1990), considerable discussion has taken place on what this is (see Jaros 2005 for a detailed review). The core claims of LPT tend to be abstract rather than contingent. Or put it another way, whereas HRM claims focus on specific changes to, for example, skill or control, LPT proceeds from higher-order statements about the structural properties of the capitalist labor process that shape skills and control (Thompson 1990). This is important because many observers wrongly associate LPT with contingent claims (in this case made by Braverman) such as the deskilling thesis or the ubiquity of Taylorism as a control system.

So what are these core propositions? The starting point is the indeterminacy of labor—the unique character of labor as a commodity requires its conversion from labor power (the potential for work) into labor (actual work effort) in order for the accumulation of capital to take place. Incomplete labor contracts are a commonplace observation from a variety of perspectives, but the difference is in cause and consequences. This struggle over 'conversion' is located in the constant renewal of the forces of production under the impact of the competitive accumulation of capital. Amongst the central consequences is the control imperative. As market mechanisms alone cannot regulate the labor process, systems of management are utilized to reduce the indeterminacy gap between labor power and actual labor. Given divergent positions in the social relations of production and therefore potentially conflicting interests, that imperative does not go unchallenged. The notion of the workplace as a contested terrain is a central motif of LPT, which is often described as a 'control and resistance model' of workplace relations. This is not wholly accurate. It has long been recognized that although the workplace relations between capital and labor are ones of 'structured antagonism' (Edwards 1990), capital, in order to constantly revolutionize the work process, must seek some level of creativity and cooperation from labor. LPT has therefore long recognized that there is a continuum of possible, situationally driven, and over-lapping worker responses to relations of ownership and control in the workplace— from resistance to accommodation, compliance, and consent.

Despite the fact that this approach does not seek to explain or predict specific outcomes (such as deskilling) from more general imperatives, it has still left many writers more sympathetic to HRM unhappy. In essence, core LPT is still seen as a structuralist straitjacket. Particular objection is made to the control imperative and the idea of managers as 'agents of capital' (Storey 1985: Watson 1994). However, this confuses a James Bond notion of agent—people given orders and sent out into the world to execute them—with a more general notion of particular groups of managers who must interpret and enact their agency role on behalf of capital within specific institutional, market, and workplace conditions. As Elger (2001) observes, post-Braverman LPT came to accept a 'relative autonomy' of the work-place within capitalism. Whilst some on the more Marxist wing demur, most contributors accept that though there is an inherent struggle between capital and labor at work, this has no necessary links with any wider class struggle.

HRM theory, unlike LPT, does not appear to conceptualize capitalism as setting structural limits to the degree to which the interests of labor and capital can converge. The latter is inherently more skeptical about managerial ideology, pes-simistic about the progressive character of workplace change and the capacity to reconcile competing interests. However, the two 'sides' should be capable of debating and attempting to resolve the status of empirical claims about trends in the workplace and the wider economy.

There are no significant methodological barriers. It is true that LPT writers have a preference for qualitative approaches that can reach beneath the surface of managerial rhetoric and conventional survey evidence on worker attitudes and dominant narratives of workplace change to identify the reality of practices on the ground and uncover worker voice and action. However, though most LPT research has been based on case studies or ethnographies, it is not in principle hostile to quantitative approaches. Indeed, the core propositions of LPT cannot be addressed through qualitative case studies alone. Survey and related methods can also be used to test dominant rhetorics against worker voice and management practice (e.g. Harley 1999). As Thursfield and Hamblett note, because of its realist epistemology, LPT thus differs from the influential idealist critique that focuses on HRM as 'a cultural construction that is made up of a number of metaphors and myths' (2004: 114). LPT and HRM can therefore fish in the same waters, testing different propositions through identical datasets.

In sum, LPT 'has tried to account for the variations and complexity of workplace relations and identify key trends across sectors, companies and nation states, whilst setting out the systemic features of the capitalist labor process that shape and constrain those relations' (Thompson and Newsome 2004: 135). While LPT only has indirect interest in some areas of concern to HRM, notably labor market issues, its research programs have incrementally generated some key propositions and findings and the rest of the chapter sets those out in relation to parallel claims made within HRM literatures.

# 8.4 INTERROGATING HRM

We now move to consider what insights LPT can provide into the core propositions of HRM through examining three sets of closely related issues which LPT can elucidate and challenge. Each of the issues is addressed by considering empirical studies which have been undertaken, informed by a LPT perspective, showing how these studies have generated conclusions which are different from those which the core propositions of HRM would suggest.

## 8.4.1 Control

As we indicated earlier, HRM claims have been made that there has been from the 1980s onwards a move from *control to commitment*. Influential articles from Walton (1985) and Bowen and Lawler (1992) sought to locate these changes in new competitive pressures and the enhanced demands of a service-oriented, knowledge-based economy. As a result, 'command and control' was no longer seen as an option for successful businesses, and coercion and rules were displaced by values, trust, and self-direction as a means of coordination.

It has to be said that such conceptualizations of control are very weak. Walton refers to *the* control strategy as if there were a single disposition of management or context within which to operate. Explicitly or implicitly, control is treated as coterminous with Taylorism, bureaucracy, and adversarial industrial relations systems. In his view, new strategic contingencies (take your pick from post-Fordism to the knowledge economy) mean that control is not required. A more credible proposition offered by some HRM writers is that there has been a shift towards soft controls: in other words, towards practices intended to *generate* commitment through a combination of culture-led changes and delegation of authority. Soft controls tend to be presented as part of a package of high-commitment practices sustained by a strategic orientation and a high level of integration between corporate, functional, and operational levels of the business (Kochan et al. 1986).

LPT had already anticipated the idea of a shift to soft(er) controls. Burawoy (1985) argued that modern production regimes combined coercive mechanisms with those directed at consent and limited forms of workplace citizenship. This was followed by an influential paper by Ray (1986) that presented corporate culture as the last frontier of control, enabling organizations to internalize controls and generate emotional identification—though she qualified this by admitting that new controls operated alongside traditional ones, were internally contradictory, and may not work or work outside particular contexts.

HRM propositions on changing controls have had wider resonance because they share some characteristics with overlapping claims about the intent and outcomes of new management practices made by some critical researchers with links to LPT such as Willmott (1993) and Sewell (1998). Associated with 'post-structuralist' or Foucauldian perspectives, the main argument sees corporate culture as an effective means of extending managerial control more congruent with postmodern times and their emphasis on consumption and identity. Though the language of governance of the employee's soul is critical, the HRM claim is repeated that modern management focuses on the 'insides' or subjectivity of workers rather than their manifest behaviors (Deetz 1992). Such arguments countered the optimistic gloss of HRM notions of empowerment and teamwork, but reinforced the view that new normative controls were seen *to work*. Whilst, from Burawoy (1979, 1985) onwards, LPT recognized that consent can be generated from both worker and managerial practices, what is implicitly shared across some HRM and post-structuralist commentators is an assumption that management can shape identities in a way that overcomes traditional bases of interest formation. Yet without an acknowledgement of structured antagonism and divergent interests one is left *only* with consent and accommodation, and not control and resistance.

A double critique—of claims made on behalf of HRM and by post-structuralists—was the explicit starting point of Thompson and Ackroyd's (1995) influential article. But this critique developed into a more ambitious attempt to systematically map contemporary worker actions across the domains of time, effort, product, and identity (Ackroyd and Thompson 1999). The concept of employee misbehavior, though not without dispute within LPT, meant that LPT was better equipped to address and move beyond the partial decline of formal organization and collectivist industrial relations. Issues of culture and identity are not denied, but are seen as new contested terrains, as illustrated in Taylor and Bain's (2003) account of how call center workers use humor and other informal action as a tool of resistance.

The conceptual weaknesses of soft control arguments have often been compounded by a tendency to draw evidence primarily from managerial sources and to confuse the formal capacities of technological and managerial systems with their actual usage and effectiveness. Such observations have been shared by a wide range of more mainstream commentators on HRM. Survey and case study evidence demonstrates limited attitudinal transformation and a predominance of behavioral compliance in the face of adverse conditions for employees created by corporate restructuring and change programs (Cooper 1995; Hope and Hendry 1995; Korczynski et al. 1995; Rosenthal et al. 1997). We will return to the broader issue of the sustainability of soft controls in the last section.

### 8.4.1.1  *LPT: Key Propositions on Control*

One of the key propositions of LPT with respect to contemporary trends in managerial control is *the persistence of worker resistance*, even to new normative forms of control that focus on worker attitudes and emotions. In part this is an a priori theoretical argument—given the indeterminacy of labor, control can never be complete and is always contestable. But it is also derived from the evidence discussed in the last section: of continued informal misbehavior by employees (revealed in qualitative case studies) and of limited buy-in to managerial norms (as revealed in surveys and case studies).

Three other propositions can be identified. First, there is a claim concerning *continuity in combination*. In other words, LPT research has sought to challenge the displacement argument of HRM writers—that when new practices expand, others by definition contract or disappear. It accepted that the normative sphere has been an expanding area of managerial practice, without endorsing the view that these have replaced or even marginalized the more traditional mechanisms of bureaucratic rationalization, work intensification, and aspects of scientific management.

Much of the continuity evidence comes from European and North American critiques of claims about lean production. The rhetoric of devolved decision-making and 'working smarter not harder' was countered by qualitative research showing work intensification and multi-tasking under modified traditional methods, dubbed variously democratic Taylorism or participative rationalization (see for example Delbridge 2000; Parker and Slaughter 1995). At the same time, it was recognized that under lean production regimes, management focuses more on the normative sphere in order to bypass trade union representation and secure worker identification with broader organizational norms (Danford 1998).

New practices such as control through customers were identified by labor process writers as 'borrowing heavily from and extending traditional management paradigms' (Fuller and Smith 1991). A later generation of researchers have been in the forefront of studies of the expanded realm of call center work, noting how surveillance and monitoring is intended to create an 'assembly line in the head' (Taylor and Bain 1999). To gain competitive advantage through interactive service work, companies frequently seek to generate high commitment and shared identity, but these interventions are built on top of traditional controls. Korczynski et al. (1995) refer to the continuing rationalizing logics that management seek to reconcile with service quality, producing a form of customer-oriented bureaucracy. Nor are such tendencies confined to routine work.

Within these studies we can identify a second proposition—*the extension of controls* into new territories. Not only are new controls being added to old ones, old forms of control are being applied to new territories. The classic example is the scripting of service interactions, originally popularized by Ritzer (1993), but linked to the development of a variety of feelings' rules for the mobilization of emotional labor by writers working within a labor process tradition such as Bolton (2004). LPT sees knowledge management as, in part, an extension of controls into what were hitherto areas of limited regulation. Companies employing expert labor are under increased competitive pressure to speed up the product development cycle, prompting management to try to identify, monitor, and standardize the tacit knowledge of such workers (McKinlay 2005).

We would also identify an emergent final proposition. As has been noted, LPT has long pointed to the existence of combinations of controls, but a clear trend seems to be evident—towards the *increased hybridity* of control structures as environments and organizational structures become more complex (Alvesson and Thompson 2005). In call centers that trend is towards integrated systems of technical, bureaucratic, and normative controls (Callaghan and Thompson 2001). The significance of such developments is highlighted by Houlihan (2002), who shows that whilst work and markets vary in the industry, there is a characteristic high-commitment, low-discretion model of call center work and management.

LPT needs to specify the drivers in a more credible way, but hybridity of this kind—where conventional soft HRM practices coexist alongside neo-Taylorist work organization—poses a significant challenge to HRM. Whether with respect to call centers (Batt and Moynihan 2002) or more generally (Watson 2004), HRM writers tend to rely on contrasting ideal types of high-commitment and low-commitment HRM strategies, In other words, even where HRM writers argue for the existence of contingent strategies, they are conceived as coherent packages—high *or* low trust, high *or* low skill and so on. This is not *a* stable hybrid. Capital still has to manage the tensions and trade-offs, resulting in shifting and precarious sets of choices and adjustments across different sectors, but this is a long way from control *or* commitment.

## 8.4.2 Work Organization

Claims of a move to non-Taylorist or humanistic work organization are hardly new (Harley 2005). Nevertheless, HRM literatures make a number of claims about these approaches to work organization. First, it is argued that they are increasingly common. Second, organizations that employ such approaches to work organization, particularly in a systematic and strategic fashion, can foster high levels of satisfaction, commitment, and mutual gains among their employees (Guest 2002). Finally, largely as a result of their impact on employees, these approaches to work organization contribute to superior organizational performance in terms of measures such as labor productivity and turnover (Huselid 1995). Thus, if we wish to assess the strength of LPT as a means to interrogate key claims of HRM, we should look to existing empirical studies and ask what they tell us about these claims.

Most labor process literature in this area has sought to assess the impact of work organization, and particularly work teams, on employees utilizing qualitative data (see for example: Danford 1998; Parker and Slaughter 1995; Sewell 1998). Detailed case studies that access employee voice have tended to emphasize the 'dark side of flexibility' and added 'mean' to lean production. In particular, this research indicates that new forms of work organization not only fail to enhance employee discretion, but lead to enhanced, though modified managerial control through peer- and self-monitoring, thereby contributing to work intensification (e.g. Findlay et al. 2000). As we have discussed this body of research in the previous section, albeit briefly, we will not dwell on it here (see also Thompson and Newsome 2004 for more detail). However, implicitly or explicitly, most of these studies assume that new forms of work organization do indeed lead to performance gains, albeit through negative impacts on employees.

If LPT has questioned the assumptions of a new 'high road' in the workplace through qualitative studies, there is broader support for a skeptical view. The evidence concerning the diffusion of participative work practices is limited and fragmentary, but it is possible to piece together evidence and assess their prevalence. In the United States, a number of nationally based studies have reported substantial take-up of such practices (Appelbaum et al. 2000: 11; Osterman 2000). Analysis of data from the British 1998 Workplace Employee Relations Survey (WERS98) shows that use of individual practices is widespread, but varies considerably across industry (Harley et al. 1999). Geary's (1999) research in Ireland shows a high take-up of teamwork. Edwards et al. review the evidence in France, Italy, Germany, and Sweden and report that the level of participative work practices is significant, limitations of the data notwithstanding (2002: 88–92). Evidence from the 1995 Australian Workplace Industrial Relations Survey suggests that participative practices tend to be taken up unevenly across workplaces, industries, and sectors (Harley et al. 1999). It is clear that Taylorist or neo-Taylorist approaches to work remain widespread and that new forms of work organization have not necessarily displaced traditional approaches. Just as there has been hybridization of control strategies, there may well have been hybridization in work organization.

Given the volume of evidence it seems difficult to dispute the proposition that new forms of work organization are associated with superior performance (see for example Appelbaum et al. 2000). Indeed, one of the few British studies which explicitly adopts a LPT perspective found such positive associations (Ramsay et al. 2000). As we indicated above, the central concern of LPT is not *whether* such associations exist. Rather, the concern of LPT is primarily with *why*, and it is here that LPT and HRM part company in theoretical terms.

As noted earlier, it is common in HRM literature to *assume* that performance gains from new forms of work organization accrue by virtue of their positive impact on employees. It is noteworthy that, unlike LPT, there have been few HRM studies which have sought to test this assumption (for an exception see Guest 2002). A small body of work explicitly draws on LPT and has utilized survey data to test associations between work organization and employee outcomes. A series of papers by Harley (1999, 2001), utilizing the Australian Workplace Industrial Relations Survey (AWIRS) and the British WERS98 survey, examines links between work organization and employee outcomes including discretion, satisfaction, commitment, stress, and work intensity. These analyses, which seek to assess both LPT and HRM claims, consistently fail to find associations between 'empowering' forms of work and team-based work on one hand and employee outcomes, either positive or negative, on the other. Ramsay et al. (2000) also explicitly adopt a LPT perspective and seek to test both LPT-inspired and HRM-inspired models of the impact of work organization on employees. This study, utilizing the WERS98 dataset, found that while some progressive labor management practices were associated with positive employee outcomes (supporting the conventional HRM view), some were also associated with negative employee outcomes (supporting the LPT view).

### 8.4.2.1 *Insights from Labor Process Theory*

To summarize LPT-informed research on work organization—the qualitative studies have generally found negative impacts on employees, while the quantitative studies have found either no effect or mixed effects. From a methodological perspective, the differences between the results of qualitative and quantitative studies are not difficult to square. In terms of making generalizations about the impact of work organization, we must fall back on the large-scale quantitative studies. The fact that the quantitative studies show that there are sometimes positive outcomes as well as negative outcomes, and sometimes none at all, suggests that the impact of new forms of work organization varies. The strength of qualitative studies is that they allow us to understand *how* work organization has an impact on employees. We cannot generalize as far from the results, but these studies provide us with a way of understanding the potential for and nature of negative outcomes. There is nothing in LPT which says that there will necessarily be a simple logic of opposition in which anything management does will necessarily have a negative impact on employees, although it does suggest that while production takes place within capitalism, there are constraints on the extent to which work organization can lead to 'win-win' outcomes. The concept of 'structured antagonism' (Edwards 1990), discussed earlier, recognizes that in the employment relationship there will always be (actual or potential) conflict, but simultaneously there may be shared interests. If we accept this, then there is no inconsistency between the findings of quantitative and qualitative studies—the latter simply illustrate causal processes in some of the instances which have been identified by the former.

It may also be the case that in some instances there are simultaneously positive *and* negative impacts on employees. Work reform may, for example, increase employee discretion while simultaneously increasing stress by shifting responsibility for decisions to employees. How does LPT account for these patterns? In the case of 'no impact', a plausible argument is that new forms of work organization simply do not replace existing hierarchical management structures and thus do not challenge managerial prerogative (see Harley 1999). For example, a 'foreman' may become a 'team leader' and a shift in a plant be redesignated a 'team', without any change to actual practice. From an LPT perspective, in many cases management will be unwilling to undertake genuine changes to management structures, precisely because this would be seen as compromising managerial prerogative. In other instances, new forms of work organization are likely to have negative impacts because they are used as new control mechanisms, in which peer- and self-monitoring intensify work (Sewell 1998). In such cases, it may also be that employees experience a mixture of positive and negative impacts. For example, an increase in employee discretion may also involve an increase in responsibility for meeting production targets, thereby contributing to work intensification and heightened levels of stress.

LPT has sought to challenge a naive optimism which expects new forms of work always or mainly to have positive outcomes. Nevertheless, it recognizes that within the constraints of capitalist production, there is room for struggle and negotiation over the organization of work and its outcomes. The extent to which new forms of work organization lead to win–lose or win–win, or some combination, will depend largely on struggles between management and employees or their trade unions, within broader market constraints.

## 8.4.3 Skill Formation and Human Capital

The formation of skills occupies a central role in HRM and LPT. As we argued earlier, the latter does not claim that deskilling is an inherent law of capitalism. However, if skill is 'knowledgeable practice within elements of (job) control' (Thompson 1989: 92), LPT sees cost and control imperatives as placing constraints on the development of workforce skills and is inherently skeptical of claims for long-term upskilling. HRM tends to be sympathetic to, but not dependent on, such claims. Human Capital theory had already shifted the terms of debate about competitive advantage by emphasizing that the quality and skills of the workforce can have a significant effect on productivity (Becker 1964). HRM theorists emphasize a more contingent argument that changes in the external environment have made the internal assets of the firm more significant and strategic. In particular, human assets—the skills, knowledge, and attitudes of employees—become the crucial competitive advantage.

In this context, the dominant HRM model is a human capital/high-involvement one (Kaufman 2004: 324–5). We would expect a strategic approach to HRM to be marked, above all, by investment in the workforce and this would be associated with enhanced skills, training, career structures, and skill- and knowledge-based reward systems. Indeed, such an approach was the underlying basis of the 'bargain' for employees to buy into high-performance work systems or new transactional psychological contracts (Herriot and Pemberton 1995). As one of the most authoritative studies supporting HPWSs argued, workers need incentives to acquire new skills and engage in discretionary effort, whilst for employers, 'increasing training, employment security, and pay incentives for non-managerial employees has the greatest effect on plant performance' (Appelbaum et al. 2000: 8).

Such arguments have been augmented by claims from two other sources. Resource-based views of the firm see human capital as a key invisible asset that is increasingly valuable and hard to imitate (Barney 1991). At a more popular level, academic and policy discourse is now dominated by reference to the growth of a knowledge economy in which the (thinking) skills and knowledge of the employee are displacing the traditional factors of production as the key asset for firms.

Research undertaken within LPT and related perspectives, however, demonstrates that this is a hugely flawed account of the dynamics of skill formation. First, there is the inconvenient fact that the largest actual and projected job growth in the USA and UK is at the lower end of the labor market. Most are in routine jobs in hospitality and retail, or in personal services in the private and public sectors, and few have any relation to high-tech employment (Brown et al. 2001, Thompson 2004). Where does that leave high-skill or knowledge work? Despite repeated optimistic claims that the majority of jobs fall into this category, more rigorous analysis of official occupational data indicates that those that could be classified as knowledge workers with substantial 'thinking skills' are a relatively small minority in the USA and UK (Brown and Hesketh 2004), and Australia (Fleming et al. 2004).

Second, there is limited evidence that employers, at least in Anglo-Saxon economies, are delivering on the commitment to invest in other aspects of human capital. Even the mainstream business literature frequently bemoans the violation of the traditional psychological contract as employees are exhorted to take over responsibility for skill and career development and abandon any hope of stable, long-term employment (Deal and Kennedy 1999). Whilst the outcomes of studies are sometimes contradictory, there is evidence of long-term decline in traditional career structures and internal labor markets, and falling investment in training (Cappelli 2001). Some of this is a result of fear that such investment will be lost through redundancy or exit from their firm, or lack of incentives to invest due to greater permeability in organizational boundaries as a result of perpetual restructuring and outsourcing (Rubery et al. 2000). The outcome, however, is, contrary to HRM forecasts, an emergent 'de-knowledging' of the firm (Littler and Innes 2003).

### 8.4.3.1 *Alternative Propositions*

Though the above critique has been produced by writers of varying perspectives, contemporary LPT has made a distinctive contribution to explaining what *has* happened to skill formation and why. The most common conclusion of critics of human capital and knowledge economy arguments is to return to the concept of a polarization of high-skill 'knowledge work' and low-skill 'routine' jobs—perhaps an 'hourglass economy' (Fleming et al. 2004: 733). Whilst this is useful, it doesn't adequately address the dynamics in the content of skills. Three key trends can be identified from recent LPT research. First, that a partial break with Taylorism and Fordism from the mid–1980s onwards relied primarily on a *qualitative intensification of labor* (Thompson 2003: 362–4). Initially, LPT developed a critique of flexibility models by highlighting employer moves to multi-tasking rather than multi-skilling. This was linked to work intensification through lean production (Parker and Slaughter 1995) and teamworking (Danford 1998; Findlay et al. 2000). There is now a considerable body of wider evidence supporting a work intensification thesis (e.g. Green 2001). But this intensification required the mobilization of something new, whether described as 'knowledgeability' (Thompson et al. 2000), knowledge worked (Brown and Hesketh 2004), or the 'extra-functional skills' of the 'new model worker' (Flecker and Hofbauer 1998). It can be seen that these arguments do not lead back to a simple notion of deskilling. In fact, such observations critically recast the HRM insight that contemporary work systems are dependent on the 'full utilization of labor.'

Second, that there has been a decisive shift in the skill requirements of employers, but one that rests more on 'capitalizing on humanity' than investing in human capital (Thompson et al. 2000). As the introduction to a recent volume from the labor process book series sets out, paralleling the shift from explicit to tacit knowledge has been one from *technical to social skills* (Warhurst et al. 2004). Whilst employers may have in the past thought 'positive attitudes' were desirable, they were not regarded as *skills* integral to the job. Today, in much service and other work, 'person-to-person' social competencies are prized above all. This has been confirmed in wider research in France and the USA which has found that attitudes, dispositions, and appearance are frequently more important than level of education and training (Mounier 2001). With respect to appearance, LPT has been at the forefront of developing the concept of 'aesthetic labor' to describe how more employers are drawing on the embodied capacities of employees in the service encounter. Such trends are reflected in the language of social policy and vocational training such as 'transferable skills,' 'generic skills,' and 'employability.' The latter marks the transfer of responsibility for investment in human capital from employers to employees.

It might be argued that these trends confirm an upskilling trajectory, albeit by a different, non-technological route. But an expanded conception of skill is not the same as a deepening. The palette of skills has been widening, but it has not been accompanied for most workers by the two other crucial ingredients—task autonomy and knowledgeable practice. More and more jobs depend on IT-driven expert systems and scripted encounters. And whilst the cognitive, emotional, and cultural demands of the 'new' soft skill currencies will differ across the range of jobs, competencies such as positive attitudes, ability to work as a team, and communication *are* generic and therefore hard to connect to any notion of high skills/knowledge (Brown et al. 2001: 40).

Third, we have to reconsider the locus of the 'investment' made through HRM practices. Increasingly managerial practice is to *identify the social and personal capital* held by the actual or potential employee. As a result, employers may be choosing to invest more in recruitment and selection processes that can identify workers with the appropriate personal characteristics, than in skill development and learning (Brown and Hesketh 2004; Callaghan and Thompson 2001).

Overall, the message of this section has been that whilst investment in human capital is important, it is not as important as and is more different in character than one would expect from the core HRM assumptions outlined earlier. No existing society has attained the modest target of at least 50 percent of occupations categorized as technical, managerial, and professional. Moreover, an increasingly attractive alternative to investment in training as a means of raising productivity is to increase the use of immigrant labor (Brown et al. 2001: 50). The continued dominance of a 'low-skills equilibrium' can partly be explained through a contingency or comparative capitalisms approach. In other words, that either the wrong strategic choices are being made by employers in low-road Anglo-Saxon economies—or that large parts of the service sector do not require a human capital/high-involvement approach in any type of economy. Whilst there is some truth in both of these observations, an attention to political economy directs us to the significance of other contextual changes that we discuss in our final section.

# 8.5 Taking Stock and Moving On

When the evidence is examined for the core optimistic claims on control, work organization, and skills, it is patchy at best and absent at worst. It is commonly held that, particularly at the populist end, HRM scholars have tended to mix up their predictions and their prescriptions. Our concern, however, is with another kind of confusion. Of particular note is that the core claims are largely contingent on particular changes in economic and social context. These consist of either the general argument of a paradigm break from some species of Fordist capitalism or a more diffuse idea that market expansion, volatility, and speed of technical change have decisively altered the rules of the game.

Whilst mainstream perspectives have never exactly been realistic about the nature of capitalism, it seems to us that, if anything, recent years have seen global political economy shift away from, rather than towards, the configuration predicted by HRM theorists. There is a growing body of evidence that in financialized economies capital markets rather than product or labor markets are the dominant drivers of firm behavior (Thompson 2003). In circumstances where downsizing and perpetual restructuring are the norm in many sectors, progressive objectives in work and employment spheres are difficult to sustain and increasingly disconnected from wider trends in corporate governance. Crucially, those firms that have achieved gains in productivity and market share through the appropriate HPWS measures are not immune from destructive effects of enhanced demands for shareholder value.

HR managers may want to pursue higher performance and high-commitment policies, at least in some sectors, but the levers they are pulling are often outweighed or countermanded by corporate decision makers in thrall to financial markets. As Kunda and Ailon-Souday (2005) demonstrate, the dominant form of market rationalism has little time for culture and is more interested in reducing than transforming the workforce. One crucial conclusion to be drawn from these observations is that the 1990s are a more significant decade for transformative change than the 1980s that shaped the assumptions of HRM. In this context, whilst many of the prescriptions of HRM are laudable, they are increasingly out of step with reality.

HRM not only needs to reconsider some of its core concepts, it needs to address some methodological limitations. To date, research has been characterized by a narrow focus on the individual firm, largely separate from analysis of any bigger picture (Thompson 2003: 372). At the same time as ignoring the 'big picture,' HRM can also be criticized for overlooking the experiences of employees within workplaces. Whilst LPT has been guilty of too many qualitative case studies, it is theoretically predisposed to locate work relations within the broader political economy. We are not for a moment suggesting that if such an approach were adopted HRM and LPT would converge—clearly the theoretical differences remain significant—but there would be much greater scope for fruitful engagement between the two approaches.

The final question which our chapter raises is why, in the face of compelling counter-evidence, core propositions of HRM continue to hold sway in significant sections of the academic community, as well as among practitioners. As Harley and Hardy (2004: 393) argue, mainstream HRM scholarship is characterized by an increasing convergence of meaning among researchers as to what HRM is and how it should be researched, while at the same time the practice of HRM remains ambiguous and variable. This means that managers can use the language of HRM to establish the legitimacy of their practices, even if the latter bear little resemblance to the former. Less cynically, perhaps the key appeal of HRM lies in its optimism about the capacity of capitalism to become more humanistic. We share many of the goals, but part company on analysis and agency. Gramsci's nostrum—pessimism of the intellect, optimism of the will—remains the best starting point for confronting the possibilities of workplace reform.

## References

Ackroyd, S., and Thompson, P. (1999). *Organizational Misbehaviour.* London: Sage.

Alvesson, M., and Thompson, P. (2005). 'Post-Bureaucracy?' In S. Ackroyd, R. Batt, P. Thompson, and P. Tolbert (eds.), *A Handbook of Work and Organization.* Oxford: Oxford University Press.

Appelbaum, E., Bailey, T., Berg, P., and Kalleberg, A. I. (2000). *Manufacturing Advantage: Why High Performance Work Systems Pay off.* Ithaca, NY: ILR Press.

Barney, G. (1991). 'Firm Resources and Sustained Competitive Advantage.' *Journal of Management,* 17/11: 99–120.

Batt, R., and Moynihan, L. (2002). 'The Viability of Alternative Call Centre Production Models.' *Human Resource Management Journal,* 12/4: 14–34.

Becker, G. (1964). *Human Capital.* New York: Columbia University Press.

Bolton, S. (2004). *Emotion Management.* London: Palgrave.

Bowen, D. E., and Lawler, E. E., III (1992). 'The Empowerment of Service Workers: What, Why, How, and When.' *Sloan Management Review,* 33/3: 31–9.

Boxall, P., and Purcell, J. (2003). *Strategy and Human Resource Management.* London: Palgrave.

Braverman, H. (1974). *Labor and Monopoly Capital: The Degradation of Work in the Twentieth Century.* New York: Monthly Review Press.

Brown, P., and Hesketh, A. (2004). *Playing to Win: Managing Employability in the Knowledge-Based Economy.* Oxford: Oxford University Press.

—— Green, A., and Lauder, H. (2001). *High Skills: Globalization, Competitiveness, and Skill Formation.* Oxford: Oxford University Press.

Burawoy, M. (1979). *Manufacturing Consent: Changes in the Labor Process under Monopoly Capitalism.* Chicago: University of Chicago Press.

—— (1985). *The Politics of Production.* London: Verso.

Callaghan, G., and Thompson, P. (2001). 'Edwards Revisited: Technical Control in Call Centers.' *Economic and Industrial Democracy,* 22/1: 13–37.

Cappelli, P. (2001). 'Assessing the Decline of Internal Labor Markets.' In I. Berg and A. Kalleberg (eds.), *Sourcebook of Labor Markets: Evolving Structures and Processes.* New York: Plenum.

Cooper, J. (1995). 'Managerial Culture and the Stillbirth of Organizational Commitment.' *Human Resource Management Journal,* 5/3: 56–76.

DANFORD, A. (1998). *Japanese Management Techniques and British Workers.* London: Mansell.

DEAL, T., and KENNEDY, A. (1999). *The New Corporate Cultures: Revitalizing the Workplace after Downsizing, Mergers and Reengineering.* New York: Texere.

DEETZ, S. (1992). 'Disciplinary Power in the Modern Corporation.' In M. Alvesson and H. Willmott (eds.), *Critical Management Studies.* London: Sage.

DELBRIDGE, R. (2000). *Life on the Line in Contemporary Manufacturing.* Oxford: Oxford University Press.

EDWARDS, P. K. (1990). 'Understanding Conflict in the Labor Process: The Logic and Autonomy of Struggle.' In D. Knights and H. Willmott (eds.), *Labor Process Theory.* London: Macmillan.

EDWARDS, P. K., BÉLANGER, J., and WRIGHT, M. R. (2002). 'The Social Relations of Productivity: A Longitudinal and Comparative Study of Aluminum Smelters.' *Relations industrielles/Industrial Relations,* 57: 309–30.

EDWARDS, R. (1979). *Contested Terrain: The Transformation of the Workplace in the Twentieth Century.* London: Heinemann.

ELGER, T. (2001). 'Critical Materialist Analyses of Work and Employment: A Third Way?' Paper prepared for the International Workshop 'Between Sociology of Work and Organisation Studies: The State of the Debate in Italy and in the United Kingdom' (Bologna, 16–17 November).

FINDLAY, P., HINE, J. A., McKINLAY, A., MARKS, A., and THOMPSON, P. (2000). ' "Flexible When it Suits Them": The Use and Abuse of Teamwork Skills.' In S. Proctor and F. Mueller (eds.), *Teamworking.* London: Macmillan.

FLECKER, J., and HOFBAUER, J. (1998). 'Capitalizing on Subjectivity: The "New Model Worker" and the Importance of Being Useful.' In P. Thompson and C. Warhurst (eds.), *Workplaces of the Future.* London: Macmillan.

FLEMING, P., HARLEY, B., and SEWELL, G. (2004). 'A Little Knowledge is a Dangerous Thing: Getting below the Surface of the Growth of "Knowledge Work" in Australia.' *Work, Employment and Society,* 18/4: 725–47.

FULLER, L., and SMITH L. (1991). 'Consumers' Reports: Management by Customers in a Changing Economy.' *Work, Employment and Society,* 5/1: 1–16.

GEARY, J. (1999). 'The New Workplace: Change at Work in Ireland.' *International Journal of Human Resource Management,* 10/5: 870–90.

GREEN, F. (2001). 'It's Been a Hard Day's Night: The Concentration and Intensification of Work in Late Twentieth Century Britain.' *British Journal of Industrial Relations,* 39/1: 53–80.

GUEST, D. (1987). 'Human Resource Management and Industrial Relations.' *Journal of Management Studies,* 8/3: 503–21.

—— (2002). 'Human Resource Management, Corporate Performance and Employee Well-Being: Building the Worker into HRM.' *Journal of Industrial Relations,* 44/3: 335–58.

HARLEY, B. (1999). 'The Myth of Empowerment: Work Organization, Hierarchy and Employee Autonomy in Contemporary Australian Workplaces.' *Work Employment and Society,* March/13/1: 41–66.

—— (2001). 'Team Membership and the Experience of Work in Britain: An Analysis of the WERS98 Data.' *Work, Employment and Society,* 15/4: 721–42.

—— (2005). 'Hope or Hype? High Performance Work Systems.' In B. Harley, J. Hyman, and P. Thompson (eds.), *Participation and Democracy at Work.* London: Palgrave Publishing.

HARLEY, B., and HARDY, C. (2004). 'Firing Blanks? An Analysis of Discursive Struggle in HRM.' *Journal of Management Studies*, 41/3: 377–400.

—— RAMSAY, H., and SCHOLARIOS, D. (1999). *High Tide and Green Grass: Employee Experience in High Commitment Work Systems*. Critical Management Studies Workshop, Academy of Management Conference, 7 August, Chicago.

HERRIOT, P., and PEMBERTON, C. (1995). *New Deals*. Chichester: John Wiley and Sons.

HOCHSCHILD, A. R. (1983). *The Managed Heart: Commercialization of Human Feeling*. London: University of California Press.

HOPE, V., and HENDRY, J. (1995). 'Corporate Culture: Is it Relevant for the Organizations of the 1990s.' *Human Resource Management Journal*, 5/4: 61–73.

HOULIHAN, M. (2002). 'Tensions and Variations in Call Centre Management Strategies.' *Human Resource Management Journal*, 12/4: 67–85.

HUSELID, M. (1995). 'The Impact of Human Resource Management Practices on Turnover, Production and Corporate Financial Performance.' *Academy of Management Journal*, 38: 635–72.

JAROS, J. (2005). 'Marxian Critiques of Thompson's (1990) "Core" Labor Process Theory: An Evaluation and Extension.' *ephemera*, 5/1: 5–25.

KAUFMAN, B. E. (2004). 'Toward an Integrative Theory of Human Resource Management.' In B. E. Kaufman (ed.), *Theoretical Perspectives on Work and the Employment Relationship*. Ithaca, NY: Cornell University Press.

KNIGHTS, D., and WILLMOTT, H. (eds.) (1990). *Labor Process Theory*. London: Macmillan.

KOCHAN, T. A., KATZ, H. C., and McKERSIE, R. B. (1986). *The Transformation of American Industrial Relations*. New York: Basic Books.

KORCZYNSKI, M., SHIRE, K., FRENKEL, S., and TAM, M. (1995). 'Service Work in Consumer Capitalism: Customers, Control and Contradictions.' *Work, Employment & Society*, 14/4: 669–87.

KUNDA, G., and AILON-SOUDAY, G. (2005). 'New Designs: Design and Devotion Revisited.' In S. Ackroyd, R. Batt, P. Thompson, and P. Tolbert (eds.), *The Oxford Handbook of Work and Organization*. Oxford: Oxford University Press.

LITTLER, C. R., and INNES, P. (2003). 'Downsizing and Deknowledging the Firm.' *Work, Employment and Society*, 17/1: 73–100.

McKINLAY, A. (2005). 'Knowledge Management.' In S. Ackroyd, R. Batt, P. Thompson, and P. Tolbert (eds.), *The Oxford Handbook of Work and Organization*. Oxford: Oxford University Press.

MOUNIER, A. (2001). *The Three Logics of Skill in French Literature*. Sydney: NSW Board of Vocational Education and Training.

OSTERMAN, P. (2000). 'Work Reorganization in an Era of Restructuring: Trends in Diffusion and Effects on Employee Welfare.' *Industrial and Labor Relations Review*, 53/2: 179–96.

PARKER, M., and SLAUGHTER, J. (1995). 'Unions and Management by Stress.' In S. Babson (ed.), *Lean Work: Empowerment and Exploitation in the Global Auto Industry*. Detroit: Wayne State University Press.

RAMSAY, H., HARLEY, B., and SCHOLARIOS, D. (2000). 'Employees and High Performance Work Systems: Testing inside the Black Box.' *British Journal of Industrial Relations*, 38/4: 501–32.

RAY, C. A. (1986). 'Corporate Culture: The Last Frontier of Control?' *Journal of Management Studies*, 23/3: 287–97.

RITZER, G. (1993). *The McDonaldization of Society*. London: Pine Forge Press.

ROSENTHAL, P., HILL, S., and PECCEI, R. (1997). 'Checking out Service: Evaluating Excellence, HRM and TQM in Retailing.' *Work, Employment and Society,* 11/3: 481–503.

RUBERY, J., EARNSHAW, J., MARCHINGTON, M., and COOKE, F. L. (2000). 'Changing Organisational Forms and the Employment Relationship.' Manchester Business School Working Paper 14.

SEWELL, G. (1998). 'The Discipline of Teams: The Control of Team-Based Industrial Work through Electronic and Peer Surveillance.' *Administrative Science Quarterly,* 43/2: 406–69.

STOREY, J. (1985). 'The Means of Management Control.' *Sociology,* 19/2: 193–211.

TAYLOR, P., and BAIN, P. (1999). ' "An Assembly Line in the Head": Work and Employee Relations in the Call Centre.' *Industrial Relations Journal,* 30/2: 101–17.

—— —— (2003). 'Subterranean Worksick Blues: Humor as Subversion in Two Call Centers.' *Organization Studies,* 24/9: 1487–509.

THOMPSON, P. (1989). *The Nature of Work,* 2nd edn. London: Macmillan.

—— (1990). 'Crawling from the Wreckage: The Labor Process and the Politics of Production.' In D. Knights and H. Willmott (eds.), *Labor Process Theory.* London: Macmillan.

—— (2003). 'Disconnected Capitalism: or Why Employers Can't Keep their Side of the Bargain.' *Work, Employment and Society,* 17/2: 359–78.

—— (2004). *The Knowledge Economy Myth.* Glasgow: Big Thinking

—— and ACKROYD, S. (1995). 'All Quiet on the Workplace Front?' *Sociology,* 29/4: 19–33.

—— and NEWSOME, K. (2004). 'Labor Process Theory, Work and the Employment Relation.' In B. E. Kaufman (ed.), *Theoretical Perspectives on Work and the Employment Relationship.* Ithaca, NY: Cornell University Press.

—— WARHURST, C., and CALLAGHAN, G. (2000). 'Human Capital or Capitalising on Humanity? Knowledge, Skills and Competencies in Interactive Service Work.' In C. Prichard, R. Hull, M. Chumer, and H. Willmott (eds.), *Managing Knowledge.* London: Palgrave.

THURSFIELD, D., and HAMBLETT, J. (2004). 'Human Resource Management and Realism: A Morphogenetic Approach.' In S. Fleetwood and S. Ackroyd (eds.), *Critical Realism in Action in Organization and Management Studies.* London: Routledge.

WALTON, R. E. (1985). 'Towards a Strategy of Eliciting Employee Commitment Based on Policies of Mutuality.' In R. E. Walton and P. R. Lawrence (eds.), *Human Resource Management: Trends and Challenges.* Boston: Harvard Business School Press.

WARHURST, C., GRUGULIS, I., and KEEP, E. (eds.) (2004). *The Skills that Matter.* London: Palgrave.

WATSON, T. J. (1994). *In Search of Management: Culture, Chaos and Control in Managerial Work.* London: Routledge.

—— (2004). 'Human Resource Management and Critical Social Science Analysis.' *Journal of Management Studies,* 41/3: 447–67.

WILLMOTT, H. (1993). 'Strength is Ignorance; Slavery is Freedom: Managing Culture in Modern Organization.' *Journal of Management Studies,* 30/5: 515–52.

CHAPTER 9

# HRM AND SOCIETAL EMBEDDEDNESS

JAAP PAAUWE

PAUL BOSELIE

## 9.1 INTRODUCTION

ONE of the more fundamental aspects of the ongoing debate about the added value of HRM relates to 'best practice' versus 'best fit.' 'Best practice' argues for the universal success of certain HR practices while 'best fit' acknowledges the relevance of contextual factors. We argue that differences in institutional settings (for example, across countries) affect the nature of HRM. To understand this phenomenon, HRM needs additional theory. In this chapter, we use 'new institutionalism' (DiMaggio and Powell 1983) and the theoretical notions of organizational justice (Greenberg 1990) and organizational legitimacy (Suchman 1995) as a better way to understand the shaping of HR policies and practices in different settings.

Strategic HRM has gained both credibility and popularity over the last decade, especially with respect to the impact of HRM on organizational performance (see Paauwe 2004 and Boselie et al. 2005 for overviews). More than 100 papers have been published in the last decade on this topic. However, these papers have often neglected the importance of the societal embeddedness of HRM. In contrast, in the 1980s, a much greater emphasis on social context in explaining HR practices was evident.

The starting point for most HRM approaches in the 1980s was the external environment: models typically had an 'outside-in' character (see, for example, the work of Beer et al. 1984 and Schuler and Jackson 1987). These works appeared to have been heavily influenced by industrial relations (IR) perspectives (e.g. Dunlop 1958; Kochan et al. 1984) or by 'strategic contingency' models (e.g. Woodward 1965; Lawrence and Lorsch 1967). A radical change from outside-in approaches to 'inside-out' models was introduced during the late 1980s and early 1990s as a result of the increased popularity of the resource-based view of the firm (e.g. Wernerfelt 1984; Barney 1991). This radical change resulted in less attention to the organizational context and the external environment, simply because the implicit assumption was made that the context mattered less than valuable, scarce, inimitable, and difficult-to-substitute internal resources (e.g. unique human resources) for creating sustained competitive advantage (Paauwe and Boselie 2003).

Moreover, in the 1980s, the academic disciplines of HRM and industrial relations were more closely aligned with many academics being active in both fields (for example, authors like Kochan, Katz, Boudreau, Keenoy, Guest, Poole, Sisson, and Purcell). Nowadays, consideration of context is mainly limited to 'control variables' like age, sector, technology, and rate of unionization.

This chapter aims to restore the balance by offering a more explicit account of the importance of societal embeddedness in HRM. As an independent variable, societal embeddedness can have an important influence on the shaping of HR policies and practices and their subsequent effect on performance. As Karen Legge remarks: 'Just at the time when the key ideas of resource-based value theory penetrate the thinking (if not necessarily, the practice) of practitioners, I would predict that the academic debates, while not abandoning the RBV perspective, will tend to refocus *outward* to explore more fully the institutionalist approaches' (Legge 2005: 40).

The chapter starts with a short overview of the different institutional settings in which the shaping of HR policies and practices takes place (section 9.2). We next take a closer look at the field of HRM itself (section 9.3), especially focusing on strategic contingency approaches in HRM. Do different HRM models take the importance of the societal context into account? In section 9.4, we explain how researchers in the field of IR have much to offer the contextual analysis of HRM. This motivates us to use institutional theory (section 9.5) to build a theoretical base that can encompass context in the study of HRM. Finally, in section 9.6, we pay attention to the need to achieve a balance between market and institutional pressures if firms are to simultaneously pursue competitive advantage, legitimacy, and long-term viability (Boxall and Purcell 2003; Paauwe 2004).

## 9.2 DIFFERENT INSTITUTIONAL SETTINGS

Organizations worldwide are confronted with different environmental constraints. These may be the result of fundamental differences between countries (Gospel and Pendleton 2003) or between regions. 'Anglo-Saxon' countries such as the USA are less institutionalized with respect to employment relationships, including industrial relations and HR issues, than 'Rhineland' countries such as Germany, France, and the Netherlands. For example, in the Netherlands, institutional mechanisms include the influence of the 'social partners' (including the trade unions and works councils) and of labor legislation relating to works councils, conditions of employment, collective bargaining, flexible employment, and security. At national level, the social partners and government reach agreements on how to fight unemployment, how to reduce the number of people entitled to disability benefits, and so on (e.g. Paauwe and Boselie 2003). Several items in Pfeffer's (1994) well-known list of 'best practices' are institutionalized in Rhineland settings. For example, employee benefits—one can think of health care insurance, pension schemes, and security with respect to unemployment and disability—are almost completely collectively determined in the Netherlands (Visser and Hemerijck 1997). Differences between the environmental constraints that companies face can also be a consequence of sectoral differences (Peccei et al. 2005): for example, differences between traditional manufacturing and knowledge-intensive services.

Within Europe, there are differences between regional groupings (for example the 'Nordic cluster' of Norway, Denmark, Sweden, and Finland, the 'Germanic cluster' of Germany, Switzerland, and Austria, and the 'Latin European cluster' of Italy, Spain, Portugal, France, and Belgium) as well as differences among nations (Brewster 2004: 365). This has led a number of European academics to make a plea for a more contextual perspective on HRM models in order to correct for, and counteract, the universalistic nature of US-based HRM approaches (e.g. Brewster 2004). Those subscribing to this stream of analysis assume that US approaches cannot be applied in European settings and that, therefore, each institutional setting requires its own unique HRM model (Brewster 2004: 367). However, we strongly believe it is more useful to develop an approach, as in the field of comparative IR (e.g. Kochan et al. 1984; Poole 1986), that suits, and can be adapted to, different institutional settings. This approach implies that we need to refine the analysis of HRM in order to take account of the shaping of HR practices in different institutional settings. This refinement can be built on new institutionalism (DiMaggio and Powell 1983; Scott and Meyer 1994). But before we elaborate this point, we will discuss traditional strategic HRM approaches.

# 9.3 HRM AND STRATEGIC CONTINGENCY APPROACHES

Looking back at the classic HRM models of Beer et al. (1984) and Fombrun et al. (1984), we see that they paid attention to how context has an impact on HRM policies and practices. Fombrun's model (the so-called 'Michigan approach') refers to context in terms of economic, political, and cultural forces. Beer et al.'s model (the so-called 'Harvard model') is more explicit in that it recognizes a wide range of contextual factors ranging from stakeholder interests to situational factors. Next to shareholders and management, Beer et al. (1984) take stakeholders such as employees, government, community, and unions into account. Situational factors that have an impact on the stakeholders include the labor market, task technology, laws, and societal values. Since Fombrun et al. (1984) and Beer et al. (1984), research has moved forward to testing the added value of human resource management: the HRM and performance debate. Empirical studies on the added value of HRM include contextual features such as the degree of unionization and industry or sector as control variables but little or no attention is actually paid to how these factors affect HRM or how they interact (Boselie et al. 2005).

In terms of the HRM theories of the last two decades, Delery and Doty (1996) distinguish between universalistic, configurational, and contingent approaches. The last one is especially interesting for our purposes. Contingency theory[1] states that the relationship between relevant independent variables (like HRM practices) and the dependent variable (performance) will vary according to influences such as company size, age, and technology, strategy, capital intensity, the degree of unionization, industry/sector, ownership, and location. Strategic contingency approaches were the most popular theoretical approaches used in empirical HRM-performance research in the period 1994–2003, exceeding the number of studies which used either the RBV or high-performance/high-commitment HRM approaches (Boselie et al. 2005).

Strategic contingency approaches gained popularity in HRM in the 1980s through the work of a number of authors. Miles and Snow (1984) developed a model for linking HR strategy to competitive strategy using three basic types of

---

[1] The Essex studies (Woodward 1965), the famous work by Lawrence and Lorsch (1967), the Aston Programme (e.g. Pugh and Hickson 1976), and the work of Mintzberg (1979) represent a stream in organization theory known as strategic contingency approaches. Their empirical research findings suggest that contingencies (e.g. firm size, branch of industry, firm age, capital intensity, trade union influence, technology) affect strategic decision-making, organizational goals, organizational structure, systems, and culture. Contingency approaches stress the relevance of the 'organization–environment interface' (Lawrence and Lorsch 1967) and the notion of situation-determined problems. The contingency school covers a range of models, which advocate fitting business strategy to its surrounding (external) context.

strategic behavior (defenders, prospectors, and analyzers). Schuler and Jackson (1987) connected Porter's (1985) competitive strategies to desired employee behaviors and HR practices. Baird and Meshoulam (1988) aligned HR activities and the organization's stage of development. These early approaches provided clear and understandable frameworks for linking the external environment or context to supportive HR practices. In Schuler and Jackson's (1987) model, Porter's generic strategies were the point of departure for a repertoire of role behaviors in each case. HR practices were to be used to stimulate, or even enforce, the role behaviors seen as relevant to different competitive strategies. However, this model did not take into account societal embeddedness. It dealt with the competitive marketplace and with how different strategies in combination with different employee role behaviors could help to realize competitive advantage.

Boxall and Purcell (2003) provide an extensive overview of critiques of this kind of contingency theory in HRM research. First, these models tend to overlook employee interests in their attempts to align strategy and HRM. 'They generally fail to recognize the need to align employee interests with the firm or comply with prevailing social norms and legal requirements' (Boxall and Purcell 2003: 54). Second, making a distinction between, for example, only three competitive strategies (see Porter's (1985) typology) lacks sophistication and does not reflect the more varied nature of organizational strategies in practice. Large firms (e.g. MNCs) apply a whole range of different strategies in order to create performance outcomes, varying from cost reduction strategies in, for example, product storage and logistics through to high-quality differentiation strategies (for example, seeking to satisfy customers through excellent services). A third criticism by Boxall and Purcell (2003) concerns the problem that these models do not pay much attention to dynamics. In other words, contingency approaches rarely consider change processes and pressures, in terms of both contextual and organizational changes.

On the one hand, we conclude that strategic contingency approaches provide understandable and insightful frameworks on strategy, HRM, and context. On the other, these models are oversimplified, lacking sufficient depth to capture the complexity and dynamics necessary for understanding the relationship between HRM and its environment.

We need further theory to assess the relationships within a set of HRM practices and explore how these relate to, interact with, and are influenced by context. How are HRM practices embedded in society at large? Moreover, how do we define 'context'? How can we develop a theory that will make it possible to generate hypotheses about the relationships within the enormous variety of HRM practices as well as the various contextual factors involved (Paauwe and Boselie 2003)? Poole (1990) criticizes a number of HRM models, Beer et al.'s among others, and suggests the need to include globalization, power, and strategic choice. Hendry and Pettigrew (1990) want to broaden HRM models by including economic, technical and socio-political topics, which incorporate a range of factors that influence strategic decision-making in HRM. Of course, these authors emphasize that they do not want to fall into the trap of contingent determinism. There is always leeway for the actors involved to make strategic choices. The importance of context is recognized in the field of IR, which has a tradition and a well-developed range of theoretical models for carrying out internationally oriented research. Much can be learnt from these approaches.

# 9.4 HRM and Industrial Relations: Societal Embeddedness, Strategic Choice, and Different Rationalities

The relationship between IR and HRM received a lot of attention as HRM emerged as an area of study (e.g. Guest 1987; Storey 1989; Poole 1986; Storey and Sisson 1993; de Nijs 1996). We are especially interested in what we can learn from IR theory, and IR modeling in particular, in order to shed light on the societal embeddedness of HRM. The early models of IR theory (e.g. Dunlop 1958) focused on the process of rule-making in the employment relationship (Clegg 1979) and emphasized the adaptive nature of IR systems and their actors to the economic, technological and political context. They were, however, rather deterministic. Walker (1969), Poole (1986) and Kochan et al. (1984) were among the first to recognize that variations in IR institutions and practices had their roots in the strategic choices (Child 1972) of the parties to the employment relationship.

Kochan et al. (1986) extensively adapted and added to Dunlop's original framework. They saw a more active, as opposed to a merely adaptive, role for management, emphasizing the idea of strategic choice. Of course, all parties involved can make strategic decisions but Kochan et al. (1984: 17) considered management to be the dominant party in this respect. They also included interrelated levels of industrial relations. Next to the functional level of collective bargaining, they included strategic and workplace levels in their analysis. The strategic level, by definition, concerns long-term, high-level planning and encompasses, from a management point of view, the strategic role of human resources. Kochan et al. (1984: 21) stress that theory should allow an exploration of both the content and the process of strategy formation. The concept of strategy in industrial relations is only useful if actors have some discretion over decisions.

Poole (1986: 13) suggests that the concept of strategy encapsulates, at a more abstract level, the idea of overall design within social action, which is based upon various forms of rationality. He associates the concept of strategy with the following general categories of social action:

- *Instrumental-rational*, which refers to the means needed to achieve utilitarian ends (reflecting material interests and the will to power). Weber (1946) labels this 'Zweckrationalität'.
- *Value-rational*, which refers to ethical, aesthetic, religious, political, or other ideals (involving identification and commitment). Weber (1946) labels this 'Wertrationalität'.
- *Affectual/emotional*, which refers to the actor's specific affects and feelings (sentiments and emotions can enhance value-rational commitments).
- *Traditional*, which refers to ingrained habits (the institutionalization of previous strategic decisions of either a utilitarian or idealistic character).

In the field of HRM, these four kinds of social action are particularly relevant in shaping HR practices. From an economic and managerial perspective, it is usual for only the instrumental-rational perspective to be taken into account. However, especially when decisions relate to the shaping of employment relationships, other categories of social action, based on values, emotions, and traditions, are at stake. Kochan et al. (1986) also attach importance to the role of values, which stem from different rationalities, the role of history, and processes of institutionalization. The framework presented in Fig. 9.1 summarizes their approach.

This brings us into the realm of new institutionalism, a strand of theorizing which gives us a sound basis for the inclusion of context in the study of HRM and a way to explore the societal embeddedness of HR practices.

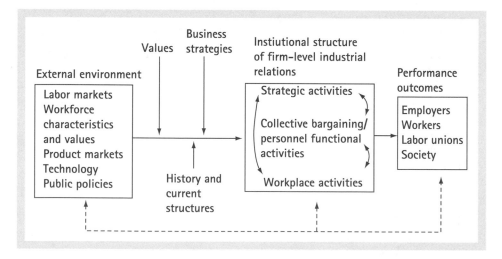

**Fig. 9.1. General framework for analyzing industrial relations issues**

*Source:* Kochan et al. 1986.

# 9.5 HRM and New Institutionalism

The idea that organizations are deeply embedded in wider institutional environments suggests, according to Powell (1998: 301), that organizational practices are often either direct reflections of, or responses to, rules and structures existing in the wider environment (Meyer and Rowan 1977). Jaffee (2001: 227) states that:

viewing organisations as institutions means that organisations have a history, a culture, a set of values, traditions, habits, routines and interests. This contrasts with the economic or bureaucratic view of organisations that views organisations as formally rational instruments for the realization of clearly defined objectives. Calling organisations 'institutions' means that they are not simply black boxes that produce goods and services, but human organisations driven by emotion and tradition.

Thus, institutional theory combines a rejection of the optimization assumptions of the rational actor models popular in economics with an interest in institutions as independent variables (Powell 1998: 301). Processes of institutionalization can be defined as those 'by which societal expectations of appropriate organizational action influence the structuring and behaviour of organizations in given ways' (Dacin 1997: 48). Selznick (1957), one of the founders of institutional theory, used the term institutionalization, to refer to the organizational policies and practices that become 'infused with value beyond the technical requirements of the task at hand' (Jaffee 2001: 227). In general, institutional theory shows how the behavior of organizations is not solely a response to market pressures, but also to institutional pressures. These include those emanating from regulatory agencies such as the state and the professions, from general social expectations, and from the actions of leading organizations (Greenwood and Hinings 1996).

At the beginning of the 1980s, a group of US-based sociologists presented themselves as *new* institutionalists. Academics such as Selznick, Meyer, Rowan, Scott, DiMaggio, Powell, and Zucker can be considered as the founding fathers (and in Lynne Zucker's case, founding mother) of the new institutionalism. According to Greenwood and Hinings (1996), the new institutionalism assumes that organizations conform to contextual expectations in order to gain legitimacy and to increase their probability of survival. (For an extensive treatment of the differences between old and new institutionalism, we refer readers to DiMaggio and Powell 1991).

In respect of the societal embeddedness of HRM, the contribution made by DiMaggio and Powell (1983, 1991) is particularly important. They state that organizations become more similar with respect to practices and systems within an organizational field, not only because of market mechanisms, but also as a result of institutionalization or 'structuration.' The concept that best captures the process of homogenization is *isomorphism*. DiMaggio and Powell (1983) define isomorphism as a constraining process that forces one unit in a population (or organizational field) to resemble other units that are exposed to the same set of environmental conditions. There are two types of isomorphism: competitive and institutional. Competitive isomorphism assumes a system of rationality emphasizing market competition, niche change, and 'fit,' and is most relevant where free and open competition exists. However, for a more complete understanding of organizational change, DiMaggio and Powell (1983) focus more on an alternative perspective, that of institutional isomorphism. Three institutional mechanisms are said to influence decision-making in organizations: *coercive* mechanisms, which stem from political influence and the problem of legitimacy; *mimetic* mechanisms, which result from standard responses to uncertainty; and *normative* mechanisms, which are associated with professionalization. Coercive influence refers to the formal and informal pressures exerted by organizations on which a firm is dependent, as well as to the cultural expectations held in wider society.

According to Lammers et al. (2000), new institutionalism criticizes the 'functionalistic contingency approaches' of the 1960s, which assume that actors are rational. In contrast, new institutionalists believe in the 'non-rationality' of processes at all levels in society—the micro (individual and organizational), meso (branch or industry), and macro levels (national or international). The central theme in new institutionalist approaches is the study of processes of cognitive and normative institutionalism, whereby people and organizations conform *without thinking* to social and cultural influences (Lammers et al. 2000). These normative influences are taken-for-granted assumptions (Zucker 1977) that actors perceive as being part of their objective reality.

Coercive mechanisms in HRM include, amongst others, the influence of labor legislation and government and, in some societies, the 'social partners' (including trade unions and works councils). Mimetic mechanisms refer to imitations of the strategies and practices of competitors as a result of uncertainty or fashion in the field of management. The current interest in developing and implementing HR scorecards (e.g. Becker et al. 2001) is an example. Normative mechanisms include the impact of professional networks on management policies. According to DiMaggio and Powell (1991), these networks, in particular, encourage isomorphism. Professional networks are influenced by the way universities and professional training institutes develop and reproduce taken-for-granted organizational norms among professional managers and staff specialists in the different functional areas of finance, marketing, accounting, and HRM. To give an example, it is now very common to assert that HRM should be business oriented and must add value. Other aims are subservient to this dominant goal. Thirty years ago, in the Netherlands at least, one of the central purposes of HRM was the support of industrial or organizational democracy. In Fig. 9.2, we give an overview of the way in which the three mechanisms identified by DiMaggio and Powell (1991) have impacts on HRM.

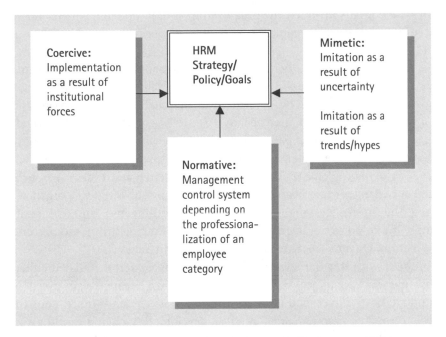

**Fig. 9.2. Impacts of DiMaggio and Powell's three mechanisms on HRM**

## 9.5.1 Institutional Theory and Change

Institutional theory has been criticized for only being able to explain the persistence and homogeneity of phenomena and being unable to deal with the role of interests and agency in shaping action (e.g. Dacin et al. 2002: 45–7). The work of DiMaggio and Powell (1991), just discussed, shows how organizations change due to the influence of coercive mechanisms, mimetic forces, and normative pressures. However, these processes imply that organizations, in a specific organizational field, such as a sector or industry, will become more alike. Although DiMaggio and Powell are able to account for change, it is change in the *same* direction within an organizational field. Their approach does not take into account the possibility of uniqueness due to specific interests and human agency. Greenwood and Hinings (1996) tackle this problem by starting from the premiss that a major source of organizational resistance to change derives from the normative embeddedness of an organization within its institutional context. In order to be able to account for change, they explore the interaction between context and strategic choice, arguing that unique change can occur if an organization decouples itself from the institutional context and reformulates its internal 'interpretative scheme.' An organization's interpretative scheme consists of assumptions about the appropriate domain in which the organization should operate, beliefs and values about the principles of organizing, and defined performance criteria to assess success.

The extent to which an organization can be decoupled from the institutional context depends on its internal dynamics, which include the kind and degree of commitment to change, the power structures and coalitions favoring or opposing organizational change, and the capacity to implement change. Greenwood and Hinings (1996) define this capacity as the ability to manage the transition process from one template to another.

Oliver (1991) complements this dynamic perspective and makes it possible to account for change in the institutional framework by showing how organizations can respond to institutional processes. Organizations use different strategies (options) to respond to institutional processes, ranging from acquiescence to manipulation. Oliver's (1991) framework is shown in Table 9.1.

A problem with this framework is that the responses are formulated either in a conforming way ('acquiesce' and 'compromise') or in a negative way ('avoid,' 'defy,' 'manipulate'). If Oliver had also formulated positive and more constructive strategic responses such as 'lead,' 'initiate,' 'develop,' the scheme would provide a more complete overview of strategic responses (Paauwe 2004: 45).

Oliver (1992: 564) went on to introduce the idea of deinstitutionalization and defined it as the process by which the legitimacy of an established or institutionalized

### Table 9.1  Strategic responses to institutional processes

| Strategies | Tactics | Examples |
| --- | --- | --- |
| | Habit | Following invisible, taken-for-granted norms |
| Acquiesce | Imitate | Mimicking institutional models |
| | Comply | Obeying rules and accepting norms |
| | Balance | Balancing the expectations of multiple constituents |
| Compromise | Pacify | Placating and accommodating institutional elements |
| | Bargain | Negotiating with institutional stakeholders |
| | Conceal | Disguising nonconformity |
| Avoid | Buffer | Loosening institutional attachments |
| | Escape | Changing goals, activities, or domains |
| | Dismiss | Ignoring explicit norms and values |
| Defy | Challenge | Contesting rules and requirements |
| | Attack | Assaulting the sources of institutional pressure |
| | Co-opt | Importing influential constituents |
| Manipulate | Influence | Shaping values and criteria |
| | Control | Dominating institutional constituents and process |

*Source*: Oliver 1991.

practice erodes or discontinues. In identifying the various factors that contribute to this process, and thus to change, she distinguishes intra-organizational determinants from external environmental forces:

*Intra-organizational determinants.* 'Pressures may arise within the organization as new members are recruited, performance declines, power alignments shift, goals are more clearly defined or the organizational structure is transformed owing to diversification or mergers. These rather common events can conceivably threaten, or at least call into question, institutionalised patterns of organization and behaviour and stimulate change' (Jaffee 2001: 235 based on Oliver 1992: 579).

*External environmental forces.* 'These might include increasing competition or environmental turbulence, changes in government regulations, shifts in public opinion, dramatic events or crises and changes in task environment relationships' (Jaffee 2001: 235 based on Oliver 1992: 579). In principle, these forces will cause change in the same direction for all organizations involved in the same organizational field. However, due to human agency and strategic choice, organizations can and will differ in their response to these kinds of forces.

In a similar way to Oliver, Colomy (1998) draws attention to the role of human agency in transforming the normative, cognitive, and regulative aspects of institutions (see also Jaffee 2001: 236). Moreover, Dacin et al. (2002) summarize a range of studies (for example Kraatz and Moore 2002; Sherer and Lee 2002; Townley 2002; Zilber 2002) that explicitly pay attention to the role of power, interests, and agency in determining how organizations interpret and respond to institutions: actors are not passive, they make choices as they interpret their environments (Dacin et al. 2002: 47). In summary, then, a range of authors have worked on building a new institutionalist approach which recognizes both forces for sameness and forces which stimulate idiosyncratic change.

## 9.6 HRM AND STRATEGIC BALANCING

In the previous section, we outlined how institutional theory can help us account for the societal embeddedness of HR practices. New institutionalism enables us to identify the underlying reasons why organizations in the same sector or industry become increasingly alike, while still allowing for change on the basis of human agency and strategic choice. Environmental determinism is thus avoided. However, we have only dealt with one side of the coin of social embeddedness. Organizations find themselves amidst *two* forces in the environment. On the one hand, there are competitive forces, based on economic rationality, which lead to decisions to differentiate from competitors in an effort to achieve or maintain sustained competitive advantage. On the other hand, there are isomorphic pressures based on normative rationality, which lead organizations to become increasingly alike in order to achieve legitimacy in their organizational field. Legitimacy is needed in order to acquire resources from potential exchange partners such as customers, suppliers, and regulators. A legitimate firm will manage to obtain resources of higher quality and at more favorable terms than a firm whose legitimacy is challenged (Deephouse 1999: 152).

These two forces are examined in research undertaken by Deephouse (1999). In a longitudinal study of commercial banks, he finds empirical support for his *strategic balance theory*. This states that moderately differentiated firms, which achieve a balance between a focus on legitimacy and a market focus, tend to have higher performance than either highly conforming firms, which emphasize meeting legitimacy requirements, or highly differentiated firms maximizing the economic/ market dimension.

Within the field of HRM, Paauwe (2004) uses the theory of strategic balance in his contextually based human resource theory. Here, long-term viability can only be achieved if a balance is realized between economic and relational rationalities. Organizations need to pursue economic rationality with an emphasis on creating added value, but they are also confronted with the challenge of relational or normative rationality. This implies establishing sustainable and trustworthy relationships with all relevant stakeholders (not just customers and shareholders) based on criteria of legitimacy and fairness as moral values (Paauwe 2004: 67).

The strategic tension in achieving a balance between sometimes competing or conflicting forces is recognized by Boxall and Purcell (2003: 7). They distinguish goals of labor productivity, organizational flexibility, and social legitimacy that need to be met, to some degree, in order to achieve organizational viability. They emphasize the 'harsh' reality of strategic tensions among these three critical goals: seen, for example, when companies transfer activities to low-cost countries to achieve productivity/efficiency goals at the expense of societal legitimacy in the high-wage countries where mass lay-offs occur.

Relatively little attention has been paid to the challenge of simultaneously achieving the goals of productivity/flexibility and social legitimacy despite the fact that reconciling opposing goals is extremely important for the long-term survival of organizations. With increasing international competition, organizations are forced to implement work systems that place increasing demands on employees to work smarter, better, or faster. This may require the implementation of lean manufacturing work systems or, more generally, high-performance or high-involvement work systems. In a growing number of cases, the need is to achieve an agile work system, which emphasizes fast and efficient learning, encouraging multi-skilling, empowerment, and reconfigurable teams and work designs (Dyer and Shafer 1999; Sharp et al. 1999). If these forms of work reorganization are not paralleled or balanced by a sufficient degree of trust, legitimacy, and fairness, the enforced changes will be likely in the long run to result in dissatisfaction, burn-out, and stress. Hence, a single-minded pursuit of economic rationality to the exclusion of other factors carries the seeds of its own destruction. Recognition of relational rationality means that social goals have to be considered, especially those concerning organizational justice and social legitimacy.

## 9.6.1 Organizational Justice/Fairness

Failing to meet objectives of legitimacy and fairness will lead to perceived injustice by those involved (e.g. employees, managers, works council representatives, trade union officers) and affects employee behavior and social relations within an organization (Greenberg 1990). A meta-analysis of organizational justice by Colquitt et al. (2001) shows positive effects of perceived justice (both procedural and distributive) on job satisfaction, organizational commitment, employee trust, and organizational citizenship behavior (OCB), underlining the relevance of fairness and legitimacy in organizations. Meeting the criterion of relational rationality means that managers need to 'treat their people well.'

The term 'justice' is generally used to connote 'oughtness' and is focused on the way people evaluate the fairness of a decision (Boxall and Purcell 2003). Baron and Kreps (1999) present two implicit assumptions that represent the starting point for organizational justice approaches. First, they make the assumption that individual employees evaluate their personal position relative to others in a process of social comparison (encompassing upward comparison, downward comparison, and horizontal comparison). Second, individual employees not only attend to the absolute rewards they receive, but also to the fairness of the allocation decisions.

There are two basic forms of organizational justice: distributive and procedural. Distributive justice concerns people's perception of outcomes or rewards and the way they are allocated (Baron and Kreps 1999: 107). This form of justice is relevant for workers' satisfaction with decisions concerning their jobs and pay. Typical issues related to distributive justice are: 'How am I being paid in comparison to my colleagues?' and 'How much effort do I have to put into my job in comparison to colleagues with similar responsibilities?' Procedural justice, on the other hand, deals with the fairness of the procedures used to determine outcome distributions or allocations (Colquitt et al. 2001). Procedural justice is often related to workers' perception of the supervisor, their attachment to the organization, and their willingness to engage in various kinds of 'organizational citizenship behavior.' Colquitt et al. (2001) show that perceptions of distributive justice tend to be correlated with perceptions of procedural justice. They add two other forms of organizational justice based on interactions: interpersonal justice and informational justice. Interpersonal justice is concerned with whether people are treated in a polite, dignified, and respectful way by authorities (Colquitt et al. 2001: 427). Informational justice points to the role of information flows and the way people perceive these flows: in particular, information about why certain procedures are used and why certain outcomes are distributed (Colquitt et al. 2001: 427). All four forms of justice affect employee motivation.

## 9.6.2  Organizational Legitimacy

Organizational legitimacy relates to the organization as a whole. It can be defined as 'a generalized perception or assumption that the actions of an entity are desirable, proper, or appropriate within some socially constructed system of norms, values, beliefs, and definitions' (Suchman 1995: 574). Suchman (1995) provides an excellent overview of organizational legitimacy and distinguishes two overall traditions. The first tradition, seen in the work of Pfeffer and Salancik (1978), among others, adopts a managerial view and stresses the instrumental ways in which an organization can manifest itself: for example, by using evocative symbols to gain societal support (Suchman 1995: 572). This approach can be characterized as organizational managers 'looking out.' The second comes from studies in the institutional tradition like that of DiMaggio and Powell (1983). These emphasize the sector-wide structuration dynamics that put pressures on organizations to meet or adopt legitimacy expectations set at sectoral or societal levels. These pressures can limit the organization's room to maneuver in decision-making (Suchman 1995). This viewpoint reflects society 'looking in.' Each tradition is further subdivided among researchers who focus on legitimacy grounded in pragmatic assessments of stakeholder relations (a superficial way of looking at legitimacy), legitimacy grounded in normative evaluations of moral propriety, and legitimacy grounded in cognitive definitions of appropriateness and interpretability (Suchman 1995). Pragmatic legitimacy mainly rests on the self-interested calculations of an organization's most immediate audiences. Moral legitimacy builds on the question of whether a given activity is the right thing to do and not on judgements about whether a given activity benefits the evaluator. Cognitive legitimacy is based on acceptance of the organization as necessary or inevitable based on some taken-for-granted cultural account. It does not involve evaluation on moral grounds.

In summary, strategic balancing involves taking into account both market principles (economic value) and institutional principles (moral values). In our view, the viability of an organization can only be secured by meeting contextual economic demands (e.g. for efficiency, flexibility, innovativeness) and institutional demands both at the societal level (reflected in the concept of organizational legitimacy) and at the individual employee level (reflected in the concept of organizational justice).

## 9.7 CONCLUSIONS

The starting point of this chapter was to explore HRM in its societal embeddedness. Our first key aim was to emphasize the value of new institutionalism as an additional theoretical perspective explaining the shaping of HRM in different environments. Our second key aim was to develop the idea of 'strategic balance' theory concerned with economic and relational rationalities—with the latter involving organizational justice at the individual level and organizational legitimacy at the organization level.

Institutional theory has been criticized for putting too much emphasis on stability, for being deterministic, and for placing too much emphasis on the conservative and conserving nature of institutions. In response to these criticisms, we showed how institutional theory is able to encompass change, the role of agency, and processes of deinstitutionalization. The interplay between, on the one hand, institutional factors which force an organization to comply with rules and regulations in order to bring about legitimacy and, on the other, the competitive market place, where strategic choice and leeway will allow an organization to position itself differently (in order to achieve a competitive advantage), led us finally to the importance of strategic balancing (Deephouse 1999). Not only is fit between HR and competitive strategy a necessary condition for organizational success, but so too is institutional fit.

The advantage of our approach is that we can complement the present academic interest in the linkage between HRM and performance with wider institutional factors influencing the choice of HR practices. The theoretical concepts used in this chapter shift the attention from internal organizational resources to a more interactive level, relating the organization to its environment, and making us more conscious of the role of taken-for-granted assumptions and mimetic, normative, and regulatory mechanisms in the wider context. Our approach can be used in different institutional settings, including regions, countries, and sectors (see, for example, Paauwe 2004). The approach offers a fruitful perspective for cross-national and cross-sectoral comparative research into the effects of various institutional mechanisms on the shaping of HR practices and their possible relationship with performance. HR practices should meet the demands of the market place (e.g. for efficiency and agility) and the institutional setting (for social legitimacy), while at the same time being perceived as fair and just by employees.

## REFERENCES

BAIRD, L., and MESHOULAM, I. (1988). 'Managing Two Fits of Strategic Human Resource Management.' *Academy of Management Review*, 13/1: 116–28.

BARNEY, J. B. (1991). 'Firm Resources and Sustainable Competitive Advantage.' *Journal of Management*, 17: 99–120.

BARON, J. N., and KREPS, D. M. (1999). *Strategic Human Resources: Frameworks for General Managers.* New York: John Wiley & Sons.

BECKER, B. E., HUSELID, M. A., and ULRICH, D. (2001). *The HR Scorecard: Linking People, Strategy and Performance.* Boston: Harvard Business School Press.

BEER, M., SPECTOR, B., LAWRENCE, P. R., MILLS, D. Q., and WALTON, R. E. (1984). *Managing Human Assets.* New York: The Free Press.

BOSELIE, P., DIETZ, G., and BOON, C. (2005). 'Commonalities and Contradictions in HRM and Performance Research.' *Human Resource Management Journal*, 15/3: 67–94.

BOXALL, P., and PURCELL, J. (2003). *Strategy and Human Resource Management.* New York: Palgrave Macmillan.

BREWSTER, C. (2004). 'European Perspectives on Human Resource Management.' *Human Resource Management Review*, 14: 365–82.

CHILD, J. (1972). 'Organisational Structure, Environment and Performance: The Role of Strategic Choice.' *Sociology*, 6/1: 1–22.

CLEGG, H. A. (1979). *The Changing System of Industrial Relations in Great Britain.* Oxford: Blackwell.

COLOMY, P. (1998). 'Neofunctionalism and Neoinstitutionalism: Human Agency and Interest in Institutional Change.' *Sociological Forum*, 13/2: 265–300.

COLQUITT, J. A., CONLON, D. E., WESSON, M. J., PORTER, C. O. L. H., and NG, K. Y. (2001). 'Justice at the Millennium: A Meta-analytic Review of 25 Years of Organizational Justice Research.' *Journal of Applied Psychology*, 86/3: 425–45.

DACIN, M. T. (1997). 'Isomorphism in Context: The Power and Prescription of Institutional Norms.' *Academy of Management Journal*, 40/1: 46–81.

—— GOODSTEIN, J., and SCOTT, W. R. (2002). 'Institutional Theory and Institutional Change: Introduction to Special Research Forum.' *Academy of Management Journal*, 45/1: 45–57.

DEEPHOUSE, D. L. (1999). 'To be Different, or be the Same? It's a Question (and Theory) of Strategic Balance.' *Strategic Management Journal*, 20: 147–66.

DELERY, J. E., and DOTY, D. H. (1996). 'Modes of Theorizing in Strategic Human Resource Management: Tests of Universalistics, Contingency, and Configurational Performance Predictions.' *Academy of Management Journal*, 39/4: 802–35.

DIMAGGIO, P. J., and POWELL, W. W. (1983). 'The Iron Cage Revisited: Institutional Isomorphism and Collective Rationality in Organizational Fields.' *American Sociological Review*, 48/2: 147–60.

—— —— (eds.) (1991). *The New Institutionalism in Organizational Analysis.* Chicago: University of Chicago Press.

DUNLOP, J. T. (1958). *Industrial Relations Systems.* Boston: Harvard Business School Press.

DYER, L., and SHAFER, R. A. (1999). 'From Human Resource Strategy to Organizational Effectiveness: Lessons from Research on Organizational Agility.' *Research in Personnel and Human Resource Management*, 4: 145–74.

FOMBRUN, C., TICHY, N. M., and DEVANNA, M. A. (eds.) (1984). *Strategic Human Resource Management.* New York: John Wiley and Sons.

GOSPEL, H., and PENDLETON, A. (2003). 'Financial Markets, Corporate Governance, and the Management of Labour.' *British Journal of Industrial Relations*, 41/3: 557–82.

GREENBERG, J. (1990). 'Organizational Justice: Yesterday, Today, and Tomorrow.' *Journal of Management*, 16: 399–432.

GREENWOOD, R., and HININGS, C. R. (1996). 'Understanding Radical Organizational Change: Bringing Together the Old and the New Institutionalism.' *Academy of Management Review*, 21/4: 1022–55.

GUEST, D. E. (1987). 'Human Resource Management and Industrial Relations.' *Journal of Management Studies*, 24/5: 503–21.

HENDRY, C., and PETTIGREW, A. (1990). 'Human Resource Management: An Agenda for the 1990s.' *International Journal of Human Resource Management*, 1/1: 17–43.

JAFFEE, D. (2001). *Organization Theory: Tension and Change*. Boston: McGraw-Hill.

KOCHAN, T. A., MCKERSIE, R. B., and Capelli, P. (1984). 'Strategic Choice and Industrial Relations Theory.' *Industrial Relations*, 23/1: 16–39.

—— KATZ, H. C., and MCKERSIE, R. B. (1986). *The Transformation of American Industrial Relations*. New York: Basic Books.

KRAATZ, M. S., and MOORE, J. H. (2002). 'Executive Migration and Institutional Change.' *Academy of Management Journal*, 45/1: 120–43.

LAMMERS, C. J., MIJS, A. A., and NOORT, W. J. VAN (2000). *Organisaties vergelijkender wijs: ontwikkeling en relevantie van het sociologisch denken over organisaties*. Utrecht: Het Spectrum.

LAWRENCE, J. W., and LORSCH, P. R. (1967). *Organization and Environment*. Cambridge, Mass.: Harvard University Press.

LEGGE, K. (2005). *Human Resource Management, Rhetorics and Realities*. London: Macmillan Business.

MEYER, J. W., and ROWAN, B. (1977). 'Institutionalized Organizations: Formal Structures as Myth and Ceremony.' Reprinted in W. W. Powell and P. J. DiMaggio (eds.), *The New Institutionalism in Organizational Analysis*. Chicago: University of Chicago Press, 1991.

MILES, R., and SNOW, C. (1984). 'Designing Strategic Human Resources Systems.' *Organizational Dynamics*, Summer: 36–52.

MINTZBERG, H. (1979). *The Structuring of Organizations*. London: Prentice Hall.

NIJS, W. F. DE (1996). 'Arbeidsverhoudingen en personeelsmanagement.' In A. G. Nagelkerke and W. F. de Nijs (eds.), *Regels rond arbeid*. Leiden: Stenfert Kroese.

OLIVER, C. (1991). 'Strategic Responses to Institutional Processes.' *Academy of Management Review*, 16/1: 145–79.

—— (1992). 'The Antecedents of Deinstitutionalization.' *Organization Studies*, 13/4: 563–88.

PAAUWE, J. (2004). *HRM and Performance: Unique Approaches for Achieving Long-Term Viability*. Oxford: Oxford University Press.

—— and BOSELIE, P. (2003). 'Challenging "Strategic HRM" and the Relevance of the Institutional Setting.' *Human Resource Management Journal*, 13/3: 56–70.

PECCEI, R., BOSELIE, P., and PAAUWE, J. (2005). 'Human Resource Practices and Isomorphism.' Working paper presented at the 4th Dutch HRM Network Conference November 2005 in Enschede, the Netherlands.

PFEFFER, J. (1994). *Competitive Advantage through People*. Boston: Harvard Business School Press.

—— and SALANCIK, G. (1978). *The External Control of Organizations: A Resource Dependence Perspective*. New York: Harper and Row.

POOLE, M. (1986). *Industrial Relations: Origins and Patterns of National Diversity*. London: Routledge.

POOLE, M., (1990). 'Editorial: HRM in an International Perspective.' *International Journal of Human Resource Management*, 1/1: 1–15.

PORTER, M. E. (1985). *Competitive Advantage*. New York: Free Press.

POWELL, W. W. (1998). 'Institutional Theory.' In C. L. Cooper and C. Argyris (eds.), *Encyclopaedia of Management*. Oxford: Blackwell Business.

PUGH, D. S. and HICKSON, D. J. (1976). *Organizational Structure in its Context: The Aston Programme I*. Westmead: Saxon House.

SCHULER, R. S., and JACKSON, S. E. (1987). 'Linking Competitive Strategies with Human Resource Management Practices.' *Academy of Management Executive*, 1: 207–19.

SCOTT, W. R., and MEYER, J. W. (1994). *Institutional Environments and Organizations*. Thousand Oaks, Calif.: Sage.

SELZNICK, P. (1957). *Leadership in Administration: A Sociological Perspective*. New York: Harper and Row.

SHARP, J. M., IRANI, Z., and DESAI, S. (1999). 'Working towards Agile Manufacturing in the UK Industry.' *International Journal of Production Economics*, 62/1–2: 155–69.

SHERER, P. D., and LEE, K. (2002). 'Institutional Change in Large Law Firms: A Resource Dependency and Institutional Perspective.' *Academy of Management Journal*, 45/1: 102–19.

STOREY, J. (ed.) (1989). *New Perspectives on Human Resource Management*. London: Routledge.

—— and SISSON, K. (1993). *Managing Human Resources and Industrial Relations*. Milton Keynes: Open University Press.

SUCHMAN, M. C. (1995). 'Managing Legitimacy: Strategic and Institutional Approaches.' *Academy of Management Review*, 20: 571–610.

TOWNLEY, B. (2002). 'The Role of Competing Rationalities in Institutional Change.' *Academy of Management Journal*, 45/1: 163–79.

VISSER, J., and HEMERIJCK, A. (1997). *'A Dutch Miracle': Job Growth, Welfare Reform and Corporatism in the Netherlands*. Amsterdam: Amsterdam University Press.

WALKER, K. F. (1969). 'Strategic Factors in Industrial Relations Systems: A Programme of International Comparative Industry Studies.' *International Institute for Labour Studies Bulletin*, 6/June: 187–209.

WEBER, M. (1946). *From Max Weber: Essays in Sociology*. Oxford: Oxford University Press.

WERNERFELT, B. (1984). 'A Resource Based View of the Firm.' *Strategic Management Journal*, 5: 171–80.

WOODWARD, J. (1965). *Industrial Organization: Theory and Practice*. London: Oxford University Press.

ZILBER, T. (2002). 'Institutionalization as an Interplay between Actions, Meanings and Actors: The Case of a Rape Crisis Center in Israel.' *Academy of Management Journal*, 45/1: 234–54.

ZUCKER, L. (1977). 'The Role of Institutionalisation in Cultural Persistence.' *American Sociological Review*, 42: 726–43.

# PART II

# CORE PROCESSES AND FUNCTIONS

CHAPTER 10

....................................................................................................

# WORK ORGANIZATION

....................................................................................................

## JOHN CORDERY

## SHARON K. PARKER

## 10.1 INTRODUCTION

....................................................................................................

THE greatest improvement in the productive powers of labour, and the greater part of the skill, dexterity and judgement with which it is any where directed, or applied, seem to have been the effects of the division of labour.

(Adam Smith 1776, quoted in Davis and Taylor 1972: 25)

Perhaps the most prominent single element in modern scientific management is the task idea. The work of every workman is fully planned out by the management at least one day in advance, and each man receives in most cases complete written instructions, describing in detail the task which he is to accomplish, as well as the means to be used in doing the work ... the average workman will work with the greatest satisfaction, both to himself and his employer, when he is given each day a definite task which he is to perform in a given time.

(Taylor 1947: 297, 300)

... workers respond best—and most creatively—not when they are tightly controlled by management, placed in narrowly defined jobs, and treated like an unwelcome necessity, but, instead, when they are given broader responsibilities, encouraged to contribute, and helped to take satisfaction in their work.

(Walton 1985: 77)

> ... organizations are beginning to make the more radical move of abandoning the concept of the job altogether. One factor contributing to the demise of traditional jobs is the growing use of self-managing teams ... Although management typically plays a key role in deciding which skills the team requires and selecting the individuals who have these competencies, it is usually left to the team to decide how the work should be divided among its members. As the team evolves and team members become more multiskilled, the work that each individual performs often shifts to accommodate personal as well as work requirements.
>
> (Lawler and Finegold 2000: 7–8)

As the above quotations suggest, opinions as to the best ways to organize and manage work activities within the operating core of an organization have varied widely over the past 250 years. The past three decades, in particular, have witnessed major changes to organizations and the work that is performed by their members, brought about in the main by technological changes and global competition. Terms such as lean production, manufacturing business process re-engineering, outsourcing, team-based working, *kaizen*, just-in-time production, empowerment, call centers, contingent workers, virtual teams, tele-work and the learning organization are just some of the words that have entered the lingua franca of management, denoting ways in which organizations have attempted to respond to such changes.

This chapter outlines a systems framework for describing the ways in which work activities are structured and coordinated by organizations in response to technological, economic, and social imperatives. In doing so, we are particularly mindful of the impact that evolving work configurations have upon an organization, its members, and the broader environment within which that organization operates.

## 10.2 A SYSTEMS PERSPECTIVE ON WORK ORGANIZATION

The frequency with which such terms as task design, job design, work organization, and work system are used synonymously suggests that some conceptual clarification might be fruitful. According to Wall and Clegg (1998: 337), job design refers to 'the specification of the content and methods of jobs,' while work organization 'usually signifies a broader perspective linking jobs more explicitly to their organizational context.' Accordingly, we define work organization as *the way tasks are organized and coordinated within the context of an overarching work system*. A work system, in turn, may be viewed as a particular configuration of interacting subsystems, including work content, technology, employee capabilities, leadership style,

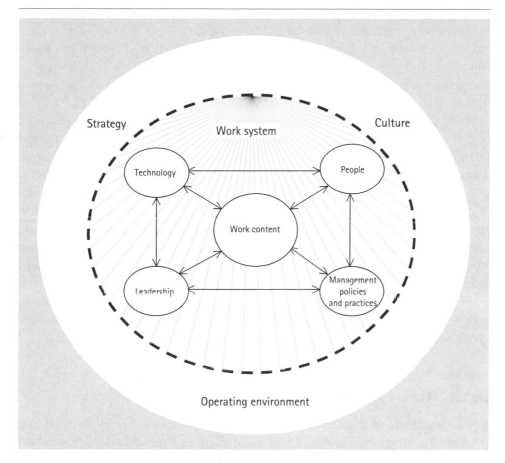

**Fig. 10.1. The organization of a work system**

*Source:* After Beer et al. 1985: 570.

and management policies and practices (Beer et al. 1985; Sinha and Van de Ven 2005). This conceptual framework is presented in Fig. 10.1.

Adopting a systems perspective on work organization has a number of advantages. First, it provides a common framework for describing the myriad ways of organizing and coordinating work processes that have evolved over time and in different contexts and which attract different labels or terminologies. For example, it can be used to differentiate, say, between different approaches to teamworking that might evolve in two different call centers. It can also be used to describe the working arrangements involved in practices as apparently diverse as lean production and empowerment.

Second, the work systems perspective recognizes that the productive work of an enterprise arises as a result of a complex interplay between a number of work subsystems. For example, increases in the complexity of tasks performed by employees or in their role responsibilities are likely to be either facilitated or inhibited by the existing knowledge, skills, and abilities they already possess, their attitudes towards such changes, and/or by the organization's capacity to deliver education and training. Such changes are also likely to necessitate changes to remuneration practices, as well as requiring first-line managers to delegate some of their tasks.

Finally, as is the case with open systems perspectives on organizations generally (e.g. Katz and Kahn 1966), the work systems approach recognizes that such a system interacts with (imports from, exports to) an environment that is defined, in large part, by such factors as the organization's overarching corporate strategy, its culture, and the broader operating environment of the organization, one that is defined by societal, economic, political, and legal considerations. While work systems can have an impact on such environments, for example by exporting skill, products, or services, it is more likely that the effectiveness of a given work system configuration will depend on the degree to which it is compatible with its operating environment.

In the sections that follow, we describe the main components (subsystems) of a work system and their interrelationship. We then go on to discuss different criteria used to judge the effectiveness of work systems, and to review three generic work system configurations.

## 10.2.1 Work Content

At the core of any work system's configuration are the tasks and roles performed by employees in their jobs—'the set of activities that are undertaken to develop, produce and deliver a product—that is, a physical and/or information good and service' (Sinha and Van de Ven 2005). The content of that work/those jobs may be described in terms of a number of design parameters or characteristics, the range of which is considerable and reflects the predominant interests of those analysing or designing the work (e.g. Campion 1988). We choose here to focus on a limited set of core features of work content, commonly identified in the work design literature, which are not encapsulated by other aspects of the work system (e.g. rewards), and which are important from the perspective of *both* organizations and job incumbents (Baron and Kreps 1999; Hackman and Oldham 1976, 1980; Parker and Wall 1998; Parker et al. 2001; Sinha and Van de Ven 2005). These characteristics include the scope, control, variability, demands, and feedback directly associated with tasks and duties.

*Scope*. The breadth and level of tasks and responsibilities exercised by an incumbent represents a major work design parameter. Some jobs are highly specialized horizontally, that is to say, the range of tasks they contain is very small. This is frequently reflected in low cycle times for completion of units of work. Jobs can also be 'vertically' specialized, to the extent that more complex tasks, such as those involving planning, scheduling, and decision-making, and high-level skills, are separated out. This is sometimes referred to as work simplification.

*Discretion.* In some work systems, employees have a high degree of control over operational aspects of work performance, such as the pace and timing of tasks or the performance strategies adopted, whereas in others no such discretion is permitted. The level of autonomy or discretion a job affords is generally regarded as being of considerable psychological significance to job incumbents, in respect of their motivation and satisfaction.

*Variability.* This aspect of job content relates to the degree of stability that exists in tasks and roles over time. In some work systems, for example, employees rotate between jobs or functional task groupings, whereas in others the content of the work remains fairly constant. Job rotation provides the employer with some benefits, in terms of flexibility of labor allocation, and potentially enables employees to utilize a greater proportion of their skills and talents. However, rotation may also interfere with the development of task proficiency and performance-relevant mental models (Hackman 2002).

*Demands.* Workload is also a key factor associated with jobs. Workloads can take the form of physical demands, though the growing prevalence of knowledge-based work means that increasingly such demands are intellectual (or cognitive) in character. In the case of service jobs, there has been increasing recognition that work can involve emotional labor, and that the emotional demands this creates can be extremely stressful (Brief and Weiss 2002; Grandey 2000)—particularly in jobs that are also cognitively demanding (Glomb et al. 2004). Demands can also arise as a consequence of role conflict, where job incumbents are required to perform multiple roles with conflicting objectives (e.g. Frenkel et al. 1999). Demand is also experienced as a consequence of conflict between job and non-job roles (Raghuram and Weisenfeld 2004), particularly where work involves long hours (MacInnes 2005).

*Feedback.* Some jobs and tasks automatically generate information that enables the person performing them to judge how well he or she is performing. Performance feedback is an important determinant of the capacity to self-regulate within a job (Locke and Latham 2002), though the performance-monitoring capabilities provided by modern information technologies can generate both positive and negative consequences for organizations and employees alike (Frenkel et al. 1999; Stanton 2000).

*Interdependence.* Finally, work content varies according to whether tasks/roles are performed individually or are assigned to a group (or team) of employees. It has become increasingly common for organizations to formulate and manage work content at the level of a team of employees, such as through the creation of self-managing work teams (Cordery et al. 1991), creating strong behavioral and outcome interdependencies between employees in the process (Wageman 1995).

While the content of tasks, activities, and roles is at the core of the work system, it is critically dependent on other four other work subsystems: technology, leadership, workforce capabilities, and management policies and practices. Each of these subsystems, and their relationship to work content, is now briefly discussed.

## 10.2.2 Technology

The content of work activities and responsibilities is strongly influenced by the technical subsystem. In the first instance, task technology may directly influence the 'locus of control' in respect of work activities (Mintzberg 1979). In highly regulated or automated technical systems, such as provided by some assembly line and call center technologies, the opportunities for people to exercise discretion in respect of the way they perform the work (e.g. pace, order) is virtually non-existent.

Furthermore, some technologies have a degree of sophistication and complexity that automatically generates cognitive demands within an operator's work role, and the inherent unreliability of many complex technologies may also generate variability and uncertainty in work tasks and role requirements (Wall et al. 2002). Varying levels of technologically derived uncertainty means that, for some jobs, it is possible to prescribe in great detail the manner of task execution using rules and standard operating procedures, while in others, the nature of task requirements and demands is not able to be specified in advance of their execution.

Technical systems also affect interdependence. Continuous process technologies, for example, generate complex levels of interdependence between tasks that favor the allocation of some coordination and control responsibilities to a group of employees. In other situations (e.g. some customer service roles), an employee is able to perform all required tasks independently of others, and the requirement to define collective work content is less acute.

## 10.2.3 Leadership

The leadership behaviors of managers and supervisors are also likely to help shape the content of work activities and to interact with other elements of the work system. For example, high levels of job discretion may act as a substitute for, or neutralize, the effects of some aspects of transactional and transformational leader behaviors (Whittington et al. 2004). Conversely, the direct involvement of a manager or supervisor in the process of allocating tasks to employees, setting the pace of work, and in decisions over the choice of work methods will invariably reduce the level of scope and discretion experienced by job incumbents (Cordery and Wall 1985).

Where jobs and tasks are highly specialized, there is likely to be a need for first-level management to act as the linking mechanism, coordinating activities across individuals. However, where interdependent tasks are grouped within the one job, or within a responsible work team, then such coordinative behaviors on the part of first-level management are likely to be less necessary.

## 10.2.4  People

The successful performance of any set of work activities is clearly dependent on the level of commitment and capability demonstrated by the extant workforce (Ulrich et al. 1999). The knowledge, skills, and abilities the workforce possess, are capable of attaining, or are willing to engage create both opportunities and constraints in respect of the specialization or enlargement of job content. Work roles frequently fail to capitalize fully on the existing knowledge, skills, and talents of employees (Morrison et al. 2005), employees can also differ in the confidence with which they approach expanded or enriched work roles (Burr and Cordery 2001; Parker 1998), and cultural values and beliefs may also shape attitudes about (and acceptance of) different forms of work organization (Kirkman and Shapiro 1997).

## 10.2.5  Management Policies and Practices

Ultimately, any set of work roles and responsibilities must be supported by a set of sympathetic and appropriate management policies and practices. It has long been recognized that different approaches to work organization are frequently associated with different 'bundles' of human resource management practices (e.g. Pil and MacDuffie 1996). Models of team effectiveness generally specify elements of a supportive organizational context (training, information, and reward systems) as being a key input to the effectiveness of teamworking (e.g. Hackman 2002). Elsewhere in the human resource management literature, the value of rigorous selection techniques, pay contingent on collective output, intensive training and development, job security guarantees, low status differentials, and widespread information sharing in supporting 'high-involvement' work designs has been strongly advocated (e.g. Pfeffer 1998; O'Reilly and Pfeffer 2000).

# 10.3  ARCHETYPAL WORK SYSTEM CONFIGURATIONS

The effectiveness of any given work system design needs to be assessed against multiple criteria, given the potentially divergent interests of those associated with it (e.g. employees, employers, customers). The following six main criteria have been identified from the literature (Beer et al. 1985; Campion and Thayer 1987; Baron and Kreps 1999; Parker et al. 2001):

- the work system's capacity to generate high levels of work performance and goal attainment on the part of those working within it;
- the degree to which the work system develops, produces, and delivers its designated product or service in an efficient and cost-effective manner;
- the extent that work system is able to sustain and build on human capital and performance capabilities;
- the work system's capability of effective adaptation to changes in the organization's strategic direction (e.g. cost leadership vs. innovation) and in operating environment (e.g. economic and labor market changes);
- the degree to which the work system generates rewards (intrinsic and extrinsic) for those who operate it; and
- its sustainability, in terms of its impact on the physical and psychological health of employees, the degree to which it builds positive social relationships, and effects a healthy work–life balance.

With these criteria in mind, we now compare and contrast three archetypal work systems. These are archetypes, in the sense that they represent idealized configurations of work subsystems that may be found in organizational settings. Table 10.1 summarizes the work content characteristics associated with different work system archetypes.

## 10.3.1 'Mechanistic' Work Systems

The configuration of work subsystems we label 'mechanistic' represents a long-established tradition in work organization, and has arguably provided the dominant model for the organization of work over the past century. Its development may be traced forward from the writings of Adam Smith (1776) and Charles Babbage (1835) on the advantages associated with the division of labor, to the work of

Table 10.1 A taxonomy of work content characteristics associated with different work system archetypes

| Work system | Scope | Discretion | Variability | Demands | Interdependence | Feedback |
|---|---|---|---|---|---|---|
| Mechanistic | Low | Low | Low | Physical demands | Low | Low |
| Motivational | High | High | Moderate | Cognitive | Moderate | High |
| Concertive | High | High | High | Cognitive and affective demands | High | High |

Frank Gilbreth (1911) and, more famously, Frederick Taylor (1911)'s scientific management treatise (Locke 1982).

The content of work activities within the mechanistic work system is typically characterized by high levels of horizontal and vertical job specialization (low scope), tight constraints on the manner in which work is performed (low discretion), and little variation in the tasks performed (low variability). For these reasons, jobs that arise within such configurations are frequently described using adjectives such as 'simplified,' 'narrow,' 'deskilled,' 'fragmented,' or 'standardized.' Furthermore, work activities are invariably organised with an individual (rather than a group) as the focus of task performance and accountability (low interdependence).

In terms of the other elements of the work system identified in Fig. 10.1, work activities within mechanistic work systems are typically controlled and coordinated by close and direct task supervision, supported by the use of formal rules and standard operating procedures. Technology tends to be highly routinized, designed to deliver high predictability and low variability in task requirements. The simplified work content tends to generate (and attract) an operating workforce whose skill levels are highly specialized and who have limited flexibility. Human resource policies and practices tend to manage performance at the individual level, with pay based on individual job evaluation and/or performance output. Training is limited to creating proficiency in those tasks contained within a fixed job definition.

A contemporary illustration of the operation of mechanistic work systems can be found in Holman's (2005) description of call centers that adopt a 'mass service' model of service management. One way for such a call center to cut costs is to employ cheaper, low-skilled customer service representatives (CSRs). To do this, it becomes necessary to simplify the tasks they perform, and to 'embed' these tasks in the technology by means of preordained scripts and/or standard procedures governing customer–employee interaction. The work content in these systems can be characterized as low scope (CSRs mostly answer calls, usually of a similar type, whilst supervisors deal with any problems), low discretion (tightly defined scripts specify what should be said throughout the call), low variability (CSRs usually do not rotate jobs), low interdependence (CSRs usually work on their own), and sometimes high demand (e.g. pressure to complete calls within certain times).

Mechanistic work systems clearly have the primary objective of delivering efficiency-related outcomes (Morgeson and Campion 2002). Amongst the benefits that they have been seen as generating (especially in the operating core of the organization) are reductions in training costs, improvements in productivity associated with reductions in the time taken to switch between different tasks, and increased task proficiency as job complexity is reduced. Job simplification may also mean that it becomes easier to find employees with the requisite base levels of skills in the labor market, and make it more feasible to automate some tasks.

On the debit side, however, it seems clear that the low discretion combined with high demands and low skill utilization frequently associated with job content in such work systems may generate negative psychological and behavioral outcomes, such as anxiety, depression, lower performance motivation, job dissatisfaction, absenteeism, and turnover (Holman 2002; Marchand et al. 2005). For example, Parker (2003) found that mechanistic forms of work organization associated with lean production practices generated reduced commitment, less willingness to accept broadened role responsibilities, and increased job depression.

## 10.3.2 'Motivational' Work Systems

In contrast to the mechanistic archetype, 'motivational' work system configurations are founded upon prescriptions for work content that are seen as being intrinsically motivating or psychologically empowering for those performing the work—that is, the work involved satisfies innate psychological needs such as those for autonomy, competence, and relatedness (Ryan and Deci 2000). The origins of 'motivational' work system configurations can be found in the writings of mid-twentieth-century management theorists such as Douglas McGregor and Frederick Herzberg. McGregor, for example, argued that mechanistic work systems invariably underutilized employee capabilities, particularly in respect of the exercise of 'imagination, ingenuity, and creativity in the solution of organizational problems' (1960: 48), as well as their capacity to find work enjoyable and satisfying in and of itself.

McGregor's theorizing finds practical application in the 'vertical job loading' practices advocated by Herzberg (1968), in the subsequent development of the Job Characteristics Model of motivation (Hackman and Oldham 1976), and in the more recent concept of employee psychological empowerment (Spreitzer 1995; Seibert et al. 2004; Thomas and Velthouse 1990).

Over time, a set of prescriptions for enhancing the motivational properties of jobs have been developed (see Table 10.2). Of central importance is the perceived need to create individual work roles that contain a reasonable breadth and depth of job tasks, as well as a fair degree of autonomy. Frequently, this approach is described as job enrichment or empowerment (Parker and Wall 1998). To continue our earlier illustration with respect to customer service call centers, Holman (2005: 116) described an 'empowered' CSR job in which, for example, CSRs have higher scope (e.g. carry out a variety of calls, solve problems themselves, and use a range of high-level skills), higher discretion (e.g. calls are usually unscripted), and greater interdependence (CSRs need to share information and draw on others' knowledge). Such empowered CSR jobs are more prevalent in high-value-added market segments because customers demand professional attention, which is facilitated by a motivational work design. Interestingly, however, it is in the low-value-added and

## Table 10.2 Recommended job design strategies

'Motivational' strategies

1. Arrange work in a way that allows the individual employee to influence his or her own working situation, work methods, and pace. Devise methods to eliminate or minimize pacing.

2. Where possible, combine interdependent tasks into a job.

3. Aim to group tasks into a meaningful job that allows for an overview and understanding of the work process as a whole. Employees should be able to perceive the end product or service as contributing to some part of the organization's objectives.

4. Provide a sufficient variety of tasks within the job, and include tasks that offer some degree of employee responsibility and make use of the skills and knowledge valued by the individual.

5. Arrange work in a way that makes it possible for the individual employee to satisfy time claims from roles and obligations outside work (e.g. family commitments).

6. Provide opportunities for an employee to achieve outcomes that he or she perceives as desirable (e.g. personal advancement in the form of increased salary, scope for development of expertise, improved status within a work group, and a more challenging job).

7. Ensure that employees get feedback on their performance, ideally from the task as well as from the supervisor. Provide internal and external customer feedback directly to employees.

8. Provide employees with the information they need to make decisions.

*Source*: Parker and Wall 1998: 20.

more cost-conscious market segments where high-involvement work practices appear to have most impact on sales growth: they not only add value, but they are also rarer and therefore confer competitive advantage (Batt 2002).

In terms of the four other elements of the work system, the motivational configuration typically seems to work best when the associated technology is non-regulatory, providing reasonable scope and opportunity for operator discretion, and moderately complex, so that there exist meaningful opportunities for problem-solving and a variety of tasks to be performed. In other words, there needs to be a degree of non-routineness associated with the technical system if real empowerment is to exist, and for motivational advantages to accrue (Wall et al. 2002). Wright and Cordery (1999) found that performance motivation and job satisfaction were higher for wastewater treatment plant operators in high-discretion job roles where the complexity and unpredictability (operational uncertainty) of the technical system was high, but not where the technology was relatively simple and predictable. In the latter situations, 'empowered' jobs proved less satisfying and motivating than those designed according to more mechanistic principles.

The sort of leadership practices that are typically advocated in association with empowered work content are those that involve less direct supervision of task performance, employee involvement in decision-making and 'transformational' leadership (Avolio et al. 2004; Cordery and Wall 1985; Whittington et al. 2004). Transformational leaders motivate employees to perform at the highest levels through a range of supportive practices, such as inspirational communication, role modeling, and coaching.

Workforce characteristics also play a role in supporting empowered work content. For example, individual differences in knowledge and ability, growth need strength, and extrinsic satisfaction of individual employees can moderate the strength of the relationship between empowered/enriched job content and motivational, affective, and performance outcomes (Oldham 1996). Cultural values can also influence responses to empowerment. For instance, Eylon and Au (1999) found that individuals from a high power distance culture did not perform as well in a simulation exercise when they were empowered relative to when they were not empowered. High-power distance cultures are those in which inequalities amongst people are seen as appropriate and acceptable, such as in the form of centralized or paternal leadership. Such findings suggest cultural factors can shape the relative benefits of empowered work systems.

Finally, empowered work content is frequently 'bundled' with other supporting management and human resource management practices, including flexible or 'fuzzy' role descriptions, information systems that have the job holder as the focal point for the delivery of performance information, increased investment in training to support expanded role content, an emphasis on career development, and skill-based pay (Oldham and Hackman 1980).

Studies of the impact of motivational work systems on a range of effectiveness criteria have generated mixed results. Evidence is consistently supportive that the work content produced by such configurations (relative to more mechanistic systems) generates a sustained willingness to expend effort, positive work attitudes (e.g. job satisfaction, commitment), and lower levels of absenteeism and turnover on the part of employees (Parker and Wall 1998). Where such work designs afford the incumbent the opportunity to self-regulate in response to exposure to the demands (physical, cognitive, emotional) associated with work, they may also reduce the stressful effects of demanding jobs (Terry and Jimmieson 1999). Empowered work designs have also been associated with increased knowledge and perspective-taking (Parker and Axtell 2001; Wall et al. 1992), the development of greater role breadth self-efficacy, or employees' confidence in their ability to carry out proactive, interpersonal, and integrative tasks (Parker 1998), and a more flexible and proactive role orientation on the part of job incumbents (Parker et al. 1997; Morgeson, et al. 2005).

To the extent that task performance is potentially directly affected by motivated effort, self-efficacy, and positive work orientations, such work design configurations appear likely to generate high levels of both task and contextual performance (Langfred and Moye 2004). For example, Griffin (1991) showed that a motivational work redesign increased, over the longer term, the performance (assessed via supervisory ratings) of over 500 bank tellers. Workman and Bomber (2004) similarly found that increasing employee involvement in work process decision-making within a call center led to significant improvements in customer satisfaction, fewer repeat calls, and better problem resolution, along with improvements in job satisfaction and organizational commitment. Overall, however, the evidence in respect of the impact on productivity is equivocal (Wall et al. 2002), leading to calls for various methodological improvements in this research area (e.g. Parker and Turner 2002), as well as the suggestion that there may be some degree of trade-off between work systems that are motivating and satisfying, versus 'mechanistic' work systems that are productive and efficient (Morgeson and Campion 2002).

Common criticisms of motivational work systems include the observation that they frequently fail to deliver any real increase in autonomy to employees (Argyris 1998; Forrester 2000), and that the expanded work roles may simply translate into more demanding work and longer hours (Yates et al. 2001). As we discuss later, these criticisms reflect more on the implementation of motivational work systems, rather than the effects of work content per se.

## 10.3.3 'Concertive' Work Systems

Concertive work systems are sometimes referred to as team-based or commitment models of work organization, and represent a substantial component of what has come to be known a high-commitment human resource management approach (Boxall and Purcell 2003). The aim of the 'concertive' work system is to put in place a pattern of working arrangements that maximizes the likelihood of employees working in concert with each other, whilst expending high levels of effort in the effective pursuit of organizational goals. The first full and coherent expression of the characteristics of this work system configuration, which evolved from the work of socio-technical systems theorists at the Tavistock Institute of Human Relations (e.g. Trist and Bamforth 1951; Pasmore 1988), was provided by scholars at the Harvard Business School (Beer et al. 1985; Walton 1985) and has since received strong advocacy through the writings of Pfeffer and colleagues at Stanford University (e.g. Pfeffer 1998; O'Reilly and Pfeffer 2000).

At the core of the concertive work system, work activities are assigned to self-managed work teams rather than individuals. This involves a group of employees being allocated a relatively whole task to perform, where group members are (at least partially) multi-skilled in respect of the overall set of group tasks, have substantial discretion over decisions relating to the performance of the work, and where performance is managed at the level of the group, rather than the individual (Cordery 2005). The increased discretion/responsibility is extended beyond the immediate production/service task, to aspects of the management of the broader work role. Thus, for example, the work team as a whole might also exercise responsibility for developing performance goals and standards, allocating tasks and workloads, performance monitoring, initiating and/or conducting training and development activities, liaising directly with customers, and hiring new team members (Cohen and Bailey 1997; Kirkman and Rosen 2000).

With the self-managed work team defining the characteristic work content, the concertive system accommodates such arrangements by virtue of a supportive configuration of technical, leadership, workforce, and human resource management subsystems. In the first place, it has been argued that the variability and unpredictability associated with the technology are a desirable, if not essential, precondition for the creation of self-managing work teams (Wall et al. 2002). Furthermore, research has shown that moderate to high levels of technological interdependence are key determinants of the desirability both of the decision to allocate work to teams in the first place and of the level of self-management they are afforded (Hackman 2002; Langfred and Moye 2004). The viability of team-based work is also affected by leadership style. Some have argued that the key to the maintenance of effective self-management within teams is the absence of a formal external leadership role (Beekun 1989), pointing out that managers often struggle to adapt to their introduction (Douglas and Gardner 2004; Vallas 2003), while others have advocated various forms of leader coaching (Hackman and Wageman 2005; Morgeson 2005).

Models of team effectiveness routinely identify management practices in respect of rewards, training, and information-sharing as being necessary to support team-based tasks and roles (e.g. Hackman 1987). Both team-based pay and skill-based pay are strongly advocated (Bartol and Srivastava 2002; Kirkman and Rosen 2000; Walton 1985). Training systems need to help teams develop the depth, breadth, and flexibility of skills needed for effective self-managed team performance (Ellis et al. 2005; Marks et al. 2002). In addition, adequate, directed, and shared information and feedback are critically important to a team's capacity to exercise effective self-determination (DeShon et al. 2004). Other management policies that have been identified as supportive of the concertive model of work organization include job security guarantees, the reduction of status differentials, and team-level work role descriptions (Pfeffer 1998; Kirkman and Rosen 2000).

Finally, it has long been recognized that the composition of work teams is a determinant of their effectiveness, and that the level of knowledge, skill, and ability available within the team is critical (Hackman 2002). It appears that some individuals are better suited to working in self-managed work teams than others, by virtue of possessing knowledge, skills, and abilities (KSAs) related to conflict resolution, collaborative problem-solving, communication, goal-setting and performance management, and planning and task coordination (Stevens and Campion 1999; Leach et al. 2005; Morgeson et al. 2005).

The apparent popularity of concertive team-based work systems over recent decades has been well documented (Lawler et al. 1995; Staw and Epstein 2000), with several potential benefits having been identified (Cordery 2004, 2005). First, the use of self-managed work teams may enable more direct forms of control to be exercised over critical interdependencies within the work process. Second, teams increase the range of knowledge and expertise potentially available for problem-solving. Third, they may generate administrative efficiencies and greater flexibility in labor allocation. Finally, to the extent that they incorporate elements of the motivational configuration described earlier, team-based work systems are also seen as generating a range of socio-psychological outcomes, such as improved opportunities for meaningful social interaction, and improvements in job charac-teristics (variety, autonomy, etc.). This may act as an important attractant for talent in the external labor market (Pfeffer 1998).

As with motivational work systems, research findings as to the effects and success of concertive team-based work systems are mixed. In general, as with empowered work, the evidence seems stronger and more consistent that they generate positive motivational and affective outcomes (e.g. Batt 2004; Cordery et al. 1991; Hunter et al. 2002) than that they enhance performance and productivity (Allen and Hecht 2004). This is not to say that significant performance benefits haven't been obtained via the introduction of such systems (e.g. Banker et al. 1996; Macy and Izumi 1993); it's just that the findings are inconsistent (e.g. Spreitzer et al. 1999). Even when it comes to employee reactions to work within concertive systems, not all employees are seen to react favorably, and workloads may be intensified leading to increased stress (Hutchinson et al. 2000) and increased conflict between work and non-work roles (Knights and McCabe 2003). Furthermore, the particular nature and strength of behavioral norms developed by highly cohesive self-managed work teams may impact negatively on both performance and the well-being of individual team members (Barker 1993).

In the next section, we conclude with some of the possible reasons for the inconsistent findings in respect of this and other work system configurations.

# 10.4 CONSISTENCY, FIT, AND TRADE-OFFS IN WORK SYSTEM EFFECTIVENESS

Several questions arise out of our review of the mechanistic, motivational, and concertive configurations. First, why is it that there are such divergent findings in relation to the predicted outcomes for each work organization archetype and, second, do these models represent points on an evolutionary scale of improvement in the design of work systems? In other words, are concertive models better suited to contemporary organizational settings than mechanistic (and motivational) approaches?

In answering the first question, we have suggested that the effectiveness of any particular work system will be determined by the degree of consistency amongst its constituent elements. If team working or empowerment is not supported by appropriate changes to supervisory leadership, or the reward system continues to only reward individual performance, or if the technology either overdetermines the manner of task performance or generates few real opportunities for collective decision and action, then concertive configurations are obviously less likely to flourish (see, for example, Sprigg et al. 2000, who showed negative effects of teamwork when introduced in an incompatible setting). That such internal consistency is hard to achieve and maintain may help to explain the sometimes weak and inconsistent effects we have noted for several work configurations, and is one reason why it has been suggested that the operation of a work system, along with its supporting human resource management architecture, can act as a source of competitive advantage for some firms (Baron and Kreps 1999; Pfeffer 1998).

In respect of the relative merits of the various approaches, this point is still a matter of considerable discussion and debate. One position is that the mechanistic, motivational, and concertive work systems are effective to the extent that they provide a well-integrated match with what the organization is trying to achieve, its culture, and the broader societal context within which the organization is located. This is analogous to the 'best fit' perspective that has been advanced elsewhere in respect of strategic human resource management (Boxall and Purcell 2003; Wright and Snell 1998; Youndt et al. 1996). Baron and Kreps (1999), for example, question whether or not a high-commitment model (with its embedded 'concertive' work system) is likely to be as effective in situations where the corporate strategy is competing on cost, where process improvements are unlikely to be found, where there are high levels of mobility in the labor market, where there is a declining market, where the level of skill in the current workforce is very low, and where competition exists in the form of another employer operating a similar work design configuration. Implicit in this view is the notion of a trade-off between criteria such as cost effectiveness and efficiency on the one hand, and others such as innovation, flexibility, and employee motivation and commitment on the other (Morgeson and Campion 2002).

A contrasting view to that of Baron and Kreps (1999) is that any corporate strategy, including cost leadership, is best effected by a motivated and committed workforce (Pfeffer 1998; O'Reilly and Pfeffer 2000), and that concertive systems are best suited to attracting and retaining talent, meeting contemporary societal expectations in respect of the rewards work should offer, and sustaining the high levels of organizational performance required for success in today's highly competitive global business environment. These contrasting views partly reflect different meanings of effectiveness (e.g. Pfeffer and colleagues' perspective incorporates broader societal criteria). Nevertheless, they do diverge in their vision of how work systems affect organizational performance; an issue which is perhaps best served by further empirical inquiry.

# 10.5 SUMMARY AND CONCLUSIONS

In this chapter, we outlined a systems framework that captures the essential characteristics of the myriad ways in which work activities can be organized. The three major ways that work has been organized map onto the quotations that we introduced at the outset. Both Smith and Taylor advocated as the most efficient and motivating the mechanistic work system, characterized by 'simplified' jobs that are low in scope, discretion, variability, feedback, and interdependence. Walton described the value of the motivational work system, characterized by enriched jobs with high scope and discretion. The final quotation by Lawler and Finegold (2000) recommended the concertive work system, which particularly emphasizes high levels of interdependence between jobs, or teamworking. All of these three archetype work systems can be seen within today's workplace, each offering advantages and disadvantages for individuals and organizations. The mechanistic work system can offer efficiency gains (at least in some contexts) but few motivational or humanistic benefits. Both the motivational and concertive approach offer the latter, as well as potential benefits for flexibility, innovation, and other such performance outcomes, but their overall effect on organizational effectiveness has been less consistently demonstrated.

In large part, the inconsistent demonstration of positive organizational effects of motivational and concertive work systems reflects the interdependence between work organization and other organizational subsystems. As our systems perspective suggests, work content affects, and is affected by, technology, leadership, people's skills and attributes, and management policies and practices. Aligning these subsystems to be coherent and internally consistent is difficult, especially when implementing motivational and concertive work systems that often require a quite radical departure from traditional mechanistic practices.

The systems approach to work design means that, although choices often exist in how to organize work, one must consider and manage those choices in conjunction with other organizational subsystems. The systems approach also has implications for research, suggesting the need for more explicit consideration of the interrelationships between subsystems when evaluating alternative work configurations, as well as the need to further assess the impact on effectiveness of fit between the internal work system and the broader organizational and strategic environment.

## REFERENCES

ALLEN, N. J. and HECHT, T. D. (2004). 'The "Romance of Teams": Toward an Understanding of its Psychological Underpinnings and Implications.' *Journal of Occupational and Organizational Psychology*, 77: 439–61.

ARGYRIS, C. (1998). 'Empowerment: The Emperor's New Clothes.' *Harvard Business Review*, 76: 98–105.

AVOLIO, B. J., ZHU, W., KOH, W., and BHATIA, P. (2004). 'Transformational Leadership and Organizational Commitment: Mediating Role of Psychological Empowerment and Moderating Role of Structural Distance.' *Journal of Organizational Behavior*, 25: 951–69.

BABBAGE, C. (1835). *On the Economy of Machinery and Manufacturers*. London: Charles Knight.

BANKER, R. D., FIELD, J. M., SCHROEDER, R. G., and SINHA, K. K. (1996). 'Impact of Work Teams on Manufacturing Performance: A Longitudinal Field Study.' *Academy of Management Journal*, 39: 867–90.

BARKER, J. R. (1993). 'Tightening the Iron Cage: Concertive Control in Self-Managing Teams.' *Administrative Science Quarterly*, 38: 408–37.

BARON, J. N., and KREPS, D. M. (1999). *Strategic Human Resources: Frameworks for General Managers*. New York: John Wiley and Sons.

BARTOL, K. M., and SRIVASTAVA, A. (2002). 'Encouraging Knowledge Sharing: The Role of Organizational Reward Systems.' *Journal of Leadership and Organization Studies*, 9: 64–76.

BATT, R. (2002). 'Managing Customer Services: Human Resource Practices, Quit Rates, and Sales Growth.' *Academy of Management Journal*, 45: 587–97.

—— (2004). 'Who Benefits from Teams? Comparing Workers, Supervisors, and Managers.' *Industrial Relations*, 43: 183–212.

BEEKUN, R. I. (1989). 'Assessing the Effectiveness of Socio-technical Interventions: Antidote or Fad?' *Human Relations*, 102: 877–97.

BEER, M., SPECTOR, B., LAWRENCE, P. R., MILLS, D. Q., and WALTON, R. E. (1985). *Human Resource Management: A General Manager's Perspective*. New York: Free Press.

BOXALL, P., and PURCELL, J. (2003). *Strategy and Human Resource Management*. New York: Palgrave Macmillan.

BRIEF, A., and WEISS, H. M. (2002). 'Organizational Behavior: Affect in the Workplace.' *Annual Review of Psychology*, 53: 279–307.

BURR, R., and CORDERY, J. L. (2001). 'Self-Management Efficacy as a Mediator of the Relation between Job Design and Employee Motivation.' *Human Performance*, 14: 27–44.

CAMPION, M. A. (1988). 'Interdisciplinary Approaches to Job Design: A Constructive Replication with Extensions.' *Journal of Applied Psychology*, 73: 467–81.

—— and THAYER, P. W. (1987). 'Job Design: Approaches, Outcomes, and Trade-offs.' *Organizational Dynamics*, 15: 66–79.

COHEN, S. G., and BAILEY, D. E. (1997). 'What Makes Teams Work: Group Effectiveness Research from the Shop Floor to the Executive Suite.' *Journal of Management*, 23: 239–90.

CORDERY, J. (2004). 'Another Case of the Emperor's New Clothes?' *Journal of Occupational and Organizational Psychology*, 77: 481–4.

—— (2005). 'Team Work.' In D. Holman, T. D. Wall, C. W. Clegg, P. Sparrow, and A. Howard (eds.), *The Essentials of the New Workplace: A Guide to the Human Impact of Modern Working Practices*. Chichester: John Wiley.

—— and WALL, T. D. (1985). 'Work Design and Supervisory Practices: A Model.' *Human Relations*, 38: 425–41.

—— MUELLER, W. S., and SMITH, L. M. (1991). 'Attitudinal and Behavioral Effects of Autonomous Group Working: A Longitudinal Field Study.' *Academy of Management Journal*, 43: 464–76.

DAVIS, L. E., and TAYLOR, J. C. (1972). *Design of Jobs*. Baltimore: Penguin.

DeSHON, R. P., KOZLOWSKI, S. W. J., SCHMIDT, A. M., MILNER, K. R., and WIECHMANN, D. (2004). 'A Multiple-Goal, Multi-level Model of Feedback Effects on the Regulation of Individual and Team Performance.' *Journal of Applied Psychology*, 89: 1035–56.

DOUGLAS, C., and GARDNER, W. L. (2004). 'Transition to Self-Directed Work Teams: Implications of Transition Time and Self-Monitoring for Managers' Use of Influence Tactics.' *Journal of Organizational Behavior*, 25: 47–65.

ELLIS, A. P. J., BELL, B. S., PLOYHART, R. E., HOLLENBECK, J. R., and ILGEN, D. R. (2005). 'An Evaluation of Generic Teamwork Skills Training with Action Teams: Effects on Cognitive and Skill-Based Outcomes.' *Personnel Psychology*, 58: 641–72.

EYLON, D., and AU, K. Y. (1999). 'Exploring Empowerment Cross-cultural Differences along the Power-Distance Dimension.' *International Journal of Intercultural Relations*, 23/3: 373–85.

FORRESTER, R. (2000). 'Empowerment: Rejuvenating a Potent Idea.' *Academy of Management Executive*, 14/3: 67–80.

FRENKEL, S. J., KORCZYNSKI, M., SHIRE, K. A., and TAM, M. (1999). *On the Front Line: Organization of Work in the Information Economy*. London: Cornell University Press.

GILBRETH, F. B. (1911). *Brick Laying System*. New York: Clark.

GLOMB, T. M., KAMMEYER-MUELLER, J. D., and ROTUNDO, M. (2004). 'Emotional Labor Demands and Compensating Wage Differentials.' *Journal of Applied Psychology*, 89: 700–14.

GRANDEY, A. A. (2000). 'Emotion Regulation in the Workplace: A New Way to Conceptualize Emotional Labor.' *Journal of Occupational Health Psychology*, 5: 95–100.

GRIFFIN, R. W. (1991). 'Effects of Work Redesign on Employee Perceptions, Attitudes and Behaviours: A Long-Term Investigation.' *Academy of Management Journal*, 34: 425–35.

HACKMAN, J. R. (1987). 'The Design of Work Teams.' In J. W. Lorsch (ed.), *Handbook of Organizational Behaviour*. Englewood Cliffs, NJ.: Prentice Hall.

—— (2002). *Leading Teams: Setting the Stage for Great Performances*. Boston: Harvard Business School Press.

—— and OLDHAM, G. R. (1976). 'Motivation through the Design of Work: Test of a Theory.' *Organisational Behaviour and Human Performance*, 15: 250–79.

—— —— (1980). *Work Redesign*. Reading, Mass.: Addison-Wesley.

—— and WAGEMAN, R. (2005). 'A Theory of Team Coaching.' *Academy of Management Review*, 30: 269–87.

HERZBERG, F. (1968). 'One More Time: How do you Motivate Employees?' *Harvard Business Review*, 46: 53–63.

HOLMAN, D. (2002). 'Employee Well-Being in Call Centres.' *Human Resource Management Journal*, 12: 35–50.

—— (2005). 'Call Centres.' In D. Holman, T. D. Wall, C. W. Clegg, P. Sparrow, and A. Howard (eds.), *The Essentials of the New Workplace: A Guide to the Human Impact of Modern Working Practices*. Chichester: John Wiley.

HUNTER, L. W., MacDUFFIE, J. P., and DOUCET, L. (2002). 'What Makes Teams Take: Employee Reactions to Work Reforms.' *Industrial and Labor Relations Review*, 55: 448–72.

HUTCHINSON, S., PURCELL, J., and KINNIE, N. (2000). 'Evolving High Commitment Management and the Experience of the RAC Call Centre.' *Human Resource Management Journal*, 10: 63–78.

KATZ, D., and KAHN, R. L. (1966). *The Social Psychology of Organizations*. New York: Wiley.

KIRKMAN, B. L., and ROSEN, B. (2000). 'Powering up Teams.' *Organizational Dynamics*, 28: 48–66.

—— and SHAPIRO, D. L. (1997). 'The Impact of Cultural Values on Employee Resistance to Teams: Toward a Model of Globalized Self-Managing Work Team Effectiveness.' *Academy of Management Review*, 22: 730–57.

KNIGHTS, D., and McCABE, D. (2000). 'Bewitched, Bothered and Bewildered: The Meaning and Experience of Teamworking for Employees in an Automobile Company.' *Human Relations*, 53: 1481–517.

—— —— (2003). 'Governing through Teamwork: Reconstituting Subjectivity in a Call Centre.' *Journal of Management Studies*, 40: 1587–619.

LANGFRED, C. W., and MOYE, N. A. (2004). 'Effects of Task Autonomy on Performance: An Extended Model Considering Motivational, Informational, and Structural Mechanisms.' *Journal of Applied Psychology*, 89: 934–45.

LAWLER, E. E., and FINEGOLD, D. (2000). 'Individualizing the Organization: Past, Present and Future.' *Organizational Dynamics*, 29: 1–15.

—— MOHRMAN, S. A., and LEDFORD, G. E. 1995. *Employee Involvement and Total Quality Management: Practices and Results in Fortune 1000 Companies*. San Francisco: Jossey-Bass.

LEACH, D. J., WALL, T. D., ROGELBERG, S. G., and JACKSON, P. R. (2005). 'Team Autonomy, Performance, and Member Job Strain: Uncovering the Teamwork KSA Link.' *Applied Psychology: An International Review*, 54/1: 1–24.

LOCKE, E. A. (1982). 'The Ideas of Frederick W. Taylor: An Evaluation.' *Academy of Management Review*, 7: 14–24.

—— and LATHAM, G. P. (2002). 'Building a Practically Useful Theory of Goal Setting and Task Motivation: A 35-Year Odyssey.' *American Psychologist*, 57: 705–17.

McGREGOR, D. (1960). *The Human Side of Enterprise*. New York: McGraw-Hill.

MacINNES, J. (2005). 'Work–Life Balance and the Demand for Reduction in Working Hours: Evidence from the British Social Attitudes Survey 2002.' *British Journal of Industrial Relations*, 43: 273–95.

MACY, B. A., and IZUMI, H. (1993). 'Organizational Change, Design, and Work Innovation: A Meta-analysis of 131 North American Field Studies 1961–1991.' *Research in Organizational Change and Development*, 7: 235–313.

MARCHAND, A., DEMERS, A., and DURAND, P. (2005). 'Does Work Really Cause Distress? The Contribution of Occupational Structure and Work Organization to the Experience of Psychological Distress.' *Social Science and Medicine*, 61: 1–14.

MARKS, M. A., SABELLA, M. J., BURKE, C. S., and ZACCARO, S. J. (2002). 'The Impact of Cross-Training on Team Effectiveness.' *Journal of Applied Psychology*, 87: 3–13.

MINTZBERG, H. (1979). *The Structuring of Organizations*. Englewood Cliffs, NJ: Prentice Hall.

MORGESON, F. P. (2005). 'The External Leadership of Self-Managing Teams: Intervening in the Context of Novel and Disruptive Events.' *Journal of Applied Psychology*, 90: 497–508.

—— and CAMPION, M. A. (2002). 'Minimizing Tradeoffs when Redesigning Work: Evidence From a Longitudinal Quasi-experiment.' *Personnel Psychology*, 55: 589–612.

—— DELANEY-KLINGER, K., and HEMINGWAY, M. A. (2005). 'THE Importance of Job Autonomy, Cognitive Ability, and Job-Related Skill for Predicting Role Breadth and Job Performance.' *Journal of Applied Psychology*, 90: 399–406.

MORRISON, D. L., CORDERY, J. L., GIRARDI, A., and PAYNE, R. (2005). 'Job Design, Opportunities for Skill Utilisation and Job-Related Affective Well-Being.' *European Journal of Work and Organisational Psychology*, 14: 59–80.

OLDHAM, G. R. (1996). 'Job Design.' In C. L. Cooper and I. T. Robertson (eds.), *International Review of Industrial and Organizational Psychology*, vol. xi. New York: John Wiley.

—— and HACKMAN, J. R. (1980). 'Work Design in the Organizational Context.' In B. M. Staw and L. L. Cummings (eds.), *Research in Organizational Behavior*, vol. ii. Greenwich, Conn.: JAI Press.

O'REILLY, C. A., and PFEFFER, J. (2000). *Hidden Value: How Great Companies Achieve Extraordinary Results with Ordinary People*. Boston: Harvard Business School Press.

PARKER, S. K. (1998). 'Role Breadth Self-Efficacy: Relationship with Work Enrichment and Other Practices.' *Journal of Applied Psychology*, 83: 835–52.

—— (2003). 'Longitudinal Effects of Lean Production on Employee Outcomes and the Mediating Role of Work Characteristics.' *Journal of Applied Psychology*, 88: 620–34.

—— and AXTELL, C. M. (2001). 'Seeing Another Viewpoint: Antecedents and Outcomes of Employee Perspective Taking.' *Academy of Management Journal*, 44: 1085–101.

—— and TURNER, N. (2002). 'Work Design and Individual Job Performance: Research Findings and an Agenda for Future Inquiry.' In S. Sonnentag (ed.), *Psychological Management of Individual Performance: A Handbook in the Psychology of Management in Organizations*. Chichester: John Wiley and Sons.

—— and WALL, T. (1998). *Job and Work Design: Organizing Work to Promote Well-Being and Effectiveness*. Thousand Oaks, Calif.: Sage Publications.

—— —— and JACKSON, P. R. (1997). ' "That's not my Job": Developing Flexible Employee Work Orientations.' *Academy of Management Journal*, 40: 899–929.

—— —— and CORDERY, J. L. (2001). 'Future Work Design Research and Practice: An Elaborated Work Characteristics Model.' *Journal of Occupational and Organizational Psychology*, 73: 414–40.

PASMORE, W. A. (1988). *Designing Effective Organizations: The Sociotechnical Systems Perspective*. New York: Wiley.

PFEFFER, J. (1998). *The Human Equation: Building Profits by Putting People First*. Boston: Harvard Business School Press.

PIL, F. K., and MacDUFFIE, J. P. (1996). 'The Adoption of High-Involvement Work Practices.' *Industrial Relations*, 35: 423–55.

RAGHURAM, S., and WEISENFELD, B. (2004). 'Work–Nonwork Conflict and Job Stress among Virtual Workers.' *Human Resource Management*, 43: 259–77.

RYAN, R. M., and DECI, E. L. (2000). 'Self-Determination Theory and the Facilitation of Intrinsic Motivation, Social Development, and Well-Being.' *American Psychologist*, 55: 68–78.

SEIBERT, S. E., SILVER, S. R., and RANDOLPH, W. A. (2004). 'Taking Empowerment to the Next Level: A Multiple-Level Model of Empowerment, Performance and Satisfaction.' *Academy of Management Journal*, 47: 332–49.

SINHA, K. K., and VAN de VEN, A. H. (2005). 'Designing Work within and between Organizations.' *Organization Science*, 16: 389–408.

SPREITZER, G. M. (1995). 'Individual Empowerment in the Workplace: Dimensions, Measurement, Validation.' *Academy of Management Journal*, 38: 1442–65.

—— COHEN, S. G., and LEDFORD, G. E., Jr. (1999). 'Developing Effective Self-Managing Work Teams in Service Organizations.' *Group and Organization Management*, 24: 340–66.

SPRIGG, C. A., JACKSON, P. R., and PARKER, S. K. (2000). 'Production Teamworking: The Importance of Interdependence and Autonomy for Employee Strain and Satisfaction.' *Human Relations*, 53: 1519–43.

STANTON, J. M. (2000). 'Reactions to Employee Performance Monitoring: Framework, Review and Research Directions.' *Human Performance*, 13: 85–113.

STAW, B. M., and EPSTEIN, L. D. (2000). 'What Bandwagons Bring: Effects of Popular Management Techniques on Corporate Performance, Reputation and CEO Pay.' *Administrative Science Quarterly*, 45: 523–56.

STEVENS, M. J., and CAMPION, M. A. (1999). 'Staffing Work Teams: Development and Validation of a Selection Test for Teamwork Settings.' *Journal of Management*, 25: 207–28.

TAYLOR, F. W. (1911). *The Principles of Scientific Management*. New York: Harper.

—— (1947). 'The Principles of Scientific Management.' Reprinted in V. H. Vroom and E. L. Deci (eds.), *Management and Motivation*. Harmondsworth: Penguin, 1978.

TERRY, D., and JIMMIESON, N., (1999). 'Work Control and Well-Being: A Decade Review.' In C. L. Cooper, and I. T. Robertson (eds.), *International Review of Industrial and Organizational Psychology*, vol. xiv. Chichester: Wiley.

THOMAS, K. W., and VELTHOUSE, B. A. (1990). 'Cognitive Elements of Empowerment: An Interpretive Model of Intrinsic Motivation.' *Academy of Management Review*, 15: 666–81.

TRIST, E. L., and BAMFORTH, K. W. (1951). 'Some Social and Psychological Consequences of the Long-Wall Method of Coal-Getting.' *Human Relations*, 4: 3–38.

ULRICH, D., ZENGER, J., and SMALLWOOD, N. (1999). *Results-Based Leadership*. Boston: Harvard Business School Press.

VALLAS, S. P. (2003). 'Why Teamwork Fails: Obstacles to Workplace Change in Four Manufacturing Plants.' *American Sociological Review*, 68: 223–50.

WAGEMAN, R. (1995). 'Interdependence and Group Effectiveness.' *Administrative Science Quarterly*, 40: 145–80.

WALL, T. D., and CLEGG, C. W. (1998). 'Job Design.' In C. L. Cooper and C. Argyris (eds.), *The Concise Blackwell Encyclopedia of Management*. Oxford: Blackwell.

—— JACKSON, P. R., and DAVIDS, K. (1992). 'Operator Work Design and Robotics System Performance: A Serendipitous Field Study.' *Journal of Applied Psychology*, 77: 353–62.

—— CORDERY, J. L. and CLEGG, C. W. (2002). 'Empowerment, Performance and Operational Uncertainty: A Theoretical Integration.' *Applied Psychology: An International Review*, 51: 146–69.

WALTON, R. E. (1985). 'From Control to Commitment.' *Harvard Business Review*, March–April: 77–84.

WHITTINGTON, J. L., GOODWIN, V. L., and MORRAY, B. (2004). 'Transformational Leadership, Goal Difficulty, and Job Design: Independent and Interactive Effects on Employee Outcomes.' *Leadership Quarterly*, 15: 593–606.

WORKMAN, M., and BOMBER, W. (2004). 'Redesigning Computer Call Centre Work: A Longitudinal Field Experiment.' *Journal of Organizational Behavior*, 25: 317–37.

WRIGHT, B. M., and CORDERY, J. L. (1999). 'Production Uncertainty as a Contextual Moderator of Employee Reactions to Job Design.' *Journal of Applied Psychology*, 84: 456–63.

WRIGHT, P. M., and SNELL, S. A. (1998). 'Toward a Unifying Framework for Exploring Fit and Flexibility in Strategic Human Resource Management.' *Academy of Management Review*, 23: 756–72.

YATES, C., LEWCHUK, W., and STEWART, P. (2001). 'Empowerment as Trojan Horse: New Systems of Work Organization in the North American Automobile Industry.' *Economic and Industrial Democracy*, 22: 517–41.

YOUNDT, M. A., SNELL, S. A., DEAN, J. W., and LEPAK, D. P. (1996). 'Human Resource Management, Manufacturing Strategy, and Firm Performance.' *Academy of Management Journal*, 39: 836–66.

CHAPTER 11

# EMPLOYMENT SUBSYSTEMS AND THE 'HR ARCHITECTURE'

DAVID LEPAK

SCOTT A. SNELL

## 11.1 INTRODUCTION

THERE is an interesting tension that exists within the HRM literature with regard to employment subsystems. On the one hand, a clear pattern is emerging in strategic HRM research that suggests that HR systems geared toward increased commitment and employee involvement can have a dramatic impact on organizational outcomes (Becker and Gerhart 1996). Terms such as commitment-oriented HR systems (Arthur 1992; Lepak and Snell 2002), high-performance work systems (Huselid 1995), high-involvement HRM (Guthrie 2001), and the like exude a connotation of extensive investment in, and reliance on, employees. In fact, many researchers have suggested that people (human capital), more so that other organizational resources, may be a strong potential source for achieving a sustainable competitive advantage (Pfeffer 1994).

At the same time, many firms are increasing their use of externalized employment (e.g. temporary employees, independent contractors) as well as implementing employment subsystems within their organizations. Proponents of externalization suggest that relying on different forms of external labor may enable firms to be responsive to changes in labor demands, lower labor costs, and increase access to skills their employees do not possess (Matusik and Hill 1998). And arguments for establishing subsystems within organizations are based on the logic that not all employees make equivalent strategic contributions to competitive success. As a result, the nature of the employment arrangement and associated HR system designs should differentiate core versus non-core employees (Delery and Shaw 2001) or between A players, B players, and C players (Huselid et al. 2005).

At first glance, the trend of increased outsourcing of human capital and employment subsystems, and their implied economic benefits, may be viewed as standing in direct contrast to a high-commitment approach towards managing people (cf. Boxall 1998; Rubery et al. 2004). If people are one of a company's key sources of competitive advantage, how can companies simultaneously be committed to employees and use contingent labor?

In some ways, this tension runs in parallel to—or is indicative of—the distinction between managing people and managing jobs. Organizations do both, and the crux of this issue depends upon where critical knowledge resides. In some cases, say extreme instances of Taylorism (Fordism), core knowledge is embedded in the design of tasks and standard operating procedures/routines. In these situations, discretion is neither required nor desired from employees, and the key managerial objective would likely be finding suitable labor that can (reliably) perform these tasks at the lowest possible cost. In other cases, where critical knowledge cannot be codified or standardized, creativity and innovation are perhaps required. As a consequence, the key knowledge asset shifts toward employee human capital (rather than the job). In these instances, effective performance requires discretionary and/or proactive behavior on the part of employees. Accordingly, the key managerial objective would likely be fully engaging employee involvement and commitment to organizational goals and performance.

Historically, HRM practices have been based on the management of jobs. As much as anything, this derives from the fact that the profession matured under an era of large-scale manufacturing. But the increasing reality is that the knowledge that companies rely on for competitive success not only resides in the minds of their employees but also in the minds of contractors, consultants, and other external workers with whom they collaborate. In many ways, the trend toward a differentiated workforce is a response to the increasing importance of knowledge management. Certain employees are hired to perform a relatively standardized job while others are sought for what they know and their potential.

In addition, the use of employment subsystems continues to evolve based on factors related to globalization, strategic considerations, and managing both the stocks and flow of knowledge. First, companies are increasingly turning to employment options on a global level. The trends toward offshoring (Reich 2005) and 24/7 or 'follow the sun' employment strategies (Solomon 2001) exemplify the growing trend toward a global approach to managing human capital. While global employment subsystems may certainly be driven by cost considerations, on the one hand, they are also driven by knowledge-based motivations on the other. How does globalization influence the use of employment subsystems? Second, a typical argument is that companies (should) internalize their core employees and outsource peripheral work. While this general approach has received some support (Delery and Shaw 2001; Lepak and Snell 1999), the reality is that what is peripheral to one firm may be core to another (and vice versa). Companies vary in how they compete, and variations in strategic priorities are likely to influence choices among employment systems for different groups of employees. Finally, a central challenge for companies that compete based on knowledge is not only to have a clear sense of what knowledge its employees presently hold and need in order to achieve its business goals, it is equally important to promote exchange of knowledge, innovation, and learning to maintain competitive distinction. That is, it is not knowledge per se that make a competitive edge possible, but rather the extent to which the company can effectively manage knowledge to create value over time. This distinction reflects the difference between managing knowledge stocks and managing the flow of knowledge among employees within as well as across employment subsystems (cf. Boxall 1998; Dierickx and Cool 1989; Kang et al. in press).

The rest of this chapter is structured as follows. First, we review the 'HR architecture' to provide a backdrop for our discussion of employment subsystems and changing forms of employment. Second, we examine the implications of globalization, strategy, and managing knowledge flows for how companies structure their portfolio of employment subsystems. Throughout our discussion we offer suggestions for future research.

## 11.2 THE HR ARCHITECTURE

Researchers such as Boxall (1998), Osterman (1987), and Purcell (1999) note that different employment systems exist within firms. For instance, Osterman (1987) argued that firms choose among different HR practices when triggered by events such as technological change, reduced labor supply, and rising wages. These forces contribute to the creation of different employment subsystems within firms. Boxall (1998: 268) suggested that firms differentiate between an inner core of employees who are 'responsible for valuable innovations or for successful imitations' and an outer core of employees who are instrumental in maintaining process efficiencies and capacity. While the terms may differ, a common theme is that firms may heavily invest in a core group of employees while also maintaining a peripheral group of employees from whom they prefer to remain relatively detached. Going beyond internal subsystems, many organizations have increased their use of externalized employment arrangements as well. Long-term partnerships, consultancy arrangements, and contract work represent employment subsystems that exist on the periphery of, or completely external to, an organization's workforce.

From a strategic HRM perspective, a key point for understanding employment subsystems is that these work arrangements have direct implications for how companies structure their HR systems to manage them. For example, Rousseau (1995) as well as Tsui et al. (1995) argued not only that employment subsystems differ, but also that the employment relationships or psychological contracts may differ as well. In general, firms might emphasize either a long-term, relational approach or a short-term, transactional approach for internal and external workers. These choices directly impact how employees are managed.

Lepak and Snell (1999) suggested that by juxtaposing two dimensions—strategic value and uniqueness—it is possible to derive a matrix of four groups of human capital (and associated types of knowledge) that differ in terms of employment subsystems, employment relationships, and the HR systems used to manage employee groups. *Strategic value* is determined by the skill sets of employees that enable a firm to enact strategies that improve efficiency and effectiveness, exploit market opportunities, and/or neutralize potential threats (Barney 1991; Wright and McMahan 1992). Accordingly, value is derived from the ability of these skills to increase the ratio of benefits to customers relative to their associated costs (i.e. value = benefits/costs). *Uniqueness* refers to the extent to which knowledge and skills are specialized or firm specific (e.g. Williamson 1975). Unique human capital may consist of tacit knowledge or deep experience that cannot be found in an open labor market, thereby reducing the extent to which it may be transferred to other firms. Figure 11.1 summarizes the HR architecture.

## 11.2.1 Core Knowledge (Knowledge-Based Employment)

Given their high strategic value and uniqueness, core knowledge workers are most likely to contribute directly to a firm's core competencies on the basis of what they know and how they use their knowledge (Snell et al. 1999; Purcell 1999). As a result, firms have financial and strategic incentives to internally develop and invest in these employees. To do so, companies tend to implement a commitment-based HR system (e.g. Lepak and Snell 2002) that invests in the development of employee competencies, empowers employees, and encourages participation in decision-making and discretion on the job. Likewise, long-term incentives (e.g. stock ownership, extensive benefits, or knowledge-based pay systems) may be offered to ensure that core employees receive continued and useful feedback and adopt

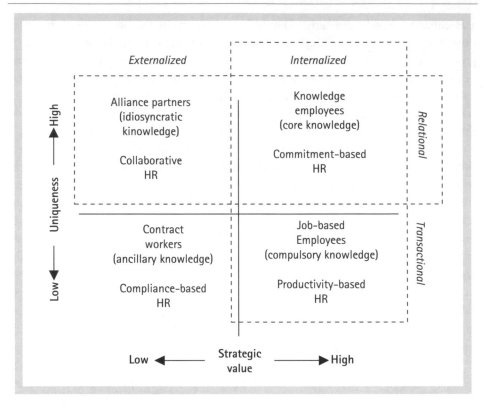

**Fig. 11.1. HR architectural perspective**

*Source:* Adapted from Lepak and Snell, 1999, 2002; Snell et al. 1999.

a long-term orientation (Snell and Dean 1992). Such practices are designed to help firms maintain unique knowledge that leads to strategic advantage.

## 11.2.2 Compulsory Knowledge (Job-Based Employment)

Similar to core knowledge, compulsory knowledge is important for value creation and strategic advantage. Given strategic value, employment for these individuals tends to be internalized, provided there is sufficient supply of labor. However, because this form of human capital is not unique, it is mobile and firms may suffer a capital loss if their investments transfer to a competitor. As a result, organizations tend to de-emphasize development, and the employment relationship tends to adhere to a more traditional job-based orientation focused on immediate performance (Lepak and Snell 2002). Managers are likely to rely more on a productivity-based HR configuration that focuses on standardized jobs and selecting people from the external labor market who can contribute immediately (cf. Tsui et al. 1995). Incentives for these employees tend to focus on efficiency and productivity through a results-based approach and performance appraisals are likely to emphasize a short-term, results-oriented component (Snell 1992; Snell and Youndt 1995).

## 11.2.3 Ancillary Knowledge (Contract Work Arrangements)

Lepak and Snell (1999) suggested that firms are most likely to establish short-term contractual arrangements for tasks that are of limited strategic value and uniqueness. When the requisite knowledge is of limited strategic value, there is no strong incentive to internalize employment. And because the knowledge is of limited uniqueness, companies tend to adopt a more transactional rather than a relational employment relationship. Similar to compulsory knowledge, managing ancillary knowledge tends to focus on short-term productivity and efficiency for tasks of limited scope, purpose, or duration (Lepak and Snell 2002). This is done by focusing on compliance with preset rules, regulations, and/or procedures. For example, job descriptions are likely to be standardized and training and performance management, if conducted, is likely to be limited to ensuring that company policies, systems, and procedures are carried out. In addition, compensation for these employees is likely to be based on an hourly wage and the accomplishment of specific tasks or goals.

## 11.2.4 Idiosyncratic Knowledge (Alliances/Partnerships)

Employees with idiosyncratic knowledge possess unique know-how but their know-how is of limited strategic value. Because their knowledge is not as central to value creation and strategy, employees with this type of human capital may be externalized. However, these external partners have specialized knowledge that is not easy to find in the market. As a consequence, long-term partnerships are likely to be fostered that preserve continuity over time, ensure trust among partners, and engender reciprocity and collaboration (Lepak and Snell 2002). While there tends not to be investment in the human capital itself, there is substantial investment in the relationship with these individuals. Given the need for ongoing exchange, alliance partners are more likely to be managed by a collaborative HR configuration characterized by group incentives, cross-functional teams, and the like. Such practices may ensure greater integration and stronger relationships with the firm and the partner employees.

Though still in its infancy, an architectural perspective of employment subsystems has received some empirical support. For example, Lepak and Snell (2002) demonstrated that companies use different HR systems to manage different employee groups, depending on their strategic value and uniqueness. Similarly, in a study of 375 companies in Spain, Gonzales and Tacorante (2004) showed that over 70 percent of the companies in their sample relied on all four modes of employment,

27 percent used three of the four employment modes, and 2 percent used only two employment modes. Like Lepak and Snell (2002), Gonzales and Tacorante (2004) also found consistent differences in the HRM practices used among each employee group. Looking beyond the extent of their use, Lepak et al. (2003) found that a more extensive reliance on core knowledge employees and/or short-term contract workers was positively associated with firm performance (ROA and market-to-book value) while an increased reliance on non-core, job-based employees and external alliance partners was associated with diminished firm performance.

Interestingly, while research indicates that companies do adopt a differentiated approach to their employment portfolio and there are performance implications for how the portfolio is structured, there are potentially additional implications (both positive and negative) related to adopting a mixed approach to employment. For example, while a differentiated approach may result in improved performance by targeting high investments in critical skills sets, it is also possible that such an approach may trigger equity concerns among different groups, depending on the spillover of the HR systems used across employee groups. Groups that receive lower levels of investment, though possibly justified in terms of their potential strategic contributions, may experience inequity and display less than desired attitudes and behaviors as a result. At the same time, treating all employees equally might involve over-investing in non-critical employees and under-investing in critical employees. While such an approach may alleviate equity concerns among non-core employees, it may not be cost effective for the firm and might actually result in expending unnecessary costs without reaping the benefits. These tensions may be magnified in situations where employees in different employee groups (and exposed to different HR systems) perform tasks and activities that are highly interdependent (Boxall 1998; Rubery et al. 2004).

To complicate matters further, researchers examining employment subsystems in general, and the HR architecture in particular, have not focused on the three emerging issues noted above—the globalization of employment, the importance of strategy, and balancing both knowledge stocks and flows within and across employment groups—for both the use and effectiveness of implementing alternative employment options for their workforce. In the remainder of this chapter, we extend the HR architecture to examine these issues.

# 11.3 GLOBALIZATION AND THE HR ARCHITECTURE

One of the most pervasive trends regarding employment subsystems is directly related to the globalization of companies. In particular, offshoring—sending work to other countries—has received considerable attention and raised a number of issues for how companies structure their HR architecture. In many ways, the increased use of international employment subsystems is a natural extension of the HR architecture. Pressures for the continued pursuit of lower costs, increased expertise, and flexibility have encouraged many managers to think beyond country boundaries for the most efficient and/or effective source of labor.

In the context of the HR architecture, one could imagine an extension of employment subsystems to include short-term outsourcing arrangements as well as more long-term offshoring arrangements and alliance partnerships. If a task or service that is of low strategic value and limited uniqueness may be performed at a lower cost in another country, and there is a viable organization in that country to deliver that task or service, there is a strong incentive for companies to consider outsourcing this work. By doing so, the company may be able to recoup those costs, access greater efficiencies and/or expertise in the performance of the tasks by the outsourcing provider, and divert their investments to more value-added core employees. In these scenarios, international outsourcing is a logical extension of more traditional domestic-based outsourcing or contractual arrangements.

Investments in offshoring are intended to gain cost advantages from maintaining operations in another country with internal employees (rather than another company's employees) as part of a broader global sourcing strategy. On the one hand, offshoring may be pursued to achieve similar benefits to those derived from outsourcing; namely cost advantages. Ultimately, however, the costs advantages may go away as wages inevitably increase in developing countries such as China, India, and Hungary that are frequent centers of offshoring activities (Aron and Singh 2005). So the challenge is to offshore initially for cost and flexibility, but then focus on increasing productivity/expertise faster than wages increase. On the other hand, offshoring is a logical extension of more long-term partnerships, although for perhaps different reasons. In China, for example, companies typically enter via joint ventures that involve alliances (rather than, say, subsidiaries). The government requires it. And while costs may certainly be a consideration, it may also be the case that the labor force in another country excels in certain areas of expertise such as science or medicine or simply has a greater supply of labor for a particular expertise (Purcell et al. 2004).

Although international partnerships present a challenge in terms of distance, they present an opportunity for '24/7' or 'follow the sun' workforce arrangements that allow for work to be continuously performed around the world without any downtime. A partner of a US firm in India, for example, may conceivably start their work day just as the employees in the USA are completing their work day. By doing so, companies may be able to decrease the time to completion of new products or services while dramatically increasing their labor pool. Given the continual pressures for innovation and/or cost considerations, it is logical that companies are exploring these work arrangements. However, the long-term performance benefits (or costs) are not well known.

## 11.3.1 Research Implications

Most of the literature focusing on international HRM has focused on managing employees within a specific country or on expatriate management. Yet, managing the portfolio of global sourcing options, including offshoring, outsourcing, alliances, and the like, on a global level is likely to be equally challenging. The picture is further complicated when researchers consider the implications of global markets. Much of the controversy about outsourcing and offshoring manufacturing jobs, for example, needs to be couched within the context of where the work is done relative to where the products and services are sold. Many firms argue that their international employees are producing for international markets. Critics charge that the international work is too often devised to exploit low-cost labor, and then the goods/services are shipped back to the host country. These issues have political as well as competitive implications and much more research is needed to understand them fully.

Relatedly, while these different arrangements are typically argued to facilitate cost savings and company flexibility, the question remains as to how these arrangements relate to other facets of value creation. For example, faced with customer concerns stemming from dealing with customer service representatives in India, Dell reconsidered its sourcing strategy for its call centers. Though simplistic, this example highlights the fact that organizations must balance tensions for cost savings with achieving strategic objectives such as quality enhancements, operational performance, market access, innovation, customer service, and the like (Aron and Singh 2005). Saving costs at the expense of other performance outcomes is unlikely to prove a sustainable strategy over time. A related issue focuses directly on which jobs or tasks and activities are most appropriate candidates for these global sourcing options. If we shift our focus away from solely cost considerations, the key question becomes which employee talent pools drive value creation within organizations and how should those talent pools be employed to maximize value creation while capitalizing on cost-saving options?

Viewing the HR architecture from a global perspective also requires greater attention to environmental factors. Countries vary in the quality of their human capital, the relative supply and demand of different occupational skill sets, labor costs as well as labor laws, unionization, and worker preferences. It may be the case that the use of temporary employees, for example, reflects country regulatory and environmental factors as much as consideration of strategic value and uniqueness. Companies operating in countries with restrictive labor laws regarding employee terminations may be more willing to choose externalized employment options, rather than commit to long-term employment, even for critical or core employee groups, compared to companies operating in environments that are more employer friendly. Relatedly, the supply of labor in different occupational groups may influence which employment options are most beneficial to pursue in different regions or countries. In some countries, occupational specialists may be in such short supply or high demand that they have considerable leverage or bargaining power in determining which type of employment option they are willing to work within (Purcell et al. 2004).

Finally, how does a global HR architecture impact the composition of the HR systems used to manage these subsystems? While outsourcing or offshoring arrangements may be managed sufficiently with a compliance-oriented HR system, long-term alliance partners must be coordinated. Given cultural differences, and in many cases considerable distance, what should be the composition of the HR systems for these global partners? How should companies design HR systems for these different countries that simultaneously meet a company's strategic needs while addressing the local country's requirements? Researchers have struggled with the distinction between global efficiency and local responsiveness at the strategy level. The unique challenge here is that these are often not completely independent entities that may be managed differently. From an architectural perspective, these employment subsystems must be integrated and coordinated to prove effective.

## 11.4 STRATEGY AND THE HR ARCHITECTURE

Although our discussion so far has focused on the relationships among human capital, employment, and HR systems, it is important to explore how a company's strategic direction may impact how they structure their HR architecture. Much of the strategic HRM research has focused on the direct linkage between a firm's strategy and its dominant orientation toward HR (e.g. Arthur 1992; Miles and Snow 1984). The underlying logic for this focus is that different organizational strategies have certain behavioral requirements for their successful implementation (Jackson et al. 1989; Miles and Snow 1984). To elicit these behaviors, organizations design and deploy HR practices that motivate certain employee attitudes and behaviors while discouraging others.

Building on this behavioral perspective, one might anticipate that firms pursuing different strategic orientations would be likely to utilize different HR configurations for their employee groups. For example, in the case of firms pursuing innovation, it may be that the entire workforce needs to be more oriented toward knowledge creation and transfer (Leonard-Barton 1995; Schuler and Jackson 1987). As noted by Jackson and colleagues (1989), firms that compete in the market place by being more innovative than their competitors must have employees that are willing to take risks and experiment with new ideas. Achieving this requires that firms implement HR practices that encourage employees to engage in creative behavior, cooperate and share ideas with others, and retain a long-term focus (Wright and McMahan 1992). Based on this, we might expect to see more pervasive use of the commitment-based and collaborative HR systems for all employees as these HR configurations focus on creating and transferring knowledge whereas productivity-based and compliance-based HR systems do not.

In contrast, a low-cost strategy is likely to involve firms orienting their workforce more toward productivity and efficiency concerns (Miles and Snow 1984; Porter 1985; Schuler 1992). As noted by Wright and McMahan (1992: 304), a cost strategy 'requires such things as repetitive behaviors, a short-term focus, autonomous activity, high concern for quantity, moderate concern for quality, and low risk taking.' If managers are focused on efficiency and productivity maximization for all employees, they might establish more short-term performance horizons for individuals in the top two quadrants of the matrix than is normally anticipated (i.e. managing them more like employees in the bottom quadrants). Further, managers focused on low costs may not be willing to expend the resources necessary for training and knowledge development (an expense that might diminish profit margins in the short run). In this case, we might expect to see more reliance on productivity-based and compliance-based HR configurations for all employee groups than commitment and collaborative HRM.

While organizations may adopt an overarching orientation toward managing all employees via higher levels of commitment and collaboration or productivity and compliance, we anticipate that adopting an HR architecture perspective adds additional complexity to the influence of strategy. Rather than focusing solely on which overarching HR orientation to adopt, an architectural perspective also directly raises the issue of how different employee groups add value. In the HR architecture, there are two key issues that emerge that complicate this discussion. First, different strategies emphasize different internal business processes for competitive advantage. Second, not all skill sets groups are equally critical for value creation among different internal business processes and, ultimately, competitive differentiation.

Differences in the strategic objectives firms pursue directly influence the relative role and value of different business processes in the value chain. For example, firms focused on product leadership (and innovation) are likely to depend most critically on different processes from firms focused on operational excellence (cost). And firms focused on customer intimacy compete on a different set of processes as well. While there certainly may be many more strategic objectives firms may pursue, the key point is that the pursuit of different strategic objectives influences which processes within the value chain are most critical for a competitive advantage based on the strategic objective.

By extension, the relative employee groups oriented toward various business processes are likely to vary in their potential contributions toward critical value creation activities. As a result, an employee group possessing certain skill sets may be particularly critical in one company but may be less critical in another company pursuing a different source of competitive advantage, even when performing the same job. And if the nature of the contribution varies, the HR systems that are most effective in leveraging their potential are likely to vary as well. For example, pursuit of innovation does not mean everyone has to be managed with a high-commitment HR system. What it does is increase the importance of product development and marketing skills as a core skill set for competitive advantage. Similarly, low cost does not require that everyone be managed for efficiency and cost savings. Rather, it requires continuous improvement to drive productivity that may potentially be realized through more commitment-oriented or high-performance work systems rather than solely through productivity and compliance-oriented HR systems. At the same time, however, at the margins, low-cost firms probably emphasize standardized processes more than innovative firms.

## 11.4.1 Research Implications

Conceptually, an architectural perspective may provide some insights into the mixed findings in the literature regarding the notion of external fit or alignment between strategy and HR systems. It may be the case that the external fit hypothesis only holds for specific skill sets within organizations; that is, companies may vary their HR systems for core skill sets to realize alignment with strategic priorities but adopt a more general or efficiency-oriented approach for other, non-critical skill sets. As suggested by Delery and Shaw (2001), using high-performance HR systems may be most important for an organization's strategic core workforce. If this reflects organizational reality, research that fails to differentiate the alignment between strategy and HR systems for core employees versus the alignment between strategy and the management of an entire workforce may provide an inappropriate assessment of how external fit operates.

If companies rely on different skills sets for various strategic objectives, this certainly has implications for how we conceptualize the effectiveness of employment options and HR systems. Rather than focusing on the overall performance benefits related to the use of a single HR system across an entire workforce, it may be more appropriate to more narrowly examine the use of HR systems for specific employees that are instrumental for a company's source of competitive advantage. Moreover, if different business processes are more important than others for various sources of competitive advantage, and different skill sets are emphasized for different processes, the metrics we choose to assess HR system effectiveness might have to be more fine grained as well. For example, focusing on ROA or ROE or market-based performance may fail to truly reflect how the management of sales employees relates to sales growth or customer satisfaction. There may be a strong relationship between HR system use for critical employees with more narrow performance metrics than with organization-wide metrics that are influenced by a variety of factors, many of which may have nothing to do with how employees are managed.

A related issue emerges when we consider that different skills sets within organizations must often be combined to realize strategic priorities (Boxall 1996, 1998; Purcell et al. 2004) and these interactions may extend to employee groups outside of organizations as well (Lepak and Snell 2003; Rubery et al. 2004). While different employee groups are likely to vary in how they add value, or the extent of their value added, we have to also consider the technical and social interdependencies that exist between employee groups (Baron and Kreps 1999). While the independent contributions of some employee groups toward value-creating activities may admittedly be fairly low, it is conceivable that they serve an important supportive role that facilitates valuable and unique contributions of other employee groups or organizational processes that are vital to a company's strategic objectives. This possibility highlights the importance of managing both each individual employment subsystem as well as the coordination of employee efforts across employee subsystems.

One of the underlying arguments for an architectural perspective is that companies may adjust their level of investment in different employee groups based on their potential contribution toward competitive advantage. Conceptually, this suggests that understanding the impact of HR on firm performance requires examination of appropriate performance metrics to reflect how employee groups add value as well as how multiple employee groups are managed simultaneously— rather than focusing on the use of a particular HR system across employees or focusing solely on one employee group.

# 11.5 KNOWLEDGE FLOWS AND THE HR ARCHITECTURE

According to the resource-based view of the firm, a sustained competitive advantage is created 'when implementing a value creating strategy not simultaneously implemented by any current or potential competitor *and* when these other firms are unable to duplicate the benefits of this strategy' (Barney 1991: 102). This is achieved by basing competition on internal resources that are valuable, rare, inimitable, and non-substitutable. While there are many different resources that may serve as a source of competitive advantage, a frequently cited source is the knowledge embedded in their people (Jackson et al. 2003). Such knowledge

(*knowledge stocks*) helps firms create competitive advantage through the effective use, manipulation, and transformation of various organizational resources required to perform a task (Nonaka 1994; Kogut and Zander 1992; Grant 1996).

In addition to knowledge stocks, Dierickx and Cool (1989) noted that *knowledge flows* are vital for the creation of new knowledge, as well as recombination of existing knowledge. While a company's knowledge stocks provides a foundation for competitive advantage (Grant 1996), what differentiates successful companies from others may very well be how companies manage knowledge flows; that is, how companies effectively leverage, integrate, and create knowledge among individuals within and across different employment modes.

Recently, several researchers have directly addressed this issue and have shifted our attention to the broader domain of intellectual capital with a key focus on the importance of social capital. As noted by Youndt et al. (2004: 337), intellectual capital can be broadly conceptualized as 'the sum of all knowledge an organization is able to leverage in the process of conducting business to gain competitive advantage' and consists of human, social, and organizational capital. Human capital refers to individual employee capabilities—their knowledge, skills, and abilities. Nahapiet and Ghoshal (1998) define social capital as the aggregate of resources embedded within, available through, and derived from the network of relationships possessed by an individual or organization (Brass et al. 2004). Finally, organizational capital refers to 'institutionalized knowledge and codified experience stored in databases, routines, patents, manuals, structures, and the like' (Youndt et al. 2004: 338).

Subramanian and Youndt (2005) examined the relationships between these three types of intellectual capital and innovation, and found that organizational capital was positively associated with incremental innovative capability and social capital was related to both incremental and radical capabilities. Interestingly, they also found that human and social capital interacted positively to influence radical innovative capability. One direct implication of this is that it suggests that human capital provides the most value for innovative capabilities when employee knowledge is shared among employees. Relatedly, Collins and Clark (2003) explored the relationships among network-building HRM practices, internal and external social networks of top management teams, and firm sales growth and stock growth. Their results provide support for a mediating effect of top managers' social networks. As these findings suggest, knowledge stocks (human capital) are most valuable when paired with appropriate knowledge flow (social capital).

The importance of social capital and managing knowledge flow highlights a limitation of the HR architecture. While an architectural perspective helps to create an overall picture of how an organization's portfolio of knowledge stocks is managed, differentiating employees based on their uniqueness and strategic value does not account for how to promote knowledge flow within and across different employment modes. Put simply, it does not take into account interactions and

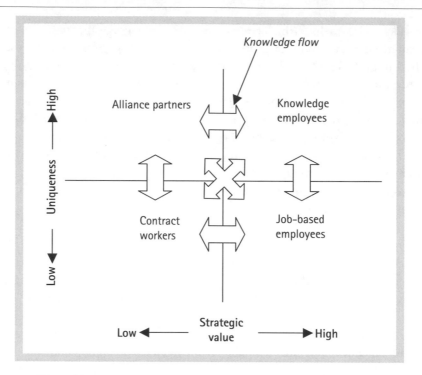

**Fig. 11.2. HR architectural perspective and knowledge flows**

interdependencies across employment systems. In an attempt to overcome this limitation, Kang et al. (in press) focus directly on the implications of managing both knowledge stocks and flows in the HR architecture. According to Kang et al. (in press), success in creating customer value requires that firms are successful in both exploitative and exploratory innovation based on employee knowledge. Recognizing that different employee groups within the HR architecture possess different levels and types of knowledge, leveraging that knowledge requires that organizations design HR systems in a way to encourage entrepreneurial activity among employees for exploratory innovation as well as cooperative activity among employees to exploit and extend existing knowledge for competitive advantage.

Two relational HR archetypes are proposed to accomplish these goals. A *cooperative* relational archetype is characterized by a dense social network with strong ties among members, generalized trust based on shared norms of reciprocity, and a common architectural knowledge that provides the basis for coordination and integration among different sources of employee knowledge. This tightly coordinated network structure is anticipated to allow employees to exchange, combine, and integrate in-depth knowledge with all members of the network to exploit and extend existing knowledge to create customer value. The primary HR activities that support a cooperative relational archetype are interdependent work structures, clan-fostering initiatives, and broader skill development initiatives. An *entrepreneurial* archetype is characterized by more sparse and non-redundant networks, relatively weak and intermittent ties among employees, based on dyadic trust among some members of the network. This looser and more fluid network structure is anticipated to allow employees to pursue more novel and diverse knowledge exchanges necessary for exploratory learning and innovation. The primary HR activities that support an entrepreneurial archetype are flexible work structures, results-based incentives, and trans-specialist development.

## 11.5.1 Research Implications

One of the underlying rationales for using different employment subsystems is that they afford firms different types of flexibility (Lepak et al. 2003; Wright and Snell 1998). Core knowledge workers provide organizations with a greater degree of *resource flexibility*—the ability to perform a wide assortment of tasks—compared to traditional employees. With regard to external or contingent workers, contract arrangements provide organizations with more *coordination flexibility*—the ability to adjust the number and types of skills in use—as compared to more long-term alliances. In contrast, while short-term contractual arrangement and many offshoring arrangements provide companies with coordination flexibility, long-term partnerships may provide an additional benefit—*knowledge access flexibility*.

The increasing reality is that the knowledge that companies rely on for competitive success not only resides in the minds of their employees but also in the minds of contractors, consultants, and other external workers with whom they collaborate. Of course, realizing these benefits requires a concerted effort by organizations for managing the flow of knowledge across these subsystems, both within and outside of the organization.

A key challenge is that employment subsystems directly impact the opportunities and patterns of interactions among internal and external employees as well as the knowledge foundation that each group possesses (cf. Boxall 1996, 1998). By influencing how different employment groups interact, the structure of the HR architecture influences the nature of the network structure. Some HR architectures, with a greater reliance on internal employment and possibly long-term partnerships, may be characterized by dense network connections. In contrast, HR architectures with a greater use of external employee groups and more fluid alliance partnerships may be characterized by sparse networks with relative weak ties. An important research question is if, and how, the overarching structure of employment subsystems impacts the flow of knowledge within the HR architecture. Are there certain structural patterns that are more appropriate for exploration of new sources of value creation versus exploitation of current knowledge bases to leverage and extend existing sources of value creation? Are there other architectural structures that are ideal for less innovative outcomes such as organizational efficiency or customer service? If different structural patterns of employment subsystems offer different organizational benefits, research is needed to examine which architectural patterns are ideal to achieve these disparate objectives.

Relatedly, research is needed that examines the importance of the direction of knowledge flows. For example, is it more important to have knowledge flow equally in all directions or flow toward critical or core employees? It is conceivable that companies may be able to realize knowledge advantages to the extent to which they are able to increase the flow of knowledge from external employment arrangements across their organizational boundaries while decreasing the flow of knowledge in the other direction (cf. Matusik and Hill 1998). Focusing on the direction and flow of knowledge also raises the issue of willingness to share knowledge (Lepak and Snell 2003). Companies are only able to realize benefits of knowledge flow to the extent that employees are willing to cooperate (Coff 1997). If certain employees perceive a personal benefit in hoarding their knowledge, or a perceived risk of sharing what they know, what HR practices are able to encourage employees to share their knowledge with the appropriate people?

An additional important research question focuses on relationships between HR systems for employees within each employment system and the higher-level relational archetypes that are expected to facilitate knowledge exchange across employment subsystems. While implementing HR practices across employee groups to facilitate greater knowledge flow is viable, does it diminish the uniqueness, and perhaps the effectiveness, of the HR systems used for managing the knowledge stocks within each employment mode? Do some of the relational archetype HR practices send conflicting messages to employees on their role within the company? Also, what are the relative costs, benefits, and challenges for implementing multiple HR practices within a company? Research that investigates the impact of implementing higher-level relational archetypes on the effectiveness of HR systems for employment subsystems would provide insights into the viability and effectiveness of the potential value of relational archetypes for facilitating knowledge flow across employee groups.

# 11.6 CONCLUSION

As the outset of this chapter we raised an apparent tension within organizations. On the one hand, researchers and practitioners continue to claim that employees are a key source of a company's competitive advantage. At the same time, however, many firms are increasing their use of both internal and external employment subsystems among their workforce. The key question is: if people matter so much for competitive success, how can companies continue to turn to contingent labor, outsourcing arrangements, as well as selectively invest in subgroups of employees. Our view on this tension is that it is a natural outgrowth of some significant changes that companies are dealing with that stem from an increasing need to distinguish managing jobs and managing knowledge. Adopting an architectural perspective recognizes that companies must do both. Some employees add value by efficiently performing well-defined tasks while others add value for their unique role or critical contributions toward competitive advantage.

While the ultimate decision as to whether or not companies pursue one or more of these employment subsystems is influenced by numerous factors, we focused on several factors that are likely to be particularly important. First, while globalization certainly increases the options that companies have at their disposal for employing their workforce to pursue lower costs, increased expertise, and workforce flexibility, countries vary significantly in the quality of their human capital, the relative supply and demand of different occupational skill sets, labor costs, as well as legal and logistical considerations that influence the potential benefits of relying on alternative employment options. Second, we considered the notion that companies differentiate their employees, not based on job titles, but on the value added of their knowledge and skill sets for internal business processes necessary to realize a competitive advantage. By focusing on knowledge and skill sets rather than jobs, firms may be in a position to focus their investments on those employees that are most critical to their competitive success while leveraging the capabilities of external providers, domestically or internationally, for other tasks or services wherever they may be located around the globe. Of course, a central challenge that companies face is to have a clear sense of what knowledge employees presently hold and need in order to achieve business goals as well as the need to understand how to promote the exchange of knowledge, innovation, and learning to maintain competitive distinction; a task that is increasingly difficult with a globalized sourcing strategy and further differentiated workforce.

Clearly, there are many research questions that remain to be addressed regarding the implications for the use of various forms of employment by organizations. Boxall and Purcell (2003) suggested that firms' choices among employment options are not based solely on economic rationality. Echoing this sentiment, we encourage research that explores factors such as the role of the legal, social, and institutional environments in employment decisions. Relatedly, we still do not have a firm grasp on the performance implications of differentiating employment systems. In particular, research is needed that examines individual reactions to working within a company simultaneously using multiple employment subsystems as well as the role of social and technical interdependencies between employee groups for knowledge flow and competitive success (Purcell et al. 2004).

Moving forward, a key challenge for strategic HRM research is to better understand the nature of knowledge work, the trade-offs among employment options, and how to develop HR systems that are appropriate for managing employees with specific skills sets as well as to identify mechanisms to facilitate knowledge-sharing, transfer, and exchange across employee groups. And while we have probably raised more questions than we have answered, we hope this chapter has provided some ideas to stimulate additional research in this area.

# References

ARON, R., and SINGH, J. V. (2005). 'Getting Offshoring Right.' *Harvard Business Review*, December: 135–43.

ARTHUR, J. B. (1992). 'The Link between Business Strategy and Industrial Relations Systems in American Steel Minimills.' *Industrial and Labor Relations Review*, 45: 488–506.

BARNEY, J. (1991). 'Firm Resources and Sustained Competitive Advantage.' *Journal of Management*, 17: 99–120.

BARON, J. N., and KREPS, D. M. (1999). *Strategic Human Resources: Frameworks for General Managers*. New York: John Wiley.

BECKER, B. E., and GERHART, B. (1996). 'The Impact of Human Resource Management on Organizational Performance: Progress and Prospects.' *Academy of Management Journal*, 39: 779–801.

BOXALL, P. (1996). 'The Strategic HRM Debate and the Resource Based View of the Firm.' *Human Resource Management Journal*, 6: 59–75.

—— (1998). 'Achieving Competitive Advantage through Human Resource Strategy: Towards a Theory of Industry Dynamics.' *Human Resource Management Review*, 8: 265–88.

—— and PURCELL, J. (2003). *Strategy and Human Resource Management*. Basingstoke: Palgrave Macmillan.

BRASS, D. J., GALASKIEWICZ, J., GREVE, H. R., and TSAI, W. (2004). 'Taking Stock of Networks and Organizations: A Multilevel Perspective.' *Academy of Management Journal*, 47: 795–817.

COFF, R. W. (1997). 'Human Assets and Management Dilemmas: Coping with Hazards on the Road to Resource-Based Theory.' *Academy of Management Review*, 22: 374–402.

COLLINS, C. J., and CLARK, K. D. (2003). 'Strategic Human Resources Practices, Top Management Team Social Networks, and Firm Performance: The Role of HR Practices in Creating Organizational Competitive Advantage.' *Academy of Management Journal*, 46: 740–52.

DELERY, J. E., and SHAW, J. D. (2001). 'The Strategic Management of People in Work Organizations: Review, Synthesis, and Extension.' In G. Ferris (ed.), *Research in Personnel and Human Resource Management*. Greenwich, Conn.: JAI Press.

DIERICKX, I., and COOL, K. (1989). 'Asset Stock Accumulation and Sustainability of Competitive Advantage.' *Management Science*, 35: 1504–13.

GONZALEZ, S. M., and TACORANTE, D. V. (2004). 'A New Approach to the Best Practices Debate: Are Best Practices Applied to All Employees in the Same Way?' *International Journal of Human Resource Management*, 15: 56–75.

GRANT, R. M. (1996). 'Toward a Knowledge-Based Theory of the Firm.' *Strategic Management Journal*, 17 (Winter Special Issue): 109–22.

GUTHRIE, J. (2001). 'High Involvement Work Practices, Turnover, and Productivity: Evidence from New Zealand.' *Academy of Management Journal*, 44: 180–92.

HUSELID, M. A. (1995). 'The Impact of Human Resource Management Practices on Turnover, Productivity, and Corporate Financial Performance.' *Academy of Management Journal*, 38: 635–72.

HUSELID, M. A., BECKER, B. E., and BEATTY, D. (2005). *The Workforce Scorecard: Managing and Measuring Human Capital to Drive Strategy Execution*. Boston: Harvard Business School Press.

JACKSON, S., SCHULER, R., and RIVERO, J. (1989). 'Organizational Characteristics as Predictors of Personnel Practices.' *Personnel Psychology*, 42: 727–86.

—— HITT, M. A., and DeNISI, A. S. (2003). *Managing Knowledge for Sustained Competitive Advantage: Designing Strategies for Effective Human Resource Management*. San Francisco: Jossey-Bass.

KANG, S. C., MORRIS, S., and SNELL, S. A. (in press). 'Relational Archetypes, Organizational Learning, and Value Creation: Extending the Human Resource Architecture.' *Academy of Management Review*.

KOGUT, B., and ZANDER, U. (1992). 'Knowledge of the Firm, Combinative Capabilities, and the Replication of Technology.' *Organization Science*, 3: 383–97.

LEONARD-BARTON, D. (1995). *Wellsprings of Knowledge: Building and Sustaining the Sources of Innovation*. Boston: Harvard Business School Press.

LEPAK, D. P., and SNELL, S. A. (1999). 'The Human Resource Architecture: Toward a Theory of Human Capital Allocation and Development.' *Academy of Management Review*, 24: 31–48.

—— —— (2002). 'Examining the Human Resource Architecture: The Relationships among Human Capital, Employment, and Human Resource Configurations.' *Journal of Management*, 28: 517–43.

—— —— (2003). 'Managing the Human Resource Architecture for Knowledge-Based Competition.' In S. Jackson, M. Hitt, and A. DeNisi (eds.), *Managing Knowledge for Sustained Competitive Advantage: Designing Strategies for Effective Human Resource Management*. Frontiers in Industrial Organizational Psychology. Greenwich, Conn.: JAI Series.

—— TAKEUCHI, R., and SNELL, S. A. (2003). 'Employment Flexibility and Firm Performance: Examining the Interaction Effects of Employment Mode, Environmental Dynamism, and Technological Intensity.' *Journal of Management*, 29: 681–703.

MATUSIK, S. F., and HILL, C. W. L. (1998). 'The Utilization of Contingent Work, Knowledge Creation, and Competitive Advantage.' *Academy of Management Review*, 23: 680–97.

MILES, R. E., and SNOW, C. C. (1984). 'Designing Strategic Human Resources Systems.' *Organizational Dynamics*, Summer: 36–52.

MORRIS, S., SNELL, S. A., and LEPAK, D. P. (in press). 'An Architectural Approach to Managing Knowledge Stocks and Flows: Implications for Reinventing the HR Function.' To appear in R. Burke and C. Cooper (eds.), *Reinventing HR*. London: Routledge Press.

NAHAPIET, J., and GHOSHAL, S. (1998). 'Social Capital, Intellectual Capital, and the Organizational Advantage.' *Academy of Management Review*, 23: 242–66.

NONAKA, I. (1994). 'A Dynamic Theory of Organizational Knowledge Creation.' *Organization Science*, 5: 14–37.

OSTERMAN, P. (1987). 'Choice of Employment Systems in Internal Labor Markets.' *Industrial Relations*, 26: 46–67.

PFEFFER, J. (1994). *Competitive Advantage through People*. Boston: Harvard Business School Press.

PORTER, M. (1985). *Competitive Advantage: Creating and Sustaining Superior Performance*. New York: Free Press.

PURCELL, J. (1999). 'High Commitment Management and the Link with Contingent Workers: Implications for Strategic Human Resource Management.' In P. M. Wright, L. D. Dyer, J. W. Boudreau, and G. T. Milkovich (eds.), *Research in Personnel and Human Resource Management*. Greenwich, Conn.: JAI Press.

—— PURCELL, K., and TAILBY, S. (2004). 'Temporary Work Agencies: Here Today, Gone Tomorrow?' *British Journal of Industrial Relations*, 42/4: 705–25.

REICH, R. B. (2005). 'Plenty of Knowledge Work to Go Around.' *Harvard Business Review*, April: 17.

ROUSSEAU, D. M. (1995). *Psychological Contracts in Organizations: Understanding Written and Unwritten Agreements*. Thousand Oaks, Calif.: Sage.

RUBERY, J., CARROLL, M., COOKE, F. L., GRUGULIS, I., and EARNSHAW, J. (2004). 'Human Resource Management and the Permeable Organization: The Case of the Multi-Client Call Centre.' *Journal of Management Studies*, 41: 1199–222.

SCHULER, R. (1992). 'Linking the People with the Strategic Needs of the Business.' *Organisational Dynamics*, Summer: 18–32.

—— and JACKSON, S. E. (1987). 'Linking Competitive Strategies with Human Resource Management Practices.' *Academy of Management Executive*, 1: 207–19.

SNELL, S. A. (1992). 'Control Theory in Strategic Human Resource Management: The Mediating Effects of Administrative Information.' *Journal of Management*, 35: 292–328.

—— and DEAN, J., Jr. (1992). 'Integrated Manufacturing and Human Resource Management: A Human Capital Perspective.' *Academy of Management Journal*, 35: 467–504.

—— and YOUNDT, M. A. (1995). 'Human Resource Management and Firm Performance: Testing a Contingency Model of Executive Controls.' *Journal of Management*, 21: 711–37.

—— LEPAK, D. P., and YOUNDT, M. A. (1999). 'Managing the Architecture of Intellectual Capital: Implications for Strategic Human Resource Management.' In P. M. Wright, L. D. Dyer, J. W. Boudreau, and G. T. Milkovich (eds.), *Research in Personnel and Human Resource Management*. Greenwich, Conn.: JAI Press.

SOLOMON, C. M. (2001). 'Managing Virtual Teams.' *Workforce*, 80/June: 60–5.

SUBRAMANIAN, M., and YOUNDT, M. A. (2005). 'The Influence of Intellectual Capital on the Types of Innovative Capabilities.' *Academy of Management Journal*, 48/3: 450–63.

TSUI, A. S., PEARCE, J. L., PORTER, L. W., and HITE, J. P. (1995). 'Choice of Employee–Organization Relationship: Influence of External and Internal Organizational factors.' In G. R. Ferris (ed.), *Research in Personnel and Human Resources Management*. Greenwich, Conn.: JAI Press.

WILLIAMSON, O. E. (1975). *Markets and Hierarchies: Analysis and Antitrust Implications*. New York: Free Press.

WRIGHT, P. M., and McMAHAN, G. C. (1992). 'Theoretical Perspectives for Strategic Human Resource Management.' *Journal of Management*, 18: 295–320.

—— and Snell, S. A. (1998). 'Toward a Unifying Framework for Exploring Fit and Flexibility in Strategic Human Resource Management.' *Academy of Management Review*, 23: 756–72.

YOUNDT, M. A., SUBRAMANIAN, O., and SNELL, S. A. (2004). 'Intellectual Capital Profiles: An Examination of Investments and Returns.' *Journal of Management Studies*, 41: 335–61.

CHAPTER 12

........................................................................................

# EMPLOYEE VOICE SYSTEMS

........................................................................................

## MICK MARCHINGTON

## 12.1 INTRODUCTION

........................................................................................

EMPLOYEE voice appears to be the latest in a long line of terms used to describe employment practices designed to allow workers some 'say' in how their organizations are run; previous variants include worker participation, industrial democracy, employee involvement, and empowerment. The term is rarely defined precisely, and voice tends to incorporate HR practices of both a direct and an indirect form, in unionized and non-union settings, and in task-related and off-line teams (Millward et al. 2000; Bryson 2004). Others have used the term to refer to grievance processes and employee complaints about management (Boroff and Lewin 1997; Luchak 2003), and even so-called 'silent' forms of voice such as sabotage, absence from work, or shirking (Benson 2000; Hyman 2005). This wide range of uses makes it difficult to assess whether 'voice' actually marks a departure from the initiatives that have gone before or whether it is nothing more than 'old wine in new bottles.'

Traditionally, voice has been used primarily in relation to union-based and broader forms of participation, rather than direct employee involvement, because this was seen as the principal way in which workers could gain influence at work (Freeman and Medoff 1984; Millward et al. 2000). More recently, analysis has shifted to examine non-union models of indirect voice, such as through joint consultative committees and works councils (Dundon et al. 2004; Haynes et al. 2005). Given space limitations, rather than provide yet another review of indirect voice, this chapter focuses primarily on direct voice for several reasons. First, union and non-union collective voice has been analyzed at length in many other publications (for example, Osterman et al. 2001; Gospel and Wood 2003), and it was felt impossible to develop this material without a proper analysis of different national legal systems or cultures. Second, the decline in union density in most developed countries has meant that direct forms of voice—both through upward problem-solving and through new forms of work organization—are likely to offer workers greater opportunities for influence than they did in the past. Indeed there is evidence that direct forms of voice are associated, by workers, with more positive perceptions of managerial responsiveness than either union or non-union forms of indirect representation (Bryson 2004). Third, as direct voice mechanisms impact more immediately on workers than indirect representation, they are seen as more relevant to worker needs (Freeman and Rogers 1999; Osterman et al. 2001). Changes at work group level can make a major difference to people's daily lives, and direct, personal involvement can seem more meaningful than higher-level discussions about long-term plans (Purcell and Georgiadis 2006). Of course, it is recognized that direct voice may offer opportunities for change only at the margins of managerial decision-making (Ramsay et al. 2000) because key strategic choices are made way beyond the confines of the participative process (Strauss 1998). Finally, concentrating on direct voice allows a sharper focus on the *processes* accompanying informal participation at the workplace, and it is acknowledged that few surveys have captured workers' views. If we are to understand better how HRM impacts on workers, the so-called 'black box' needs to be opened up in order to discern how workers interpret managerial practices (Wright and Boswell 2002; Benson and Lawler 2003). This is especially important when examining the interaction effects of a number of different voice mechanisms, both direct and indirect, and the extent to which they are embedded within the workplace (Marchington 2005).

The focus on direct voice should not be interpreted as a sign that indirect and union voice is unimportant for the achievement of worker influence in organizations; far from it. Evidence from Purcell and Georgiadis (2006) indicates that combinations of direct and indirect voice have the strongest relationship with worker commitment, satisfaction, and discretion. In a later section of this chapter we return to the question of how indirect voice systems can shape the development of direct voice, particularly in societies where strong institutional pressures or influential trade unions create frameworks at national and organizational levels within which voice can flourish.

Three broad versions of direct voice are considered in this chapter. These are *task-based participation*, such as redesigned work operations, teamworking, and self-managed teams; *upward problem-solving* techniques such as off-line teams, quality circles, suggestion schemes, and worker input into briefing groups; and *complaints about fair treatment*, such as grievance procedures, speak-up programs, and whistle-blowing. The first two of these typically appear within discussions of HRM as they are explicitly aimed at 'adding value' within the context of organizational goals. They are designed to give workers a chance to contribute to managerial decision-making, either in their day-to-day work or through formal and managerially instigated processes that tap into employees' skills and ideas. However, this overlooks the role that voice plays in articulating employee concerns about management style and practice beyond the relatively limited confines of how their own work is organized. Whilst it may not be immediately apparent how this contributes to organizational goals, voice can be seen as an alternative to exit and thus, amongst other things, to reduced levels of labor turnover (Hirschmann 1970). It may also help to weed out supervisors who treat workers badly or are poor at communications, and so help to improve productivity through the provision of a fairer deal at work.

This chapter does not presuppose the dominance of any single style of people management—such as high commitment—nor does it assume that voice is likely to operate in precisely the same way in different countries or sectors. The interplay of forces between nation states, large multinational corporations, and product and labor markets means that forms of voice vary depending on institutional, organizational, and workplace contexts (Katz and Darbyshire 2000; Rubery and Grimshaw 2003). Even forms of voice sharing the same title may differ because of the rationale for their introduction, how they have been implemented, and the influence of broader social systems. Workers' expectations from voice also differ depending on the legal and vocational education systems, the state of the product and labor markets, and the type of work on which they are employed (Marchington et al. 1994; Kessler et al. 2004). Voice is probably the area of HRM where tensions between organizational and worker goals, and between shareholder and stakeholder views, are most apparent because it connects with the question of managerial prerogative and social legitimacy. This becomes even more complex when voice operates across organizational boundaries as workers effectively operate under the direction of two or more sets of employers within a culture of contracting relations (Marchington et al. 2004).

The remainder of the chapter is structured as follows. First we develop a framework within which different forms of voice can be considered. Second, we discuss links between embedded voice and worker perceptions, focusing on the use of multiple and 'deep' techniques. Third, we analyze a number of factors promoting or impeding voice at national, organizational, and workplace levels, in so doing noting the tensions surrounding the concept. Finally, some conclusions are drawn.

## 12.2 A FRAMEWORK FOR ANALYZING DIRECT VOICE SYSTEMS

Having outlined the contrasting ways in which worker voice has been used in previous literature, in this section we construct a threefold framework for analyzing direct voice which draws upon earlier work by the author and colleagues. The three elements are task-based participation, upward problem-solving, and complaints about fair treatment; the framework is presented in Table 12.1.

Interest in *task-based participation* has grown enormously over the last decade, along with the emergence of the high-commitment model and high-performance work systems (HPWS). Voice through mechanisms such as team working, self-managed teams, and autonomous work groups is now seen as a major component of the HPWS model, largely because these forms of work organization provide workers with an opportunity to use their discretion at work rather than be subject to close supervision by managers (Appelbaum et al. 2000). Task-based participation has a long history, especially under the guise of Quality of Work Life Programs in the USA and Sweden in the 1960s and 1970s (Heller et al. 1998).

Employee voice through task-based participation is where workers have a direct say in how work is organized. As such it is integral to the job, forming a part of everyday working life, rather than being bolted on in the shape of off-line teams or only experienced through union representatives or managers who choose to involve workers. It can occur both horizontally and vertically. The former refers to the number and variety of tasks which workers perform at the same skill level in an organization. Provided workers are given greater opportunities to exercise discretion at work and gain some control over their working lives, this enhances voice. In some cases task-based participation may offer little more than a way in which to alleviate the boredom associated with repetitive routines, and at least offer the opportunity to do something different, if only for a short period of time. In terms of voice, however, the improvements may be minimal. Vertical task-based participation comprises two different forms. Employees may be trained to undertake tasks at a higher skill level or they may be given some managerial and supervisory responsibilities, such as taking over the planning and design of work as well as its execution. Teamworking combines both horizontal and vertical task-based participation, and may even offer workers the chance to manage their own teams (Benders 2005). Again, these forms of work redesign can give workers greater influence and control over their daily working lives, and in the case of self-managed teams the opportunity to organize their own activities in line with broader departmental targets.

Managers are interested in this form of voice to improve levels of quality, productivity, and customer service through the more effective deployment of front-line workers. Under the high-commitment model, managements hope

**Table 12.1 Framework for analyzing direct voice**

| Worker goals | Type of voice system | Typical voice mechanisms | Managerial goals | Tensions inherent in the system | Links with other components of HRM |
|---|---|---|---|---|---|
| More interesting work | Task-based participation | High-performance work systems | Improvements in quality and customer service | Contested notions of autonomy and responsibility | Job design and organizational structures |
| Greater control and discretion over job performance | | Self-managed teams Autonomous work groups | Enhanced worker commitment and satisfaction | Self-control and increased managerial surveillance | Pay and rewards Training and skill upgrading |
| Opportunity to contribute ideas to improve work | Upward problem-solving | Off-line teams  Quality circles | Improvements in quality and customer service | Employment security and lean production | Communication, consultation and representation |
| Recognition of worker skills | | Suggestions schemes  Two-way briefings | Appropriation of worker skills and expertise | Distribution of rewards from increased productivity | Rewards and recognition  Training and career development |
| Chance to express dissatisfaction about issues | Complaints to management | Grievance procedures Direct complaint to supervisor | Allowing workers to let off steam Desire to remove problems | Managerial prerogatives and employee rights Fairness at work | Disputes procedures and industrial relations Equal opportunities |
| Desire to rectify problems | | | | | Recruitment and retention |

that these forms of work organization will add value over and above more traditional methods where workers merely responded to management instructions (Appelbaum et al. 2000). Whilst there is substantial evidence that task-based participation provides organizational benefits, there are also claims that even if workers feel they are working harder under a teamworking regime they are also more satisfied with their jobs (Wilkinson et al. 1997; Osterman 2000). Although much depends on the organizational and managerial context, teamwork does have the potential to deliver autonomy and responsibility, satisfaction and control. It can also provide more interesting work if managements are serious about making jobs larger and more meaningful. However, some tasks offer little opportunity for job enlargement because strict safety rules have to be followed or there are difficulties in finding ways of redesigning jobs without major technical change.

Although some commentators would regard task-based participation, and especially teamworking, as the ultimate in direct voice, others see it merely as increasing pressure on workers to perform. For example, Barker (1993: 408) suggests that self-managing teams produce 'a form of control more powerful, less apparent and more difficult to resist than that of the former bureaucracy.' Under a teamworking regime, pressure for performance comes from peers rather than from managers, and whilst some would see this as liberating and genuinely positive, others view it as management control at its most subversive and unethical as team members take over responsibility for peer surveillance (Sewell 2005).

*Upward Problem-Solving* incorporates a range of voice mechanisms which tap into employee knowledge and ideas, typically through individual suggestions or through ad hoc or semi-permanent groups brought together for the specific purpose of resolving problems or generating ideas. These off-line schemes tend to be 'bolted on' rather than integral to the work process (Batt 2004) but they have become much more extensive over the last decade in most developed economies (Benson and Lawler 2003; Kessler et al. 2004). They are central to notions of high-commitment HRM because upward problem-solving is predicated on assumptions that employees are a major source of competitive advantage. Not only are these practices designed to increase the stock of ideas, they are also expected to increase cooperation at work and evidence suggests that workers like being involved (Freeman and Rogers 1999). Despite offering a greater degree of active voice than communications cascaded down the management hierarchy, critics view these practices as problematic precisely because they encourage employees to collaborate with management in helping resolve work-related problems.

There are two types of upward problem-solving scheme. First, there are suggestion schemes whereby employees receive financial rewards for suggestions that are outside the domain of their own specific job. These schemes have the potential to create bad feelings as well as good, especially if the workers making suggestions feel that their idea merits higher rewards. There is a danger, moreover, that paying for suggestions encourages an instrumental approach to work (Marchington and Wilkinson 2005).

Problem-solving groups/quality circles and two-way briefings constitute the second and much more extensive type of upward communications. Typically the former comprise small groups of workers who meet on a regular basis to identify, analyze, and solve quality and work-related problems. Members may be drawn either from the same team or from a range of different work areas, meeting under the guidance of a leader, sometimes with assistance from one or more facilitators. Upward problem-solving groups are designed to achieve explicit production, quality, or service goals through the appropriation of workers' ideas but they can also enhance employee morale and commitment if it is felt their views have been taken seriously. However, there are problems in sustaining problem-solving groups beyond the initial phase of active involvement as groups question whether or not gains will be maintained (Handel and Levine 2004). Briefing groups which are designed to encourage feedback from workers can also fall within this category; evidence from the UK indicates this is now a regular feature of schemes initially designed to foster downward communications.

Workers and trade unions have questioned managements' motives for introducing upward problem-solving groups, fearing that they will be used merely to achieve improvements in productivity that will result in job losses (Osterman 2000). Even if employers agree not to cut jobs, workers are criticized for acting as management stooges, helping organizations to improve performance without any commensurate increase in rewards. Tensions are particularly inherent with this form of direct worker voice because upward problem-solving operates at the interface between management and non-managerial workers, and some would advise workers not to take part in such groups, arguing that employers should be forced to pay for any ideas offered by workers that are beyond their 'normal' job. Similarly, employers that are subject to extensive product market pressures might disapprove of any activity allowing workers productive time away from their work station due to cost implications (Cappelli and Neumark 2001).

The final category of direct voice is where workers *complain*, either directly or through formal grievance procedures, to management about its behavior and performance at work. This category is quite different from those that have just been discussed, but it is also the one that is most commonly associated with the term 'voice' itself, largely through the work of Hirschmann (1970). He defined voice as 'any attempt at all to change, rather than escape from, an objectionable state of affairs, whether through individual or collective petition to management' (Hirschmann 1970: 30). It was assumed that workers would only stay to fight for improvements in their working lives (voice) if they were loyal enough to the organization, otherwise they would leave (exit). From management's perspective therefore, voice can be seen as a useful way of letting off steam, a safety valve, as well as a desire to improve the situation. Workers, on the other hand, value the chance to articulate their concerns directly to managers or through union representatives with the hope this will lead to changes in behavior. Freeman and Medoff (1984) in following up this idea argued that the voice option made sense for both parties, rather than allowing things to degenerate to the point where workers decided to leave. They felt unions offered the best opportunity for workers to exercise their voice because of their independence from management.

Some recent literature has examined the voice-loyalty-exit concept in relation to grievance-raising by workers in the USA. Boroff and Lewin (1997) found that, contrary to Hirschmann's thesis, it was the workers who expressed lower levels of loyalty to the organization that were more likely to complain—that is, use voice— whilst loyal workers were more prone to 'suffer in silence.' Workers who complained to management were more likely to suffer adverse consequences subsequent to raising their grievance. Indeed, Lewin and Peterson (1999) found that workers who filed grievances had significantly lower promotion rates, and there was some evidence they had higher rates of labor turnover and lower performance ratings. In societies where grievance-raising does not have legal backing, workers may be anxious that raising grievances will lead to future retribution, but where this is buttressed by legal regulations and societal support voice may offer a more viable option (Malos et al. 2003).

Luchak (2003) suggests we need to differentiate between direct and representative voice. Whilst the latter tends to lead to more hostile reactions from management, the former tends to be seen in a more preventive light. Accordingly, loyal employees with a strong affective bond with the organization are more prone to use direct and more flexible channels to make their complaints, with the consequence that they are willing to 'go the extra distance to ensure that problems are settled before they have a chance to escalate' (Luchak 2003: 128). However, he acknowledges the success of this route depends largely on management's willingness to act on employee suggestions, as well as on the seriousness of the grievance and the extent to which it challenges managerial prerogative. This shows the importance of locating voice within the context of wider HR policies and industrial relations systems because some employers would probably prefer anyone with a grievance to quit the organization rather than stay and be an irritant in the future. Alternatively, employers adopting a pluralist perspective might be inclined to see the potential value of complaints as a source of feedback that complements well-developed representative arrangements.

## 12.3 EMBEDDING VOICE AT WORK

One problem with existing studies of voice is that they focus on the first two elements in this framework, broadly under the heading of employee involvement, but they also tend to draw on management respondents to assess the extensiveness of voice. Accordingly, these measure 'intended' practices (Wright and Boswell 2002) rather than those experienced by workers themselves. These studies lack sensitivity to the complexities of voice, and it is apparent from case studies that managerial claims to have implemented particular practices do not necessarily square with organizational reality (Van den Berg et al. 1999). For example, ideas generated by problem-solving groups may not be implemented or managers may fail to respond to concerns raised by workers, perhaps due to pressure of work, lack of interest, or cost. Data on coverage of voice provided by senior managers probably overestimates the impact on workers because of failures to implement practice effectively at the workplace (Paauwe and Boselie 2005).

Fortunately, some studies have considered the type, quality, and combinations of voice in evaluating its impact, and assess the opportunities workers are given to exercise influence at work. For example, Batt (2004:189) argues that workers find participation in self-managed teams much more significant than involvement in problem-solving groups, commenting that 'off-line' teams 'do not sufficiently influence the organization of work and daily routines of employees to dramatically affect their attitudes and self-interests.' Bryson (2004) analyzed the effects of union, non-union, and individual voice on employee perceptions of managers' responsiveness to them. He found that some forms of voice yield a higher-quality response from managers than others—meetings of the whole workforce being more effective than problem-solving groups, for example. Moreover, the effectiveness of methods depends on whether they are used individually or in combination, and the most effective voice mechanisms are a combination of direct and non-union voice (Bryson 2004). Purcell and Georgiadis (2006: 12) suggest the use of both direct and indirect systems of voice 'has the capacity both to limit the number of issues or problems listed by employees as matters they want resolved, and to deal with them when they arise.'

Much depends on how voice is implemented and sustained. For example, whilst most organizations are likely to have in place a variety of formal and informal mechanisms for dealing with employee grievances, workers' willingness to use these can vary depending on their own manager's style and attitudes. As we have seen, research on grievance-filing in the USA shows workers may be disinclined to use voice if they believe managers will respond negatively to complaints about fair treatment (Luchak 2003). For voice to be effective and meaningful, it needs to operate within a climate that is seen as supportive and 'strong,' utilizing principles of legitimacy, consistency, and fairness (Bowen and Ostroff 2004).

The extent to which voice is embedded within the workplace can be assessed by its breadth and depth. *Breadth* can be measured by the number of voice components operating at the workplace on the principle that several practices operating together provide greater reinforcement than any single practice alone.

# 12.4 FACTORS SHAPING VOICE AT THE WORKPLACE

Much of the literature on voice, particularly on direct employee involvement, assumes it is part of a high-commitment culture. Accordingly, this emphasizes how voice can be developed to ensure it contributes to performance outcomes, either directly or through mediating factors such as satisfaction or commitment. However, we have already noted voice is absent from some workplaces and that not all employers believe it is a key component of HRM. Whilst they might be able to see value investing in sophisticated selection processes or employment law training because this can be seen directly to add value (through better-quality staff) or reduce costs (through avoidance of tribunals), the impact of voice on bottom-line performance is less clear. Similarly, given the wide range of circumstances in which they operate, employers have some degree of choice about whether or not to implement voice systems; indeed, some do all they can to prevent workers from having any independent voice at work.

Responding to the challenge set by Benson and Lawler (2003) that little is known about why organizations adopt voice systems, Table 12.2 sets out the major factors at a societal, organizational, and workplace level that shape voice. The table presents two polar positions, one articulating factors that facilitate and promote voice whilst the other outlines factors that discourage and impede voice. These are labeled 'promoting voice' and 'impeding voice' respectively. These factors are not assumed to be deterministic as, even in a highly regulated system, managers retain some flexibility in how they implement HRM. It is also acknowledged that forces may operate in different directions, with some pointing towards the adoption of voice and others not. Although Table 12.2 inevitably oversimplifies the situation, it does offer points of comparison. Furthermore, it recognizes there are finer shades of gradation between the two extremes, but space does not permit a full discussion of these.

## 12.4.1 Policy Framework and Financial System

Debates continue about whether employment systems in different countries are converging given the degree to which multinational companies operate on a global basis (see, for example, Katz and Darbyshire 2000; Quintanilla and Ferner 2003). However, it is broadly acknowledged that some countries—for example, much of Europe other than the UK and Ireland—tend towards a coordinated market economy that is governed by the principles of stakeholder interests. In this situation, voice is likely to be promoted by the presence of national institutions and

Table 12.2 Factors influencing the adoption of voice systems

| Factor shaping voice | Voice culture | |
|---|---|---|
| | Promoting voice | Impeding voice |
| Policy framework and financial system | Coordinated market economies<br>Legislation supporting worker rights and voice<br>Stakeholder perspective predominant | Liberal market economies<br>Voluntarist approach to worker rights and voice<br>Shareholder perspective predominant |
| Product markets | Oligopolistic and stable product markets<br>Long-term partnerships between organizations<br>Employer dominates markets | Highly competitive and unstable product markets<br>Market driven by a contracting culture/spot markets<br>Employer marginal within markets |
| Technology, skill, and staffing levels | Capital-intensive systems<br>High staff to customer ratios | Labour-intensive systems<br>Low staff to customer ratios |
| Labor markets and industrial relations | High skill levels/workers hard to replace<br>Strong cooperative management–union relations | Low skill levels/workers easy to replace<br>Hostile management–union relations or non-union organization |
| Supervisory skills and management style | Employer support for high-commitment HRM<br>Supervisors trained in people management skills | Employer not interested in high-commitment HRM<br>Supervisors not trained in people management skills |
| Worker interests | High levels of commitment from workers<br>Anticipation of long-term career in organization | High levels of apathy from workers<br>Fragmented work, little expectation of long-term career in organization |

employment laws that support worker voice in the context of stakeholder needs. This appears to impact on the take-up of voice systems (Kessler et al. 2004; Paauwe 2004). At the other extreme are countries tending towards a liberal market economy where there is less legislation on workers' rights and employers have greater freedom to choose HR systems they feel are appropriate for business needs. In this latter situation, given little societal or legal pressure to implement particular forms of voice there might be a broader range of voice systems, but in the absence of direct intervention it is unlikely to be promoted, and may even be impeded. Of course, the situation is complicated by the interrelationship between multinationals, national business systems, and models of indirect voice (Rubery and Grimshaw 2003).

## 12.4.2 Product Markets

A number of authors have analyzed how product markets might impact on HRM by relating the market orientation or the strategic position of the organization to its management style (for example, Schuler and Jackson 1987; Marchington 1990). Broadly, voice is more likely to be promoted when employers dominate product markets because they feel there is room for maneuver when developing HRM and voice systems. Being engaged in long-term deals with other organizations for the supply of a relatively rare product or being known for the high quality of their products or service makes it easier to establish the link between voice and product market success. Task-based participation, teamworking, and upward problem-solving can all be seen to contribute directly to improved performance. The links are less clear for grievance processes, but line managers would probably prefer staff to express their concerns directly rather than venting their frustration on customers. Conversely, voice is likely to be impeded if market pressures appear to allow managers little time to make decisions, so causing them to doubt the value of voice. Instability in product markets can mean that employers such as small subcontractors feel at the mercy of the market and argue there is no time or need to develop voice (Marchington et al. 2004).

## 12.4.3 Technology, Skill, and Staffing Levels

Similar sets of arguments apply in relation to levels of technology and skills (Benson and Lawler 2003), especially where labor costs form a major component of controllable costs. This can mean organizations operate with skeleton staffing levels, allowing little opportunity for voice during working hours because of service or production pressures. Moreover, employers may feel little incentive to develop voice if labor turnover is high because any benefits gained by giving employees greater discretion or engaging in upward problem-solving are lost when they quit.

Whilst the above factors hinder voice, it is likely to be promoted when labor costs form a small part of overall costs, workers routinely operate in teams, and direct worker voice is a critical part of the employment relationship. In this situation, employers are more likely to derive benefits from voice through greater levels of worker commitment, whilst employees may gain from the opportunity to use their discretion (Appelbaum et al. 2000). However, as Korczynski (2002) notes, voice in the service sector often occurs when front-line staff are encouraged to speak-up merely in order to convey the views of customers rather than their own concerns.

## 12.4.4 Labor Markets and Industrial Relations

Voice is likely to be promoted when workers have high levels of technical or other skills because employers want to reduce 'exit' due to the time it takes to train new staff. With knowledge workers in particular, the opportunity to exercise discretion is thought to be a key factor impacting on satisfaction and retention levels (Allen et al. 2003; Kinnie et al. 2005). Moreover, the prompt settlement of grievances might reduce labor turnover and help to retain staff when skills are in short supply (Osterman et al. 2001). By contrast, given the ease with which low-skilled workers can generally be replaced, employers have less incentive to encourage voice, either to reduce the likelihood of exit or to improve product quality.

Voice can also be shaped by employer policies towards industrial relations and trade unions (Purcell and Ahlstrand 1994). In a non-union environment, for example, there is little pressure on employers to ensure the adoption of effective voice systems unless management feels it is worthwhile for other reasons. Similarly, if trade unions are hostile to direct voice, viewing it as a device to undermine collective organization, it is likely to be impeded. On the other hand, organizations with partnership deals are more likely to work together to promote direct voice as part of a drive to increase mutuality and the promotion of trust within organizations (Kochan and Osterman 1994; Guest and Peccei 2001). Furthermore, several authors find representative and direct forms of voice interact positively with one another, and that voice is more effective if it is developed across dual channels (Sako 1998; Delbridge and Whitfield 2001; Purcell and Georgiadis 2006).

## 12.4.5 Management Style and Supervisory Skills

The extent to which line managers are able and willing to use people management skills is critical in making voice meaningful at workplace level (Marchington and Wilkinson 2005). However, their ability in this area depends crucially on the approach taken by employers and their preparedness to recruit, develop, and promote supervisors with the confidence to encourage voice. Employers need to recognize that voice can be seen as challenging to supervisors; for example, the creation of autonomous teams can dispense with supervisors altogether (Batt 2004) and grievances may threaten their authority (Marchington and Wilkinson 2005). Supervisors are more likely to be positive if they are trained and developed in HR skills rather than being blamed for failing to develop voice (Fenton-O'Creevy 2001). As we saw in the previous section, the more that voice fits with the rest of the HR system the more likely it is to make a meaningful impact on organizations.

### 12.4.6 Worker Interests

Voice is critically dependent on workers being willing to contribute through upward problem-solving and active membership of a team as well as choosing to raise grievances through procedures rather than working without enthusiasm or quitting the organization (Noon and Blyton 1997). The high-commitment model assumes workers want to contribute to organizational success, and whilst there are examples when this does happen it cannot be taken for granted. Workers are more inclined to use their voice if they believe something will change as a result of their involvement or they will remain with the organization long enough to reap the benefits of their efforts. Consequently, voice is more likely to flourish if workers are committed to organizational goals (Allen et al. 2003). Conversely, voice is unlikely to develop if workers see little point in putting forward ideas or raising issues with their manager because they feel nothing will be happen or, worse still, they will be bullied or harassed for articulating their views (Ramsay et al. 2000). When workers are employed on short-term or insecure contracts, say through agencies or sub-contracting arrangements, there may be little incentive to make their voice heard (Marchington et al. 2004). Godard's (2004) distinction between 'involving' and 'intensifying' cultures is critically important here. This argues that even with high-commitment HR practices in place, there are differences in how these are applied by employers and how they are perceived by workers. Employers that appear to take voice seriously and ensure managers are trained in how it should operate are likely to be very different from those where it is applied partially or uses the labels as a device to intensify work. Worker interest in voice will soon disappear if benefits are not shared (Osterman 2000).

## 12.5 SUMMARY AND CONCLUSIONS

The main points made in this chapter can be summarized briefly. There are two points relating to methodology. First, whilst there are powerful arguments that voice can contribute to the achievement of improved performance, there is also the alternative perspective that organizations with high levels of performance, or those operating in favorable product market circumstances (reverse causality), are more able to afford the costs of implementing voice (Boxall and Purcell 2003; Schneider et al. 2003). Second, as voice has a processual as well as a substantive component, we need to focus on interactions between line managers and staff at workplace level rather than on grand HR strategies or 'counts' of how many HR practices are supposedly in place. If we wish to understand why workers might work harder or smarter, it is valuable to know how voice impacts on them directly.

In relation to perspective and philosophy there are also two points. Voice is an essential component of HRM for those who believe it should serve more than employer goals alone. This is not just in terms of engaging employees' contributions and reaping the benefits of constructive conflict—managerial goals—but also it acknowledges mutuality in the employment relationship. Second, whilst voice may be important to satisfy management goals, it also includes opportunities to ensure fair treatment at work, either through direct or indirect union voice. Unless employers accept this form of voice, it is hard to see why workers should bother contributing their ideas to enhance organizational goals. Analysis should therefore include the idea that voice relates to a range of stakeholder interests (Paauwe 2004).

Finally, in relation to context there are two points. First, voice is not something that can be prescribed in detail for every workplace irrespective of country, sector, or organization. Further research needs to consider the forms voice might take in quite contrasting circumstances, and the influence that a range of shaping factors may have over its structures and processes. Second, however, we cannot ignore the possibility that some employers may want HR systems without any room for voice. Such an approach might appeal to employers that care only about exploiting workers or believe high shareholder returns in the short term are more important than sustained product quality or a reputation for good customer service. However, even if there might be a business case for rejecting voice, its absence raises major questions about how organizations operate in so-called democratic societies. In this situation, as Godard (2004: 370) argues, if employers are not prepared to change their behavior voluntarily, legislation might be the only way to achieve progressive employment policies, meaningful representation, and voice.

# REFERENCES

ALLEN, D. G., SHORE, L. M., and GRIFFEN, R. W. (2003). 'The Role of Perceived Organizational Support and Supportive Human Resource Practices in the Turnover Process.' *Journal of Management*, 29/1: 99–118.

APPELBAUM, E., BAILEY, T., BERG, P., and KALLEBERG, A. (2000). *Manufacturing Advantage: Why High Performance Work Systems Pay off.* Ithaca, NY: Cornell University Press.

BARKER, J. (1993). 'Tightening the Iron Cage: Coercive Control in Self-Managing Teams.' *Administrative Science Quarterly*, 38/3: 408–37.

BATT, R. (2004). 'Who Benefits from Teams: Comparing Workers, Supervisors, Managers.' *Industrial Relations*, 43/1: 183–212.

BENDERS, J. (2005). 'Team Working: A Tale of Partial Participation.' In B. Harley, J. Hyman, and P. Thompson (eds.), *Participation and Democracy at Work: Essays in Memory of Harvie Ramsay.* Basingstoke: Palgrave.

BENSON, G., and LAWLER, E. (2003). 'Employee Involvement: Utilization, Impacts and Future Prospects.' In D. Holman, T. Wall, C. Clegg, P. Sparrow, and A. Howard (eds.), *The New Workplace: A Guide to the Human Impact of Modern Working Practices.* Chichester: Wiley.

BENSON, J. (2000). 'Employee Voice in Union and Non-union Australian Workplaces.' *British Journal of Industrial Relations*, 38/3: 453–59.

BOROFF, K. E., and LEWIN, D. (1997). 'Loyalty, Voice and Intent to Exit a Union Firm: A Conceptual and Empirical Analysis.' *Industrial and Labor Relations Review*, 51/1: 50–63.

BOWEN, D. E., and OSTROFF, C. (2004). 'Understanding HRM–Firm Performance Linkages: The Role of the "Strength" of the HRM System.' *Academy of Management Review*, 29/2: 203–21.

BOXALL, P., and PURCELL, J. (2003). *Strategy and Human Resource Management.* Basingstoke: Palgrave Macmillan.

BRYSON, A. (2004). 'Managerial Responsiveness to Union and Nonunion Worker Voice in Britain.' *Industrial Relations*, 43/1: 213–41.

CAPPELLI, P., and NEUMARK, D. (2001). 'Do "High-Performance" Work Practices Improve Establishment-Level Outcomes?' *Industrial and Labor Relations Review*, 54/4: 737–75.

COX, A., ZAGELMEYER, S., and MARCHINGTON, M. (2003). 'The Embeddedness of Employee Involvement and Participation and its Impact on Employee Outcomes: An Analysis of WERS 1998.' Paper presented to the EGOS conference, Copenhagen.

DELBRIDGE, R., and WHITFIELD, K. (2001). 'Employee Perceptions of Job Influence and Organizational Participation.' *Industrial Relations*, 40/3: 472–89.

DUNDON, T., WILKINSON, A., MARCHINGTON, M., and ACKERS, P. (2004). 'The Meanings and Purpose of Employee Voice.' *International Journal of Human Resource Management*, 15/6: 1149–70.

FENTON-O'CREEVY, M. (2001). 'Employee Involvement and the Middle Manager: Saboteur or Scapegoat?' *Human Resource Management Journal*, 11/1: 24–40.

FREEMAN, R., and MEDOFF, J. (1984). *What Do Unions Do?* New York: Basic Books.

—— and Rogers, J. (1999). *What Workers Want.* Ithaca, NY: Cornell University Press.

GILL, C., and KRIEGER, H. (1999). 'Direct and Representative Participation in Europe: Recent Survey Evidence.' *International Journal of Human Resource Management*, 10/1: 572–91.

GODARD, J. (2004). 'A Critical Assessment of the High Performance Paradigm.' *British Journal of Industrial Relations*, 42/2: 349–78.

GOSPEL, H., and WOOD, S. (eds.) (2003). *Representing Workers: Union Recognition and Membership in Britain.* London: Routledge.

GUEST, D., and PECCEI, R. (2001). 'Partnership at Work: Mutuality and the Balance of Advantage.' *British Journal of Industrial Relations*, 39/1: 207–36.

HANDEL, M., and LEVINE, D. (2004). 'The Effects of New Work Practices on Workers.' *Industrial Relations*, 43/1: 1–43.

HAYNES, P., BOXALL, P., and MACKY, K. (2005). 'Non-union Voice and the Effectiveness of Joint Consultation in New Zealand.' *Economic and Industrial Democracy*, 26/2: 225–52.

HELLER, F., PUSIĆ, E., STRAUSS, G., and WILPERT, B. (1998). *Organizational Participation: Myth and Reality*. Oxford: Oxford University Press.

HIRSCHMANN, A. O. (1970). *Exit, Voice and Loyalty: Responses to Decline in Firms, Organizations, and States*. Cambridge, Mass.: Harvard University Press.

HYMAN, R. (2005). 'Whose (Social) Partnership?' In M. Stuart and M. Martinez-Lucio (eds.), *Partnership and Modernisation in Employment Relations*. London: Routledge.

KATZ, H. C., and DARBISHIRE, O. (2000). *Converging Divergences: Worldwide Change in Employment System*. Ithaca, NY: Cornell University Press.

KAUFMAN, B. E. (2003). 'High-Level Employee Involvement at Delta Air Lines.' *Human Resource Management*, 42/2: 175–90.

KESSLER, I., UNDY, R., and HERON, P. (2004). 'Employee Perspectives on Communication and Consultation: Findings from a Cross-National Survey.' *International Journal of Human Resource Management*, 15/3: 512–32.

KINNIE, N., HUTCHINSON, S., PURCELL, J., RAYTON, B., and SWART, J. (2005). 'One Size Does Not Fit All: Employee Satisfaction with HR Practices and the Link with Organizational Commitment.' *Human Resource Management Journal*, 15/4: 9–29.

KOCHAN, T., and OSTERMAN, P. (1994). *The Mutual Gains Enterprise*. Boston: Harvard Business School Press.

KORCZYNSKI, M. (2002). *Human Resource Management in Service Work*. Basingstoke: Palgrave Macmillan.

LEWIN, D., and PETERSON, R. (1999). 'Behavioural Outcomes of Grievance Activity.' *Industrial Relations*, 38/4: 554–76.

LIDEN, R., BAUER, T., and ERDOGAN, B. (2004). 'The Role of Leader–Member Exchange in the Dynamic Relationship between Employer and Employee: Implications for Employee Socialisation, Leaders and Organizations.' In J. Coyle-Shapiro, L. Shore, S. Taylor, and L. Tetrick (eds.), *The Employment Relationship: Examining Psychological and Contextual Perspectives*. Oxford: Oxford University Press.

LUCHAK, A. (2003). 'What Kind of Voice do Loyal Employees Use?' *British Journal of Industrial Relations*, 41/1: 115–35.

MALOS, S., HAYNES, P., and BOWAL, P. (2003). 'A Contingency Approach to the Employment Relationship: Form, Function and Effectiveness Implications.' *Employee Responsibilities and Rights Journal*, 15/3: 149–67.

MARCHINGTON, M. (1990). 'Analysing the Links between Product Markets and the Management of Employee Relations.' *Journal of Management Studies*, 27/2: 111–32.

—— (2005). 'Employee Involvement: Patterns and Explanations.' In B. Harley, J. Hyman, and P. THOMPSON (eds.), *Participation and Democracy at Work: Essays in Memory of Harvie Ramsay*. Basingstoke: Palgrave.

—— and WILKINSON, A. (2005). 'Direct Participation and Involvement.' In S. Bach (ed.), *Managing Human Resources: Personnel Management in Transition*, 4th edn. Oxford: Blackwell.

—— —— ACKERS, P., and GOODMAN, J. (1994). 'Understanding the Meaning of Participation: Views from the Workplace.' *Human Relations*, 47/8: 867–94.

—— —— —— and DUNDON, T. (2001). *Management Choice and Employee Voice*. London: Chartered Institute of Personnel and Development.

MARCHINGTON, M., GRIMSHAW, D., RUBERY, J., and WILLMOTT, H. (eds.) (2004). *Fragmenting Work: Blurring Organizational Boundaries and Disordering Hierarchies.* Oxford: Oxford University Press.

MILLWARD, N., BRYSON, A., and FORTH, J. (2000). *All Change at Work?* London: Routledge.

NOON, M., and BLYTON, P. (1997). *The Realities of Work.* London: Macmillan Press.

OSTERMAN, P. (2000). 'Work Restructuring in an Era of Restructuring: Trends in Diffusion and Effect on Employee Welfare.' *Industrial and Labor Relations Review,* 53/2: 179–96.

—— KOCHAN, T. A., LOCKE, R. M., and PIORE, M. J. (2001). *Working in America: A Blueprint for the New Labor Market.* Boston: MIT Press.

PAAUWE, J. (2004). *HRM and Performance: Unique Approaches for Achieving Long-Term Viability.* Oxford: Oxford University Press.

—— and BOSELIE, P. (2005). 'HRM and Performance: What's Next?' *Human Resource Management Journal,* 15/4: 68–83.

PURCELL, J., and AHLSTRAND, B. (1994). *Human Resource Management in the Multi-divisional Company.* Oxford: Oxford University Press.

—— and GEORGIADIS, K. (2006). 'Why Should Employers Bother with Worker Voice?' In R. Freeman, P. Boxall, and P. Haynes (eds.), *What Workers Say: Employee Voice in the Anglo-American World.* Ithaca, NY: Cornell University Press.

QUINTANILLA, J., and FERNER, A. (2003). 'Multinationals and Human Resource Management: Between Global Convergence and National Identity.' *International Journal of Human Resource Management,* 14/3: 363–8.

RAMSAY, H., SCHOLARIOS, D., and HARLEY, B. (2000). 'Employees and High-Performance Work Systems: Testing inside the Black Box.' *British Journal of Industrial Relations,* 38/4: 501–31.

RUBERY, J., and GRIMSHAW, D. (2003). *The Organization of Employment: An International Perspective.* Basingstoke: Palgrave Macmillan.

SAKO, M. (1998). 'The Nature and Meaning of Employee "Voice" in the European Car Components Industry.' *Human Resource Management Journal,* 8/2: 5–18.

SCHNEIDER, B., HANGES, P. J., SMITH, B., and SALVAGGIO, A. N. (2003). 'Which Comes First: Employee Attitudes or Organizational Financial and Market Performance?' *Journal of Applied Psychology,* 88: 836–51.

SCHULER, R., and JACKSON, S. (1987). 'Linking Competitive Strategies with Human Resource Management.' *Academy of Management Executive,* 1/3: 207–19.

SEWELL, G. (2005). 'Doing What Comes Naturally? Why We Need a Practical Ethics of Teamwork.' *International Journal of Human Resource Management,* 16/2: 202–18.

STRAUSS, G. (1998). 'An Overview.' In F. Heller, E. Pusić, G. Strauss, and B. Wilpert (eds.), *Organizational Participation: Myth and Reality.* Oxford: Oxford University Press.

VAN den BERG, R. J., RICHARDSON, H. A., and EASTMAN, L. J. (1999). 'The Impact of High Involvement Work Processes on Organizational Effectiveness.' *Group and Organization Management,* 24/3: 300–39.

WILKINSON, A, GODFREY, G., and MARCHINGTON, M. (1997). 'Bouquets, Brickbats and Blinkers: Total Quality Management and Employee Involvement in Practice.' *Organization Studies,* 18/5: 799–819.

WRIGHT, P. M., and BOSWELL, W. R. (2002). 'Desegregating HRM: A Review and Synthesis of Micro and Macro Human Resource Management Research.' *Journal of Management,* 28/3: 247–76.

# EEO AND THE MANAGEMENT OF DIVERSITY

ELLEN ERNST KOSSEK

SHAUN PICHLER

## 13.1 INTRODUCTION

HUMAN resource management of Equal Employment Opportunity (EEO) and workforce diversity involves the development and implementation of employer policies and practices that not only create a diverse workplace, but foster a supportive culture to enable individuals from different backgrounds to be able to productively work together to achieve organizational goals.

Ensuring EEO, and the creation of a work environment that capitalizes on the benefits of a diverse workforce, are of growing importance for organizational effectiveness. Most employees around the globe work in organizations with a diversity and multicultural dimension to their business. They work with customers, co-workers, suppliers, and business units with many different cultural and social identities, ethnicities, and nationalities. The 'flattening' of the economic work world and growing widespread Internet access (Friedman 2005) have heightened the multiculturalism of many workplaces. New and evolving virtual work systems are developing around the globe. Reduction of employment and national trade barriers between nations in the European Community and among the former

Soviet states illustrate social and political changes towards increasing levels of workplace diversity within and across continents. These external environmental shifts have created such mega-trends as: the emergence of new and expanded roles for women, people of color, immigrants, and offshore workers; heightened work–life stress from a 24/7 work day; and growing cultural clashes over workplace values.

The objective of this chapter is to discuss the HRM perspective regarding EEO and diversity. Towards this end, we define core concepts, and then examine labor force shifts and other rationales for managing EEO/diversity. We conclude by discussing 'how' firms are managing these issues. Future research implications are integrated at the end of relevant sections.

The HRM perspective assumes that along with financial, physical, and techno-logical resources, employees represent another set of important organizational resources—its human resources (Tayeb 1995). Consistent with other chapters, we see managing human resources as requiring employment policies and practices to attract, retain, develop, and reward individuals so that they perform tasks efficiently and effectively to meet job objectives and organizational goals. A key aspect of HRM is an increased focus on how to secure employees' commitment and dedication to the firm's goals via practices that jointly enhance employee job satisfaction and performance (Guest 1999).

Historically, HRM systems were designed to promote homogeneity such as selecting individuals similar to those who have been successful in the past or assuming that individuals would have similar career paths and motivations (Jackson 1992). Emphasizing EEO and diversity management requires employers to re-view existing practices in new ways to effectively support a more heteroge-neous population. These goals require a fundamental philosophical and practical shift in HR strategies to account for more variance and openness to diversity in employee characteristics and ways of working than when members' demographic backgrounds are highly similar. HRM policies affect the degree of indirect and direct *employment discrimination* by regulating the fairness of under-represented groups' (1) *access* to organizational opportunities and rewards, and (2) *treatment* as organizational members (Gelfand et al. 2005). Fairness has two dimensions: (1) procedural fairness (the same procedures are followed in recruitment, selection, and development), and (2) outcome fairness (majority and minority groups receive equal pay and promotion). Below we define core concepts underlying HRM to promote fairness and equal treatment in employment.

# 13.2 EEO AND DIVERSITY CORE CONCEPTS

In this section, we define the following key concepts: discrimination, EEO, affirmative action, diversity, inclusion, and multiculturalism.

## 13.2.1  EEO Concepts

*Employment discrimination* is defined as unjust actions against individuals or groups that deny them equality of treatment in employment (Dovidio and Hebl 2005). It can involve processes of *prejudice*, defined as attitudinal biases; and *stereotyping*, defined as cognitive distortions and ascription of characteristics to persons or groups who differ from one's own (Dipboye and Colella 2005). EEO activities focus on preventing job-related discrimination, prejudice, and stereotyping.

For exemplary purposes, we draw on definitions from the USA, as it was one of the earliest countries to pass comprehensive anti-discrimination legislation. The USA was also an early adopter of diversity initiatives that first became widespread in the late 1980s. The overall goal of *equal employment opportunity* policies and practices is to prevent job discrimination at all stages of the employment relationship including recruitment, hiring, promotion, and lay-offs. For example, the main Equal Employment Opportunity Law in the USA is Title VII. Found in the 1964 Civil Rights Act, Title VII makes workplace discrimination illegal on the basis of sex, age, race, color, religion, and national origin. Although no direct definition of discrimination is actually found in Title VII, the courts have defined it in two main ways (Wolkinson 2000): adverse treatment and impact. *Disparate or adverse treatment* involves unequal treatment of a person on the basis on their race, sex, national origin, age, or religion. Also referred to as *direct discrimination*, here the employer in some way treats minority members of protected classes differently from majority members. In the USA, the plaintiff has the burden of proving intentional direct discrimination. Evidence might include statements made that reference an individual's demographic background as in some way being linked to their qualifications to do the job. An example is job advertisements that expressly require an applicant to be a certain gender or age, a practice that is legal in some countries unlike the USA and UK (Lawler and Bae 1998). The 1973 US Supreme Court ruling in *McDonnell Douglas* v. *Green* codified the conditions needed to establish a prima facie case of disparate treatment. First, the individual must be a member of a protected class and be qualified for the job for which she or he applied. Second, the position must have remained open with the employer continuing to take applications from people with qualifications similar to the rejected applicant.

The second main type of employment discrimination under Title VII is *disparate* or *adverse impact*. Also referred to as *indirect discrimination, adverse impact* occurs when seemingly neutral organizational policies, requirements, or practices that are not inherently job related have a disproportionately negative effect on employment access or outcomes of protected groups. For example, if a firm has a culture of only promoting managers who are able to participate in regular early morning golfing outings, it may find fewer qualified working parents with young school-age children to promote. This practice in and of itself would not be illegal, unless the practice was shown to have adverse impact on a protected class, such as more adversely affecting women than men; and such a practice was shown to not be inherently job related in order to be a good manager. There need not be employer intent to discriminate to prove adverse impact. In the 1971 US Supreme Court case that developed this principle, *Griggs* v. *Duke Power*, the company required first-line supervisors to have a high school diploma and pass some additional employment tests (Wolkinson 2000). Although these selection tools disproportionately eliminated more African Americans than other individuals, the company did not validate these selection criteria as being predictive of supervisor performance.

Several years after Title VII was passed, Executive Order 11246 was adopted mandating that US government contractors take *affirmative action* to hire and promote a workforce that mirrored relevant labor markets. Affirmative action requires employers who have contracts with the federal government to take action to reduce historical discrimination barriers, identify job groups where members of protected classes are underutilized or under-represented in comparison to labor market prevalence, and to formulate timetables and goals for remedying barriers and underutilization. Examples of practices might include designating positions to be targeted to members of specific demographic groups, or giving temporary 'plus factors' in hiring evaluations if certain groups have been severely under-represented in jobs compared to their representation in the labor market. Such remedies must be temporary.

It should be noted that many other nations and NGOs have adopted legislation and practices that are similar to US EEO concepts. For example, the UK enacted the Equal Pay Act in 1970 and the Race Relations Act in 1976, and also established a Commission for Racial Equality and the Equal Opportunities Commission (Goodman et al. 1998). Ratified in 2003, the European Union has adopted an equal treatment directive that delineates a binding framework for prohibiting racial and gender discrimination in employment (Diamantopoulou 2001). The International Labor Organization's Discrimination (Employment and Occupation) Convention 1958 (No. 111) prohibits direct and indirect employment discrimination similar to the EEO concepts described under Title VII. In addition to race, color, sex, religion, and national origin, it also protects political minorities and has been ratified by nearly all of the 178 countries in the ILO (Tomei 2003).

A key issue for multinationals to determine is how to implement EEO systems that legally comply with the specific laws of the many countries of operation. As a rule of thumb, employers generally should follow local laws. For example, Savage and Wenner (2001) note that globalization has dramatically increased the number of foreign employers operating in the USA and that, despite some exceptions, US anti-discrimination laws generally apply to foreign companies and their subsidiaries. Similarly, Posthuma et al. (in press) develop guidelines for multinationals to use to help determine when US employment laws apply when operating across national boundaries. Based on a review of federal court cases, they identify key factors such as whether the location of work is inside or outside the USA, the employer's home country and number of employees, whether the employee is a US citizen or authorized to work in the USA, and international law defenses. Overall, US multinationals should be concerned about US anti-discrimination laws applying abroad to US citizens and foreign companies should be concerned about US laws when operating within the boundaries of the USA. Although the USA is used as an example here, these same types of analyses could be conducted for multinationals of other nations around the globe.

## 13.2.2 Creating Diversity, Inclusion, and Multicultural Organizations

In the late 1980s and early 1990s, as firms increased global operations and national workforces became more diverse, many leading multinationals began to realize that complying with legal mandates was not enough; getting people of many different backgrounds in the employment door was only the first step. Organizations that had HR systems designed to manage a generally white male employee population needed cultural change to better integrate women and racial and ethnic minorities (Kochan et al. 2003). Management of diversity, multiculturalism, and workforce inclusion strategies are viewed as a proactive approach to EEO management. EEO historically has been more focused on legal compliance, or reacting to remedying past discrimination.

The fundamental challenge employers face in implementing EEO practices is to not only ensure legal compliance but also to foster productivity, and to effectively link EEO activities to environmental changes such as demographic labor market shifts, globalization, and strategic business goals. This entails developing and implementing HRM initiatives that not only (1) increase and retain the numerical representation of historically excluded groups for legal compliance; but (2) manage diversity to ensure the inclusion of a diverse workforce throughout the firm, and (3) create a positive multicultural social system where members of different backgrounds participate fully in decision-making (Kossek et al. 2006).

*Workforce diversity* is defined as variation of social and cultural identities among people existing together in a defined employment or market setting (Cox 1993). It is important to note that a firm can be diverse–have numerical representation of individuals from different backgrounds–but not necessarily be inclusive or multicultural. An *inclusive workplace* is one that values individual and group workforce differences, cooperates by addressing the needs of disadvantaged groups in the surrounding community, and collaborates with other entities across national and cultural boundaries (Mor Barak 2005). These attributes build on each other to develop a higher stage of inclusion. An employer's capability to develop EEO strategies that foster an 'inclusive workplace' is the current trend in fostering diversity effectiveness. Kossek (2006) argues that the objective is 'how do we enable each employee to bring the best of themselves to work when they are there, feel like they are included in the workplace culture, and able to focus and care about work outcomes?'

Cox (1993, 2001) holds that there are six characteristics of a *multicultural organization* that distinguish this type from firms that are monolithic (homogeneous) or only heterogeneous in representation, merely tolerating diversity. His characteristics include: (1) pluralism, where socialization is a two-way process that enables minorities to shape organizational norms and values; (2) full structural integration, where key labor market groups are represented at all levels of the organization; (3) integration in informal networks, where all members have access; (4) absence of cultural bias, where discrimination and prejudice in the workplace is eliminated; (5) widespread organizational identification, which enables all to be equally committed to and identify with the firm; and (6) minimal inter-group conflict due to different identity group memberships. His definition provides concrete measures that scholars and employers can use to measure the effectiveness of HRM strategies.

Some studies have looked at Cox's criteria separately, such as Ibarra's (1995) research on the degree to which minorities had equal opportunity to be integrated into informal managerial networks, or Ely's (1995) study on how the lower structural integration and representation of senior women leaders negatively affected gender relations and climate at lower organizational levels. Future research should not only include studies that examine these as individual criteria in cross-sectional studies, but should examine them longitudinally in an integrative fashion. Studies should also look at effective employer practices promoting inclusion for emerging forms of diversity that merit protection. This might include studies of domestic partner benefits for individuals of varying sexual orientations or studies of flexibility to care for one's family without facing backlash or hurting job security, or promotion prospects. Like Equal Employment Opportunity research on the adverse impact of seemingly neutral employment practices on classes protected under Title VII and similar legislation, employers can help foster an inclusive workplace by conducting an audit of the adverse impact of seemingly 'neutral' employment policies and job conditions on these new diversity groups.

In the next two sections, we discuss the growing importance for employers not only to hire a diverse workforce but to develop HR systems that foster formal and informal equal workplace opportunity.

# 13.3 INTERNATIONAL LABOR FORCE TRENDS

A critical rationale for employers to implement EEO and diversity management strategies emanates from dramatic shifts in labor force demographics.

Across a wide majority of nations, women's workforce participation rates continue to increase. In 2000, female labor force participation rates were 63 percent in the USA and averaged 45 percent in Europe, although with high variation across countries (UN 2000). In the USA, the participation rate of women is expected to grow faster than that of men over the period from 2002 to 2012: a 1 percent increase in the representation of women compared to a 1 percent decline for men (Labor Force 2003). In developing nations, however, lower educational opportunities for women remain barriers to higher labor force participation (Weichselbaumer and Winter-Ebmer 2003).

In the USA and other developed countries, the problem of reconciling work and family life is a growing issue affecting both men and women's employment experiences. Employers will need to be able to move beyond adopting formal work and family policies to create cultures that allow for workers with caregiving demands to be included in mainstream corporate cultures (Kossek 2006).

Although workforce diversity will increase for employers in both developing and developed countries, the nature and sources of diversity will generally differ. Riche and Mor Barak (2005) note that, overall, in developed countries, increased workforce diversity will largely come from the ageing of the population, and the increased hiring of minorities and immigrants. For example, in the USA from 2002 to 2012, the labor force participation of Hispanic or Latino workers is predicted to grow by 33 percent—three times faster than the growth rate for all non-Hispanic workers. Participation rates of Asians are also expected to increase dramatically—by 51 percent—making them the fastest-growing labor force group. Labor force participation rates for white non-Hispanics are expected to decrease, while those for blacks are expected to rise slightly (BLS 2005; Toosi 2004). In contrast, in developing countries, increased diversity will largely emanate from foreign employers seeking to hire unemployed and under-employed native workers. Employers who can effectively manage the distinct EEO and diversity issues related to demographic shifts in different labor markets in their domestic and global operations are likely to be regarded as employers of choice and attract the best talent.

Variation in labor shortage rates will differentially affect employers' EEO recruitment efforts in developed and developing countries. In general, less developed countries are experiencing a proportional and absolute jump in their working-age (15–64) populations, while industrialized countries are experiencing a slowing or even a decline (Riche and Mor Barak 2005). For example, statistics show that the population growth rate of North America is expected to decrease from 2005 to 2025, while the population growth rate of Africa is expected to rise significantly in the same period (UN 2005). Riche and Mor Barak (2005) argue that employers in countries with shortages of young people will need to use immigration and the employment of non-traditional workers (such as older workers, women, and minorities) in order to maintain healthy ratios between workers and retirees. Healthy ratios imply there are sufficient numbers of workers in the labor force to support pensions and health care and other social programs for retirees. While some scholars have argued that these demographic shifts will create a severe labor shortage in developed countries like the USA, others contend that the ageing of the US workforce, increased life expectancy, and delayed retirement will largely prevent such a shortage, as many older workers will remain active in the labor force (Cappelli 2003).

In developed nations, low rates of population increase among nationals have resulted in migrants making a significant contribution to national population growth. The UK, the USA and Japan, in particular, are increasingly dependent on immigrant labor to fill labor shortages, both in high-and low-skilled jobs (*The Economist* 2000). Since the 1990s, the USA has steadily increased the amount of H1–B visas granted, including a 67 percent annual jump in 2001 just prior to 9/11. The UK has similarly relaxed recruitment requirements for foreign-born employees in certain high-skill industries. OECD member countries have witnessed a substantial increase in foreign-born temporary workers in the agricultural, household services, and other low-wage sectors (OECD 2003). Immigrants from Latin America and Asia currently make up the bulk of recent immigrants to what are referred to as 'settlement countries' (e.g. Australia, Canada, the USA and New Zealand) (OECD 2003). While these population trends have been effectively documented at the labor market level, future research should be focused on assessing the effectiveness of employer HRM practices in providing EEO in this context. For example, studies should examine effective strategies for integrating immigrants.

# 13.4 HRM BENEFITS OF MANAGING EEO AND DIVERSITY

Besides adapting to labor market developments in order to attract and retain necessary talent, there are many other employer benefits from managing EEO well. The challenge for employers is to be able to link EEO objectives to HR strategies being enacted at different levels of the firm, and to goals that are widely valued for organizational effectiveness. For illustrative purposes, Table 13.1 provides

## Table 13.1 Definitions of employer objectives of EEO and diversity strategies

| HRM activity and strategy | Level of HRM strategy | Definition | Desired outcome |
| --- | --- | --- | --- |
| HR and organizational vision, mission and goal alignment | Organizational | The ideal reason that the organization exists and the HR roadmap for how HR activities will fulfill its stated reason for existence in consideration of EEO | • Organizational unity and commitment and productivity<br>• Employee focus on organization's goals |
| Organizational learning | Organizational | Shared organizational vocabulary, practices and venues that encourage open discussion among employees of different backgrounds, training and orientation programs, mentoring programs, conflict management programs, resources and materials that are adapted to workers of many backgrounds | • Increased understanding of how EEO and diversity issues affect organizational effectiveness<br>• Enhanced interpersonal relations among employees<br>• Enhanced learning among employees and organizational groups<br>• Increased number of employees across demographic backgrounds ready for advancement |
| Organizational inclusion and culture change toward multiculturalism | Organizational | Organizational norms espousing equality, collectivism, the value of human resources, flexibility, creativity, and participation | • Organizational unity and commitment<br>• Cooperation |
| Team-building | Group | Integration of traditional power holders in the organization with non-traditional workers from different backgrounds who are emerging as leaders | • Enhanced interpersonal skills<br>• Enhanced integration of diverse points of view into organization's processes and decisions |
| HR planning | Individual | Procedures designed to recruit and select women and people of color, clear articulation of the organization's recruitment and selection processes based on job-related criteria, clear articulation of organization's commitment to diversity in recruitment and selection | • Increased representation of women and people of color<br>• Perceptions of fair procedures by all employees<br>• Employee support of organization |
| Individual learning and mentoring strategies | Individual | Individuals are paired with others who are dissimilar in one or more characteristics | • Enhanced interpersonal understanding<br>• Eradication of entrenched stereotypes<br>• Develop talent pool depth |

(continued)

**Table 13.1  (continued)**

| HRM activity and strategy | Level of HRM strategy | Definition | Desired outcome |
|---|---|---|---|
| Widespread employee participative management and involvement | Individual and group | Employee meetings, employee committees, suggestion boxes, climate surveys, open-door policies, grievance procedures. Although these are tailored to address core workplace issues, the degree to which employees of all backgrounds are integrated fosters an inclusive workplace. | • Employee participation and voice<br>• Employee involvement in organizational decisions<br>• Creative approaches to organizational opportunities<br>• Improved organizational processes and performance |

*Source*: Adapted from Kossek et al. 2006.

examples of some general HR strategies and activities, ranging from organizational learning to team-building. These HR strategies have particular objectives, such as promoting organizational unity and commitment to organizational goals or greater employee involvement in organizational decision-making. Some of these strategies are directed primarily at the organizational level; others primarily target groups or individuals within the organization. In order for EEO activities to be effective, it is critical to clearly identify benefits and outcomes from HR strategies such as those depicted in Table 13.1, and assess the organizational implications of EEO and diversity activities and linkages to general HR strategies (Kossek and Lobel 1996).

Figure 13.1 shows three ways to directly link EEO strategies to organizational effectiveness. Building on work by Kossek et al. (2006), the first objective of many EEO practices is to jointly increase the capability of employees and the actual diversity of the employee population. For example, one study recently found that if employers emphasize promotion and developmental opportunities for all workers as part of efforts to create a learning organization, there is also an increase in the representation of women in the organization as a whole (Goodman et al. 2003).

Increasing the diversity of the workforce, fostering creativity, reducing daily conflict, improving attitudes, commitment, and the cultural experiences of members are what employers should view as process-oriented or intermediate outcomes. These should be considered as intermediate outcomes in order to emphasize the importance of employers recognizing that they should not stop with the creation of diversity or the reduction of conflict as the only end products of EEO strategies. As the second link in Fig. 13.1 suggests, it is equally critical for employers to learn how to effectively link the presence of diversity and positive

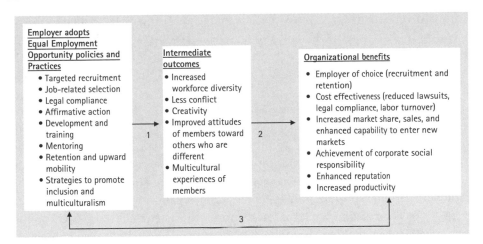

**Fig. 13.1. Goals of EEO and managing workforce diversity policies and practices**

social processes, such as the increased representation of many viewpoints, to key organizational outcomes (cf. Cox 1993, 2001; Kossek and Lobel 1996). These include being an employer of choice, increased cost effectiveness from reduced lawsuits and turnover, increased market share, enhanced capability to enter new markets, positive corporate reputations from being viewed as socially responsible, and higher productivity. A key challenge for employers is to actually evaluate the effectiveness of specific HR practices relative to these outcomes. Employers are sometimes reluctant to open up EEO and diversity activities to formal scrutiny given the sensitivity and important legal ramifications of these initiatives.

One exception is research by Rynes and Rosen (1995) on diversity training activities which finds that while diversity training is effective in improving inter-mediate outcomes, enhancing positive attitudes towards those who are different, training activities did not produce lasting change and were not well linked to organizational outcomes.

Employer objectives and rhetoric regarding EEO and diversity activities evolve over time and can be classified across stages of development. Early on in EEO efforts, most employers focus on compliance with legal mandates. Then, leading firms move on to more progressive goals, embracing diversity as a moral perspec-tive. Beyond legal and moral imperatives, progressive employers eventually recog-nize that they need to learn how to leverage increased diversity to promote a competitive advantage over other businesses (Cox 2001; Tayeb 1995). Focusing on competitive advantage moves the effective implementation of EEO and diversity management into the strategic HRM domain, where policies and practices are linked to an organization's strategic goals in order to improve business perform-ance. The SHRM argument derives from resource-based theory: employers with a more diverse workforce have the advantage of being able to better mirror increasingly diverse markets, and unique social resources to enhance capability in competitive business environments (Richard 2000). Studies have related the presence of a diverse labor force to customer demand for products and services (Richard et al. 2002).

Yet many firms are still striving to better link EEO efforts to organizational performance. Currently, there is a spectrum of employers' levels of development. Some are still responding to, or minimally complying with, legal mandates. Other firms focus efforts on incremental programs and policies as discrete ends. Yet, as the research reviewed in the next section shows, some studies have shown that employers can link EEO to clear outcomes, and organizational change and effectiveness. As Thomas and Ely (1996) note, under this later stage, employers are not only successful in making the unitary change of hiring employees who mirror customers' demographics, but they also are able to achieve an interactive organizational change toward greater multiculturalism and learning. At these higher stages of sophistication, employers have majority members who value learning from minority employees, and a culture that fosters interactive adaptation and learning. Thus, organizational change is ongoing and dynamic, involves mutual ongoing learning and adaptation where individuals not only adapt to the corporate culture, but the organizational culture is also receptive to adaptation and learning from these newer members. Thus, the assimilation process is not just one way, where individuals must always adapt to the dominant corporate culture, but is generally collaborative—the corporate culture changes and is shaped as well by the heterogeneous workforce.

## 13.5 BEST PRACTICES AND STRATEGIES

Table 13.2 summarizes some of the research on 'best practices' in EEO strategies with future research implications. We have organized these studies into three groups: practices that promote perceptions of organizational inclusion and justice, practices that reduce discrimination through HR practices, and practices that improve financial competitiveness. Workplace inclusion is most enhanced when targeted recruitment and selection efforts incorporate multiple methods. By this we mean that recruitment objectives are not just based on any single recruitment method, in order to limit the risk of overly relying on a method that does not effectively tap into ethnically and racially diverse talent pools. For example, if one only advertised in the *New York Times*, perhaps one might not reach as many members of under-represented groups as if one advertised on the Internet and

## Table 13.2  EEO HR practices and organizational effectiveness: representative studies

| EEO practice | Representative studies | Research findings | Organizational implications | Future research |
|---|---|---|---|---|
| *Selection practices to enhance organizational inclusiveness and justice perceptions* | | | | |
| Targeted recruitment | Highhouse et al. (1999) Kim and Gelfand (2003) Rau and Adams (2005) Thomas and Wise (1999) | Minority candidates and other targeted group members are more attracted to firms with minority recruiters and firms with an EEO/ diversity statement, which can be affected by the presence of other supportive organizational policies. | Targeted recruitment should focus on the combined, mutually reinforcing effects of recruiter characteristics and organizational policies on applicant attraction. | Past research has often used student subjects in experimental laboratory research. This could be extended to field research using more relevant samples. |
| Affirmative action in hiring | Heilman et al. (1992) Heilman et al. (1997) | Individuals hired through affirmative action programs (AAPs) are rated as less competent because they are perceived to be hired on the basis of their identity group membership, not qualifications. This effect is mitigated only when explicit performance information is available. | Organizational practices intended to benefit underrepresented groups may actually have unintended negative consequences. In order to remediate negative stigmas attached to beneficiaries, management can disseminate information about merit components of AAPs. | The effects observed in these studies are robust and replicable across student and managerial samples. Research could investigate predictors of positive associations with AAP in organizations, and management strategies for preventing stigmatization. |
| Focusing EEO on formalized affirmative action policies | Leck and Saunders (1992) French (2001) | More formalized AA policies were found to be more effective in improving the representation of women, disabled persons, and minorities in Canada. Australian employers with AA were the most effective in increasing diversity, compared to other EEO policies. | Organizations should be open to using formal AA programs when informal methods are ineffective and severe under-representation exists of members of protected classes. | Studies need to identify how to help firms make the transition from formalized AA to non-mandated approaches over time, and understand how to reduce backlash against AA recipients, as well as identify new emerging diversity groups that could benefit from AA. |

(continued)

## Table 13.2 (continued)

| EEO practice | Representative studies | Research findings | Organizational implications | Future research |
|---|---|---|---|---|
| Structured interviews | Chapman and Zwieg (2005) Gollub-Williamson et al. (1997) Huffcut and Arthur (1994) Terpstra and Rozell (1997) | Although use is limited in practice, selection interviews generally increase in validity with increased structure. While structured interviews have been found to have no impact on procedural justice perceptions, they have been linked to an effective defense against discrimination litigation. | Structured interviews can facilitate selection of high-performing candidates and can also increase legal defensibility. | Since interviewee reactions to structured interviews are often negative, and use varies by training of HRM practitioners, more research is needed into the conditions under which structured interviews have high acceptability and legal effectiveness. |

*EEO socialization, training and appraisal practices to reduce discrimination*

| EEO practice | Representative studies | Research findings | Organizational implications | Future research |
|---|---|---|---|---|
| Non-discrimination policy | Morrison and Von Glinow (1990) Ragins and Cornwell (2001) | The communication of a non-discrimination policy stating employment discrimination is prohibited reduces perceptions of discrimination among minorities, both visible and invisible. | A non-discrimination policy can indirectly lead to improvements in job attitudes among minority group members. | While a non-discrimination policy acts as a signal, research is needed to establish the effectiveness of such policies for reducing actual discrimination. |
| Due process performance appraisal | Folger et al. (1992) Taylor et al. (1995) | Due process performance appraisal results in more favorable reactions (e.g. perceptions of fairness of appraisal procedures) among both managers and employees even when ratings are lower. | Reactions to performance appraisal and general job attitudes among employees can be improved through implementing due process performance appraisal. | Research could examine alternative outcomes beyond perceptions of appraisal fairness, such as turnover, performance improvement, and satisfaction. |
| Diversity training | Hanover and Cellar (1998) King et al. (2005) Rynes and Rosen (1995) Sanchez and Medkik (2004) | Research indicates that participants have generally favorable reactions towards diversity training, but product-ivity effects are | Diversity training can raise cultural awareness as well as awareness of inclusive organizational policies and prac-tices. Management | More research is needed which examines the effects of diversity training on transfer of training to the job, actual behavioral change |

| EEO practice | Representative studies | Research findings | Organizational implications | Future research |
|---|---|---|---|---|
| | | not always evaluated. Diversity training has been shown to positively influence participants' attitudes and self-ratings of behavior towards minority group members. | support is important for training success. | and productivity outcomes as well as looking at inter-active relationships with supportive organizational policies and practices. |
| *EEO practices and financial effectiveness* | | | | |
| | Hersch (1991) Pruitt and Nethercutt (2002) Wright et al. (1995) Bierman (2001) | Announcements of award-winning AAPs are related to short-run stock price increases, whereas announcements of guilty discrimination verdicts are related to short-run decreases in stock price. | Financial losses associated with the announcement of an EEO violation can be extensive. Effective diversity management may be a source of competitive advantage. | Implication that investors attribute awards and settlements to effective human resource management needs further investigation. Researchers caution that using secondary media sources may overestimate financial losses. |

radio and other more widely accessible sources. Similarly, selection decisions should not be made on the basis of performance in a single selection method, which may have adverse impact against a particular group. It is far better to make decisions based on good performance as evinced from several selection data sources. In this way, one does not weed out a member of a protected class simply because of a lower performance on a single method that may not be all that predictive of on-the-job performance.

There are many 'best practices' in developing a selection and recruitment process that promotes diversity and EEO effectiveness. Some examples are using minority recruiters who mirror a more diverse applicant pool. Structured interview protocols are also effective because they ensure procedural consistency in the data collected from each applicant, and similarity in the interview experience. Publicizing statements of an organization's commitment to diversity in recruitment materials is also important to send a message of openness to individuals of many backgrounds. In order to prevent stereotyping of hires under affirmative action, it is critical to show explicit performance information indicating the competence of hires. Formal affirmative action programs have also been shown to be more effective than less formal efforts in countries ranging from Australia to the USA and Canada (Leck and Saunders 1992). This finding holds up as long as these policies are sincerely backed by management cultural support.

Regarding preventing discriminatory practice, one particularly effective practice is using due process performance appraisals. These aim to ensure that employees experience fair and structured procedures in evaluation. Making selection and evaluation processes transparent and allowing for voice can increase perceptions of fairness of hiring activities and reduce lawsuits and perceptions of injustice. Anti-discrimination policies can decrease discrimination not only for visible minorities (e.g. those associated with gender, race, or ethnicity), but also invisible minorities (e.g. those associated with sexual orientation or religion).

One of the most popular HR strategies, diversity training, has been found to be most effective when not only linked to general attitudinal change, such as understanding and valuing diversity, but also operationalized in terms of specific HR practices such as interviewing techniques or performance appraisals. Other effective practices include visible Diversity Advisory Committees comprised of respected leaders, mandatory training, and targeted communications to specific minority members (Jackson 2002).

One particularly effective practice involves mentoring programs that enable formal and informal knowledge to be shared and support leadership development socialization processes. Same-race and gender mentoring programs have the advantage of enabling individuals of similar background to share common workplace experiences and learn about what works well in the particular organizational culture. Cross-gender and race programs serve different goals. When, for example, a Hispanic female new college hire is paired with a senior vice president who is a white male, the new recruit is aided by having greater high-level visibility and also increased access to important tacit knowledge—things that a new hire may find difficult to obtain on their own. One caveat, however, for mentoring programs is that they should not be forced (e.g. mentors and mentees should have some choice in the matching process), and there should be mutual rewards for participation.

As Table 13.2 notes in the third section, studies have shown that not only can EEO activities lead to the creation of a workforce mirroring increasingly diverse labor markets, but having award-winning affirmative action programs is associated with short-run stock price increases.

One particularly promising area for future research and practice involves the development of statistical measures that enable researchers and firms to empirically investigate relationships between anti-discrimination policies and employment-related outcomes across international contexts. Some studies suggest that MNCs are attracted to low-regulation countries with good workforce skills (Cooke and

Noble 1998): for example, a study by Bognanno et al. (2005) who use restrictions on lay-offs as proxies for the measurement of labor standards. Other studies find contradictory evidence. For example, the ILO's Institute of Labor Studies has used the language of conventions 100 and 111 to develop five measures of gender discrimination (Kucera 2001, 2002). Three of the discrimination measures involve wage discrimination, whereas the other measures involve occupational and skill attainment. These measures have been used to assess relationships between discrimination at the national level and foreign direct investment. While 'conventional wisdom' would suggest that foreign direct investment would tend to flow into countries with lower labor standards, no such relationship was found in a cross-country analysis of 127 countries (Kucera 2002). Rather, the data indicated that countries with greater worker rights received more FDI, which is consistent with research that has found ratification of ILO standards to be positively related to FDI (Cooke 1997): for instance, a positive relationship between FDI and gender equality, although this relationship is partly dependent on which regions of the world are analyzed. It is important that future studies investigate different ways of capturing labor regulation and employment policy progressiveness across countries and firms. Additional analyses need to be conducted across minority groups to assess progress, the degree of policy implementation, and at the employer level, to assess profitability, growth, and productivity.

A final growing area for study of best practices emanates from comparative studies of EEO practices across countries. Far more research on HR strategies to manage EEO and diversity has been conducted in Western and developing countries than in developed and Eastern cultures. As the economic fulcrum shifts toward the new markets and labor forces in such countries as China, India, Latin America, and Africa, it will be increasingly critical to triangulate studies on national culture with studies of employer practices and organizational cultural implementation (see this Handbook, Chapter 25). For example, Ryan et al. (1999) sent surveys to several hundred employers in twenty-two countries. Employers in countries higher on uncertainty avoidance tended to use more selection tests and use them more frequently, conducted more interviews for a position, were more likely to use standardized interview questions, and more frequently audited selection processes than countries low on uncertainty avoidance. Organizations in countries higher on power distance were less likely to use peers as interviewers. This study suggests major barriers to implementing HR practices that have been shown to reduce discrimination in cultures low on uncertainty avoidance or high on power distance. It also underlines the importance of studying linkages between organizational and cross-cultural behavior and preferences for EEO and HR practices in the same study.

Similarly, Lawler and Bae (1998), in a study of Thailand where gender discrimination is legal, found that national culture had effects on the recruitment practices of multinational corporations. They investigated the relationship between economic growth, factors related to national culture, and the discriminatory nature of job advertisements for professional jobs. Multinationals from countries that were more individualistic were less likely to require that job applicants be male and were more likely to use gender-neutral advertisements. Economic growth was not related to whether or not job advertisements were discriminatory.

Both of these studies suggest that national culture has a strong influence on the discriminatory behavior of multinational corporations when operating in foreign countries. The degree to which the national culture is open to valuing heterogeneity may have an influence on the degree to which selection and recruitment and other EEO practices are implemented in a non-discriminatory fashion.

## 13.6 CONCLUSION

In this chapter, we have defined core concepts in EEO and diversity management, and employer rationales, HR strategies, and outcomes from these activities. Because workforce diversity management, discrimination, and EEO involve different meanings and assumptions across countries and cultures, employers in different countries often define EEO and diversity differently (Wrench 2003). Variation in how diversity management is socially constructed may lead to different HR strategies to solve different types of perceived problems and affects the perceived valence of preferred solutions. The research reviewed in this chapter suggests that EEO 'best practices' tend to involve clear and transparent HR procedures and decision-making processes, which are grounded in the core concepts of prevention of adverse treatment and impact. We argue that such goals are universal ones that should be aspired to across employment settings.

We have also argued that adopting EEO policies to comply with legal standards is a critical first step in effective diversity management. However, at the same time, the presence of policies on paper does not necessarily foster deep cultural change and commitment to widespread implementation and integration of diversity initiatives with other HR and business systems without top management commitment and leadership. Leaders must buy into the belief that effective EEO management is not only the socially responsible thing for employers to do; it is critical for organizational effectiveness, learning, and productivity. Employers accrue the greatest benefits from EEO activities the more that they learn to hire, effectively develop, and utilize the potential of individuals from the many different backgrounds that mirror the increasing diversity of the labor markets in which they operate, linking these HR initiatives to their overarching strategic and business objectives.

# REFERENCES

BIERMAN, L. (2001). 'OFCCP Affirmative Action Awards and Stock Market Reaction.' *Labor Law Journal*, 57: 572–7.

BLS (2005). United States Department of Labor, Bureau of Labor Statistics. BLS releases 2002–12 employment projections. (www.bls.gov/news.release/pdf/ecopro.pdf). Accessed 9 July 2005.

BOGNANNO, M. F., KEANE, M. P., and YANG, D. (2005). 'The Influence of Wages and Industrial Relations Environments on the Production Location Decisions of US Multinational Corporations.' *Industrial and Labor Relations Review*, 58/2: 171–201.

CAPPELLI, P. (2003). 'Will There Really be a Labor Shortage?' *Organizational Dynamics*, 32/3: 221–34.

CHAPMAN, D. S., and ZWIEG, D. L. (2005). 'Developing a Nomological Network for Interview Structure: Antecedents and Consequences of the Structured Selection Interview.' *Personnel Psychology*, 58: 673–702.

COOKE, W. (1997). 'The Influence of Industrial Relations Factors on US Foreign Direct Investment Abroad.' *Industrial and Labor Relations Review*, 51/1: 3–17.

—— and NOBLE, D. (1998). 'Industrial Relations Systems and US Foreign Direct Investment Abroad.' *British Journal of Industrial Relations*, 36/4: 581–609.

COX, T. (1993). *Cultural Diversity in Organizations: Theory, Research and Practice*. San Francisco: Berrett-Koehler.

—— (2001). *Creating the Multicultural Organization: A Strategy for Capturing the Power of Diversity*. San Francisco: Jossey Bass.

DIAMANTOPOULOU, A. (2001). 'European Union Action to Combat Racism.' *European Commission Contribution to the World Conference against Racism, Racial Discrimination, Xenophobia and Related Intolerance*. Luxembourg: European Commission, Office for Official Publications of the European Communities, at http://europa.eu.int, 4–5.

DIPBOYE, R., and COLELLA, A. (2005). 'An Introduction.' In R. Dipboye and A. Collela (eds.), *Discrimination at Work: The Psychological and Organizational Bases*. Mahwah, NJ: LEA Press.

DOVIDIO, J., and HEBL, M. (2005). 'Discrimination at the Individual Level: Cognitive and Affective Factors.' In R. Dipboye and A. Colella (eds.), *Discrimination at Work: The Psychological and Organizational Bases*. Mahwah, NJ: LEA Press.

*The Economist* (2000). 'A Continent on the Move.' 6 May: 25–8.

ELY, R. (1995). 'The Power in Demography: Women's Social Construction of Gender Identity at Work.' *Academy of Management Journal*, 38: 589–634.

FOLGER, R., KONOVSKY, M. A., and CROPANZANO, R. (1992). 'A Due Process Metaphor for Performance Appraisal.' In B. M. Staw and L. L. Cummings (eds.), *Research in Organizational Behavior*. Greenwich, Conn.: JAI Press.

FRENCH, E. (2001). 'Approaches to Equity Management and their Relationship to Women in Management.' *British Journal of Management*, 12: 267–85.

FRIEDMAN, F. (2005). *A Brief History of the 21st Century: The World is Flat*. New York: Farrar, Strauss, & Giroux.

GELFAND, M. J., NISHII, L. H., RAVER, J. L., and SCHNEIDER, B. (2005). 'Discrimination in Organizations: An Organization Level Systems Perspective.' In B. L. Diptoye and A. Colella (eds.), *Discrimination at Work: The Psychological and Organizational Bases*. Mahwah, NJ: Lawrence Erlbaum.

Gollub-Williamson, L., Campion, J. E., Malos, S. B., Roehling, M. V., and Campion, M. A. (1997). 'Employment Interview on Trial: Linking Interview Structure with Litigation Outcomes.' *Journal of Applied Psychology*, 82/6: 900–12.

Goodman, J., Marchington, M., Berridge, J., Snape, E., and Bamber, G. (1998). 'Employment Relations in Britain.' In G. Bamber and R. D. Lansbury (eds.), *International and Comparative Employment Relations: A Study of Industrialized Market Economies*. Sydney: Allen & Unwin.

—— Fields, D., and Blum, T. (2003). 'Cracks in the Glass Ceiling: In What Kind of Organizations do Women Make it to the Top?' *Group and Organization Management*, 28: 475–501.

Guest, D. E. (1999). 'Human Resource Management: The Worker's Verdict.' *Human Resource Management*, 9/3: 6.

Hanover, J. M. B., and Cellar, D. F. (1998). 'Environmental Factors and the Effectiveness of Workforce Diversity Training.' *Human Resource Development Quarterly*, 9/2: 105–24.

Heilman, M. E., Block, C. J., and Lucas, J. A. (1992). 'Presumed Incompetent? Stigmatization and Affirmative Action Efforts.' *Journal of Applied Psychology*, 77: 536–44.

—— —— and Stathatos, P. (1997). 'The Affirmative Action Stigma of Incompetence: Effects of Performance Information Ambiguity.' *Academy of Management Journal*, 40: 603–25.

Hersch, J. (1991). 'Equal Opportunity Law and Firm Profitability.' *Journal of Human Resources*, 26/1: 139–53.

Highhouse, S., Stierwalt, S. L., Bachiochi, P., Elder, A. E., and Fisher, G. (1999). 'Effects of Advertised Human Resource Management Practices on Attraction of African American Applicants.' *Personnel Psychology*, 52: 425–42.

Huffcut, A. I., and Arthur, W., Jr. (1994). 'Hunter & Hunter (1984) Revisited: Interview Validity for Entry-Level Jobs.' *Journal of Applied Psychology*, 79/2: 184–90.

Ibarra, H. (1995). 'Race, Opportunity and Diversity of Social Circles in Managerial Networks.' *Academy of Management Journal*, 38: 673–703.

Ilo (2005). International Labour Organization (www.ilo.org/ilolex/english/docs/declworld.htm). Accessed 5 July.

Jackson, A. (2002). 'Competitive Practices in Diversity.' www.shrm.org/diversity/hottopics/compprac.asp, accessed 5 February 2004.

Jackson, S. E. (1992). *Diversity in the Workplace: Human Resource Initiatives*. New York: Guilford Press.

Kim, S. S., and Gelfand, M. J. (2003). 'The Influence of Ethnic Identity on Perceptions of Organizational Recruitment.' *Journal of Vocational Behavior*, 63: 396–419.

King, E. B., Hebl, M. R., Turner, S., and DeChermont, K. (2005). 'The Influence of Goal-Setting and Leader Support in Diversity Training: Integrating Gay and Lesbian Topics.' In E. King and M. Hebl (co-chairs), *Overcoming Barriers to Equality among Diverse Sexual Orientations at Work*. Symposium presented at the annual meeting of the Academy of Management Meeting, Honolulu, Hawaii.

Kochan, T., Bezrukova, K., Ely, R., Jackson, S. E., Joshi, A., Jehn, K. E., Leonard, D., Levine, D., and Thomas, D. (2003). 'The Effects of Diversity on Business Performance: Report of a Feasibility Study of the Diversity Research Network.' *Human Resource Management*. 42/3: 3–21.

Kossek, E. (2006). 'Work and Family in America: Growing Tensions between Employment Policy and a Transformed Workforce.' In E. Lawler and J. O'Toole (eds.), *The New American Workplace*. New York: Palgrave Macmillan.

—— and LOBEL, S. (1996). *Managing Diversity: Human Resource Strategies for Transforming the Workplace*. Oxford: Blackwell.

—— —— and BROWN, J. (2006). 'Human Resource Strategies to Manage Work Force Diversity: Examining "The Business Case".' In A. Konrad, P. Prasad, and J. Pringle (eds.), *Handbook of Workplace Diversity*. London: Sage.

KUCERA, D. (2001). 'Measuring Fundamental Rights at Work.' *Statistical Journal of the United Nations*, 18/3: 175–86.

—— (2002). 'Core Labour Standards and Foreign Direct Investment.' *International Labour Review*, 141/1–2: 31–71.

Labor Force (2003). *Occupational Outlook Quarterly*, Winter 2003/2004.

LAWLER, J. J., and BAE, J. (1998). 'Overt Employment Discrimination by Multinational Firms: Cultural and Economic Influences in a Developing Country.' *Industrial Relations*, 37/2: 126–53.

LECK, J., and SAUNDERS, G. (1992). 'Hiring Women: The Effects of Canada's Equity Employment Act.' *Canadian Public Policy*, 18: 203–21.

MOR BARAK, M. (2005). *Managing Diversity: Toward a Globally Inclusive Workplace*. Thousand Oaks, Calif.: Sage.

MORRISON, A. M., and VON GLINOW, M. A. (1990). 'Women and Minorities in Management.' *American Psychologist*, 4: 200–8.

OECD (2003). 'Trends in International Migration.' *Organization for Economic Cooperation and Development*. Paris: OECD.

POSTHUMA, R. A., ROEHLING, M. V., and CAMPION, M. A. (in press). 'Applying U.S. Employment Discrimination Laws to International Employers: Advice for Scientists and Practitioners.' *Personnel Psychology*.

PRUITT, S. W., and NETHERCUTT, L. L. (2002). 'The Texaco Racial Discrimination Case and Shareholder Wealth.' *Journal of Labor Research*, 23/4: 687–93.

RAGINS, B. R., and CORNWELL, J. M. (2001). 'Pink Triangles: Antecedents and Consequences of Perceived Workplace Discrimination against Gay and Lesbian Employees.' *Journal of Applied Psychology*, 86: 1244–61.

RAU, B. L., and ADAMS, G. A. (2005). 'Attracting Retirees to Apply: Desired Organizational Characteristics of Bridge Employment.' *Journal of Organizational Behavior*, 26: 648–60.

RICHARD, O. C. (2000). 'Racial Diversity, Business Strategy, and Firm Performance: A Resource-Based View.' *Academy of Management Journal*, 43: 164–77.

—— KOCHAN, T., and McMILLAN-CAPEHART, A. (2002). 'The Impact of Visible Diversity on Organizational Effectiveness: Disclosing the Contents in Pandora's Black Box.' *Journal of Business and Management*, 8/3: 1–26.

RICHE, M., and MOR BARAK, M. (2005). 'Global Demographic Trends: Impact on Workforce Diversity.' In M. Mor Barak (ed.), *Managing Diversity: Toward a Globally Inclusive Workplace*. Thousand Oaks, Calif.: Sage.

RYAN, A. M., McFARLAND, L., SHL, H. B., and PAGE, R. (1999). 'An International Look at Selection Practices: Nation and Culture as Explanations for Variability in Practice.' *Personnel Psychology*, 52: 359–91.

RYNES, S., and ROSEN, B. (1995). 'A Field Study of Factors Affecting the Adoption and Perceived Success of Diversity Training.' *Personnel Psychology*, 48: 247–70.

SANCHEZ, J. I., and MEDKIK, N. (2004). 'The Effects of Diversity Awareness Training on Differential Treatment.' *Group & Organization Management*, 29/4: 517–36.

SAVAGE, E., and WENNER, S. (2001). 'Impact of U.S. Anti-discrimination Laws on Foreign Corporations: Part 2.' *Benefits and Compensation International*, 32/4: 8–12.

TAYEB, M. (1995). *The Management of a Multicultural Workforce*. New York: John Wiley & Sons.

TAYLOR, M. S., TRACY, K. B., RENARD, M. K. HARRISON, J. K., and CARROLL, S. J. (1995). 'Due Process in Performance Appraisal: A Quasi-experiment in Procedural Justice.' *Administrative Science Quarterly*, 40: 495–523.

TERPSTRA, D. E., and ROZELL, E. J. (1997). 'Why Some Potentially Effective Staffing Practices are Seldom Used.' *Public Personnel Management*, 26/4: 483–95.

THOMAS, D., and ELY, R. (1996). 'Making Differences Matter: A New Paradigm for Managing Diversity.' *Harvard Business Review*, September/October: 79–90.

THOMAS, K. M., and WISE, P. G. (1999). 'Organizational Attractiveness and Individual Differences: Are Diverse Applicants Attracted by Different Factors?' *Journal of Business and Psychology*, 13/3: 375–90.

TOMEI, M. (2003). 'Discrimination and Equality at Work: A Review of the Concepts.' *International Labour Review*, 142/4: 401–20.

TOOSI, M. (2004). 'Labor Force Projections to 2012: The Graying of the U.S. Workforce.' *Monthly Labor Review*, 127/2: 37–58.

UNITED Nations (2000). *The World's Women 2000: Trends and Statistics*. Geneva: United Nations.

—— (2005). 'World Population Prospects: The 2004 Revision.' *Population Division of the Department of Economic and Social Affairs of the United Nations Secretariat*. www.un.org/esa/population/publications/WPP2004/2004Highlights_finalrevised.pdf.

WEICHSELBAUMER, D., and WINTER-EBMER, R. (2003). *A Meta-analysis of the International Gender Wage Gap*. Economics working papers, 2003–11, Department of Economics, Johannes Kepler University, Linz.

WOLKINSON, B. (2000). 'EEO in the Workplace: Employment Law Challenges.' In E. E. Kossek and R. Block (eds.), *Managing Human Resources in the 21st Century: From Core Concepts to Strategic Choice*. Cincinnati: South-Western Publishing.

WRENCH, J. (2003). *Managing Diversity, Fighting Racism, or Combating Discrimination? A Crucial Exploration*. Council of Europe and European Commission Seminar. Resituating Culture: Reflections on Diversity, Racism, Gender, and Identity on the Context of Youth. Budapest, June.

WRIGHT, P., FERRIS, S. P., HILLER, J. S., and KROLL, M. (1995). 'Competitiveness through Management of Diversity: Effects on Stock Price Valuation.' *Academy of Management Journal*, 38/1: 272–87.

C H A P T E R   1 4

# RECRUITMENT STRATEGY

## MARC ORLITZKY

## 14.1 INTRODUCTION

INTERNAL labor markets seem to have become noticeably weaker (Cappelli 1999). The 'new deal at work' entails the increasing externalization of human resource processes that large organizations had traditionally internalized. Thus, organizations now face a strategic mandate to improve, if not optimize, their recruiting practices because, in today's increasingly market-based human resource management (HRM), effective recruitment is likely to be the 'most critical human resource function for organizational success and survival' (Taylor and Collins 2000: 304).

This chapter provides an overview of the theoretical and empirical contributions that have been made to the literature on recruitment strategy.[1] Recruitment can usefully be defined as 'those practices and activities carried out by the organization with the primary purpose of identifying and attracting potential employees' (Barber 1998: 5). This definition highlights the important difference between two HR functions that are typically seen as indivisible, or at least difficult to distinguish, namely recruitment and selection. Whereas selection is the HR function that pares down the number of applicants, recruitment consists of those HR practices and processes that make this paring down possible—by expanding the pool of firm-specific candidates from whom new employees will be selected.[2] Thus, as the first

---

[1] I am grateful to Mark Stephens, who helped with the collection of articles and development of tables.
[2] Of course, these conceptual boundaries between recruitment and selection become more fluid in practice.

stage in the strategic HRM value chain, recruitment controls and limits the potential value of such 'downstream' HR processes as employee selection or training and development. When the 'pattern of planned human resource deployments and activities [is] intended to enable an organization to achieve its goals' (Wright and McMahan 1992: 298), HRM can be said to be strategic. More specifically, for recruitment to become strategic, HR practitioners must find effective answers to the following five questions (Breaugh 1992; Breaugh and Starke 2000): (1) Whom to recruit? (2) Where to recruit? (3) What recruitment sources to use (e.g. the web, newspapers, job fairs, on campus, etc.)? (4) When to recruit? (5) What message to communicate?

Surveying the organizational recruitment literature, this review builds on and extends previous reviews (such as Breaugh and Starke 2000; Rynes 1991; Rynes and Barber 1990; Rynes and Cable 2003; Taylor and Collins 2000). At the same time, it highlights the importance of contextual variables at the *organizational* level of analysis. Mirroring the tension between general 'best practice' approaches and contingency approaches (cf. Boxall and Purcell 2003), the chapter has a dual focus: (1) How, or why, does recruitment affect organizational performance? (2) Under what conditions (in what contexts) does recruitment matter? First, it reviews current knowledge with respect to the main effects *of* recruitment on organization-level outcomes. Then, it discusses organization-level contingencies *on* recruitment. In both sections, I critically appraise the state of knowledge about recruitment strategy. Adopting Rynes's (1991) practice, I present key findings chronologically in two summary tables for a quick overview. I conclude my review with some important trajectories for theoretical development, future research, and management practice and summarize the conclusions of the literature review.

In taking a strategic perspective on recruitment, I assume that HR laws and regulations function as sectoral, regional, or national 'table stakes' (Boxall and Purcell 2003), which entire industry sectors might have in common. Thus, 'table stakes' might present strategic implications for levels of analysis higher than the individual organization, but do not, and cannot, serve as organization-level differentiating factors. Because adherence to laws regulating the recruitment function (e.g. affirmative action) cannot strategically differentiate effective from ineffective employers, in my view a legal focus would be misplaced theoretically. In addition, a focus on HR rules and regulations would be impractical as they often represent nationally or regionally specific baselines for organizational activities. Of course, the lack of discussion of cultural differences in regulating recruitment does not imply at all that employment rules and regulations are unimportant (far from it!), but only that they are unlikely to create a competitive advantage for *individual firms*. One could in fact conclude that abiding by legal and ethical rules, which are often culturally specific, is the price of admission that a firm will have to pay in order to identify, pursue, and attract talented individuals who are able and willing to contribute to its bottom line.

Another important assumption is about the level of analysis to which this review applies. Anything in the empirical recruitment literature that explicitly analyzes recruitment inputs, processes, and outcomes from an individual-level perspective is omitted from this review. In some cases, this scope delimitation has resulted in the exclusion of seminal studies in the recruitment literature. For example, Boudreau and Rynes (1985) made a landmark contribution in their development of recruitment utility. They prescriptively modeled the extent to which recruitment might make positive financial contributions to a firm's performance. Utility models represent a mathematically complex application of decision theory to assess the economic impact of recruitment activities and practices on organizations (Boudreau 1991). Recruitment utility models can deepen organizations' understanding of why a particular recruitment practice may have firm-specific net benefits rather than net costs. Through these utility calculations, it can be shown, for example, that organizations should not always aim to attract applicants with outstanding credentials or aim to maximize applicant pool size (Breaugh 1992: 12–13). However, utility analysis has a number of drawbacks, including problems with its computational and measurement complexities (see, e.g., Carlson et al. 2002) and research showing that practitioners are incredulous towards the utility estimates used (Latham and Whyte 1994). Although utility analysis remains one path toward the systematic, analytically precise evaluation of the general pay-offs from different recruitment strategies and practices, a more systemic answer to the question of *why* and *under what conditions* recruitment and recruitment strategy can enhance organizational success has been attempted through the resource-based view of the firm (RBV).

## 14.2 KEY INSIGHTS FROM LANDMARK STUDIES

### 14.2.1 Why and How Does Recruitment Matter? The Resource-Based View of the Firm

In the 1990s, the RBV, as a mathematically less complex framework, supplanted utility analysis in the evaluation of possible organization-level benefits of recruitment. Taylor and Collins (2000: 317–21) argue that recruitment satisfies Barney and Wright's (1998) five RBV criteria, which might offer a competitive advantage. First, recruitment might add *value* by enhancing labor cost efficiencies and/or spilling over to customer perceptions of the firm's products or services. Second, recruitment strategy might identify and tap talent that is *rare* in the labor market. Third, an organization's set of recruitment practices might be such a complex bundle of tactics that it is virtually *inimitable*. Fourth, recruitment may be a *non-substitutable* organizational practice to the extent that the recruitment strategy is innovative and idiosyncratic to one organization. Fifth, for maximum leverage, recruitment must be *aligned* with other HR practices, so that recruitment might support and enhance the benefits of the other HR functions, such as compensation, selection, or performance appraisal. When these five conditions are met, recruitment would be expected to make a contribution to a firm's financial performance.

Albeit small in number, there are a few studies that examine recruitment at the organizational level of analysis and suggest ways in which recruitment might affect organizational effectiveness. Some details about these studies are listed in Table 14.1 and discussed in the following section. In general, these studies point to the strategic importance of several recruitment-related practices.

Two studies found that the extent to which firms analyze and evaluate recruitment practices may be associated with higher organizational performance. Koch and McGrath (1996) combined an item about the formal evaluation of recruitment and selection practices with an item about HR planning. Of the three HR indexes they examined (see Table 14.1), this first measure showed the largest association with labor productivity. Similarly, Terpstra and Rozell (1993) found that firms that analyzed recruiting sources for their effectiveness in generating high-performance applicants had greater annual profitability in manufacturing and wholesale/retail industries, greater overall performance in service and wholesale/retail industries, and greater sales growth in service industries.

A set of studies by Huselid and his colleagues showed relationships between recruitment intensity and a few indicators of organizational performance. Recruitment intensity is defined as the number of applicants per position and may also be called the 'selection ratio.' Huselid (1995) found that when recruitment intensity was combined with other items measuring employee motivation, it was related to productivity (logarithm of sales per employee) and one measure of financial performance (Tobin's $q$), but not to another financial performance measure (gross rate of return on capital) or employee turnover. Delaney and Huselid (1996) examined the same predictor, staffing selectivity, separately and showed that, while it was not associated with perceived organizational performance, it was linked to perceived *market* performance. Though not reported in the article, Delaney and Huselid mentioned the general robustness of their results, showing no differences between for-profit and non-profit organizations.

Investigating the impact of organizational characteristics *on* recruitment effectiveness, two other organization-level studies had a slightly different focus from the studies mentioned so far. One organization-level study focused on compensation policy as a predictor of recruiting effectiveness (Williams and Dreher 1992). Because pecuniary inducements may be considered one of the three basic applicant attraction strategies (Rynes and Barber 1990), it is pertinent to this review.

**Table 14.1 Summary of previous research investigating the main effects of recruitment on organizational effectiveness**

| Study | Sample | Independent variables (IV) | Dependent variables (DV) | Results |
|---|---|---|---|---|
| Williams and Dreher (1992) | 352 US banks | Compensation policies | Recruitment outcomes: 1. Applicant pool size 2. Acceptance rate 3. Length of position vacancy | 1. % of compensation allocated for benefits was positively associated with applicant pool size. 2. Pay level was positively associated with acceptance rates. 3. Benefits level was negatively associated with days required to fill a position. 4. (Contrary to expectations) benefit flexibility was negatively related to applicant pool size. 5. (Contrary to expectations) pay level was positively associated with days required to fill a position. |
| Terpstra and Rozell (1993) | 201 US companies with over 200 employees (for a 23% response rate) | Companies' analysis of recruiting sources for effectiveness in generating high-performance employees | 1. Annual profitability 2. Profit growth 3. Sales growth 4. Overall performance | 1. IV was not, or only to a minor extent, correlated (in zero-order correlations) with DVs 1–4 overall. However, study also showed moderator effects: 2. In manufacturing firms, IV and profitability were related ($\beta = .23$). 3. In service industry firms, IV was associated with sales growth ($\beta = .53$ and $r = .50$) and overall performance ($\beta = .35$). 4. In wholesale/retail firms, IV was associated with profitability ($\beta = .79$) and overall performance ($\beta = .73$). |
| Huselid (1995) | 968 publicly held firms from Compact Disclosure (28% response rate) | Intensity of recruiting efforts (selection ratio) part of one of two factors constituting High Performance Work Practices (Factor = Employee Motivation) | 1. Turnover 2. Productivity 3. Tobin's q (financial performance) 4. Gross rate of return on capital | 1. Factor Employee Motivation related to productivity and Tobin's q, but not to turnover or return on capital. 2. Some evidence of horizontal/internal systems fit with other Factor of Employee Skills and Org. Structures. |

(continued)

**Table 14.1 (continued)**

| Study | Sample | Independent variables (IV) | Dependent variables (DV) | Results |
|---|---|---|---|---|
| Delaney and Huselid (1996) | 727 US organizations drawn from National Organizations Survey (51% response rate) | Number of applicants considered for each position (staffing selectivity): 3 items for 3 different positions ($\alpha = .66$) | 1. Perceived org. performance<br>2. Perceived market performance | 1. Staffing selectivity generally not related to perceived org. performance, but to perceived market performance.<br>2. Generally robust results: no moderator effects differentiating for-profit and non-profit organizations. |
| Koch and McGrath (1996) | 495 US business units (for a 7% response rate) | Recruitment practices included in 2 of 3 HR indexes:<br>1. HR planning index: Staffing plans and evaluation of hiring practices<br>2. Investments in hiring: Recruitment intensity and evaluation of recruitment sources | Labor productivity: Net sales per employee | 1. HR planning index positively associated ($\beta = .36$ and .27, respectively) with productivity.<br>2. Hiring index positively associated ($\beta = .10$ and .07, respectively) with productivity.<br>3. Both indexes interacted with capital intensity (betas of interaction terms were .29 and .04, respectively). |
| Turban and Greening (1996) | 189 US companies | Corporate social performance (CSP) | Employer attractiveness | CSP—especially the dimensions of employee relations ($\beta = .16$) and product quality ($\beta = .19$)—positively predicted employer attractiveness, above and beyond the effects of asset size ($\beta = .14$) and profitability ($\beta = .19$). |

| Study | Sample | Predictor measures | Dependent variables | Findings |
|---|---|---|---|---|
| Becker and Huselid (1998) | 691 US firms | Two items (selection ratio and formal HR planning that considers recruitment and succession) combined with 22 other items forming an HR system latent construct | 1. Market value (ln)<br>2. Market value/book value (ln)<br>3. Sales/employee (ln)<br>4. Gross rate of return<br>5. Turnover | Generally—in both manufacturing and non-manufacturing sectors—positively related with first four DVs and negatively with turnover (as expected). |
| Collins and Han (2004) | 99 companies recruiting on US campuses (response rate of 43%) | 1. Early recruitment practices: High– vs. low-involvement strategies<br>2. Corporate advertising<br>3. Firm reputation | Applicant pool quantity and quality | 1. Corporate advertising and firm reputation are positively related to number of applicants and perceived applicant quality.<br>2. Corporate advertising was directly related to organization-level average applicant GPA ($\beta = .24$) and applicants' work experience ($\beta = .29$).<br>3. Effects of high– and low-involvement recruitment strategies variable ($\beta$s ranging from $-.09$ to $.29$).<br>4. Interactions between advertising and recruitment strategies as well as reputation and recruitment strategies. |

As shown in Table 14.1, a number of observations were consistent with Williams and Dreher's hypotheses, while others were unexpected. The study provided evidence that pay level was positively associated with measures of (proximate) recruitment effectiveness, but also suggested that the commercial banks studied might have used compensation in a reactive fashion. In other words, organizations may adjust pay levels as a response to prior difficulties with recruitment, which would explain the study's surprising fifth finding listed in Table 14.1.

Another study (Turban and Greening 1996) showed that high pay or benefits levels may not be the only variables increasing an organization's ability to attract applicants. Rather, corporate social performance, the extent to which a firm's policies and programs exhibit a social and environmental concern with a variety of stakeholder issues, may enhance corporate reputation, which in turn will attract more employees. Product quality and employee relations have been identified as the two elements of social performance particularly pertinent to recruitment at the organizational level of analysis (Turban and Greening 1996). While several individual-level studies found evidence supportive of brand equity in attracting applicants (e.g. Collins and Stevens 2002; Gatewood et al. 1993), there has been no research stressing the strategic importance of applicants' perceptions of 'employer of choice' for *organization*-level outcomes. In fact, some of these individual-level studies (e.g. Turban and Cable 2003) questioned the generalizability and practical applicability of a lot of previous research on organizational reputation, employee branding, and applicant attraction. However, in general, the findings of this research stream, in combination with the findings by Trank and colleagues (2002), suggest that pay may not be the only leverage that organizations can use in attracting high-quality applicants.

In the most recent study of recruitment effectiveness, Collins and Han (2004) showed that the amount of corporate advertising, as measured by the firm's selling, general, and administrative costs, had the greatest and most consistent statistical effect on the prehire outcomes of applicant pool quantity and quality. While both corporate advertising and firm reputation were related to the number of applicants and applicant quality, only advertising was associated with positions filled, applicants' work experience, and applicants' grade point average (GPA). Early recruitment strategies, whether low-involvement practices (i.e. general recruitment ads, sponsorship) or high-involvement practices (i.e. detailed recruitment ads, employee endorsements), showed variable main effects on prehire outcomes. Interestingly, high-involvement generally did not have greater impact than low-involvement recruitment practices. In fact, one of the largest effects ($\beta = .28$) between recruitment practices and prehire outcomes was between corporate sponsorships (e.g. scholarships, donations to universities from which they recruit) and interview ratio, which is the number of applicants divided by number of interviews a company conducted. Only employee endorsements had a greater association with one other prehire outcome, applicant GPA ($\beta = .29$).

In summary, to some extent the few studies that investigated recruitment in relation to organizational effectiveness are reassuring because they point to a number of potential general benefits of recruitment and predictors of recruitment effectiveness. Recruitment intensity may enhance labor productivity and several different financial performance outcomes. In turn, organizations can attract more applicants (and, thus, increase recruitment intensity) by highlighting their reputation for social responsibility, high pay, or generous benefits in their recruitment practices. At the same time, the studies also showed considerable variability suggestive of a range of contingencies, which will be explored in the next section.

Yet, there are also several theoretical and methodological problems with this research stream. One problem concerns the theoretical framework. Most of the aforementioned studies either explicitly (e.g. Becker and Huselid 1998; Koch and McGrath 1996) or implicitly adopted the RBV as the main causal explanation of the postulated relationships. Such a perspective ignores the major theoretical problems inherent in this economic perspective. One criticism is the charge that the RBV does not capture the complexity inherent in HR systems and, therefore, must be developed further (Colbert 2004). More importantly, various statements in the RBV can be shown to be true by definition (tautological) and, thus, cannot be disconfirmed empirically (Powell 2001; Priem and Butler 2001). In other words, the RBV seems to fall short with respect to core criteria of theory evaluation. Hence, scholars in HRM should not uncritically adopt any theoretical framework whose validity has fundamentally been questioned by the field that generated it.

Additional methodological problems with organization-level research of the kind reviewed above include the lack of attention to path models that specify both proximate and distal dependent variables that might capture the effectiveness of given recruitment practices more fully. Most recruitment research has omitted any detailed descriptions of such direct and indirect path effects. The only exception is Huselid (1995), who tested his expectation that turnover and productivity—as more proximate endogenous variables—would mediate the impact of recruitment practices (and other 'high-performance work practices') on financial performance. However, as Fig. 14.1 indicates, the HR variable that included recruitment intensity was not related to one mediator and one dependent variable, so the only mediation effect found was through productivity (as mediator) to Tobin's $q$, the ratio of a firm's market value to the replacement cost of its assets. Of course, one way to circumvent this problem of the causal uncertainty inherent in the links of recruitment to distal organizational outcomes is a greater focus on proximate, prehire outcomes. More specifically, analyzing proximate recruitment prehire outcomes in an organization-level study, Collins and Han (2004) did heed this important advice by Rynes (1991) for more meaningful recruitment research.

Other methodological problems concern the measurement of recruitment-related variables. Often recruitment is combined with other variables to form a latent construct, when in fact the factor structure was quite ambiguous with respect

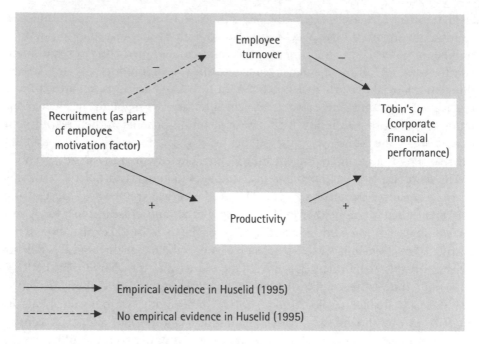

**Fig. 14.1. Mediation effects of recruitment on organizational effectiveness**

to the recruitment item (see table 1 in Huselid 1995). This makes it difficult to discern the separate effect of recruitment. In addition, the meaning of the recruitment items can often be questioned (Rynes and Cable 2003) because they may, in fact, be confounded with unmeasured influences such as company reputation or visibility.

## 14.2.2 Organizational Contingencies of Recruitment Strategies

Based on various theoretical and practical perspectives, it would be unrealistic to expect particular recruitment strategies to be superior to all others, regardless of contextual influences. Even the most ardent proponents of 'best practice' models in strategic HRM acknowledge the importance of a variety of contingency factors (e.g. Pfeffer 1998). Although there are no studies investigating the effect of the fit between recruitment and context on organizational effectiveness (Rynes and Cable 2003), we can, to an admittedly limited extent, use descriptive research on organizational context and recruitment to speculate about the possibly strategic imperative of such context-aligned recruitment practices.[3]

---

[3] The approach covered in section 14.2.2 assumes that, to be effective, company processes and structures must be aligned with a number of contingency factors. Thus, although the contingency approach may not be explicitly prescriptive, it implicitly is most certainly so. Generally, neoclassical economics, contingency theory, and neo-institutional theory highlight the effectiveness of organizational adaptation to organizational contexts.

The studies reviewed in the previous section point to the existence of several contextual and contingency factors affecting both the practice and effectiveness of recruitment. Some of these contingencies have already been highlighted above, first and foremost sectoral or industry moderators. The following section expands on this review and adds other studies that have a descriptive focus, examining how the practice of recruitment may be influenced by several contextual variables. Although other contextual variables (such as institutional norms) may be important (Rynes and Cable 2003), organizational attributes and strategies tend to be the variables that have been investigated the most, as shown in Table 14.2.

The most clearly articulated description of the impact of organizational context on recruitment strategy is in Windolf's (1986) seminal article. Windolf proposed five distinct recruitment strategies, which can be placed in a parsimonious two-by-two matrix of contingency variables, as depicted in Fig. 14.2. The two variables, classified as either high or low, are the firm's labor market power and the firm's 'organizational intelligence,' which is defined as the 'capacity of the firm to use professional knowledge, to collect and process information, and to work out complex labour market strategies' (Windolf 1986: 239). In this model, the *innovative* recruitment strategy is concerned with attracting a heterogeneous group of creative applicants, drawing on a wide range of recruitment sources. A second recruitment strategy occupying the same high-high quadrant is the *autonomous* strategy, which starts with a precise definition of the ideal candidate in terms of skills, age, or sex. Therefore, autonomous firms, isolated from labor market

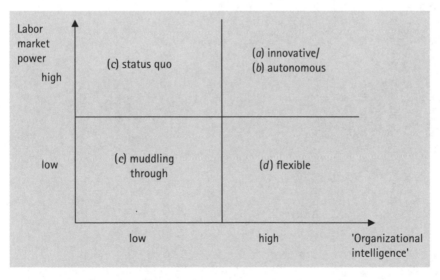

**Fig. 14.2. Windolf's typology of recruitment strategies**
*Source:* Windolf 1986.

**Table 14.2 Summary of previous research investigating contingency effects of/on recruitment practices and strategy**

| Study | Sample | Contextual variables investigated | Independent variables | Dependent variables |
|---|---|---|---|---|
| Windolf (1986) | Case studies of about 75 UK firms, about 85 (West) German firms | 1. Labor market power (environment)<br>2. Organizational intelligence (internal resources)<br>3. Nationality<br>4. Firm size | 1. Labor market power (environment)<br>2. Organizational intelligence (internal resources)<br>3. Technical complexity of product and production process | Recruitment strategies:<br>(a) innovative<br>(b) autonomous<br>(c) status quo<br>(d) flexible<br>(e) muddling through |
| Rynes and Boudreau (1986) | 145 large organizations that engage in campus recruiting | Industry | Organizational characteristics, including perceived competitive advantage, accuracy of communications, importance of recruiter selection, information recorded about colleges, extent to which recruiter informed, etc. | Recruiting practices<br>Perceived recruiting effectiveness |
| Terpstra and Rozell (1993) | 201 US companies with over 200 employees (for a 23% response rate) | Industry | Companies' analysis of recruiting sources for effectiveness in generating high-performance employees | 1. Annual profit<br>2. Profit growth<br>3. Sales growth<br>4. Overall performance |
| Schwan and Soeters (1994) | 4 Dutch organizations (962 vacancies) | Industry<br>Organization type | Organization type (à la Mintzberg) | External versus internal recruitment strategy |
| Koch and McGrath (1996) | 495 US business units (for a 7% response rate) | Industry<br>Capital intensity | Recruitment practices included in 2 of 3 HR indexes:<br>1. HR planning index: staffing plans and evaluation of hiring practices<br>2. Investments in hiring: recruitment intensity and evaluation of recruitment sources | Labor productivity: net sales per employee |

| Study | Sample | Firm characteristics / Industry | Independent variables | Dependent variables |
| --- | --- | --- | --- | --- |
| Rynes et al. (1997) | 251 organizations from population of National Association of Colleges and Employers (for a 21% response rate) | Firm characteristics Industry | 1. Long-term staffing strategies<br>2. Median age of workforce<br>3. Environmental dynamism<br>4. Use of effective recruitment sources (as defined by respondents)<br>5. Competitive offers | Hiring of experienced employees (extent and success) |
| Barber et al. (1999) | 119 small organizations, 184 large organizations (for an overall response rate of 19%) | Firm size (small firms = firms with less than 500 employees; large firms = firms with over 1,000 employees) | Firm size | 1. Recruitment management: (a) Dedicated HR staff (b) Recruiter training<br>2. Recruitment planning and timing<br>3. Recruitment source use<br>4. Metrics of recruitment effectiveness |
| Rao and Drazin (2002) | 588 US mutual fund families | 1. Organizational age<br>2. Organization's external linkages | 1. Organizational age<br>2. Organization's external linkages<br>3. Performance of rivals from which new hires have been recruited<br>4. Size of rival fund family<br>5. Age of rival fund family | 1. Product innovation<br>2. Recruitment of talent from rivals<br>3. Industry tenure of new recruits |
| Williamson and Cable (2003) | 505 firms from various Fortune datasets | 1. Board interlocks (network ties)<br>2. Number of other firms hiring from source firm (frequency-based imitation)<br>3. Size of other firms hiring (trait-based imitation) | 1. Board interlocks (network ties)<br>2. Number of other firms hiring from source firm (frequency-based imitation) | Sources of an employer's top management team hires in 1990–4 (organizational hiring patterns) |

(continued)

**Table 14.2 (continued)**

| Study | Sample | Contextual variables investigated | Independent variables | Dependent variables |
|---|---|---|---|---|
| | | 4. Financial performance of other firms hiring from source firm (outcome-based imitation)<br>5. Industry<br>6. Organization size<br>7. Source prestige<br>8. Source ROA | 3. Size of other firms hiring (trait-based imitation)<br>4. Financial performance of other firms hiring from source firm (outcome-based imitation)<br>5. Industry<br>6. Organization size<br>7. Source prestige<br>8. Source ROA | |
| Collins and Han (2004) | 99 companies recruiting on US campuses (response rate of 43%) | 1. Corporate advertising<br>2. Firm reputation | 1. Early recruitment practices: High- vs. low-involvement strategies<br>2. Corporate advertising<br>3. Firm reputation | Applicant pool quantity and quality |
| Gardner (2005) | 661 US software firms (response rate of 73%) | 1. Product–market overlap<br>2. Locality of labor market<br>3. Value of human capital<br>4. Transferability of targeted human capital<br>5. Interaction of value and human capital | 1. Degree of threat (poaching)<br>2. Locality of hiring firm outside the target firm's local labor market<br>3. Value of human capital | Retaliatory-defensive recruitment activities (as part of a larger set of retaliatory-defensive reactions to poaching) |

fluctuations, tend to use narrow and specific recruitment channels (either the Job Centre or professional journals and newspapers). As innovative and autonomous firms do not differ with respect to labor market power and organizational intelligence, Windolf invokes a third variable, the technical complexity of the product and the production process, to differentiate these two recruitment strategies. According to Windolf, innovative recruitment strategies are more appropriate for organizations scoring high in technical complexity, while autonomous strategies fit with relatively low levels of technical complexity.

The three remaining recruitment strategies occupy the other three quadrants. The *status quo* strategy is focused on attracting a homogeneous set of applicants, especially as far as demographics and socio-economic status are concerned, and, thus, deliberately relies on social networks and referrals. In status quo firms, even changes in technology or job requirements will not change recruitment practices. Status quo firms are characterized by low organizational intelligence and high labor market power and have a traditional, or conservative, strategic stance rather than an innovative one or one defined by scientific management (which is characteristic of *autonomous* recruitment). *Flexible* recruitment strategies are adopted by firms with weak market positions, thus being forced to adapt to changing environmental conditions. Strategic control is typically well thought out and centralized in these firms which have low market power (e.g. because of low wages or unpleasant working conditions) yet high organizational intelligence. *Muddling-through* recruiters, located in the low-low quadrant, draw on less strategic thinking or professional expertise than flexible employers. Their recruitment and selection techniques are often unsophisticated. Therefore, *muddling-through* firms generally have higher employee turnover than firms located in the other quadrants.

Empirically, Windolf (1986) examined the differential use of recruitment channels for firms located in the four quadrants of his typology. For unskilled workers, status quo firms clearly relied most on social networks to attract new employees (53 percent); for white-collar workers, innovative/autonomous firms and status quo firms equally relied on social networks (45 and 44 percent, respectively). This set of findings, inconsistent with the typology, can be explained by the fact that autonomous firms are typically very large and embedded in vast personnel networks, which in turn may be used to reinforce a sense of community. Overall, Windolf's study shows that the reliance on internal labor markets for recruiting is typically a function of increasing organizational size and geographic location (West Germany vs. UK).

Another European study confirmed the impact of (Mintzbergian) organization type on internal versus external recruitment strategies. Schwan and Soeters (1994) conceptualized organizational boundary crossing as vacancy-filling and connected it to overarching organizational strategies and configurations. The four cases they investigated were generally consistent with the authors' expectation that in 'machine bureaucracies,' internal recruitment would be more frequent than external recruitment. In the production plant studied, a private sector machine bureaucracy, 78 percent of positions were filled internally. Similarly, in the social security office, a public sector machine bureaucracy, 66 percent of all positions were filled through internal recruitment. In contrast, the two types of professional bureaucracies, an accounting firm and a hospital, relied more on external recruitment (used as vacancy-filling method for 76 percent and 64 percent of open positions, respectively). So, to some extent, this empirical analysis showed internal versus external recruitment to be dependent on configurational types of organization. However, Schwan and Soeters also provided cross-type generalizations in that new positions tended to be filled through external recruitment channels (except in the hospital). Similarly, when labor turnover was high, external recruitment was the generally preferred method in the three-year study period.

Unsurprisingly, Schwan and Soeters's (1994) study confirms previous findings from econometric studies, which have highlighted the interdependence between labor market conditions and recruitment strategies. For example, Hanssens and Levien (1983) showed that in times of tight labor supply, organizations are forced to use more expensive and intensive recruitment methods. Earlier studies also demonstrated that tight labor supply often causes organizations to cast a wider geographic net in recruitment (Malm 1955) or reduce hiring standards (Thurow 1975). Hence, the research reviewed so far clearly suggests that recruitment strategy is influenced by broader strategic and environmental contingencies.

Less theoretically grounded, but statistically more sophisticated research has highlighted the importance of considering other contextual factors. Rynes et al. (1997) showed that greater focus on the recruitment of experienced employees (i.e. individuals with two or more years of post-college work experience) was associated with greater organizational growth, a short-term focus in staffing strategies, older current employees, and less dynamic environments. Unlike Rynes et al. (1997), who did not find statistically significant associations for firm size, Barber and her colleagues showed how firm size affected a range of recruitment practices, including number of recruitment sources, planning, and timing, as well as recruiter training (Barber et al. 1999). One of the most interesting of their findings was that smaller firms were slightly more likely to use internal recruitment sources (employee referrals and networking). Conversely, larger firms were less likely to use external agencies and advertising in their recruitment. Instead, large firms were far more likely to rely on campus recruiting than small firms.

It is important to note that the *existence* of these contextual influences does not allow us to draw any conclusions about the *effectiveness* of considering a variety of organizational contingencies in recruitment practice. In fact, there is a dearth of research investigating the effectiveness of fit between recruitment strategies and features of the environment. The little, inconclusive evidence we do have is generally based on survey respondents' perceptions of recruitment success. For example, Rynes and her colleagues (1997) found very few organizational factors related to the success of recruitment (of experienced employees)—only the use of effective sources[4] (where effectiveness of source use was defined by one respondent within each firm), median employee age, and relatively high salary offers. In addition, Barber and her colleagues (1999) found evidence that organizational size affected firms' definitions of recruitment success. Compared to small firms, relatively large firms were more likely to invoke goal attainment (i.e. meeting of preset organizational goals in their recruitment efforts—whatever these goals were) and less likely to use new hire performance or retention as metrics that define recruitment effectiveness. Thus, any future theory of the context dependence of recruitment strategy must not only pay tribute to the wide variety of contingency factors, but also to the fact that different organizations may define recruitment success differently, which invariably adds conceptual complexity.

Focusing on the organization-level consequences of recruitment activities, two studies (which have already been reviewed in section 14.2.1) examined the impact of industry context from a slightly different contingency perspective. First, Terpstra and Rozell (1993) showed that, in manufacturing firms, the systematic evaluation of recruiting sources was related to annual profitability, but not to other organizational performance measures. In service firms, organizations' systematic evaluation of recruitment was associated with sales growth and overall performance, whereas in wholesale/retail firms recruitment evaluation was shown to have a large impact on profitability and overall performance. In financial companies, no statistically significant effect was found for any of the four observed organizational performance criteria. In sum, Terpstra and Rozell found that the systematic evaluation of organizational recruiting practices may not matter across the board, but is most likely moderated by several industry contingencies. Second, Koch and McGrath (1996) showed how the capital intensity of a firm might positively interact with HR (including recruitment) planning to bring about greater labor productivity. That is, recruitment planning and assessment were more important in capital-intensive industries, possibly because any labor effect may be leveraged by costly capital assets (for which Koch and McGrath derived an economic proof in the appendix of their article).

Another study shows that industry effects are not the only contextual factors affecting recruitment. Analyzing the recruitment of top managers, Williamson and Cable (2003) drew on social contagion and institutional theory to demonstrate that firms' network ties, the number of other firms hiring from the source firm, and the organizational size of those other firms affected top-management hiring patterns.

---

[4] Respondents were asked questions about nine recruitment sources (listed in decreasing order of perceived effectiveness): informal referrals, newspaper ads, private search firms, formal referrals from other companies/business units, direct applications, college (alumni) placement services, professional associations, temp agencies, and on-line recruitment. Today, this last source perceived to be least effective in the mid-1990s would presumably be seen as much more useful with the rapid spread of the Internet.

In general, the study suggests that, descriptively, institutional determinants often accompany rational influences—in recruitment as much as in other areas of HRM (see, e.g., Gooderham et al. 1999). Specifically, firms were more likely to recruit top managers from other firms with which they shared network ties. Mimetic iso-morphism shaped recruitment activities, with previous hiring and other firms' size being more important predictors of top management recruiting than other firms' financial performance, that is, outcome imitation. Unfortunately, because the authors only reported unstandardized regression coefficients, the magnitude of the different effect sizes found cannot be compared directly. Also, future research will have to investigate whether these institutional influences are also prescriptively meaningful (that is, have an impact on either recruitment or organizational effectiveness of top managers *and* other employee groups) and morally defensible.[5]

Sometimes, the lack of generalizability of direct effects presents an impetus for the search for moderator, contingency, or interaction effects. In an interesting study which has already been discussed above, Collins and Han (2004) found strong support for the hypothesis that low-involvement recruitment practices (i.e. general recruitment ads and company sponsorships of scholarships, etc.) only mattered when applicants were not aware of firm image, that is, when companies had not previously invested in advertising or reputation enhancement. Conversely, there was also strong evidence that high-involvement practices (i.e. detailed recruitment ads and employee endorsements) only mattered when a company had already established awareness of itself through company advertising or reputation. In combination, these two findings indicate that company advertising and reputation represent contingency factors in the organizational context shaping recruitment strategies.

Other interesting research connects recruitment to competitive strategy. Rao and Drazin (2002) found that young and poorly connected investment fund firms may use recruitment from competitors as a strategic response to their lack of product innovation. To some extent, this response in hiring new talent makes strategic sense because external recruitment of talent generally was shown to be associated with investment funds' greater product innovation. When firms were particularly isolated, the effects of recruitment on product innovation were more pronounced. All in all, this study shows that recruitment can be used as a strategic response to overcome organizational resource constraints.

In a related vein, Gardner's (2005) study showed that poaching of talent by competitors may often set in motion retaliatory-defensive strategy dynamics. Results showed that recruitment by competitors outside the target firm's local

---

[5] The existence of these environmental-institutional factors does not imply researchers or managers can use this evidence to justify hiring patterns that reduce employee diversity and may even constitute prima facie evidence of discrimination against network outsiders. That is, the ethical implications of Williamson and Cable's (2003) findings must be scrutinized.

labor market, as well as the value and transferability of human capital, exacerbated retaliatory-defensive actions. Contrary to predictions, however, overlapping product markets were not significantly associated with retaliatory-defensive recruiting actions. Probably the most interesting finding was the interaction between the value and transferability of human capital. When both are high, the likelihood of defensive retaliation (e.g. retaliatory recruitment of employees from previous 'poacher') increased dramatically. On the other hand, when human capital is non-transferable, its value did not make a difference in defensive retaliation (compared to no response). This study suggests that recruitment can represent, in a broad repertoire of organizational actions, an activity that is used to defend against, or retaliate for, talent raiding—in particular when other companies' 'poaching' involves highly transferable and valuable employee skills.

In summary, this review of the literature on recruitment strategy shows that there is little consensus on the meaning of the term. Definitions and contexts of recruitment strategy vary widely, so that not a lot of knowledge has been accumulated—despite many commendable attempts to heed Rynes and Barber's (1990) call for elevating the level of analysis from the individual to the organization. Although the direct effects of recruitment practices are either non-generalizable, modest in size, or uncertain in terms of causal attribution (Rynes 1991; Rynes and Cable 2003), research has made major advances in identifying organization-level contingencies of recruitment. However, as long as there is no generally accepted typology of recruitment strategies, it is difficult to determine the theoretical importance of these empirically verified contingencies.

# 14.3 IMPLICATIONS OF THE RECRUITMENT STRATEGY LITERATURE

The lack of theoretical integration points to needed trajectories for future theory development, research, and management policy. Future research could ameliorate the lack of solid knowledge, which is due to three root causes: insufficient theoretical development, little organization-level prescriptive research, and the academic–practitioner gap (see also Taylor and Collins 2000).

## 14.3.1 Future Theory Development

More sophisticated theory development is required to clarify the dimensions of recruitment strategy. One obvious dimension is internal versus external recruitment, which is supported by two seminal European, small-$n$ studies of recruitment strategy (Schwan and Soeters 1994; Windolf 1986). Barber's (1998: 6–13) five 'dimensions of recruitment' are not so much dimensions of recruitment strategy as a unifying framework for categorizing both individual- and organization-level research on recruitment or assessing the state of knowledge. The dimensions or categories are actors (applicants, organization, organizational agents, and outsiders), activities, outcomes, context, and phases. As no study can focus on all five dimensions, Barber (1998) used the last dimension, recruitment phases, in her detailed overview of the recruitment literature. However, to advance recruitment research further, recruitment scholars need to develop a comprehensive, theoretically coherent, and succinct model of recruitment strategies. Such a model could then be used to circumscribe more definitively our knowledge of *how* and *why* recruitment works.

Whereas Barber's (1998) framework may be too broad to be useful as defining the dimensions of recruitment strategy, an earlier framework (namely, Rynes and Barber 1990) might need more detailed conceptual development. Rynes and Barber's model broadly conceptualized applicant attraction strategies as comprising (1) recruitment, (2) targeting different applicant pools (i.e. non-traditional applicants or less-qualified applicants), and (3) pecuniary and non-pecuniary inducements. Thus, in a way, this model anticipated Boxall and Purcell's (2003: 141) concern that Windolf's (1986) typology omitted inducements as a key dimension of recruitment strategy. Within the first 'strategy,' Rynes and Barber mention elements of recruitment (namely, organizational actors, messages, sources, timing), but not really strategies that explicitly differentiate one firm from another economically. Also, the distinction between 'strategies' (1) and (2) may be helpful from an expositional perspective, but it is not entirely clear why HR directors would not think about recruitment strategy and applicant pools simultaneously. That is, changes in (1) typically result in changes in (2), and (2) might in fact be conceptually subsumed under (1).

There is no dearth of approaches from which theoretical inspiration may emerge, and some approaches may be more fruitful avenues to pursue than others. Although the resource-based view of the firm (RBV) is currently one of the most popular theories among HR scholars, it may have a number of theory-inherent flaws, as discussed before. In addition, because recruitment is an HR function that is situated at the boundary between labor markets and organizations, a primarily internal theory of organizational advantage and competitiveness, such as the RBV, may not be as useful for clarifying causalities as theories that focus on the market/organization boundary. Kaufman's (2004) argument that transaction cost economics promises theoretical traction might be particularly applicable to the HR function of recruitment. Related theoretical work has been advanced by Lepak and Snell (1999), who integrate transaction cost economics with the RBV and human capital theory to build a typology of organizations' HR configurations.

Economic theories may help us determine under what conditions internal recruitment or external recruitment matter more. However, they may also leave out important considerations of cognitive-psychological processes, communication, and language in social systems (Boje et al. 2004; Luhmann 1995). Because an effective recruitment strategy would, most likely, have to create language-based mental models of 'employer of choice' (see, e.g., Allen et al. 2004), greater focus on sociological-linguistic theories may be important in the future to build micro–macro theory bridges. Prescriptively, we must study which features of recruitment communications have the greatest organizational impact. At the same time, we must descriptively examine how line managers and HR professionals actually make decisions about the aforementioned five central questions related to recruitment strategy (Breaugh 1992; Breaugh and Starke 2000; Rynes and Cable 2003).

## 14.3.2 Future Empirical Research

Recruitment researchers must work toward greater accumulation of knowledge. In most cases this will mean more empirical replications must be performed (Tsang and Kwan 1999), which generally are not valued as much in academic circles as completely new research. Unfortunately, the academic obsession with empirical and theoretical novelty may stunt paradigm development (Donaldson 1995; Pfeffer 1993). With more cumulative research, we could examine empirically how much the findings vary across samples and study settings and whether such variability is due to sampling error, measurement error, and a variety of other study artifacts rather than theoretically important contingency factors (Hunter and Schmidt 2004). Because of the lack of cumulative knowledge (Rynes 1991; Rynes and Cable 2003), the only recruitment-related studies that integratively investigated mediators, moderators, and artifacts were four meta-analyses on realistic job previews (McEvoy and Cascio 1985; Phillips 1998; Premack and Wanous 1985; Reilly et al. 1979). Ultimately, similar meta-analyses will be required on other organization-level determinants and outcomes of recruitment strategies, but they can only happen if empirical knowledge is generated cumulatively. To facilitate this cumulative knowledge growth, more programmatic recruitment research will be necessary (cf. Berger et al. 2005).

Future empirical research must also address the dramatic changes in organizational recruitment practices (Rynes and Cable 2003; Taylor and Collins 2000). For example, the Internet may present opportunities *and* threats for organizational recruitment (Cappelli 2001). Although there have been some early, fairly sophisticated studies from the perspective of web applicants (e.g. Dineen et al. 2002), research on the use and usefulness from the organization's perspective should be conducted with the same methodological rigor as this individual-level research. Moreover, organization-level research on Internet recruitment should add a prescriptive angle to its so far more descriptive research questions (e.g. Backhaus 2004). Future research should examine to what extent innovative recruitment practices are in fact related to recruiting effectiveness and organizational effectiveness. Most importantly, although there is an integrative organization-level model of broad applicant attraction strategies (i.e. Rynes and Barber 1990), its propositions have largely remained untested (Barber 1998; Taylor and Collins 2000). In addition, Rynes and Cable (2003: 70–2) have suggested many other fruitful areas for future research, covering a wide variety of topics ranging from recruitment sources to organizational characteristics to various recruitment-related processes. Many of these proposed research questions will affect recruitment strategy.

Any empirical investigation of the contribution of recruitment to strategic HRM and overall organizational effectiveness requires simultaneous attention to the multidimensionality of effectiveness (Boxall and Purcell 2003), organizational contingencies, and such general workplace trends as the demise of internal labor markets (Cappelli 1999, 2000). To evaluate the effectiveness of recruitment, researchers should not only examine its cost effectiveness and effects on labor productivity. Rather, recruitment, like other HR functions, can also serve the purpose of greater organizational flexibility (Boxall and Purcell 2003; Wright and Snell 1998). Finally, social legitimacy and corporate social performance should not only be treated as antecedents of recruitment success, but should also be investigated as possible outcomes of recruitment (Orlitzky and Swanson in press).

## 14.3.3 IMPLICATIONS FOR MANAGEMENT PRACTICE

For practitioners, there is little evidence about any generalizable 'best practice' takeaway from the recruitment literature. Staffing professionals at many large companies such as DuPont seem to have realized this a long time ago (see, for example, an HR executive expressing the sentiment that 'there is no best way to recruit new employees' in Breaugh 1992: 39). Even positive effects of recruitment practices that logically should be superior to their alternatives, such as realistic job previews, have been found to be either inconsistent across studies or only modest in magnitude (in the meta-analyses cited above). At the organizational level, prescriptions that are seemingly sensible across the board, such as maximizing applicant pools, may have to be qualified because any apparent benefits must be weighed against their costs. In turn, benefits and costs depend on a number of contextual influences or contingencies. High recruitment intensity, for example, might be one of the myths that should not be implemented uncritically by organizations (see Breaugh 1992: 12–13 for other examples of such questionable assumptions). The only generalizable advice in which we can have fairly high confidence comes from individual-level research (not reviewed in this chapter): recruiters that possess greater interpersonal skills and warmth seem to be an important reason why applicants decide to accept job offers (Barber 1998; Taylor and Collins 2000).

Reviewers of the recruitment literature usually bemoan the fact that academic research has had little relevance for recruiting practice (Breaugh and Starke 2000; Rynes 1991; Rynes and Cable 2003). Relevance might be enhanced by more attention to prescriptive organization-level issues and processes (Rynes and Cable 2003; Taylor and Collins 2000), and also a cross-disciplinary widening of the research lens. Practitioners need knowledge that is not narrowly defined by disciplinary boundaries. Particularly informative for practice would be studies by research teams that rely on cross-disciplinary and practitioner–academic dialogues (see also Rynes et al. 2001). This way, researchers could discern whether practitioners believe the dramatic changes in labor markets and organizations over the last decade (Cappelli 1999) are here to stay—and what important questions these changes may raise with respect to recruitment and recruitment strategy. As mentioned before, what is regarded as one of the most sophisticated approaches to the evaluation of recruitment strategy by scholars, namely utility analysis (cf. Barber 1998: 128), may be ignored or even rejected by practitioners (Latham and Whyte 1994). The use of cross-disciplinary research teams would most likely highlight the need for parsimony and simplicity counterbalancing the ever increasing complexity of academic frameworks.

# 14.4 CONCLUSION

This review has shown the context dependence and contingent nature of recruitment practices. The studies seem to suggest that whatever works for one organization may not work for others in terms of recruitment strategy. The chapter structure reflected the tension between possible 'best practice' principles (section 14.2.1) and contingency factors (section 14.2.2). As it shows, there are unlikely to be any recruitment practices that will always 'work' or matter. Instead, some of the best recruitment research has shown that the adoption of recruitment strategies may depend on the hiring practices of other firms, labor market conditions, and industry context, among other variables.

However, this conclusion about the existence of several contingency effects (as shown in Table 14.2) may have to be qualified by two caveats. First, study artifacts (e.g. sampling error) may mask generalizable effects. Second, the mere existence of contingencies does not prove the superiority of a contingency approach to recruitment. Only psychometric meta-analysis can investigate the former caveat about study artifacts, but a future meta-analysis in recruitment requires a research program whose theoretical foundation is less piecemeal than recruitment research so far. The second caveat requires a more in-depth examination of the causal mechanisms linking recruitment, its prehire outcomes, and posthire consequences. Broad strategic HR frameworks that have integrated a variety of theories (e.g. Lepak and Snell 1999; Wright and Snell 1998) may be valuable starting points for the development of theoretically persuasive research programs in recruitment. The first step in that direction would be the development of a parsimonious model of recruitment strategy whose effectiveness criteria are theoretically connected to these broader strategic HR frameworks. Without a comprehensive yet parsimonious typology and theory of recruitment strategy, academics and practitioners will not have any criteria by which to judge the effectiveness of new activities such as Internet recruiting.

## References

ALLEN, D. G., VAN SCOTTER, J. R., and OTONDO, R. F. (2004). 'Recruitment Communication Media: Impact on Prehire Outcomes.' *Personnel Psychology*, 57/1: 143–71.

BACKHAUS, K. B. (2004). 'An Exploration of Corporate Recruitment Descriptions on Monster.Com.' *Journal of Business Communication*, 41/2: 115–36.

BARBER, A. E. (1998). *Recruiting Employees: Individual and Organizational Perspectives*. Thousand Oaks, Calif.: Sage.

—— WESSON, M. J., ROBERSON, Q. M., and TAYLOR, M. S. (1999). 'A Tale of Two Job Markets: Organizational Size and its Effects on Hiring Practices and Job Search Behavior.' *Personnel Psychology*, 52: 841–67.

BARNEY, J., and WRIGHT, P. M. (1998). 'On Becoming a Strategic Partner: The Role of Human Resources in Gaining Competitive Advantage.' *Human Resource Management*, 37/1: 31–46.

BECKER, B. E., and HUSELID, M. A. (1998). 'High Performance Work Systems and Firm Performance: A Synthesis of Research and Managerial Implications.' *Research in Personnel and Human Resources Management*, 16: 53–101.

BERGER, J., WILLER, D., and ZELDITCH, M. (2005). 'Theory Programs and Theoretical Problems.' *Sociological Theory*, 23/2: 127–55.

BOJE, D. M., OSWICK, C., and FORD, J. D. (2004). 'Language and Organization: The Doing of Discourse.' *Academy of Management Review*, 29/4: 571–7.

BOUDREAU, J. W. (1991). 'Utility Analysis for Decisions in Human Resource Management.' In M. D. Dunnette and L. M. Hough (eds.), *Handbook of Industrial and Organizational Psychology*, vol. ii. Palo Alto, Calif.: Consulting Psychologists Press.

—— and RYNES, S. L. (1985). 'Role of Recruitment in Staffing Utility Analysis.' *Journal of Applied Psychology*, 70/2: 354–66.

BOXALL, P., and PURCELL, J. (2003). *Strategy and Human Resource Management.* New York: Palgrave Macmillan.

BREAUGH, J. A. (1992). *Recruitment: Science and Practice.* Boston: PWS-Kent.

—— and STARKE, M. (2000). 'Research on Employee Recruitment: So Many Studies, So Many Remaining Questions.' *Journal of Management,* 26/3: 405–34.

CAPPELLI, P. (1999). *The New Deal at Work: Managing the Market-Driven Workforce.* Cambridge, Mass.: Harvard Business School Press.

—— (2000). 'A Market-Driven Approach to Retaining Talent.' *Harvard Business Review,* 78/1: 103–11.

—— (2001). 'Making the Most of On-Line Recruiting.' *Harvard Business Review,* 79/3: 139–46.

CARLSON, K. D., CONNERLEY, M. L., and MECHAM, R. L. (2002). 'Recruitment Evaluation: The Case for Assessing the Quality of Applicants Attracted.' *Personnel Psychology,* 55: 461–90.

COLBERT, B. A. (2004). 'The Complex Resource-Based View: Implications for Theory and Practice in Strategic Human Resource Management.' *Academy of Management Review,* 29/3: 341–58.

COLLINS, C. J., and HAN, J. (2004). 'Exploring Applicant Pool Quantity and Quality: The Effects of Early Recruitment Practice Strategies, Corporate Advertising, and Firm Reputation.' *Personnel Psychology,* 57/3: 658–717.

—— —— and STEVENS, C. K. (2002). 'The Relationship between Early Recruitment-Related Activities and the Application Decisions of New Labor-Market Entrants: A Brand Equity Approach to Recruitment.' *Journal of Applied Psychology,* 87: 1121–33.

DELANEY, J. T., and HUSELID, M. A. (1996). 'The Impact of Human Resource Management Practice on Perceptions of Organizational Performance.' *Academy of Management Journal,* 39: 949–69.

DINEEN, B. R., ASH, S. R., and NOE, R. A. (2002). 'A Web of Applicant Attraction: Person–Organization Fit in the Context of Web-Based Recruitment.' *Journal of Applied Psychology,* 87/4: 723–34.

DONALDSON, L. (1995). *American Anti-Management Theories of Organization: A Critique of Paradigm Proliferation.* Cambridge: Cambridge University Press.

GARDNER, T. M. (2005). 'Interfirm Competition for Human Resources: Evidence from the Software Industry.' *Academy of Management Journal,* 48/2: 237–56.

GATEWOOD, R. D., GOWAN, M. A., and LAUTENSCHLAGER, G. J. (1993). 'Corporate Image, Recruitment Image, and Initial Job Choice Decisions.' *Academy of Management Journal,* 36/2: 414–27.

GOODERHAM, P. N., NORDHAUG, O., and RINGDAL, K. (1999). 'Institutional and Rational Determinants of Organizational Practices: Human Resource Management in European Firms.' *Administrative Science Quarterly,* 44: 507–31.

HANSSENS, D. M., and LEVIEN, H. A. (1983). 'An Econometric Study of Recruitment Marketing in the U.S. Navy.' *Management Science,* 29/10: 1167–84.

HUNTER, J. E., and SCHMIDT, F. L. (2004). *Methods of Meta-analysis: Correcting Error and Bias in Research Findings.* Thousand Oaks, Calif.: Sage.

HUSELID, M. A. (1995). 'The Impact of Human Resource Management Practices on Turnover, Productivity, and Corporate Financial Performance.' *Academy of Management Journal,* 38: 635–72.

KAUFMAN, B. E. (2004). 'Toward an Integrative Theory of Human Resource Management.' In B. E. Kaufman (ed.), *Theoretical Perspectives on Work and the Employment Relationship.* Champaign, Ill: Industrial Relations Research Association.

Koch, M. J., and McGrath, R. G. (1996). 'Improving Labor Productivity: Human Resource Management Policies Do Matter.' *Strategic Management Journal*, 17: 335–54.

Latham, G. P., and Whyte, G. (1994). 'The Futility of Utility Analysis.' *Personnel Psychology*, 47: 31–46.

Lepak, D. P., and Snell, S. A. (1999). 'The Human Resource Architecture: Toward a Theory of Human Capital Allocation and Development.' *Academy of Management Review*, 24: 31–48.

Luhmann, N. (1995). *Social Systems*. Stanford, Calif: Stanford University Press.

McEvoy, G. M., and Cascio, W. F. (1985). 'Strategies for Reducing Employee Turnover: A Meta-analysis.' *Journal of Applied Psychology*, 70: 342–53.

Malm, F. T. (1955). 'Hiring Procedures and Selection Standards in the San Francisco Bay Area.' *Industrial Labor Relations Review*, 8: 231–52.

Orlitzky, M., and Swanson, D. (in press). 'Socially Responsible Human Resource Management: Charting New Territory.' In J. R. Deckop (ed.), *Human Resource Management Ethics*. Greenwich, Conn.: Information Age Publishing.

Pfeffer, J. (1993). 'Barriers to the Advance of Organizational Science: Paradigm Development as a Dependent Variable.' *Academy of Management Review*, 18/4: 599–620.

—— (1998). *The Human Equation: Building Profits by Putting People First*. Boston: Harvard Business School Press.

Phillips, J. M. (1998). 'Effects of Realistic Job Previews on Multiple Organizational Outcomes: A Meta-analysis.' *Academy of Management Journal*, 41: 673–90.

Powell, T. C. (2001). 'Competitive Advantage: Logical and Philosophical Considerations.' *Strategic Management Journal*, 22: 875–88.

Premack, S. L., and Wanous, J. P. (1985). 'A Meta-analysis of Realistic Job Preview Experiments.' *Journal of Applied Psychology*, 70: 706–19.

Priem, R. L., and Butler, J. E. (2001). 'Is the Resource-Based "View" a Useful Perspective for Strategic Management Research?' *Academy of Management Review*, 26: 22–40.

Rao, H., and Drazin, R. (2002). 'Overcoming Resource Constraints on Product Innovation by Recruiting Talent from Rivals: A Study of the Mutual Fund Industry, 1986–94.' *Academy of Management Journal*, 45/3: 491–507.

Reilly, R. R., Brown, B., Blood, M. R., and Malatesta, C. Z. (1979). 'The Effects of Realistic Previews: A Study and Discussion of the Literature.' *Personnel Psychology*, 34: 823–34.

Rynes, S. L. (1991). 'Recruitment, Job Choice, and Post-Hire Consequences: A Call for New Research Directions.' In M. D. Dunnette and L. M. Hough (eds.), *Handbook of Industrial and Organizational Psychology*, vol. ii. Palo Alto, Calif.: Consulting Psychologists Press.

—— and Barber, A. E. (1990). 'Applicant Attraction Strategies: An Organizational Perspective.' *Academy of Management Review*, 15: 286–310.

—— and Boudreau, J. (1986). 'College Recniting in Large Organizations: Practice, Graluation, and Research Implications.' *Personal Psychology*, 39: 729–57.

—— and Cable, D. M. (2003). 'Recruitment Research in the Twenty-First Century.' In W. Borman, D. R. Ilgen, and R. Klimoski (eds.), *Handbook of Psychology, Industrial and Organizational Psychology*, vol. xii. New York: Wiley.

—— Orlitzky, M., and Bretz, R. D., Jr. (1997). 'Experienced Hiring Versus College Recruiting: Practices and Emerging Trends.' *Personnel Psychology*, 50: 309–39.

—— Bartunek, J. M., and Daft, R. L. (2001). 'Across the Great Divide: Knowledge Creation and Transfer between Practitioners and Academics.' *Academy of Management Journal*, 44/2: 340–55.

SCHWAN, R., and SOETERS, J. (1994). 'The Strategy of Vacancy-Filling from Internal and External Labor Market Sources: An Empirical Assessment of the Recruitment Strategy of Different Types of Organization.' *Scandinavian Journal of Management*, 10/1: 69–85.

TAYLOR, M. S., and COLLINS, C. (2000). 'Organizational Recruitment: Enhancing the Intersection of Research and Practice.' In C. Cooper and E. A. Locke (eds.), *Industrial and Organizational Psychology*. Oxford: Blackwell.

TERPSTRA, D. E., and ROZELL, E. J. (1993). 'The Relationship of Staffing Practices to Organizational Level Measures of Performance.' *Personnel Psychology*, 46: 27–48.

THUROW, L. (1975). *Generating Inequality*. New York: Basic.

TRANK, C. Q., RYNES, S. L., and BRETZ, R. D., Jr. (2002). 'Attracting Applicants in the War for Talent: Differences in Work Preferences among High Achievers.' *Journal of Business & Psychology*, 16/3: 331–45.

TSANG, E. W. K., and KWAN, K.-M. (1999). 'Replication and Theory Development in Organizational Science: A Critical Realist Perspective.' *Academy of Management Review*, 24/4: 759–80.

TURBAN, D. B., and CABLE, D. M. (2003). 'Firm Reputation and Applicant Pool Characteristics.' *Journal of Organizational Behavior*, 24/6: 733–51.

—— and GREENING, D. W. (1996). 'Corporate Social Performance and Organizational Attractiveness to Prospective Employees.' *Academy of Management Journal*, 40/3: 658–72.

WILLIAMS, M. L., and DREHER, G. F. (1992). 'Compensation System Attributes and Applicant Pool Characteristics.' *Academy of Management Journal*, 35: 571–95.

WILLIAMSON, I. O., and CABLE, D. M. (2003). 'Organizational Hiring Patterns, Interfirm Network Ties, and Interorganizational Imitation.' *Academy of Management Journal*, 46: 349–58.

WINDOLF, P. (1986). 'Recruitment, Selection, and Internal Labour Markets in Britain and Germany.' *Organization Studies*, 7/3: 235–54.

WRIGHT, P. M., and MCMAHAN, G. C. (1992). 'Theoretical Perspectives for Strategic Human Resource Management.' *Journal of Management*, 18/2: 295–320.

—— and SNELL, S. A. (1998). 'Toward a Unifying Framework for Exploring Fit and Flexibility in Strategic Human Resource Management.' *Academy of Management Review*, 23: 756–72.

# CHAPTER 15

# SELECTION DECISION-MAKING

NEAL SCHMITT

BRIAN KIM

## 15.1 INTRODUCTION

CERTAINLY, one of the most important sets of decisions an organization makes is the decision to employ personnel. All aspects of an organization's activities are directed and enacted by the people that comprise the organization. It is also not the case that just any person's activity will optimize organizational functioning. Nearly a century of work on the use of various employment procedures has documented that there are substantial individual differences in job performance and that the use of good selection procedures results in the employment of better performing individuals (Schmidt and Hunter 1998) and greater practical utility for organizations (Boudreau and Ramstad 2003).

## 15.2 METHODS USED

Probably the most extensive set of published data on the use of various methods by which firms in different countries make decisions is provided by Ryan et al. (1999).

Nine hundred and fifty-nine firms in twenty different countries responded to their survey on the manner in which hiring decisions are made. Extensive use of interviews was reported in all countries ranging from an average of two per applicant to nearly four per applicant in France. Across all countries, these firms reported using just under five test types to evaluate job applicants. Of those who used tests, work samples, medical screens, and cognitive ability tests were most frequently used. Physical ability tests, integrity/honesty tests, video-based tests, projective tests, drug tests, and graphology were infrequently or never used. There were some relatively large differences across countries also; respondents in Japan and Malaysia reported no test use. Firms in all parts of the world report that they often or always use application blanks, educational qualifications, references from previous employers, and, to a somewhat lesser extent, personal references as a means to make decisions about prospective employees. While the Ryan et al. study does provide descriptive data on the methods used and the extent of their use, it does not inform us as to the manner or sequence in which such data are collected. In US companies, it is probably the case that educational qualifications, application letters, and letters of reference are used as initial screens followed by interviews and more formal, quantifiable data collection using tests. However, the use of tests is by no means universal. On average, approximately 30 percent of US organizations indicated using these devices, with a slightly greater use reported across organizations in all countries.

The constructs measured by these various methods are often categorized into 'can do' measures indicating the ability to perform important work tasks and 'will do' measures that reflect a person's motivation or willingness to perform work well. Measures of both sets of constructs prove to be valid predictors of subsequent job performance, as described in the next section.

## 15.2.1 Validity of Methods Used

One common way in which test use is justified is to correlate test scores or other methods of evaluating applicant potential with subsequent measures of job performance. A recent summary of these criterion-related validation studies conducted over an eighty-five-year period has been provided by Schmidt and Hunter (1998). They report average correlations above .50 for general mental ability tests, work sample tests, and structured interviews. The average validity reported for job knowledge tests is .48. Somewhat lower validities are reported for measures of personality constructs such as conscientiousness and integrity and for methods such as job experience measures, unstructured interviews, and reference checks. Assessment centers which include multiple methods of data collection display validities of .37. The manner in which organizations assess criterion-related validity (and the type of study that is the source of the Schmidt and Hunter meta-analytic review) is summarized in the next section of our chapter. Guidelines for validation research and test use in general are provided in the SIOP Principles (2003).

## 15.2.2 Validation of Test Use

The manner in which organizations proceed to develop and validate their selection procedures has followed a relatively well-defined set of steps that is enshrined in scientific (AERA, APA, and NCME 1999; SIOP 2003) and legal guidelines (Uniform Guidelines 1978). This process begins with a job analysis that seeks to define the tasks required of job incumbents and the knowledge, skills, abilities, and other characteristics (KSAOs) required for accomplishing those tasks effectively. Information regarding specific organizational objectives or work conditions that influence the capability of job incumbents to do their jobs is also sought during the job analysis. Armed with this information, selection experts develop or select measures by which they can gauge the effectiveness of applicants who seek to occupy these jobs. After the measurement of applicant KSAOs and their subsequent performance, data regarding KSAOs and job performance measures is correlated to assess the validity of the procedures. This information is also used to inform the implementation of the selection procedures and to determine their worth or utility to the organization. This process has been described in numerous textbooks for decades (e.g. Guion 1998; Ployhart et al. in press; Schmitt and Chan 1998), and the effectiveness of this decision-making process is well documented.

# 15.3 DEVELOPMENTS IN SELECTION DECISION-MAKING

In this chapter we attempt to describe five developments during the last several years that have extended this decision-making model or required adaptations of this model to new circumstances and concerns. The following list comprises this set of 'new' developments. First, increasing attention has been directed towards determining the role of selection practices in overall organizational effectiveness (e.g. Huselid 1995) and the use of selection to further strategic organizational goals (Boudreau and Ramstad 2003). This contrasts with earlier utility models (e.g. Cascio 2000) that aggregated individual impact to assess organizational level impact. Second, much work and writing on personnel selection has reconsidered the criteria against which we validate measures of KSAOs. Campbell and his colleagues (Campbell et al. 1993) proposed a popular, multidimensional perform-ance model, as have Borman and Motowidlo (Motowidlo 2003), who are con-cerned with contextual performance. In addition, Organ (1997) and others have written about citizenship behavior, and Pulakos and colleagues (Pulakos et al. 2000) have investigated adaptive performance. A third area that continues to receive attention both in legal venues and psychological research is affirmative action and its impact on organizations and their members (Aguinis 2004; Bell et al. 2000). Fourth, some small amount of attention is being directed to the consider-ation of how individual differences in the aggregate contribute to organizational effectiveness. This requires that we build and evaluate theories of staffing that link individual, intermediate, and organizational levels (Ployhart 2004; Ployhart and Schneider in press). The need for multilevel theories of job performance and organizational effectiveness is underscored by the increasing use of teams and by research on team composition and effectiveness (e.g. Carpenter et al. 2004). Perhaps spurred in part by the 9/11 tragedy and recent corporate scandals, a fifth topic that organizations have become increasingly concerned about is employee deviance and counterproductivity (Ones 2002).

The traditional selection model outlined at the beginning of this chapter has served organizational researchers well over most of the first century in the appli-cation of personnel selection research. The five issues mentioned above complicate or expand the concerns inherent in this traditional approach to selection decision-making. The remainder of this chapter is devoted to each of these concerns in more detail and the relevant, recent research (primarily studies published since 2000). The concluding section of the chapter outlines the implications for organizations and describes some of the questions that we believe warrant more attention.

## 15.3.1 Selection and Organizational Effectiveness

In the past decade, there has been a growing interest in establishing that selection procedures and the human capital attracted by an organization have an impact on organizational-level outcomes such as profitability and productivity. Studies have also attempted to show what combinations of human resource interventions, as well as other organizational inputs, have such impact. Early approaches that examined the impact of selection decision practices at the organizational level did so in isolation of other human resource (HR) functions (e.g. Terpstra and Rozell 1993). These studies were soon replaced by studies looking at the effect of multiple HR functions (Huselid 1995) and specific combinations of functions, sometimes thought to represent 'high-performance work systems' (Becker and Huselid 1998).

Terpstra and Rozell (1993) reported correlational data supporting the conclusion that organizations using a wide variety of selection procedures (such as interviews, cognitive ability tests, biodata, and the evaluation of recruiting sources) had higher levels of overall performance, annual profit, and growth in profit. Huselid (1995) reported small ($< .10$) correlations between different HR functions and corporate financial performance, and a set of similar studies followed shortly after (Delaney and Huselid 1996; Delery and Doty 1996; Huselid et al. 1997). Wright and Boswell (2002) have provided an informative review of this work. In more recent and more sophisticated work, Hitt et al. (2001) and Batt (2002) examined the degree to which the performance of law firms, as indexed by the ratio of net income to total firm revenue, was influenced by various aspects of human capital. They found a curvilinear relationship between human capital and performance reflecting the fact that the early expenses associated with capturing the best talent only paid off later in the firm's history. They also reported an interaction between human capital and strategy, as reflected in service and geographic diversification. Batt (2002) found that quit rates were lower and sales growth measures were higher in telephone call centers that emphasized high skills, employee participation, teams, high pay, and security.

It is not hard to criticize the methodological rigor of these studies as some have done (Boxall and Purcell 2000; Wright et al. 2001b). Senior-level personnel usually provide responses to single-item measures of HR functioning, sometimes about issues of which they could not be well informed. Questions are often superficial, perhaps resulting from an effort to keep survey instruments short and maximize return rates. Wright et al. (2001b) point out that these measures cannot possibly be very reliable; this lack of reliability may be one reason why the relationship with firm outcomes is often so very low.

Even with the potential limitations of the database on the relationships between HR functions and firm performance, there seems to be consensus on several issues. First, it is not productive to consider HR functions or human capital in isolation of other aspects of the organization or even of the society in which the organization functions. Most representative of this position is the work of Lepak and Snell (2002) who describe configurations of HR activities that are most often associated with particular types of employment modes (i.e. knowledge-based, job-based, contract work, and alliance or partnerships). Second, successful organizations, or systems, must have human capital (knowledge, skills, and abilities, or KSAs), the social capital (internal and external relationships), and organizational capital (processes, technologies, and databases) to be successful. Firms must have the KSAs, but also develop practices that motivate people. This resource-based view (Wright et al. 2001a) and a more theoretical view of firm performance, strategy, and the role of human resources appear to be the direction in which this area of study is now headed. Finally, Wright et al. (2005) show that HR practices are strongly related to future performance as well as past performance. This finding challenges the prevailing assumption that HR practices cause organizational performance rather than the reverse, or that both are caused by some external variable(s).

Third, there is also recognition among selection researchers that multilevel theorizing and research must be motivated by levels of conceptualization and construct operationalization that may involve more than simply aggregating individual-level data. We turn to this specific issue in a later section.

## 15.3.2  Reconceptualization of the Performance Domain

The meaning of job performance has changed throughout the decades, but it has changed radically in recent years. Austin and Villanova (1992) chronicled the early history of job performance concepts, operational definitions, and measures from 1917–92 and noted that a major limitation of the research conducted prior to 1990 was the *criterion problem*. Job performance was often treated too narrowly (i.e. deficient) and sometimes inappropriately when applied to a particular context (i.e. contaminated), with a large focus on the technical aspects of a person's production or service delivery. However, a confluence of events beginning in the late 1980s, including drastic changes to the nature of work in organizations and societal pressures toward fair evaluations of individual effectiveness, fostered the growth of new performance theories that have added structure to an expanding criterion domain.

Largely consistent with emerging theories of job performance (e.g. Borman et al. 1983; Brief and Motowidlo 1986; Organ 1988), Campbell (1990; Campbell et al. 1996) proposed a comprehensive performance model consisting of eight work behavior categories, with (job-specific and non-job-specific) task proficiency and communication task proficiency central to all jobs. He strongly emphasized defining performance in terms of behavior, but limited the domain to behaviors that are relevant to organizational goals. Empirical work from Project A (see Campbell et al. 1990; McCloy et al. 1994; McHenry et al. 1990) supported aspects of the Campbell model, as well as related models like Borman and Motowidlo's (1993) task and contextual performance notions (e.g. Borman et al. 1995; Van Scotter et al. 2000). At the same time, the dimensions proposed by different models have received varying degrees of support (see reviews by Coleman and Borman 2000; Motowidlo 2003; Viswesvaran and Ones 2000). Viswesvaran et al. (2005) recently argued that a single, construct-level factor accounts for 60.3 percent of the variance in performance ratings across the 303 studies in their meta-analysis, but also acknowledge that certain assumptions about true score and error underlie their interpretations. Additionally, the majority of the studies in the Viswesvaran meta-analysis were not guided by the recent conceptual definitions of performance and often did not include measures of the dimensions suggested by Campbell and others.

Part of the impetus for research on non-task performance behaviors, particularly 'citizenship behaviors' (LePine et al. 2002; Organ 1997; Rotundo and Sackett 2002), stems from the adverse impact created against racial minorities by cognitive ability tests (Hough et al. 2001). While research clearly shows that cognitive ability validly predicts overall job performance better than any other single characteristic (Schmidt 2002), some question whether the historical focus on task behaviors as performance (Austin and Villanova 1992) has led to the dubious conclusion that other person characteristics are *necessarily* weaker predictors of all types of performance, especially if one considers citizenship behaviors (Motowidlo et al. 1997). Using personality, biodata, interviews, and other predictors of organizational citizenship (Borman et al. 2001; Organ and Ryan 1995) in conjunction with cognitive ability, researchers have attempted to reduce adverse impact (e.g. Bobko et al. 1999; De Corte 1999; Hattrup et al. 1997; Murphy and Shiarella 1997). Unfortunately, such efforts typically fail to reduce impact by a practically meaningful degree while retaining criterion-related validity (Hough et al. 2001; Sackett et al. 2001).

Still, researchers have studied non-task behaviors in their own right for two different reasons. Regarding extra-role (Van Dyne et al. 1995) and citizenship behaviors (which are distinct; Organ 1997; Rotundo and Sackett 2002), selecting job applicants for these types of behaviors can, in theory, lead to greater organizational effectiveness that is more consistent over time since citizenship supports the environment in which core job tasks are performed, by definition. For instance, employees who are always willing to assist each other can reduce disruptions in the flow of production. The second reason for selecting applicants to perform non-task behaviors is that today's organizations often hold multiple goals (e.g. Oswald et al. 2004; Rotundo and Sackett 2002). The production of raw goods must be balanced with other concerns such as demonstrating corporate responsibility, for example. Counterproductive performance behaviors are also related to organizational interests apart from production or service delivery because they can incur costly damage (Bennett and Robinson 2003; Kelloway et al. 2002). Selecting people who will not engage in absenteeism, theft, sexual harassment, and violence may be critical to effective organizational functioning. Although it is evident that such concerns have existed for years (e.g. most job applications request statements about applicants' past criminal records), selection theories and practices are now explicitly linking these goals to individual employee requirements.

Recent notions of performance have also gained depth and complexity with the inclusion of a time dimension. Theories about adaptive work behaviors attempt to explain how people can perform well in new or continually changing contexts (e.g. Pulakos et al. 2000) and why the rank order of individuals might change with experience (Viswesvaran and Ones 2000). The selection of adaptive employees is also gaining usefulness as organizations abandon formal job structures (Cascio 1995). With cross-trained teams (Marks et al. 2002), employees may need certain adaptive KSAs that help them decide when and how to perform back-up behaviors (Dickinson and McIntyre 1997) when routine processes are disrupted.

Viewing performance over time has also led to the development of more general theories. Ployhart et al. (2001) provided additional support for Sackett and colleagues' early work on typical and maximum performance (DuBois et al. 1993; Sackett et al. 1988) and found that different personality dimensions best predicted each of the performance constructs. Others have concluded that performance should be regarded as a dynamic process rather than as a set of static behaviors that people perform at any given time (e.g. Kozlowski et al. 1999; Ployhart and Hakel 1998; Sackett et al. 1988).

Regardless of one's view of performance, these recent advances in theory and research have emphasized the importance of selecting employees who will be able to contribute to a wide range of organizational functions, some of which are not directly related to the tasks for which the employee's job description holds them responsible.

## 15.3.3 Concerns about Subgroup Representation and Remedies

Reconciling the use of valid selection devices and the desire that the workforce be representative of societal demographics continues to be of concern among practitioners, researchers, the legal profession, and the public at large (AERA et al. 1999; Barrett and Luecke 2004; *Grutter* v. *Bollinger et al.* 2003; Sharf and Jones 1999; SIOP 2003). Research on this issue over the last forty years has clarified several points. First, the tests that have been examined (most frequently cognitive ability tests) are not psychometrically biased in that predicted outcomes for protected groups are not less than similar outcomes predicted for the majority group. Second, there are large minority–majority group differences favoring Caucasians over African American groups and to a lesser extent Hispanic American groups on cognitive ability tests (Roth et al. 2001) and favoring men over women on physical ability tests (Hogan 1991). Smaller differences occur in some instances on other tests (Bobko et al. 1999; Hough 1998). Third, various attempts to remove these subgroup differences in cognitive ability may serve to diminish them by a small amount, but large subgroup differences remain and often produce legally defined levels of adverse impact on minority groups (Sackett et al. 2001).

There have been some new developments in this arena. Statistically, consideration of the impact of reliability and the precision of measurement has resulted in proposals to band test scores, reflecting the notion that differences within bands are not reliably discriminable. Decisions about test scores within a band are then made on other bases including ethnic status. An edited book (Aguinis 2004) provides a discussion of various approaches to banding including their mechanisms, the degree to which social values are implicit in these methods of test use, and their legal status. The impact of banding on minority hiring varies considerably given the situation and the particular banding remedy employed. The appropriateness of banding continues to be hotly debated in the scientific and legal communities.

Lack of predictive bias in ability tests and large subgroup differences in test scores produce a projected loss in utility when test scores are used in a less than optimal manner, as would be the case with banding (Laczo and Sackett 2004; Sackett and Roth 1991). Whether these differences translate into differences in organizational functioning or not is less clear, as is evidence that the proportion of members of one subgroup or another in the workforce impacts performance. The popular view (Doyle 2000) is that a well-educated, highly diverse workforce composed of people working productively and creatively with members of diverse races, religious backgrounds, and cultural histories is important to maintaining organizational competitiveness. This view is best represented by an amicus brief filed by a large number of Fortune 500 companies in support of the University of Michigan admissions policies (*Grutter* v. *Bollinger et al.* 2003). Leonard (1990) and Steel and Lovrich (1987) failed to find a relationship between the proportion of minorities or women in organizations and organizational efficiency. Nonetheless, affirmative action policies do improve employment opportunities for minority groups and women (Kravitz et al. 1997), and Holzer and Neumark (1996) reported little evidence of substantially weaker job performance among most groups of minority and female affirmative action hires. Sacco and Schmitt (2005), however, found evidence for a negative relationship between racial diversity and change in profitability among 3,454 quick service restaurants. The whole question of the impact of organizational diversity on organizational performance merits further investigation. Like many other performance phenomena, this relationship is likely moderated and mediated by the past relational histories and attitudes of the employees and organizations involved as well as the societal context.

Researchers have also examined employee attitudes toward affirmative action policies and the people that benefit from these policies. Heilman et al. (1998) reported that affirmative action programs seem to have negative consequences for perceptions of employees who are thought to be hired based on group membership rather than merit. Bell et al. (2000) reported both negative and positive reactions to affirmative action programs among manager and student groups. On the negative side, these people believed that such programs led to employers hiring less qualified employees, were responsible for reverse discrimination, created the perception that minorities and women could not succeed on their own, and required a lot of paperwork and resources. On the positive side, these people felt that affirmative action improved the job opportunities of women and minorities, gave everyone an equal opportunity, and reduced discrimination and conflict among employees. Using the theory of reasoned action (Fishbein and Ajzen 1975), they also found that relatively simple attempts to change attitudes toward affirmative action programs caused white attitudes to be more negative in response to negative information; minority attitudes became more favorable as a function of positive communications. Thus attitudes became more polarized. Attitudes and intentions based on the Fishbein–Ajzen formulations were related to overt behavior in the form of sending postcards to congressional representatives espousing their view of affirmative action. While attitudes toward affirmative action do not change the composition of the workforce themselves, they are critically important for the societal acceptance of such remedies and for determining the degree to which organizations can form fully functioning and collaborative work teams when affirmative action programs are used.

One area about which we have seen very little information is comparative international data. At least among Americans, there appears to be little information as to how other societies resolve diversity dilemmas or if they even perceive a problem. Cross-cultural studies of these issues might reveal data and solutions that could be more widely applied.

## 15.3.4 Team-based Performance and Multilevel Issues

Ideally, it would be simplest for organizations to conduct selection at the highest possible level. Organizations would scour the world for the best intact department or team rather than try and assemble one with a random collection of individuals. In reality, organizations add individuals (i.e. line workers, team members, executives, etc.) to their existing system structures (i.e. positions or roles) that are presumably designed in such a way as to enable individuals to fulfill organizational needs optimally at multiple levels (Ployhart and Schneider 2002a; also see Kozlowski and Klein 2000, for an overview of general multilevel issues). Today, a large number of employees must not only perform their own job, but also assist team members, endorse management practices, and represent their organization within the community. At best, a failure to consider the multilevel nature of work phenomena in selection decisions will reduce organizational effectiveness. At worst, employees will be devoting their energy towards tasks that are useless or even harmful towards the organization.

The principle underlying typical selection practices is that individual difference characteristics will determine who will be of greatest value to the organization based on their job performance (cf. Motowidlo 2003). In *appropriately designed* jobs that take organizational needs into consideration, employees will improve organizational effectiveness simply by performing their duties well, where duties might include citizenship performance and other supportive behaviors, as well as task performance. Alas, many jobs are designed imperfectly. Consequently, Ployhart and Schneider (2002a) emphasize the potential need to conduct team-work analyses or organizational needs assessments, in addition to traditional job analyses, to ensure that individuals' performance will be adding value to an organization.

From a multilevel perspective, individual work behaviors can then be divided into those that accomplish individual job tasks and those that lead to the fulfillment of higher-level needs. Although the first section of this chapter suggested that selection decisions and general HR practices must be compatible, this section provides a closer look at how individuals can be selected to fulfill needs beyond their specific job.

From a selection perspective, some theories imply that individuals perform behaviors (e.g. citizenship; Borman and Motowidlo 1997) both to increase the effectiveness of higher-level units and to accomplish specific job tasks. Ehrhart and Naumann (2004) offered one way of viewing citizenship behaviors in the aggregate to explain how norms of cooperation and altruistic behavior are developed. Having similar objectives, DeShon et al. (2004) proposed a multilevel model of goal-setting as it moves from the individual to the team level, and Stewart et al. (2005) explored the use of team member roles for explaining how individual personality traits affect team cohesion and performance.

From the perspective of team performance researchers, the vast literature on team/group processes shows that communication and coordination, culture and norms, fit, and many other behaviors and attitudes are important for group effectiveness. However, only a few studies have directly linked individual characteristics to team-level processes. Miller (2001) and McClough and Rogelberg (2003) provided evidence to support earlier validation work (Stevens and Campion 1994) that a test of teamwork KSAs could predict group effectiveness and individual performance within teams, respectively. The most recent study using the test showed that teamwork KSAs mediated the effect of job autonomy on team performance and job strain (Leach et al. 2005).

Still, more work on the generalizability of such characteristics is needed, especially considering the many types of teams that exist (Sundstrom et al. 1990) and the varied tasks (i.e. disjunctive and conjunctive) they must accomplish. Once valid individual- and team-level KSAs are identified, multilevel perspectives also suggest that the configuration of existing personnel may determine group effectiveness. Work on team configurations and the distribution of member KSAs (e.g. structural contingency theory; Hollenbeck et al. 2002) suggests that gaps in team capabilities can be filled either by selecting replacement personnel or by reconfiguring team processes or structures.

Perhaps the most important implication of adopting a multilevel perspective for selection is that incompatibilities between organizational subsystems can reduce overall effectiveness. Ostroff (2002) notes that plant-level practices may conflict with organization-wide policies. Similarly, Ployhart and Schneider (2002a) use an example of the trade-off between validity and diversity to illustrate how maximizing individual performance with cognitive selection measures can have harmful effects on organizational policies regarding diversity. Hence, higher-level outcomes (like diversity) may result only when lower-level units perform at a subpar level, particularly when the units are competing for the same organizational resources. Yet, this assertion also implies that organizations can achieve certain outcomes by hiring individuals who perform sufficiently well so as to add unique value to the system, but who are not necessarily the top applicants, thereby reducing selection costs.

Another interesting pattern in the current literature is the differential growth of team composition and 'compilation' models. Composition models seek to explain the aggregation of lower-level behaviors that are similar while compilation models seek to explain group-level phenomena that result from specialized individual behaviors (Kozlowski and Klein 2000). As Chan's (1998) typology of aggregation models suggests, compilation models require complex theoretical justifications for aggregation rather than simple demonstrations of agreement or similarity, as do most composition models. The consequence of this distinction is that we still lack standard methods for combining performance behaviors when each person in a team or organization has a specialized function. The problem becomes further complicated when team membership is continually shifting and the selection of a new member depends on the current team composition/compilation.

Regardless of whether aggregation occurs through composition or compilation, it is always important to establish that individual-level predictors of performance will also predict higher-level outcomes, over which the individual has some control. Ployhart and Schneider (2002a) elaborated on the classic validity model depicted by Binning and Barrett (1989) to show how the validity of individual-level predictors translates into validity at multiple, higher levels.

Despite the progress made by multilevel theorists and the evident costs of failing to consider relevant issues, it appears that future researchers will encounter difficulties in defining and measuring tasks and KSAs that have meaning across multiple levels of organizational structures (Schmitt 2002). The necessary but daunting task of weighting predictors across levels will also be an obstacle to the development of appropriate selection systems (Ployhart and Schneider 2002b). Establishing validity at multiple levels also carries with it practical concerns about how to find sufficiently large sample sizes that contain variance (e.g. at the plant level).

## 15.3.5 Deviance and Counterproductivity

Given the tradition of pathology and dysfunction in psychology, it is somewhat surprising that critical examinations of organizational deviance and counterproductive work behaviors began just over a decade ago. The 'dark side behaviors,' as Griffin and O'Leary-Kelly (2004) label them, range from the mildly annoying to the criminal, but often pose serious threats to an organization's resources and productivity, social system, or public image even when the base rate is low (Harris and Ogbonna 2002). As such, organizations should be concerned not only with selecting productive employees, but also with selecting out employees who will harm the organization.

Negative work behaviors can generally be characterized by their intentional nature and detrimental consequences, and be classified according to the recipient(s) of the negative consequences and the severity of harm incurred (Griffin and O'Leary-Kelly 2004; Robinson and Bennett 1995). The labels 'deviance' and 'counterproductivity', in particular, have been used to refer to acts like absenteeism, withholding effort, theft, sabotage, spreading rumors, sexual harassment, and physical violence (Miles et al. 2002; Robinson and Bennett 1997). Yet, there is a lack of consistent support for the parsing of negative behaviors into specific dimensions, partly because hypothesized facets tend to be correlated (Lim and Cortina 2005; Sackett 2002; Viswesvaran and Ones 2000). Bennett and Robinson (2003) noted that past research has been plagued with definitional problems. They concluded (p. 251): 'What matters most is not whose definition of workplace deviance [and other related concepts] is used in a given study, but only that the definition matches the theory and the operationalizations used in question.'

Although *deviance* can be defined narrowly as behaviors departing from the norm, the broader concept of *counterproductivity* appears to clash with the concept of prosocial behaviors, as well as with general definitions of performance. The fundamental question is: Are positive and negative organizational behaviors merely two ends of the spectrum? If they are, organizations need only be concerned with selecting people based on their propensity and ability to perform positive, helpful behaviors. If the two concepts are distinct, then additional predictors will be needed to select the best applicants. From a theoretical standpoint, it would be much simpler to examine employee behaviors without attaching value to them, as Campbell (1990) suggests, since the same behavior may be seen as positive in one context and negative or neutral in another (Heilman and Chen 2005; Rotundo and Sackett 2002).

Miles et al. (2002) provided data showing different patterns of relationships for counterproductive and citizenship behaviors with environmental working conditions, affect, and trait anger and a weak negative correlation between the two types of performance, suggesting that these concepts represent distinct dimensions. Kelloway et al. (2002) came to the same conclusion after conducting confirmatory factor analyses of citizenship and counterproductivity. Still, additional theory is needed to justify this conceptual distinction. For example, Sackett (2002) provided evidence of a strong negative relationship between counterproductivity and citizenship, but still concluded that the concepts were mutually exclusive on the premise that an employee can engage in all types of performance (i.e. task, citizenship, *and* counterproductive performance).

Beyond strict behaviorism, a focus on intentions can make an examination of both positive and negative work behaviors more meaningful, given a particular context (Brief and Motowidlo 1986; Griffin and O'Leary-Kelly 2004; Harris and Ogbonna 2002). Motivational determinants of counterproductive behaviors such as coercion by a superior, attempts to resolve injustice, mental illness, whistle-blowing, and the need to fit in with a culture that happens to be harmful might cause behaviors to be condoned while intentions related to selfishness, aggressive tendencies toward resolving conflict, and a lack of integrity might create blame. Some organizational (change) practices can attempt to control these motivational factors, but selection devices may also help by identifying people with characteristics that moderate or neutralize the factors naturally.

In an early meta-analysis, Ones et al. (1993) showed that integrity tests predict counterproductive work behaviors, although validities were better for broader outcome measures than theft alone. More recent work has also shown that integrity tests are generally valid predictors of counterproductive outcomes (e.g. Fortmann et al. 2002). Bennett et al. (2005) describe moral identity as a self-regulating mechanism that prevents the pursuit of unethical behaviors. At the same time, Sackett and Wanek (1996) point out a number of issues that may limit the successful use of integrity tests, including overlap with personality constructs and legal rights to privacy.

As suggested by Robinson and Bennett (1997), visible deviance could also serve as an emotional or instrumental expression aimed at remedying an injustice (Neuman 2004). Spector and Fox (2002, 2004) introduced formal models in which affect, stress, and perceptions of control mediate the influence of affective dispositions and situational factors on counterproductive behaviors. Penney and Spector (2002) found evidence supporting a model of trait anger expressed as aggression, where trait anger was triggered by threats to one's narcissistic view. However, college students who were not necessarily working comprised their sample, necessitating future investigations. Marcus et al. (2002) validated a counterproductive behavior scale and later used it to show that self-control (i.e. the higher-level ability to consider and weigh short- and long-term consequences and to delay gratification) predicted general counterproductive behaviors in a German organization (Marcus and Schuler 2004). In any case, the implication of such research is that organizations may wish to select individuals who are able and willing to express themselves in a constructive or mature manner, and who will remedy injustices through formally sanctioned means (e.g. communicating with the supervisor directly).

Other predictors of negative work behaviors include attitudes toward risk-taking and career orientation (Harris and Ogbonna 2002). In applying the General Affective Aggression Model (Anderson 1997) to work behaviors, Neuman (2004) suggests that personality, self-monitoring, beliefs and values regarding aggression, and self-esteem are indirect determinants of aggression. Although aspects of personality have typically shown small relationships with deviance (Bennett and Robinson 2003), Colbert et al. (2004) found, in four samples, that conscientiousness, agreeableness, and emotional stability moderated the effect of environmental work factors (i.e., developmental opportunities and support) on organizational deviance. Interestingly, Bennett and Robinson (2003) propose that ethnic cultural variables related to ethnocentrism, cooperation, and collectivism might identify employees who avoid deviant behaviors.

Before concluding this section, we also note that the progress in research on deviance/counterproductivity occurs at a relatively slow pace partly because of 'the Achilles' heel of counterproductivity research' (Sackett 2002: 7). While some forms of counterproductive behavior are public (e.g. absence), many are acts by employees who do not wish to be detected (e.g. theft, sabotage, harassment). This means that employees' status on the criterion of interest is very difficult to determine and that some instances of counterproductive behavior go undetected. Despite this barrier, continual efforts to understand negative work behaviors will undoubtedly improve the capability of future selection systems to increase organizational effectiveness.

## 15.3.6 Additional Current Issues

Those familiar with the selection literature would undoubtedly add other complexities to traditional concerns of criterion-related validity. The following are some other issues that we believe are important, but for which space considerations preclude a more extensive discussion. Today's workforce is often geographically dispersed and people often work very different schedules (e.g. Martins et al. 2004). This flexibility in the manner, time, and place of work require new considerations when organizations hire people into these positions. Technology has also brought changes in the way in which selection devices are administered (Potosky and Bobko 2004), which in turn has produced interesting research on measurement equivalency and validity, applicant reactions, and test security. The rapid globalization of major organizations has meant that their staffs are often assigned to work in foreign countries. Concerns about expatriate selection often involve spousal issues (e.g. Takeuchi et al. 2002) and training to cope in cultures very different from one's home country (Lievens et al. 2003). Mergers and acquisitions (e.g. Coff 2002) often create a situation in which the new organizational entity has surplus talent in some areas, or the merger creates the need for individuals with a new combination of KSAOs. In the last fifteen years, interest in the reactions of the employees or applicants that are the targets of organizations' selection decisions has burgeoned (Gilliland 1993).

## 15.4 CONCLUSION

We began with a brief summary of the traditional test validation model that has guided selection decision-making for over 100 years. While this model is still relevant, there is no dearth of new issues to consider when an organization makes decisions about selecting its human resources. We briefly summarized five of these issues that appeared to be generating the most attention in the research literature during the last decade. Some of these issues require the integration of individual differences literature with the macro literature on organizational strategy (i.e. relating human resource practices or capabilities to organizational or team effectiveness). There are also developments that change the manner in which data on human resource capabilities are measured (e.g. technological advances), the types of people assessed (e.g. expatriates, people working in virtual environments or with flexible schedules), what is being predicted with our decision tools, and concerns of the audience to which our methods are directed (e.g. reactions to selection procedures and issues of bias). All of these issues serve to ensure an exciting and intellectually challenging environment for human resource practitioners and researchers alike.

# REFERENCES

AGUINIS, H. (2004). *Test Score Banding in Human Resource Selection*. Westport, Conn.: Praeger.

American Educational Research Association, American Psychological Association, and National Council of Measurement in Education (1999). *Standards for Educational and Psychological Testing*. Washington: American Educational Research Association.

ANDERSON, C. A. (1997). 'Effects of Violent Movies and Trait Hostility on Hostile Feelings and Aggressive Thoughts.' *Aggressive Behavior*, 23: 161–78.

AUSTIN, J. T., and VILLANOVA, P. (1992). 'The Criterion Problem: 1917–1992.' *Journal of Applied Psychology*, 77: 836–74.

BARRETT, G. V., and LUECKE, S. B. (2004). 'Legal and Practical Implications of Banding for Personnel Selection.' In H. Aguinis (ed.), *Test-Score Banding in Human Resource Selection*. Westport, Conn.: Praeger.

BATT, R. (2002). 'Managing Customer Services: Human Resource Practices, Quit Rates, and Sales Growth.' *Academy of Management Journal*, 45: 587–97.

BECKER, B. E., and HUSELID, M. A. (1998). 'High Performance Work Systems and Firm Performance: A Synthesis of Research and Managerial Applications.' *Research in Personnel and Human Resource Management*, 16: 53–101.

BELL, M. P., HARRISON, D. A., and McLAUGHLIN, M. E. (2000). 'Forming, Changing, and Acting on Attitude Toward Affirmative Action Programs in Employment: A Theory Driven Approach.' *Journal of Applied Psychology*, 85: 784–98.

BENNETT, R. J., and ROBINSON, S. L. (2003). 'The Past, Present, and Future of Workplace Deviance Research.' In J. Greenberg (ed.), *Organizational Behavior: The State of the Science*, 2nd edn. Mahwah, NJ: Erlbaum.

—— AQUINO, K., REED, A., II., and THAU, S. (2005). 'The Normative Nature of Employee Deviance and the Impact of Moral Identity.' In S. Fox and P. E. Spector (eds.), *Counterproductive Work Behavior: Investigations of Actors and Targets*. Washington: APA Press.

BINNING, J. F., and BARRETT, G. V. (1989). 'Validity of Personnel Decisions: A Conceptual Analysis of the Inferential and Evidential Bases.' *Journal of Applied Psychology*, 74: 478–94.

BOBKO, P., ROTH, P. L., and POTOSKY, D. (1999). 'Derivation and Implications of a Meta-analytic Matrix Incorporating Cognitive Ability, Alternative Predictors, and Job Performance.' *Personnel Psychology*, 52: 561–89.

BORMAN, W. C., and MOTOWIDLO, S. J. (1993). 'Expanding the Criterion Domain to Include Elements of Contextual Performance.' In N. Schmitt and W. Borman (eds.), *Personnel Selection in Organizations*. San Francisco: Jossey-Bass.

—— —— (1997). 'Task Performance and Contextual Performance: The Meaning for Personnel Selection Research.' *Human Performance*, 10: 99–109.

—— —— and HANSER, L. M. (1983). 'A Model of Individual Performance Effectiveness: Thoughts about Expanding the Criterion Space.' Paper presented as part of symposium, 'Integrated Criterion Measurement for Large Scale Computerized Selection and Classification,' 91st annual American Psychological Association conference, (August).

—— WHITE, L. A., and DORSEY, D. W. (1995). 'Effects of Ratee Task Performance and Interpersonal Factors on Supervisor and Peer Performance Ratings.' *Journal of Applied Psychology*, 80: 168–77.

—— PENNER, L. A., ALLEN, T. D., and MOTOWIDLO, S. J. (2001). 'Personality Predictors of Citizenship Performance.' *International Journal of Selection and Assessment*, 9: 52–69.

BOUDREAU, J. W., and RAMSTAD, P. M. (2003). 'Strategic Industrial and Organizational Psychology and the Role of Utility Analysis Models.' In W. C. Borman, D. R. Ilgen, and R. J. Klimoski (eds.), *Handbook of Psychology*, vol. xii. New York: Wiley.

BOXALL, P., and PURCELL, J. (2000). 'Strategic Human Resource Management: Where have we Come from and Where should we be Going?' *International Journal of Management Reviews*, 2: 183–203.

BRIEF, A. P., and MOTOWIDLO, S. J. (1986). 'Prosocial Organizational Behaviors.' *Academy of Management Review*, 11: 710–25.

CAMPBELL, J. P. (1990). 'Modeling the Performance Prediction Problem in Industrial and Organizational Psychology.' In M. D. Dunnette and L. M. Hough (eds.), *Handbook of Industrial and Organizational Psychology*, vol. i. Palo Alto, Calif.: Consulting Psychologists Press.

—— McHENRY, J. J., and WISE, L. L. (1990). 'Analyses of Criterion Measures: The Modeling of Performance.' *Personnel Psychology*, 43: 313–43.

—— McCLOY, R. A., OPPLER, S. H., and SAGER, C. E. (1993). 'A Theory of Performance.' In N. Schmitt and W. C. Borman (eds.), *Personnel Selection in Organizations*. San Francisco: Jossey-Bass.

—— GASSER, M. B., and OSWALD, F. L. (1996). 'The Substantive Nature of Job Performance Variability.' In K. R. Murphy (ed.), *Individual Differences and Behavior in Organizations*. San Francisco: Jossey-Bass.

CARPENTER, M. A., GELETKANYCZ, M. A., and SANDERS, W. G. (2004). 'Upper Echelons Research Revisited: Antecedents, Elements, and Consequences of Top Management Team Composition.' *Journal of Management*, 30: 749–58.

CASCIO, W. F. (1995). 'Whither Industrial and Organizational Psychology in a Changing World of Work?' *American Psychologist*, 50: 928–39.

—— (2000). 'Managing a Virtual Workplace.' *Academy of Management Executive*, 14: 81–90.

CHAN, D. (1998). 'Functional Relations among Constructs in the Same Content Domain at Different Levels of Analysis: A Typology of Composition Models.' *Journal of Applied Psychology*, 83: 234–46.

COFF, R. W. (2002). 'Human Capital, Shared Expertise, and the Likelihood of Impasse in Corporate Acquisitions.' *Journal of Management*, 28: 107–28.

COLBERT, A. E., MOUNT, M. K., HARTER, J. K., WITT, L. A., and BARRICK, M. R. (2004). 'Interactive Effects of Personality and Perceptions of the Work Situation on Workplace Deviance.' *Journal of Applied Psychology*, 89: 599–609.

COLEMAN, V. I., and BORMAN, W. C. (2000). 'Investigating the Underlying Structure of the Citizenship Performance Domain.' *Human Resource Management Review*, 10: 25–44.

DE CORTE, W. (1999). 'Weighing Job Performance Predictors to Both Maximize Quality of the Selected Workforce and Control the Level of Adverse Impact.' *Journal of Applied Psychology*, 84: 695–702.

DELANEY, J. T., and HUSELID, M. A. (1996). 'The Impact of Human Resource Management Practices on Perceptions of Organizational Performance.' *Academy of Management Journal*, 39: 949–69.

DELERY, J. E., and DOTY, D. H. (1996). 'Modes of Theorizing in Strategic Human Resource Management: Tests of Universalistic, Contingency, and Configurational Performance Predictions.' *Academy of Management Journal*, 39: 802–35.

DESHON, R. P., KOZLOWSKI, S. W. J., SCHMIDT, A. M., MILNER, K. R., and WIECHMANN, D. (2004). 'A Multiple-Goal, Multilevel Model of Feedback Effects on the Regulation of Individual and Team Performance.' *Journal of Applied Psychology*, 89: 1035–56.

DICKINSON, T. L., and McINTYRE, R. M. (1997). 'A Conceptual Framework for Teamwork Measurement.' In M. T. Brannick, E. Salas, and C. Prince (eds.), *Team Performance Assessment and Measurement*. Mahwah, NJ: Erlbaum.

DOYLE, R. A. (2000). 'GM Supports University's Stand on Affirmative Action.' *University Record*, 37. Ann Arbor: University of Michigan.

DUBOIS, C. L. Z., SACKETT, P. R., ZEDECK, S., and FOGLI, L. (1993). 'Further Exploration of Typical and Maximum Performance Criteria: Definitional Issues, Prediction, and Black–White Differences.' *Journal of Applied Psychology*, 78: 205–11.

EHRHART, M. G., and NAUMANN, S. E. (2004). 'Organizational Citizenship Behavior in Work Groups: A Group Norms Approach.' *Journal of Applied Psychology*, 89: 960–74.

FISHBEIN, M., and AJZEN, I. (1975). *Belief, Attitudes, Intention, and Behavior*. Reading, Mass.: Addison-Wesley.

FORTMANN, K., LESLIE, C., and CUNNINGHAM, M. (2002). 'Cross-cultural Comparisons of the Reid Integrity Scale in Latin America and South Africa.' *International Journal of Selection and Assessment*, 10: 98–108.

GILLILAND, S. W. (1993). 'The Perceived Fairness of Selection Systems: An Organizational Justice Perspective.' *Academy of Management Review*, 18: 694–734.

GRIFFIN, R. W., and O'LEARY-KELLY, A. M. (2004). 'An Introduction to the Dark Side.' In R. W. Griffin and A. M. O'Leary-Kelly (eds.), *The Dark Side of Organizational Behavior*. San Francisco: Jossey-Bass.

GRUTTER v. BOLLINGER et al. (2003). 539 US Supreme Court. Docket No. 02–241. 23 June.

GUION, R. M. (1998). *Assessment, Measurement, and Prediction for Personnel Decisions*. Mahwah, NJ: Erlbaum.

HARRIS, L. C., and OGBONNA, E. (2002). 'Exploring Service Sabotage: The Antecedents, Types and Consequences of Frontline, Deviant, and Antiservice Behaviors.' *Journal of Service Research*, 4: 163–83.

HATTRUP, K., ROCK, J., and SCALIA, C. (1997). 'The Effects of Varying Conceptualizations of Job Performance on Adverse Impact, Minority Hiring, and Predicted Performance.' *Journal of Applied Psychology,* 82: 656–64.

HEILMAN, M. E., and CHEN, J. J. (2005). 'Same Behavior, Different Consequences: Reactions to Men's and Women's Altruistic Citizenship Behavior.' *Journal of Applied Psychology,* 90: 431–41.

—— BATTLE, W. S., KELLER, C. E., and LEE, R. A. (1998). 'Type of Affirmative Action Policy: A Determination of Reaction to Sex-Based Preferential Selection.' *Journal of Applied Psychology,* 83: 190–205.

HITT, M. A., BIERMAN, L., SHIMIZU, K., and KOCHHAR, R. (2001). 'Direct and Moderating Effects of Human Capital on Strategy and Performance in Professional Service Firms: A Resource-Based Perspective.' *Academy of Management Journal,* 44: 13–28.

HOGAN, J. C. (1991). 'Physical Abilities.' In M. D. Dunnette and L. M. Hough (eds.), *Handbook of Industrial and Organizational Psychology,* vol. ii. Palo Alto, Calif.: Consulting Psychologists Press.

HOLLENBECK, J. R., MOON, H., ELLIS, A. P. J., WEST, B. J., ILGEN, D. R., SHEPPARD, L., PORTER, O. L. H., and WAGNER, J. A., III. (2002). 'Structural Contingency Theory and Individual Differences: Examination of External and Internal Person-Team Fit.' *Journal of Applied Psychology,* 87: 599–606.

HOLZER, H., and NEUMARK, D. (1996). *Are Affirmative Action Hires Less Qualified: Evidence from Employer–Employee Data on New Hires.* Cambridge, Mass.: National Bureau of Economic Research.

HOUGH, L. M. (1998). 'Personality at Work: Issues and Evidence.' In M. D. Hakel (ed.), *Beyond Multiple Choice: Evaluating Alternatives to Traditional Testing for Selection.* Mahwah, NJ: Erlbaum.

—— OSWALD, F. L., and PLOYHART, R. E. (2001). 'Determinants, Detection and Amelioration of Adverse Impact in Personnel Selection Procedures: Issues, Evidence and Lessons Learned.' *International Journal of Selection and Assessment,* 9: 152–94.

HUSELID, M. A. (1995). 'The Impact of Human Resource Management Practices on Turnover, Productivity, and Corporate Financial Performance.' *Academy of Management Journal,* 38: 635–72.

—— JACKSON, S. E., and SCHULER, R. A. (1997). 'Technical and Strategic Human Resource Management Effectiveness as Determinants of Firm Performance.' *Academy of Management Journal,* 40: 171–88.

KELLOWAY, E. K., LOUGHLIN, C., BARLING, J., and NAULT, A. (2002). 'Self-Reported Counterproductive Behaviors and Organizational Citizenship Behaviors: Separate but Related Constructs.' *International Journal of Selection & Assessment,* 10: 143–51.

KOZLOWSKI, S. W. J., and KLEIN, K. J. (2000). 'A Multilevel Approach to Theory and Research in Organizations: Contextual, Temporal, and Emergent Processes.' In K. J. Klein and S. W. J. KOZLOWSKI (eds.), *Multilevel Theory, Research, and Methods in Organizations.* San Francisco: Jossey-Bass.

—— GULLY, S. M., NASON, E. R., and SMITH, E. M. (1999). 'Developing Adaptive Teams: A Theory of Compilation and Performance across Levels and Time.' In D. R. Ilgen and E. D. Pulakos (eds.), *The Changing Nature of Performance: Implications for Staffing, Personnel Actions, and Development.* San Francisco: Jossey-Bass.

KRAVITZ, D. A., HARRISON, D. A., TURNER, M. E., LEVINE, E. L., CHAVES, W., BRANNICK, M. T., DENNING, D. L., RUSSELL, C. J., and CONARD, M. A. (1997). *Affirmative Action:*

*A Review of Psychological and Behavioral Research.* Bowling Green, Oh.: Society for Industrial and Organizational Psychology.

LACZO, R. M., and SACKETT, P. R. (2004). 'Effects of Banding on Performance and Minority Hiring: Further Monte Carlo Simulations.' In H. Aguinis (ed.), *Test Score Banding in Human Resource Selection.* Westport, Conn.: Praeger.

LEACH, D. J., WALL, T. D., ROGELBERG, S. G., and JACKSON, P. R. (2005). 'Team Autonomy, Performance, and Member Job Strain: Uncovering the Teamwork KSA Link.' *Applied Psychology: An International Review,* 54: 1–24.

LEONARD, J. S. (1990). 'The Impact of Affirmative Action Regulation and Equal Employment Law on Black Employment.' *Journal of Economic Perspectives,* 4: 47–63.

LEPAK, D. P., and SNELL, S. A. (2002). 'Examining the Human Resource Architecture: The Relationships among Human Capital, Employment, and Human Resource Configurations.' *Journal of Management,* 28: 517–43.

LEPINE, J. A., EREZ, A., and JOHNSON, D. E. (2002). 'The Nature and Dimensionality of Organizational Citizenship Behavior: A Critical Review and Meta-analysis.' *Journal of Applied Psychology,* 87: 52–65.

LIEVENS, F., HARRIS, M. M., VAN KEER, E., and BISQUERET, C. (2003). 'Predicting Cross-Cultural Training Performance: The Validity of Personality, Cognitive Ability, and Dimensions Measured by an Assessment Center and a Behavior Description Interview.' *Journal of Applied Psychology,* 88: 476–89.

LIM, S., and CORTINA, L. M. (2005). 'Interpersonal Mistreatment in the Workplace: The Interface and Impact of General Incivility and Sexual Harassment.' *Journal of Applied Psychology,* 90: 483–96.

McCLOUGH, A. C., and ROGELBERG, S. G. (2003). 'Selection in Teams: An Exploration of the Teamwork Knowledge, Skills, and Ability Test.' *International Journal of Selection and Assessment,* 11: 56–66.

McCLOY, R. A., CAMPBELL, J. P., and CUDECK, R. (1994). 'A Confirmatory Test of a Model of Performance Determinants.' *Journal of Applied Psychology,* 79: 493–505.

McHENRY, J. J., HOUGH, L. M., TOQUAM, J. L., HANSON, M. A., and ASHWORTH, S. (1990). 'Project A Validity Results: The Relationship between Predictor and Criterion Domains.' *Personnel Psychology,* 43: 335–54.

MARCUS, B., and SCHULER, H. (2004). 'Antecedents of Counterproductive Behavior at Work: A General Perspective.' *Journal of Applied Psychology,* 89: 647–660.

—— —— QUELL, P., and HÜMPFNER, G. (2002). 'Measuring Counterproductivity: Development and Initial Validation of a German Self-Report Questionnaire.' *International Journal of Selection and Assessment,* 10: 18–35.

MARKS, M. A., SABELLA, M. J., BURKE, C. S., and ZACCARO, S. J. (2002). 'The Impact of Cross-Training on Team Effectiveness.' *Journal of Applied Psychology,* 87: 1–13.

MARTINS, L. L., GILSON, L. L., and MAYNARD, M. T. (2004). 'Virtual Teams: What do we Know and Where do we Go from Here?' *Journal of Management,* 30: 805–36.

MILES, D. E., BORMAN, W. E., SPECTOR, P. E., and FOX, S. (2002). 'Building an Integrative Model of Extra Role Work Behaviors: A Comparison of Counterproductive Work Behavior with Organizational Citizenship Behavior.' *International Journal of Selection and Assessment,* 10: 51–7.

MILLER, D. L. (2001). 'Reexamining Teamwork KSAs and Team Performance.' *Small Group Research,* 32: 745–66.

MOTOWIDLO, S. J. (2003). 'Job Performance.' In W. C. Borman, D. R. Ilgen, and R. J. Klimoski (eds.), *Comprehensive Handbook of Psychology*, xii: *Industrial and Organizational Psychology*. New York: Wiley.

—— BORMAN, W. C., and SCHMIT, M. J. (1997). 'A Theory of Individual Differences in Task and Contextual Performance.' *Human Performance*, 10: 71–83.

MURPHY, K. R., and SHIARELLA, A. H. (1997). 'Implications of the Multidimensional Nature of Job Performance for the Validity of Selection Tests: Multivariate Frameworks for Studying Test Validity.' *Personnel Psychology*, 50: 823–54.

NEUMAN, J. H. (2004). 'Injustice, Stress, and Aggression in Organizations.' In R. W. Griffin and A. M. O'Leary-Kelly (eds.), *The Dark Side of Organizational Behavior*. San Francisco: Jossey-Bass.

ONES, D. (2002). 'Introduction to the Special Issue on Counterproductive Behaviors at Work.' *International Journal of Selection and Assessment*, 10: 1–4.

—— VISWESVARAN, C., and SCHMIDT, F. L. (1993). 'Comprehensive Meta-analysis of Integrity Test Validities: Findings and Implications for Personnel Selection and Theories of Job Performance.' *Journal of Applied Psychology*, 78: 679–703.

ORGAN, D. W. (1988). *Organizational Citizenship Behavior: The Good Soldier Syndrome*. Lexington, Mass.: Lexington Books.

—— (1997). 'Organizational Citizenship Behavior: It's Construct Clean-up Time.' *Human Performance*, 10: 85–97.

—— and RYAN, K. (1995). 'A Meta-analytic Review of Attitudinal and Dispositional Predictors of Organizational Citizenship Behavior.' *Personnel Psychology*, 48: 775–802.

OSTROFF, C. (2002). 'Leveling the Selection Field.' In F. J. Yammarino and F. Dansereau (eds.), *The Many Faces of Multi-level Issues*. Amsterdam: JAI.

OSWALD, F. L., SCHMITT, N., KIM, B. H., RAMSAY, L. J., and GILLESPIE, M. A. (2004). 'Developing a Biodata Measure and Situational Judgment Inventory as Predictors of College Student Performance.' *Journal of Applied Psychology*, 89: 187–207.

PENNEY, L. M., and SPECTOR, P. E. (2002). 'Narcissism and Counterproductive Work Behavior: Do Bigger Egos mean Bigger Problems?' *International Journal of Selection and Assessment*, 10: 126–34.

PLOYHART, R. E. (2004). 'Organizational Staffing: A Multilevel Review, Synthesis, and Model.' In J. J. Martocchio (ed.), *Research in Personnel and Human Resource Management*. Oxford: Elsevier.

—— and HAKEL, M. D. (1998). 'The Substantive Nature of Performance Variability: Predicting Interindividual Differences in Intraindividual Performance.' *Personnel Psychology*, 51: 859–901.

—— and SCHNEIDER, B. (2002a). 'A Multi-level Perspective on Personnel Selection Research and Practice: Implications for Selection System Design, Assessment, and Construct Validation.' In F. J. Yammarino and F. Dansereau (eds.), *The Many Faces of Multi-level Issues*. Amsterdam: JAI.

—— —— (2002b). 'A Multi-level Perspective on Personnel Selection: When Will Practice Catch up?' In F. J. Yammarino and F. Dansereau (eds.), *The Many Faces of Multi-level Issues*. Amsterdam: JAI.

—— —— (in press). 'Multilevel Selection and Prediction: Theories, Methods, and Models.' In A. Evers, O. Smit-Voskuyl, and N. R. Anderson (eds.), *Handbook of Personnel Selection*. Chichester: Wiley.

—— LIM, B., and CHAN, K. (2001). 'Exploring Relations between Typical and Maximum Performance Ratings and the Five Factor Model of Personality.' *Personnel Psychology*, 54: 809–43.

—— SCHNEIDER, B., and SCHMITT, N. (in press). *Organizational Staffing: Contemporary Practice and Theory*. Mahwah, NJ: Erlbaum.

POTOSKY, D., and BOBKO, P. (2004). 'Selection Testing via the Internet: Practical Considerations and Exploratory Empirical Findings.' *Personnel Psychology*, 57: 1003–34.

PULAKOS, E. D., ARAD, S., DONOVAN, M. A., and PLAMONDON, K. E. (2000). 'Adaptability in the Workplace: Development of a Taxonomy of Adaptive Performance.' *Journal of Applied Psychology*, 85: 612–24.

ROBINSON, S. L., and BENNETT, R. J. (1995). 'A Typology of Deviant Workplace Behaviors: A Multi-dimensional Scaling Study.' *Academy of Management Journal*, 38: 555–72.

—— —— (1997). 'Workplace Deviance: Its Definitions, its Manifestations, and its Causes.' *Research on Negotiations in Organizations*, 6: 3–27.

ROTH, P. L., BEVIER, C. A., BOBKO, O., SWITZER, F. S., III., and TYLER, P. (2001). 'Ethnic Group Differences in Cognitive Ability in Employment and Educational Settings: A Meta-analysis.' *Personnel Psychology*, 54: 297–330.

ROTUNDO, M., and SACKETT, P. R. (2002). 'The Relative Importance of Task, Citizenship, and Counterproductive Performance to Global Ratings of Job Performance: A Policy-Capturing Approach.' *Journal of Applied Psychology*, 87: 66–80.

RYAN, A. M., McFARLAND, L., BARON, H., and PAGE, R. (1999). 'An International Look at Selection Practices: Nation and Culture as Explanations for Variability in Practice.' *Personnel Psychology*, 52: 359–92.

SACCO, J. M., and SCHMITT, N. (2005). 'A Dynamic Multilevel Model of Demographic Diversity and Misfit Effects. *Journal of Applied Psychology*, 90: 203–31.

SACKETT, P. R. (2002). 'The Structure of Counterproductive Work Behaviors: Dimensionality and Relationships with Facets of Job Performance.' *International Journal of Selection and Assessment*, 10: 5–11.

—— and ROTH, L. (1991). 'A Monte Carlo Examination of Banding and Rank Order Methods of Test Score Use in Personnel Selection.' *Human Performance*, 4: 279–95.

—— and WANEK, J. E. (1996). 'New Developments in the Use of Measures of Honesty, Integrity, Conscientiousness, Dependability, Trustworthiness, and Reliability for Personnel Selection.' *Personnel Psychology*, 49: 787–829.

—— ZEDECK, S., and FOGLI, L. (1988). 'Relations between Measures of Typical and Maximum Job Performance.' *Journal of Applied Psychology*, 73: 482–6.

—— SCHMITT, N., ELLINGSON, J. E., and KABIN, M. B. (2001). 'High-Stakes Testing Employment, Credentialing, and Higher Education: Prospects in a Post-Affirmative-Action World.' *American Psychologist*, 56: 302–18.

SCHMIDT, F. L. (2002). 'The Role of General Cognitive Ability and Job Performance: Why There Cannot be a Debate.' *Human Performance*, 15: 187–210.

—— and HUNTER, J. E. (1998). 'The Validity and Utility of Selection Methods: Practical and Theoretical Implications of 85 Years of Research Findings.' *Psychological Bulletin*, 124: 262–74.

SCHMITT, N. (2002). 'A Multi-level Perspective on Personnel Selection: Are we Ready?' In F. J. Yammarino and F. Dansereau (eds.), *The Many Faces of Multi-level Issues*. Amsterdam: JAI.

SCHMITT, N., and CHAN, D. (1998). *Personnel Selection: A Theoretical Approach.* Thousand Oaks, Calif.: Sage.

SHARF, J. C., and JONES, D. P. (1999). 'Employment Risk Management.' In J. F. Kehoe (ed.), *Managing Selection Strategies in Changing Organizations.* San Francisco: Jossey-Bass.

Society for Industrial and Organizational Psychology (2003). *Principles for the Validation and Use of Personnel Selection Procedures.* Bowling Green, Oh.: SIOP.

SPECTOR, P. E., and FOX, S. (2002). 'The Emotion-Centered Model of Voluntary Work Behavior: Some Parallels between Counterproductive Work Behavior and Organizational Citizenship Behavior.' *Human Resource Management Review,* 12: 269–92.

—— —— (2004). 'The Stressor-Emotion Model of Counterproductive Work Behavior (CWB).' In S. Fox and P. E. Spector (eds.), *Counterproductive Work Behavior: Investigations of Actors and Targets.* Washington, DC: APA Press.

STEEL B. S., and LOVRICH, N. P. (1987). 'Equality and Efficiency Tradeoffs in Affirmative Action—Real or Imagined? The Case of Women in Policing.' *Social Science Journal,* 24: 53–70.

STEVENS, M. J., and CAMPION, M. A. (1994). 'The Knowledge, Skill, and Ability Requirements for Teamwork: Implications for Human Resource Management.' *Journal of Management,* 20: 503–30.

STEWART, G. L., FULMER, I. S., and BARRICK, M. R. (2005). 'An Exploration of Member Roles as a Multilevel Linking Mechanism for Individual Traits and Team Outcomes.' *Personnel Psychology,* 58: 343–65.

SUNDSTROM, E., DE MEUSE, K. P. and FUTRELL, D. (1990). 'Work Teams: Application and Effectiveness.' *American Psychologist,* 45: 120–33.

TAKEUCHI, R., YUN, S., and TESLUK, P. (2002). 'An Examination of Crossover and Spillover Effects of Spousal and Expatriate Cross-Cultural Adjustment on Expatriate Outcomes.' *Journal of Applied Psychology,* 87: 655–66.

TERPSTRA, D. E., and ROZELL, E. J. (1993). 'The Relationship of Staffing Practices to Organizational Level Measures of Performance.' *Personnel Psychology,* 46: 27–48.

'Uniform Guidelines on Employee Selection Procedures' (1978). *Federal Register,* 43: 38290–315.

VAN DYNE, L., CUMMINGS, L. L., and PARKS, J. M. (1995). 'Extra-Role Behaviors: In Pursuit of Construct and Definitional Clarity (a Bridge over Muddied Waters).' *Research in Organizational Behavior,* 17: 215–85.

VAN SCOTTER, J. R., MOTOWIDLO, S. J., and CROSS, T. C. (2000). 'Effects of Task Performance and Contextual Performance on Systemic Rewards.' *Journal of Applied Psychology,* 85: 526–35.

VISWESVARAN, C., and ONES, D. S. (2000). 'Perspectives on Models of Job Performance.' *International Journal of Selection and Assessment,* 8: 216–26.

—— SCHMIDT, F. L., and ONES, D. S. (2005). 'Is there a General Factor in Ratings of Job Performance? A Meta-analytic Framework for Disentangling Substantive and Error Influences.' *Journal of Applied Psychology,* 90: 108–31.

WRIGHT, P. M., and BOSWELL, W. R. (2002). 'Desegregating HRM: A Review and Synthesis of Micro and Macro Human Resource Management Research.' *Journal of Management,* 28: 247–76.

—— DUNFORD, B., and SNELL, S. A. (2001a). 'Human Resources and the Resource Based View of the Firm.' *Journal of Management,* 27: 701–21.

—— GARDNER, T. M., MOYNIHAN, L. M., PARK, H., GERHART, B., and DELERY, J. (2001*b*). 'Measurement Error in Research on Human Resources and Firm Performance: Additional Data and Suggestions for Future Research.' *Personnel Psychology*, 54: 875–902.

—— —— —— and ALLEN, M. R. (2005). 'The Relationship between HR Practices and Firm Performance: Examining Causal Order.' *Personnel Psychology*, 58: 409–46.

CHAPTER 16

# TRAINING, DEVELOPMENT, AND COMPETENCE

## JONATHAN WINTERTON

## 16.1 INTRODUCTION

ACCORDING to the conventional wisdom of 'nuts and bolts' personnel management, having established personnel requirements (taking into account labor turnover, retirements, sales forecasts, and the impact of technological changes on productivity), recruitment, selection, and training follow as a linear trilogy. A workforce with the requisite skills is the logical end result, enabling the personnel team to focus on appraisal, remuneration, and motivation until the next round of 'manpower planning' (a term that surprisingly endured well beyond the advent of gender-free language in the profession). Of course this is a caricature of the standard personnel texts that some of us are old enough to remember, but barely an exaggerated one despite its distance from the reality of workplace practice. Modern HRM might emphasize the need for continuous training, and development to maintain the dynamic capabilities supporting organizational strategy and make endless caveats about choices to be made between recruitment, training, and outsourcing. The rhetoric is more sophisticated, but is it any closer to reality? In practice, there are innumerable possible combinations for solving the workforce capability problem. Organizations may provide training and development internally, externally, or in combination to 'make' a competent workforce, attempt to 'buy' by recruiting or poaching skilled labor, paying attractive premium rates with what is saved on training expenditure, or endeavor to reduce dependence on skilled labor altogether through particular choices of technology, work organization, and outsourcing. Where organizations do train, the overriding objective is to develop the competence or ability of employees, but in such a generalization, axiomatic perhaps to the point of tautology, the complex diversity of approaches is lost.

Why are there such differences in approaches to training and development given that all organizations need a competent workforce? Decisions on whether or not to provide training, and if so whether to do so internally or externally, are not made in a vacuum but are influenced by national and sectoral cultures, institutional arrangements, and state policies on education and training. This chapter seeks to explore the diversity of approaches and offer some explanations by situating the policy and practice of training and development within different national and supranational contexts. To this end, the chapter first addresses the political economy of skill formation, tracing the influence of the Organization for Economic Cooperation and Development (OECD) and International Labor Office (ILO) policies on the strategies developed by regional supra-state bodies such as the European Union (EU) and the Asia-Pacific Economic Cooperation (APEC) countries and the implementation of these strategies at the level of nation states.

This review provides the context for the subsequent sections which address in turn training, development, and competence. In the training section, theory, policy, and practice are considered, including the diversity of national systems for vocational education and training (VET) and the relationship between work organization and workplace learning. The development section is distinguished from training in terms of objectives and scope, while the emergence of Human Resource Development (HRD) is explained not only in terms of a more strategic focus but also in relation to initiatives like corporate universities. The competence section addresses the confusion surrounding the term, contrasting four predominant approaches derived from the USA, the UK, France, and Germany, each of which has influenced other countries to varying degrees. Drawing on these four traditions, a more holistic approach to competence is presented as the model currently being used to structure learning outcomes within the European Qualifications Framework. Section 16.6 considers the major trajectories of theory, policy, and practice in this domain, while the final section offers an overall summary and conclusion, drawing out the major issues for theory and management practice.

# 16.2 THE POLITICAL ECONOMY
## OF SKILL FORMATION

While there is substantial diversity in national systems and traditions of training and development, the globalization of markets and the internationalization of production represent common driving forces that have led international organizations like the ILO and OECD to emphasize training and development. The OECD *Jobs Study* (1994*a*, 1994*b*) was particularly influential, arguing that the major cause of rising unemployment and the incidence of low-wage jobs was the gap between the need of OECD economies to adapt and the ability of governments to implement the necessary changes. The *Jobs Study* recommended measures to combat unemployment including macroeconomic policies promoting growth and job creation; technological development and entrepreneurship; increasing labor market flexibility; strengthening active labor market policies; and improving labor force skills. Subsequent OECD reports called for increasing the knowledge base and innovative capacity through upgrading workforce skills, noting that on average in OECD countries between 15 and 20 percent of school leavers have no qualification and 20 percent of the working population is functionally illiterate, whilst skill thresholds and earnings differentials (related to educational attainment) continue to rise.

Strongly influenced by the OECD *Jobs Strategy*, supra-state organizations have developed and coordinated regional training strategies. A comparison of the training strategies of the EU and APEC shows very different political structures adopted in the two organizations and contrasting approaches to supranational coordination of training (Haworth and Winterton 2004). The two regions face common challenges arising from globalization and both the EU and APEC identified training as an essential component of raising competitiveness. Each region has considerable diversity in terms of the economies of member countries which gives the global challenges different meanings in different contexts and restricts the development of uniform strategies across the regions. Despite these apparent similarities, there are fundamental differences in organization and underlying objectives. APEC's organization is based on consensual decision-making, essential for the Asian economies, while EU policy is directive to create an integrated market. The means by which training policies are developed and implemented also differ. Social dialogue is a defining principle of the EU policy approach that combines economic and social objectives whereas in APEC the trade unions play no role in developing regional training policy.

The strategies of the OECD, ILO, and supra-state organizations give the impression of a universal consensus that training is the essential component for developing modern competitive economies. Yet at the level of nation states not only is there wide diversity in the approaches to training and development, but also substantial differences in the skills equilibrium which are not explained by differences in the sectoral composition of economies. Several sector studies by the National Institute for Economic and Social Research have compared the UK and Germany (Steedman and Wagner 1987), confirming the UK economy as having a 'low skills equilibrium' (Finegold and Soskice 1988). While the higher skill level of the German workforce is generally seen as a source of competitive advantage, permitting German firms to focus on higher-value-added market niches, the narrow specialization of skilled workers in Germany has also restricted the development of cross-functional adaptability necessary for the lean production and quick response associated with the USA and UK (Herrigel 1996).

Anglo-American approaches to skill formation share a high proportion of low-skilled workers and a higher proportion of high-skilled than those at the intermediate skills level (in the USA case, a much higher proportion of graduates). This approach contrasts with the 'typical' EU approach, where there are fewer low-skilled and a highly formalized apprenticeship system that creates a higher proportion of those with intermediate skills. The differences reflect prevailing labor market conditions: the Anglo-American model is associated with low unemployment but more casual and precarious employment, while the European model is associated with highly regulated labor markets with high employment security but high levels of unemployment. The OECD agenda is concerned with encouraging the Anglo-American approach to labor market flexibility but also with raising skills overall.

The 'Americanization' of labor markets is tied to a belief that training to raise skills is a panacea permitting economic growth, higher employment, and lower unemployment (the one is not the dual of the other since labor market participation rates vary enormously, especially for women) as well as (in Europe at least) promoting social cohesion. Despite the apparent consensus among policy makers, there are academic critiques. Crouch et al. (2001) offer the most comprehensive critique, whilst accepting key elements of the OECD analysis: the acquisition of knowledge and skills is the main challenge and opportunity for full employment; low skilled work, rural and domestic, is disappearing; and some countries (like Sweden) have succeeded in a high-skills strategy. However, they have serious reservations with this essentially supply-side approach: public service employment, a major source of high-skill and entry-level jobs is contracting; improvements in productivity stem job growth; new secure high-skill jobs are insufficient to absorb those displaced in low-skill sectors; labor markets are becoming polarized into high-skill and peripheral jobs; labor market deregulation reduces living standards to reduce unemployment; lifelong learning devolves responsibility to the individual and reduces state obligations. If everyone becomes educationally successful, then the criteria of success shift to a higher level and improving the educational level of a potential workforce does not immediately create new jobs. There is evidence from many countries (including France, Italy, Spain, and the USA) of over-education, with rising graduate unemployment and the use of a university degree as a sorting device, producing the paradoxical, and in the long run unstable, situation whereby young people find prolonged education increasingly unsatisfactory but increasingly demand it.

Since New Labour was elected in 1997, the UK government has been a keen advocate of this skills discourse, establishing the Skills Task Force to develop a national agenda for skills development, and the National Advisory Group for Continuing Education and Lifelong Learning to advise on developing a culture of lifelong learning and widening participation. The UK backed the EU economic reform agenda agreed at the Lisbon summit in March 2000, which set the goal for Europe to become by 2010 'the most competitive and knowledge-based economy in the world capable of sustainable growth and better jobs and greater social cohesion.' The Barcelona summit (March 2002) set the further objective of making 'European education and training systems a world quality reference by 2010.' In 2001, the UK government restructured post-compulsory education under the newly created Learning and Skills Council and in 2003 published a White Paper outlining the government's skills strategy, *21st Century Skills: Realising our Potential*, establishing Sector Skills Councils to align training with labor market needs.

The discourse is different in economies facing economic transformation (as in the former Soviet Union), restructuring (everywhere, but especially in those economies with a high proportion of agriculture or primary industries), reconstruction (as in South Africa), and modernization (in degrees ranging from Vietnam to Turkey). Skill formation is inevitably central to these processes and some economists see the development of human capital as more important in explaining patterns of long-term economic growth than physical capital (Briggs 1987). Nevertheless, the same problem is manifest as in the OECD countries: skills mismatches are common as a result of employer reluctance to provide training and educational provision insufficiently adapted to the needs of the labor market. Hence it is important to resist the temptation of seeing training as 'good' and more training as 'better.' Training must be adapted to the needs of the individual and the organization if it is to deliver the benefits intended and it is to this issue that the next section is addressed.

## 16.3 TRAINING

The objective of training is to ensure that all employees have and maintain the requisite competences to perform in their roles at work. While the state is typically involved in ensuring that new entrants to the labor market are adequately trained, continuing training is mainly the concern of the enterprise and the individual. This section seeks to provide an overview of the theory, policy, and practice of training, drawing out different approaches associated with different national contexts.

Theories of training are based on theories of learning since training effectiveness is measured by the extent to which the individuals concerned learn what they need to know, can do what they need to do, and adopt the behaviors intended; i.e. the acquisition of knowledge, skills, and attitudes. Cognitive learning, related to the understanding and use of new concepts (knowledge), may be contrasted with behavioral learning, related to the physical ability to act (skill). Welford (1968: 12–13), who defined skill as a combination of factors resulting in 'competent, expert, rapid and accurate performance,' regarded this as equally applicable to manual operations and mental activities. Welford's (1968, 1976) work demonstrates how actions are selected and coordinated at different levels of skilled performance and the conditions of practice and training that facilitate the acquisition and transfer of skill. Fitts and colleagues (Fitts et al. 1961; Fitts and Posner 1967) developed a three-stage framework for skill acquisition involving (i) a cognitive phase of understanding the nature of the task and how it should be performed; (ii) an associative phase involving inputs linked more directly to appropriate actions and reduced interference from outside demands; and finally (iii) an autonomous phase when actions are 'automatic' requiring no conscious control. Anderson (1981, 1983) developed a framework for the acquisition of cognitive skill in which the declarative and procedural phases correspond with Fitts's cognitive and autonomous phases. In place of an intermediary associative phase, Anderson argued that there is a continuous process of 'knowledge compilation' involving the conversion of declarative knowledge into procedural knowledge. Proctor and Dutta (1995: 18), in what is arguably the most authoritative text on skill acquisition, define skill as 'goal-directed, well-organized behavior that is acquired through practice and performed with economy of effort.'

Training policies and practices are, or should be, informed by these and other underpinning theories of learning. Training cannot be considered independently of context, and different national systems of VET reflect different economic, social, political, and cultural conditions and traditions. Various typologies of systems of skill formation have been proposed to distinguish the different families of VET systems (Ashton et al. 2000; ILO 1998; OECD 1998). These variously distinguish the 'schooling model' where VET provision may be integrated within general education or delivered through separate VET institutions, the consensual 'dual model' where the emphasis is on apprenticeship, and voluntarist market led or enterprise led models, which may be associated with high or low skills strategies. With some simplification, two key dimensions of VET systems allow an adequate typology: the *focus* of skill formation (workplace or school) and the *regulation* of the VET system (state or market). Within Europe, four countries illustrate the differences. In terms of its focus, VET is mostly industry led and centered on the workplace in the UK and Germany, whereas training is education led and centered on vocational training schools in Italy and France. The German dual system entails instruction in VET schools in parallel with work-based training, but the curricula focus on workplace needs. Whereas VET is regulated by the state in Germany and France, in the UK and Italy arrangements are market led, with responsibility for training largely devolved to employers (Winterton 2000).

Whatever the system, training policy should ensure that labor market needs are met. Some have questioned employers' ability adequately to identify future skills needs, asking whether employers really need the skills they want (Stasz 1997) and, equally, if they want the skills they need. In the UK, it was argued that employers recruit graduates because they are plentiful, but then use them in intermediate functions to remedy labor market skills deficiencies at this level. Recent evidence disputes this hypothesis, showing that the vast majority of graduates in England are employed within three years in positions that demand graduate skills, despite the doubling of university entrants in a little over a decade (Elias and Purcell 2004).

In market-led training systems like the UK, some employers have been tempted to focus on narrow job-related skills, wanting to 'pick and mix' modules of vocational qualifications to suit their needs for flexibility, rather than respecting the integrity of qualifications that improve employability. In the state-led German system, modularization has been resisted in the interests of maintaining the integrity of 'Beruf', usually translated as occupation but embracing the culture and traditions of a craft. State regulation facilitates a higher level of skill development, which explains why vocational qualifications are almost as extensive in France as in Germany, but the French system is focused on state vocational schools and employers complain that the training is inappropriate, a problem not apparent in the German dual system where the curriculum is focused on workplace needs.

Turning to practice, training involves three processes: analysis of needs, development of provision, and evaluation. Training needs analysis compares existing competences with those required and can be undertaken at the level of the organization, the work team, and the individual. At the organizational level, the purpose is to establish training priorities in the light of organizational strategy and associated core competences. At team level, the purpose is to ensure that teams possess the complementary skills required for effective performance and functional flexibility. At the individual level, a development review aims to match career aspirations with organizational needs. A comparison of the attributes required for a particular job (in the job profile) with those of the current job holder provides a starting point; more detail is obtained by task or functional analysis which identifies specific knowledge, skills, and attitudes needed.

In the development phase, the training content is determined from the needs analysis and appropriate modes of delivery identified for the different elements. Training is invariably more structured for new employees because the induction period is crucial in reducing dysfunctional labor turnover; job training should only begin after induction. Operative training involves explaining why a task is performed, how it should be performed, and providing an opportunity for practice. Two methods were traditionally employed: 'sitting by Nellie' (Crichton 1968) and training centers. Sitting by Nellie (learning with an experienced employee) is still widely used and effective where experienced employees are taught training techniques. The advantage of training centers using full-time professional trainers may be offset by problems of training transfer when the trainee moves to the work station, either because of the exigencies of the work process or differences between theory and practice.

Evaluation is intended to provide feedback for improving future provision, informing senior management for strategic decisions on training expenditure, and encouraging trainees to reflect on their experiences. According to the seminal work of Kirkpatrick (1967), training can be evaluated at four levels. Reaction-level evaluation provides information on what participants thought of a training program and is of limited value. Learning-level evaluation is concerned with the effectiveness of the acquisition of knowledge, skills, and attitudes through training. Behavioral-level evaluation is concerned with how well skills or behaviors have been transferred to the job, according to participants, superiors, and subordinates. Results-level evaluation, measuring the impact of training on the organization's return on investment, cost savings, quality changes, and improvements in work output, is the most valuable but most challenging due to difficulties in attributing performance improvements to training interventions.

# 16.4 DEVELOPMENT

The key distinction between development and training is that development involves a wider range of activities with less specific ends than training. Training is designed with specific learning outcomes that form the basis for examination of the skills acquired: an operator who has received the requisite training *should be able to* use a milling machine to produce test pieces within the tolerance required, for example. Development is focused more on the individual than the occupation and is concerned with longer-term personal growth and career movement: in France, the term *évolution professionnelle* is used in preference to *développement*, hence emphasizing the ends rather than the means.

Development is also related to the idea of social and economic progress because developing workforce skills has a major impact on national economies (Zidan 2001); where economies are undergoing a process of development, transition, or

such recognition of competence, irrespective of the route of acquisition, for those who have had fewer opportunities for formal education and training (Rainbird 2000a); and the potential of a competence-based approach for integrating education and training, whilst aligning both with the needs of the labor market (Winterton 2005).

Despite the central role of competence, there is such confusion surrounding the concept that it is impossible to identify or impute a coherent theory or to arrive at a definition capable of accommodating and reconciling all the different ways that the term is used. Different cultural contexts profoundly influence the understanding of competence and four dominant approaches can be distinguished that developed more or less independently in the USA, the UK, France, and Germany (Delamare Le Deist and Winterton 2005). These four approaches have variously influenced policy and practice worldwide.

The competence movement began in the USA where White (1959) is credited with having introduced the term to describe those personality characteristics associated with superior performance and high motivation. White defined competence as an 'effective interaction (of the individual) with the environment' and argued that there is a 'competence motivation' in addition to competence as 'achieved capacity.' McClelland (1976) followed this approach and developed tests to predict competence as opposed to intelligence, subsequently describing this as 'competency' and marketing the approach through the consulting firm that became Hay McBer. Because of skepticism regarding the predictive value of cognitive ability tests, the competency approach started from the opposite end, observing effective job performers to determine how these individuals differ from less successful performers. Competency thus captures skills and dispositions beyond cognitive ability, such as self-awareness, self-regulation, and social skills; while some of these may also be found in personality taxonomies (Barrick and Mount 1991), competencies are fundamentally behavioral and susceptible to learning (McClelland 1998). This tradition has remained particularly influential in the USA, with competency defined in terms of 'underlying characteristics of people' that are 'causally related to effective or superior performance in a job,' 'generalizing across situations, and enduring for a reasonably long period of time' (Boyatzis 1982; Hay Group et al. 1996; Klemp and Spencer 1982; Spencer and Spencer 1993). It is worth noting that others have defended the predictive power of intelligence tests (Hunter and Hunter 1984; Barrett and Depinet 1991).

Since the end of the 1990s, competence-based HRM has become widespread in the USA, not only in relation to HRD, but also in selection, retention, remuneration, and leadership (Athey and Orth 1999; Dubois and Rothwell 2004; Foxan 1998; Rodriguez et al. 2002). In this renaissance, competency has a much broader conception than hitherto, including knowledge and skills alongside the behavioral or psycho-social characteristics in the McClelland tradition. Even within the predominantly behavioral approach, many conceptions of competency now include knowledge and skills alongside attitudes, behaviors, work habits, abilities, and personal characteristics (Gangani et al. 2004; Lucia and Lepsinger 1999; Naquin and Wilson 2002; Nitardy and McLean 2002; Russ-Eft 1995).

A different approach was developed during the 1980s in the UK when a competence-based, unified system of work-based, vocational qualifications (National Vocational Qualifications in England and Wales, Scottish Vocational Qualifications in Scotland) was adopted. Occupational standards of competence, grounded in functional analysis of occupations in a variety of contexts, identify key roles, broken down into units of competence and further subdivided into elements with associated performance criteria and range indicators for assessment. The emphasis is on functional competence: the ability to demonstrate performance to the standards required of employment in a work context. While this is still the dominant approach in the UK, some employers developed their own competence frameworks or adopted other generic models combining functional and behavioural factors to create hybrid competence models.

The competence movement started later in France (Klarsfeld and Oiry 2003) and became particularly influential from 1993 when the Agence Nationale Pour l'Emploi (National Employment Agency) adopted a competence framework and HRM professionals began replacing the logic of qualification with competence. In the 1990s, the state introduced a right for individuals to have a *bilan de compétences* (assessment of competences) undertaken by educational organizations to provide a basis for personal development. Competence featured increasingly in HRM practice from the mid-1990s, further encouraged by the initiative, *Objectif compétences* (Objective: competence), of the employers' association MEDEF (Mouvement des Entreprises de France) in 2002. The French approach makes an analytical distinction between *savoir* (*compétences théoriques*, i.e. knowledge), *savoir-faire* (*compétences pratiques*, i.e. functional competences), and *savoir être* (*compétences sociales et comportementales*, i.e. behavioral competences).

While competence (*Kompetenz*) was implicit in the German system, the main emphasis is on the concept of *Beruf Qualifikation*, the mastery of all the tasks specific to an occupation. In the 1980s, 'key qualifications' (*Schlüsselqualifikationen*) were introduced, relating to individual characteristics, experience, and knowledge. In 1996, the German education system moved from subject (inputs) to competence (outcomes) and curricula specifying learning fields (*Lernfelder*). *Kompetenz* is concerned with capacity to act (*Handlungsvermögen*) and, in the occupational sense, this is expressed as vocational action competence (*Handlungskompetenz*). A standard typology of competences now appears at the beginning of every new vocational training curriculum, elaborating domain competence (*Fachkompetenz*), personal competence (*Personalkompetenz*), and social competence (*Sozialekompetenz*). General cognitive competence (*Sachkompetenz*), the ability to think and act in an insightful and problem-solving way, is a prerequisite for developing *Fachkompetenz*. A balance of subject, personal, and social competence is the prerequisite for 'method and learning competence' (*Methodenkompetenz und Lernkompetenz*).

In recent years, many countries have adopted competence-based qualifications, usually following quite closely one of the above models or hybrid forms. Competence-based occupational profiles and/or qualification frameworks already exist or are under development in most of the fifteen 'old' EU member states and are being promoted in those of the ten 'new' EU member states that had not already adopted this approach. The UK approach had a major impact on the Commonwealth countries, while the German approach reappears in Austria and Slovenia. Portugal has adopted the French model in revising the secondary education system with curricula designed to achieve learning outcomes specified in terms of cognitive competences (*competências cognitivas*), functional competences (*competências funcionais*), and social competences (*competências sociais*).

Competence-based approaches have been criticized for neglecting socio-cultural contexts, and are accused of creating abstract, narrow, and oversimplified descriptions of competence that fail adequately to reflect the complexity of work performance in different organizational cultures and workplace contexts (Attewell 1990; Norris 1991; Sandberg 1994). Competences are centered on the individual, but constructivist and interpretative approaches derived from phenomenology view competence as a function of the context in which it is applied (Dreyfus and Dreyfus 1986). Interpretative approaches acknowledge workers' tacit knowledge and skills (Polanyi 1967), overlooked if competence is treated as context free because work practice seldom accords with formal job descriptions. Tacit competences, even of so-called 'unskilled workers' (Kusterer 1978), can have a determining impact on the success of an enterprise (Flanagan et al. 1993).

It can be concluded that while competence-based training and development is gaining ground, the earlier American psycho-social approach and the narrow functional approach pioneered in the UK are giving way to more holistic approaches, particularly along the lines of the French and German models. The new recognition of the importance of informal and experiential learning is likely to broaden the concept of competence even further from the abstract, mechanistic approaches, to legitimize tacit knowledge and skills, and to capture more adequately the complexity of actual work processes.

## 16.6 FUTURE DIRECTIONS

Given the difficulties of forecasting future skill needs, any attempt to forecast future directions of training, development, and competence must carry the usual caveats.

The best that can be done is to make some rather general observations on emerging trends and some intelligent guesses as to the extent they are likely to continue. This is done with respect to the politics of skill formation, training policy and practice, development, and competence.

In terms of the politics of skill formation, it is clear that there is a global consensus involving governments and international organizations on the need to increase the level of workforce skills in line with technological developments and the emergence of a global knowledge-based economy. However, several critics have noted that supply-side solutions are not a panacea for labor demand deficiencies. Moreover, Keep (2005) warns that the idea of high skills for all, often coupled with 'best practice' models of HRM, can be viewed as a search for happy endings to counteract the challenges of mounting welfare burdens, declining sectors, and growing inequalities. The analysis is flawed, he argues, because 'knowledge workers' only exist in parts of some economies and low-paid, low-skilled occupations prevail in many sectors. Moreover, the associated best practice model of HRM is a 'mirage,' at best a 'minority sport,' since organizations are inclined to adopt partially those elements of the model that fit their strategy. The persistence of Taylorist work organization, enthusiastically adopted in many service sector enterprises that optimists associate with the knowledge-based economy, means that we are likely to see an increasing polarization of skills.

As for training policy, there is growing criticism that formal training in vocational schools is failing to meet the needs of the labor market as economic restructuring and technological changes are making traditional skills obsolete. In Turkey, for example, graduate unemployment is 10 percentage points higher than unemployment among unqualified young people and employers prefer to recruit untrained workers than those from state-run vocational schools. In sectors like textiles and metalworking, employers have established foundations to deliver training suited to labor market needs but the certificates awarded are not recognized by the state, whereas the officially recognized qualifications of the vocational schools do not meet employers' needs. Efforts are in place with the support of the European Commission to bring education closer to the labor market but this case illustrates some of the difficulties of ensuring training is appropriate. There is also increasing recognition that the Anglo-American hegemony in HRM (Boxall 1995: 6) produces inappropriate training solutions for the specific needs of developing and transition economies. In recent years, there has been a spectacular increase in interest in HRD in the Asian, Arab, and African economies, which offer different paradigms of skill formation (Ashton et al. 2000).

In terms of practice, the distinction between training and development appears to be diminishing as there is increasing acceptance that most learning is informal, and even accidental. Training is giving way to learning and development, which implies individuals taking responsibility for learning and provision being more adapted to individual needs, in terms of both content and learning style. For organizations, training and development are becoming intimately linked to organizational strategy, with a focus on adaptability and flexibility for both the developmental objectives and the delivery of training opportunities. For states, the need for co-investment by employers and individuals is high on the agenda and formal education is becoming more focused on core skills and engaging with learning. In this transformation, the role of the HRD specialist is becoming one of facilitating learning opportunities rather than providing the formally structured training provision of the past. This tendency is also reflected in the policy emphasis on lifelong learning with the aim of integrating education, training, and adult and community learning. Moves within the EU to create a European Qualifications System, for example, are driven by a concern not only to promote labor mobility between member states but also to integrate higher education, vocational training, and experiential routes of skills acquisition. While there is a continued emphasis on external qualifications for initial training, internal initiatives for continuing and adaptive training are increasingly important, with the establishment of workplace learning facilities and the use of Accreditation of Prior Learning (*Validation des Acquis Expérientielles*) for validation of non-formal experiential learning.

Development is in the ascendant and voices of modernization advocate changing the focus from training individuals to facilitating learning by individuals, teams, and organizations, some even claiming that already 'the development process has overtaken the training event at individual, group and organization level' (Mabey and Iles 1994: 1). Using Engestrom's (2001) concept of 'expansive learning,' recent analyses of employee development have distinguished expansive and restrictive workplace environments in terms of the extent to which they promote or inhibit opportunities for learning (Rainbird et al. 2003). Some organizations are responding to the need for continuous development by establishing Workplace Learning Environments, ranging from a few computers in a quiet corner to immense Corporate Universities. Companies such as Ford have introduced schemes to encourage employees to return to learning, and similar initiatives have been led by trade unions in the UK (Rainbird 1990, 2000*b*), particularly since the introduction of Union Learning Representatives (Rodgers et al. 2003).

As for competence, there are again signs that American hegemony on competency is being challenged by multidimensional competence frameworks, along the lines of the French and German models. Significantly, a holistic approach to competence has been recommended for the European Credit Transfer System for VET and in the European Qualifications Framework that was being developed during 2006. The holistic competence model recognizes the unity of competence, as in the *Beruf* tradition, and the difficulty of breaking specific competences into the analytically distinct cognitive, functional, and social dimensions in practice. Meta-competence (learning to learn, for example) is presented as an overarching input that facilitates the acquisition of output competences.

# 16.7 SUMMARY AND CONCLUSIONS

This chapter has considered the politics of skill formation, the policies and practices of training and development, and approaches to building competence. The question was posed at the outset as to why, given that all organizations need a competent workforce, there are significant differences in approaches to training and development between different economies and different enterprises. There is no simple answer: different contexts evidently demand different approaches to training and development but even in the same context different approaches may be adopted. As with approaches to HRM in general, 'one size fits all' is not a serious option for HRD.

According to international organizations like the OECD, the need to develop new skills for the emerging knowledge-based economy represents a policy priority that has clearly influenced supranational bodies like the EU and APEC. Despite this consensus, shared by most national governments, the focus on supply-side issues can be criticized for neglecting the demand side. Are the jobs being created that demand these skills and do employers really need the skills they want?

There are extensive national differences in VET systems even within the EU and, when we look beyond to transition economies like the former Soviet states, to developing economies like South Africa, and to the dynamic Asian and Middle Eastern countries, there are approaches to national HRD strategies that challenge the Anglo-American dominance so evident in the literature. Development, in particular, in these cases may have broader objectives associated not only with personal and professional evolution but also clear socio-economic objectives.

In suggesting scenarios for the future, two divergent trends are apparent simultaneously, often in the same environment. The first concerns the increasingly strategic focus of training and development on the competences needed to support organizational strategy, typified by the UK *Investor in People Standard*. This approach may become more widespread as organizations seek to justify investment in training and development with a return on performance improvements. The fundamental objective of training and development is to ensure individuals have the skills or competences needed for their work performance, whether part of a high-skill, high-performance HRM model or simply the basic skills demanded of a Taylorist work process. The second trend is the widespread, but not universal, tendency for training to give way to development and for both to give way to learning, implying the individual taking more responsibility and the HRD role becoming one of facilitating learning opportunities. In policy terms, this trend is also apparent in initiatives to create 'joined-up' lifelong learning, where the experiences of school, college, university, workplace, and community are seen as contributing in complementary ways to individual development. While the two trends may seem contradictory, the first focused on narrow organizational performance needs and the second on broader individual development, they should perhaps be seen as complementary and part of the inherent challenge of balancing the needs of the organization and the individual.

## REFERENCES

ANDERSON, J. R. (ed.) (1981). *Cognitive Skills and their Acquisition*. Hilldale, NJ: Lawrence Erlbaum.

—— (1983). *The Architecture of Cognition*. Cambridge, Mass.: Harvard University Press.

ASHTON, D., SUNG, J., and TURBIN, J. (2000). 'Towards a Framework for the Comparative Analysis of National Systems of Skill Formation.' *International Journal of Training and Development*, 4/1: 8–25.

—— GREEN, F., SUNG, J., and JAMES, D. (2002). 'The Evolution of Education and Training Strategies in Singapore, Taiwan, and South Korea: A Development Model of Skill Formation.' *Journal of Education and Work*, 15/1: 5–30.

ATHEY, T. R., and ORTH, M. S. (1999). 'Emerging Competency Methods for the Future.' *Human Resource Management*, 38/3: 215–26.

ATTEWELL, P. (1990). 'What is Skill?' *Work and Occupations*, 4: 422–48.

BARRETT, G. V., and DEPINET, R. L. (1991). 'A Reconsideration of Testing for Competence rather than for Intelligence.' *American Psychologist*, 46/10: 1012–24.

BARRICK, M. R., and MOUNT, M. K. (1991). 'The Big Five Personality Dimensions and Job Performance: A Meta-analysis.' *Personnel Psychology*, 44: 1–26.

BJØRNÅVOLD, J. (2000). *Making Learning Visible*. Thessaloniki: CEDEFOP.

BOXALL, P. (1995). 'Building the Theory of Comparative HRM.' *Human Resource Management Journal*, 5/5: 5–17.

BOYATZIS, R. E. (1982). *The Competent Manager: A Model for Effective Performance*. New York: Wiley.

BRIGGS, V. M. (1987). 'Human Resource Development and the Formulation of National Economic Policy.' *Journal of Economic Issues*, 21/3: 1207–40.

CRICHTON, A. (1968). *Personnel Management in Context*. London: Batsford.

CROUCH, C., FINEGOLD, D., and SAKO, M. (1999). *Are Skills the Answer? The Political Economy of Skills Creation in Advanced Industrial Countries*. Oxford: Oxford University Press.

DELAMARE LE DEIST, F., and WINTERTON, J. (2005). 'What is Competence?' *Human Resource Development International*, 8/1: 27–46.

DREYFUS, H. L., and DREYFUS, S. E. (1986) *Mind over Machine: The Power of Human Intuition and Expertise in the Era of the Computer*. New York: Free Press.

DUBOIS, D. A., and ROTHWELL, W. J. (2004). *Competency-Based Human Resource Management*. Palo Alto, Calif.: Davies-Black.

EC (1996). *Teaching and Learning: Towards the Learning Society*. Luxembourg: European Commission Publications Office.

—— (2000a). *Lisbon European Council: Presidency conclusions*. http://ue.eu.int/newsroom/NewMain.asp?LANG=1

—— (2000*b*). *Memorandum from the Commission: Lifelong Learning.* Brussels: Commission of the European Communities.

—— (2001*a*). *Communication from the Commission: Making a European Area of Lifelong Learning a Reality.* Brussels: Commission of the European Communities.

ELIAS, P., and PURCELL, K. (2004). 'Is Mass Higher Education Working? Evidence from the Labour Market Experiences of Recent Graduates.' *National Institute Economic Review,* 190: 60–74.

ENGESTROM, Y. (2001). 'Expansive Learning at Work: Toward an Activity Theoretical Reconceptualization.' *Journal of Education and Work,* 14/1: 133–55.

FINEGOLD, D., and SOSKICE, D. (1988). 'The Failure of Training in Britain: Analysis and Prescription.' *Oxford Review of Economic Policy,* 4/3: 21–53.

FITTS, P. M., and POSNER, M. I. (1967). *Human Performance.* Belmont, Calif.: Brooks/Cole.

—— BAHRICK, H. P., NOBLE, M. E., and BRIGGS, G. E. (1961). *Skilled Performance.* New York: John Wiley.

FLANAGAN, M., McGINN, I., and THORNHILL, A. (1993). *Because no Bastard ever Asked Me.* Canberra: Stakeholder.

FOXAN, M. J. (1998). 'Closing the Global Leadership Competency Gap: The Motorola GOLD Process.' *Organization Development Journal,* 16: 5–12.

GANGANI, N T., McLEAN, G. N., and BRADEN, R. A. (2004). 'Competency-Based Human Resource Development Strategy.' *Academy of Human Resource Development Annual Conference, Austin, TX, 4–7 March, Proceedings,* ii. 1111–18.

HAWORTH, N., and WINTERTON, J. (2004). 'HRD Policies and the Supra-state: A Comparative Analysis of EU and APEC Experience.' 'Fifth Conference on HRD Research and Practice: International Comparative and Cross Cultural Dimensions of HRD', Limerick, 27–8 May.

Hay Group, Towers Perrin, Hewitt Associates Llc, M. William Mercer Inc., and American Compensation Association (1996). *Raising the Bar: Using Competencies to Enhance Employee Performance.* Scottsdale, Ariz.: American Compensation Association.

HERRIGEL, G. B. (1996). 'Crisis in German Decentralized Production.' *European Urban and Regional Studies,* 3/1: 33–52.

HUNTER, J. E., and HUNTER, R. F. (1984). 'Validity and Utility of Alternate Predictors of Job Performance.' *Psychological Bulletin,* 96: 72–98.

HUSSEY, D. E. (1988). *Management Training and Corporate Strategy: How to Improve Competitive Performance.* Oxford: Pergamon.

ILO (1998). *World Employment Report 1998–1999. Employability in the Global Economy: How Training Matters.* Geneva: International Labor Office.

IoM (1994). *Management Development to the Millennium: The Cannon and Taylor Working Party Reports.* London: Institute of Management.

JOHNSON, S., and WINTERTON, J. (1999). *Management Skills.* Skills Task Force Research Paper 3. London: Department for Education and Employment.

KEEP. E. (2005). Keynote presentation to 'Sixth International Conference on HRD Research and Practice', Leeds, 26–7 May.

KIRKPATRICK, D. (1967). 'Evaluation of Training.' In R. Craig and L. Bittell (eds.), *Training and Education Handbook.* New York: McGraw-Hill.

KLARSFELD, A., and OIRY, E. (eds.) (2003). *Gérer les compétences: des instruments aux processus.* Paris: Vuibert.

KLEMP, G. O., and SPENCER, L. M. (1982). *Job Competence Assessment*. Reading, Mass.: Addison-Wesley.

KUSTERER, K. C. (1978). *Know-How on the Job: The Important Working Knowledge of 'Unskilled' Workers*. Boulder, Colo.: Westview.

LUCIA, A. D., and LEPSINGER, R. (1999). *The Art and Science of Competency Models: Pinpointing Critical Success Factors in an Organization*. San Francisco: Jossey-Bass/ Pfeiffer.

MABEY, C., and ILES, P. (eds.) (1994). *Managing Learning*. London: Thomson.

McCLELLAND, D. (1976). *A Guide to Job Competency Assessment*. Boston: McBer & Co.

—— (1998). 'Identifying Competencies with Behavioural-Event Interviews.' *Psychological Science*, 9/5: 331–9.

McGIVNEY, V. (1999). *Excluded Men: Men Who are Missing from Education and Training*. Leicester: NIACE.

McLAGAN, R. A., and SUHADOLNIK, D. (1989). *Models for HRD Practice*. Alexandra, Va.: American Society of Training and Development.

MANSFIELD, B. (2004). 'Competence in Transition.' *Journal of European Industrial Training*, 28/2/3/4: 296–309.

MOLANDER, C., and WINTERTON, J. (1994). *Managing Human Resources*. London: Routledge.

NAQUIN, S. S., and WILSON, J. (2002). 'Creating Competency Standards, Assessments and Certification.' *Advances in Developing Human Resources*, 4/2: 180–7.

NITARDY, C. N., and McLEAN, G. N. (2002). 'Project Management Competencies Needed by HRD Professionals: A Literature Review.' *Academy of Human Resource Development Conference, Honolulu, HA, 27 February–3 March, Proceedings*, ii. 956–63.

NORDHAUG, O. (1993). *Human Capital in Organizations*. Oslo: Scandinavian University Press.

NORRIS, N. (1991). 'The Trouble with Competence.' *Cambridge Journal of Education*, 21/3: 1–11.

OECD (1994a). *The OECD Jobs Study: Evidence and Explanations. Part I: Labour Market Trends and Underlying Forces of Change*. Paris: Organization for Economic Cooperation and Development.

—— (1994b). *The OECD Jobs Study: Evidence and Explanations. Part II: The Adjustment Potential of the Labour Market*. Paris: Organization for Economic Cooperation and Development.

—— (1998). *Technology, Productivity and Job Creation: Best Policy Practices*. OECD Jobs Strategy 1998 Edition. Paris: Organization for Economic Cooperation and Development.

PFEFFER, J. (1999). *Competitive Advantage through People*. Cambridge, Mass.: Harvard University Press.

POLANYI, M. (1967). *The Tacit Dimension*. London: Routledge and Kegan Paul.

PRAHALAD, C. K., and HAMEL, G. (1990). 'The Core Competence of the Corporation.' *Harvard Business Review*, May–June: 79–91.

PROCTOR, R. W., and DUTTA, A. (1995). *Skill Acquisition and Human Performance*. London: Sage.

RAINBIRD, H. (1990). *Training Matters: Union Perspectives on Industrial Restructuring and Training*. Oxford: Blackwell.

—— (2000a). 'Skilling the Unskilled: Access to Work-Based Learning and the Lifelong Learning Agenda.' *Journal of Education and Work*, 13/2: 183–97.

—— (ed.) (2000b). *Training in the Workplace.* Basingstoke: Macmillan.

—— FULLER, A., and MUNRO, A. (eds.) (2003). *Workplace Learning in Context.* London: Routledge.

RODGERS, J., WALLIS, E., and WINTERTON, J. (2003). 'Union Learning Representatives: Making the European Area of Lifelong Learning a Reality?' Fourth Conference on HRD Research and Practice: Lifelong Learning for a Knowledge-Based Society, Toulouse, 23–4 May.

RODRIGUEZ, D., PATEL, R., BRIGHT, A., GREGORY, D., and GOWING, M. K. (2002). 'Developing Competency Model to Promote Integrated Human Resource Practices.' *Human Resource Management*, 41: 309–24.

RUSS-EFT, D. (1995). 'Defining Competencies: A Critique.' *Human Resource Development Quarterly*, 6/4: 329–35.

SANDBERG, J. (1994). *Human Competence at Work: An Interpretive Approach.* Göteburg: Bas.

SPENCER, L., and SPENCER, S. (1993). *Competence at Work: A Model for Superior Performance.* New York: Wiley.

STASZ, C. (1997). 'Do Employers Need the Skills they Want? Evidence from Technical Work.' *Journal of Education and Work*, 10/3: 205–33.

STEEDMAN, H., and WAGNER, K. (1987). 'A Second Look at Productivity, Machinery and Skills in Britain and Germany.' *National Institute Economic Review*, 122: 84–95.

STEWART, J., and McGOLDRICK, J. (eds.) (1996). *Human Resource Development: Perspectives, Strategies and Practice.* London: Pitman.

STF (1998). *Towards a National Skills Agenda.* First Report of the National Skills Task Force, SKT1, London: Department for Education and Employment.

UNDP (1990). *Human Development Report: Defining and Measuring Human Development.* New York: United Nations Development Program Publications.

—— (2003). *Arab Human Development Report.* New York: United Nations Development Program Publications.

WALTON, J. S. (1999). *Strategic Human Resource Development.* London: Pearson Education.

WELFORD, A. T. (1968). *Fundamentals of Skill.* London: Methuen.

—— (1976). *Skilled Performance: Perceptual and Motor Skills.* Glenview, Ill.: Scott, Foresman.

WHITE, R. H. (1959). 'Motivation Reconsidered: The Concept of Competence.' *Psychological Review*, 66: 279–333.

WINTERTON, J. (2000). 'Social Dialogue over Vocational Training in Market-Led Systems.' *International Journal of Training and Development*, 4/1: 8–23.

—— (2005). 'From Bologna to Copenhagen: Developing a European System for Credit Transfer in VET.' *International Journal of Training Research*, forthcoming.

—— and WINTERTON, R. (1997). 'Workplace Training and Enskilling.' In S. Walters (ed.), *Globalization, Adult Education and Training: Impacts and Issues.* London: Zed Books.

—— (1999). *Developing Managerial Competence.* London: Routledge.

World Bank (1997). *World Development Report 1997: The State in a Changing World.* New York: Oxford University Press.

ZIDAN, S. S. (2001). 'The Role of HRD in Economic Development.' *Human Resource Development Quarterly*, 12/4: 437–43.

# REMUNERATION: PAY EFFECTS AT WORK

## JAMES P. GUTHRIE

## 17.1 INTRODUCTION

COSTCO Wholesale Corporation is a 'warehouse retailer' with over 60,000 employees working in stores spread across the USA, Canada, Taiwan, Japan, Mexico, and the UK Costco is the market leader in the US warehouse retailer segment, but they have a fierce rival in Sam's Club, a division of Wal-Mart Stores. While Costco and Sam's Club share a number of similarities, their approach to employee compensation is strikingly different. The average hourly wage of Costco's full-time employees is 42 percent higher than the average hourly wage of Sam's Club employees. In addition, Costco's health care, retirement, and other benefits are also markedly superior. Although the data specific to Sam's Club is not available, Wal-Mart covers 66.6 percent of employee health care premiums while Costco pays 92 percent. Jim Sinegal, Costco's CEO, maintains, 'This is not altruistic. This is good business.' Costco's CFO agrees, saying, 'Paying higher wages translates into more efficiency.' Deutsche Bank financial analyst Bill Dreher disagrees with these sentiments: 'At Costco, it's better to be an employee or a customer than a shareholder.' Emme Kozloff, an analyst at Sanford C. Bernstein & Company, also disagrees with Costco's pay strategy, complaining that CEO Sinegal 'has been too benevolent.' In addition to being 'different' in terms of pay level, Costco also differentiates itself with its relatively egalitarian approach to pay. Jim Sinegal's total pay package in 2004 was $550,000, an amount much less than those found in his industry peer group (Costco was 29th in total revenues among all US companies in 2004). According to Sinegal, this again represents good business sense: 'I just think that if you're going to try to run an organization that's very cost-conscious, then you can't have those disparities. Having an individual who is making 100 or 200 or 300 times more than the average person working on the floor is wrong.'[1]

As illustrated in the above passage, executives and other stakeholders consider compensation policies to be important business decisions. This passage also serves to illustrate deep-seated disagreement as to what represents 'best practice' in compensation management. In the academic literature, there is a similar diversity of perspectives, opinions, and conclusions. While this chapter will incorporate and review some of this vast literature, it is not intended to be an exhaustive review of all compensation research.[2] Instead, the goal of this chapter is to review, summarize, and discuss academic research as it pertains to *pay effects* or consequences associated with a set of limited, yet fundamentally important compensation policy issues and decisions: *pay level, pay structure*, and *pay form or payment system*. Prior to beginning the review of relevant research, I first provide a brief description of these policy issues.

*Pay level* refers to an organization's pay position relative to other product/service and labor market competitors. Broadly, firms can lead, lag, or match the market. As described above, Costco has chosen to be a market leader. What are the likely implications of this decision? Costco executives believe that organizational effectiveness will be enhanced, whereas the financial analysts quoted above are somewhat less optimistic. This chapter reviews studies that inform this debate.

While pay level refers to 'how much' employees are paid, *pay form* or *payment system* refers to 'how' they are paid—the manner in which compensation is distributed. Most generally, 'form' or 'payment system' refers to the relative amount of pay that is fixed, as opposed to variable. As reviewed below, pay-for-performance is one of the more controversial areas of compensation research. There has been significant disagreement as to whether paying for performance enhances or decreases employee motivation and individual and organizational effectiveness. In addressing this topic, I review and discuss studies examining the influence of individual and group-based pay-for-performance plans on motivation and performance.

---

[1] Data on Costco, Sam's Club, and Wal-Mart is obtained from Greenhouse 2005; Holmes and Zellner 2004; and Zimmerman 2004.

[2] For a more complete treatment of compensation research, interested readers are especially encouraged to consult Gerhart and Rynes 2003.

In this chapter, I also review effects associated with two dimensions of *pay structure*. The first dimension, the extent to which a firm's pay structure is relatively hierarchical or flat (also referred to as 'pay dispersion'), is specifically mentioned by Jim Sinegal, CEO of Costco. He states that a pay structure in which top executives make '100 or 200 or 300 times more than the average person working on the floor is wrong' and intimates that Costco's egalitarian pay structure promotes organizational effectiveness. Another aspect of pay structure is the basis of pay. Along with research on pay dispersion effects, I also review a limited number of studies examining the use of person-based, as opposed to job-based, pay systems. I begin with *pay form*, then review *pay structure*, followed by a discussion of *pay level* effects.

# 17.2 EFFECTS OF PAY FORM/PAYMENT SYSTEM

> With money, you can make the devil push a millstone.
>
> (Chinese proverb)

One of the more interesting—and controversial—issues in compensation has been delineating the manner and magnitude in which pay influences employee motivation and performance. The focus in this debate has been on whether or not monetary (i.e. 'extrinsic') rewards have 'incentive effects' or positively affect employees' attitudes and performance. While this is undeniably an important topic, pay policies may also broadly affect organizational functioning by impacting the talent level and mix of a firm's workforce. This can occur through reward systems' influence on the entry (i.e. attraction, recruiting, hiring) and exit (turnover) of employees. This point is emphasized by Rynes (1987: 190): 'compensation systems are capable of attracting (or repelling) the right kinds of people because they communicate so much about an organization's philosophy, values, and practice.' In this section, I first review evidence related to 'incentive effects' followed by a review of research on the influence of reward systems on workforce composition and competence ('sorting' effects).

*Incentive effects.* A number of theoretical perspectives have been used to explain and understand the mechanisms by which monetary rewards may positively influence individual and group performance. Chief among these are expectancy theory (Vroom 1964), goal-setting theory (Locke 1968), reinforcement theory (Skinner 1969), and agency theory (Jensen and Meckling 1976). Another theory, cognitive evaluation theory, or CET (Deci and Ryan 1985), has been used to challenge the basic assumption that pay positively impacts employee performance.

CET suggests that rewards may be harmful to employee performance due to detrimental effects on intrinsic task motivation. Intrinsic motivation is experienced when a person performs an activity that is of interest to them even when no apparent reward is received. Extrinsic motivation refers to motivation to perform an activity strictly for the rewards themselves (Daniel and Esser 1980). CET suggests that intrinsic motivation is adversely affected by rewards when reward recipients perceive the reward as controlling or as a challenge to competence. This suggestion has spurred a number of studies to test propositions of the theory, with mixed results.

A series of meta-analyses (Cameron and Pierce 1994, 1997; Deci et al. 1999; Eisenberger and Cameron 1996; Wiersma 1992) suggests that the extent to which rewards undermine intrinsic motivation is limited and circumscribed. The most supportive of these meta-analyses is Deci et al. (1999), but as pointed out by Gerhart and Rynes (2003), Deci et al.'s study found no support for detrimental effects on attitudes; moreover, their findings suggesting negative effects for the 'free-time' measure of intrinsic motivation were much more pronounced in school-aged children as opposed to an adult (college-age) population. Finally, some studies (e.g. Fang and Gerhart 1999) have reported *positive* relationships between pay and intrinsic motivation. Thus, although the CET literature has generated a provocative and healthy dialogue on the motivational value of incentives (e.g. Gupta and Shaw 1998; Kohn 1998), research does not overwhelmingly support the assertion that incentives and rewards undermine individuals' motivation or task interest. Moreover, even if Deci and colleagues are more right than wrong—even if incentives and rewards have the deleterious effects they suggest—the cumulative evidence (reviewed below) belies the claim that 'incentive plans cannot work' (Kohn 1993).

An early meta-analysis by Guzzo et al. (1985) examined the productivity effects of a number of organizational initiatives, including 'financial compensation', in studies published during the 1971–81 time period. While financial initiatives had no effect on employee withdrawal, the effect on productivity was both statistically and practically significant. In fact, the effect size associated with financial compensation initiatives was more than twice that of any of the other classes of initiatives (e.g. training, appraisal and feedback, goal-setting, etc.).

Jenkins et al. (1998) conducted a more recent meta-analysis of studies published from 1960 to 1996. Jenkins et al. (1998) only analyzed individual-level research that used experimental or quasi-experimental designs. Of the forty-seven separate studies, forty-one focused on performance quantity and six on performance quality. While the cumulative results across the six studies focusing on performance quality found no relationship between incentives and quality (the effect was positive, but small and insignificant), the effect size for performance quantity was substantial (.34). While incentive effects were evident in all settings, the effect sizes in both field (.48) and simulations (.56) were much higher than those reported in laboratory settings (.24). Since the majority of studies are conducted in lab settings, this may indicate that many studies underestimate the performance effects of incentives. Jenkins et al. speculate that weaker laboratory results may be partly attributable to the smaller incentives typically used in these settings. Jenkins et al. conclude by saying: 'These results also question the ... argument that people do not value money. If money is not important, financial incentives should show no systematic relationship with performance. Obviously, the research evidence amassed over three and a half decades shows otherwise' (1998: 783).

Other important studies include Lazear (1999) (reviewed below) and Gerhart and Milkovich (1990). Using data on approximately 14,000 top and middle-level executives and managers across a five-year time frame, Gerhart and Milkovich (1990) examined a number of research questions related to managerial base and contingent pay. The first important finding of this study is that organizations appear to be 'strategic'—they exhibit stable and systematic differences across time in terms of both pay level and pay mix (relative use of base vs. contingent pay). The second important finding from this study is that organizational differences in contingent pay (but not pay level) predict organizational profitability.

Research evidence also suggests that group-based pay-for-performance plans can be effective. In general, group incentive systems include plans in which payouts are contingent upon the achievement of group or unit goals. The best-known forms of these types of pay plans are profit-sharing and gain-sharing plans. Gain-sharing plans are group-based reward plans which pay a bonus based upon productivity improvements or cost reduction. These plans also often include a formal employee involvement component. Profit-sharing plans are another group-based reward option. While all profit-sharing plans pay a bonus based upon the achievement of profitability, these plans vary substantially in terms of frequency of payout, deferred versus cash payouts, size of the profit share, etc. Other forms of group-based pay plans include goal- or win-sharing plans and employee stock ownership plans (ESOPs).

While the mechanics of plans such as gain-sharing, profit-sharing, and ESOPs are obviously distinct, from an economic or psychological perspective they are generically more similar than different (Weitzman and Kruse 1990). They seek to enhance productivity by aligning employer and employee interests and motivating employees to contribute to organizational effectiveness. As with individual pay-for-performance plans, group pay plans can be viewed from a variety of theoretical perspectives, including goal-setting theory (Guthrie and Hollensbe 2004; Hollensbe and Guthrie 2000) and expectancy theory (Lawler 2000). Although generally applied to executive compensation, agency theory can also be applied, with group-based pay plans designed to align managers and employees' interests (Welbourne and Gomez-Mejia 1995).

Studies indicate that group performance-based pay plans can positively impact organizational outcomes (e.g. Kruse 1993; Mangan and St-Onge 2005; Pritchard et al. 1988). Due to concerns with 'line of sight' and instrumentality perceptions (e.g. Lawler 2000), profit-sharing plans are often viewed as a less effective form of group-based pay plan. Studies have shown, however, that these plans can impact firm performance, especially when they include mechanisms eliciting employee participation, rewards for individual contributions, cash payouts instead of deferred monies, and payouts of a significant increment based on relatively small profit centers (e.g. Kruse 1993; Long 2000; Mangan and St-Onge 2005).

In a series of well-designed field studies of gain-sharing plans, Arthur and colleagues (Arthur and Jelf 1999; Arthur and Aiman-Smith 2001; Arthur and Huntley forthcoming) have illuminated some of the intermediary mechanisms underlying these plans' effectiveness. These studies found that gain-sharing plans can improve labor relations (Arthur and Jelf 1999), organizational learning (Arthur and Aiman-Smith 2001), and efficiency via employees' suggestions (Arthur and Huntley forthcoming).

Intriguing evidence also suggests that the aggregate productivity effects observed for group-based pay plans may be partly due to their effects on lower performing employees. Studies by Weiss (1987) and Hansen (1997) suggest the move from individual incentive to group incentive plans results in employee performance converging to a standard: the lowest performing employees show substantial improvement following the introduction of the group plan, while the performance of the most able workers tends to decrease. These results await further replication and specification.

*Sorting effects.* The effects of pay-for-performance plans may be enhanced by what labor economists label as 'sorting'—the influence that incentives have on employee attraction and attrition. In perhaps the best examination of sorting effects to date, Lazear (1999) provides compelling results from a study of windshield installers at Safelite Glass Corporation. Defined in terms of units installed per day per worker, he found that worker productivity increased by 44 percent following implementation of a piece-rate incentive plan, with about one-half due to incentive effects, and the remainder due to sorting.

Research grounded in the person–organization fit paradigm also provides evidence related to sorting. Per Rynes (1987), compensation sends signals to prospective applicants regarding organizational culture and values. These 'signals' may impact workforce composition in the form of ability and/or disposition. Using experimental and/or policy-capturing studies, research has shown that the attractiveness of pay-at-risk and individual vs. group-based contingent pay depends on individual differences such as cognitive ability, risk preference, self-efficacy, and other aspects of personality (cf. Bretz et al. 1989; Cable and Judge 1994; Stevens and Ash 1998; Trank et al. 2002).

Research also suggests sorting effects through turnover. A meta-analysis performed by Williams and Livingstone (1994) found that pay-for-performance reward contingencies magnified the inverse relationship between performance and turnover. A more precise illustration is provided by Harrison, Virick, and William

(1996). In this field study of home telecommunications sales representatives, at the two-month mark on the job, new employees transitioned from a relatively fixed pay scheme to a system where 100 percent of pay depended upon sales performance. During the first two months of employment the correlation between sales performance and turnover was very modest, but under the commission-based system, this correlation increased dramatically.

Another supportive example is Trevor et al.'s (1997) study of managerial and professional employees of a petroleum company. Of interest here, turnover rates among top performers reduced substantially if they experienced significant salary growth. According to Trevor et al.:

> The greatest differences in retention under conditions of low and high salary growth were by far in the top two performance categories. We contend that the fate of these few employees is disproportionately important to the organization. ... Tomorrow's stars and perhaps even franchise players may be among today's few top performers; their retention, at least in part, appears to depend on paying them according to their performance. (1997: 57)

Sturman et al. (2003) analyzed the economic benefit of 'winning the talent war'— retaining higher performers through the use of individual pay-for-performance plans. Even under the most conservative assumptions regarding the value associated with employee performance variability, Sturman et al. demonstrate that performance contingent pay yields substantial financial benefits over the non-contingent pay strategy.

Group–based pay plans have interesting implications for voluntary turnover. While some evidence suggests reductions in voluntary turnover (e.g. Azfar and Danninger 2001; Wilson and Peel 1991), group-based pay plans are also imbued with the 'free rider' problem, where incentive effects are diluted by peers' attempts to free-ride off others' contribution. The free-rider problem should be particularly disturbing to higher-performing workers (Hansen 1997; Weiss 1987), leading to greater dissatisfaction and turnover among this group (see Park et al. 1994). Further, if group incentive plans are particularly dissatisfying for employees who perceive themselves as 'high performers,' then this problem may be magnified by the 'Lake Wobegone effect:' the statistical anomaly that almost all employees perceive their performance to be above average (Meyer 1975). Moreover, increases in group size may exacerbate this problem. Described as the $1/n$ problem (where $n =$ group size), direct returns to individuals in group settings are diluted by a factor of $1/n$ (Hansen 1997; Kruse 1993; Weitzman and Kruse 1990). Guthrie (2000) reported results consistent with this argument, showing that organizational turnover rates under group incentive plans increased as a function of group size.

*Pay form/payment system effects: summary.* A review of the literature suggests strongly that pay-for-performance plans, both at the individual and group levels, can have both statistically and practically significant effects. Research also suggests that effects of pay-for-performance are due to both incentive and sorting effects. Research examining pay-for-performance issues needs to especially be aware of bias that may be introduced when designs do not allow for sorting effects. In fact, the lower effects sizes for laboratory studies reported by Jenkins et al. (1998) may partly be attributable to this phenomenon. Lab studies or simulations are needed that allow subjects to 'sort' into different pay conditions in order to more precisely elucidate the contributions of sorting versus incentive effects.

In addition to observing increases in mean productivity, Lazear (1999) also documents increased dispersion around the mean following the introduction of the Safelite incentive plan. According to Lazear, once the incentive system was implemented, workers performed closer to their actual abilities, leading to both higher and more dispersed performance. This is mindful of discussions of 'typical' versus 'maximum' performance (Sackett et al. 1988). The use of intense pay-for-performance schemes may partially mimic 'maximum performance' conditions. If pay-for-performance practices have the potential to draw employees closer to 'maximum' performance, then these schemes may also have significant implications for employee selection. Specifically, these pay plans may call for increased emphasis on ability or dispositional selection criteria, as opposed to behavioral criteria.

Group-based pay-for-performance plans are arguably more complex than plans based on individual performance and, as such, more research is needed to flesh out our understanding of the effects and effectiveness of various plan features. For example, as noted earlier, evidence suggests that group-based pay plans are effective despite the potential negative impact on the most able employees (Hansen 1997; Park et al. 1994; Weiss 1987). What precise mechanisms are at work here? Preliminary evidence suggests that the mutual monitoring and peer pressure under group-based pay plans may serve to raise the performance of below-average and average employees so as to offset any losses among the top performing employees. What is the magnitude of the effect on top performers? What design elements will most effectively cause top performers to maintain their contributions? While research evidence suggests that larger incentives and rewards for individual contributions to group performance may counteract this problem (Long 2000), much more research is needed on these and other group pay phenomena.

# 17.3 EFFECTS OF PAY STRUCTURE

Inequality, rather than want, is the cause of trouble.

(Chinese saying)

In this section, I review research related to two aspects of pay 'structure'—pay dispersion and pay basis. In terms of dispersion, pay structures can range from being relatively flat or egalitarian, with limited differences across levels and positions, to those that are steep or hierarchical, displaying large differences across levels and positions. With respect to pay basis, I review a limited number of studies that have examined the use of person-based, as opposed to job-based, pay systems.

*Pay dispersion.* A starting point for this research stream is tournament theory, which seeks to both explain and inform pay structures. Developed by Lazear and Rosen (1981), tournament theory suggests that it may be efficient (i.e. it makes economic sense) to pay those at the top of a pay structure a wage that exceeds their marginal contributions. Steep differentials will benefit organizations if these pay structures serve to attract a talented pool of employees and entice them to perform at high levels in a contest for the top 'prizes.' A number of studies have examined tournament theory in the context of sports, with supportive evidence provided by studies such as Ehrenberg and Bognanno's (1990) study of golf tournaments and Becker and Huselid's (1992) study of auto racing.

In a study of professional baseball teams, Bloom suggests that more egalitarian pay structures 'can be beneficial for *group* performance because they may inculcate feelings of fairness and common purpose, foster cooperative, team-oriented behavior, and support common goal orientations' (1999: 26). Bloom examines the impact of pay dispersion on individual and team performance and finds that more egalitarian pay structures are associated with higher levels of individual and team performance. Bloom's results for baseball are consistent with several other studies of this sport (e.g. DeBrock et al. 2004; Jewell and Molina 2004).

What about the 'real' world? A number of studies have looked at pay dispersion effects at the executive level. When compared to other nations, US companies have often been described as (and criticized for) having pay structures that are 'overly' hierarchical. This suggests that tournament structures may be an American phenomenon, but this is belied by international evidence (e.g. Conyon et al. 2001; Eriksson 1999). Other tournament features that have been supported using executive pay data include greater pay dispersion associated with fewer promotions (Leonard 1990), more dynamic industry environments (Bloom and Michel 2002; Leonard 1990), greater numbers of tournament 'participants' (e.g. Conyon et al. 2001; Leonard 1990; Main et al. 1993), and higher executive turnover (Bloom and Michel 2002).

Consistent with the conclusion of Gerhart and Rynes (2003), it does appear that the bulk of the evidence from studies at this level has established the existence of tournament-like structures within the executive ranks. While evidence is generally supportive that these structures exist at this level, are tournament structures 'efficient'? Do more dispersed executive pay structures positively impact firm performance? The evidence in this regard is mixed (cf. Conyon et al. 2001; Eriksson 1999; Leonard 1990; Main et al. 1993).

Researchers have also examined performance outcomes associated with pay dispersion among workers outside of the executive ranks. These studies are generally more challenging since this pay data is often not publicly available. At the same time, these studies are arguably more important because they broaden the focus beyond the rarefied air of the executive suite to include those more directly responsible for making products and/or delivering services.

Similar to Bloom (1999), Cowherd and Levine note that organizations are 'both economic exchange systems that produce goods and services and emotional hot-beds fueled by continual social comparison' (1992: 305). These researchers argued that inter-class pay dispersion may negatively affect product quality through detrimental effects on employees' discretionary effort, cooperation, commitment, or, more formally, organizational citizenship behavior (Organ 1990). Results were consistent with these arguments.

Another study focusing on pay dispersion effects among non-executives is Shaw et al. (2002). They first make the point that intra-class wage dispersion (or hori-zontal dispersion) likely has more powerful effects on employee attitudes and behavior than inter-class dispersion (vertical dispersion): 'Horizontal pay distribu-tions hold constant many potentially confounding factors (e.g., differences in status, social class, job titles) that could reasonably explain variations in pay levels' (2002: 509). Second, they argue that pay dispersion cannot be judged as helpful or harmful to organizational effectiveness in the abstract. One consideration is the existence of individual pay-for-performance practices, which will strengthen individual motivation and, importantly, legitimize pay differences. Results across two samples largely support their arguments.

Shaw et al. also note that when authors make normative arguments for the effectiveness of pay compression, they do so by arguing that more egalitarian pay structures will enhance cooperation and teamwork toward the completion of interdependent tasks. This implies a contingency argument, wherein task interde-pendency should moderate the performance impact of pay structure. In fact, one of the original proponents of tournament theory has made similar arguments: 'If harmony is important, pay compression is optimal on strict efficiency grounds' (Lazear 1989: 579). Supporting this contingency argument, Shaw et al. find that performance is poorest when pay dispersion and work interdependence are both high.

Another relevant study is Pfeffer and Langton's (1993) examination of the effects of pay dispersion on a sample of over 17,000 faculty from more than 600 US academic departments. Their main finding was that wage dispersion within de-partments is associated with lower satisfaction, productivity, and collaboration on the part of individual faculty.[3] Similar to Shaw et al. (2002), Pfeffer and Langton report that the impact of pay dispersion on satisfaction is reduced in departments where the dispersion is more 'justified' (i.e. more strongly correlated with experi-ence, education, or productivity).

---

[3] Gerhart and Rynes 2003 provide an interesting critique of this study.

Brown et al. (2003) examined the implications of pay dispersion for organizational performance (efficiency, patient care, financial performance) within 333 acute care hospitals in the state of California. They find the effect of pay dispersion on organizational performance depends on an organization's pay market position. Egalitarian structures were more effective when paired with below-market wages and hierarchical structures more effective in tandem with above-market pay.

*Pay basis.* Traditional job-based pay systems (e.g. point factor systems) are structured so that pay is attached to the jobs that employees perform. The internal value of jobs is often determined by job evaluation, a process wherein value is assigned based on the assessment of jobs vis-à-vis a set of compensable factors (e.g. skills, responsibility, effort, working conditions). Jobs of similar value are assigned to the same pay grades. Lower pay grades represent jobs of lower value; higher pay grades contain jobs of higher value. In job-based systems, jobs and pay grades are often 'priced' through the use of market survey data. While job evaluation helps determine the internal pay structure ('internal equity'), collecting representative market pay data helps firms assign wages and ensure external competitiveness ('external equity'). In job-based pay systems, while there may be pay adjustments (e.g. merit increases) associated with performance, pay is largely determined by the value of the job that one holds. Thus, large pay increases occur primarily as a function of progressing up the hierarchy of pay grades into jobs deemed to have more organizational value.

In contrast to job-based pay structures, person-based pay structures attach pay to individual employees' skills, knowledge, or competencies. Under person-based pay systems, the basis for pay is largely a function of the breadth and/or depth of knowledge, skills, or competencies possessed by an employee. The knowledge or skills required for work process or task completion are typically broken down into skill or knowledge 'blocks' which are, in turn, often further broken down into skill or knowledge 'levels.' Under person-based pay systems, pay adjustments are made when individuals are certified as having acquired additional skills or knowledge specific to the particular system. As with job-based systems, market pay data is often used to help 'price' the pay structure, although the pricing is often complicated by the lack of comparable person-based systems in other organizations.

Advocates of person-based reward systems believe these pay systems hold many advantages over job-based systems (Lawler 2000). Job-based systems are thought to incent upward promotion, reinforce hierarchical structures, and to be more consistent with a 'command and control,' top-down management style. Moreover, job-based systems are deemed less compatible with interdependent tasks and team-based structures. In contrast, person-based systems, with their emphasis on skill and knowledge acquisition, are argued to be a better fit with the need for a lean, flexible, and multi-skilled workforce able to adjust their roles as dictated by changing market and organizational demands. For all of these reasons, proponents of person-based pay systems believe they should be a central component of 'high performance' or 'high involvement' work organizations (Lawler 2000).

Despite the strong interest and growth in the use of the person-based alternative as a basis for pay, relatively few studies have empirically examined the consequences of these plans. The exceptions include work by McNabb and Whitfield (2001) who found that British firms using more of a 'high-performance' approach to management were less likely to utilize job evaluation and performed more poorly if they did. Other research suggests that use of person-based pay systems may reduce organization-level turnover (Guthrie 2000).

To date, the best evidence of the organizational-level performance impacts of person-based pay plans is provided by Murray and Gerhart (1998). These authors obtained thirty-seven months of time series data from a production facility's records to examine the impact of skill-based plan adoption on three fundamentally important indicators of performance: product quality (scrap percentage), productivity (labor hours per part), and labor cost (wages divided by number of good parts produced). The time series data indicates that productivity increased dramatically following adoption of skill-based pay, with labor hours per part reduced by 58 percent. Despite the fact that hourly wages increased during the study period, the increased productivity resulted in a 16 percent reduction in labor costs. Also, the skill-base pay facility's scrap rate was 82 percent; better than a comparison control facility.

*Pay structure effects: summary.* Research results on pay dispersion effects are unequivocally equivocal. This may be logical since, in a general way, both overly hierarchical and overly egalitarian pay structures are likely to violate equity theory principles. Moreover, it is apparent that definitions of 'egalitarian' and 'hierarchical' will depend on a host of contingencies, including—but certainly not limited to—the nature of the task (e.g. Bloom, 1999; Shaw et al. 2002), market pay position (Brown et al. 2003), use of 'legitimate' bases for pay dispersion (Shaw et al. 2002) and industry (Bloom and Michel 2002). Even though we are beginning to understand these issues, much remains unexplored. For example, even in the case of baseball, where a number of studies have shown negative effects for pay dispersion on team performance, it is still not clear why this occurs. This is especially true given that the opposite finding has been reported in studies of other professional team sports (DeBrock et al. 2004). Moreover, while much of the criticisms of hierarchical pay are directed toward ratios of executive pay to 'average' workers, Shaw et al. (2002) make the point that intra-class pay dispersion is probably more impactful than inter-class dispersion. This seems intuitive, but requires empirical examination.

Research on the person-based pay alternative is fairly undeveloped at present. The only tightly designed study of organizational consequences associated with this approach to pay was quite promising (Murray and Gerhart 1998). Along with other studies of 'main effects,' more studies are needed on the contextual conditions that make the person-based alternative a better 'fit.'

# 17.4 EFFECTS OF PAY LEVEL

It's not money that brings happiness, it's lots of money.

(Russian proverb)

Viewed from the perspective of neoclassical economic theory, individual employers are assumed to be wage-*takers*, as opposed to wage-*makers*. In this view, wages are determined by the market-level supply and demand for workers and, as price-takers and profit-maximizers, individual firms will hire workers until the marginal revenue generated by additional hires equals the cost of the market-determined wage. From this traditional perspective, there is no advantage for firms to deviate from the 'market' rate. In fact, doing so would always negatively impact firm profits. Both anecdotal and empirical evidence suggests, however, that firms vary substantially in the amount of compensation offered to employees. The Costco example in the beginning of this chapter is one example. More formally, Leonard (1989) showed that wages for a similar job can vary by as much as 50 percent within a given city. Moreover, while the economics literature tends to focus on human capital and industry characteristics in explaining pay-level differences, research suggests that organizations adopt distinct, stable market pay positions (Gerhart and Milkovich 1990). What are the consequences associated with these different pay-level positions? As detailed below, the relevant body of work remains incomplete and somewhat inconsistent.

The 'efficiency wage hypothesis' (Akerlof and Yellen 1986) was developed to help understand pay market positioning effects and outlines several mechanisms to help understand why paying above-market wages may sometimes be 'efficient' or, more colloquially, improve firm effectiveness. First, since workers will want to maintain employment with their above-market employer, it will reduce the likelihood of 'shirking' or performance problems. Second, above-market wages may help by reducing turnover. Third, similar to equity theory arguments, employees may increase their effort and performance out of a sense of fairness. Fourth, above-market employers may enjoy an advantage in terms of their ability to attract a more talented pool of applicants. Several studies appear to validate a number of these arguments.

A clever study of the efficiency wage hypothesis was conducted by Cappelli and Chauvin (1991). They used data on seventy-eight plants from a single US firm to examine the relationship of wage rates with employee dismissal for disciplinary reasons (e.g. due to low performance, absenteeism, tardiness, etc.). While all plants were under the same national contract, cost-of-living differences in different locations led to significant differences in employees' 'real wages.' Consistent with efficiency wage predictions, Cappelli and Chauvin found that higher (real) wages reduced 'shirking' and discipline-related dismissals, with the effect magnified with increases in local unemployment rates.

Other research supports the conclusion that above-market wage rates tend to reduce employees' turnover intentions or actual turnover (e.g. Guthrie 2001; Levine 1993; Shaw et al. 1998). In one of the few studies to link relative pay rates with employee attitudes, Levine (1993) found that higher plant wage rates in their US and Japanese sample improved employee outcomes on a number of measures, including job and pay satisfaction levels, intentions to stay with the company, and reports of willingness to 'work harder.' In addition to affecting turnover, it is perhaps unsurprising that potential employees are also attracted to firms paying higher wages (e.g. Barber and Bretz 2000; Cable and Judge 1994).

In sum, research suggests that higher relative wages improve the ability to both attract and retain employees. This is again illustrated by Costco. For example, after the first year of employment, Costco has a 6 percent employee turnover rate, as compared to 21 percent at Sam's Club (Holmes and Zellner 2004). Does this ability to retain employees yield economic benefits? Costco believes that its higher market wage helps account for its comparative productivity advantage in terms of sales revenue ($795 sales/square foot per employee vs. $516 at Sam's) and operating profits ($13,643 per employee vs. $11,034 at Sam's). Because of this productivity advantage—and despite the fact that their per capita wage rates are higher—Costco's labor costs as a percentage of revenue are significantly lower than Sam's Club.

The research evidence, however, is a bit more mixed. Supportive evidence for the efficiency wage argument is found in a study of UK manufacturing plants (Wadhwani and Wall 1991), where higher relative wages were positively associated with both output and value added per employee. However, Gerhart and Milkovich (1990) found that while use of contingency pay for managers positively influenced firm performance (ROA), managerial pay-level position did not affect performance. And, in Brown et al.'s (2003) study of pay practices in California hospitals, while pay level had direct, positive impacts on organizational performance in terms of both patient care quality and efficiency, there were non-linear, diminishing returns to increases in market pay position, prompting the authors to assert that 'there exist limits as to how much selection can be improved, turnover can be reduced, and motivation can be increased with pay' (p. 760).

Finally, the set of studies on pay effects in the professional sports arena discussed earlier is also relevant. While Bloom (1999) finds strong negative effects on baseball team performance for pay dispersion, he finds no pay-level effects (in fact, his bivariate correlations indicate that relative team payroll has a significant, *negative* correlation with teams' finishing positions). His results stand in contrast with those of Frick et al. (2003) who find strong positive effects for total team pay in four different US professional leagues: baseball, basketball, hockey, and football.

These mixed results underscore the need for firms to consider a host of firm-specific variables that may moderate consequences associated with pay-level policy decisions. This is highlighted by Klaas and McClendon, who applied utility analysis to pay-level policy decisions and concluded that firms must determine the 'financial impact that pay level has on turnover (both quantity and quality), applicant pool characteristics, acceptance rates, selections costs, and equity reactions and then compare the sum total of these effects to discounted wage costs' (1996: 136–7).

*Pay level effects: summary.* Based on available evidence, it seems reasonably clear that higher pay levels are attractive to both prospective and current employees. Applicants find above-market employers appealing and current employees are less likely to depart. Thus, higher pay levels put employers in a strong position vis-à-vis labor market competitors. Whether or not this translates into competitive success, however, is not straightforward. As Brown et al. (2003) point out, there are diminishing returns to increasing wages—and specifying the inflection point will likely prove challenging. In addition, the problem an above-market employer will face is a challenge shared by any 'employer of choice'—they will be attractive to *all* members of the labor market. Thus, rigorous and valid selection systems should moderate the relationship between above-market pay strategies and firm success.

Combining other pay design elements may also prove beneficial. Specifically, utilizing strong pay-for-performance elements in tandem with above-market wages may magnify the 'efficiency' advantage with the benefits of 'sorting.' This may help explain Brown et al.'s (2003) results, where high pay dispersion coupled with above-market wages yielded superior profitability. That is, if the wage dispersion was the result of paying for performance, then the combined benefits may have been in place. Moreover, if the pay dispersion resulted from a pay-for-performance system perceived as 'legitimate,' then firms may benefit from both sorting effects and employees' perceptions of equity and justice (Shaw et al. 2002). These notions are inferred from previous research and require empirical examination.

Costco's executives believe that higher employee pay is 'efficient' in the sense that high wages attract and retain a talented, committed, and productive workforce. However, studies are needed to verify the validity and generalizability of this claim, including research examining the causal pathway between pay levels, applicant and employee attitudes, intermediary outcomes such as absenteeism, turnover, productivity, and, ultimately, financial success.

# 17.5 CONCLUSION

This brief review of extant compensation research highlights what makes this topic so interesting—despite a plethora of studies, there are many fundamental issues that remain unresolved. Stated another way, it is not clear what constitutes 'best practice' in many aspects of compensation policy and practice. In each of the areas addressed in this chapter—pay form, structure, and level—there are a myriad of issues that require the proverbial 'additional future research.' While evidence clearly suggests that 'money matters,' in the sense that it affects many aspects of individual and organizational behavior and performance, it is often unclear as to 'how' or 'why' this occurs.

As one example, while paying an above-market wage can improve organizational effectiveness (e.g. Brown et al. 2003), this is not always true (Gerhart and Milkovich 1990). In part this is because pay-level effects depend on contingencies such as, for example, use of contingent pay and pay structure. In fact, the uncertainty about this issue may lead firms to 'play it safe' and attempt to conform to market pay norms: 'the consequences associated with paying too little or too much may be so serious that organizations avoid risky experimentation with pay level strategies' (Gerhart and Milkovich 1990: 685).

Although compensation practice remains imbued with ambiguity, it *is* important—the vast array of research and writing devoted to compensation issues is a testament to this fact. Recent years have witnessed significant progress; future research can inform practice by continuing to reduce uncertainty surrounding organizational reward systems.

# REFERENCES

AKERLOF, G. A., and YELLEN, J. L. (1986). *Efficiency Wage Models of the Labor Market.* Cambridge: Cambridge University Press.

ARTHUR, J. B., and AIMAN-SMITH, L. (2001). 'Gainsharing and Organizational Learning: An Analysis of Employee Suggestions over Time.' *Academy of Management Journal*, 44: 737–54.

—— and HUNTLEY, C. L. (forthcoming). 'Ramping up the Organizational Learning Curve: Assessing the Impact of Deliberate Learning on Organizational Performance under Gainsharing.' *Academy of Management Journal.*

—— and JELF, G. S. (1999). 'The Effects of Gainsharing on Grievance Rates and Absenteeism over Time.' *Journal of Labor Research*, 20: 133–45.

AZFAR, O., and DANNINGER, S. (2001). 'Profit-Sharing, Employment Stability and Wage Growth.' *Industrial and Labor Relations Review*, 54: 619–30.

BARBER, A. E., and BRETZ, R. D. (2000). 'Compensation, Attraction and Retention.' In S. L. Rynes and B. Gerhart (eds.), *Compensation in Organizations: Current Research and Practice.* San Francisco: Jossey-Bass.

BECKER, B. E., and HUSELID, M. A. (1992). 'The Incentive Effects of Tournament Compensation Systems.' *Administrative Science Quarterly*, 37: 336–50.

BLOOM, M. (1999). 'The Performance Effects of Pay Dispersion on Individuals and Organizations.' *Academy of Management Journal*, 42: 25–40.

—— and MICHEL, J. G. (2002). 'The Relationship among Organizational Context, Pay Dispersion and Managerial Turnover.' *Academy of Management Journal*, 45: 33–42.

BRETZ, R. D., and BOUDREAU, J. W. (1994). 'Job Search Behavior of Employed Managers.' *Personnel Psychology*, 47: 275–301.

—— ASH, R. A., and DREHER, G. F. (1989). 'Do People Make the Place? An Examination of the Attraction-Selection-Attrition Hypothesis.' *Personnel Psychology*, 42: 561–81.

BROWN, M. P., STURMAN, M. C., and SIMMERING, M. J. (2003). 'Compensation Policy and Organizational Performance: The Efficiency, Operational, and Financial Implications of Pay Levels and Pay Structure.' *Academy of Management Journal*, 46: 752–62.

CABLE, D., and JUDGE, T. A. (1994). 'Pay Preferences and Job Search Decisions: A Person–Organization Fit Perspective.' *Personnel Psychology*, 47: 317–48.

CAMERON, J., and PIERCE, W. D. (1994). 'Reinforcement, Reward, and Intrinsic Motivation: A Meta-analysis.' *Review of Educational Research*, 64: 363–423.

—— —— (1997). 'Rewards, Interest and Performance: An Graluation of Experimental Findings.' *ACA Journal*, 6: 6–15.

CAPPELLI, P., and CHAUVIN, K., (1991). 'An Interplant Test of the Efficiency Wage Hypothesis.' *Quarterly Journal of Economics*, August: 769–87.

CONYON, M. J., PECK, S. L., and SADLER, G. V. (2001). 'Corporate Tournaments and Executive Compensation: Evidence from the U.K.' *Strategic Management Journal*, 22: 805–15.

COWHERD, D. M., and LEVINE, D. L. (1992). 'Product Quality and Pay Equity between Lower-Level Employees and Top Management: An Investigation of Distributive Justice Theory.' *Administrative Science Quarterly*, 37: 302–20.

DANIEL, T. L., and ESSER, J. K. (1980). 'Intrinsic Motivation as Influenced by Rewards, Task Interest, and Task Structure.' *Journal of Applied Psychology*, 65: 566–73.

DEBROCK, L., HENDRICKS, W., and KOENKER, R. (2004). 'Pay and Performance: The Impact of Salary Distribution on Firm-Level Outcomes in Baseball.' *Journal of Sports Economics*, 5: 243–61.

DECI, E. L. (1971). 'Effects of Externally Mediated Rewards on Intrinsic Motivation.' *Journal of Personality and Social Psychology*, 18: 105–15.

—— and RYAN, R. M. (1985). *Intrinsic Motivation and Self-Determination in Human Behavior.* New York: Plenum Press.

—— KOESTNER, R., and RYAN, R. M. (1999). 'A Meta-analytic Review of Experiments Examining the Effects of Extrinsic Rewards an Intrinsic Motivation.' *Psychological Bulletin*, 25: 627–68.

EHRENBERG, R. G., and BOGNANNO, M. L. (1990). 'Do Tournaments have Incentive Effects?' *Journal of Political Economy*, 98: 1307–24.

EISENBERGER, R., and CAMERON, J. (1996). 'Detrimental Effects of Reward: Reality or Myth?' *American Psychologist*, 51: 1153–66.

ERIKSSON, T. (1999). 'Executive Compensation and Tournament Theory: Compirical Tests on Danish Data.' *Journal of Labor Economics*, 17: 262–80.

FANG, M., and GERHART, B. (1999). 'How do Company Differences in Pay for Performance Strategy Influence Intrinsic Motivation, Extrinsic Motivation and Overall Motivation?' Paper presented at the annual meeting of the Academy of Management, Chicago.

FRICK, B., PRINZ, J., and WIKELMANN, K. (2003). 'Pay Inequalities and Team Performance: Empirical Evidence from the North American Major Leagues.' *International Journal of Manpower*, 24: 472–88.

GERHART, B., and MILKOVICH, G. T. (1990). 'Organizational Differences in Managerial Compensation and Financial Performance.' *Academy of Management Journal*, 33: 663–91.

—— and RYNES. S. L. (2003). *Compensation: Theory, Evidence, and Strategic Implications.* Thousand Oaks, Calif.: Sage Publications.

GOMEZ-MEJIA, L. R., and BALKIN, D. B. (1992). 'Determinants of Faculty Pay: An Agency Theory Perspective.' *Academy of Management Review*, 35: 921–55.

GREENHOUSE, S. (2005). 'How Costco Became the Anti-Wal-Mart.' *New York Times*, 17 July.

GUPTA, N., and SHAW, J. (1998). 'Let the Evidence Speak: Financial Incentives *are* Effective!!' *Compensation and Benefits Review*, 30/2: 26, 28–32.

GUTHRIE, J. P. (2000). 'Alternative Pay Practices and Employee Turnover: An Organization Economics Perspective.' *Group and Organization Management*, 25: 219–39.

—— (2001). 'High Involvement Work Practices, Turnover and Productivity: Evidence from New Zealand.' *Academy of Management Journal*, 44: 180–90.

—— and HOLLENSBE, E. C. (2004). 'Group Incentives and Performance: A Study of Spontaneous Goal Setting, Goal Choice, and Goal Commitment.' *Journal of Management*, 30/2: 263–84.

GUZZO, R. A., JETTE, R. D., and KATZELL, R. A. (1985). 'The Effects of Psychologically Based Interventions on Worker Productivity: A Meta-analysis.' *Personnel Psychology*, 38: 275–91.

HANSEN, D. G. (1997). 'Worker Performance and Group Incentives: A Case Study.' *Industrial and Labor Relations Review*, 51: 37–49.

HARRISON, D. A., VIRICK, M., and WILLIAM, S. (1996). 'Working without a Net: Time, Performance, and Turnover under Maximally Contingent Rewards.' *Journal of Applied Psychology*, 81: 331–45.

HOLLENSBE, E. C., and GUTHRIE, J. P. (2000). 'Group Pay-for-Performance Plans: The Role of Spontaneous Goal-Setting.' *Academy of Management Review*, 25: 864–72.

HOLMES, S., and ZELLNER, W. (2004). 'Commentary: The Costco Way.' *BusinessWeek online*, 12 April.

JENKINS, D. G., MITRA, A., GUPTA, N., and SHAW, J. D. (1998). 'Are Financial Incentives Related to Performance? A Meta-analytic Review of Empirical Research.' *Journal of Applied Pscychology*, 83: 777–87.

JENSEN, M. C., and MECKLING, W. N. (1976). 'Theory of the Firm: Managerial Behavior, Agency Costs and Ownership Structure.' *Journal of Financial Economics*, 3: 305–60.

JEWELL, R. T., and MOLINA, D. J. (2004). 'Productive Efficiency and Salary Distribution: The Case of US Major League Baseball.' *Scottish Journal of Political Economy*, 51: 127–42.

KLAAS, B. S., and McCLENDON, J. A. (1996). 'To Lead, Lag or Match: Estimating the Financial Impact of Pay Level Policies.' *Personnel Psychology*, 49: 121–40.

KOHN, A. (1993). 'Why Incentives Cannot Work.' *Harvard Business Review*, September–October: 54–63.

—— (1998). 'Challenging Behaviorist Dogma: Myths about Money and Motivation.' *Compensation and Benefits Review*, 30: 27–33.

KRUSE, D. L. (1993). *Profit Sharing: Does it Make a Difference?* Kalamazoo, Mich.: W. E. Upjohn Institute.

LAWLER, E. (2000). *Rewarding Excellence.* San Francisco: Jossey-Bass.

LAZEAR, E. P. (1989). 'Pay Equality and Industrial Politics.' *Journal of Political Economy*, 97: 561–80.

—— (1999). 'Performance Pay and Productivity.' *American Economic Review*, 90: 1346–61.

—— and ROSEN, S. (1981). 'Rank Order Tournaments as an Optimum Labor Contract.' *Journal of Political Economy*, 89: 841–64.

LEONARD, J. S. (1989). 'Wage Structure and Dynamics in the Electronics Industry.' *Industrial Relations*, 28: 251–75.

—— (1990). 'Executive Pay and Firm Performance.' *Industrial and Labor Relations Review*, 43: 13S–29S.

LERINE, D. I. (1993). 'What do Wages Buy?' *Administrative Science Quarterly*, 38: 462–83.

LOCKE, E. A. (1968). 'Toward a Theory of Task Motivation and Incentives.' *Organizational Behavior and Human Performance*, 3: 157–89.

LONG, R. J. (2000). 'Employee Profit Sharing: Consequences and Moderators.' *Relations industrielles/Industrial Relations*, 55: 477–504.

McNABB, R., and WHITFIELD, K. (2001). 'Job Gratuation and High Performance Work Practices: Compatible or Contuctual?' *Journal of Management Studies*, 38: 293–312.

MAIN, B., O'REILLY, C., and WADE, J. (1993). 'Top Executive Pay: Tournament or Teamwork.' *Journal of Labor Economics*, 11: 606–28.

MANGAN, M., and ST-ONGE, S. (2005). 'The Impact of Profit Sharing on the Performance of Financial Services Firms.' *Journal of Management Studies*, 42: 761–91.

MEYER, H. H. (1975). 'The Pay for Performance Dilemma.' *Organizational Dynamics*, 3: 39–50.

MURRAY, B. C., and GERHART, B. (1998). 'An Empirical Analysis of a Skill-Based Pay Program and Plant Performance Outcomes.' *Academy of Management Journal*, 41: 68–78.

ORGAN, D. W. (1990). 'The Motivational Basis of Organizational Citizenship Behavior.' In B. M. Staw and L. L. Cummings (eds.), *Research in Organizational Behavior*. Greenwich, Conn.: JAI Press.

PARK, H. Y., OFORI-DANKWA, J., and BISHOP, D. R. (1994). 'Organizational and Environmental Determinants of Functional and Dysfunctional Turnover: Practice and Research Implications.' *Human Relations*, 47: 353–66.

PFEFFER, J., and LANGTON, N. (1993). 'The Effect of Wage Dispersion on Satisfaction, Productivity, and Working Collaboratively: Evidence from College and University Faculty.' *Administrative Science Quarterly*, 38: 382–407.

PRITCHARD, R. D., JONES, S. D., ROTH, P. L., STUEBING, K. K., and EKEBERG, S. E. (1988). 'Effects of Group Feedback, Goal Setting and Incentives on Organizational Productivity [Monograph].' *Journal of Applied Psychology*, 73: 337–58.

RYNES, S. (1987). 'Compensation Strategies for Recruiting.' *Topics in Total Compensation*, 2: 185–96.

—— and BOUDREAU, J. W. (1986). 'College Recruiting in Large Organizations: Practice, Evaluation, and Research Implications.' *Personnel Psychology*, 39: 729–57.

SACKETT, P. R., ZEDECK, S., and FOGLI, L. (1988). 'Relations between Measues of Typical and Maximum Job Performance.' *Journal of Applied Psychology*, 73: 482–6.

SHAW, J. D., DELERY, J. E., JENKINS, G. D., Jr., and GUPTA, N. (1998). 'An Organizational-Level Analysis of Voluntary and Involuntary Turnover.' *Academy of Management Journal*, 41: 511–25.

—— GUPTA, N., and DELERY, J. E. (2002). 'Pay Dispersion and Workforce Performance: Moderating Effects of Incentives and Interdependence.' *Strategic Management Journal*, 23: 491–512.

SKINNER, B. F. (1969). *Contingencies of Reinforcement*. Englewood Cliffs, NJ: Prentice-Hall.

STEVENS, C. D., and ASH, R. A. (1998). 'Personality and Pay Preferences: A Person–Organization Fit Perspective.' Paper presented to the conference of the Society for Industrial and Organizational Psychology, Dallas, Tex.

STURMAN, M. C., TREVOR, C. O., BOUDREAU, J. W., and GERHART, B. (2003). 'Is it Worth it to Win the Talent War? Evaluating the Utility of Performance-Based Pay.' *Personnel Psychology*, 56: 997–1035.

TRANK, C. Q., RYNES, S. L., and BRETZ, R. D., Jr. (2002). 'Attracting Applicants in the War for Talent: Differences in Work Preferences Among High Achievers.' *Journal of Business Psychology*, 17: 331–45.

TREVOR, C., GERHART, B., and BOUDREAU, J. (1997). 'Voluntary Turnover and Job Performance: Curvilinearity and the Moderating Influences of Salary Growth and Promotions.' *Journal of Applied Psychology*, 82: 44–61.

VROOM, V. H. (1964). *Work and Motivation*. New York: Wiley.

WADHWANI, S. B., and WALL, M. (1991). 'A Direct Test of the Efficiency Wage Model Using U.K. Micro-data.' *Oxford Economic Papers*, 43: 529–48.

WEISS, A. (1987). 'Incentives and Worker Behavior: Some Evidence.' In H. R. Nalbandian (ed.), *Incentives, Cooperation and Risk Sharing*. Totowa, NJ: Rowman & Littlefield.

WEITZMAN, M. L., and KRUSE, D. L. (1990). 'Profit sharing and Productivity.' In A. S. Blinder (ed.), *Paying for Productivity: A Look at the Evidence*. Washington: The Brookings Institution.

WELBOURNE, T. M., and GOMEZ-MEJIA, L. R. (1995). 'Gainsharing: A Critical Review and a Future Research Agenda.' *Journal of Management*, 21: 559–609.

WIERSMA, U. J. (1992). 'The Effects of Extrinsic Rewards in Intrinsic Motivation: A Meta-analysis.' *Journal of Occupational and Organizational Psychology*, 65: 101–14.

WILLIAMS, C. R., and LIVINGSTONE, L. P. (1994). 'Another Look at the Relationship between Performance and Voluntary Turnover.' *Academy of Management Journal*, 37: 269–98.

WILSON, N., and PEEL, M. J. (1991). 'The Impact on Absenteeism and Quits of Profit-Sharing and Other Forms of Employee Participation.' *Industrial and Labor Relations Review*, 44: 454–68.

ZIMMERMAN, Z. (2004). 'Costco's Dilemma: Be Kind to its Workers, or Wall Street?' *Wall Street Journal*, 16 March, p. B1.

CHAPTER 18

# PERFORMANCE MANAGEMENT

GARY LATHAM

LORNE M. SULSKY

HEATHER MACDONALD

## 18.1 INTRODUCTION

JACK Welch, the former CEO of General Electric (GE), repeatedly emphasized the necessity of a boundaryless organization. This is because GE could not afford its divisions hoarding rather than sharing information if it was to remain competitive in a global market place. Similarly, Latham and Heslin (2003) argued the necessity of a boundaryless psychology. I/O psychology cannot afford to have significant advances in knowledge in one subfield go unnoticed in other subfields if it wishes to remain relevant in the public domain. In both GE and I/O psychology, information languishing within a division or subdiscipline can lead to fractionization, which is the peeling away of one or more parts that in turn can lead to the formation of a separate entity. The danger for this to occur in I/O psychology is inherent in its very name.

That a dichotomy between industrial vs. organizational psychology is false is evident in the science and practice of performance appraisal/management. The appraisal and management of an employee's and a team's performance are core requirements of leadership. A cornerstone of the appraisal and management of both an employee's and a team's performance is the inculcation of a desire for continuous improvement, i.e. the motivation of people in the workplace to choose to perform, to choose to exert effort in doing so, and to choose to persist until the organization's goals are attained. A cornerstone of leadership is to provide feedback in relation to the goals that have been set in ways that increase self and collective efficacy so that even higher goals can and should be attained. Thus it is foolhardy to view the subdomains of leadership and motivation on one continuum and performance appraisal/management on another. Another central role of leadership is to make administrative decisions regarding a person, as well as the team in which the person is a member. Yet decision-making issues and team performance have yet to receive the attention in the performance appraisal/management literature that they deserve.

A distinguishing feature of performance management relative to performance appraisal is that the former is an ongoing process whereas the latter is done at discrete time intervals (e.g. annually). Ongoing coaching is an integral aspect of performance management (Latham et al. 2005). Performance appraisal is the time period in which to summarize the overall progress that an individual or team has made as a result of being coached, and to agree on the new goals that should be set.

Common to the performance management/appraisal process are the four following steps. First, desired job performance must be defined. Second, an individual's performance on the job must be observed. Is the person or team's performance excellent, superior, satisfactory, or unacceptable? Third, feedback is provided and specific challenging goals are set as to what the person or team should start doing, stop doing, or be doing differently. Fourth, a decision is made regarding retaining, rewarding, training, transferring, promoting, demoting, or terminating an individual. Although this four-step process appears simple, it is ripe for interpersonal conflict, and hence is likely to lead to the demotivation rather than the motivation of employees. Employees often question the dimensions of performance on which they are being appraised (e.g. 'you are evaluating me on the wrong things') as well as the objectivity of the appraiser. The purpose of this chapter is to review the literature for answers to these issues and in doing so to pose questions that have yet to be addressed.

## 18.2 STEP 1: DEFINE JOB PERFORMANCE

This first step includes clarifying the performance domain for which employees are accountable. Inherent in this step are decisions regarding the choice of a coaching appraisal instrument, the technology if any that should be used to supplement the appraisal process, and the importance of context to all of the above. This section addresses these issues and, in addition, describes two theories for defining and rating performance.

The initial question that has to be addressed is what should supervisors be looking for when observing and appraising an employee on the job? That is, what behavioral items should constitute an appraisal/diagnostic performance instrument? A clear articulation of what is meant by performance is necessary for the development of valid performance diagnostic tools. Moreover, an appropriate definition of perform-ance is a prerequisite for the feedback delivery and goal-setting process. In short, a performance theory is needed that stipulates (*a*) the relevant performance dimen-sions, (*b*) the performance standards or expectations associated with alternative performance levels, (*c*) how situational constraints should be weighted (if at all) when evaluating performance, (*d*) the number of performance levels or gradients (see Cardy and Keefe 1994), and (*e*) the extent to which performance should be based upon absolute vs. relative comparison standards (Austin and Villanova 1992; Wagner and Goffin 1997). A request by the United States Army for a project, subsequently known as Project A, to address these issues led to the formation of a performance theory (Campbell et al. 1993).

Campbell et al.'s theory defines performance as behavior or action relevant to the attainment of an organization's goals that can be scaled, that is, measured. More-over, job performance is defined as what one is paid to do, or what one should be paid to do. The theory states that the measurement options, be they ratings from a supervisor, peer, or self, a simulated work sample, or hard criteria (e.g. tallying revenue generated, costs saved, customer complaints, or some variant of a com-puterized performance assessment) besides being valid, reliable, and not deficient should be free of contamination from sources of variation that are not under the control of the individual (e.g. differences in technology impacting a person's performance). Situational enhancers or constraints, if not taken into account in an appraisal, can contaminate the mean, variance, or both with regard to an individual's performance.

Campbell et al.'s theory further states that performance is multidimensional, and that each dimension is represented by a category of similar behaviors or actions. The theory posits a taxonomy of higher-order performance components, namely, (1) job-specific task proficiency, (2) non-job-specific task proficiency (i.e. organ-izational citizenship behavior), (3) written and oral communication proficiency, (4) demonstration of effort, (5) maintenance of personal discipline, (6) facilitation of peer and team performance, (7) supervision/leadership, and (8) management/administration. This theory provides a framework for any scientist who wants to study performance and any practitioner who wants to improve it. Among the determinants of performance are three types of choices an individual makes, namely, the choice to perform, choice of effort level, and choice of duration of effort, that is, a person's persistence.

## 18.2.1 Appraisal Instruments

Inherent in the definition of job performance is the development of an instrument for assessing it. Hence, the appraisal instrument is more than a form to be completed 'after the fact' at the request of the HR department. It is a diagnostic tool to be used on an a priori basis to facilitate self-coaching and the coaching of others as to what a person needs to start, stop, or continue doing on the job. In short, it specifies for both the manager and the employee what should be observed for attaining organizationally desired outcomes.

In practice, many organizations focus on the outcomes themselves such as measures of goal attainment. The dangers in doing so are at least fivefold. First, outcome measures are often affected by factors beyond a person's control (e.g. the economy). Consequently, a person receives a high or low evaluation undeservedly. Second, outcome measures are often deficient in that they do not take into account factors for which a manager should be held accountable (e.g. sharing information with other divisions; team playing). Third, they can encourage a 'results at all costs' mentality where 'winning the game is perceived to be more important for one's career than how one plays the game.' Fourth, a focus on outcomes is counter to the coaching process inherent in performance management. A focus on outcomes keeps people informed of the score, but it does not tell them by what means and to what extent they have influenced their rate of promotion, salary increase, or their team's production. Fifth, outcome measures increase the probability of hindsight bias, a decision-making error discussed subsequently. Behavioral instruments, on the other hand, should be designed to specify how an organization's strategy is to be implemented in order to attain its goals.

Behaviorally anchored rating scales or BARS (Smith and Kendall 1963) provide the rater with behavioral illustrations of the different points on the rating scale (i.e. 'behavioral anchors' for defining a 1, 5, or a 7 rating of an employee). Behavioral observation scales or BOS (Latham and Wexley 1977) require appraisers to rate the frequency with which they have observed an employee demonstrate specific behaviors. In contrast to these two instruments are trait-based scales which require the rater to make inferences from behavioral observations to personality dispositions (e.g. integrity, dependability). This inferential leap makes it difficult to calibrate specific ratings to actual employee behaviors. Hence inter-observer reliability between two or more appraisers is usually low. Giving an employee constructive feedback without defining each trait behaviorally can cause confusion: 'What did she mean when she said I need to be more assertive with peers?' Thus, it is not surprising that the North American courts take a dim view of them (Latham and Wexley 1994).

BARS are based on the assumption by Smith and Kendall (1963) that it is helpful to give raters a frame of reference in the form of behavioral illustrations of what constitutes unacceptable, acceptable, and highly acceptable performance.

These illustrations, or behavioral anchors, are derived from a job analysis, namely, the critical incident technique or CIT (Flanagan 1954). The appraiser keeps a diary of what each employee is observed doing on the job. At the time of a formal appraisal, the person reads the diary and then rates the employee, typically on a 7–9 point scale, using the behavioral anchors as a guide for determining whether the performance is highly acceptable, highly unacceptable, or somewhere in between.

BOS are algebraic, summated, five-point Likert scales where the items comprising a scale, originally derived from the CIT, are item or factor analyzed. As noted earlier, an appraiser records the frequency with which an employee was observed engaging in the behaviors listed on the scale (e.g. 'praises a person for performing well' Almost Never 0 1 2 3 4 Almost Always).

Despite the care that goes into developing BARS, subsequent studies have found no evidence that they are superior to trait scales with regard to minimizing rating errors (Schwab et al. 1975; DeCotiis 1977). In addition, no significant differences have been found between BARS and BOS with regard to minimizing halo and leniency error, or increasing inter-observer reliability.

These findings finally led to the hypothesis that perhaps more important than the rating scale that is used is the training that appraisers receive in using it. Fay and Latham (1982) found that rating errors were reduced significantly regardless of whether BARS, BOS, or trait scales were used when people received rater error training (Latham et al. 1975). However, behavioral scales, following rater training, were more resistant to rating errors than trait scales. BOS and BARS were equally resistant to rating errors. With regard to practicality, BOS were evaluated as significantly better than BARS and trait scales by the users.

## 18.2.2 Practicality

Practicality is important because to the extent that a manager feels the appraisal scale is useful, it is likely to be used as the basis for setting goals which in turn directly affect an employee's motivation (Locke and Latham 2002). In too many instances, psychometrically sound instruments either are not used or are soon abandoned because of failure on the part of researchers to take user reactions into account.

Consequently, Wiersma and Latham (1986) examined the practicality of BOS, BARS, and trait scales. American managers and their white-collar subordinates preferred BOS to BARS in all cases, and in all but two cases to the use of trait scales. Lawyers who specialize in human resource litigation also preferred BOS to the two alternatives in terms of defensibility in the courtroom. These results have been replicated in the Netherlands (Wiersma et al. 1995). BOS were preferred by Dutch managers over the other two methods for providing feedback, differentiating among employees, determining training needs, setting goals, objectivity, and overall ease of use. The trait scale was viewed by the Dutch managers as good or as slightly better than the BARS.

Working in Israel, Tziner and Kopelman (1988) found that the use of BOS was rated as significantly higher by appraisers than were trait scales on three goal-setting dimensions, namely, goal clarity, goal acceptance, and goal commitment. These results were due to the behavioral specificity provided by the BOS. In a subsequent study in Israel, appraisals based on BOS resulted in higher subsequent job satisfaction and organizational commitment than appraisals based on trait scales (Tziner and Latham 1989). The specificity of the BOS strengthened employees' feelings of control over their work, and minimized feelings of ambiguity regarding expectations of them. Thus, both Tziner and Kopelman (2002), as well as Bernardin (2005), concluded that BOS are preferable to BARS and trait scales because they convey what the person 'must do,' feedback is perceived as factual, objective, and unbiased; and the feedback is conducive to setting specific challenging goals. Similar findings have been obtained with Canadian managers regarding perceptions of fairness in the appraisal process (Latham and Seijts 1997).

The superiority of the BOS to other appraisal scales likely reflects the fact that they are based on Wherry and Bartlett's (1982) theory of rating. Among the theorems and corollaries are the following: (1) rating scales which assess behaviors that are maximally controlled by the ratee lead to more accurate ratings than those which refer to the tasks affected primarily by the situation; (2) raters vary in the accuracy of ratings given in direct proportion to the relevancy of their previous contacts with the ratee; (3) rating items which refer to frequently performed acts are rated more accurately than those which refer to acts performed rarely; (4) the rater makes more accurate ratings when forewarned of the behaviors to be rated because this focuses attention on the pertinent behaviors; (5) deliberate direction of attention to the behaviors to be assessed reduces rating bias; (6) physical features of a scale which facilitate recall of the actual perception of behavior increase rating accuracy (e.g. larger descriptive behavioral statements are preferable to single value words or simple phrases); (7) keeping a written record between rating periods of specifically observed critical incidents improves the objectivity of recall; (8) stressing the importance of appraisals to the organization or society as a whole decreases bias and increases rater accuracy; (9) observation with intention to remember facilitates recall; (10) behaviors which are readily classified by an observer within a special category have smaller overall bias components; similarly, rating items that are factorially unidimensional result in relatively less overall bias than items which have a complex factor pattern.

In developing BOS, consistent with this theory, Latham and Wexley (1994) stressed that appraisers must be individuals who are aware of the aims and objectives of an employee's job, frequently observe the person's behavior on the job, and are capable of discerning competent from inappropriate performance. The BOS forewarn the appraiser and the appraisee of the specific behaviors that are to be appraised. Hence the BOS focuses both a supervisor's and a subordinate's attention on the same critical behaviors. The BOS are comprised of complete behavioral statements (e.g. 'Gives performance appraisals on time,' 'Involves employees in the appraisal process'). Appraisers, as is the case with BARS, are encouraged to keep an ongoing record of their observations. The BOS should consist of the behaviors required to implement an organization's strategy (Latham and Latham 2000). The individual items on a scale are derived from an item or a factor analysis. A category label is given for each scale (e.g. Interactions with Clients; Development of Subordinates; Service to Firm).

## 18.2.3 Technology

Advances in technology raise a question for which currently there is no answer: *How should appraisal formats using the latest technologies be designed to best facilitate feedback/development and goal-setting?*

An emerging trend in performance management is to bypass appraisal formats altogether and rely instead on electronic performance monitoring or EPM (Alge 2001). EPM is viewed positively by many organizations because it allegedly enforces performance standards and decreases negative behaviors such as theft, absenteeism, or tardiness. Moreover, it allegedly lessens the necessity of daily supervision devoted to inspection and discipline through its second-by-second tracking of a person's behavior. Finally, the fact that employee performance data is collected and stored leads to fact-based performance appraisals. Nevertheless, a review of the literature revealed that the use of EPM usually results in an increase in job-related stress, which can lead to illness, which in turn leads to absenteeism, job dissatisfaction, and employee turnover (Zweig 2005). Two studies by Zweig and Webster (2002) explain why. EPM violates the basic psychological boundary between the employer and employee—one that is predicated on privacy, autonomy, and respect. 'It appears that a technology that removes control over the type and scope of information we share with others, changes the fundamental nature of personal relationships, and drives people to question their own and others' behaviors will trigger strong negative reactions' (Zweig and Webster 2002: 627). In addition, EPM narrows the performance domain to only those behaviors that can be tracked by a computer (Sulsky and Keown 1998).

Alder and Ambrose (2005) suggested that adverse employee reactions to EPM stem from ways in which the technology is implemented, rather than from the technology itself. EPM might be acceptable to employees if it is not used as the basis for the subsequent goals that are set; rather, EPM is used solely to assist a coach and an employee to track goal progress, and revise goals when necessary. In addition, employees would receive feedback directly from their supervisor/coach, rather than from the EPM system. This should promote perceptions of procedural justice, by giving employees a voice in the interpretation of the data. These ideas suggest a second question for which there is currently no answer: *How might we best integrate EPM into a performance management system?*

Employees improve their performance on simple tasks when EPM is present, yet performance decreases with difficult tasks in the presence of EPM (Davidson and Henderson 2000). A social facilitation explanation for this result is that performance tends to increase for relatively simple tasks because the worker is aware of the monitoring and motivation is heightened as a result. If the task is perceived to be too difficult, however, the presence of monitoring may create some degree of internal anxiety (due to being observed by others)—leading to performance decrements.

Moreover, the employees may not have been committed to performing well on the difficult task. If a difficult goal is set, and progress is tracked via EPM, performance should lead to goal attainment, given commitment (Locke and Latham 2002). Thus, a third research question that has yet to be addressed: *Does EPM facilitate goal attainment when goal commitment is high?*

## 18.2.4 Context

Raters and ratees have different definitions of an effective appraisal system. Balzer and Sulsky (1990) found that raters perceive appraisal instruments effective if they are easy to use, and effective in helping them change employee attitudes and behavior. Alternately, an effective appraisal system from the lens of employees is one that clarifies linkages between behavior and rewards, and is seen as fair in terms of process and outcome (e.g. rewards) allocation.

A second contextual variable that is potentially relevant to appraisal formats is an organization's culture. An organization that values internal competition and hence is concerned with identifying high-potential individuals may be inclined to use rankings rather than ratings of employees. Wagner and Goffin (1997) showed in a laboratory setting that comparative rating formats yield ratings that are significantly higher in accuracy than ratings of absolute performance. Because the generalizability of this finding to organizational settings is not known, a fourth research question needs to be addressed: *Are comparative rating scales preferred in organizations that value internal competition?* The downsides to a positive answer to this question are at least twofold. First, rankings are prohibited by the 1978 Carter Civil Service Reform Act in the United States. This legislation applies to Federal Government employees. Second, a comparative rating may make it difficult to provide an employee feedback for setting goals to substantively improve performance.

# 18.3 STEP 2: OBSERVE PERFORMANCE

As Smith (1976: 367) noted: 'Observation and interpretation hold the key to the establishment of effective criteria.' Yet, an ongoing problem in appraising people is the lack of reliability in the observation of their behavior (Ronan and Prien 1971; Spool 1978). This unreliability is largely attributed to well-known rating errors such as 'first impressions,' 'halo,' and 'similar-to-me.' Lifson (1953) found that up to one-third of performance measurement variance is due to rater differences despite the fact that the observers had considerable experience in observing and evaluating people in the workplace. Lance (1994) corroborated this finding. Experience, however, is not a substitute for training. To solve the problem regarding lack of reliability, an observer must be trained. In this section, training programs that have been shown to be effective are described, and the necessity of taking context into account is explained.

Latham et al. (1975) developed a workshop based on three principles of learning, namely, active participation, knowledge of results, and practice. In brief, managers were given job descriptions, observed people on videotape, made an appraisal, received feedback on their accuracy, discussed the rating error that was made (e.g. 'central tendency'), ways of overcoming each error (e.g. contrast effects), and then observed and appraised subsequent people on videotape. The trained supervisors made significantly more accurate ratings than those in the control group.

The benefit of this training on rating accuracy for the company where it was conducted was shown in a subsequent study (Pursell et al. 1980). An extensive job analysis had been conducted for use in selecting predictors for a validation study. Yet no evidence of validity was subsequently found for any of the five tests. This was surprising because the tests were developed and/or selected to correspond directly with the skills required by job incumbents. Moreover, the supervisors themselves were involved in the development of the appraisal instrument. They even stated that this was an excellent way of assessing an employee's effectiveness and that the approach would be uncomplicated for them. This suggested that the absence of significant validity coefficients was due to rating errors in the use of the appraisal scale rather than to technical inadequacies in either the choice of predictors or the appraisal instrument. Therefore, the above training program was used to minimize rating errors. Twelve months after the initial performance evaluations, and one month after the rater training program, the supervisors re-evaluated the same employees. The result was significant validity coefficients for four of the five predictors. These correlations were significantly different from those that were previously obtained. Additional evidence that the training of the observers was effective was shown in the respective distribution of ratings before and after the training. The range of criterion ratings at Time 1 was 4–9 while that at Time 2 encompassed the entire nine-point appraisal scale. The distribution in ratings between the two time periods was significant.

Still another training approach, consistent with the cognitive processes required in a performance appraisal, is frame-of-reference training or FOR (Bernardin et al. 2000). The purpose of FOR training is to calibrate raters so that they agree on (*a*) how to match specific ratee behaviors to the appropriate performance dimensions, (*b*) the effectiveness levels of alternative behaviors, and (*c*) the rules for combining individual judgements into a summary evaluation for each performance dimension (Sulsky and Day 1992). To the extent that FOR training helps raters formulate correct impressions of a ratee's performance on each performance dimension, rating accuracy increases. This occurs even if raters forget specific performance information and rely upon their overall impressions of a ratee's performance, as is predicted by cognitive processing models (Sulsky and Day 1994; Noonan and Sulsky 2001).

Implicit person theory (IPT), that is, beliefs regarding the malleability of behavior, affects appraisals of others (Heslin et al. 2005). Entity theorists believe that an individual's personal attributes are largely fixed. This leads them to quickly form strong impressions of an individual that they resist reversing, despite subsequent contradictory information. The IPT of incrementalists, on the other hand, is that personal and situational determinants of an employee's behavior are dynamic. Thus they reconsider their initial impressions if new information warrants it.

Failure to recognize a significant decrease in the performance of a surgeon or a pilot, for example, could be catastrophic. Similarly, a failure to acknowledge a significant improvement in behavior can lead to employee resentment and withdrawal. Heslin et al. showed how Pratkanis and Aronson's (2001) self-persuasion methodology can be used to train entity theorists to adopt an incremental IPT that is sustained over time.

Martell et al. (1995) found that memory of job-related behavior is affected by performance expectations. Raters who believe that a person has performed well vs. poorly report observing more effective and less ineffective behaviors regardless of whether the behaviors actually occurred. Source monitoring training corrects this error. Martell and Evans (2005) trained raters to report only behaviors that evoke detailed memories and to suppress reporting behaviors that are based on feelings of familiarity when completing a behavioral checklist. Consequently, raters were capable of identifying how they remember what they remember in doing a performance appraisal. Distinguishing between the two sources of memory judgements reduced the biasing effect of rater expectations of an employee.

## 18.3.1 Context

Often overlooked in training programs is the social and political context of appraisal. Training focuses primarily on ability rather than the motivation of appraisers. An appraiser's behavior is a product of both. Consequently, future training programs on maximizing objectivity should focus on the motivational underpinnings of appraisal errors. Discovering ways of overcoming various social and political factors that cause raters to intentionally give an inaccurate appraisal would lead to a 'quantum' advance in the practical benefits derived from appraisal research.

In addition to a person's age, race, sex, and ethnicity affecting an appraisal (Latham and Mann 2006), organizational politics are a factor (Tziner et al. 1996). A supervisor's positive regard for subordinates often results in leniency and halo errors, and less inclination to punish poor performance (Lefkowitz 2000). This is especially true with regard to perceived similarities regarding extroversion, conscientiousness, and emotional stability (Strauss et al. 2001).

One of the most studied motivational drivers is ratee gender. A review of objective and subjective indicators of performance as a leader revealed that men are usually evaluated as more effective than women (Eagly et al. 1995). Societal culture as a possible contextual variable (Fletcher 2001; Fletcher and Perry 2002) that affects an appraiser's rating of an employee also needs to be considered. It seems likely that societal values affect ways in which performance is both conceptualized and appraised. A collectivist culture may strongly weight competencies (e.g. cooperation) relating to team performance (McIntyre and Salas 1995) when evaluating a person's overall performance. It may also favor intentionally committing a positive leniency error. Similarly, an individualistic culture that values competition might promote the use of a comparative appraisal scale.

## 18.4 STEP 3: GIVE FEEDBACK AND SET GOALS

Before taking this step, one must realize that different stakeholders use different referents when evaluating performance. Schrader and Steiner (1996) suggested that when making an appraisal, a manager may evaluate performance against an absolute standard (e.g. the behavioral anchors on a BARS scale), a comparative standard (e.g. other employees), or an individual standard (e.g. how performance has changed within the individual over time). Moreover, they found evidence suggesting that individuals prefer the standards that are most accessible and available. For instance, a manager may decide an employee will be given negative feedback based upon absolute standards, while the employee expects positive feedback on the basis of constantly seeing how poorly their co-workers are performing, and because the employee thinks his or her performance has improved since the last appraisal period.

To the extent that a manager and subordinate hold differing views concerning what constitutes job performance, conflict is likely to occur. The solution is to adapt/tie Campbell et al.'s (1993) theory of performance to an organization's strategy, as suggested by Wherry and Bartlett's (1982) theory. Further, BOS should be used to make explicit to all parties 'the rules of the game' for earning a high appraisal. The basis for an evaluation must be made explicit prior to the appraisal period (e.g. absolute vs. comparative vs. relative improvement).

The appraisal system includes the training of observers, the development and use of an appraisal scale, and the definition of performance that is to be assessed by the scale. In contrast, the appraisal process includes providing feedback to an employee and setting goals to be attained based on this feedback. Hence there is a direct linkage between the performance appraisal literature and the literature on motivation, particularly in regard to feedback and goal-setting theory (Locke and Latham 1990, 2002). The integration of these two linkages is the essence of a performance management system (Williams 1998; Latham and Mann 2006) because the feedback is given on an ongoing basis for the purpose of developing and motivating an individual. Consistent with both Wherry and Bartlett's, as well as Campbell et al.'s theories, the feedback is likely to be acted upon, and the commitment to goals based on this feedback is likely to be high, if the appraisal scale assesses the behaviors necessary for implementing the organization's strategy. That is, the scale makes explicit what employees must do to implement it effectively (Latham and Latham 2000). This was shown in a study by Wright (2004). He employed a cognitive mapping strategy to identify issues of concern to both raters and ratees when considering what constitutes an effective appraisal system. Consistent with Wherry and Bartlett's theory, the results showed that raters want to see that the appraisal system adds value to the organization, and is linked to business strategy. Ratees emphasized that the system should be specific and easy to understand. These results reinforce Balzer and Sulsky's (1990) conclusion that the perception of an appraisal's effectiveness is likely to vary across constituent groups.

Studies on the effectiveness of training programs on ways to provide ongoing feedback, and set challenging goals for an employee based on this feedback, are absent from the literature. Nevertheless, frameworks for the design of training programs do exist. DeNisi and Kluger (2000) reported that feedback is effective when it (a) focuses on the behavior rather than the person, (b) is selective so as not to overwhelm the person, (c) focuses on the behavior that is desired, and the way to demonstrate it, and (d) is used as the basis for setting specific goals. Similarly, Frese's (2005) research shows that people can be taught through instructions to embrace negative feedback when errors are framed as beneficial to the learning process, and to be resilient subsequent to making errors, through systematic exploration. Goal-setting research suggests when to set performance outcome versus learning versus behavioral goals (Brown and Latham 2002; Seijts and Latham 2001). Keown-Gerrard and Sulsky (2001) demonstrated that it is possible to train raters to take into account situational constraints when making perform-ance evaluations.

### 18.4.1 Teams

People rarely work alone. Invariably they are members of one or more teams. Hence, effective performance management requires coaching and appraising both the individual and the team as a whole. For example, in the current dynamic environment in which most individuals and teams operate, both the individual and the team as a whole must possess the knowledge, skills, and efficacy beliefs that enable adaptability (Chen et al. 2005).

It is likely that Wherry and Bartlett's (1982) theory of rating is as applicable to the appraisal of a team as it is to appraising an individual. However, the metrics for evaluating a team may differ from those used for appraising an individual member. For instance at the individual level, mental models involve knowledge coherence, or the extent to which the relatedness among pairs of concepts reflects a consistent structure. On the other hand, team mental models reflect inter-member similarity in terms of the extent to which the same knowledge base is shared and embraced. Both Chen et al. (2004) and Kozlowski and Klein (2000) argued that team mental models capture qualitatively different constructs from their individual-level ana-logues. Performance ratings of the adaptive performance may not capture the same construct as do objective performance ratings of an individual's outputs used to assess a team's adaptive performance (Chen et al. 2005).

## 18.5 STEP 4: MAKE A DECISION

Yet to be incorporated into performance management is the decision-making literature. The necessity for doing so is that decision-making is embedded in appraisals of employees. What rating should be assigned? What aspects of a person's performance could benefit from coaching? Who should be given add-itional responsibility? Who should be given a salary increase? Who should be removed from the team, transferred, or promoted to a new team?

The decision-making literature is replete with empirical demonstrations of heuristics or 'rules of thumb' that entrap decision makers (Kahneman and Frederick 2002). For example, knowledge of performance outcomes strongly affects how an employee is appraised. Positive outcomes, in contrast to negative ones, increase the probability that an employee's past decisions/behaviors will be evaluated as good ones. This 'hindsight bias' reflects the fact that most people view the outcome of performance as the most important criterion for making a judgement of an employee, even though the outcome may have been affected positively or negatively by factors beyond a person's control.

This hindsight bias also affects evaluations of one's own team. Staw (1975) found that individuals who were led to believe erroneously that they had performed well rather than poorly evaluated the cohesiveness within their teams more favorably than those who were told the opposite. In short, performance outcomes serve as potent cues to infer or 'see' various work behaviors that may exist only in the imagination of the appraiser.

The 'availability bias' is a heuristic whereby appraisers form a judgement on the basis of what is readily brought to mind. Hence, salient events are likely to bias an overall appraisal of a person's performance. A 'confirmation bias' is the tendency to seek information that conforms to one's own definition of a solution to a problem. Hence, appraisers sometimes look for data to support their preconceived evaluation of an employee. Still another decision-making error is the illusion of manageability. Das and Teng (1999) found that managers are prone to the erroneous belief that outcomes can be contained, corrected, or reversed, given extra effort on the part of an employee.

Bazerman (1994) has identified thirteen of these types of errors. Ways to keep these errors from contaminating the performance management process have yet to be discovered.

## 18.6 Conclusions

In this chapter, we hopefully make clear that the answers required to move the field of performance management forward are much less straightforward than the questions. We know a great deal more about ways to manage the performance of an individual than about ways to manage a team. We know what to observe and how to observe an individual objectively. We are at a loss as to how to overcome political considerations that lead people not to do so. Advances in knowledge have been made with regard to technology that managers embrace to assist them in the appraisal process, and that in the eyes of employees their managers misuse. We know that making decisions is inherent in performance management, yet solutions to decision-making errors remain a mystery. Two great strides in this domain include recognition that ongoing performance management is more effective than an annual appraisal in bringing about a positive change in an employee's behavior, and that context must be taken into account in doing so.

# REFERENCES

ALDER, G. S., and AMBROSE, M. L. (2005). 'An Examination of the Effect of Computerized Performance Monitoring Feedback on Monitoring Fairness, Performance, and Satisfaction.' *Organizational Behavior and Human Decision Processes*, 97: 161–77.

ALGE, B. J. (2001). 'Effects of Computer Surveillance on Perceptions of Privacy and Procedural Justice.' *Journal of Applied Psychology*, 86: 797–804.

AUSTIN, J. T., and VILLANOVA, P. (1992). 'The Criterion Problem: 1917–1992.' *Journal of Applied Psychology*, 77: 836–74.

BALZER, W. K., and SULSKY, L. M. (1990). 'Performance Appraisal Effectiveness.' In K. R. Murphy and F. E. Saal (eds.), *Psychology in Organizations: Integrating Science and Practice*. Series in Applied Psychology. Hillsdale, NJ,: Lawrence Erlbaum Associates.

BAZERMAN, M. H. (1994). *Judgment in Managerial Decision Making*, 3rd edn. New York: Wiley.

BERNARDIN, H. J. (2005). 'Behavioral Observation Scales.' In S. Cartwright (ed.), *Human Resource Management*, v: *The Blackwell Encyclopedia of Management*, 2nd edn. Malden, Mass.: Blackwell Publishing.

—— BUCKLEY, M. R., TYLER, C. L., and WIESE, D. S. (2000). 'A Reconsideration of Strategies in Rater Training.' *Research in Personnel and Human Resources Management*, 18: 221–74.

BROWN, T. C., and LATHAM, G. P. (2002). 'The Effects of Behavioural Outcome Goals, Learning Goals and Urging People to do their Best on an Individual's Teamwork Behaviour in a Group Problem Solving Task.' *Canadian Journal of Behavioural Science*, 34: 276–85.

CAMPBELL, J. P., McCLOY, R. A., OPPLER, S. H., and SAGER, C. E. (1993). 'A Theory of Performance.' In N. Schmitt and W. Borman (eds.), *Personnel Selection in Organizations*. San Francisco: Jossey-Bass.

CARDY, R. L., and KEEFE, T. J. (1994). 'Observational Purpose and Evaluative Articulation in Frame-of-Reference Training: The Effects of Alternative Processing Modes on Rating Accuracy.' *Organizational Behavior and Human Decision Processes*, 57: 338–57.

CHEN, G., MATHIEU, J. E., and BLIESE, P. D. (2004). 'A Framework for Conducting Multilevel Construct Validation.' In F. J. Yammarino and F. Dansereau (eds.), *Research in Multilevel Issues: Multilevel Issues in Organizational Behavior and Processes*, vol. iii. Oxford: Elsevier.

—— THOMAS, B., and WALLACE, J. C. (2005). 'A Multilevel Examination of the Relationships among Training Outcomes, Mediating Regulatory Processes, and Adaptive Performance.' *Journal of Applied Psychology*, 90: 827–41.

DAS, T. K., and TENG, B. (1999). 'Cognitive Biases and Strategic Decision Processes: An Integrative Perspective.' *Journal of Management Studies*, 36: 757–78.

DAVIDSON, R., and HENDERSON, R. (2000). 'Electronic Performance Monitoring: A Laboratory Investigation of the Influence of Monitoring and Difficulty on Task Performance, Mood State, and Self-Reported Stress Levels.' *Electronic Performance Monitoring*, 30: 906–20.

DeCOTIIS, T. A. (1977). 'An Analysis of the External Validity and Applied Relevance of Three Rating Formats.' *Organizational Behavior and Human Performance*, 19: 247–66.

DeNISI, A. S., and KLUGER, A. N. (2000). 'Feedback Effectiveness: Can 360-Degree Appraisals be Improved?' *Academy of Management Executive*, 14: 129, 139.

EAGLY, A. H., KARAU, S. J., and MAKHIJANI, M. G. (1995). 'Gender and the Effectiveness of Leaders: A Meta-analysis.' *Psychological Bulletin*, 117: 125–45.

FAY, C. H., and LATHAM, G. P. (1982). 'Effects of Training and Rating Scales on Rating Errors.' *Personnel Psychology*, 35: 105–16.

FLANAGAN, J. C. (1954). 'The Critical Incident Technique.' *Psychological Bulletin*, 51: 327–58.

FLETCHER, C. (2001). 'Performance Appraisal and Management: The Developing Research Agenda.' *Journal of Occupational and Organizational Psychology*, 74: 473–87.

—— and PERRY, E. L. (2002). 'Performance Appraisal and Feedback: A Consideration of National Culture and a Review of Contemporary Research and Future Trends.' In N. Anderson, D. S. Ones, H. K. Sinangil, and C. Viswesvaran (eds.), *Handbook of Industrial, Work and Organizational Psychology*, vol. i. Thousand Oaks, Calif: Sage.

FRESE, M. (2005). 'Grand Theories and Midrange Theories: Cultural Effects on Theorizing and the Attempt to Understand Active Approaches to Work.' In K. G. Smith and M. Hitt (eds.), *The Oxford Handbook of Management Theory: The Process of Theory Development*. Oxford: Oxford University Press.

HESLIN, P., LATHAM, G. P., and VAN DE WALLE, D. (2005). 'The Effect of Implicit Person Theory on Performance Appraisals.' *Journal of Applied Psychology*, 90: 842–56.

KAHNEMAN, D., and FREDERICK, S. (2002). 'Representativeness Revisited: Attribute Substitution in Intuitive Judgment.' In T. Gilovich, D. Griffin, and D. Kahneman (eds.), *Heuristics and Biases: The Psychology of Intuitive Judgment*. New York: Cambridge University Press.

KEOWN-GERRARD, J. L., and SULSKY, L. M. (2001). 'The Effects of Task Information Training and Frame-of-Reference Training with Situational Constraints on Rating Accuracy.' *Human Performance*, 14: 305–20.

KOZLOWSKI, S. W. J., and KLEIN, K. J. (2000). 'A Multilevel Approach to Theory and Research in Organizations: Contextual, Temporal, and Emergent Processes.' In K. J. Klein and S. W. J. Kozlowski (eds.), *Multilevel Theory, Research, and Methods in Organizations: Foundations, Extensions, and New Directions*. San Francisco: Jossey-Bass.

LANCE, C. E. (1994). 'Test of a Latent Structure of Performance Ratings Derived from Wherry's (1952) Theory of Ratings.' *Journal of Management*, 20: 757–71.

LATHAM, G. P., and HESLIN, P. (2003). 'Training the Trainee as Well as the Trainer: Lessons to be Learned from Clinical Psychology.' *Canadian Psychology*, 44: 218–31.

—— and LATHAM, S. D. (2000). 'Overlooking Theory and Research in Performance Appraisal at One's Peril: Much Done, More to Do.' In C. Cooper and E. A. Locke (eds.), *International Review of Industrial-Organizational Psychology*. Chichester: Wiley.

—— and MANN, S. (2006). 'Advances in the Science of Performance Appraisal: Implications for Practice.' In G. P. Hodgkinson and J. K. Ford (eds.), *International Review of Industrial and Organizational Psychology*, 21: 295–338.

—— and SEIJTS, G. H. (1997). 'The Effect of Appraisal Instrument on Managerial Perceptions of Fairness and Satisfaction with Appraisals from their Peers.' *Canadian Journal of Behavioural Science*, 29: 275–82.

—— and WEXLEY, K. N. (1977). 'Behavioral Observation Scales.' *Personnel Psychology*, 30: 255–68.

—— —— (1994). *Increasing Productivity through Performance Appraisal*, 2nd edn. Reading, Mass.: Addison-Wesley.

—— —— and PURSELL, E. D. (1975). 'Training Managers to Minimize Rating Errors in the Observation of Behavior.' *Journal of Applied Psychology*, 60: 550–5.

LATHAM, G. P., ALMOST, J., MANN, S., and MOORE, C. (2005). 'New Developments in Performance Management.' *Organizational Dynamics*, 34: 77–87.

LEFKOWITZ, J. (2000). 'The Role of Interpersonal Affective Regard in Supervisory Performance Ratings: A Literature Review and Proposed Causal Model.' *Journal of Occupational and Organizational Psychology*, 73: 67–85.

LIFSON, K. A. (1953). 'Errors in Time-Study Judgments of Industrial Work Pace.' *Psychological Monographs*, 67, whole no. 355.

LOCKE, E. A., and LATHAM, G. P. (1990). *A Theory of Goal Setting and Task Performance.* Englewood Cliffs, NJ: Prentice Hall.

—— —— (2002). 'Building a Practically Useful Theory of Goal Setting and Task Motivation: A 35-Year Odyssey.' *American Psychologist*, 57: 705–17.

McINTYRE, R. M., and SALAS, E. (1995). 'Measuring and Managing for Team Performance: Emerging Principles from Complex Environments.' In R. A. Guzzo, E. Salas, et al. (eds.), *Team Effectiveness and Decision Making in an Organization.* San Francisco: Jossey-Bass.

MARTELL, R. F., and EVANS, D. P. (2005). 'Source Monitoring Training: Toward Reducing Rater Expectancy Effects in Behavioral Measurement.' *Journal of Applied Psychology*, 90: 956–63.

—— GUZZO, R. A., and WILLIS, C. E. (1995). 'A Methodological and Substantive Note on the Performance-Cue Effect in Ratings of Work-Group Behavior.' *Journal of Applied Psychology*, 80: 191–5.

NOONAN, L. E., and SULSKY, L. M. (2001). 'The Impact of Frame-of-Reference Training on Alternative Training Effectiveness Criteria in a Canadian Military Sample.' *Human Performance*, 14: 3–26.

PRATKANIS, A., and ARONSON, E. (2001). *Age of Propaganda: The Everyday Use and Abuse of Persuasion.* New York: Freeman.

PURSELL, E. D., DOSSETT, D. L., and LATHAM, G. P. (1980). 'Obtaining Valid Predictors by Minimizing Rating Errors in the Criteria.' *Personnel Psychology*, 33: 91–6.

RONAN, W. W., and PRIEN, E. P. (1971). *Perspectives on the Measurement of Human Performance.* New York: Appleton-Century-Crofts.

SCHRADER, B. W., and STEINER, D. D. (1996). 'Common Comparison Standards: An Approach to Improving Agreement between Self and Supervisory Performance Ratings.' *Journal of Applied Psychology*, 81: 813–20.

SCHWAB, D. P., HENEMAN, H. G., and DeCOTIIS, T. A. (1975). 'Behaviorally Anchored Rating Scales: A Review of the Literature.' *Personnel Psychology*, 28: 549–62.

SEIJTS, G. H., and LATHAM, G. P. (2001). 'The Effect of Learning, Outcome and Proximal Goals on a Moderately Complex Task.' *Journal of Organizational Behavior*, 22: 291–307.

SMITH, P. C. (1976). 'Behaviors, Results and Organizational Effectiveness.' In M. Dunnette (ed.), *Handbook of Industrial and Organizational Psychology.* Chicago: Rand-McNally.

—— and KENDALL, L. M. (1963). 'Retranslation of Expectations: An Approach to the Construction of Unambiguous Anchors for Rating Scales.' *Journal of Applied Psychology*, 47: 149–55.

SPOOL, M. D. (1978). 'Training Programs of Observers of Behavior: A Review.' *Personnel Psychology*, 31: 853–85.

STAW, B. M. (1975). 'Attributions of the "Causes" of Performance: A General Alternative Interpretation of Cross-sectional Research on Organizations.' *Organizational Behavior and Human Processes*, 13: 414–32.

STRAUSS, J. P., BARRICK, M. R., and CONNERLEY, M. L. (2001). 'An Investigation of Personality Similarity Effects (Relational and Perceived) on Peer and Supervisor Ratings and the Role of Familiarity and Liking.' *Journal of Occupational and Organizational Psychology*, 74: 637–57.

SULSKY, L. M., and DAY, D. V. (1992). 'Frame of Reference Training and Cognitive Categorization: An Empirical Investigation of Rater Memory Issues.' *Journal of Applied Psychology*, 77: 501–10.

—— —— (1994). 'An Examination of the Effects of Frame-of-Reference Training on Rating Accuracy under Alternative Time Delays.' *Journal of Applied Psychology*, 79: 535–43.

—— and KEOWN, J. L. (1998). 'Performance Appraisal in the Changing World of Work: Implications for the Meaning and Measurement of Work Performance.' *Canadian Psychology*, 39: 52–9.

TZINER, A., and KOPELMAN, R. (1988). 'Effects of Rating Format on Goal-Setting Dimensions: A Field Experiment.' *Journal of Applied Psychology*, 73: 323–6.

—— —— (2002). 'Is there a Preferred Performance Rating Format? A Non-Psychometric Perspective.' *Applied Psychology: An International Review*, 51: 479–503.

—— and LATHAM, G. P. (1989). 'The Effects of Appraisal Instrument, Feedback and Goal Setting on Worker Satisfaction and Commitment.' *Journal of Organizational Behavior*, 10: 145–53.

—— —— PRICE, B. S., and HACCOUN, R. (1996). 'Development and Validation of a Questionnaire for Measuring Perceived Political Considerations in Performance Appraisal.' *Journal of Organizational Behavior*, 17: 179–90.

WAGNER, S. H., and GOFFIN, R. D. (1997). 'Differences in Accuracy of Absolute and Comparative Performance Appraisal Methods.' *Organizational Behavior and Human Decision Processes*, 70: 95–103.

WHERRY, R. J., and BARTLETT, C. J. (1982). 'The Control of Bias in Ratings: A Theory of Rating.' *Personnel Psychology*, 35: 521–51.

WIERSMA, U., and LATHAM, G. P. (1986). 'The Practicality of Behavior Observation Scales, Behavioral Expectation Scales, and Trait Scales.' *Personnel Psychology*, 39: 619–28.

—— VAN DEN BERG, P., and LATHAM, G. P. (1995). 'Dutch Reactions to Behavioral Observation Expectation, and Trait Scales.' *Group and Organization Management*, 20: 297–309.

WILLIAMS, R. (1998). *Performance Management*. London: International Thomson Business Press (Essential Business Psychology Series).

WRIGHT, R. P. (2004). 'Mapping Cognitions to Better Understand Attitudinal and Behavioral Responses in Appraisal Research.' *Journal of Organizational Behavior*, 25: 339–74.

ZWEIG, D. (2005). 'Beyond Privacy and Fairness Concerns: Examining Psychological Boundary Violations as a Consequence of Electronic Performance Monitoring.' In J. Weckert (ed.), *Electronic Monitoring in the Workplace: Controversies and Solutions*. Hershey, Pa.: Ida Group.

—— and WEBSTER, J. (2002). 'Where is the Line between Benign and Invasive? An Examination of Psychological Fairness to the Acceptance of Awareness Monitoring Systems.' *Journal of Organizational Behavior*, 23: 605–33.

# PART III

## PATTERNS AND DYNAMICS

# CHAPTER 19

# HRM SYSTEMS AND THE PROBLEM OF INTERNAL FIT

SVEN KEPES

JOHN E. DELERY

## 19.1 INTRODUCTION

THE field of strategic human resource management (SHRM) has received increasing attention that has resulted in a flurry of innovative research, which has greatly expanded our knowledge of the relationship between human resource management (HRM) activities (e.g. policies or practices) and organizational-level outcomes (e.g. turnover, productivity, and performance). One of the defining characteristics of SHRM has been the proposition that HRM systems and not individual HRM practices are the source of competitive advantage. Specifically, it is proposed that coherent and internally aligned HRM practices form 'powerful connections' that create positive synergistic effects on organizational outcomes, while inconsistent HRM practices form 'deadly combinations,' which create negative synergistic effects that harm organizational effectiveness (Becker and Huselid 1998; Becker et al. 1997; Delery 1998; Delery and Shaw 2001). Previous reviews of the fit perspectives in SHRM have had a pessimistic tone and concluded that there was little evidence of the assumption that 'fit' leads to organizational success, although most reviews did not specifically focus on internal fit (e.g. Gerhart in press; Wright and Sherman 1999; Wright and Snell 1998). For example, Gerhart (in press), in a review of HRM systems, concluded that research has produced only 'weak or, at best, mixed' support for the internal fit perspective.

The purpose of this chapter is to revisit the theoretical foundation of internal fit and provide a review of the literature addressing this issue. Specifically, we set out to explore the theory and research behind the internal fit perspective in an attempt to summarize and advance our knowledge behind HRM systems and internal fit. In doing so, we address the theory behind 'fit', the interplay between external and internal fit, issues of the level of abstraction (e.g. focus on HRM philosophies, policies, or practices in measuring HRM systems), different types of internal fit, problems stemming from levels of analysis issues, and the empirical evidence, before summarizing and concluding.

## 19.2 THE THEORY BEHIND INTERNAL FIT

The idea of fit or alignment and synergistic effects of internal fit has been explicit in almost all SHRM research (e.g. Delery and Doty 1996; Delery and Shaw 2001; Ichniowski et al. 1997; MacDuffie 1995). Delery and Doty (1996) outlined three theoretical frameworks that were being used to describe the relationship between HRM practices and organizational performance. The universalistic approach, which was described as arguing for a universal relationship between individual 'best' HRM practices and firm performance, was perhaps the only framework that explicitly did not argue for positive 'fit' effects. A close examination of the work most often attributed as arguing for universalistic relationships between single HRM practices and firm performance reveals that there was an acknowledgement even there that practices might be more effective when combined with supporting practices (e.g. Pfeffer 1994). For instance, Pfeffer (1994: 31), when discussing sixteen best HRM practices, stated that 'it is important to recognize that practices are interrelated—it is difficult to do one thing by itself with much positive result.'

The other perspectives identified by Delery and Doty (1996), the contingency and configurational, have dealt more directly with at least two forms of fit. The SHRM literature distinguishes between what has been termed vertical or external fit and horizontal or internal fit. While external fit denotes the alignment between HRM practices and the specific organizational context (e.g. organizational strategy), internal fit refers to the coherent configuration of individual HRM practices that support each other (Becker et al. 1997; Delery 1998). When researchers talk about 'internal fit,' they are usually referring to an arrangement of HRM activities (e.g. HRM policies or practices) that work in concert, whether they call these arrangements 'systems' (e.g. Delery and Doty 1996), 'bundles' (e.g. MacDuffie 1995), or 'clusters' (e.g. Arthur 1992). The *contingency perspective* of SHRM captures the ideas of external fit and predicts that the relationship between HRM practices and organizational effectiveness is contingent upon an organization's strategy (Delery and Doty 1996). The *configurational perspective*, on the other hand, takes a more holistic view that is aligned with the concept of equifinality and highlights the importance of fit and complementarity among HRM practices in predicting organizational effectiveness (Delery and Doty 1996). According to the concept of equifinality, different HRM practices that fit together can yield identical outcomes. It appears that most SHRM researchers today take a combination of the contingency and configurational perspectives in that it is proposed that different internally consistent HRM systems are effective for either different parts of the workforce or under different strategic considerations (Lepak and Snell 1999). Coming from this combined perspective, it is clear that internal and external fit are in a constant interplay. While not attempting to downplay this interplay, in the remainder of this review, we focus most attention on the notion of internal fit and only highlight certain external fit issues where appropriate.

Using the configurational perspective and drawing on research concerning the HRM architecture (Kepes and Delery in press; Lepak and Snell 1999) and individual HRM practice areas, we show that it is vital to differentiate between different types of internal fit. We believe that it is partly a lack of consideration of these distinctions that may have led previous researchers to conclude that there is only limited evidence for the importance of internal fit.

Regardless of the type of internal fit, the basic assumption of this perspective is that 'the effectiveness of any [individual HRM] practice depends on the other practices in place' (Delery 1998: 291); that a coherent system of supporting HRM practices has greater effects on organizational effectiveness than the sum of each individual practice effect (Ichniowski et al. 1997). As we will show, there is substantial empirical evidence that supports the importance of complementary practices and the notion of synergistic effects.

## 19.2.1 Fit and the Resource-based View of the Firm

One of the most widely cited definitions of strategic human resource management highlights the importance of fit by emphasizing the 'coordination or congruence among the various human resource management practices' in influencing organizational outcomes (Wright and McMahan 1992: 298). The resource-based view (Barney 1991) provides the backdrop for understanding the relationship between HRM systems and organizational effectiveness. This view takes an implicit systems perspective and suggests that combinations of complementary resources enable a firm to realize their full potential and help in achieving a sustainable competitive advantage. Individual resources, on the other hand, have a limited ability to realize this. Inherent in this perspective is also the concept of fit and equifinality (Delery and Doty 1996) in that different internally consistent configurations of distinct resources may provide the source of a sustainable competitive advantage.

Wright et al. (1994) and Barney and Wright (1998) investigated the role that HRM plays in developing a competitive advantage in much detail. Wright et al. (1994: 318) concluded that HRM practices themselves cannot be a source of a sustainable competitive advantage, but that they may play an essential role in 'developing the sustained competitive advantage through the development of the human capital pool, and through moderating the relationship between this pool and sustained competitive advantage by affecting HR behavior.' Barney and Wright (1998) broadened this somewhat narrow view and discussed in more depth how systems of HRM practices and the administrative HRM function itself could become sources of sustainable competitive advantage. These authors examined whether HRM systems and the HRM function meet the criteria set forth by Barney (1991) and suggested that systems of HRM practices that create synergistic effects are indeed a source of a sustainable competitive advantage. These integrated HRM systems are rare, valuable, and, contrary to physical and organizational capital, 'difficult, if not impossible for competitors to identify and copy' due to the interrelatedness of the individual HRM practices in the interdependent HRM system (Barney and Wright 1998: 40). Hence, it is the internal fit between HRM practices that may provide a significant source of sustainable competitive advantage.

# 19.3 THE COMPLEXITY OF INTERNAL FIT

In the previous section, we presented the foundation of the theory supporting the importance of internal fit, whether HRM systems in and of themselves (Barney and Wright 1998; Delery and Shaw 2001) or the human capital that they create (Wright et al. 1994) are the source of organizational effectiveness. While it is argued that strong internal fit of HRM practices can provide a sustainable competitive advantage, in part due to causal ambiguity and social complexity (Barney 1991; Barney and Wright 1998), these factors make it very difficult to specify a priori which sets of HRM practices actually fit together and create the desired 'invisible capability' that leads to organizational success (Becker and Huselid 1998). There are, thus, significant challenges, which range from actually designing and implementing internally consistent HRM systems to empirically specifying and measuring internal fit. We expand on this in the next section.

## 19.3.1  Designing Internally Coherent HRM Systems

It is a very difficult task to actually design an internally consistent HRM system in which all HRM practices are internally aligned and reflect the policies and overall HRM philosophy of the organization. First, any HRM system must be appropriate for the organization's competitive strategy: helping the organization achieve its strategic and tactical goals. As many researchers have pointed out, different environments and contextual settings require distinct sets of practices (e.g. Becker and Huselid 1998; Delery and Doty 1996). While this problem is often seen to relate more to external rather than internal fit, we believe that it has significant implications for internal fit.

Several internal and external factors influence an organization's strategy and the external fit, which, in turn, influences the effectiveness of internal fit (Boxall and Purcell 2003; Wright and Snell 1998); there is clearly a reciprocal relationship between external and internal fit. Ignoring external fit can lead to an overly rigid HRM system and may cause inertia. Also, the critical HRM goals (e.g. labor productivity, social legitimacy, and organizational flexibility) create complex and possibly paradoxical demands with regard to the HRM system, leading to 'strategic tension' (Boxall and Purcell 2003). These demands need to be managed and balanced in an efficient way. An organization's flexibility or agility with regard to its HRM system is, thus, essential for internal fit over time and long-term organizational success (Boxall and Purcell 2003; Dyer and Shafer 1999; Wright and Snell 1998).

Abell's concept of 'dual strategies' highlights the fact that successful organizations have to adapt by 'mastering the present and pre-empting the future' (Abell 1993: 296). In the context of HRM, this indicates that organizations have to adjust their HRM systems over time for them to remain effective in light of changing external and internal forces (Dyer and Shafer 1999). For instance, changes in the environment, in the firm's strategy, or their workforce needs should trigger modifications in a firm's HRM system. Otherwise, these systems, internally aligned or not, could become misaligned with contextual forces (Boxall and Purcell 2003). The detailed examination of these dynamics, however, is beyond the scope of this chapter. We concentrate on internal fit per se but want to emphasize the fact that internal fit is dynamic, not static.

Second, the entire HRM strategy must dictate a coherent bundle of HRM practices and policies which align and support each other. As mentioned previously, however, there are different types of internal fit. To date, most researchers have focused only on what we term inter-practice area fit within an HRM system (fit across different HRM practices within one HRM system). This is just one type of internal fit and may be an overly simplistic view of this concept. As Lepak and Snell (1999) highlighted with their HRM architecture, organizations likely have distinct HRM systems for different groups of employees, reflecting the employee groups' uniqueness and value to the organization. This HRM architecture has been defined as 'the HRM activities (philosophy, policies, practices, and processes) within different HRM systems that organizations must do today to manage and prepare themselves to develop the human capital required for achieving a competitive advantage in current or emerging opportunity areas' (Kepes and Delery in press). It is, therefore, the organization and management of several different HRM systems within an organization. Each system, in turn, has different levels of abstraction (Wright 1998); it is comprised of distinct HRM philosophies, policies, practices, and processes (Becker and Gerhart 1996; Schuler 1992).

Kepes and Delery (in press) described in detail the components of the HRM architecture. These include the organizational climate, HRM system philosophies, HRM system policies, HRM system practices, and HRM system processes. *Organizational climate* (or the overarching HRM philosophy) reflects all formal and informal HRM activities and serves as the glue that holds an organization together (Reichers and Schneider 1990; Schneider and Brief 1996). *HRM system philosophies* refer to the guiding principles that identify and characterize the value and treatment of employees covered within a particular HRM system. They represent the shared perceptions among certain groups of employees. *HRM system policies* serve as guidelines and benchmarks for specific HRM activities (e.g. compensation practices and processes). Hence, policies reflect *what* an organization is trying to achieve, not *how* it will achieve its goals. *HRM system practices* identify broad HRM activities and techniques to ensure the implementation of the HRM policies. Finally, through *HRM system processes*, the actual implementation of the HRM practices takes place. They denote detailed explanations of *how* the HRM practices are executed. In the following discussions we use the term HRM activities to refer to HRM philosophies, policies, practices, and processes.

These complexities within the HRM architecture with its HRM systems and HRM activities illustrate that there is not only internal fit between HRM policies or practices within a particular HRM system but also within-HRM system vertical fit (or internal vertical fit) between each component (or level of abstraction) of the HRM system and different types of internal horizontal fit. In an attempt to add structure to this discussion, we describe different types of internal fit in the following section.

## 19.3.2 Types of Internal Fit

We distinguish between four different types of internal fit. The first three denote fit within a particular HRM system while the last one signifies internal fit between different HRM systems within one HRM architecture. *Within-HRM system vertical fit* refers to the degree of fit between different HRM activities on diverse levels of abstraction (e.g. fit between compensation policies, practices, and processes). This type of fit and its consequences are rarely explored in the literature although it is often indirectly acknowledged. For instance, conventional wisdom suggests that, while most companies *report* using merit pay and having merit pay policies, in actuality few have valid practices and processes that pay their employees based on merit (Heneman 1990). This represents a misfit between the policy and the practice level, which could result in a negative synergistic effect. A policy that stresses compensation based on merit is likely to be ineffective or even counterproductive without proper practices and processes that implement that policy. Processes more directly affect employees, their behaviors, and attitudes than do policies. When policies and processes are not aligned, dysfunctional behaviors may arise due to perceptions of injustice, which are likely to harm organizational effectiveness (Simons and Roberson 2003).

What has been often called internal horizontal fit, we divide into intra-HRM and inter-HRM activity area fit. *Inter-HRM activity area fit* denotes the fit *between* different HRM activity areas. By and large, HRM researchers have focused on inter-practice area fit (e.g. Arthur 1992; Delery and Doty 1996; Ichniowski et al. 1997; MacDuffie 1995; Shaw et al. 2002). This type of internal fit was also the focus of Delery's (1998) review and the level of abstraction where Becker et al. (1997) first theorized about 'powerful connections' and 'deadly combinations.' *Intra-HRM activity area fit*, on the other hand, is the alignment between specific HRM activities *within* a certain set of HRM activities (e.g. HRM practices within the compensation practice area). Not only do distinct HRM activity areas need to be aligned but also the elements within each HRM activity area. For example, specific HRM activities within the compensation activity area (e.g. pay level, pay dispersion, pay basis, and pay structure) need to fit in order to achieve synergistic effects. When discussing the empirical evidence later in this chapter, we address both of these types of fit in more detail.

Finally, there is also internal fit between different HRM systems within the HRM architecture (internal *between-HRM system fit*). While the previous types of internal fit are within a particular HRM system (e.g. the system used to manage a particular employee group), the various HRM activities within one system may also have to fit their counterparts in other HRM systems within the HRM architecture (Kepes and Delery in press). Following Lepak and Snell's (1999) discussion of the different types of HRM systems used to manage different types of employees within the firm, it is essential to discuss the degree to which these different HRM systems within an organization actually fit together to support the overall HRM strategy. This type of fit has been neglected in the SHRM literature. Theoretically, it has been indirectly addressed with concepts such as 'buffering of the strategic core' (e.g. Pfeffer and Baron 1988) and the 'flexible firm' (e.g. Atkinson 1984). Empirical examinations, however, are rare (but see e.g. Hakim 1990), especially from an internal fit perspective.

Within this particular type of fit, 'strategic tensions' between differing HRM systems could arise due to, for example, different workforce needs or goals for labor productivity and social legitimacy (Boxall and Purcell 2003). Any organization has to balance these possibly conflicting demands with its aspirations of achieving between-HRM system fit while remaining flexible in the competitive landscape. Having vastly different HRM systems within the firm could bring with it negative consequences, including perceptions of injustice and inequity within the workforce and legitimacy dilemmas with external constituencies. The first issue (e.g. injustice and inequity within the workforce) was briefly discussed by Kepes and Delery (in press); however, we have only begun to develop conceptual frameworks dealing with this type of fit (which is similar to Baron and Kreps's (1999) 'among employee consistency'). At present, we would argue that internal between-HRM system fit may be assessed by the degree to which the different HRM systems are linked by a common system philosophy or the degree to which they support an organization's culture and climate. This, however, may disregard and even contradict external demands (e.g. social legitimacy). Managing the 'strategic tensions' between differing HRM goals and other internal/external demands is, hence, as critical for long-term organizational success as internal fit per se (e.g. Boxall and Purcell 2003; Wright and Snell 1998).

In sum, the overall HRM architecture with various HRM systems and different HRM activities and components or levels of abstraction is a complex system, composed of multiple elements, which likely interact in complex ways. We visually depict this in Fig. 19.1. A misfit on or between any of these levels is likely to cause

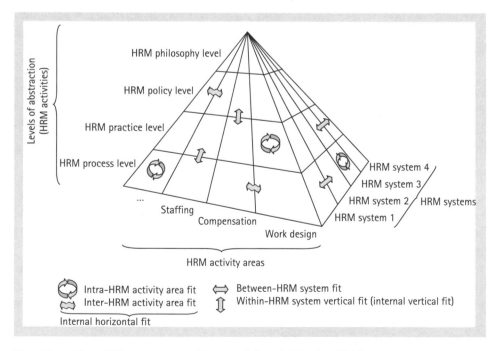

Fig. 19.1. The different types of internal fit within the HRM architecture

problems within the HRM architecture and the respective HRM system(s). Without this complex alignment, the HRM system may not be embedded within the organization and cannot create the 'invisible capability' that enhances organizational effectiveness (Becker and Huselid 1998). This multidimensional view further highlights the fact that identical HRM policies but different HRM practices or the same HRM practices but distinct HRM processes may result in the same outcome if they are aligned, which is consistent with the configurational perspective (Delery and Doty 1996). Such a complex interactive view is not new to SHRM, although these complexities have traditionally been scantly treated. Recently, Colbert (2004) extended the current perspectives in SHRM by bringing complexity theory into the field. We do not wish to simply repeat Colbert's complexity perspective. Instead, we believe it is important to discuss the types of internal fit in more detail, and to highlight the complexity of the HRM architecture and the need for more rigorous research in SHRM.

## 19.3.3 Internal Fit and Possible Effects (Additive and Synergistic Effects)

After discussing the different types of internal fit, it is necessary to describe the different ways in which HRM activities could 'fit' together. This discussion is specifically related to the two most discussed types of fit in the literature: intra-HRM and inter-HRM activity area fit. In this literature, it is rare for much attention to be given to precisely describing how practices actually fit together and the consequences of non-fit. Often, researchers simply list a number of 'best' HRM activities and suggest that, because they are 'best' activities, they must fit together. Delery (1998), however, provided an in-depth overview of internal fit and the different relationships between HRM practices. Here, we want to briefly review this conceptual work linking various HRM activities with each other.

The internal relationships between HRM activities (both intra-HRM and inter-HRM activity area) can take many different forms (see Delery 1998). First, simple *additive effects* are possible. Here, the combination of two HRM activities on the same level of abstraction results in the sum of the separate effects of each individual HRM activity (e.g. a personality and a work sample test in the staffing area at the process level). Additive effects come about if the individual HRM activities have independent, non-overlapping effects on the outcome. HRM activities that simply have additive effects do not actually show 'fit' in the way that term has been used in the SHRM literature. It is wise for organizations to combine such practices, however, because the combination results in better performance than using either activity alone.

Second, *interactive* or *synergistic effects* are possible. These are more consistent with the way many SHRM researchers have presented the idea of 'fit' in that the effect of one activity is actually contingent on the other activities present. These effects can be further distinguished into three separate categories. *Substitutable effects* occur if the HRM activities are substitutes for each other in that each activity results in an identical outcome (e.g. two different personality tests that assess the Big Five personality traits in the staffing area). Having two activities that are substitutes results in outcomes equal to one practice alone. Thus, nothing is gained from an organizational effectiveness perspective. In fact, financial performance eventually decreases due to the additional costs of having two HRM activities that yield identical outcomes.

The most interesting synergistic effects, and the ones most commonly associated with the internal fit perspective of SHRM, are 'powerful connections' and 'deadly combinations' (Becker et al. 1997). They get to the core of fit, alignment, and synergy in that it is proposed that complementary HRM activities have greater effects on organizational effectiveness than the sum of the effects of each individual activity (Ichniowski et al. 1997). *Positive synergistic effects* ('powerful connections') are those where the combination of two individual HRM activities has a more positive effect than the sum of each HRM activity's individual effects. An example might be the combination of valid performance appraisals and a pay-for-perform- ance system. Together these activities should have a much greater positive effect than using either activity alone. On the other hand, *negative synergistic effects* ('deadly combinations') refer to the situation where HRM activities actually work against each other, undermining each other's effects. This could be the case, for instance, if team-oriented work structures are combined with individual incen- tives. Either of these activities alone may produce positive outcomes, but when combined they could actually harm performance.

In any theoretical development focusing on either intra-HRM or inter-HRM activity area fit, it is essential that researchers develop specific hypotheses about the nature of that fit—something that has rarely been done in the SHRM literature. It is not enough to simply say that a system of practices should have greater influence on performance than the individual practices. Researchers must specify which practices must fit with each other and discuss the negative consequences, if any, of misfit. It is unlikely that all HRM activities typically thought of as components of a 'high- performance work system' have positive synergistic relationships with each other. Some may have independent additive effects, while others may have the positive synergistic effects so often discussed.

## 19.3.4 Levels of Analysis

The different types of internal fit discussed above illustrate the complexities in designing and measuring effective HRM systems. Yet, they also highlight a related issue that further increases the inherent complexities of measuring internal fit. The basic assumptions of SHRM are based on multilevel theory (Kozlowski and Klein 2000; Ostroff and Bowen 2000). The SHRM paradigm holds that HRM systems affect the characteristics (e.g. attitudes, KSAs, motivation, and empowerment) of organizational actors (individual level) and groups of actors (group level). These characteristics, in turn, affect workforce productivity and organizational performance (plant and/or organizational level). Inherent in this perspective are cross-level and multilevel models (Kozlowski and Klein 2000). This further complicates the design and measurement of HRM systems. Even if HRM managers use valid selection tools to select the best possible applicants, there is virtually no research that specifically establishes a link between selection techniques at the individual level and group or organizational performance (Ployhart 2004). Similar observations can be made for virtually every other HRM activity area. There is only very limited research that uses data from multiple levels of analysis to investigate these complex relationships.

For researchers, besides the obvious data collection problems, there are theoretical and methodological problems and challenges of this multilevel perspective (Kozlowski and Klein 2000). Besides some well-known measurement problems (e.g. Gerhart in press; Gerhart et al. 2000), simple abstractions from lower-level to higher-level relationships and vice versa are likely to be inappropriate. Combining the issues of levels of abstraction and analysis, we can make the predictions that the HRM philosophy may affect an organization, that the HRM policies have the potential to affect large parts of the workforce (all employees who are covered by the specific policies), and that HRM practices and processes may affect specific work groups, those that the practices and processes target. This has important implications for SHRM research. Collecting data on HRM practices that cover the entire workforce may be inappropriate since individual practices are unlikely to target an entire workforce (Delery and Shaw 2001; Kepes and Delery in press; Lepak and Snell 1999). HRM measures must match the level on which outcome measures are collected. Measuring HRM practices (level of abstraction) and organizational performance (level of analysis), for example, may denote a misalignment and the empirical results could be a methodological artifact rather than a true relationship (Kozlowski and Klein 2000).

There is a critical need in this research area to match levels of abstraction and levels of analysis. Theory should guide the appropriate determination of the different levels. Only then can the effects of internally consistent or inconsistent HRM systems on individual, group, or organizational effectiveness be understood. Recently, Ostroff and Bowen (2000) proposed a multilevel framework that links HRM systems to firm effectiveness (see also Bowen and Ostroff 2004). Their model illustrates the need to take a multilevel perspective when investigating HRM systems and the fit between the different elements within it.

# 19.4 RESEARCH AND EVIDENCE ON INTERNAL FIT

Now that we have discussed the theory and complexities behind the internal fit perspective, we turn to the empirical evidence. Until now, Delery's (1998) review is the only one that devoted considerable space to measurement issues and empirical evidence of internal fit. Other review articles center around the strategy—HRM system relationship or external fit (e.g. Wright and Sherman 1999) or fit in relation to a specific activity area (e.g. compensation, Gerhart 2000). There is therefore a need to describe and evaluate the empirical results related to the different types of internal fit. This section centers around inter-practice and intra-practice area fit since most of the research to date has investigated only these types of internal fit. We could not find studies that specifically addressed within-HRM system vertical fit or between-HRM system fit. The lack of studies in both of these areas is troublesome.

## 19.4.1 Inter-HRM Activity Area Fit

As previously conceptualized, inter-HRM activity area fit denotes the fit *across* different HRM activities at the same level of abstraction (e.g. the alignment between compensation and work design HRM practices). In a first step to investigate this type of fit, several authors have examined whether certain HRM activities hang together and make up a theoretically coherent HRM system. In one of the earliest studies following this line of thought, Arthur (1992) used a cluster analysis approach and grouped organizations based on ten HRM policy and practice variables that made up a HRM system. As predicted, Arthur found that organizations with a cost leadership strategy had substantially different HRM systems from organizations with a differentiation strategy.

Empirical researchers seem to have followed Becker and Gerhart's (1996) call for more research using cluster analytic techniques (e.g. De Saá-Pérez and García-Falcón 2002; Delery et al. 1997; Ordiz-Fuertes and Fernández-Sánchez 2003; Ostroff 2000). In general, these studies support the notion that there are separate HRM systems, comprised of distinct HRM activities (mostly at the policy and practice levels of abstraction). For example, Ostroff (2000) found five, De Saá-Pérez and García-Falcón (2002) four, and Ordiz-Fuertes and Fernández-Sánchez (2003) two clusters of distinct HRM systems. There are likely to be many reasons for the different numbers of clusters found, ranging from sample characteristics, HRM activities included in the survey, a mixture of policy *and* practice items, through to shortcomings of cluster analysis, which are well documented (see Delery 1998).

Nevertheless, all studies using cluster analysis support Arthur's (1992) finding that different organizations have distinct, theoretically internally consistent HRM activities, supporting indirectly the notion of internal fit. With a similar theoretical approach, applying pattern analysis, Verburg et al. (2004) concluded that fit per se was not associated with superior performance. Instead, certain types of HRM systems were related to better organizational performance, a finding aligned with previous research (e.g. Arthur 1992; Becker and Huselid 1998).

Several empirical studies have used factor analytic techniques and scales or indices as measures of HRM systems (e.g. De Saá-Pérez and García-Falcón 2002; Huselid 1995; MacDuffie 1995; Vandenberg et al. 1999; Zacharatos et al. 2005), possibly due to the familiarity and acceptance of these techniques in the social sciences. While the studies reviewed by Delery (1998) only employed exploratory factor analysis, more recent studies have used a confirmatory approach. The paper by Zacharatos et al. (2005) is most notable. In their first study, the authors measured ten high-performance HRM practices with several items on Likert-type scales. Fit measures supported their prediction and all parameter estimates were significant. In a second study, using almost identical scales and items, Zacharatos et al. (2005) further showed that their high-performance HRM system had convergent and discriminant validity when affective commitment was included in a two-factor model; both factors were positively correlated as theory would predict (Arthur 1992; Meyer and Smith 2000).

Taken together, the results of all the above cited studies clearly demonstrate that certain HRM activities fit with each other and form a coherent 'bundle.' However, all of the studies only investigated fit at the policy and practice levels. Some studies even combine the policy and practice levels, which is possibly a serious shortcoming. Further, although most studies conclude that their results show coherent HRM systems, they really show only that organizations have internally aligned HRM policies and/or practices. No study actually looks at the fit of an entire HRM system, the fit between different HRM activity areas across several levels of abstraction, or even the fit of a complete HRM architecture. Nevertheless, all of these studies provide some support for the notion of inter-HRM activity area fit.

Another shortcoming of these studies is that they do not necessarily account for synergistic effects, one of the hallmarks of internal fit. Hence, while the studies show support for the presence of 'bundles' of HRM activities, they do not prove the existence of 'powerful connections' or 'deadly combinations.' The interaction approach using regression analysis allows for a better test of synergistic effects, although it only allows for testing fit between a limited number of practices. Adopting this approach, Delery et al. (1997) used broadly measured HRM practices (e.g. selective staffing, performance-based pay, and participative decision-making) and performed multiple two- and three-way interactions that unmistakably support the notion of fit *and* synergies.

Shaw et al. (2002), using a similar approach, found that individual performance-based pay that results in pay dispersion is only effective in an independent work setting whereas more equally distributed pay allocations are more effective in interdependent working arrangements. The dependent variables in the study were measures of workforce effectiveness and the results indicate the need to align the two practice areas of compensation and work design, and, more importantly, that alignment leads to positive synergistic effects whereas misalignment is detrimental. A study by Kruse et al. (2004) supports these findings, showing that employee ownership alone does not improve organizational performance. Combining employee ownership plans with policies and practices that involve employees and give them a voice, however, has a significant effect on workforce productivity and firm performance (see also Blasi et al. 2003). In a study investigating the joint effects of top management team (TMT) compensation and firm internationalization on organizational performance, Carpenter and Sanders (2004) also found 'powerful connections' and 'deadly combinations.' Firm performance was amplified for conditions of high TMT pay level and TMT long-term incentives when a firm's degree of internationalization (DOI) was high while performance diminished for firms with low DOIs. The opposite was true for the pay gap between TMT members and their CEO.

The findings and conclusions of these studies are clearly supportive of the theory behind internal fit, specifically inter-HRM activity area fit. Further, their results are generally consistent with Lawler's (1986) high-involvement approach to management and illustrate perhaps most clearly the effects of 'powerful connections' and 'deadly combinations.' Many researchers have criticized the field of SHRM for its lack of a strong theory, particularly when it comes to the conceptualization of performance enhancing HRM systems (e.g. Becker and Gerhart 1996; Wright and Sherman 1999). Using the high-involvement management approach as the foundation may thus provide the basis to develop a theoretically grounded framework for SHRM.

## 19.4.2 Intra-HRM Activity Area Fit

Research on intra-practice area fit has taken off during the last few years. The findings from this stream of research add critically to our knowledge by showing that different HRM activities in a specific HRM activity area are more effective when aligned. As with the fit between different sets of activity areas within the overall HRM system, individual activities within a HRM activity area create synergistic effects that can either enhance or suppress effectiveness.

From research in the selection and staffing areas, it has long been known that individual selection devices have incremental validity and, thus, additive effects on individual performance. Recent studies are also supportive of synergistic effects.

All of these studies have used the interaction approach with regression analysis. In a study predicting turnover, Shaw et al. (1998) found that the selection ratio interacts with valid selection techniques. The lowest discharge rate was found when firms use valid selection techniques and have a low selection ratio, an effect that was stronger than the individual main effects. When the selection ratio was high, however, valid selection techniques were associated with high discharge rates. Also, the effect of the selection ratio (low or high) on quit rates was relatively stable when the use of selection procedures was low. These findings clearly show that there are 'powerful connections' and 'deadly combinations' within the selection activity area.

More fit-supporting findings on intra-HRM activity area fit come from compensation research. Studies at the individual level of analysis by Pfeffer and colleagues (e.g. Pfeffer and Davis-Blake 1992; Pfeffer and Langton 1993) found that certain combinations of specific compensation activities (e.g. pay dispersion and pay level, pay dispersion and pay structure knowledge) interact with each other and influence satisfaction as well as individual and collective performance. Certain combinations yield 'powerful connections' while others are 'deadly combinations' and result in less satisfied and productive employees.

At the organizational level, Shaw and Gupta (2001) found that pay system communication interacts with performance-based pay and seniority-based pay in predicting quit rates. Pay system communication was critical when pay dispersion was high and significantly reduced turnover. A combination of low pay system communication, however, showed different effects. More recently, Brown et al. (2003) investigated the interaction between pay level and pay dispersion. As predicted, the interaction of both sets of compensation practices predicted workforce productivity and organizational performance. Specifically, the authors observed an inverted U-shaped relationship between pay level and financial performance that varied with the degree of pay dispersion. For example, low degrees of pay dispersion and low pay levels as well as high pay levels and high degrees of pay dispersion were 'powerful connections' and resulted in equally high levels of organizational performance. The opposite arrangements were 'deadly combinations.' It should be noted, however, that Brown and colleagues treated pay dispersion as a 'within-job category' variable (horizontal pay dispersion) but operationalized it across the organizational hierarchy (vertical pay dispersion). This may have led to spurious outcomes and misleading conclusions (see Pfeffer and Langton 1993).

As with inter-HRM activity area fit, a serious shortcoming in the research on intra-HRM activity area fit is that nearly all studies have focused on only two levels of abstraction (e.g. policy and practice levels). Research at the process level is desirable since it is at this level where employees interact with HRM activities and experience their direct impact. It seems thus likely that the synergistic effects found at higher levels of abstraction are even more dramatic.

## 19.5 CONCLUSION

The basic idea behind internal fit is that coherent systems of HRM activities create positive synergistic effects that enhance organizational effectiveness, while conflicting sets of HRM activities create negative synergistic effects and harm organizational effectiveness. The concept of internal fit is important to SHRM research because it is at the heart of the arguments linking HRM activities and sustained competitive advantage. It is very difficult for poorly performing organizations to imitate the HRM systems of more successful ones. In resource-based terminology, these systems are relatively inimitable in part because of the causal ambiguity surrounding the interaction of the individual HRM activities. Researchers and practitioners have become more cognizant of the issue of internal fit and work has begun to enhance our understanding of this very complex issue. In this chapter, we set out to provide an overview of the main theoretical issues involving the internal fit of HRM activities. In doing so, we also briefly reviewed the recent academic work.

There is now some agreement that there is a multilevel HRM architecture within organizations. Drawing on this research, we identified and described four different types of internal fit (within-HRM system vertical fit, intra-HRM activity area fit, inter-HRM activity area fit, and between-HRM system fit). We did this not simply to provide the field with yet another typology. It is truly our hope that this explication of the types of fit will have a beneficial impact on research. It is clear to us that researchers must be more explicit in specifying and explaining the proposed relationships between HRM activities than they have to date. It must be clearly specified which HRM activities fit with each other and the particular type of fit since it seems unlikely that the theoretical arguments for all types are identical. With more complete conceptual arguments, researchers should be better able to choose appropriate measurement and statistical tools. It should not be enough to justify the use of an index as a measure of the HRM system simply because previous research has done so. More attention to these details can only advance the state of SHRM and address previous calls for more theory and rigorous empirical studies (e.g. Becker and Gerhart 1996; Delery and Shaw 2001).

Based on our review of the empirical literature, we dispute claims that there is a scarcity of empirical evidence that supports the notion of internal fit. There is a great deal of research that supports the general theoretical conception of internal fit and the different types of fit, including synergistic 'powerful connections.' However, virtually all of the research to date has focused on intra- and inter-HRM activity area fits. Research on within-HRM system vertical fit and between-HRM system fit is clearly desirable and would advance our knowledge of the alignment between different levels of abstraction and between different HRM systems within the HRM architecture. Research will benefit from more carefully structured and systematic thinking about internal fit within and across HRM systems.

# REFERENCES

ABELL, D. F. (1993). *Managing with Dual Strategies: Mastering the Present, Preempting the Future*. New York: Free Press.

ARTHUR, J. B. (1992). 'The Link between Business Strategy and Industrial Relations Systems in American Steel Minimills.' *Industrial and Labor Relations Review*, 45/3: 488–506.

ATKINSON, J. (1984). 'Manpower Strategies for Flexible Organizations.' *Personnel Management*, 16/8: 28–31.

BARNEY, J. B. (1991). 'Firm Resources and Sustained Competitive Advantage.' *Journal of Management*, 17/1: 99–120.

—— and WRIGHT, P. M. (1998). 'On Becoming a Strategic Partner: The Role of Human Resources in Gaining Competitive Advantage.' *Human Resource Management*, 37/1: 31–46.

BARON, J. N., and KREPS, D. M. (1999). *Strategic Human Resources: Frameworks for General Managers*. New York: John Wiley.

BECKER, B. E., and GERHART, B. (1996). 'The Impact of Human Resource Management on Organizational Performance: Progress and Prospects.' *Academy of Management Journal*, 39/4: 779–801.

—— and HUSELID, M. A. (1998). 'High Performance Work Systems and Firm Performance: A Synthesis of Research and Managerial Implications.' In G. R. Ferris (ed.), *Research in Personnel and Human Resources Management*, vol. xvi. Greenwich, Conn.: JAI Press.

—— —— PICKUS, P. S., and SPRATT, M. F. (1997). 'HR as a Source of Shareholder Value: Research and Recommendations.' *Human Resource Management*, 36/1: 39–47.

BLASI, J. R., KRUSE, D., and BERNSTEIN, A. (2003). *In the Company of Owners: The Truth about Stock Options (and Why Every Employee Should Have Them)*. New York: Basic Books.

BOWEN, D. E., and OSTROFF, C. (2004). 'Understanding HRM–Firm Performance Linkages: The Role of the "Strength" of the HRM System.' *Academy of Management Review*, 29/2: 203–21.

BOXALL, P. F., and PURCELL, J. (2003). *Strategy and Human Resource Management*. Basingstoke: Palgrave Macmillan.

BROWN, M. P., STURMAN, M. C., and SIMMERING, M. J. (2003). 'Compensation Policy and Organizational Performance: The Efficiency, Operational, and Financial Implications of Pay Levels and Pay Structure.' *Academy of Management Journal*, 46/6: 752–62.

CARPENTER, M. A., and SANDERS, W. G. (2004). 'The Effects of Top Management Team Pay and Firm Internationalization on Mnc Performance.' *Journal of Management*, 30/4: 509–28.

COLBERT, B. A. (2004). 'The Complex Resource-Based View: Implications for Theory and Practice in Strategic Human Resource Management.' *Academy of Management Review*, 29/3: 341–58.

DELERY, J. E. (1998). 'Issues of Fit in Strategic Human Resource Management: Implications for Research.' *Human Resource Management Review*, 8/3: 289–309.

DELERY, J. E., and DOTY, D. H. (1996). 'Modes of Theorizing in Strategic Human Resource Management: Tests of Universalistic, Contingency, and Configurational Performance Predictions.' *Academy of Management Journal*, 39/4: 802–35.

—— and SHAW, J. D. (2001). 'The Strategic Management of People in Work Organizations: Review, Synthesis, and Extension.' In G. R. Ferris (ed.), *Research in Personnel and Human Resource Management*, vol. xx. New York: JAI Press.

—— GUPTA, N., and SHAW, J. D. (1997). 'Human Resource Management and Firm Performance: A Systems Perspective.' Paper presented at the Southern Management Association Meeting; Atlanta, Ga.

DE SAÁ-PÉREZ, P., and GARCÍA-FALCÓN, J. M. (2002). 'A Resource-Based View of Human Resource Management and Organizational Capabilities Development.' *International Journal of Human Resource Management*, 13/1: 123–40.

DYER, L., and SHAFER, R. A. (1999). 'From Human Resource Strategy to Organizational Effectiveness: Lessons from Research on Organizational Agility.' In P. M. Wright, L. Dyer, J. W. Boudreau, and G. T. Milkovich (eds.), *Research in Personnel and Human Resource Management.* Supplement 4: *Strategic Human Resource Management in the 21st Century.* Stamford, Conn.: JAI Press.

GERHART, B. (2000). 'Compensation Strategy and Organizational Performance.' In S. L. Rynes and B. Gerhart (eds.), *Compensation in Organizations.* San Francisco: Jossey-Bass.

—— (in press). 'Human Resource Systems.' In C. Ostroff and T. Judge (eds.), *Perspectives on Organizational Fit.* Mahwah, NJ: L. Erlbaum Associates.

—— WRIGHT, P. M., MCMAHAN, G. C., and SNELL, S. A. (2000). 'Measurement Error in Research on Human Resources and Firm Performance: How Much Error is There and How Does it Influence Effect Size Estimates?' *Personnel Psychology*, 53/4: 803–34.

HAKIM, C. (1990). 'Core and Periphery in Employers' Workforce Strategies: Evidence from the 1987 E.L.U.S. Survey.' *Work, Employment and Society*, 4/2: 157–88.

HENEMAN, R. L. (1990). 'Merit Pay Research.' In K. M. Rowland and G. R. Ferris (eds.), *Research in Personnel and Human Resource Management.* vol. viii. Greenwich, Conn.: JAI Press.

HUSELID, M. A. (1995). 'The Impact of Human-Resource Management-Practices on Turnover, Productivity, and Corporate Financial Performance.' *Academy of Management Journal*, 38/3: 635–72.

ICHNIOWSKI, C., SHAW, K., and PRENNUSHI, G. (1997). 'The Effects of Human Resource Management Practices on Productivity: A Study of Steel Finishing Lines.' *American Economic Review*, 87/3: 291–313.

KEPES, S., and DELERY, J. E. (in press). 'Designing Effective HRM Systems: The Issue of HRM Strategy.' In C. Cooper and R. Burke (eds.), *The Human Resources Revolution: Research and Practice.* Amsterdam: Elsevier.

KOZLOWSKI, S. W. J., and KLEIN, K. J. (2000). 'A Multilevel Approach to Theory and Research in Organizations: Contextual, Temporal, and Emergent Processes.' In K. J. KLEIN and S. W. J. Kozlowski (eds.), *Multilevel Theory, Research, and Methods in Organizations: Foundations, Extensions, and New Directions.* San Francisco: Jossey-Bass.

KRUSE, D., FREEMAN, R. B., BLASI, J. R., BUCHELE, R., SCHARF, A., RODGERS, L., and Macklin, C. (2004). 'Motivating Employee-Owners in ESOP Firms: Human Resource Policies and Company Performance.' Centre of Economic Performance, London School of Economics and Political Science, CEP Discussion Paper No. 658, November.

LAWLER, E. E. (1986). *High-Involvement Management.* San Francisco: Jossey-Bass.

LEPAK, D. P., and SNELL, S. A. (1999). 'The Human Resource Architecture: Toward a Theory of Human Capital Allocation and Development.' *Academy of Management Review*, 24/1: 31–48.

MacDUFFIE, J. P. (1995). 'Human-Resource Bundles and Manufacturing Performance: Organizational Logic and Flexible Production Systems in the World Auto Industry.' *Industrial and Labor Relations Review*, 48/2: 197–221.

MEYER, J. P., and SMITH, C. A. (2000). 'HRM Practices and Organizational Commitment: Test of a Mediation Model.' *Canadian Journal of Administrative Sciences*, 17/4: 319–31.

ORDIZ-FUERTES, M., and FERNÁNDEZ-SÁNCHEZ, E. (2003). 'High-Involvement Practices in Human Resource Management: Concept and Factors that Motivate their Adoption.' *International Journal of Human Resource Management*, 14/4: 511–29.

OSTROFF, C. (2000). 'Human Resource Management and Firm Performance: Practices, Systems, and Contingencies.' Working paper, Arizona State University.

—— and BOWEN, D. E. (2000). 'Moving HR to a Higher Level: HR Practices and Organizational Effectiveness.' In K. J. Klein and S. W. J. Kozlowski (eds.), *Multilevel Theory, Research, and Methods in Organizations: Foundations, Extensions, and New Directions*. San Francisco: Jossey-Bass.

PFEFFER, J. (1994). *Competitive Advantage through People: Unleashing the Power of the Work Force*. Boston: Harvard Business School Press.

—— and BARON, J. N. (1988). 'Taking the Workers Back out: Recent Trends in the Structuring of Employment.' In B. M. Staw and L. L. Cummings (eds.), *Research in Organizational Behavior*, vol. x. Greenwich, Conn.: JAI Press.

—— and DAVIS-BLAKE, A. (1992). 'Salary Dispersion, Location in the Salary Distribution, and Turnover among College Administrators.' *Industrial and Labor Relations Review*, 45/4: 753–63.

—— and LANGTON, N. (1993). 'The Effect of Wage Dispersion on Satisfaction, Productivity, and Working Collaboratively: Evidence from College and University Faculty.' *Administrative Science Quarterly*, 38/3: 382–407.

PLOYHART, R. E. (2004). 'Organizational Staffing: A Multilevel Review, Synthesis, and Model.' In J. J. Martocchio (ed.), *Research in Personnel and Human Resources Management*, vol. xxiii. Greenwich, Conn.: JAI Press.

REICHERS, A. E., and SCHNEIDER, B. (1990). 'Climate and Culture: An Evolution of Constructs.' In B. Schneider (ed.), *Organizational Climate and Culture*. San Francisco: Jossey-Bass.

SCHNEIDER, B., and BRIEF, A. P. (1996). 'Creating a Climate and Culture for Sustainable Organizational Change.' *Organizational Dynamics*, 24/4: 6–19.

SCHULER, R. S. (1992). 'Strategic Human Resources Management: Linking the People with the Strategic Needs of the Business.' *Organizational Dynamics*, 21/1: 18–32.

SHAW, J. D., and GUPTA, N. (2001). 'Does Money Make Good Employees Leave? Organizational Pay Decisions, Performance, and Employee Quit Patterns.' Paper presented at the Southern Management Association Meeting, New Orleans. (Best Paper, Human Resources, Careers, and Conflict Management Track).

—— DELERY, J. E., JENKINS, G. D., and GUPTA, N. (1998). 'An Organization-Level Analysis of Voluntary and Involuntary Turnover.' *Academy of Management Journal*, 41/5: 511–25.

—— GUPTA, N., and DELERY, J. E. (2002). 'Pay Dispersion and Workforce Performance: Moderating Effects of Incentives and Interdependence.' *Strategic Management Journal*, 23/6: 491–512.

SIMONS, T., and ROBERSON, Q. (2003). 'Why Managers Should Care about Fairness: The Effects of Aggregate Justice Perceptions on Organizational Outcomes.' *Journal of Applied Psychology*, 88/3: 432–43.

VANDENBERG, R. J., RICHARDSON, H. A., and EASTMAN, L. J. (1999). 'The Impact of High Involvement Work Processes on Organizational Effectiveness: A Second-Order Latent Variable Approach.' *Group & Organization Management*, 24/3: 300–39.

VERBURG, R. M., DEN HARTOG, D. N., and KOOPMAN, P. L. (2004). 'Configurations of Human Resource Management Practices: A Theoretical Model and Empirical Test.' Paper presented at the Academy of Management Meeting, New Orleans.

WRIGHT, P. M. (1998). 'Strategy-HR Fit: Does It Really Matter?' *Human Resource Planning*, 21/4: 56–7.

—— and McMAHAN, G. C. (1992). 'Theoretical Perspectives for Strategic Human Resource Management.' *Journal of Management*, 18/2: 295–320.

—— and SHERMAN, W. S. (1999). 'Failing to Find Fit in Strategic Human Resource Management: Theoretical and Empirical Problems.' In G. R. Ferris (ed.), *Research in Personnel and Human Resource Management*. Greenwich, Conn.: JAI Press.

—— and SNELL, S. A. (1998). 'Toward a Unifying Framework for Exploring Fit and Flexibility in Strategic Human Resource Management.' *Academy of Management Review*, 23/4: 756–72.

—— McMAHAN, G. C., and McWILLIAMS, A. (1994). 'Human Resources and Sustained Competitive Advantage: A Resource-Based Perspective.' *International Journal of Human Resource Management*, 5/2: 301–26.

ZACHARATOS, A., BARLING, J., and IVERSON, R. D. (2005). 'High-Performance Work Systems and Occupational Safety.' *Journal of Applied Psychology*, 90/1: 77–93.

CHAPTER 20

................................................................

# HRM AND CONTEMPORARY MANUFACTURING

................................................................

## RICK DELBRIDGE

## 20.1 INTRODUCTION

................................................................

THE relative importance of manufacturing to advanced mature economies has become one of intense debate. There are those of the view that the very marked decline in employment numbers in manufacturing in countries such as France, Germany, Japan, the UK, and the USA is an appropriate and efficient response to the increasing globalization of the supply of manufactured products.[1] Nevertheless, it remains the case that the world's leading economies retain strengths in key industrial sectors and are actively seeking to further develop their presence in emergent markets such as, for example, biotechnology and communications technologies.

The world's major industrial companies are increasingly hybrid enterprises, providing a range of services but retaining control over the manufacture of goods. Multinational corporations have sought out cheaper locations for their

Thanks to the editors and colleagues, in particular Paul Edwards and Jon Morris, for comments and advice. The support of the ESRC/EPSRC Advanced Institute of Management Research is also gratefully acknowledged.

[1] Figures for OECD countries show that two-thirds of employees work in the service sector (OECD 2000). Fewer than one in seven UK workers is employed in manufacturing.

manufacturing operations, looking in particular to benefit from lower labor costs. These MNCs have also had to contend with the emergence of manufacturing companies from newly industrializing economies in South America, Eastern Europe, and South-East Asia. This has resulted in intense cost-based competition in mature industrial and consumer product markets. The challenge of meeting low-cost competition has contributed to an increasing emphasis on labor productivity in manufacturing. The management of manufacturing operations has been heavily influenced over the last twenty years by the advent of the 'lean manufacturing' model of organization, operations, and management, initially associated with the successful emergence of Japanese firms into mature high-volume markets. This chapter concerns itself primarily with developments in advanced mature economies but there is evidence that the model is increasingly influential in manufacturing throughout the world.[2] Thus, the model has been the 'dominant system' (Smith and Meiksins 1995) of manufacturing in recent times and is the start point for this chapter.

Along with cost pressures, technological advances, an increasing sophistication of consumer markets, product differentiation, and the proliferation of market niches have placed an onus on innovation in terms of new product development and ongoing product and process improvement. These have arisen as particularly pressing concerns for the future of manufacturing organizations in advanced economies which require greater levels of innovation and higher value added in order to remain competitive against lower-cost rivals. These pressures have combined to question the extent to which the lean manufacturing model, with its focus on volume, standardization, efficiency, and incremental continuous improvement, can meet the challenges facing manufacturers operating in mature economies. Recognition of these shifts has prompted an increasingly holistic view of strategy and organization, with implications for corporate governance, corporate business unit links, and the nature of work and employment relations. In combination, these features of the context of contemporary manufacturing have resulted in a number of key developments in organization that have important implications for human resource management: an emphasis on skill and creativity throughout the firm, the incorporation of learning and improvement into ongoing operational activities, an emphasis on the creation and application of knowledge for product and process improvement, and greater inter-organizational and network-level participation in both operations and innovation.

---

[2] See, for example, the overview of developments in the world auto industry in Kochan et al. 1997. And evidence is not restricted to the motor industry; see the interesting case comparison of LG Electronics and Samsung in South Korea provided by Kim and Bae 2005. There is also an increasing body of research that documents the nature of ongoing reforms in HRM in China that is critical to understanding the future in manufacturing but this lies outside the concerns of the current chapter (for an overview see Warner 2004 and *International Journal of Human Resource Management*, 15/4–5 (2004)).

Such developments have led to recognition that employment systems are increasingly centered on the organization rather than on an industry or occupational basis (Katz and Darbishire 2000). Blyton and Turnbull (2004: 81) suggest that this represents an attempt by management to insulate the organization from the external labor market but not the product market; workers are encouraged to identify with their employer and its struggle with competitor firms. It has been further suggested that this indicates a move 'from control to commitment' (Legge 1995) with managers seeking to establish mutual obligation with their employees rather than authoritarian direct control. And the rise of human resource management in manufacturing firms has been closely associated with these attempts to engender greater employee commitment, particularly in association with so-called 'high-performance' work systems, such as teamworking, and lean production practices (Appelbaum et al. 2000; MacDuffie 1995a). However, the empirical evidence on the extent to which such practices have been successfully adopted is mixed and their likely impact on workers has been the subject of considerable debate. It is suggested here that the disconnections between spheres of economic activity and business organization that increasingly characterize contemporary capitalism (Thompson 2003) result in tensions at the workplace which undermine the prospects for local managers and employees to secure and maintain the effort and job security bargains that are key. This confirms the significance of local conditions, workplace–corporate organization, institutional context, and political economy in understanding the challenges confronting human resource management in contemporary manufacturing (Godard 2004).

The first sections of this chapter outline the key elements of organization and HRM associated with contemporary high-volume production, in particular the key arguments and characteristics of lean manufacturing. Lean manufacturing and the associated high-performance work system model has been influential in the development of management practices throughout manufacturing sectors and beyond. However, they are primarily premised on labor efficiencies and incremental improvement. The chapter reviews the evidence on the implementation and outcomes of lean adoption. The second main section reviews alternatives to 'lean.' The requirement for innovation and higher value added noted above has meant that a greater emphasis on creating and managing knowledge than that associated with lean manufacturing has become central. One insightful, and increasingly influential, way of conceiving of this challenge has been developed from the concept of 'communities of practice,' i.e. groups of largely autonomous and self-organizing experts. The notion of communities of practice is introduced and the implications for organization and management are considered. In the final sections we argue for the importance of situating the management of manufacturing workers in context.

## 20.2 WORKERS IN CONTEMPORARY MANUFACTURING

The nature of competition in mature product markets has prompted a revision to traditional Taylorist views of job design and work organization in manufacturing operations. While anticipation of 'post-Taylorist' and 'post-Fordist' new worlds has run ahead of empirical evidence of radical shopfloor transformation, the dynamic and unpredictable context of manufacturing has led to a reassessment of the extent to which design and execution can be separated (Kenney and Florida 1993; Cooke and Morgan 1998; Appelbaum et al. 2000). Drives to reduce cost and improve efficiencies on the shop floor now rely heavily on the input of operator-level employees responsible for the jobs; shopfloor employees are seen as *sources of ideas* for improvement (Adler 1993; Fruin 1992). This has given rise to discussion of plants as 'learning factories' (Leonard Barton 1992; Fruin 1997), sites of knowledge creation and application as well as the production of physical objects, where workers think as well as do (Snell and Dean 1992). Delbridge et al. (1998) outline the key attributes of such an approach. In particular, they emphasize continuous improvement activities 'that are driven by internal sources of information such as the tacit knowledge of shopfloor workers, the "contextual" knowledge of technicians, and the "formal" knowledge of professionals and craft workers' (Delbridge et al. 1998: 227).

Such expectations require the organization and management of workers in order that discretionary effort and employees' skills and knowledge be developed and appropriated. Thus, the role of HRM has been a key feature in research and debates regarding the 'learning factory.' In particular, it has been argued that the effective implementation of specific bundles of 'progressive' HR practices and 'high-involvement' work practices, known as High-Performance Work Systems (HPWSs), positively affect individual, team and organizational performance (Arthur 1994; MacDuffie 1995a; MacDuffie and Pil 1999; Appelbaum et al. 2000). These practices relate to the organization of work and the emergence of new manufacturing and management practices such as teamworking, multi-skilling, and the encouragement of employee involvement in which continuous improvement is seen as central in sustaining competitive advantage (Cappelli and Neumark 2001). A number of studies have reported positive associations between firm-level measures of HRM and work systems and organizational performance (for example, Arthur 1994; Becker and Gerhart 1996; Huselid 1995; MacDuffie 1995a).

The exact relationships between workers, management practices, and organizational performance have been conceptualized through a number of divergent theoretical frameworks (Jackson and Schuler 1995). Numerous quantitative studies have found evidence that employee involvement, complemented by appropriate

HR practices, increases organizational performance, but the exact nature of such relationships remains unclear (for recent reviews see Appelbaum 2002; Benson and Lawler 2003). There has been considerable variety in the detail of these studies,[3] indicating the absence of a widely accepted set of measures of 'progressive' or 'high-performance' HRM (Barton and Delbridge 2004), and making comparisons problematic. In seeking to distill the essence of these studies, Cappelli and Neumark (2001) conclude that the central feature of this literature is the link between employee involvement and high performance. This is consistent with Florida et al.'s (1998: 199) conclusion that the defining characteristic of new work regimes is the attempt to promote knowledge mobilization and organizational learning, founded on the dimensions of teamwork, employee involvement, and training.

## 20.3 LEAN MANUFACTURING

### 20.3.1 The Key Argument of the Lean Model

Rather as the Fordist production system presented a coherent and rounded model of consumption, production, and organization, so the lean model provides an integrated system linking markets, organization, production, and employment relations. Early advocates of lean production (also called 'just-in-time production') made direct and favorable comparisons with Fordism in advancing the superiority of this alternative model (Ohno 1988; Womack et al. 1990). It is the systemic linking of market demand, technical and operational features, and work organization with the role of workers underpinned by appropriate HR practices which is fundamental. The empirical research of MacDuffie (1995a) provides the strongest example of the key arguments regarding the integration of management practices.

MacDuffie's work has been highly influential, especially in advocating the 'bundling' of mutually constitutive and supportive practices. His conclusions stem from detailed analysis of quantitative data gathered from car assemblers across the world and his central argument is that it is the *combination* of lean production practices with high-involvement work systems and complementary HR practices that creates the necessary organizational environment for high-performance manufacturing (see also MacDuffie and Pil 1997). He underscores the central role of a participative workforce and argues that the potential technological superiority of lean production is only realized through the active participation of shopfloor workers. Management seeks to ensure workers contribute discretionary

---

[3] Becker and Gerhart 1996 note twenty seven different variables that have been used as proxies for high-performance work practices across just five independent studies.

effort through a variety of HR practices which are deemed to support the employment relationship and encourage worker participation. This is consistent with the conclusion of Strauss (1998: 195) whose review of studies of organizational participation confirms that such schemes are unlikely to prove successful without 'appropriate human-resource policies.' Thus, changes in the effort bargain are to be underpinned by commitments to just rewards (Lawler 1986), job security (Kochan and Osterman 1994; Osterman 2000), and improved employment relationships through a combination of 'high-commitment' HR practices (Wood and Albanese 1995).

In practice, lean production has polarized opinion. Proponents argue that new arrangements of work and organization will lead to greater autonomy through an 'empowered', multi-skilled workforce (Wickens 1987). From this perspective, workers are the 'heart' of the lean production model (Womack et al. 1990) and will become involved in all aspects of the decision-making process as part of a participative and high-trust relationship (Walton 1985). Some proponents of this 'human-centered model' argue that organizational adaptability and learning are best served by greatly lengthened work cycles and a return to craftlike work forms that give teams 'responsible autonomy' in how they perform their tasks and authority over what have traditionally been higher-level management decisions (Adler and Cole 1993). Womack et al. (1990) argue that the potential for organizational success will be maximized in a system based on specialized work tasks supplemented by modest job rotation and greater discipline through detailed work procedures. Adler and Borys (1996) suggest that the systematization of processes can prove 'enabling' for shopfloor employees if the bureaucracy is geared toward supporting this employee involvement and creative input. These interpretations of developments in manufacturing organization have generally positive views of the implications for workers but the empirical evidence is mixed.

Critical assessments based on early examples of lean manufacturing ranged from the sceptical to the openly disapproving (Parker and Slaughter 1988; Fucini and Fucini 1990). Critiques have been founded upon both conceptual and empirical grounds. For instance, labor process theory contends that new technologies and management practices are introduced to enhance managerial control over the workforce (Delbridge et al. 1992). This, it is argued, is particularly true in the labor-intensive production of standardized products. In addition, case study research has consistently failed to find evidence that workers perceive new management practices to be beneficial to their experience of work or offer greater involvement in decision-making (Delbridge 1998; Graham 1995; Rinehart et al. 1997). Even those researchers reporting the beneficial impact of lean work for employees have recognized that these 'successes' rely on the promotion of worker identification with the enterprise, often at times when that organization faces closure (Adler 1993; Barker 1993; MacDuffie 1995b). The examples of NUMMI (Adler 1993) and ISE (Barker 1993, 1999) appear to rely heavily on a threat to the very survival of the respective plants in securing worker commitment and identification with the firm and thus run contrary to the generic argument of participation underpinned by high commitment.[4] Before considering the empirical evidence on these claims in more detail, let us articulate more precisely the key features of the lean model.

## 20.3.2  The Key Characteristics of Lean Manufacturing

The genesis of lean manufacturing can be traced to the emergence of just-in-time manufacturing at Toyota during the 1960s. One of the key architects of the Toyota Production System, Taiichi Ohno, provides a detailed account of his ideas and their implementation in his book *Just-in-Time: For Today and Tomorrow* (1988). At the outset he articulates the integrative and holistic nature of lean manufacturing, arguing that business must be seen as a 'trinity' of the market, the factory, and the company as a whole. The Toyota approach is contrasted with that of Ford, in particular in the way that production is determined by market needs and pulled through the factory rather than by schedules that push products onto the market. As the name suggests, products are manufactured 'just-in-time' to meet customer demand. This cuts waste in terms of stocks, waiting time, and over-production and places a considerable emphasis on reliable, high-quality processes and flexible workers able to work where they are required by market demands. This close coordination, reliability, and flexibility are also required of the supply chain, since the just-in-time system runs with minimal buffers with regard to time or inventory between plants as well as between work stations.

Along with internal process control and tightly integrated supply chains, the third important aspect of the Toyota system is 'innovation.' Ohno (1988: 81) makes it clear that he has higher-level innovation in mind, including the development of new products and new manufacturing techniques, though under lean manufacturing this has become understood in rather more limited terms as continuous, incremental, process improvement or *kaizen*.[5] Still, this provides a further key contrast with the Fordist production system, with workers expected to contribute to how their jobs are designed and organized. Nevertheless, along with other early assessments of the Toyota Production System (Schonberger 1982; Monden 1983; Shingo 1988), Ohno emphasizes the operational and technical aspects of the

---

[4] These examples question the significance of worker commitment and the relevance of job security within the employment relationship. In these cases, high insecurity appears to have contributed to the successful (for management) adoption of HPWSs. This contrasts with expectations that the implementation of HPWSs will be founded on reassurances over job security as a necessary element of the mutual obligations of the 'high-commitment' employment relationship.

[5] *Kaizen* is a Japanese word meaning gradual and orderly, continuous improvement and has been considered the most important concept within Japanese management (Imai 1986).

system over detailed analysis of the nature of work organization and employment relations.[6]

With the success of Japanese corporations in the 1980s and 1990s came greater interest in how Western manufacturers might learn lessons from these companies in order to improve efficiency and quality performance. There was a considerable debate around the 'transferability' of 'Japanese' manufacturing techniques and practices and an enormous interest in the so-called 'Japanization' of Western manufacturing (for example, Oliver and Wilkinson 1992; Elger and Smith 1994; Liker et al. 1999). These debates turned attention much more directly to the social processes of lean manufacturing, especially the nature of HRM practices and the employment relations required to operate a fragile and tightly integrated manufacturing system.

Early studies of Japanese factories by Abegglen (1958), Cole (1971), and Dore (1973) had outlined important elements of the uniquely Japanese approach to employment relations—the so-called 'three pillars' of lifetime employment, a seniority wage system, and enterprise unions—which derived from the socio-historical and institutional context of post-war Japan. The emphasis on transferability, however, placed the focus more squarely on work organization and management practices more appropriate to the underpinning requirements for workers to be motivated, flexible, mobile, and appropriately skilled (Thurley 1982). Proponents (for example, Wickens 1987) argued that the secret of Japanese firms' success was the combination of teamwork, quality consciousness, and flexibility which resulted in a harmonious and productive working environment. Others have questioned the harmony of Japanese workplaces (for example, Delbridge and Turnbull 1992; Gordon 1985) and empirical evidence fails to support the claims for greater worker satisfaction (see Dunphy 1986; Lincoln and Kalleberg 1990). Advocates and critics concur, though, that the systems' characteristics of lean manufacturing—minimal buffers, tight coupling of processes, the necessity of reliability and quality, and a drive for continuous improvement—place major demands on workers and present a considerable challenge to managers, particularly with regard to HR practices.

## 20.3.3 HRM and Lean Manufacturing

Recognition of the integrated nature of production, organization, and HRM has contributed significantly to advances in understanding. Previous research on new forms of work organization had tended to focus on isolated practices such as the use

---

[6] Authors such as Pascale and Athos (1982) emphasized the unique history and culture of Japan when assessing its corporate success in the 1980s and the HR practices associated with large Japanese firms at that time were influential in the emergence of Human Resource Management (see for example, Ouchi 1981).

of teams, job rotation, job design, etc. More recently there have been attempts to evaluate the *combined* effect of such practices. As introduced above, recent work suggests that such practices are most effective when used together as interrelated systems referred to variously as 'flexible,' 'high-commitment,' and 'high-performance' work systems (Florida et al. 1998). MacDuffie (1995*a*) argues for the integrated 'bundling' of high-involvement work systems, high-commitment HR practices, and lean operations. It is the mutually reinforcing nature of these bundles of practices taken together which characterizes high-performance workplaces. An underlying theme in this research is that firms should create a high degree of internal consistency, or 'fit', across their activities (Youndt et al. 1996).

MacDuffie (1995*a*) presents data from sixty-two car assembly plants[7] in support of two related arguments: (*a*) that 'innovative' HR practices affect performance as interrelated elements in an internally consistent HR bundle, and (*b*) that these bundles contribute most to manufacturing quality and productivity when they are integrated under the organizational logic of a flexible production system (his term for lean manufacturing). His findings indicate that lean production plants with team-based work systems, high-commitment HR practices, and low inventory levels consistently outperform 'mass production' plants. A key element of his argument is that these systems support employee participation and training so as to contribute to the expansion of workforce skill and the enhancement of conceptual knowledge necessary for the problem-solving and continuous improvement of the lean model.

These findings appear therefore to be consistent with those who argue that factories, specifically those located in advanced economies and seeking to compete on innovation and value added, will be sites of learning and creativity underpinned by the ongoing development of worker skills. Snell and Dean (1992) review the findings from a number of research projects into such developments and conclude that they represent 'a trend toward "upskilling" employees into "knowledge work-ers," whose responsibilities include not only physical work' (Snell and Dean 1992: 472). This returns us to the emphasis on innovation in manufacturing which has called into question the traditional division of labor under Taylorist approaches, for example as outlined by Kenney and Florida's (1993) 'innovation-mediated production.' The central features here are the reintegration of production and innovation and of intellectual and physical labor.

---

[7] The measures of high-involvement work systems which MacDuffie (1995*a*) researches are as follows: the percentage of the workforce involved in formal work teams; the percentage of the workforce involved in employee involvement groups; the number of production-related suggestions received per employee; the percentage of these suggestions implemented; the frequency of job rotation within and across teams and departments; and whether production workers are responsible for quality inspection and data-gathering. He assesses the evidence for high-commitment HR policies on the basis of the following criteria: whether hiring emphasizes an openness to learning and interpersonal skills; pay systems contingent upon performance; single status workplace (common uniform, common parking, common cafeteria, no ties); levels of initial training for new recruits (including workers, supervisors, and engineers); and levels of ongoing training for experienced employees.

Arguments in favor of skill development and employee involvement can be linked to a developing interest in the concept of 'human capital' (Lepak and Snell 1999). Put simply, there has been burgeoning interest in the prospect for the development of employees with a set of unique skills and experiences which are difficult to replicate and that may represent a source of sustainable competitive advantage for firms (Pfeffer 1994). It has been argued that the very nature of lean manufacturing and HPWSs leads to enhanced social complexity, causal ambiguity, and the development of tacit knowledge, and these combine to enhance a firm's human capital (Lepak and Snell 1999). Such arguments return us to the relationships among employee orientations and action, management practices, and organizational performance.

The overall argument at the heart of the lean model in conjunction with HPWS reflects both the skill development of individuals and the nature of how these skills are organized. It is posited that contemporary manufacturing requires both a broadening of worker skills and the combination of these skills into cross-functional, problem-solving groups. This can be seen in a number of studies that have combined both an evaluation of direct production teams and off-line problem-solving groups or 'quality circles' (Lowe et al. 1997; MacDuffie 1995a). Such studies have revitalized managerial interest in employee participation (Strauss 1998). Schemes that encourage employee participation, internal labor markets that provide opportunities for employee development and advancement, and team-based production systems are all practices that have been argued to affect both employees' experiences at work and firm performance positively (Delaney and Huselid 1996). However, Fairris's (1997) analysis of the changing nature of shopfloor labor–management relations in large US manufacturing firms over the twentieth century sounds a note of caution with regard to the extent to which such developments have altered decision-making on the shop floor. He argues that while teamwork and quality circles represent a certain decentralization of shop floor governance, they do not allow workers increased empowerment in shopfloor decision-making such as to alter fundamentally the distribution of rewards or contravene the authority of shopfloor management (Fairris 1997: 8). Indeed, research using the WERS98 dataset found that employee involvement schemes focused at the point of production, such as teams and quality circles, led to lower levels of perceived employee job influence than broader-based participation schemes such as representative participation or briefing groups (Delbridge and Whitfield 2001). The empirical evidence on how lean manufacturing has been implemented in practice carries a number of important lessons for management.

## 20.3.4 The Lean Model in Practice

A host of studies, predominantly quantitative and conducted in the USA, have found empirical support for arguments linking HPWSs and stronger economic performance of individual firms. Variations of such results have been found in a number of different manufacturing industry sectors including apparel (Appelbaum et al. 2000), auto assembly (MacDuffie 1995a), semiconductors (Appleyard and Brown 2001), and steel (Arthur 1994; Ichniowski et al 1997). As Batt and Doellgast (2005: 146) observe, these studies may differ on certain details but each finds support for the systems' approach of lean manufacturing with the performance effects of bundles of management practices measured through cluster analysis or additive indices. The details of these studies, however, reveal important context-specific elements within each sector that suggest that precisely what affects performance varies. Moreover, Appelbaum's (2002: 148) recent review of the survey evidence on the impact of HPWSs on workers ends with the conclusion that the 'jury is still out.'

The evidence on the impact of lean manufacturing and HPWSs derived from detailed case research has generally been more consistent, and negative, in its conclusions on the impact for the shopfloor workforce.[8] Batt and Doellgast (2005) suggest that this is reflected in the divergent traditions of European and US research but, while it is true that the European tradition is more consistently critical in perspective, case researchers from North America have concluded similarly. A number of qualitative studies in the motor industry (Fucini and Fucini 1990; Graham 1995; Rinehart et al. 1997) found high degrees of worker dissatisfaction with new and more demanding and stressful working conditions that were ascribed to moves toward the adoption of the lean manufacturing model. These cases argued that the primary outcome for workers was a combination of a loss of autonomy and influence with a concomitant increase in the demands placed upon them both in terms of physical effort and expectations of contributions to continuous improvement programs. More generally, the impact for employees of new workplace practices continues to be open to debate with a mixed picture emerging (Geary and Dobbins 2001; Godard 2001; Harley 2001; Anderson-Connolly et al. 2002). Understanding what lies behind this 'mixed picture' needs research that accesses the 'black box' of employee perceptions and expectations while retaining the prospect of workplace-level comparisons. While quantitative, sector-level studies are helpful (Appelbaum et al. 2000), this suggests qualitative research will continue to play a particularly important role. The impacts of lean manufacturing on workers' health (Landsbergis et al. 1999) and, in particular, stress levels (Conti and Gill 1998) have also been the subject of recent studies but good-quality data remains rare and this is another area for further research. The extent to which the inherent demands of a tightly coupled and fragile production system may be offset by the support of teamworking and complementary HR practices remains uncertain (Ramsay et al. 2000; Delbridge 2005).

A recurring problem faced in the implementation of the lean manufacturing model is that the daily demands of the production process drive out the space and

---

[8] For a fuller discussion of the evidence on the impact of lean manufacturing for workers, see Delbridge 2005.

opportunity for the innovative continuous improvement activities anticipated by Kenney and Florida (1993) and others. This is compounded when workplace relations are characterized by low trust as was found in Delbridge's (1998) study of a Japanese-owned consumer electronics plant operating in the UK. Here workers found the high levels of direct surveillance and supervision stressful and intimidating. The demands for reliable quality had led to a 'culture of blame,' dividing the workforce and exacerbating feelings of distrust. This had led to the widespread withdrawal of discretionary effort with workers failing to contribute suggestions for improvement and not participating in problem-solving group activity. Similar circumstances are reported by Rinehart et al. (1997) from their longitudinal study of a car assembly plant in Canada. They conclude that the lean production system there requires reliable and flexible workers, rather than committed ones willing to contribute discretionary effort on continuous improvement. Overall, such studies question the extent to which lean manufacturing is actually driven by an innovative learning dynamic when put into practice.

From the wealth of qualitative research that has been conducted over the last fifteen years, two key conclusions can be made: (*a*) the demands of the lean manufacturing model place a considerable strain on shopfloor workers which undermines the prospects for the deployment of discretionary effort on their part and so circumscribes the likelihood of ongoing continuous improvement; (*b*) in seeking to address the problems of (*a*), managers are confronted by important challenges over how to manage the employment relationship such that greater levels of commitment and discretionary effort may be secured. These challenges have prompted critical reflection upon universalistic notions of best practice and been framed in terms of a 'contingency' approach to strategic HRM which argues for a link between an organization's 'idiosyncratic contingencies,' business strategy, and HR practices (Boxall 1996; for an overview of these debates and the related problems of 'fit,' see Boxall and Purcell 2002 and Legge 2005). These debates have drawn greater attention to the organizational context of HR practices, work systems, and operations. In particular, there has been a growing call for an enhanced sensitivity to institutional and market context regarding the adoption and implementation of HPWSs (see Murray et al. 2002). We will reflect upon this further below, but first let us briefly consider the prospects for alternatives to the HPWS/lean manufacturing model.

## 20.4 ALTERNATIVES TO LEAN

While one should remain cautious of overly stylized patterns of organization, it is possible to recognize distinctive but relatively coherent alternatives to the lean manufacturing model. A recent international empirical study of the auto and telecommunications industries by Katz and Darbishire (2000) suggested there were four common patterns of work practices that were found to be spreading across the countries studied (Australia, Germany, Italy, Japan, Sweden, the UK, and USA). These were denoted by the authors as 'low wage,' 'HRM', 'Japanese oriented,' and 'joint team based.'

Low-wage workplace practices, according to Katz and Darbishire (2000) afford management considerable discretion and are associated with relatively high degrees of informality of process. Control is exercised through direct hierarchical relations, wages tend to be low, and there is a strong anti-trade union orientation on the part of management. Labor turnover tends to be high in such organizations but such a pattern of employment relations may prove viable in industries where competition is based upon low cost rather than high levels of quality or innovation. The position taken in this chapter is that such workplaces are likely to struggle to survive in mature economies where labor and operating costs are relatively high and susceptible to international competition. There is wider evidence, however, that these practices may be characteristic of labor-intensive manufacturing operations in low-wage economies such as China (Taylor 2001) and Malaysia (Wilkinson et al. 2001) as part of the internal and international division of labor in manufacturing multinationals.

The distinction drawn by Katz and Darbishire (2000) between HRM and Japanese-oriented workplace practices can be interpreted as two variations on lean manufacturing—the original or ideal-typical Japanese version and the version implemented by many manufacturers in the USA—in a number of regards. Both carry an emphasis on top-down corporate communication, have team-based work organization which is managed rather than self-directed, generally comparatively good levels of contingent pay, and expectations around employment stability and career development. The key distinctions are between the individualized nature of rewards and career development and management's anti-union (or union substitution) stance in the HRM pattern in contrast with the organizational career path and enterprise unionism found in the Japanese-oriented pattern.

Given our interest in how manufacturers can meet the challenge of innovativeness, creativity, and higher value added, and the evidence that lean manufacturing often fails to deliver this in practice, the joint team-based pattern seems particularly relevant. Under this approach, Katz and Darbishire (2000) find joint decision-making, semi-autonomous work groups taking a wider range of responsibilities than is typically found under lean manufacturing (and thus fewer supervisors), high pay and contingent 'pay-for-knowledge,' and a management commitment to union and employee involvement. This has considerable resonance with the 'Scandinavian' model of team-based production which has routinely been contrasted with lean manufacturing. This distinction has been rehearsed at length elsewhere (for example, Sandberg 1995) and returns us to the challenge of creating 'learning factories.'

## 20.4.1 Manufacturing Knowledge?

Our review of the evidence on contemporary manufacturing suggests expectations of highly skilled and autonomous workers populating 'learning factories' has been overly optimistic. It seems that the dynamic of continuous improvement and the re-harnessing of job design and execution anticipated by advocates of post-Fordist production systems have at best had partial effects on the nature of shopfloor decision-making and organizational control. Consequently, numerous studies have concluded that contemporary manufacturing carries forward many of the characteristics associated with Fordist production (Delbridge 1998; Danford 1998). The question of whether this is better understood as being through managerial design or failure is one we will consider below. Nevertheless, the strategic desire (necessity) for increasing levels of innovation maintains the pertinence of the challenge for manufacturing organizations to be sites of knowledge creation and application. Briefly in this section, we consider the value of the concept of 'communities of practice' and its implications in considering how HRM might address such challenges.

Commentators are increasingly recognizing the hybrid nature of organization, with stark contrasts between market and hierarchy (or mass and lean for that matter) giving way to subtler distinctions and mixed patterns of management organizational processes and control mechanisms. For instance, Adler (2001) summarizes the modes of coordination and control associated with hierarchy (authority), market (price), and community (trust) before arguing that the pressures of competition, the need for innovation, and the drive to extract and mobilize knowledge are resulting in managers adopting forms of 'soft control' with trust the key mechanism in eliciting the active consent of knowledgeable workers. Such arguments have generally been seen as pertaining to 'knowledge workers' in information technology or creative industries, but the challenges for higher creativity, innovativeness, and value added increasingly make these relevant for firms operating in mature economies in at least some manufacturing sectors.

The idea of 'community' has become a powerful one in characterizing the sense of collective social endeavor, especially in reflecting upon the importance of the hidden or tacit knowledge of workers even in highly routinized work settings (Brown and Duguid 1991, 2001; Lave and Wenger 1991). The concept draws upon anthropological concerns with the liminal spaces at the edges of formal procedures and at the intersections of organizational structures (McKinlay 2005). Such communities are only partially visible and knowable to those who are not actually members and thus they remain at the edge of management. At the same time, they are the settings for the creation and development of knowledge which lies outside the formal systems and routines but upon which the formal systems rely in order to operate efficiently.

The extent to which communities of practice can be created and managed has recently become the focus of considerable attention and debate (Contu and Willmott 2003; McKinlay 2005; Wenger et al. 2002). Wenger and colleagues (2002: 6), proponents of the organizational value of communities of practice, argue that 'cultivating communities of practice in strategic areas is a practical way to manage knowledge as an asset, just as systematically as companies manage other critical assets.' Their argument is open to criticism on a number of fronts. In particular, the conception of knowledge as 'thing' has been widely critiqued (Newell et al. 2002; Tsoukas and Vladimirou 2001) and their unitarist assumptions regarding the prospects for successfully *managing* communities of practice are reminiscent of the widely criticized way in which management texts have treated another anthropological concept—culture (see Smircich 1983; Meek 1988). Nevertheless, it is worth briefly reviewing the ways in which Wenger et al. (2002) suggest that communities of practice may be developed.

The essence of the argument is that organizations should retain an openness to participation and change that facilitates engagement within and across firm boundaries, actively develop and protect 'community spaces' that encourage voluntary and organic creativity while also retaining a management-informed focus on value and organizational design features which act as catalysts to the organic evolution of communities. This emphasizes the role of management in setting the context, tone, and focus for collective engagement which is recognized and supported as organic and self-developing:

Although communities of practice develop naturally, an appropriate amount of design can be a powerful engine for their evolution, helping members identify the knowledge, events, roles, and activities that will catalyse the community's growth. The organic nature of communities of practice challenges us to design these elements with a light hand, with an appreciation that the idea is to create liveliness, not manufacture a predetermined outcome. (Wenger et al. 2002: 64–5)

The further advantage foreseen with such organizations is that they will be popular places to work: 'one company found that employees belonging to world-class communities of practice exploring cutting-edge issues were much more likely to stick around' (Wenger et al. 2002: 7). Cohen and Prusak (2001) have also argued that the social capital and sense of belonging that employees can create at the workplace contribute to their feelings of wider company commitment and loyalty.

There is little direct and robust empirical evidence on the success or otherwise of organizational attempts at the systematic and proactive management—or 'cultivation'—of communities of practice. Conceptually, it has appeared useful in interpreting and analyzing the social interactions and knowledge-creating activities of groups of skilled and knowledgeable practitioners but the prospects of putting such ideas into practice *for management* seem questionable. Again, the debates surrounding corporate culture (as metaphor or variable; managed or otherwise) seem pertinent (for a recent review see Martin 2003). Moreover, at a fundamental level of analysis, there are developments and tensions at the heart of capitalist economic organization that must be considered in reflecting upon the management of HR in contemporary manufacturing. In so doing, we suggest that the possible reasons for the mixed evidence on the implementation and outcomes of HPWSs may also undermine the possibilities of creating and managing the organizational context suggested by Wenger et al. It is to these that we now turn.

## 20.5 SITUATING THE MANAGEMENT OF MANUFACTURING WORKERS

According to Beamish and Biggart (2006), economic sociologists have identified three major interrelated trends in market transformation that are significant to the study of work: (*a*) the overall changing shape of markets, i.e. the internationalization (spread) and globalization (integration) of economic activity (Castells 1996; Dicken 2003; Evans 1995), (*b*) the changing nature and flow of capital in markets, i.e. the sources of capital, financial expectations, and how corporations are organized (Perrow 2002; Fligstein 1990, 2001), and (*c*) the dynamic role of deregulation and technological innovation in both fomenting and reflecting these two trends. These shifts, they argue, are radically rearranging the relationships that characterize markets, especially the relations between capital, management, and labor.

These changes have major implications for the management of human resources, including assumptions regarding both the implementation and outcomes of 'models' such as HPWSs or communities of practice. At the heart of such models lies an expectation that different levels and spheres of corporate activity can be aligned. The developments summarized by Beamish and Biggart (2006) emphasize the difficulty of this, particularly in regard to the increasing (and destabilizing) influence of financial markets. Thompson (2003) has picked up on the implications of the institutional and political economic changes and recently offered a persuasive argument suggesting that 'disconnections' across spheres of business activity make it difficult for local managers to keep their side of the HPWS bargain and to implement the supportive HR practices expected by workers and their representatives. Thompson provides a realist theoretical model, outlining generative mechanisms that may explain the mixed empirical evidence that we have reported above in regard to HPWSs. In particular, he questions the extent to which there is sufficient *cohesiveness* across the realms of corporate activity to allow local management to meet the workplace bargain 'that in return for participation in the micro-management of work and expanded responsibilities ... employers will

undertake commitment and trust-building measures in the employment relationship' (Thompson 2003: 363). Unfulfilled or exploitative 'bargains' are nothing new
in capitalist economic organization but Thompson suggests that the cause may be
shifting from the long-recognized contradictions of capitalist workplace relations to
broader system-wide disconnections between the realms of corporate governance,
work organization, and employment relations. Specifically, he comments that 'there
is a massive tension between the degree of stability necessary for HRM and HPWSs
to operate effectively and the insecurity inherent in current forms of corporate
governance' (Thompson 2003: 365).

Certainly recent research has shown the tensions and difficulties faced by
workplace-level HR managers in seeking to meet corporate requirements,
manage employee expectations, and support operational performance (Barton
and Delbridge 2004). These tensions can be interpreted through the language of
strategic human resource management as the challenge of matching business
strategy and HR policy while simultaneously integrating HRM at the workplace
level. The increasing contradictions of 'external fit' between HR policy and business
strategy and 'internal fit' of HRM and workplace measures are analogous to the
breakdowns in employment bargains outlined from a different perspective by
Thompson (2003). Thus, Legge (2005: 328) has used these different terms in capturing
similar tensions: 'external fit may undermine the possibility of achieving internal fit.'
Such arguments emphasize that the management of human resources must be
situated in the wider organizational, institutional, political, and economic context
of manufacturing.

# 20.6 CONCLUDING COMMENTS

The future prospects of manufacturing industries in mature economies rely heavily
on the ability of firms to meet challenging targets for higher creativity and value
added. Such innovation is generally understood to require skilled and knowledgeable employees who are willing and able to commit discretionary effort to managerially defined tasks while also working creatively and collectively in creation of
knowledge. The role of human resource management is seen as central in contributing to the organizational contexts and sustaining the employment relationships
through which this can happen. This chapter has reviewed the empirical evidence
on work organization and HR practices in contemporary manufacturing, focusing
on high-performance work systems and lean manufacturing as the dominant
system before considering the alternatives in moving towards manufacturing
organizations as sites of knowledge creation. Our review of the empirical evidence

suggests at best a mixed picture in terms of both HPWS implementation and its outcomes.

The fragmented, disconnected, and contradictory characteristics of contemporary capitalism raise major challenges. Critical scholars from both within (Boxall and Purcell 2003; Legge 2005) and outside the field of human resource management (Thompson 2003) have identified the tensions *inter alia* between corporate and workplace spheres of economic activity, between business strategy and HR practices, and in matching the expectations of financial markets with those of employees. Such conclusions as can be drawn suggest the imperative of developing local, contingent, and reflective HR practices in support of the specific and negotiated organizational and employee goals that are germane. That these are recognized to be outcomes of negotiation upward with corporate stakeholders as well as with shopfloor employees and representatives appears crucial for any prospect of sustainable positive effects. Such conclusions should not be read as suggesting that there are not generic practices or principles that are likely to have beneficial effects, rather that the key remains the local adaptation and implementation of these.

# References

ABEGGLEN, J. (1958). *The Japanese Factory: Aspects of its Social Organization.* Glencoe, Ill.: Free Press.

ADLER, P. (1993). 'The "Learning Bureaucracy": New United Motor Manufacturing, Inc.' *Research in Organizational Behavior,* 15: 111–94.

—— (2001). 'Market, Hierarchy, and Trust: The Knowledge Economy and the Future of Capitalism.' *Organization Science,* 12/2: 215–34.

—— and BORYS, B. (1996). 'Two Types of Bureaucracy: Enabling and Coercive.' *Administrative Science Quarterly,* 41: 61–89.

—— and COLE, R. (1993). 'Designed for Learning: A Tale of Two Plants.' *Sloan Management Review,* Spring: 85–94.

ANDERSON-CONNOLLY, R., GRUNBERG, L., GREENBERG, E., and MOORE, R. (2002). 'Is Lean Mean? Workplace Transformation and Employee Well-Being.' *Work, Employment and Society,* 16/3: 389–413.

APPELBAUM, E. (2002). 'The Impact of New Forms of Work Organization on Workers.' in G. Murray, J. Belanger, A. Giles, and P.-A. Lapointe (eds.), *Work and Employment Relations in the High Performance Workplace.* London: Continuum.

—— BAILEY, T., BERG, P., and KALLEBERG, A. L. (2000). *Manufacturing Advantage: Why High-Performance Work Systems Pay off.* Ithaca, NY: Cornell University Press.

APPLEYARD, M., and BROWN, C. (2001). 'Employment Practices and Semiconductor Manufacturing Performance.' *Industrial Relations,* 40/3: 436–74.

ARTHUR, J. (1994). 'Effects of Human Resource Systems on Manufacturing Performance and Turnover.' *Academy of Management Journal,* 37: 670–87.

BARKER, J. (1993). 'Tightening the Iron Cage: Concertive Control in Self-Managing Teams.' *Administrative Science Quarterly*, 38: 408–37.

—— (1999). *The Discipline of Teamwork*. Thousand Oaks, Calif.: Sage.

BARTON, H., and DELBRIDGE, R. (2004). 'HRM in Support of the Learning Factory: Evidence from the US and UK Automotive Components Industries.' *International Journal of Human Resource Management*, 15/2, 331–45.

BATT, R., and DOELLGAST, V. (2005). 'Groups, Teams and the Division of Labor.' In S. Ackroyd, R. Batt, P. Thompson, and P. Tolbert (eds.), *The Oxford Handbook of Work and Organization*. Oxford: Oxford University Press.

BEAMISH, T., and BIGGART, N. (2006). 'Systems of Exchange and Worlds of Work: Uniting Economic Sociology with the Sociology of Work.' In M. Korczynski, R. Hodson, and P. Edwards (eds.), *Social Theories at Work*. Oxford: Oxford University Press.

BECKER, B., and GERHART, B. (1996). 'The Impact of Human Resource Management on Organizational Performance: Progress and Prospects.' *Academy of Management Journal*, 39: 779–801.

BENSON, G., and LAWLER, E. (2003). 'Employee Involvement: Utilization, Impacts and Future Prospects.' In D. Holman, T. Wall, C. Clegg, P. Sparrow, and A. Howard (eds.), *The New Workplace*. Chichester: Wiley.

BLYTON, P., and TURNBULL, P. (2004). *The Dynamics of Employee Relations*, 3rd edn. Basingstoke: Palgrave Macmillan.

BOXALL, P. (1996). 'The Strategic HRM Debate and the Resource-Based View of the Firm.' *Human Resource Management Journal*, 6/3: 59–75.

—— and PURCELL, J. (2003). *Strategy and Human Resource Management*. Basingstoke: Palgrave Macmillan.

BROWN, J., and DUGUID, P. (1991). 'Organizational Learning and Communities of Practice.' *Organization Science*, 2/1: 40–57.

—— —— (2001). 'Knowledge and Organization: A Social-Practice Perspective.' *Organization Science*, 12/2: 198–213.

CAPPELLI, P., and NEUMARK, D. (2001). 'Do "High-Performance" Work Practices Improve Establishment-Level Outcomes?' *Industrial and Labor Relations Review*, 54: 737–75.

CASTELLS, M. (1996). *The Information Age: Economy, Society, Culture*. Oxford: Blackwell.

COHEN, D., and PRUSAK, L. (2001). *In Good Company: How Social Capital Makes Organizations Work*. Boston: Harvard Business School Press.

COLE, R. (1971). *Japanese Blue Collar: The Changing Tradition*. Berkeley and Los Angeles: University of California Press.

CONTI, R., and GILL, C. (1998). 'Hypothesis Creation and Modelling in Job Stress Studies: The Effect of Just-in-Time and Lean Production.' *International Journal of Employment Studies*, 6/1: 149–73.

CONTU, A., and WILLMOTT, H. (2003). 'Re-embedding Situatedness: The Importance of Power Relations in Learning Theory.' *Organization Science*, 14/3: 283–96.

COOKE, P., and MORGAN, K. (1998). *The Associational Economy: Firms, Regions and Innovation*. Oxford: Oxford University Press.

DANFORD, A. (1998). 'Work Organisation inside Japanese Firms in South Wales: A Break from Taylorism?' In P. Thompson and C. Warhurst (eds.), *Workplaces of the Future*. London: Macmillan.

DELANEY, J., and HUSELID, M. (1996). 'The Impact of Human Resource Management Practices on Perceptions of Organizational Performance.' *Academy of Management Journal*, 39/4: 949–69.

DELBRIDGE, R. (1998). *Life on the Line in Contemporary Manufacturing*. Oxford: Oxford University Press.

—— (2005). 'Workers under Lean Manufacturing.' In D. Holman, T. Wall, C. Clegg, P. Sparrow, and A. Howard (eds.), *Essentials of the New Workplace*. Chichester: Wiley.

—— and TURNBULL, P. (1992). 'Human Resource Maximisation: The Management of Labour under a JIT System.' In P. Blyton and P. Turnbull (eds.), *Reassessing Human Resource Management*. London: Sage.

—— and WHITFIELD, K. (2001). 'Employee Perceptions of Job Influence and Organizational Participation.' *Industrial Relations*, 40/3: 472–89.

—— TURNBULL, P., and WILKINSON, B. (1992). 'Pushing Back the Frontiers: Management Control and Work Intensification under JIT/TQM Factory Regimes.' *New Technology, Work and Employment*, 7/2: 97–106.

—— KENNEY, M., and LOWE, J. (1998). 'UK Manufacturing in the 21st Century.' In R. Delbridge and J. Lowe (eds.), *Manufacturing in Transition*. London: Routledge.

DICKEN, P. (2003). *Global Shift: Reshaping the Global Economic Map in the 21st Century*, 4th edn. London: Sage.

DORE, R. (1973). *British Factory—Japanese Factory: The Origins of National Diversity in Industrial Relations*. London: Allen & Unwin.

DUNPHY, D. (1986). 'An Historical Review of the Literature on the Japanese Enterprise and its Management.' In S. Clegg, D. Dunphy, and G. Redding (eds.), *The Enterprise and Management in East Asia*. Hong Kong: Centre for Asian Studies, University of Hong Kong.

ELGER, T., and SMITH, C. (eds.) (1994). *Global Japanization? The Transnational Transformation of the Labour Process*. London: Routledge.

EVANS, P. (1995). *Embedded Autonomy: States and Industrial Transformation*. Princeton: Princeton University Press.

FAIRRIS, D. (1997). *Shopfloor Matters: Labor–Management Relations in Twentieth Century American Manufacturing*. London: Routledge.

FLIGSTEIN, N. (1990). *The Transformation of Corporate Control*. Cambridge, Mass.: Harvard University Press.

—— (2001). *The Architecture of Markets: An Economic Sociology of 21st Century Capitalist Societies*. Princeton: Princeton University Press.

FLORIDA, R., JENKINS, D., and SMITH, D. (1998). 'The Japanese Transplants in North America: Production Organization, Location, and Research and Development.' In R. Boyer, J.-J. Chanaron, U. Jurgens, and S. Tolliday (eds.), *Between Imitation and Innovation: The Transfer and Hybridization of Production Models in the International Automotive Industry*. Oxford: Oxford University Press.

FRUIN, M. (1992). *The Japanese Enterprise System*. Oxford: Oxford University Press.

—— (1997). *Knowledge Works: Managing Intellectual Capital at Toshiba*. Oxford: Oxford University Press.

FUCINI, J., and FUCINI, S. (1990). *Working for the Japanese: Inside Mazda's American Auto Plant*. New York: Free Press.

GEARY, J., and DOBBINS, A. (2001). 'Teamworking: A New Dynamic in the Pursuit of Management Control.' *Human Resource Management Journal*, 11: 3–23.

GODARD, J. (2001). 'High Performance and the Transformation of Work? The Implications of Alternative Work Practices for the Experience of Outcomes at Work.' *Industrial and Labor Relations Review*, 54: 776–805.

—— (2004). 'A Critical Assessment of the High-Performance Paradigm.' *British Journal of Industrial Relations*, 42: 349–78.

GORDON, A. (1985). *The Evolution of Labor Relations in Japan: Heavy Industry, 1853–1945.* Boston: Harvard University Press.

GRAHAM, L. (1995). *On the Line at Subaru-Isuzu: The Japanese Model and the American Worker.* Ithaca, NY: ILR and Cornell University Press.

HARLEY, B. (2001). 'Team Membership and the Experience of Work in Britain: An Analysis of the WERS98 Data.' *Work, Employment and Society*, 15: 721–42.

HUSELID, M. (1995). 'The Impact of Human Resource Management Practices on Turnover, Productivity, and Corporate Financial Performance.' *Academy of Management Journal*, 38: 635–72.

ICHNIOWSKI, C., SHAW, K., and PRENNUSHI, G. (1997). 'The Effects of Human Resource Management Practices on Productivity: A Study of Steel Finishing Lines.' *American Economic Review*, 87: 291–313.

IMAI, M. (1986). *Kaizen: The Key to Japan's Competitive Success.* New York: McGraw Hill.

JACKSON, S., and SCHULER, R. (1995). 'Understanding Human Resource Management in the Context of Organizations and their Environments.' In M. Rosenweige and L. Porter (eds.), *Annual Review of Psychology*, 46. Palo Alto, Calif.: Annual Reviews.

KATZ, H., and DARBISHIRE, O. (2000). *Converging Divergences: Worldwide Changes in Employment Systems.* Ithaca, NY: ILR and Cornell University Press.

KENNEY, M., and FLORIDA, R. (1993). *Beyond Mass Production: The Japanese System and its Transfer to the United States.* Oxford: Oxford University Press.

KIM, D.-O., and BAE, J. (2005), 'Workplace Innovation, Employment Relations and HRM: Two Electronics Companies in South Korea.' *International Journal of Human Resource Management*, 16/7: 1277–302.

KOCHAN, T., and OSTERMAN, P. (1994). *The Mutual Gains Enterprise.* Boston: Harvard Business School Press.

—— LANSBURY, R., and MacDUFFIE J. (eds.) (1997). *After Lean Production: Evolving Employment Practice in the World Auto Industry.* Ithaca, NY: ILR and Cornell University Press.

LANDSBERGIS, P., CAHILL, J., and SCHALL, P. (1999). 'The Impact of Lean Production and Related New Systems of Work Organization on Worker Health.' *Journal of Occupational Health Psychology*, 4/2: 108–30.

LAVE, J., and WENGER, E. (1991). *Situated Learning: Legitimate Peripheral Participation.* Cambridge: Cambridge University Press.

LAWLER, E. (1986). *High-Involvement Management: Participative Strategies for Improving Organizational Performance.* San Francisco: Jossey-Boss.

LEGGE, K. (1995). *Human Resource Management: Rhetorics and Realities.* Basingstoke: Macmillan.

—— (2005). 'Human Resource Management.' In S. Ackroyd, R. Batt, P. Thompson, and P. Tolbert (eds.), *The Oxford Handbook of Work and Organization.* Oxford: Oxford University Press.

LEONARD BARTON, D. (1992). 'The Factory as a Learning Laboratory.' *Sloan Management Review*, Fall: 23–38.

LEPAK, D., and SNELL, S. A. (1999). 'The Human Resource Architecture: Toward a Theory of Human Capital Allocation and Development.' *Academy of Management Review*, 24/1: 31–48.

LIKER, J., FRUIN, M., and ADLER, P. (eds.) (1999). *Remade in America: Transplanting and Transforming Japanese Management Systems*. Oxford: Oxford University Press.

LINCOLN, J., and KALLEBERG, A. (1990). *Culture, Control and Commitment*. Cambridge: Cambridge University Press.

LOWE, J., DELBRIDGE, R., and OLIVER, N. (1997). 'High Performance Manufacturing: Evidence from the Automotive Components Industry.' *Organization Studies*, 18/5: 783–98.

MACDUFFIE, J. (1995a). 'Human Resource Bundles and Manufacturing Performance: Organizational Logic and Flexible Production Systems in the World Auto Industry.' *Industrial and Labor Relations Review*, 48/2: 197–221.

—— (1995b). 'Workers' Roles in Lean Production: The Implications for Worker Representation.' In S. BABSON (ed.), *Lean Work: Empowerment and Exploitation in the Global Auto Industry*. Detroit: Wayne State University Press.

—— and PIL, F. (1997). 'Changes in Auto Industry Employment Practices: An International Overview.' In T. Kochan, R. Lansbury, and J. MacDuffie (eds.), *After Lean Production: Evolving Employment Practice in the World Auto Industry*. Ithaca, NY: ILR and Cornell University Press.

—— —— (1999). 'What Makes Transplants Thrive: Managing the Transplant of "Best Practice" at Japanese Auto Plants in North America.' *Journal of World Business*, 4: 372–92.

McKINLAY, A. (2005). 'Knowledge Management.' In S. Ackroyd, R. Batt, P. Thompson, and P. Tolbert (eds.), *The Oxford Handbook of Work and Organization*. Oxford: Oxford University Press.

MARTIN, J. (2003). 'Meta-theoretical Controversies in Studying Organizational Culture.' In H. Tsoukas and C. Knudsen (eds.), *The Oxford Handbook of Organization Theory*. Oxford: Oxford University Press.

MEEK, L. (1988). 'Organizational Culture: Origins and Weaknesses.' *Organization Studies*, 9/4: 453–73.

MONDEN, Y. (1983). *Toyota Production System: Practical Approach to Production Management*. Norcross, Ga.: Industrial Engineering and Management Press.

MURRAY, G., BÉLANGER, J., GILES, A., and LAPOINTE, P.-A. (eds.) (2002). *Work and Employment Relations in the High Performance Workplace*. London: Continuum.

NEWELL, S., ROBERTSON, M., SCARBROUGH, H., and SWAN, J. (2002). *Managing Knowledge Work*. Basingstoke: Palgrave.

OECD (2000). *OECD Employment Outlook 2000*. Paris: OECD.

OHNO, T. (1988). *Just-in-Time: For Today and Tomorrow*. Cambridge, Mass.: Productivity Press.

OLIVER, N., and WILKINSON, B. (1992). *The Japanization of British Industry: New Developments in the 1990s*. Oxford: Blackwell.

OSTERMAN, P. (2000). 'Work Restructuring in an Era of Restructuring: Trends in Diffusion and Effect on Employee Welfare.' *Industrial and Labor Relations Review*, 53: 179–96.

OUCHI, W. (1981). *Theory Z: How American Business Can Meet the Japanese Challenge*. Reading, Mass.: Addison Wesley.

PARKER, M., and SLAUGHTER, J. (1988). *Choosing Sides: Unions and the Team Concept*. Boston: Labor Notes.

PASCALE, R., and ATHOS, A. (1981). *The Art of Japanese Management*. New York: Simon and Schuster.

PERROW, C. (2002). *Organizing America: Wealth, Power, and the Origins of Corporate Capitalism*. Princeton: Princeton University Press.

PFEFFER, J. (1994). *Competitive Advantage through People*. Boston: Harvard Business School Press.

RAMSAY, H., SCHOLARIOS, D., and HARLEY, B. (2000). 'Employees and High-Performance Work Systems: Testing inside the Black Box.' *British Journal of Industrial Relations*, 38/4: 501–31.

RINEHART, J., HUXLEY, C., and ROBERTSON, D. (1997). *Just Another Car Factory? Lean Production and its Discontents*. Ithaca, NY: ILR and Cornell University Press.

SANDBERG, A. (1995). *Enriching Production*. Aldershot: Avebury.

SCHONBERGER, R. (1982). *Japanese Manufacturing Techniques: Nine Hidden Lessons in Simplicity*. New York: Free Press.

SHINGO, S. (1988). *Non-Stock Production: The Shingo System for Continuous Improvement*. Cambridge, Mass.: Productivity Press.

SMIRCICH, L. (1983). 'Concepts of Culture and Organizational Analysis.' *Administrative Science Quarterly*, 28: 339–58.

SMITH, C., and MEIKSINS, P. (1995). 'Society, System and Dominance Effects in Cross-national Organisational Analysis.' *Work, Employment and Society*, 9/2: 241–67.

SNELL, S., and DEAN, J. (1992). 'Integrated Manufacturing and Human Resource Management: A Human Capital Perspective.' *Academy of Management Journal*, 35/3: 467–504.

STRAUSS, G. (1998). 'Participation Works—if Conditions are Appropriate.' In F. Heller, E. Pusic, G. Strauss, and B. Wilpert (eds.), *Organizational Participation: Myth and Reality*. Oxford: Oxford University Press.

TAYLOR, B. (2001). 'The Management of Labour in Japanese Manufacturing Plants in China.' *International Journal of Human Resource Management*, 12/4: 601–20.

THOMPSON, P. (2003). 'Disconnected Capitalism: Or Why Employers Can't Keep their Side of the Bargain.' *Work, Employment and Society*, 17: 359–78.

THURLEY, K. (1982). 'The Japanese Model: Practical Reservations and Surprising Opportunities.' *Personnel Management*, February: 36–9.

TSOUKAS, H., and VLADIMIROU, E. (2001). 'What is Organizational Knowledge?' *Journal of Management Studies*, 38/7: 973–93.

WALTON, R. (1985). 'From Control to Commitment.' *Harvard Business Review*, 64/3: 76–84.

WARNER, M. (2004). 'Human Resource Management in China Revisited: Introduction.' *International Journal of Human Resource Management*, 15: 617–34.

WENGER, E., McDERMOTT, R., and SNYDER, W. (2002). *Cultivating Communities of Practice*. Boston: Harvard Business School Press.

WICKENS, P. (1987). *The Road to Nissan*. Basingstoke: Macmillan.

WILKINSON, B., GAMBLE, J., HUMPHREY, J., MORRIS, J., and ANTHONY, D. (2001). 'The New International Division of Labour in Asian Electronics: Work Organization and Human Resources in Japan and Malaysia.' *Journal of Management Studies*, 38/5: 675–95.

WOMACK, J., JONES, D., and ROOS, D. (1990). *The Machine that Changed the World*. New York: Rawson Macmillan.

WOOD, S., and ALBANESE, M. (1995). 'Can You Speak of a High Commitment Management on the Shopfloor?' *Journal of Management Studies*, 32: 215–47.

YOUNDT, M., SNELL, S., DEAN, J., and LEPAK, D. (1996). 'Human Resource Management, Manufacturing Strategy, and Firm Performance.' *Academy of Management Journal*, 39/4: 836–66.

CHAPTER 21

# SERVICE STRATEGIES
## MARKETING, OPERATIONS, AND HUMAN RESOURCE PRACTICES

ROSEMARY BATT

## 21.1 INTRODUCTION

OVER the last three decades, the principles of service management have become widely accepted. These call for an integrated approach to marketing, operations, and human resource management (HRM). The scholarly and business press routinely point to the importance of customer loyalty and customer relationship management for corporate profitability. Advances in marketing concepts and information systems make it possible to capture more precisely the demand characteristics of customers and to tailor solutions to meet their needs. Why is it, then, that measures of customer satisfaction have declined steadily in the last decade, websites for consumer complaints have proliferated, and media accounts of bad service appear with regularity?

In this chapter, I explore this paradox. I focus particularly on the private sector and on interactive service activities, defined as those that are produced through the interaction of employees and customers (Leidner 1993). Service management is important because the expansion of service activities and contraction of manufacturing in advanced economies means that management in services covers an ever increasing number and range of operations and employment. In addition, competing on the basis of customer service has become central to competitiveness in manufacturing as well as service industries. This is particularly true in supply chain management, where quality and productivity depends importantly on how vendor contracts with major customers are managed. However, it also applies to consumer markets, where after-sales service and service warranties and agreements have become a major source of revenues in goods production, particularly durable goods. Finally, there is growing empirical evidence that companies that compete on the basis of customer quality and customization do generate higher revenues and profits. Customer satisfaction does, in fact, matter; and the evidence is consistent with the widespread rhetoric of the importance of long-term customer relationships.

I organize this chapter into three parts. In section 21.2, I review the alternative theoretical approaches to human resource management that have been developed in the academic literature and discuss why these need to incorporate conceptual advances from services' marketing and operations management. Here, I also discuss the evidence regarding what strategies lead to better service and sales, under what conditions, and why. In section 21.3, I examine alternative organizational models that rely on outsourcing and supply chain management for customer service and sales and the arguments for and against these approaches. In section 21.4, I review real world trends: what strategies are companies actually pursuing and what are the results for consumers and employees? I close with conclusions about the future direction of service management strategies and the role of HRM in them.

# 21.2 ALTERNATIVE MODELS OF HUMAN RESOURCE MANAGEMENT

The central premiss of strategic human resource management theory is that successful organizational performance depends on a close fit or alignment between business strategy and human resource strategy. The 'fit' argument has two dimensions: a 'vertical' one (fit between business and HR strategy) and a 'horizontal' one (fit among the components of the HR system). The logic of the vertical fit argument is that effective implementation of strategy depends on having human resource policies to ensure that employees have the appropriate knowledge, skills, and abilities to carry out the strategy. The 'horizontal fit' argument assumes that the ability and motivation of workers to carry out a strategy depends on having a coherent set of policies in place—a system or bundle of complementary policies—that provide incentives for specific actions. Coherence in human resource policies includes classic functionalities: selection, training, job design, and rewards.

A number of scholars developed this line of reasoning in the 1980s (Dyer 1983), later linking it to the resource-based view of the firm (Wright et al. 1994). This approach to conceptualizing human resource management is best viewed as a framework for corporate management, designed to emphasize the importance of the human resource function and to make it an integral part of the top management team. Much of the empirical research using this framework focused on the corporate level of analysis (e.g. Delery and Doty 1996; Huselid 1995), although it expanded to include establishment-level studies as well (Youndt et al. 1996). Recent work has developed more elaborate models linking strategy and human resource management (Boxall and Purcell 2003). In general, this body of scholarship was more persuasive in demonstrating the benefits of horizontal fit (among the dimensions of human resource systems) than vertical fit (between business strategy and human resource strategy) (Wright and Sherman 1999), although there are exceptions (Arthur 1992).

## 21.2.1 Industrial Relations Approaches

A complementary approach to strategic human resource management emerged in the related field of industrial relations over a similar period of time. Compared to the SHRM literature, this perspective focused more on the productivity of whole industries and the role of institutions in shaping competitive advantage (Appelbaum and Batt 1994). Drawing on internal labor market theory (Doeringer and Piore 1971; Osterman 1984), this approach focused less on the corporate level or on the 'fit' between business and HR strategy and more on the idea of coherent employment systems at the workplace, which included human resource and labor relations practices (Kochan et al. 1986). It emphasized the need to understand the context-specific nature of technology and production processes and the complementarities between operations management and human resource systems (e.g. MacDuffie 1995).

This research incorporated insights from socio-technical systems (STS) (Trist 1981) and operations management research on quality (Deming 1984). STS theory contributes the idea of jointly maximizing the social and technical system, with employees playing a central role in work design and collaborative problem-solving. The quality literature similarly measures outcomes at the level of the production process and emphasizes employee involvement in ongoing group problem-solving to reduce variances in the production process, thereby improving first-time quality while reducing defects. Both of these approaches are in contrast to the principles of scientific management as developed by Taylor, in which the individual task is the unit of analysis and a heavy emphasis on cost reduction typically leads to a focus on improving individual efficiency at the cost of first-time quality.

The concept of high-performance work systems emerged in this line of work, which married the insights on work organization found in STS and quality management research, the insights on employee motivation from HRM and organizational behavior, and industrial relations' focus on coherent employment systems. A general proposition emerged that in current markets which demand quality and innovation, better organizational performance hinges on the adoption of coherent human resource systems that provide employees with the skills, opportunity structure, and incentives to use their discretionary effort (Appelbaum et al. 2000). Evidence to support this proposition came from a series of industry-specific studies, including automobile assembly (MacDuffie 1995), apparel and medical electronics (Appelbaum et al. 2000), computers (Bresnahan et al. 2002), semiconductors (Appleyard and Brown 2001), and steel (Appelbaum et al. 2000; Arthur 1992; Ichniowski et al. 1997).

## 21.2.2 Services Management

However, the human resource and industrial relations frameworks discussed above are insufficient for conceptualizing the management of service activities because of the important role that consumers play in the production process and, in turn, the importance of marketing in shaping interactive services. While scholars in human resource and industrial relations studies were developing a systems approach to HR strategy and employment relations, their counterparts in marketing, operations management, and organizational behavior were elaborating an integrated theory of service management. The marketing literature demonstrated how and why service marketing differs substantially from product marketing (Gronroos 1990; Lovelock 2005; Zeithaml et al. 1990). Operations management examined solutions to the problems of uncertainty and unpredictability introduced by customers in service production (Chase 1978; Mills et al. 1983), and demonstrated the extent of managerial choice in the design of service operations (Chase and Tansik 1983). Research in organizational behavior developed the implications for human resource management (Bowen 1986; Bowen and Schneider 1988). At the same time, these scholars noted the blurring of boundaries between goods and service production as technological innovations have turned some services into commodities and as competitive advantage in manufacturing has come to depend increasingly on customization in product features and after-sales service. Thus, the service management model has evolved to cover interactive services across a wide range of public and private sector settings with a mix of tangible and intangible products.

The classic assumption in the service management literature is that goods and services production differ along several dimensions. A simple classification distinguishes between the consumption of output versus the consumption of a process (Gronroos 1990). While typologies vary in degree of complexity and detail, most agree on four core differences: intangibility, heterogeneity (or variability), perishability of output (no inventory), and simultaneity of production and consumption (Lovelock 2005). Because service activities are more intangible than not, quality and productivity are difficult to measure. Because they involve co-production between a customer and provider, the heterogeneous preferences of customers make it difficult to standardize production without jeopardizing quality and customer satisfaction. Perishability of output and simultaneity of production and consumption make demand management through inventory systems more difficult and put a premium on first-time quality. These dimensions of customer contact work translate into relatively high levels of uncertainty and unpredictability.

For human resource management, the intangibility of service activities and the lack of clear measures of quality and productivity make it difficult to set specific goals for employees and evaluate and reward their performance based on those goals. The simultaneity of production and consumption implies that demand forecasting is unpredictable, and in turn, determining appropriate staffing levels is a challenge. It also suggests that first-time quality is particularly important—poor health care cannot be returned for repair—thereby putting a premium on investments in training, effective work design, and rewards to motivate responsiveness on the part of employees (Bowen and Schneider 1988). The co-production function means customers may be viewed and managed as 'human resources' (Bowen 1986). Thus, management needs to evaluate the effect of HR policies on customer behavior as well as on employee behavior and motivation. All of these characteristics imply that human resource management is particularly important in service activities and that simple command and control approaches are relatively ineffective. For example, several studies of call center workers have found that high levels of electronic monitoring and routinization are associated with anxiety, stress, emotional exhaustion, and burn-out (Carayon 1993; Deery et al. 2002; Holman et al. 2002; Singh 2000); and these, in turn, lead to absenteeism (Deery et al. 2002) and lower self-reported quality (Singh 2000). Arguably more effective are indirect methods of control—strategies that create behavioral norms and inculcate cultural values so that employees deliver the desired level of service to customers (see, for example, Peccei and Rosenthal 2000).

The characteristics of interactive services also create particular challenges for the marketing function and create incentives for it to be involved in setting human resource policies. The task of marketing is to manage customer behavior by building an understanding of the customer's characteristics and buying habits and developing a relationship that yields repeated purchases and long-term loyalty to the product or brand. The fact that customers are part of the production process opens up new avenues for marketing and decentralizes that function so that each service interaction is an opportunity to sell. Thus, marketing is not just interested in a narrowly defined 'sales force' but in any employee who comes into contact with customers. The concept of interactive marketing—the notion that service interactions provide a 'bridge to sales'—became widely accepted in the 1980s; it is viewed as the mechanism through which perceived service quality, customer satisfaction, and customer retention are achieved (Gronroos 1990). Said differently, employees are 'part of the product;' they 'enact the brand.' Every service encounter may be a 'moment of truth' that particularly satisfies or dissatisfies customers, and, in turn, shapes their future buying behavior. The fact that a negative interaction between a customer and employee has far more impact on customer behavior than a positive interaction enhances the incentives for marketing to expand its influence into human resource policies that ensure a skilled workforce capable of providing first-time quality and customizing services to fit consumer demand.

Increasingly, operations management also has influenced human resource systems in services because of heightened competition and the need to reduce costs and improve efficiencies. Historically, operations management played a limited role because of the labor-intensive nature of service work, the lack of technical solutions, and the role of the customer in the production process. Because customers introduce variability and uncertainty into the process through their heterogeneous preferences, the challenge of improving productivity is more difficult to accomplish in interactive services. This has led operations management to conceptualize customers as 'partial employees' (Mills et al. 1983), developing strategies to control customer as well as employee behavior. While many service activities involve high levels of customer contact that are difficult to standardize (such as hotels or hospitals), for many others, employers can choose a high- or low-contact approach to organizational design (Chase and Tansik 1983).

Operations management has played a critical role in transforming high-contact services into low-contact, technology-mediated ones—turning personalized interactions into impersonal 'service encounters' (Gutek 1995). While investments in computer technology were slow to yield productivity gains in the 1980s (Roach 1991), subsequent applications have helped to automate processes and reduce the labor content of transactions (Hammer and Champy 1992), improve labor productivity (Brynjolfsson and Yang 1996), and increase the speed and reliability of transaction processing by eliminating human error (Stewart and Chase 1999). Banks and insurance companies, for example, have been able to reduce the labor content of jobs by turning face-to-face interactions with bank tellers and agents into technology-mediated transactions in remote call centers.

These changes have had important implications for human resource management. On the one hand, by automating routine tasks, the remaining jobs tend to be more complex and require higher-order skills (Levy and Murnane 2002). The skill requirements of interactive service work involve three dimensions: product or substantive knowledge, knowledge of technical systems, and social interaction skills (Batt 2002). Substantive knowledge tends to be more complex than in the past because of the proliferation of product features, customization options, and product innovation; and ongoing changes in information systems require regular upgrades in computer information-processing skills and database management. Social interaction skills include not only information-gathering and processing, but negotiation skills and emotional dimensions that have been undervalued (companies have yet to figure out how to compensate emotional labor) and understudied in the research literature (see Korczynski 2005 for an excellent review of this issue).

On the other hand, advances in information systems create opportunities for increased standardization while cost pressures create incentives to compete on labor efficiency. This sets up incentives to simplify jobs by fragmenting tasks, thereby reducing the skill content of jobs and the need for training and investment in human resource systems. This standardization not only affects employee morale, absenteeism, and turnover, but irritates customers as well. For example, the widespread dissatisfaction with call centers is due in part to customer frustration with voice recognition units, elaborate menus, punching in numbers, and valuable time wasted until a service representative comes on-line. The customer's frustration spills over to the employee, whose job becomes even more difficult. Hence, operations strategies to improve efficiencies can backfire into lower service quality, customer dissatisfaction, and built-in conflict between employees and customers.

Other alternatives to improving efficiency include staff reductions, on the one hand, or shifting labor costs to consumers through self-service options, on the other. Staff reductions, however, are likely to result in poor service unless accompanied by major re-engineering of process flows. Similarly, too much reliance on self-service may create resentment among consumers or the risk of losing one's customer base. Research in marketing identifies a number of hidden costs of consumption, including not only the price in dollar terms, but in terms of search time, physical effort, psychological burdens, and follow-up or subsequent problem-solving (Lovelock 2005). In sum, while there are parallels in the effectiveness of engineering solutions in manufacturing and service activities, there are also limits to these strategies in the service arena due to the role of the customer in the process.

Several studies have pointed to the tensions between quality and cost in inter-active service settings (Frenkel et al. 1999; Korczynski 2002). In their boundary-spanning role, front-line employees are caught between the demands of customers and the demands of management, leading to role ambiguity, conflict, and stress (Bowen and Schneider 1985). Several recent empirical studies have demonstrated this problem. For example, in a study of restaurant workers, Babin and Boles (1998) found that role stress negatively affected customer–server interactions and in-creased workers' intentions to quit. Hartline and Ferrell (1996) surveyed several hundred managers, workers, and customers at 279 hotels and found that role conflict contributed significantly to employees' frustration in their attempt to fulfill their jobs. And in a major meta-analysis of research on role ambiguity and role conflict, Tubre and Collins (2000) found a significant negative relationship between role ambiguity and performance.

However, at a more fundamental level, the tension grows out of different definitions of quality, and human resource management is caught between the competing claims of marketing (focused on customers) and operations manage-ment (focused on operations efficiency and reliability). Marketing defines quality as meeting customer demands, whatever this takes (Zeithaml et al. 1990). Achiev-ing service quality entails higher labor costs because it suggests that employees take more time with customers to meet their heterogeneous needs. Operations man-agement, by contrast, focuses more on a manufacturing definition of quality, as conformance to specifications: reducing variances in transactions-processing is central, which can be achieved through process automation (Garvin 1984). By this definition, quality and efficiency can be achieved simultaneously—reminiscent of the quality management arguments found in the manufacturing studies discussed above.

Empirical research on quality in services shows that customers value several dimensions of quality. The most widely used definition (SERVQUAL) lists five dimensions: tangibles, reliability (consistency), assurance (how confident the cus-tomer is about the service being provided), responsiveness (to the customer's demands), and empathy (for the customer) (Zeithaml et al. 1990). While oper-ations management solutions can improve the quality of tangibles and the reliabil-ity of products, the remaining dimensions of service quality depend primarily on the capabilities of employees. The latter three dimensions, which account for almost 60 percent of customer satisfaction scores, are related to the ability of employees to respond effectively to customers. Moreover, research in marketing has also shown that customer experience of actual service quality (rather than customer expectations) is the strongest predictor of customer satisfaction (Appiah-Adu 1999; Cronin et al. 2000; Kane et al. 1997). Hence, strategies to improve service quality and customer satisfaction depend importantly on investment in human resource systems, including selection, training, work designed to allow discretion for employees, and rewards to induce discretionary effort.

This line of argument is central to the service climate literature (Bowen and Schneider 1988; Schneider and Bowen 1985) and the service-profit-chain argument (Heskett et al. 1997). The central insight here is that in customer contact settings, customers experience what employees experience, and negative reactions on the part of employees spill over to customers, undermining their confidence in the company and their willingness to purchase services in the future. Employee motivation or attitudes are the underlying causal theory; and human resource practices of training, discretionary work design, and appropriate rewards are thought to induce employee satisfaction and loyalty, which in turn inspire customer satisfaction and loyalty, ultimately resulting in higher profits.

Most evidence for these arguments comes from individual case studies, but some quantitative studies in the banking and retail sectors report a significant positive correlation between employee perceptions of service climate and employee commitment to service (Peccei and Rosenthal 2000), customer reports of satisfaction (Borucki and Burke 1999; Johnson 1996; Schmit and Allscheid 1995; Rogg et al. 2001), and financial performance (Borucki and Burke 1999). Gittell (2002) examined hospital management and found that stronger relationships among providers and between providers and customers produced higher levels of customer satisfaction. However, the causal story is probably more reciprocal than linear, as in Schneider et al.'s (1998) study of the reciprocal relationship between service climate and customer perceptions of quality. Moreover, to date there is little evidence of employee attitudes or satisfaction as mediating the relationship between human resource practices and customer satisfaction (see Korczynski 2002: 29–34).

Another line of argument links human resource investments to better performance, not via employee attitudes but via their effects on worker skills, knowledge, and problem-solving capabilities. For example, Batt (1999) found that sales representatives in self-directed work groups generated significantly higher sales revenues (net of labor costs), than did traditionally supervised groups, and accomplished this in part through better use of technology.

In sum, there is some growing evidence that human resource management plays an important role in the performance of service organizations, although it is less clear whether or under what conditions employee attitudes or capabilities are important as causal mechanisms. More research in this area is needed, particularly with respect to organizational and institutional contingencies. In addition, research has shown that there are unique challenges to managing service activities and that effective performance depends importantly on the coordination of marketing, operations, and human resource management in order to create a coherent approach to customers. In particular, human resource management is often caught between the marketing goal of developing customer relationships through high-contact organizational design and the operations management goal of improving reliability and efficiency through lower-contact approaches. As a result, leading experts in all three fields have called for a functionally integrated approach to service management that focuses on customer satisfaction and loyalty (Bowen et al. 1990; Lovelock 2005).

## 21.3 WHEN IS SERVICE MANAGEMENT A CORE COMPETENCY?

This brief overview of alternative human resource models developed in different disciplines in the 1980s and early 1990s shows that there were parallel arguments for a coherent systems approach to management in each case. The terminology was different, but the thrust of the arguments was similar: 'strategic fit' in human resource studies, employment systems in industrial relations, and functional integration in service management. There was also a heavy emphasis on quality and building long-term customer relations, as scholars incorporated the insights of quality management into their theories of organizational performance.

Over the last decade, however, the strategy literature has paid particular attention to the argument that firms should focus on their 'core competencies,' as articulated by Prahalad and Hamel (1990), Quinn (1992), and others. That argument posits that firms should retain functions that they consider to be their core competency while outsourcing those that are non-core. Core capabilities are defined as those that contribute value to customer benefits and end products, that provide access to a wide variety of markets, and that are difficult for competitors to imitate (Prahalad and Hamel 1990). When applied to human resource management, the theory suggests that firms should retain human capital that creates value for the firm and that is rare or unique and difficult to imitate (Barney 1991). For example, firms are likely to choose internal employment systems for operations that involve firm-specific knowledge and skills, team-based systems, or work processes that involve 'social complexity,' 'causal ambiguity,' or 'idiosyncratic learning' (Lepak and Snell 1999: 35). They are likely to externalize or subcontract work that is more generic, involves lower-order skills, or is transactional in nature.

This line of argument challenges the integrated models of human resource management discussed above and raises the question of whether, or under what conditions, service management should be considered a core competency. In the classic service management literature, the assumption was that firms should retain this function in-house because front-line employees are the marketing face to the customer and because there is need for close coordination between sales and marketing, operations, and human resource management. The argument implied that customer management should be viewed as a core competency. In the meantime, however, modularization of production emerged as a viable alternative to vertical integration across a wide range of what had been considered core activities in major industries.

Modularization allows companies to separate more complex or knowledge-intensive functions from less-intensive ones, and subcontract the latter to lower-cost producers. This process depends on the degree of separability of tasks, and it is enabled by advanced information systems that allow the coordination and management of production flows across organizational boundaries. If modular production chains can solve the problems of coordination across globally dispersed suppliers in manufacturing, then arguably the model should apply equally well to service activities. Much corporate thinking has moved in this direction in recent years.

Many service interactions are, in fact, quite separable. While place-based, high-contact services are not (hotels and hospitals), many back-office operations and low-contact services are—services that process information or goods as opposed to people. They may be separated by level of complexity, using a number of categorization strategies: by function (sales versus service; type of service enquiry (billing, repair, collections); by type of product (health insurance, home insurance, auto insurance, credit cards); by type of customer (large business, small business, high-end retail, low-end retail). Once service interactions are separated into distinct categories—by level of complexity, tacit knowledge, or asset specificity—they may be designated as core or non-core, retained in-house or outsourced to subcontractors. With the ongoing restructuring of service and sales channels into remote call centers or web-based transactions, we might expect the majority of these operations to be handled by subcontractors.

Defining what level of complexity or asset specificity should be viewed as core and 'non-core,' however, may be more problematic than it first appears. Clearly, at one extreme, customized services for corporate clients entail high levels of tacit knowledge of products and processes and deep relationships of trust with clients. At the other extreme, ad campaigns for credit card sales are generic in nature and require no personal relationships to complete. Beyond these clear dichotomies, however, decisions about what is core and non-core become more problematic. Are service and sales channels for insurance, telecommunications, and financial services simple and codifiable? Are they core or non-core for these businesses?

In addition, some competitive strategies argue against separation of tasks. Strategies based on service differentiation or branding depend on customer contact employees representing the marketing function and presenting a unique face to the customer. If customer service and sales are outsourced to a vendor who also handles the client's competitor, how will the vendor's employees provide a unique approach for one client's customers but not the competitors?

Another strategy, customer relationship management, relies on the ability of providers to create customer loyalty and long-term relations by satisfying a wide and ever-changing range of customer demands. If companies pursue this strategy, then how work is organized should revolve around the characteristics of the customer or customer segment rather than by a particular task or function. In the 1990s, many companies re-engineered service delivery channels so that business units would be organized by customer segment, with sales and marketing and customer service all reporting to one vice president. This provided a strategy of integration, with sales and marketing and customer service providing a consistent face to the customer. Once companies choose this route, their need for firm-specific knowledge of the customer and investment in human resource systems increases considerably. Employees need to manage a range of firm-specific information and knowledge in terms of substantive products, technical processes, and relationships with customers.

Empirical research supports the idea that firm-specific human capital positively affects service performance. In a study of a department store chain, for example, Sharma et al. (2000) found a significant positive relationship between sales experience and performance, and they attributed this finding to the knowledge structures of workers with greater expertise. In a meta-analysis of twenty-two studies of job experience, Quinones et al. (1995) found a .27 correlation between experience and performance. Long-term employees have the tacit firm-specific skills and knowledge—and often personal relationships with customers—to be more effective. Thus, if firms choose to compete on quality or customer service, an in-house, professional approach to human resource management appears to be the most effective route.

'Service bundling,' another strategy that is customer centric, takes advantage of economies of scope to package a number of standardized products or services. As soon as employees are responsible for packaging a number of types of products or services, the complexity of their jobs increases and the opportunities for modularization and outsourcing decline. Even separating sales and after-sales service may be problematic. While from a human resource management perspective, it is well established that sales and service activities require quite different skills, separating service and sales is often inconvenient from the customer's perspective. Moreover, this type of separation reduces opportunities for inbound service enquiries to generate sales. Thus, separating service and sales interactions typically generates trade-offs. In sum, while at first blush low-contact service interactions appear to be easily separated and outsourced, strategic considerations suggest that many companies would choose to treat service management as a core function and retain it in-house.

## 21.4 REAL WORLD TRENDS: WHY 'SERVICE STINKS'

How have customers responded to corporate service management strategies in the real world? Not very well, according to the popular media. In October 2000, *Business Week* devoted a special issue of the magazine to 'Why Service Stinks' (Brady 2000). In it, the editors provided an overwhelming series of examples of customer dissatisfaction with the *process* of service—not product *quality* or *features* or *price*. Much of the issue was devoted to the negative effects of customer relationship management. While high-value-added customers benefit from personalized attention, the flip side of the relationship coin is the poor quality of service delivered to consumers with a low profitability profile.

The importance of 'service fairness' is an idea that is catching on. Drawing on the concept of organizational justice as applied to employees in organizations, some management theorists (Seiders and Berry 1998) argue that customers expect to be treated with fairness: distributive justice (equity in treatment and outcomes), procedural justice (consistency, transparency, accuracy, freedom from bias), and interactional justice (respect, honesty, and courtesy). Customers perceive these principles to be violated in airline or hotel programs that allow frequent customers to bump other customers or in practices such as 'weblining' (Stepanek 2000)—the cyberspace equivalent of 'redlining,' in which consumers are profiled on the basis of their personal characteristics. The ability to purchase a good or service on-line depends increasingly on supplying a host of personal information that is not relevant to the transaction at hand. Consumers feel that their privacy is violated and that they are judged by their predicted, not actual behavior. Higher-value-added customers often get better discounts or treatment, while the least profitable customers may be ignored at best.

In addition to media accounts, websites such as planetfeedback.com and complaints.com have emerged as popular vehicles for customers to vent frustration at companies. Similar to the popular press articles cited above, a perusal of these sites suggests that consumers are more irritated about the service process itself than about the quality or price of goods or services. Typical complaints focus on frustration with automated response units that don't provide answers to questions, the lack of human interaction, the inability to get access to companies to resolve complaints, the failure of companies to follow through on promises, or the lack of courtesy, training, and competency of front-line staff. In sum, the source of complaints appears to reside in failures of coordination between functional departments or major deficiencies in human resource systems.

Is there any evidence that these anecdotes constitute a more general phenomenon? One of the most reliable sources is a quarterly survey of American consumers conducted by the University of Michigan (the American Customer Satisfaction Index, ASCI), which now has over ten years of trend data (Fornell et al. 1996). That survey shows two consistent trends. First, customer satisfaction with manufactured goods is consistently higher than satisfaction with service industries—averaging 10 percentage points in many cases. Second, satisfaction with manufactured goods has generally stayed the same or increased, while there has been a consistent downward trend in satisfaction with service industries. Satisfaction ratings for durable goods have hovered at 79 percent over the last ten years: for electronics, between 79 and 83 percent; automobiles, 79–80 percent; and appliances have fallen from 85 percent to 80 percent in the same period. Satisfaction with non-durable goods is also steady at about 79 to 81 percent; and personal care and cleaning products 83 to 84 percent in the same period. However, satisfaction with utilities fell from 75 percent to 72 percent; airlines from 74 percent to 66 percent; hotels from 75 to 72 percent; hospitals from 74 to 71 percent; fixed line telephones, from 80 percent to 71 percent; and wireless telephone service and cable TV hover at 65 percent and 61 percent approval, respectively. While the ASCI does not include call centers in its ratings, other surveys put satisfaction with call centers at 54 percent (Purdue University 1999).

Are these good scores or bad? Most marketing experts would argue that a 70 percent rating means that a company stands to lose 30 percent of its customer base, which suggests that both manufacturing and service industries are in trouble, but the latter more than the former. The potential loss of customers is viewed as a major problem because it is far more expensive to win new customers than maintain existing ones. Moreover, loyal customers are more profitable because over time, they buy more products and more value-added products (Reichheld 1996), and they are 'human resources' for the marketing function, through word of mouth advertising.

What accounts for these trends? Some argue that consumers' expectations are rising, and so they are demanding more. However, the ASCI data shows that company ratings vary considerably within a given product market. For example, between 2000 and 2005, satisfaction with BellSouth wireline services fell from 75 percent to 70 percent, while satisfaction with Qwest Communications rose from 64 to 69 percent. In the same time period, Continental Airlines saw its approval rating jump from 62 percent to 70 percent while that of US Airways dropped from 62 percent to 57 percent.

An alternative explanation is that service providers have shifted strategies in response to pressures associated with industry deregulation, and more recently, globalization. This holds true in sectors such as transportation (airlines, trucking), banking, utilities, telecommunications, health care, and insurance. Companies have developed differentiated strategies for serving customers according to the value of their accounts. More costly strategies based on customization, relationship management, and a professional approach to human resource management are reserved for high-value-added customers, particularly business clients, who are served through business-to-business channels. This approach is consistent with the ideas of strategic human resource management and an integrated approach to service management, and the service-profit-chain model. For the majority of customers in the mass market, however, companies have adopted more cost-driven strategies that emphasize technology solutions, de-emphasize investment in employees, outsource to low-cost providers, shift labor to consumers, and often sacrifice quality. Some management theorists even advocate segmentation strategies designed specifically to eliminate the least profitable customers (Reinartz and Kumar 2002), in essence 'firing partial employees' who do not bring in enough profits.

## 21.4.1 Customer Segmentation and Human Resource Management

Customer segmentation strategies have grown across many industries—from hotels and financial services to telecommunications and airlines. The strategies are well developed in the USA, where the national market is large. They are growing in other parts of the world as well (Boxall 2003). In the USA, a 2003 national survey of call centers found that 80 percent said they competed on the basis of service differentiation and used a targeted customer approach to organizing service. Companies were much more likely to take a professional approach to serving business customers, but a cost-driven approach to serving the mass market. In the professional model, the typical service agent had a college degree, substantial levels of discretion and involvement in problem-solving groups, and annual pay equal to $45,075. By contrast, the typical service agent in a mass market center had one year of college beyond high school, little discretion to serve customers, and earned $28,068 annually. In mass markets, where the overwhelming bulk of service transactions occur, the assumption is that competitiveness depends more on price than on quality; and hence, companies are skeptical about investing in the capabilities of front-line employees (Batt and Kwon 2005).

Customer segmentation produces differentiated outcomes for employees as well, contributing to growing wage inequality. A study of service and sales channels in telecommunications found that customer segmentation strategies coupled with variation in human resource practices lead to greater wage inequality, with workers serving large business customers enjoying a 17.5 percent wage premium over those who provided 'universal service' to consumers in any market (mixed market centers), even after controlling for human capital characteristics and human resource practices (Batt 2001). These findings held true in a replication study of a nationally random sample of call center workers across all industries in the USA (Batt and Kwon 2005).

Segmentation strategies also facilitate outsourcing and offshoring of low-skilled service work, undermining fragile job security in these settings. Once tasks are separated into distinct categories by level of complexity or value added, then simpler tasks or services for less valued customers may be outsourced at lower cost. Subcontractors, competing on costs, devise strategies to simplify tasks and further drive down skill requirements of jobs and wages, creating high turnover models of employment for employees, which often translate into low service quality as well. For example, in a comparative international study of call centers, Batt et al. (2005) found substantial differences in management practices between US in-house centers, US subcontractors, and Indian offshore subcontractors. While the in-house centers adopted a more professional approach to service, with high relative levels of skills and training, discretion, and pay, US subcontractors offered the opposite: low levels of skills, discretion, and pay. Indian subcontractors had particularly contradictory systems, hiring relatively highly educated workers with high relative pay by Indian standards, but offering the lowest levels of opportunity for discretion and problem-solving for customer service. These differences translated into significantly higher levels of turnover in the US and Indian subcontractors, compared to the in-house operations.

Segmentation strategies make two important assumptions: that there are necessary trade-offs between cost and quality and that demand in the mass market is driven primarily by price, and hence, investing in human resource systems doesn't pay off. But what evidence exists that quality strategies that invest in the workforce don't pay off in price-conscious markets? Marketing experts argue that there are ample opportunities to compete on quality and customization in mass markets— that mass customization characterizes the majority of consumer markets in advanced economies (Pine 1993). A series of case studies of low-wage service work in hospitals, hotels, banking, and telecommunications showed that investing in human resource practices could pay off in these markets (Appelbaum et al. 2003). A national study of US call centers showed that quit rates were lower and sales growth higher in centers that adopted a more professional approach to service, and that these effects were *largest* for centers serving the mass market (Batt 2002). High quit rates not only increased the costs of recruitment and selection, but negatively affected performance because new employees face a learning curve. A follow-up study of sixty-four call centers in one company, all of which served the mass market, found that centers with higher rates of training, discretion, and incentives for sales had significantly higher customer satisfaction ratings, which in turn translated into higher net revenues (net of all labor and other operating costs) (Batt and Moynihan 2005).

In sum, there is evidence that competing on quality and investing in human resource systems can pay off in price-conscious markets, but in the absence of countervailing institutional pressures such as unions or consumer organizations, companies have little incentive to make the effort.

## 21.5 CONCLUSION

In this chapter, I have argued that the unique nature of service activities poses substantial challenges for human resource management. At the level of the corporation, effective delivery of services requires a careful integration and coordination of strategies across marketing, operations, and human resource functions. At the level of the workplace, the role of human resource management is particularly important because of the powerful role that employees play in shaping consumer buying patterns, but marketing and operations management often create conflicting strategies for human resource management, leading to workplace tensions and contradictory incentives for employees.

Many companies have, indeed, created integrated systems of service delivery by targeting distinct customer segments and organizing their marketing, operations, and human resource systems around these targets. Strategies that compete on quality, customization, and innovation target high-value-added segments, typically in business-to-business channels. Strategies that compete primarily on cost are targeted towards the mass market. Hence, the alternative service management models discussed in the first two sections of this chapter are in full play, but utilized for very different market segments in the economy.

In the drive for strategic fit between business and human resource strategies in mass markets, however, it appears that companies may have put too much emphasis on cost reduction—despite the fact that there is growing evidence that strategies of mass customization do, in fact, pay off. There is also growing evidence of dissatisfaction among consumers as they put up with standardized menus and poorly trained employees or absorb the labor costs of service themselves. And managers, themselves, admit that they are uncertain about how to strike a balance between cost and quality. In sum, too much focus on cost may be the wrong business model for this market.

Consumer backlash appears to be on the rise. Consumers are not only concerned about the quality of service, but also the privacy and security of their financial information. Their jitters are exacerbated by news accounts of security leaks. The Internet has become a powerful tool for consumer voice—a major source of negative word-of-mouth marketing—or 'viral marketing,' as consumers broadcast their venom about particular experiences with companies to millions of people around the globe. And in some cases, consumer and labor organizations are working together, for example, in the recent backlash against offshoring of white-collar jobs in the USA. Legislative initiatives in over twenty states seek to limit offshoring or jobs, and most target consumers' 'right to know' where a service is originating and the right to have service provided onshore.

In sum, while there is much talk about building quality service and relationships with customers, the reality is that the construction of bad jobs and bad service is quite pervasive. The question for the future is how much consumers will complain or organize, whether consumer-labor coalitions develop around 'good jobs-good service strategies,' and how companies will respond. On the one hand, there are many opportunities to compete on quality in mass markets—through innovative uses of information technology or more sophisticated marketing research to identify opportunities for customization. Moreover, the availability of Internet databases of company-specific complaints provides opportunities for companies to identify areas that particularly need improvement. On the other hand, financial pressures push companies to continually take costs out of the business. Outsourcing, offshoring, and shifting labor to consumers are attractive quick fixes to remedy short-term profits.

In either case, it is clear that the dynamics between consumers, employees, and firms in the service economy have changed in important ways over the past few decades. Research in human resource management must be reconceptualized to take into account the influence of consumers in this process.

# REFERENCES

APPELBAUM, E., and BATT, R. (1994). *The New American Workplace: Transforming Work Systems in the United States*. Ithaca, NY: Cornell University/ILR Press.

—— BAILEY, T., BERG, P., and KALLEBERG, A. L. (2000). *Manufacturing Advantage: Why High Performance Work Systems Pay Off*. Ithaca, NY: Cornell University Press.

—— BERNHARDT, A., and MURNANE, R. J. (eds.) (2003). *Low-Wage America: How Employers Are Reshaping Opportunity in the Workplace*. New York: Russell Sage Foundation.

APPIAH-ADU, K. (1999). 'Marketing Effectiveness and Customer Retention in the Service Sector.' *Service Industries Journal*, 19/3: 26–41.

APPLEYARD, M., and BROWN, C. (2001). 'Employment Practices and Semiconductor Manufacturing Performance.' *Industrial Relations*, 40/3: 436–71.

ARTHUR, J. B. (1992). 'The Link between Business Strategy and Industrial-Relations Systems in American Steel Minimills.' *Industrial & Labor Relations Review*, 45/3: 488–506.

BABIN, B. J., and BOLES, J. S. (1998). 'Employee Behavior in a Service Environment: A Model and Test of Potential Differences between Men and Women.' *Journal of Marketing*, 62/2: 77–91.

BARNEY, J. B. (1991). 'Firm Resources and Sustained Competitive Advantage.' *Journal of Management*, 17/1: 99–120.

BATT, R. (1999). 'Work Organization, Technology, and Performance in Customer Service and Sales.' *Industrial and Labor Relations Review*, 52/4: 539–64.

—— (2001). 'Explaining Wage Inequality in Telecommunications Services: Customer Segmentation, Human Resource Practices, and Union Decline.' *Industrial and Labor Relations Review*, 54/2A: 425–49.

—— (2002). 'Managing Customer Services: Human Resource Practices, Quit Rates, and Sales Growth.' *Academy of Management Journal*, 45/3: 587–97.

—— and KWON, H. (2005). 'Management Strategies and Wage Structures among Call Center Workers.' MS.

BATT, R., and MOYNIHAN, L. M. (2005). 'Human Resource Practices, Service Quality, and Economic Performance in Call Centers.' *Cornell ILR School.*

——— DOELLGAST, V., and KWON, H. (2005). 'Service Management and Employment Systems in US and Indian Call Centers.' In *Outsourcing and Offshoring White Collar Work.* Washington, DC: The Brookings Institution.

BORUCKI, C. C., and BURKE, M. J. (1999). 'An Examination of Service-Related Antecedents to Retail Store Performance.' *Journal of Organizational Behavior,* 20/6: 943–62.

BOWEN, D. E. (1986). 'Managing Customers as Human Resources in Service Organizations.' *Human Resource Management,* 25: 371–84.

——— and SCHNEIDER, B. (1985). 'Boundary Spanning Role Employees and the Service Encounter: Some Guidelines for Management and Research.' In J. A. Czepiel, M. R. Solomon, and C. Surprenant (eds.), *The Service Encounter.* Lexington, Mass.: D. C. Heath.

——— ——— (1988). 'Services Marketing and Management: Implications for Organizational Behavior.' In B. M. Staw, and L. L. Cummings (eds.), *Research in Organizational Behavior,* vol. x. Greenwich, Conn.: JAI Press.

——— CHASE, R. B., and CUMMINGS, T. (eds.) (1990). *Service Management Effectiveness: Balancing Strategy, Organization and Human Resources, Operations, and Marketing.* Oxford: Jossey-Bass.

BOXALL, P. (2003). 'HR Strategy and Competitive Advantage in the Service Sector.' *Human Resource Management Journal,* 13/3: 1–16.

——— and PURCELL, J. (2003). *Strategy and Human Resource Management.* Basingstoke: Palgrave Macmillan.

BRADY, D. (2000). 'Why Service Stinks.' *Business Week:* 118.

BRESNAHAN, T. F., BRYNJOLFSSON, E., and HITT, L. M. (2002). 'Information Technology, Workplace Technology, and the Demand for Skilled Labor: Firm-Level Evidence.' *Quarterly Journal of Economics,* 117/1: 339–76.

BRYNJOLFSSON, E., and YANG, S. (1996). 'Information Technology and Productivity: A Review of the Literature.' *Advances in Computers,* 43: 179–214.

CARAYON, P. (1993). 'Effect of Electronic Performance Monitoring on Job Design and Worker Stress: Review of the Literature and Conceptual-Model.' *Human Factors,* 35/3: 385–95.

CHASE, R. B. (1978). 'Where Does the Customer Fit in Service Operations?' *Harvard Business Review,* 56/6: 137–42.

——— and TANSIK, D. A. (1983). 'The Customer Contact Model for Organization Design.' *Management Science,* 29/9: 1037–50.

CRONIN, J. J. J., BRADY, M. K., and HULT, G. T. (2000). 'Assessing the Effects of Quality, Value, and Customer Satisfaction on Consumer Behavioral Intentions in Service Environments.' *Journal of Retailing,* 76/2: 193–218.

DEERY, S. J., IVERSON, R. D., and WALSH, J. P. (2002). 'Work Relationships in Telephone Call Centers: Understanding Emotional Exhaustion and Employee Withdrawal.' *Journal of Management Studies,* 39/4: 471–97.

DELERY, J. E., and DOTY, D. H. (1996). 'Modes of Theorizing in Strategic Human Resource Management: Tests of Universalistic, Contingency, and Configurational Performance Predictions.' *Academy of Management Journal,* 39/4: 802–35.

DEMING, W. E. (1984). *Out of the Crisis.* Cambridge, Mass.: MIT Press.

DOERINGER, P. B., and PIORE, M. J. (1971). *Internal Labor Markets and Manpower Analysis.* Lexington, Mass.: Heath Lexington.

DYER, L. (1983). 'Bringing Human Resources into the Strategy Formulation Process.' *Human Resource Management,* 22/3: 257–71.

FORNELL, C., JOHNSON, M., ANDERSON, E., CHA, J., and BRYANT, B. (1996). 'The American Customer Satisfaction Index: Nature, Purpose, and Findings.' *Journal of Marketing,* 60/4: 7–18.

FRENKEL, S., KORCZYNSKI, M., SHIRE, K., and TAM, M. (eds.). (1999). *On the Front-Line: Organization of Work in the Information Economy.* Ithaca, NY: Cornell University Press.

GARVIN, D. (1984). 'What Does "Product Quality" Really Mean?' *Sloan Management Review,* 26/1: 25–43.

GITTELL, J. H. (2002). 'Coordinating Mechanisms in Care Provider Groups: Relational Coordination as a Mediator and Input Uncertainty as a Moderator.' *Management Science,* 48/11: 1408–26.

GRONROOS, C. (1990). *Service Management and Marketing.* Lexington, Mass.: Lexington.

GUTEK, B. (1995). *The Dynamics of Service: Reflections on the Changing Nature of Customer/ Provider Interactions.* San Francisco: Jossey-Bass.

HAMMER, M., and CHAMPY, J. (1992). *Reengineering Work: A Manifesto for Business Revolution.* New York: Warner Books.

HARTLINE, M. D., and FERRELL, O. C. (1996). 'The Management of Customer-Contact Service Employees: An Empirical Investigation.' *Journal of Marketing,* 60: 52–70.

HESKETT, J. L., SASSER, E. W., and SCHLESINGER, L. A. (1997). *The Service Profit Chain.* New York: The Free Press.

HOLMAN, D., CHISSICK, C., and TOTTERDELL, P. (2002). 'The Effects of Performance Monitoring on Emotional Labour and Well-Being in Call Centres.' *Motivation and Emotion,* 26/1: 57–81.

HUSELID, M. A. (1995). 'The Impact of Human Resource Management-Practices on Turn-over, Productivity, and Corporate Financial Performance.' *Academy of Management Journal,* 38/3: 635–72.

ICHNIOWSKI, C., SHAW, K., and PRENNUSHI, G. (1997). 'The Effects of Human Resource Management Practices on Productivity: A Study of Steel Finishing Lines.' *American Economic Revies,* 87/3/June: 291–313.

JOHNSON, J. W. (1996). 'Linking Employee Perceptions of Service Climate to Customer Satisfaction.' *Personnel Psychology,* 49/4: 831–51.

KANE, R. L., MACIEJEWSKI, M., and FINCH, M. (1997). 'The Relationship of Patient Satisfaction with Care and Clinical Outcomes.' *Medical Care,* 35/7: 714–30.

KOCHAN, T. A., KATZ, H. C., and MCERSIE, R. (1986). *The Transformation of American Industrial Relations.* New York: Basic Books.

KORCZYNSKI, M. (2002). *Human Resource Management in Service Work.* London: Palgrave.

—— (2005). 'Skills in Service Work: An Overview.' *Human Resource Management Journal,* 15/2: 3–14.

LEIDNER, R. (1993). *Fast Food, Fast Talk: Service Work and the Routinization of Everyday Life.* Berkeley and Los Angeles: University of California Press.

LEPAK, D. P., and SNELL, S. A. (1999). 'The Human Resource Architecture: Toward a Theory of Human Capital Allocation and Development.' *Academy of Management Review,* 24/1: 31–48.

LEVY, F., and MURNANE, R. J. (2002). *The New Division of Labor: How Computers Are Creating the Next Job Market.* Princeton: Princeton University Press.

LOVELOCK, C. (2005). *Services Marketing: People, Technology, Strategy,* 5th edn. Englewood Cliffs, NJ: Prentice Hall.

MACDUFFIE, J. P. (1995). 'Human Resource Bundles and Manufacturing Performance: Organizational Logic and Flexible Production Systems in the World Auto Industry.' *Industrial and Labor Relations Review,* 48/2: 197–221.

MILLS, P., CHASE, R. B., and MARGUILES, N. (1983). 'Motivating the Client/Employee System as a Service Production Strategy.' *Academy of Management Review,* 8: 301–10.

OSTERMAN, P. (1984). *Internal Labor Markets.* Cambridge, Mass.: MIT Press.

PECCEI, R., and ROSENTHAL, P. (2000). 'Front-Line Responses to Customer Orientation Programmes: A Theoretical and Empirical Analysis.' *International Journal of Human Resource Management,* 11/3: 562–90.

PINE, B. J. (1993). *Mass Customization: The New Frontier in Business Competition.* Cambridge, Mass.: Harvard Business School Press.

PRAHALAD, C. K., and HAMEL, G. (1990). 'The Core Competence of the Corporation.' *Harvard Business Review,* 68/3: 79–91.

Purdue University (1999). Call Center Benchmarking Report.

QUINN, J. B. (1992). *Intelligent Enterprise.* New York: Free Press.

QUINONES, M. A., FORD, J. K., and TEACHOUT, M. S. (1995). 'The Relationship between Work Experience and Job Performance: A Conceptual and Meta-analytic Review.' *Personnel Psychology,* 48/4: 887–910.

REICHHELD, F. F. (1996). *The Loyalty Effect.* Boston: Harvard Business School Press.

REINARTZ, W., and KUMAR, V. (2002). 'The Mismanagement of Customer Loyalty.' *Harvard Business Review:* 5–13.

ROACH, S. S. (1991). 'Services under Siege: The Restructuring Imperative.' *Harvard Business Review:* 82–91.

ROGG, K. L., SCHMIDT, D. B., SHULL, C., and SCHMITT, N. (2001) 'Human Resource Practices, Organisational Climate, and Customer Satisfaction.' *Journal of Management,* 27: 431–49.

SCHMIT, M. J., and ALLSCHEID, S. P. (1995). 'Employee Attitudes and Customer Satisfaction—Making Theoretical and Empirical Connections.' *Personnel Psychology,* 48/3: 521–36.

SCHNEIDER, B., and BOWEN, D. E. (1985). 'Employee and Customer Perceptions of Service in Banks: Replication and Extension.' *Journal of Applied Psychology,* 70/3: 423–33.

—— WHITE, S. S., and PAUL, M. C. (1998). 'Linking Service Climate and Customer Perceptions of Service Quality: Test of a Causal Model.' *Journal of Applied Psychology,* 83/2: 150–63.

SEIDERS, K., and BERRY, L. (1998). 'Service Fairness: What It Is and Why It Matters.' *Academy of Management Executive,* 12/2: 8–20.

SHARMA, A., LEVY, M., and KUMAR, A. (2000). 'Knowledge Structures and Retail Sales Performance: An Empirical Examination.' *Journal of Retailing,* 76/1: 53–69.

SINGH, J. (2000). 'Performance Productivity and Quality of Frontline Employees in Service Organizations.' *Journal of Marketing,* 64/2: 15–34.

STEPANEK, M. (2000). Weblining. *Business Week:* 14–20.

STEWART, D. M., and CHASE, R. B. (1999). 'The Impact of Human Error on Delivering Service Quality.' *Production and Operations Management Journal,* 8/3: 240–63.

TRIST, E. (1981). 'A Sociotechnical Perspective: The Evolution of Sociotechnical Systems as a Conceptual Framework and as an Action Research Program.' In A. H. van de Ven and W. Joyce (eds.), *Perspectives on Organization Design and Behavior*. New York: John Wiley and Sons.

TUBRE, T. C., and COLLINS, J. M. (2000). 'Jackson and Schuler (1985) Revisited: A Meta-analysis of the Relationships between Role Ambiguity, Role Conflict, and Job Performance.' *Journal of Management*, 26/1: 155–69.

WRIGHT, P. M., and SHERMAN, S. (1999). 'Failing to Find Fit in Strategic Human Resource Management: Theoretical and Empirical Problems.' In P. M. Wright, L. Dyer, J. W. Boudreau, and G. Milkovich (eds.), *Research in Personnel and Human Resource Management*, Supplement 4. Greenwich, Conn.: JAI Press.

—— McMAHAN, G. C., and McWILLIAMS, A. (1994). 'Human Resources and Sustained Competitive Advantage: A Resource-Based View Perspective.' *International Journal of Human Resource Management*, 5: 301–26.

YOUNDT, M. A., SNELL, S. A., DEAN, J. W., and LEPAK, D. P. (1996). 'Human Resource Management, Manufacturing Strategy, and Firm Performance.' *Academy of Management Journal*, 39/4: 836–66.

ZEITHAML, V., PARASURAMAN, A., and BERRY, L. (1990). *Delivering Quality Service: Balancing Customer Perceptions and Expectations*. New York: The Free Press.

# CHAPTER 22

# HRM AND KNOWLEDGE WORKERS

## JUANI SWART

## 22.1 INTRODUCTION

THE importance and difficulty of the management of knowledge workers has been widely acknowledged (Alvesson 2000; May et al. 2002; Scarbrough 1999; Smith et al. 2005) and knowledge worker management has now progressed beyond fad status (Drucker 1999; Scarbrough and Swan 2001). A key explanation for this development lies with the historic shift from a focus on physical and financial forms of capital as key production resources to one on human and intellectual capital (Martin and Moldoveanu 2003). Intellectual material—knowledge, information, intellectual property, experience—that can be put to use to create wealth (Stewart 1997) is at the heart of the contemporary business model (Starbuck 1992). Knowledge businesses, such as design and engineering services, computer software design, high fashion, financial services, health care, and management consulting (Lei et al. 1999), rely on the conversion of their human capital (knowledge, skills, and talent) to intellectual capital (product and service offerings in the market place).

In these environments, wealth creation is less dependent on the *control* of resources and more dependent on the exercise of specialist knowledge, or the management of organizational competencies (Blackler 1995). We can no longer blame the mismanagement of tangible resources for failures in a knowledge-based society. We now need to turn our attention to the management of the intangible. Managerial systems remain important, but it is the management of intangible assets that is now argued to be at the heart of the managerial process.

There is, however, a contradiction in what the literature offers in terms of an approach to knowledge management. On the one hand, there are theorists who uphold the knowledge-based view of the firm that knowledge is all embracing. It is in the routines, in the individual skills, and in the relationships. On the other hand, knowledge is seen as a 'possession' of an individual or a group of employees and presents a threat to knowledge-intensive firms because of the potential loss of 'intellectual capital.' A comparison of these two approaches raises the questions: 'how do we know what a knowledge-based firm is?' and 'how do we differentiate a knowledge worker from any other employee that uses knowledge in his or her everyday work?'

To address these questions, this chapter develops a definition of the knowledge worker and discusses the characteristics of knowledge workers and their work. It then shifts to the organizational level and takes a closer look at the characteristics of knowledge-based organizations and the management of knowledge work. Several managerial and theoretical challenges arise when we combine individual and organizational knowledge perspectives. Each of these challenges, together with relevant knowledge-focused HR practices, is discussed and presented in Table 22.1, which serves as a summary to the chapter. The final section looks toward the future and explores possible avenues for research, theory-building, and HRM policy and practice development.

# 22.2 DEVELOPING A DEFINITION OF KNOWLEDGE WORKERS

Galbraith suggested in 1967 that a powerful new class of technical-scientific expertise was emerging. This new class of employee or 'knowledge workers' (Zuboff 1988) are, on the whole, highly paid, high-status employees (Reich 1991) who apply their specialized knowledge, or technical-scientific expertise, to high-value-added problem solution processes. Scarbrough (1999) asserts that knowledge workers are defined primarily by the work that they do, which is relatively unstructured and organizationally contingent, and which reflects the changing demands of organizations more than occupationally defined norms and practices (p. 7). That is, having a particular set of knowledge is not enough to be recognized as a knowledge worker. It is the active application of the knowledge, through work, that is important.

This systemic notion fits with the socially constructed nature of knowledge: to understand the individual knowledge worker we need to look toward the system within which the knowledge is embedded. I suggest the following definition, paying attention to the worker, the work, and the organization, and then deconstruct it to develop linkages to managerial challenges:

> *Knowledge workers can be defined as employees who apply their valuable knowledge and skills (developed through experience) to complex, novel, and abstract problems in environments that provide rich collective knowledge and relational resources.*

## 22.2.1 Employees who Possess Valuable Knowledge and Skills: Individual Knowledge

The 'possession' of knowledge and skills (developed through experience) can best be described as 'human capital' (Bontis 1998; Davenport 1999; Lepak and Snell 1999) expressed through 'embrained' and 'embodied' knowledge (Collins 1993; Blackler 1995). Embrained knowledge represents technical-theoretical knowledge, otherwise referred to as 'know-what' (Ryle 1949) or 'knowledge about' (James 1950). Professionals are often thought to have particularly deep sets of technical-theoretical or explicit knowledge (Polanyi 1966). Knowledge workers can be seen to work from an in-depth knowledge base. However, 'knowledge of' will be of little use without experience of how to apply it.

Embodied knowledge plays an important role in the application of specialist knowledge. It refers to 'knowing how' to do something (Ryle 1949). This is illustrated by the lawyer who, with twenty-five years of experience, knows how to win a litigious case and how to apply case law to win an argument. This deeply specialist skill is often tacit, hence the notion of embodied knowledge: through application or action the knowledge worker does not focus on separate aspects or explicit parts of the skill. The embodied and embrained forms of knowledge create the foundation of knowledge *from* which the knowledge worker acts. They are part of the raw material in the knowledge conversion equation.

## 22.2.2 Knowledge Work: the Application of Knowledge to Complex, Novel, and Abstract Problems

A key characteristic of knowledge work is the capacity to solve complex problems through creative and innovative solutions: the enactment of know-what and know-how (explicit and tacit knowledge) in novel circumstances. It is therefore not the mere presence of human capital but also how it is applied that is important. Reed (1996: 585) argues that employees in this category 'specialise in complex task domains which are inherently resistant to incursions by the carriers of bureaucratic rational control.' He describes the application of the knowledge held by knowledge workers as esoteric, non-substitutable, global, and analytical.

Rather than applying deep technical knowledge to familiar situations, the crux of knowledge work is the ambiguous, the unfamiliar, or the esoteric. This does, of course, provide a useful power base for the knowledge worker to develop a market niche where his or her skills cannot be categorized and labelled. The output of the knowledge work process is often intangible (for example, consulting advice) and its quality is difficult to determine. Whether a solution is 'good' or 'no good' is often determined by factors external to the solution itself, such as changing market forces, the interpretation of the clients buying the solution, and the degree of trust that the sellers of the solution inspire.

## 22.2.3 Knowledge Production in an Environment that Provides Collective Knowledge and Social Networks

The conversion of human capital into intellectual capital is highly reliant upon the context for knowledge production. Knowledge workers interact with other knowledge workers to produce knowledge-intensive outcomes. Knowledge workers work with knowledge; their own, certainly, but also the knowledge of others as communicated through information systems and artifacts, as well as the organizational and technical knowledge encoded in programs, routines, and managerial discourse (Scarbrough 1999). Here the 'encultured' knowledge (the process of achieving shared understandings through social relationships) and embedded knowledge (systemic organizational routines) influence the production of knowledge (Blackler 1995).

This process draws on 'what others know' as well as 'how easily that knowledge is shared,' which, in turn, are influenced by the nature of the knowledge and the quality of the relationships. Smith et al. (2005), in their review of the knowledge management literature, identify three categories of organizational resources that impact on knowledge creation capability: stocks of individual knowledge, 'ego networks,' and organizational routines. These routines comprise a firm's climate. Informally, and perhaps tacitly, they establish how the firm develops and uses knowledge (p. 347). The categories of resources that make the act of knowledge work possible are sometimes seen as different forms of capital. Ego networks refer to 'social capital' (Nahapiet and Ghoshal 1998; Leana and van Buren 1999) and organizational routines are attributes of 'organizational capital.' Both social and organizational capital impact on the knowledge creation capability of an organization and the ability to conduct knowledge work.

If we look at the managerial implications of the knowledge production process, it is clear that we cannot manage knowledge workers without managing the knowledge environment within which they operate. The knowledge worker is defined by the nature of the work that she or he engages in. To be a knowledge worker is therefore not an occupational category (unlike the professions) but it is an act of producing knowledge-rich products and services. An organization cannot logically lay claim to employ knowledge workers if they are not able to engage in knowledge work. Hence, it is critically important to manage the knowledge environment to ensure that knowledge work is possible. This depends greatly on the quality of the relationships that the firm has in its network of clients and collaborating producers. Challenging and committed clients make for challenging and exciting work, which allows for the co-production of knowledge. To better understand this systemic process, it is important to be aware of both the characteristics of knowledge workers and the firms within which they operate.

## 22.3 THE CHARACTERISTICS OF KNOWLEDGE WORKERS

Knowledge workers tend, on the whole, to work exceptionally long hours (Deetz 1995), with commitment related more to the nature of the work (consulting to a client, writing software code, or solving a problem) rather than to the organization. They have a strong sense of intrinsic motivation and are mostly interested in challenging work which requires considerable creativity and initiative (Alvesson 2000). Knowledge workers also tend to identify with other like-minded professionals more than the organization for which they work (von Glinow 1988) and therefore develop strong interpersonal networks that span organizational boundaries.

Such workers, also referred to as 'symbolic-analytic' workers (Blackler 1995), tend to command high rewards, often because their know-what, know-how, and know-who is valuable and difficult to replace or imitate (Barney 1991). The core skills that they rely on to make this strong bargaining position possible include problem-solving (research, product design, fabrication), problem identification (marketing, advertising, and customer consulting), and brokerage (financing, searching, contracting) (Blackler 1995: 1027). Social skills and client relationships are also important to the process of knowledge work (Starbuck 1992) given the social nature of knowledge production. Knowledge workers therefore tend to develop their own social environments and professional networks within which they can enhance and enact their unique sets of expertise.

May et al. (2002), in their research on the job expectations of 134 knowledge workers in Australia, Japan, and the USA, found that pay was regarded as the first or second most important aspect of the job. This was followed by the intrinsic nature of the work in terms of variety, challenge, and learning opportunities. Other important factors included promotion prospects, co-worker relations, and influence over decisions that affect their work (p. 791). One of the reasons why pay and rewards were so important to the knowledge workers in this study was that, unlike the professions, status was less hierarchically or tenured based. However, the abstract nature of the knowledge worker's skills was priced on a perceptual basis: 'my client cannot do what I do (they may not even know how I do this) and because they think I'm invaluable, they'll pay a lot for my services.' This spiral of reward (perception—high reward—positive perception) is also the mechanism through which knowledge workers tend to determine their status and their 'next big career move.'

Knowledge in and of itself naturally becomes the focal point for the knowledge worker's activities. The factors that drive knowledge workers to choose some projects over others are often related to the feedback received on their knowledge outputs (often through performance management systems or client relationships) and the desire to deepen technical expertise by taking on challenging projects. Knowledge workers are often in control of the networks that they develop and the skills that they acquire and often associate their organizational commitment with the extent to which they are able to develop transferable skills (May et al. 2002). Furthermore, they feel the need to be involved in decisions that will influence their developmental opportunities and careers (more so than organization-wide decisions) and tend to have a need for a high degree of autonomy (Alvesson 1995).

One of the major factors that affects the commitment, work effort, and job satisfaction of knowledge workers is the way they are organized and relate to management (May et al. 2002). Their status is based on the mastery of unique, inimitable, and valuable skills (Barney 1991). Reed (1996) argues that, unlike traditional professionals, knowledge workers do not rely on hierarchical systems to establish credibility but rely on the intangible nature of their knowledge to create market niches for themselves. In this sense, they are 'entrepreneurial professionals' (Reed 1996). This approach to establishing political and economic power lends itself to organic or network-based organizational forms characterized by decentralized flexibility and autonomy (May et al. 2002: 777).

Knowledge workers are often found not only *inside* organizations but *across* them, drawing on their personal, professional, and expertise networks. This holds serious implications for the management of knowledge workers. Because of the prominence of individual and organizational networks, the organization has less control over how it manages 'its' knowledge workers. Non-standard forms of employment such as contracts for services and fixed-term employment can therefore be more suitable and are frequently found across knowledge-based organizations.

These characteristics of professional knowledge workers present employing organizations with some severe challenges: knowledge-based firms rely on the knowledge and skills of their employees. However, they have to create the environment for this knowledge to be developed and shared (Maister 1993). They also have to ensure that peer learning processes, which are highly valued by knowledge workers, are facilitated both through work organization and by recruiting talented and respected co-workers.

The simultaneous developing and sharing of knowledge presents a management challenge in itself because knowledge workers may hold on to their knowledge in order to secure their next career opportunity, be that within or external to the organization. Employers need to retain valuable knowledge that has been developed in order to create further value from their investment. The firm needs to appropriate value from knowledge developed (Blyer and Coff 2003), while minimizing the risk of excessive appropriation by the knowledge workers themselves. It needs to guard against excessive remuneration demands and the leakage of knowledge (in terms of innovation or clients) when employees leave the firm.

This means firms need to erect 'resource mobility barriers' (Mueller 1996) while satisfying the career needs of their knowledge workers by encouraging key employees to remain with the organization. When an organization is heavily reliant upon its human capital, the risk associated with frequent career moves between organizations is far greater and the inability to manage the leakage of knowledge across boundaries can adversely affect firm viability (Swart and Kinnie 2004).

# 22.4 THE ORGANIZATIONAL PERSPECTIVE: MANAGING KNOWLEDGE WORKERS

Organizations that facilitate knowledge production have a number of distinctive characteristics which are critical to the performance of the business. They operate in a 'pressure cooker' type of environment where product and labour markets are often unstable and technology is changing quickly. They tend to develop complex and innovative internal and external structures and forms (Frenkel et al. 1999; May et al. 2002) in comparison to other more traditional, slow-growing, and relatively bureaucratic organizations.

These organizational and environmental characteristics challenge traditional ways of organizing based on hierarchy and specialization and pose a whole series of questions about the people management practices most appropriate in these contexts. Ghoshal and Bartlett (1995: 96) suggest this may require a shift from what they term the 'strategy–structure–systems' paradigm, where the managerial task is largely concerned with allocating resources, assigning responsibilities, and then controlling the outcomes, to one based more on 'purpose–process–people.' This is where the task is to 'shape the behaviors of people and create an environment that enables them to take initiative, to co-operate and to learn.' The management of knowledge workers has been compared to conducting a symphony orchestra (Mintzberg 1998) where the key role of the manager is creating an environment for the harmonious flow of knowledge.

In many employment situations, the management of the knowledge workers is loosely structured with fluid project teams, rotation of leadership positions, and low degrees of monitoring and control being present (Alvesson 1995). This often fits with employee needs for autonomy and self-directed development (Morris 2000). May et al. (2002) argue that the knowledge worker's need for autonomy and cutting-edge skill development can best be met by creating an 'enclave' organizational form: an independent section of experts within a larger organization. Inside the enclave, a high degree of interdependence between knowledge workers with complementary forms of knowledge is likely to prevail. The authors warn that this enclave should not have absolute autonomy, but managerial control and market-based mechanisms such as performance-based reward systems should be used to focus knowledge workers' efforts on organizational and strategic objectives.

Given the fluid nature of both knowledge work and the organization of this work, managers often seek to use ideological controls and strive to create a strong sense of belonging, or a strong culture (Alvesson 1993). A process of establishing an organizational identity (Mael and Ashforth 1995) helps an organization to erect mobility barriers and goes some way toward tying valuable knowledge workers to the organization. Small to medium-sized knowledge-based firms often benefit from a strong sense of shared identity at the firm level. This is often because the owner-manager is still present in the firm and/or the majority of the original workforce is still part of the organisation. In larger firms, however, this sense of belonging needs to be 'manufactured' by using individual performance and/or organizational rewards (Alvesson 1993), establishing a variety of community-based activities (Swart et al. 2003), and engaging in some cultural manipulation to influence how knowledge workers view themselves and their relationship to the firm.

Project-based work has without any doubt become the dominant form of organizing knowledge work (Lam 2000) and a key organizational characteristic. However, project-based working presents a danger because it is often the case that knowledge workers build a strong sense of identification with their project team, which may replace their identification with their organization. Furthermore, if the team is client focused and client based, there is a strong possibility that valuable competitive knowledge may leak out to the client and remain outside the boundaries of the firm.

It is therefore important to think relationally when seeking to understand the management of knowledge workers (Gulati et al. 2000: 203; Granovetter 1973). Knowledge-based firms often operate within larger knowledge networks where they have frequent interaction with clients, partners, educators, and suppliers at many levels of organization and knowledge tends to flow relatively freely across these boundaries (Swart and Kinnie 2003). These knowledge flows are regarded as a key part of the knowledge production process. It is important to note that knowledge workers work with knowledge at an *inter*-organizational level. This phenomenon is often to the advantage of smaller firms who may be able to exploit knowledge outside the permanent employment relationship or, indeed, any employment relationship. A cluster of small biotechnology, life-science research, and law firms may work together on a larger process of knowledge production. Similarly, three or four law firms may work together on a management buyout and a life-science research firm may work closely with a pharmaceutical firm to produce compounds for further research. Such co-production of knowledge outputs focuses our attention on the quality of the knowledge network within which the firm operates.

The management of knowledge workers is influenced, and sometimes controlled, by relationships with organizations in these networks (Kinnie et al. 2005). Where firms have fewer and longer-term business-to-business relationships, we need to consider how suppliers, partners, clients, and customers influence the way in which people are managed in the focal firm.

In summary, knowledge-based firms often operate in volatile, fast-changing environments. Within this context, they need to manage ambiguous work through fluid structures. Internal (knowledge work and knowledge workers) and external (knowledge environment) forms of fluidity are put under pressure by the nature of network relationships. Networks determine the opportunities for challenging knowledge work within the firm, such as working on exciting projects, as well as the quality of knowledge outputs at the network level.

If we juxtapose the complexity of the wider environment with the characteristics of the knowledge workers themselves we are in a position to illuminate particular human resource management challenges that need to be addressed.

# 22.5 INTEGRATING INDIVIDUAL AND ORGANIZATIONAL PERSPECTIVES: MANAGEMENT DILEMMAS ASSOCIATED WITH KNOWLEDGE WORKERS

This section identifies three key themes which cut across knowledge work, knowledge workers, and knowledge-based organizations, to enable a discussion of the tensions and challenges for managing knowledge workers. Table 22.1 links the impact of each 'concurrent theme' to a particular set of HR practices. It identifies key influences on the adoption of specific sets of HR practices and then specifies a key tension that exists in relation to the particular theme, which enables identification of the managerial challenges in each area.

The first key theme is *fluidity*, or a lack of predetermined or imposed structure, which is evident in the nature of knowledge work but also in the organization of this work: the loosely structured projects in the enclave organizational form. Much of this fluidity is inherent in the application of symbolic-analytic skills to ambiguous client demands (Blackler 1995). However, the move toward fluidity is also driven by the market-based employment orientation of knowledge workers themselves (Reed 1996) wherein higher wages can more readily be negotiated because they are not subject to such strict technical-hierarchical systems and they operate in environments where less well-defined skills are sold to clients.

The fluid nature of knowledge work also influences the choice of work organization and the degree of involvement and participation. The symbolic-analytic skills which are applied to novel, complex problems necessitate organizational forms that enable fast change, flow of skills across 'project' boundaries, and high levels of discretionary decision-making. Firms need to allow knowledge workers to act in a way that they see fit at a particular moment, creating a 'leave it up to the experts' form of work organization and decision-making systems.

This creates a very specific focus for HRM. It calls for the involvement of HR practitioners in the resource allocation process, determining who should be

### Table 22.1 Concurrent themes, HR practice impact areas, and key tensions

| Concurrent themes | HR impact | Key tensions |
| --- | --- | --- |
| Fluidity | Work organization<br>Involvement and participation<br>Pay and reward | Value appropriation |
| Market-based networks:<br>Personal/professional,<br>organizational | Recruitment<br>Involvement<br>Development<br>Pay and reward<br>Retention strategies<br>Performance management | Identity fragmentation |
| Knowledge-trading | Resourcing<br>Development<br>Reward<br>Work organization<br>Career management | Skill specificity focus |

allocated to which project and for what period, as well as calling for an understanding of how work organization can be used to develop key skills. The skills development emphasis in this context is on learning-by-doing or informal learning rather than formal 'training.' This holds serious implications for talent management and the retention of key knowledge workers. If the selected work organization does not take the development of key skills into account, knowledge workers are more likely to leave the organization and seek employment with a firm that will increase their employability, or make them more attractive in the labor market.

A key tension which this theme represents is the dilemma of *value appropriation*. The firm needs to appropriate value (Blyer and Goff 2003) from knowledge developed, while minimizing the risk of excessive appropriation by knowledge workers themselves. This is difficult because not only is the nature of the knowledge that is applied to a client problem hard to specify and categorize, but the boundaries between the individual's knowledge and the final, knowledge-rich service are extremely fluid. There is a sharp contrast here between management consultants who sell their knowledge directly to a client and the shopfloor worker who is reliant on the physical capital of their employer to manufacture the final product. The knowledge worker typically has a greater sense of ownership, often expressed as intellectual property rights, over the product or service. This leads to a situation where knowledge workers themselves feel a right to appropriate value or receive high rents for their own knowledge. They may make excessive remuneration demands which the employer is unable to meet. If the employer does not manage this tension well, they can easily be in a situation where the knowledge worker leaves the organization to sell their skills directly to the same client or sets of clients. This phenomenon is frequently seen in advertising agencies, management consultancies, and brokerage firms.

The second theme noted from the characteristics of knowledge workers and the firms who employ them is that of *market-based networks*. Personal/professional networks and organizational networks influence the employment relationship. Each of these networks can be a source of identification which challenges organizational control over the management of knowledge workers (Fig. 22.1).

Personal/professional networks play a very specific role in both skill development and status-building. Individual knowledge workers often use their networks to gauge their status and may use them to put pressure on their employer to adopt certain HR practices. Often personal/professional networks are developed through independent contract arrangements. Many firms rely on, and make use of, several independent contractors who develop their own networks where they trade information about key skills and employment opportunities. These personal/professional networks can act as a market place for comparison and diffusion of management practices. For example, software developers will often meet informally and discuss their employment relationships. Comparisons of

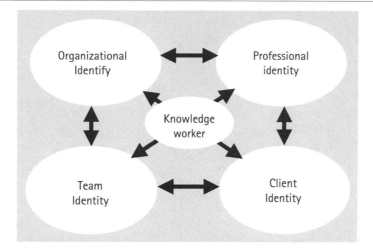

**Fig. 22.1. The multiple sources of identity of knowledge workers**
*Source:* Swart and Kinnie, 2004.

project status (what type of work for which client), pay status (the 'going rate' for a skill set), and working conditions (working hours, flexibility, involvement) can take place in these wider personal/professional networks and through them employees may put pressure on their employers to adopt particular bundles of HR practices. This pressure is very real because links within the network also represent career opportunities and employers are well aware that a 'better deal' elsewhere may result in the loss of human capital. Engagement in personal/professional networks can therefore present a threat to the firm's talent management because knowledge workers may use these networks to find alternative employment.

Organizational networks, on the other hand, largely determine the nature of the work that knowledge workers will engage in. Here, a virtuous cycle of 'great client—challenging work—great talent' can be set in motion. However, these networks are also key determinants of the nature of the employment relationship. Clients have the power to influence the employment practices (for example, pay and reward) of the firm that they contract or work with (Kinnie et al. 2005; Dyer and Nobeoka 2000). In extreme cases, the boundaries between the firm and the client can be so permeable that the client may even have an impact on the performance appraisal objectives of individual knowledge workers.

The particular set of HR practices which are influenced by the networked nature of knowledge work include recruitment, involvement, development, pay and reward, performance management, and retention. The network represents a knowledge-based labor market; it functions as a hothouse for skill development but it also communicates which skills are available and at what price. Knowledge-based organizations rely on their networks to recruit valuable and unique talent. When key skills become available in the network, organizations may contract or buy the skills, regardless of the existence of an internal vacancy. Professional networks also influence which skills are seen as valuable and are often used as vehicles for skill development.

Performance management and reward systems are particularly sensitive to network-based influences due to the permeability of the boundaries between the firm and its professional and client networks. A key reason for this influence is the abstract nature of knowledge outputs (Alvesson 2000). How can a line manager possibly judge the quality of the knowledge output without gleaning information from the users of the outputs such as the clients? However, the degree of network influence over performance management goes beyond just the nature of knowledge outputs. The business of knowledge production is an uncertain one and buyers within this market may want a greater degree of control over the ambiguous, high-cost products and services that they are buying. Attempts to gain control over the process of knowledge production may impact greatly on key performance areas within the performance management framework as well as affecting the rewards that are attached to performance outcomes.

The multiplicity of networks presents a very real challenge to the management of knowledge workers. The key tension here is with identification with, and commitment to, the organization. In essence, networks offer several sources of identification to the knowledge worker: they may identify with their occupation/profession through their professional networks, with their client through their organizational networks, and with their team through their team networks (Fig. 22.1). For most knowledge workers, their occupation is likely to be the base of their expertise, status, and economic advantage. As such, it is not surprising that knowledge workers tend to be more committed to their occupation than to their organization (May et al. 2002: 779). The alleged rivalry between occupations and organizations as the base of employee loyalty is also a common theme in the professions like law, medicine, and professional engineering. It is also likely that for knowledge workers, occupational identity drives discretionary behavior rather than organizational commitment. For example, a nurse may be motivated to 'go the extra mile' because of her belief in patient care.

The nature of knowledge work means that employees will often spend considerable periods of time on a client project or at a client site. Intricate and extended client contact most often takes place within a dedicated, client-focused project team. Once again, the opportunity to develop a strong team identity exists. This can work to the advantage of the firm if strong identification with the firm is also maintained. However, it is often the case that team identity overpowers organizational identity. This is seen in a 'them (the organization) and us (the team)' discourse.

These multiple, and sometimes competing, identities challenge the management of knowledge workers because identity is intimately linked to knowledge-sharing (Gupta and Govindarajan 2000; Nonaka et al. 2000; Strock and Hill 2000). Knowledge workers tend to share knowledge with others who 'speak the same language,' with whom they can relate. The danger lies in having strong client, team, and professional/occupational identities that pull away from organizational identity. Non-organizational identities signify a possible flow of knowledge outside the organization. In extreme cases, they also represent a possible career path. For example, a financial services team may break away from the 'parent' organization and establish a rival firm or a software developer may use his or her professional networks to explore job opportunities or a lawyer may be offered an in-house position by a client.

Successful knowledge-based firms tie occupational identity into organizational identity by facilitating professional development (Swart and Kinnie 2004). The message sent is one of: 'identify with *your* profession through *our* organization.' These successful organizations have less to fear from fluid client and team identities established through work arrangements across multiple project and client account teams.

The third theme that can be identified running through knowledge-based organizations and knowledge work is the notion of '*knowledge-trading*.' The *raison d'être* of the networks, the employment relationship and indeed the client relationship, can be seen as the development and application of human capital. This is one area where an interdependence between the firm and the knowledge worker can be identified. Individuals are often dependent on the organization for access to other knowledge workers, including those with complementary skills. They also rely on the physical and financial capital in research laboratories or technology to develop their core skills. The organization, on the other hand, relies, increasingly, on the knowledge and skills of its human capital to create a competitive advantage.

Knowledge-trading between knowledge workers and organizations has an impact on recruitment, development, work organization, and pay and reward. First, managers need to take a human capital focus in employee resourcing activities by specifying the nature of knowledge inputs that are needed within the organization: which skills need to be developed to ensure effective knowledge-trading. A human capital focus also has an impact on resource allocation. For example, if a particular skill is in demand by a client group, it is often the case that key skilled employees will be placed across project teams to allow for dispersion of the particular skill set across the organization. Here the organization needs to create tacit learning environments to ensure cost-effective skill development. Finally, the nature of knowledge-trading may have an impact on pay and reward by putting the employer in a stronger bargaining position. Knowledge workers often claim high rewards given the complexity and uniqueness of their skill, but if the interdependency of knowledge-trading is emphasized, the employer can argue that knowledge production would not be possible without access to organizational resources, networks, physical and financial capital, thereby undermining claims for excessive remuneration.

The knowledge-trading theme presents specific challenges with regard to the development of knowledge workers. First, knowledge workers are interested in knowledge-trading because they are highly focused on employability (Cappelli 1999) which enables them to move on to a career opportunity that will enable them to develop further unique skills that are attractive to other employers. The interest of the employing firm is, however, focused on retaining core skills that enable value generation and competitive advantage. The tension between employees wanting to move between organizations and the organization needing to hold on to key talent can be termed the '*retention-employability*' dilemma (Swart and Kinnie 2004). If an organization fails to address and manage this career dilemma, it will be depleted of its human capital and may create a source of competitive *dis*advantage.

A second tension that has an impact on the retention of knowledge is the specificity of skill development. Knowledge-based organizations seek to differentiate themselves by offering unique services or products and thus aim to develop organization-specific skills. Knowledge workers, on the other hand, wish to develop transferable skills that will make them attractive to prospective employers. If an organization develops predominantly firm-specific skills, the knowledge worker may sacrifice his or her employment attractiveness. Knowledge-based firms therefore need to strike a balance within their skill development agenda between organization-specific and transferable skills, which, in turn, impacts on their approach to the management of the knowledge workers' careers.

Both of these tensions speak to the need for knowledge-based firms to retain and develop valuable and unique human capital. Development often has an undesired impact on retention as employees with valuable skills become more attractive to other employers. However, if the firm does not develop the transferable as well as the organization-specific skills of their knowledge workers, they are likely to lose key employees. Most successful organizations therefore strike a 'development balance' by ensuring that they have challenging work projects in loosely structured work environments which are characterized by multiple teams. The development of a particular skill set is therefore not linked to one client or one organization-specific approach to problem solution.

## 22.6 FUTURE DIRECTIONS

The rise in importance of the knowledge worker has certainly taken center stage over the last decade. With the increasing realization that human capital is one of the key resources for sustainable competitive advantage, attention is focused on the management of knowledge workers. There has, however, been a tendency to mystify knowledge work and subsequently the management of knowledge workers. Some of this mysticism, attached to the symbolic-analytic nature of knowledge production, is justified but if we are to better understand the 'science' of knowledge worker management, we need to be a lot clearer about knowledge working and knowledge workers.

A comprehensive model of knowledge workers and knowledge working that takes the institutional environment into account is needed. One possibility is to build on the work of May et al. (2002), which takes into account the market-based model of knowledge working as well as the dual-dependent relationship between knowledge workers and the organization. This can be extended to understand the interrelationship between the nature of the knowledge environment and the process of knowledge production.

A key weakness in the current literature is the tendency to lump all knowledge workers together as if they were one big occupational category. There is a real need to disentangle the knowledge worker category. It might be beneficial to take a close look at the knowledge classification developed by Blackler (1995) for types of organizations and extend this classification to types of knowledge workers. This would mean taking account of Scarbrough's (1999) view that one can only be considered a knowledge worker if one engages in knowledge working. A more detailed approach to the possible categories of knowledge workers would be useful in understanding which HR practices have an impact on their motivation, commitment, and satisfaction.

The key tensions referred to in this chapter provide a fruitful avenue for future research and practice. We need to know more about the tensions between employer and employee in the value appropriation process. This also represents an area for research on reward practices. Are there different ways of rewarding and recognizing knowledge workers for the direct applicability of their intellectual capital to the client problem? Which reward strategies will better meet the appropriation needs of the firm and the reward goals of the individual or teams of knowledge workers?

The possible management of knowledge worker identification provides a further opportunity for research. Social identity theory can usefully be applied to knowledge-rich settings. One particular area that needs attention is the question of competing identities. How can we understand the dynamic interplay between the various identities? Should, and indeed can, organizations manage the multiple identities of the knowledge worker?

Finally, management practitioners need to both retain and develop their knowledge workers. This challenge is intimately linked to their skill development focus. Should a firm develop organization-specific skills to gain advantage in the market place or should the firm focus more on transferable skills, thereby fulfilling the employability need of its knowledge workers? To answer this question, a better understanding of the nature of the skills involved in knowledge work is needed.

## 22.7 SUMMARY AND CONCLUSIONS

This chapter has outlined the relevance and development of knowledge workers in contemporary organizations. It followed a social constructionist approach in developing a definition of knowledge workers, specifying that we need to (*a*) be clear on what type of knowledge the worker brings to the knowledge conversion process, (*b*) understand the nature of knowledge work, and (*c*) show awareness of the knowledge production environment and the social and organizational capital that it provides to the knowledge worker and the firm.

Working from this definition, the characteristics of knowledge workers were explored and juxtaposed with the characteristics of employing organizations and their managerial practices. This juxtaposition enabled the identification of three 'concurrent themes': the fluidity of the nature of knowledge work and the organization of knowledge work, the prevalence of market-based networks (personal, professional, and organizational), and the focal point of knowledge-trading. Each of these key themes influences the adoption of particular sets of HR practices. Finally, each theme and subsequent set of HR practices represents a key tension that needs to be tackled in the management of knowledge workers.

There are key messages for practice in the tensions associated with the themes of fluidity, networks, and knowledge-trading. They include the need to work on the tensions that exist around value appropriation, including negotiation of intellectual property rights and the ways in which business-to-business relationships are managed.

Managerial practice also needs to engage with how knowledge workers go about developing occupational, organizational, client, and team identities and how particular managerial practices can help to lessen tensions that exist among these identities. Among these, it is important for managers to recognize that knowledge workers often have a particularly strong need for group identity. These competing identities exist, are powerful, and influence the knowledge creation process. The managerial agenda needs to be shaped with these realities in mind.

## REFERENCES

ALVESSON, M. (1993). 'Organization as Rhetoric: Knowledge-Intensive Companies and the Struggle with Ambiguity.' *Journal of Management Studies*, 30/6: 997–1015.

—— (1995). *Management of Knowledge Intensive Companies*. Berlin: Mouton de Gruyter.

—— (2000). 'Social Identity and the Problem of Loyalty in Knowledge Intensive Companies.' *Journal of Management Studies*, 37/8: 1101–23.

BARNEY, J. B. (1991). 'Firm Resources and Sustained Competitive Advantage.' *Journal of Management*, 17/1: 99–120.

BLACKLER, F. (1995). 'Knowledge, Knowledge Work and Organizations: An Overview.' *Organization Studies,* 16/6: 1021–47.

BLYER, M., and COFF, R. W. (2003). 'Dynamic Capabilities, Social Capital, and Rent Appropriation: Ties that Split Pies.' *Strategic Management Journal,* 24: 677–86.

BONTIS, N. (1998). 'Intellectual Capital: An Exploratory Study that Develops Measures and Models.' *Management Decision,* 36/2: 63–76.

CAPPELLI, P. (1999). *The New Deal at Work.* Boston: Harvard Business School Press.

COLLINS, H. (1993). 'The Structure of Knowledge.' *Social Research,* 60: 95–116.

DAVENPORT, T. (1999). *Human Capital.* San Francisco: Jossey-Bass.

DEETZ, S. (1995). *Transforming Communication, Transforming Business: Building Responsive and Responsible Workplaces.* Cresskill, NJ: Hampton Press.

DRUCKER, P. F. (1999). 'Knowledge-Worker Productivity: The Biggest Challenge.' *Californian Management Review,* 41/2: 79–94.

DYER, J., and NOBEOKA, K. (2000). 'Creating and Managing a High-Performance Knowledge-Sharing Network: The Toyota Case.' *Strategic Management Journal,* 21: 345–67.

FRENKEL, S. J., KORCZYNSKI, M., SHIRE, K. A., and TAM, M. (1999). *On the Front Line: Organization of Work in the Information Economy.* Ithaca, NY: Cornell University Press.

GALBRAITH, J. (1967). *The New Industrial State.* Boston: Houghton Mifflin.

GHOSHAL, S., and BARTLETT, C. A. (1995). 'Changing the Role of Top Management: Beyond Structure to Process.' *Harvard Business Review,* January–February: 86–96.

GRANOVETTER, M. (1973). 'The Strength of Weak Ties.' *American Journal of Sociology,* 78: 1360–80.

GULATI, R., NOHRIA, N., and ZAHEER, A. (2000). 'Strategic Networks.' *Strategic Management Journal,* 21: 203–15.

GUPTA, A., and GOVINDARAJAN, V. (2000). 'Knowledge Management's Social Dimension: Lessons from Nucor Steel.' *Sloan Management Review,* 42/1: 71.

JAMES, W. (1950). *The Principles of Psychology.* New York: Dover.

JOHNSON, B., LORENZ, E., and LUNDVALL, B. A. (2002). 'Why All This Fuss about Codified and Explicit Knowledge?' *Industrial and Corporate Change,* 11/2: 254–62.

KINNIE, N., SWART, J., and PURCELL, J. (2005). 'Influences of the Choice of HR Systems: The Network Organisation Perspective.' *International Journal of Human Resource Management,* 16/6: 1004–28.

LAM, A. (2000). 'Tacit Knowledge, Organizational Learning and Societal Institutions: An Integrated Framework.' *Organization Studies,* 21/3: 487–513.

LEANA, C. R., and VAN BUREN, H. J. (1999). 'Organizational Social Capital and Employment Practices.' *Academy of Management Review,* 24/3: 538–55.

LEI, D., SLOCUM, J. W., and PITTS, R. A. (1999). 'Designing Organizations for Competitive Advantage: The Power of Learning and Unlearning.' *Organizational Dynamics,* Winter: 24–38.

LEPAK, D., and SNELL, S. A. (1999). 'The Human Resource Architecture: Toward a Theory of Human Capital Allocation and Development.' *Academy of Management Review,* 24/1: 31–48.

MAEL, F. A., and ASHFORTH, B. E. (1995). 'Loyal from Day One: Biodata, Organizational Identification, and Turnover among Newcomers.' *Personnel Psychology,* 48: 309–33.

MAISTER, D. (1993). *Managing the Professional Services Firm.* New York: Free Press.

MARTIN, R. L., and MOLDOVEANU, M. C. (2003). 'Capital versus Talent: The Battle That's Reshaping Business.' *Harvard Business Review,* July: 36–41.

MAY, T. Y., KORCZYNSKI, M., and FRENKEL, S. J. (2002). 'Organizational and Occupational Commitment: Knowledge Workers in Large Organisations.' *Journal of Management Studies*, 39/6: 775–801.

MINTZBERG, H. (1998). 'Covert Leadership: Notes on Managing Professionals.' *Harvard Business Review*, November–December: 140–7.

MORRIS, T. (2000). 'Promotion Policies and Knowledge Bases in the Professional Service Firm.' In M. Peiperl, M. Arthur, R. Goffee, and T. Morris (eds), *Career Frontiers: New Conceptions of Working Lives*. Oxford: Oxford University Press.

MUELLER, F. (1996). 'Human Resources as Strategic Assets: An Evolutionary Resource Based Theory.' *Journal of Management Studies*, 33/6: 757–85.

NAHAPIET, J., and GHOSHAL, S. (1998). 'Social Capital, Intellectual Capital and the Organization Advantage.' *Academy of Management Review*, 23/2: 242–66.

NONAKA, I., TOYAMA, R., and NAGATA, A. (2000). 'A Firm as a Knowledge Creating Entity: A New Perspective on the Theory of the Firm.' *Industrial and Corporate Change*, 9/1: 1–20.

POLANYI, M. (1966). *The Tacit Dimension*. London: Routledge and Kegan Paul.

REED, M. I. (1996). 'Expert Power and Control in Late Modernity: An Empirical Review and Theoretical Synthesis.' *Organization Studies*, 17/4: 573–97.

REICH, R. (1991). *The Work of Nations: Preparing Ourselves for 21st Century Capitalism*. London: Simon and Schuster.

RYLE, G. (1949). *The Concept of Mind*. London: Hutchinson.

SCARBROUGH, H. (1999). 'Knowledge as Work: Conflicts in the Management of Knowledge Workers.' *Technology Analysis and Strategic Management*, 11/1: 5–16.

—— and SWAN, J. (2001). 'Explaining the Diffusion of Knowledge Management: the Role of Fashion.' *British Journal of Management*, 12/1–3: 3–12.

SMITH, K. G., COLLINS, C. J., and CLARK, K. D. (2005). 'Existing Knowledge, Knowledge Creation Capability, and the Rate of New Product Introduction in High-Technology Firms.' *Academy of Management Journal*, 48/2: 346–57.

STARBUCK, W. H. (1992). 'Learning by Knowledge-Intensive Firms.' *Journal of Management Studies*, 29: 713–40.

STEWART, T. A. (1997). *Intellectual Capital. The New Wealth of Organizations*. New York: Doubleday.

STROCK, J., and HILL, P. A. (2000). 'Knowledge Diffusion through Strategic Communities.' *Sloan Management Review*, Winter: 63–74.

SWART, J., and KINNIE, N. (2003). 'Knowledge-Intensive Firms: The Influence of the Client on HR Systems.' *Human Resource Management Journal*, 13/3: 37–55.

—— —— (2004). *Managing the Careers of Professional Knowledge Workers*. London: CIPD.

—— —— and PURCELL, J. (2003). *People and Performance in Knowledge-Intensive Firms*. London: CIPD.

VON GLINOW, M. A. (1988). *New Professionals: Managing Today's High Technology Employees*. Boston: Addison–Wesley.

ZUBOFF, S. (1988). *In the Age of the Smart Machine: The Future of Work and Power*. New York: Basic Books.

# CHAPTER 23

# HRM AND THE NEW PUBLIC MANAGEMENT

STEPHEN BACH

IAN KESSLER

## 23.1 INTRODUCTION

As Human Resource Management (HRM) has developed as a field of study, the attention paid to public sector employment relations has been relatively limited. The preoccupation with the link between HR practice and corporate performance has been less applicable to public service organizations that are answerable to a range of stakeholders and in which HR policy has been geared to ensuring political accountability. There has been a recognition that the public sector confronts fiscal and political pressures that are altering HR practice (Boxall and Purcell 2003: 102–3). However, this observation has rarely been backed up by a sustained focus on people management in the public sector. Alvesson (2004: 12), for example, notes that many public sector organizations are knowledge intensive but, without any apparent justification, chooses to exclude them from his discussion of knowledge work.

This limited attention arises from characteristics of the sector. Defining the public sector is not straightforward because there are differences between countries in terms of the size, scope, and role of the sector. These differences reflect different patterns of ownership with processes of privatization altering the size and scope of the state sector. In many continental European countries health and education are services provided by the independent sector, but in the UK these services remain predominantly in the state sector. Along with the armed forces, the only part of the public sector which all countries share is central government administration, i.e. the core civil service which accounts for much comparative research (Pollitt and Bouckaert 2004). In addition, the relative neglect of the public sector stems from its operating according to distinctive principles and its use of employment practices that have not been viewed as especially innovative.

This analytical gap is regrettable given the size and significance of the public sector workforce. While there are variations between countries, state employees rarely constitute less than 12 percent of the workforce and, in Scandinavia, as much as a quarter or even a third (Pollitt and Bouckaert 2004: 113). Individual organizations in the UK such as the National Health Service (NHS), employ more than 1.3 million employees, five times larger than the UK's largest corporate employer, the retailer Tesco. Moreover, services that include health, education, social welfare, and defence are vital to individual well-being and societal competitiveness. The public sector in the majority of developed countries also has been at the center of a continuous programme of politically sensitive reform (Pollitt and Bouckaert 2004) with major HR implications. As a labour intensive sector the nature and outcome of any change program is inevitably dependent on how staff respond to reform initiatives.

This reform programme has typically been labeled and underpinned by a New Public Management (NPM) approach. The primary purpose of this chapter is to explore the impact of NPM on the management of human resources in the public sector. NPM corresponds to a period of public service reform which swept through many countries during the 1980s and 1990s. This observation generates supplementary questions. The first is whether there are aspects of organizational life in the public sector which combine to produce an enduring and distinctive form of HR practice under any organizational or managerial regime. The second is what form did the management of HR take before public policy attempts to pursue a NPM approach? The third relates to whether we are now entering a post-NPM era of public service reform. If this is the case, what does it mean for people management?

These questions provide the structure for the chapter. The argument presented is straightforward: enduring features of the public sector lend the conduct of HRM a distinctive form, but shifts in the prevailing organizational logic from hierarchy through markets to networks have had important implications for people management in terms of prescription, policy, and practice.

## 23.2 THE CONTEXT

Many of the characteristics of public service employment derive from the unique role of the state as employer. The degree of public scrutiny and the amount of direct and indirect political intervention in public services has no direct equivalent in the private sector. For example, in many countries, especially in southern Europe, the state has been a source of patronage and acted as 'employer of last resort' cushioning many citizens from unemployment, but with detrimental consequences for managerial accountability and efficiency (Bach 1999). The most direct influence of the state relates to the financing of public services which are funded predominantly through mechanisms linked to central or local taxation.

For the last two decades, however, governments have been concerned about the growth of public expenditure and have been reluctant to raise taxation because of the fear of the response of taxpayers and concerns about the potential adverse effect on private investment. Although there is considerable variation, most countries have attempted to exert tighter control on public expenditure and the burden of adjustment has fallen disproportionately on the public sector workforce. These pressures have been reinforced for European Union member countries by the stability and growth pact which restricts member states' fiscal freedom by establishing a 3 percent ceiling for public deficits. Additional fiscal pressures on public service providers arise from the growth in demand for services, alongside severe constraints on income generation because of the strict limits placed on user charges.

This picture is complicated by the distinction that is often made between the trading and non-trading parts of the public sector (Beaumont 1992). The latter are those services, such as education, defence, emergency services, and central government administration, which are integral to national well-being and are sheltered from the market. In contrast, organizations in the trading sector are more marketable services such as postal, telecommunications, and transport services. They often operate at 'arm's length' from central government, but, nonetheless, their presence in the public sector reflects a political judgement that they remain of societal importance and should be sheltered from market competition.

For those services that remain in the public sector, the state is a distinctive employer arising from the public accountability and transparency expected in the use of public funds. Decisions in particular relating to selection and rewards are open to public scrutiny and this has invariably encouraged standardized forms of HR practice (Morris 2000). An important aspect of this accountability concerns the pay and conditions of public sector employees; the state has to reconcile the expectation that it should be a fair employer with its duty to taxpayers as the guardian of the public purse.

In liberal democracies, this accountability occurs through elected party political representatives, found at different societal levels, typically national, regional, and/ or municipal. In federal states, for instance, the USA, Germany, and Australia, lower levels of administration have considerable autonomy compared to the more centralized control in more unified states such as the UK. Because funding is designed to give effect to party programs, representatives are concerned to ensure that their political objectives are met, lending managerial decision within public services an intrinsically political dimension. The effect of the electoral cycle is often prominent with politicians seeking to make their mark pressurizing managers to focus on the achievement of short-term targets. A high-profile example of the consequences of political intervention in public service employment concerns the establishment of the Department of Homeland Security (DHS) in the USA, in the wake of 11 September 2001. President Bush was determined that employees of the proposed DHS should not have the right to join unions or bargain collectively (Masters and Albright 2003).

These contextual features affect the character of the public service workforce. First, public services are highly labour intensive and a substantial proportion of public expenditure comprises labour costs. It is a proportion which hovers between 50 and 70 percent in developed countries (Ingraham et al. 2000: 406). Second, the proportion of women in the workforce has been increasing. Since 1995, across OECD countries, women have made up more than half the public sector workforce and there has also been a substantial growth in the proportion of women with 'high-level responsibilities,' which increased from 14 to 24 percent between 1990 and 2000/1 (OECD 2002: 5–6). In some services, particularly education, the predominance of women is particularly marked. In Italy, for instance, 75 percent of the education workforce is made up of women (Bach et al. 1999).

Third, alongside and related to the gendered nature of the workforce, there is a relatively high proportion of part-time workers. In Denmark, there are more part-time than full-time women workers in the public sector (Bach et al. 1999); in the UK, a third of women in the public services are part-time (Audit Commission 2002), compared to under a quarter in the private sector; this is a pattern repeated in France.

A fourth distinguishing feature relates to occupational composition and the general level of educational attainment. Public servants are relatively well qualified. In the UK, 44 percent have a degree or a high-level vocational qualification; this compares to barely a quarter in the private sector (Audit Commission 2002). An equally striking picture emerges in Spain, where in the public sector 56 percent of employees have a technical, professional, or university qualification, as opposed to 26 percent in the private sector (Bach et al. 1999). The level of qualifications is associated with the presence of many professions in the public sector workforce which include doctors, nurses, social workers, and teachers.

The final distinctive characteristic is associated with the values of public servants with differing views on what motivates them. It is a difference that Le Grand (2003) highlights in categorizing public servants as 'knaves' or 'knights.' Public choice theorists suggest that public servants engage in bureaucracy-maximizing 'knavish' behavior to increase their status and remuneration; a situation facilitated by the absence of competitive pressures or systems of performance management and the availability of a steady stream of public funding (Niskanen 1971). Others view public servants as 'knights' with a distinctive public service ethos comprising a strong commitment to the public interest and a willingness to sacrifice immediate personal gain in pursuing broader welfare goals (Perry and Porter 1982).

There is some evidence indicating that public sector employees are somewhat distinctive from those in the private sector. Crewson (1997) suggests that public servants in the USA are driven more by intrinsic than extrinsic rewards. It is a view which finds some support in the UK, where research amongst municipal workers indicates that a social exchange ideology is complemented by a public service orientation (Coyle Shapiro and Kessler 2004).

## 23.3 TRADITIONAL APPROACHES

These features of the public sector and its workforce have encouraged the development of approaches to public service employment regulation which are distinguishable from those in the private sector. Beaumont (1992) differentiates between two approaches, termed the 'sovereign employer' and the 'model employer' approach, which have underpinned employment relations in the public sector from at least the inception of the modern welfare state in the immediate post-Second World War period to the 1980s. The longevity of these approaches has ensured the development of embedded institutions for the regulation of the employment relationship.

The sovereign employer approach is founded on state control in shaping HR practice. Under such an approach collective bargaining, incorporating the sanction of industrial action, is often absent or modified, so removing this threat. France is an illustration of this approach with the government retaining ultimate authority to unilaterally determine pay and working conditions for established civil servants (*fonctionnaires*) (Bordogna and Winchester 2001: 54). Germany is an example of a modified sovereign employer model with a division between public employees with, and those civil servants (*Beamte*) without, collective bargaining rights.

The model employer approach is based on the state setting an example to other employers on how employees should be treated. The UK provides an example of such an approach and it is reflected in tangible benefits including high levels of job security, good pensions and sick-leave benefits, and a willingness to recognize trade unions. Indeed, more generally, one legacy of this approach is that in many countries trade union density is frequently higher amongst public than private sector employees. In Italy, public sector union density of 45 percent is around 10 percent higher than in the economy as a whole (Bach et al. 1999). The gap is substantially wider in the UK (60 percent compared to less than 20 percent in the private sector (DTI 2005)) and most marked in the USA with public sector union density of 38 percent compared to less than 9 percent in the private sector (Thomason and Burton 2003: 72).

The distinction between the sovereign and model employer approaches should not obscure shared features of public administration. There has been an enduring emphasis on 'fairness' which stems from the need for public accountability and the high degree of probity required of public servants. The search for fairness is reflected in the difficulties of establishing market rates of pay for occupations that have no equivalents in the private sector. In the UK, for many years public sector workers were paid comparable rates to those undertaking similar work in the private sector. Similar principles applied in Germany until the 1990s with changes in pay and conditions for public sector workers covered by collective bargaining agreements, usually transferred to the 38 percent of public sector employees with civil servant (*Beamte*) status (Keller 2005).

Public sector organizations are often viewed in pejorative terms as 'bureaucratic,' but the use of standardized rules enabled government policies to be implemented in a uniform manner with the intention of ensuring political accountability, preventing corruption, and facilitating equality of access for all citizens. A number of employment practices resulted from these goals. Elaborate internal labor markets, high levels of job security, and career progression based primarily on length of service and initial qualifications ensured stability and conformance to explicit procedures.

A further dimension of the public administration tradition relates to the significance of professions in shaping HR practice. Mandated by the state, professional associations have often had a considerable grip on aspects of HR practice, controlling entry into the profession, determining training standards, establishing standards of performance, and in some instances, for example amongst doctors in the UK, awarding merit payments on the basis of peer review. Consequently, the HR issues involved in managing professions were given limited attention because of the tradition of self-regulation and the assumption that public service professionals were motivated by intrinsic rather than extrinsic factors.

Finally, the existence of centralized systems of pay determination usually left little scope for managers to alter employment conditions. Involvement in HR policy was therefore confined to small groups of experts located at central level. In countries in which dedicated personnel managers existed, their role was circumscribed by detailed regulations leaving them a procedural role in implementing national employment rules (Bach 1999). For example in the USA, before the Clinton administration introduced increased devolution into federal government HR practice, the *Federal Personnel Manual* ran to over 10,000 pages of detailed personnel guidance (Moynihan 2003: 380).

This tradition was consolidated during the expansion of the public services which occurred in many countries after 1945. Governments provided their citizens with welfare services to cushion them from the type of economic crisis which emerged with such devastating social consequences in the inter-war years.

Economic growth provided the opportunity to fund the welfare state and the adoption of Keynesian demand management techniques viewed public expenditure as a tool to maintain economic stability. However, as economic and political circumstances shifted from the mid-1970s onwards, the size and scope of the public sector and the management of the workforce was increasingly questioned. The emergence of the new public management (NPM) has become associated with a radical shift in the management of the public sector workforce.

## 23.4 New Public Management and the Employment Relationship

New Public Management has been associated with a number of pressures that have been a catalyst for public sector reform. First, fiscal and social pressures on public services have arisen from the ageing of the population and advances in medical technology in OECD countries. Not only has demand for welfare services increased but there has been increased criticism of the quality of public service provision and the failure to meet citizens' expectations. Governments were confronted with the difficult challenge of 'squaring the circle' of higher demand in a context of fiscal constraint (Foster and Plowden 1996).

Second, in some countries during the 1980s, notably the UK, public service reform was underpinned by a ideological commitment to 'roll back the frontiers' of the state. Such an approach drew heavily on the assumptions underpinning public choice theory with its view of employees as 'knaves' working in inefficient state bureaucracies. Other pioneers of the NPM, especially New Zealand and Australia, with Labour governments ostensibly opposed to the New Right agenda, also vigorously implemented the NPM (Foster and Plowden 1996: 43). President Clinton was also an enthusiastic advocate of some aspects of the NPM.

This combination of pressures gave rise to a set of policy prescriptions labeled the New Public Management. Hood (1991) suggests that the term comprises the following practices:

- Hands-on professional management in the public sector
- Private sector styles of management
- Disaggregation of units
- Greater competition in service provision
- Tighter and more efficient use of resources
- Explicit standards and measures of performance
- Emphasis on output controls.

Reviews of the reform process in OECD countries reveal variation in the uptake and application of the NPM (Pollitt and Bouckaert 2004). An OECD (1996: 23) report reviewing developments in central government noted, 'in the area of human resource management . . . reform strategies are highly context specific and shaped by the cultural and institutional details of each particular country.' In some countries NPM practices were used selectively, but in others such as the UK, they were taken forward in combination. Deployed in this way there are some important linkages between the different practices. To highlight these links, the HR implications are considered under three headings: management, changing organizational structures, and resource utilization.

## 23.4.1 Management

A striking features of NPM has been its emphasis on the establishment of a cadre of managers to enforce a more 'business-like' approach. These managers are ceded greater operational control but are also more subject to centralized forms of audit. To achieve their performance goals, managers were expected to change employment practices, including tighter control of staff, through clearer performance targets linked to individual performance-related pay and more forceful management of issues such as absenteeism. In addition, pay determination was to be devolved to enhance management authority, with rewards more closely linked to local labor market conditions and organizational requirements.

These developments had implications for the career systems of managers as well as for the staff. There has been the growth of senior management roles and chief executive posts (often with experience of the private sector). The emergence of this cadre of managers was especially marked in the UK health service, and between 1985 and 1995 the number of employees categorized as NHS managers rose from 300 to over 23,000 (Kirkpatrick et al. 2005: 91). Senior managers were expected to be change agents, recruited on short-term contracts with substantially higher salaries, but required to achieve demanding performance targets (Ferlie 2002: 284). This trend signals a shift away from a predominantly career-based model of employment in which public servants remain in the public sector for their whole working life. Instead, a position-based system has emerged in which the best-suited candidate is selected for each individual position from internal or external sources. Shifts to position-based systems in the last two decades are most evident in Canada, New Zealand, Sweden, and the UK. There is a danger, however, that countries which have moved away from career-based systems for civil servants have encountered negative consequences in terms of a loss of collective responsibility and a unifying culture (OECD 2004a: 3).

A key aim of the introduction of professional managers was to curb the entrenched power of professionals. It is widely assumed that a tension exists between managers and professionals who have differing goals and orientations. The early NPM literature noted the capacity of professional groups, such as medical staff, to resist the budgetary goals associated with NPM. As these policies became more embedded it is often suggested that professional staff have fared less well in terms of their power, authority, and status (McLaughlin et al. 2002).

Evidence from the UK points to a more nuanced picture. Senior managers have become *increasingly* reliant on professionals to deliver on central government targets and professional control of services remains strong (Kirkpatrick et al. 2005). Nonetheless, professional roles have altered and in the NHS professional staff have been required to undertake more managerial work. Moreover, NPM's emphasis on the development of customer-oriented skills has altered job roles away from an exclusive focus on professionally defined norms. Pay modernization in the NHS is reinforcing this process by placing a premium on softer, interactive competencies such as oral communication; which is defined as a core skill for all health service staff (Bach 2004: 192).

The emphasis on strengthening managerial prerogatives also has implications for employee voice, with the potential to erode trade union influence. A dramatic example of this approach occurred in the UK when the Conservative government announced in 1984 that 4,000 workers at GCHQ (Government Communications Headquarters) could no longer retain their trade union membership. Given an economy-wide decline in union membership and density, it is difficult to evaluate the extent to which this has undermined the position of the public sector unions in Britain. Union density in the public sector has remained relatively high, suggesting an entrenched commitment amongst public servants to a collective voice. There are, however, other signs that union influence may have waned.

The adoption of private sector styles of management is relevant in this respect as the attention focused on performance-related pay (PRP) illustrates. Many governments including those in Canada, the Netherlands, New Zealand, Sweden, the UK, and the USA adopted PRP in some form from the 1980s. Even countries such as France, traditionally viewed as unreceptive to NPM ideas, have been experimenting with PRP for top-level civil servants in six pilot ministries since 2004 (OECD 2005). There are a number of reasons for the adoption of PRP practices. First, characterized by standard pay rates and service-related increments, traditional pay systems were perceived as weak tools for the management of employee performance. PRP was viewed as fostering individual motivation by establishing a link between achievement and rewards. Second, PRP was seen as a means to establish tighter control of the pay bill by reducing across-the-board pay increases and annual increments and, instead, targeting pay increases at high performers. Third, PRP had a political objective in demonstrating that public sector workers are not unaccountable and only receive pay increases linked to performance (OECD 2005).

In practice, the pursuit of these objectives has proved problematic. While the UK government was able to introduce PRP into the civil service where it remained the direct employer, its application to the health service and local government was limited. In the civil service, it is questionable whether PRP was effective. In terms of pay bill control, there was such a strong expectation amongst employees of an across-the-board cost-of-living increase that any attempt to use PRP to motivate employees required supplementary funding to the existing pay bill. Research that examined PRP in the UK Inland Revenue Department cast major doubts on the motivational effects of such schemes (Marsden and Richardson 1994). Adopting the tenets of expectancy theory, the authors found PRP was unlikely to motivate public servants. The setting of tangible performance objectives for public servants is difficult given the range of stakeholders they have to serve and the nature of their work; the clarity of the link between such objectives and pay is likely to be poor given various pay constraints; and typically civil servants place less weight on pay relative to other rewards, especially where the amounts of performance pay available are small.

These findings have been accepted by the OECD, formerly a leading advocate of PRP, and they conclude that 'PRP is unlikely to motivate a substantial majority of staff, irrespective of the design' (OECD 2005: 6). Nonetheless, influenced by the work of Marsden (2004), they argue that PRP has an important role to play in encouraging goal-setting and appraisal, in stimulating managerial change, and in renegotiating effort norms upwards.

## 23.4.2 Changing Organizational Structures

An important component of the NPM comprised changes in organizational structures and the breaking up of monolithic public service organizations into separate units with more devolved management practice. Apart from more direct budget responsibilities, the devolution of responsibility for HR practice to local managers allowed greater scope to alter job roles and develop other forms of flexibility. These developments also enabled line managers to play a more active role in developing workplace reforms (Bach 1999). These forms of organizational fragmentation were often accompanied by competition between service units, designed to produce an operational dynamic which was different from that underpinning the traditional state bureaucracy.

The most visible part of these reforms was a program of privatization in which most of the UK nationalized industries covering gas, water, electricity, steel, and coal had been privatized by 1997. In most cases, privatization led to substantial job losses. Collective bargaining remained the dominant form of pay determination in privatized companies, but it became more decentralized, management grades were often excluded, and the ability of trade unions to mobilize their members diminished. Senior managers experimented with new forms of HRM; some developed more abrasive styles of macho-management designed to marginalize trade unions (e.g. British Airways), whilst others (e.g. in water supply) sought to sustain cooperative relations with unions and the workforce through 'partnership agreements' (O'Connell Davidson 1993; Pendleton 1997).

In the non-trading part of the public sector, the most important component of privatization has been the contracting out or outsourcing of services; a process that has left few countries untouched (Domberger 1998). In the UK, it was mandatory in hospitals and local authorities to competitively tender for catering and cleaning services, a process which placed considerable downward pressure on terms and conditions of employment with especially detrimental effects on the employment conditions of women who tended to predominate in these services (Escott and Whitfield 1985). The process also encouraged the growth of fixed-term employment contracts because of the time-limited nature of service contracts (Corby and White 1999: 120).

Another way in which governments tried to stimulate competition was via the creation of internal markets which separated the purchasers of services from the service providers. This was the approach adopted in the UK where the government created an internal market for health care in the early 1990s, a policy emulated by other health services in countries such as Italy (Anessi-Pessina et al. 2004). While a contrived form of competition, it encouraged managers to uproot traditional patterns of HRM and experiment with changes in work organization, skill mix, and working time (Bach 2004).

A different form of structural change occurred when governments created separate 'agencies,' ministerial bodies managed under contractual arrangements, but with greater autonomy over their financial and HR management. These arrangements were adopted in civil services in Australia, Denmark, Ireland, the Netherlands, and Sweden. In the Dutch case, it was anticipated that by 2004 approximately 80 percent of civil servants would be working in departmental agencies (OECD 1996: 26; 2004b). The UK government established around 200 civil service agencies in the late 1980s. They were seen as analogous to private sector subsidiaries and better able to deliver specific services than if they were part of a larger, more integrated government department.

These new service units typically took on the employer role with a responsibility for many of the policies and practices required to manage employees. This shift in the level of responsibility for HRM had a significant impact, but it is equally apparent that the use made of these HR discretions remained constrained. In the UK, the creation of agencies and the accompanying pay devolution led to the break-up of national pay determination in the civil service and the development of agency-based pay systems. This agency set-up also fragmented career pathways, preventing the kind of seamless movement within and between departments possible under a unified civil service.

More generally, the development of local HR practices in the public services was quite limited (Kessler et al. 2000). Indeed, any local practices adopted often shared similar features, suggesting mimicking or copying. The reluctance of disaggregated service units to use their HR discretions can be related to a number of factors, as the experience of pay determination illustrates. First, the expertise of local HR specialists and trade unionists was limited, considering the legacy of centralized pay determination, which restricted their scope to take advantage of devolution. There was also inadequate specialist HR capacity and trade union organization at this level and it is not clear that general managers were always willing to involve HR specialists or union representatives in employment matters.

Second, many managers were unwilling to exercise their HR discretion because they believed that local variation would cause more problems that it would resolve. In NHS trusts and local authorities, employers successfully resisted government calls to develop local bargaining. They saw little benefit in implementing a policy that was opposed by trade unions and which would antagonize the workforce. In the absence of additional resources 'to pay for change,' they were also concerned about the administrative costs associated with local pay determination and anxious to avoid the pay 'leapfrogging' that might arise in a more 'balkanized' pay set-up (Bach and Winchester 1994).

There were also instances where employers were unable to develop local practices. In the case of the civil service executive agencies, pay devolution remained heavily constrained by Treasury control over pay mandates, limiting the money available and how it could be spent. More generally, the issue of political accountability placed limits on the risks that service units were prepared to take in the developments of new HR practices. The OECD (1996: 27) noted:

In each of the countries, traditional public sector values of merit, equity, fairness and ethical behaviour continue to influence human resource policies and practices. These values constrain the risks executives and managers are prepared to take. They remain aware that their employment policies may become subject to closer public scrutiny than would likely be applied to a private sector firm and that they must not needlessly expose their Minister or other public official to risk through unacceptable or controversial practices.

### 23.4.3 Resource Utilization

The values which the OECD Report suggests continue to underpin HR practice should not obscure the emphasis on a tighter control of resources, not least staff costs. There have been workforce reductions across a number of countries, particularly in central government. Between the mid-1980s and 1990s, employment in central government fell by around 30 percent in Germany and the UK, by 16 percent in Australia, and by 10 percent in Sweden (Ingraham et al. 2000: 395). These reductions were clearly eroding the traditional job security of public servants, particularly when allied to the growth of fixed-term working associated with the competitive pressures noted earlier.

Drawing upon some of the distinctions made in the HR literature on management styles, this focus on the efficient use of human resources has more in common with a cost minimization than a high-commitment approach to HRM (Purcell and Ahlstrand 1994). Indeed, if personnel specialists in the new disaggregated service units were involved in any activity, it was not so much devising new HR practices which met local 'business' needs but in ensuring that labor costs were reduced by tackling sickness absence and altering the composition of the workforce (Kessler et al. 2000).

The pressures faced by the public sector workforce have been exacerbated by the performance and audit regimes. In addition to encouraging a short-term approach to people management, the target culture has affected staff morale. Kirkpatrick et al. (2005: 176) highlight findings from the UK's 1998 Workplace Employment Relations Survey which showed that public sector workers were more likely than employees in the private sector to experience stress and be absent through illness. Guest and Conway (2002) reported that 'levels of satisfaction, trust and commitment are all lower in the public sector.' Most significant are the detrimental consequences for recruitment and retention, particularly for professional groups such as nurses, social workers, and teachers. Between 1995 and 1999, the number of applications to social work fell by 55 percent and, between 1996 and 2003, the vacancy rate for social workers rose from 6.4 to 11 percent (TOPSS 2003).

# 23.5 BEYOND THE NPM

In the last few years, the NPM has lost some of its potency and its contradictions have become more visible (Hood and Peters 2004). This shift of perspective is exemplified in recent OECD publications which have moved from wholesale endorsement to a much more critical stance of the key assumptions of the NPM:

While it is important to have better goals, targets and measures in government, we must recognise that such a highly formalised approach has severe limitations for complex activities. ... There is a danger that the constitutional, legal, cultural and leadership factors which together create what is important and distinctive about public services and the people who work in them, are not considered or, worse, are dismissed as the bureaucratic problem which must be 'reformed.' (OECD 2003: 4–5)

These comments reflect a belief that a 'post NPM' era is emerging. If the traditional organizational logic in the public sector was based on bureaucracy and that under NPM was founded on markets, the emergent managerial form is seen as being underpinned by networks. The emphasis represents a shift from 'government' to 'governance' which focuses on who makes public decisions and how these decisions are implemented to safeguard constitutional values. Governance signals that a wider range of agencies and stakeholders from within and beyond the public sector are becoming involved in service delivery. This raises new managerial challenges in dealing with a diverse array of stakeholders, including the workforce. Three features of this governance or network approach and their consequences for people management are analyzed:

- An emphasis on user-centered services
- The pursuit of a 'partnership' approach
- An increased emphasis on service quality and performance.

## 23.5.1 User-Centered Services

The user-centered approach to service provision marks a degree of continuity with aspects of the NPM in focusing on a shift from a producer culture to 'consumer'-sensitive services. Many governments, extending beyond the usual NPM exemplars to include Belgium and India, have introduced service charters and performance pledges designed to inculcate in employees the need to serve customers. Whereas under the NPM the emphasis was on individual citizen entitlement to services, there has been a shift of emphasis within service charters towards collective, civic obligations (Drewry 2005). In other words, the citizen has responsibilities (e.g. for their health) as well as rights, perhaps reducing a concern that aggrieved 'customers' will take out their dissatisfaction directly on public sector workers, a justifiable worry taking account of increases in violence against front-line public sector workers.

The attachment of the UK government to ratings and 'league tables' of organizational performance is integral to this approach and seeks to enhance 'choice.' Such an approach also has crucial implications for work organization. This is reflected in the establishment of 'One Stop Shops' providing the service user with a single gateway to a range of services. Often accessible by telephone or on-line, such a service not only requires different skill sets, with employees now having to deal with a wide range of queries, but it has often been provided by call centers and in a new type of working environment.

This type of user-centered approach has challenged traditional work practices. The NHS illustrates the degree to which national policy makers in the UK have continued to confront the 'privileged' position of professionals as reflected in protected job boundaries. For instance, in the UK, the power of doctors has been addressed by extending the authority of nurses to dispense certain treatments. Where recent attacks on the professions have differed from those in the past has been in the way in which they have alternated with a government willingness to engage with professional concerns. It is this more placatory government approach which can be seen as one element of the greater emphasis on 'partnership.'

## 23.5.2 Partnership

In recent debates on the reform of the public sector, the term 'partnership' has been center stage, signifying attempts to move away from adversarial relations towards mutuality. This was a key goal of President Clinton's promotion of partnership working in the federal government, a policy revoked by President Bush (Masters and Albright 2003). The term has been used in various ways. First, it reflects government attempts to ally itself with professionals by stressing its concern to try to improve their working lives. The UK government has used this rationale to justify its pursuit of more flexible work practices, notably amongst the school workforce. A workforce remodeling agreement has challenged professional job boundaries by giving whole class responsibilities to a new teaching assistant role but at the same time it has guaranteed that certain administrative 'burdens' are removed from teachers.

This new relationship with professionals is part of a broader attempt to develop a new partnership relationship with the public sector workforce. While in the UK the user is still privileged in public policy discourse, it is now recognized that user interests are best served not by the vilification of producers but by encouraging their engagement in the delivery of better services. As the British government has stressed, 'we will value public service, not denigrate it' (Cabinet Office 1999: 7). To this end, the 'model' employer approach has been resurrected, not so much as a means of setting an example to the private sector but more by 'using the example of best modern employment practice' to improve the quality of work life for its staff (Department of Health 1998: para.2.4).

How far the UK government has delivered on this rhetoric is debatable. The pay position of employees in local government and health has been improved. Survey data also suggests that public sector employees are much more likely to be communicated with and informed than those in the private sector (Kersley et al. 2005). Two-thirds of public sector workers are covered by a staff survey, while the figure is barely a third in the private sector. However, this data suggests that there has not been a major shift in levels of employee involvement across the public services over recent years.

The term partnership has also emerged in government attempts to change its relationship with the trade unions. The UK government's attitude towards the unions has vacillated, displaying a degree of ambiguity. At times the government has suggested a firm commitment to working closely with the unions. 'We recognise the contribution they [the unions] can and do make to achieving shared goals. We will continue to work in partnership with them' (Cabinet Office 1999: 55). More tangibly, recent pay agreements in health and local government have formally endorsed union partnership working at the workplace level. However, the government has continued to push through public service reforms particularly around private sector involvement in public services which has angered the unions, while at the workplace level there is evidence to suggest that partnership working is often based on a restricted form of union involvement (Bach 2004). Related concerns about management commitment, the degree of union representativeness, and the expertise of both parties have been viewed as barriers to partnership working in the US federal government (Masters and Albright 2003: 203).

The final form of partnership relates to new modes of service delivery and in particular to an approach which is based on the provision of services by a range of organizations working together. Within the public sector, this inter-organizational working has been equated with a 'joined-up' approach within government, but it has also embraced joint working between organizations in the public, independent, and private sectors. These forms of partnership mark a retreat from key elements of the NPM approach with a reliance on disaggregated service units giving way to a greater emphasis on integrated working. Moreover, the privileging of market forces and private sector practices now succumbs to a more pragmatic, mixed approach where 'what works best is used.' This approach is not confined to the UK as recent experience in the Netherlands and elsewhere testifies (Kickert 2003).

Within the public sector, a 'joined-up' approach has heralded a reaffirmation of national employment relations institutions. This is reflected in national pay agreements in health and local government which provide a framework for major pay reform. It has also been apparent in the development of more coordinated and integrated approaches to HRM in these parts of the public service with the development of national HR strategies. In addition, greater cross-organizational working raises possible tensions between HR values, systems, and practices. As agencies from different (sub) sectors come together, how do they align their deeply embedded HR approaches? For example, the UK government's attempt to develop an integrated workforce devoted to children raises questions related to how major procedural and substantives differences in pay between social workers, teachers, and various health workers are to be addressed.

## 23.5.3 Performance

Public service performance has remained central to the reform agenda across OECD countries (OECD 2003). However, there have been shifts in discourse and practice which have seen aspects of the NPM approach deepened and others given a different emphasis. Organizational performance has been increasingly related not only to the efficient but also the effective use of resources as reflected in higher-quality public services. To this end, a continued, if not greater, reliance has been placed on performance targets allied to a more explicit recognition that improved organizational performance in a service context is dependent on improved employee performance. The irony lies in the fact that a service culture still driven by performance measures has made it more difficult to elicit the type of employee performance needed to produce better-quality services.

An interest in the organizational-employee performance nexus has led to a growing concentration on employee skills. This can be seen in attempts to develop a more planned approach to service delivery, involving workforce planning and a more considered approach to the development of employee skills. While the early phases of modernization encouraged a focus on management development (Bach 1999), a wider skills deficit has forced an emphasis on targeted overseas recruitment and a focus on developing skills throughout the workforce. This emphasis is reflected in the recent agreements reached in local government and health in the UK where 'skills escalators' have been introduced to provide opportunities for employee career progression.

These attempts to develop the public sector skill base flow through to affect other HR practices. They require the creation of clear career pathways and the dedicated application of performance appraisal systems which help staff with their skills development. This is a commitment-based HR agenda which, in focusing on employee development, contrasts sharply with the cost minimization approach of the NPM era.

At the same time, such attempts are based on heroic assumptions about the willingness of employees to develop their careers in these ways. More profoundly, they sit in tension with pressures which the performance and audit framework continue to generate. In particular, performance targets continue to structure the working lives of public servants, generating cumbersome procedures and 'mountains' of paperwork which undermine morale. The principal reason for ongoing recruitment and retention difficulties relates to perceived 'burdens' associated with performance targets (Audit Commission 2002).

# 23.6 Conclusion

In recent years, the public sector in most countries has been caught up in a continuous process of reform that has major consequences for HR practice. The rise of the NPM movement signified a rejection of traditional models of HRM in the public sector. The establishment of a more assertive managerialism in conjunction with tighter control of resources, forms of marketization, and changes in organizational structures ensured that the burden of adjustment was placed squarely on the workforce. Although in many countries the public sector became more efficient, for the workforce this efficiency drive was mainly associated with more intensive working practices, downsizing, tighter control of performance, and the dilution of union influence. In terms of HR practice, there have been attempts to 'deprivilege' the employment conditions of public sector workers and there has been a degree of convergence between employment practices in the public and private sector.

In recent years, some of the unexpected consequences of the NPM have increasingly been acknowledged. These difficulties often stemmed from a failure of the NPM reforms to recognize that HR practice has both to facilitate the efficient delivery of public services and also to enshrine deeper constitutional values that make up an irreducible political core at the heart of the public sector. Ironically, some of the much derided features of the traditional 'bureaucratic' model of HR practice are being reinvented as the limitations of a fragmented and narrowly focused target approach are recognized. More emphasis is being placed on valuing the workforce and, in the UK case, the modernization agenda explicitly seeks to shift from a cost minimization approach to one modeled on the 'high-performance workplace.' The extent to which this agenda can be implemented effectively will shape HR practice in the years to come.

## REFERENCES

ALVESSON, A. (2004). *Knowledge Work and Knowledge Intensive Firms.* Oxford: Oxford University Press.

ANESSI-PESSINA, E., CANTU, E., and JOMMI, C. (2004). 'Phasing out Market Mechanisms in the Italian National Health Service.' *Public Money and Management,* August: 309–16.

Audit Commission (2002). *Recruitment and Retention.* London: Audit Commission.

BACH, S. (1999). 'Personnel Managers: Managing to Change.' In S. Corby and G. White (eds.), *Employee Relations in the Public Services.* London: Routledge.

—— (2004). *Employment Relations in the NHS: The Management of Reforms.* London: Routledge.

—— and WINCHESTER, D. (1994). 'Opting out of Pay Devolution? The Prospects for Local Pay Bargaining in UK Public Services.' *British Journal of Industrial Relations,* 32/2: 264–82.

—— BORDOGNA, L., DELLA ROCCA, G., and WINCHESTER, D. (eds.) (1999). *Public Service Employment Relations in Europe.* London: Routledge.

BEAUMONT, P. (1992). *Public Sector Industrial Relations.* London: Routledge.

BORDOGNA, L., and WINCHESTER, D. (2001). 'Collective Bargaining in Western Europe.' In C. Dell'Aringa, G. Della Rocca, and B. Keller (eds.), *Strategic Choices in Reforming Public Service Employment.* Basingstoke: Palgrave.

BOXALL, P., and PURCELL, J. (2003). *Strategy and Human Resource Management.* Basingstoke: Palgrave.

Cabinet Office (1999). *Modernising Government.* London: HMSO.

CORBY, S., and WHITE, G. (eds.) (1999). *Employee Relations in the Public Services.* London: Routledge.

COYLE SHAPIRO, J., and KESSLER, I. (2004). 'Beyond Exchange.' Paper presented to the Academy of Management, New Orleans.

CREWSON, P. (1997). 'Public Service Motivation: Building Empirical Evidence of the Incidence and Effect.' *Journal of Public Administration Research and Theory*, 7: 499–518.

Department of Health (1998). *Working Together*. London: HMSO.

DOMBERGER, S. (1998). *The Contracting Organization: A Strategic Guide to Outsourcing*. Oxford: Oxford University Press.

DREWRY, G. (2005). 'Citizen's Charters: Service Quality Chameleons.' *Public Management Review*, 7/3: 321–40.

DTI (2005). *Trade Union Membership, 2004*. London: DTI.

ESCOTT, K., and WHITFIELD, D. (1995). *The Gender Impact of CCT in Local Government*. London: HMSO.

FERLIE, E. (2002). 'Quasi Strategy: Strategic Management in the Contemporary Public Sector.' In A. Pettigrew, H. Thomas, and R. Whittington (eds.), *Handbook of Strategy and Management*. London: Sage.

FOSTER, C., and PLOWDEN, F. (1996). *The State under Stress*. Buckingham: Open University Press.

GUEST, D., and CONWAY, N. (2002). *The State of the Psychological Contract*. London: CIPD.

HOOD, C. (1991). 'A Public Management for All Seasons.' *Public Administration*, 69/1: 3–19.

—— and PETERS, G. (2004). 'The Middle Aging of New Public Management: Into the Age of Paradox.' *Journal of Public Administration Research and Theory*, 14/3: 267–82.

INGRAHAM, P., et al. (2000). 'Public Employment and the Future of Public Service.' In G. Peters and D. Savoie (eds.), *Governance in the Twenty-First Century*. Montreal: Canadian Centre for Management Development.

KELLER, B. (2005). 'Changing Employment Relations in the Public Sector.' *European Industrial Relations Review*, 376/May: 27–30.

KERSLEY, B., et al. (2005). *Inside the Workplace*. London: DTI.

KESSLER, I., and PURCELL, J. (1996). 'Strategic Choice and New Forms of Employment Relations in the Public Service Sector.' *International Journal of Human Resource Management*, 7/1: 206–29.

—— —— and COYLE SHAPIRO, J. (2000). 'New Forms of Employment Relations in the Public Services.' *Industrial Relations Journal*, 31/1: 17–34.

KICKERT, W. (2003). 'Beyond Public Management: Shifting Frames of Reference in Administrative Reforms in the Netherlands.' *Public Management Review*, 5/3: 377–99.

KIRKPATRICK, I.. ACKROYD, S., and WALKER, R. (2005). *The New Managerialism and Public Service Professions*. Basingstoke: Palgrave.

LE GRAND, J. (2003). *Motivation, Agency and Public Policy*. Oxford: Oxford University Press.

MCLAUGHLIN, K., OSBORNE, S., and FERLIE, E. (eds.) (2002). *New Public Management: Current Trends and Future Prospects*. London: Routledge.

MARSDEN, D. (2004). 'The Role of Performance-Related Pay in Renegotiating the "Effort Bargain": The Case of the British Public Sector.' *Industrial and Labor Relations Review*, 57/3: 350–70.

—— and RICHARDSON, R. (1994). 'Performance Pay: The Effects of Merit Pay on Motivation in the Public Services.' *British Journal of Industrial Relations*, 32/2: 243–61.

MASTERS, M., and ALBRIGHT, R. (2003). 'Federal Labor—Management Partnerships: Perspectives, Performance and Possibilities.' In J. Brock and D. Lipsky (eds.), *Going*

*Public: The Role of Labor Management Relations in Delivering Quality Government Services.* Urbana: University of Illinois, IRRA Series.

MORRIS, G. (2000). 'Employment in Public Services: The Case for Special Treatment.' *Oxford Journal of Legal Studies*, 20/2: 167–83.

MOYNIHAN, D. (2003). 'Public Management Policy Change in the United States during the Clinton Era.' *International Public Management Journal*, 6/3: 371–94.

NISKANEN, W. (1971). *Bureaucracy and Representative Government.* Chicago: Aldine-Atherton.

O'CONNELL DAVIDSON, J. (1993). *Privatization and Employment Relations: The Case of the Water Industry.* London: Mansell.

OECD (1996). *Integrating People Management into Public Service Reform.* Paris: OECD.

—— (2002). *Highlights of Public Sector Pay and Employment Trends: 2002 Update.* Paris: OECD.

—— (2003). *Policy Brief: Public Sector Modernization.* Paris: OECD.

—— (2004a). *Policy Brief: Public Sector Modernisation: Modernising Public Employment.* Paris: OECD.

—— (2004b). *Policy Brief: Public Sector Modernisation: Changing Organizational Structures.* Paris: OECD.

—— (2005). *Policy Brief: Paying for Performance: Policies for Government Employees.* Paris: OECD.

PENDLETON, A. (1997). 'What Impact Has Privatisation Had on Pay and Employment? A Review of the UK Experience.' *Relations industrielles*, 52/3: 554–79.

PERRY, J., and PORTER, L. (1982). 'Factors Affecting the Context for Motivation in Public Organizations.' *Academy of Management Review*, 7: 89–98.

POLLITT, C., and BOUCKAERT, G. (2004). *Public Management Reform.* Oxford: Oxford University Press.

PURCELL, J., and AHLSTRAND, B. (1994). *Human Resource Management in the Multidivisional Company.* Oxford: Oxford University Press.

RING, P., and PERRY, J. (1985). 'Strategic Management in Public and Private Organizations: Implications of Distinctive Contexts and Constraints.' *Academy of Management Review*, 10/2: 276–86.

THOMASON, T., and BURTON, J. (2003). 'Unionization Trends and Labor–Management Co-operation in the Public Sector.' In J. Brock and D. Lipsky (eds.), *Going Public: The Role of Labor Management Relations in Delivering Quality Government Services.* Urbana: University of Illinois, IRRA Series.

TOPSS (2003). *London Workforce Survey and Partnership Mapping Analysis.* London: TOPSS.

# CHAPTER 24

# MULTINATIONAL COMPANIES AND GLOBAL HUMAN RESOURCE STRATEGY

## WILLIAM N. COOKE

## 24.1 INTRODUCTION

THE growth and spread of multinational companies around the world over the last two to three decades has been nothing short of extraordinary. Indeed, since 1980 there has been a nearly twelve fold increase in foreign direct investment (FDI) and a greater than eight fold increase in the number of multinational companies (MNCs). As of 2004 there were over 61,000 MNCs with ownership in over 900,000 foreign affiliated operations worldwide. These foreign affiliates alone employed more than 54 million employees, managed over $US 31 trillion in assets, generated over $US 17 trillion in sales, and accounted for roughly 33 percent of worldwide exports and 10 percent of gross domestic product (UNCTAD 2004: 8–9

I thank Chris Brewster, Anthony Ferner, Steve Frenkel, Paul Marginson, Sully Taylor, and the editors for helpful suggestions in drafting this chapter.

and Table B.3, p. 376). The ever expanding reach of MNCs in an increasingly competitive and uncertain global market place puts the multinational enterprise at the center of a widening public debate and scrutiny regarding the impact of MNCs on the global economy, on the well-being of workers and communities across the globe, and on the earth's natural resources and environment. This broader and heated debate notwithstanding, the continual expansion of multinational operations undoubtedly raises a host of questions about the critical role of managing human resources across borders.

The focus of this chapter is on the salient human resource strategy issues and dynamics that come into play as a function of the multinational reach of companies. Although the overall objectives of formulating and implementing HR strategies as described throughout this volume are the same for national and multinational companies, global HR strategies must take into account factors germane to direct investments made abroad and the management of cross-border operations. At question herein, therefore, is: What factors or considerations are unique to companies operating across borders and what are the implications of these factors in regard to the successful development and deployment of global HR strategies?

The existing literature in regard to global HR strategies can be characterized as being in an early stage of development. To date, there have been important insights into the management of human resources on a global basis but as a body of literature it remains somewhat fragmented in its foci and suffers from the lack of attention to building a widely embraced and comprehensive analytical framework; one that pulls together the varied mix of decision-making that goes into the formulation and implementation of global HR strategies. My primary objective in this chapter, therefore, is to offer a reasonably coherent and comprehensive (albeit, highly simplified) analytical framework that captures and integrates the salient strategic decisions MNCs face in *formulating* global HR strategies. This broader focus precludes any detailed review and analyses of the various components of such a framework and underlying issues of strategy implementation. Nevertheless, my aim in venturing to articulate a fairly encompassing framework is to stimulate further discussion and debate about how we can better frame our enquiries and analyses to improve our broader theoretical and practical understanding of global strategic HR issues.

## 24.2 AN ANALYTICAL FRAMEWORK

Understanding the decision-making and choices made by MNCs in regard to global HR strategies requires understanding both the primary objectives that motivate managerial behavior and the prominent factors that influence or constrain managers as they act to achieve their primary objectives. We can begin by assuming that companies are in business to optimize profits. At a minimum, companies must achieve profitability levels sufficient to just satisfy owners and shareholders, which at any point in time may equate to mere survival. Optimization beyond this minimum threshold requires that companies create competitive advantages, which translate into a range of superior and sustainable profitability outcomes. The ability of companies to optimize profitability is bounded, of course, by constraints placed on them by the broader economic and socio-political environments within which they compete and which are never static.

Within these constraints, we can further assume that in the pursuit of optimizing profits, management *seeks to act* rationally. That is, management is calculative in weighing the benefits and costs associated with the formulation and implementation of alternative strategies. Invariably bounded by imperfect information and foresight, and facing persistent changes in the broader environment, management adjusts strategies in response to observed or anticipated changes in the broader environment, to unforeseen circumstances encountered, to trial-and-error activities that fall short of anticipated net benefits, and to mistakes invariably made. Successful companies, therefore, must be flexible and adaptable, as well as have their eyes on continuously improving performance. Although managers may not always act rationally in the pursuit of profit optimization, companies that are better able to formulate, implement, and adjust their strategies in economically rational ways are rewarded by the market place and those that are less able to do so are penalized by the market place. The socio-political contexts within which companies compete can also mete out penalties and rewards for failing to act or for acting in socially responsible ways.

With these assumptions of optimizing behavior and constraints in mind, I have attempted to diagram in Fig. 24.1 the broader context within which global HR strategies are formulated and pursued. Central to this framework, MNCs face the task of sorting through how best to formulate, implement, and adjust global HR strategies that align effectively with their more encompassing worldwide business and investment strategies. Alignment of HR and business strategies includes strategic assessments of human resource and technological capabilities in regard to MNC choices about market positioning, about where to invest, and about the diffusion of optimal HRM policies and practices; choices that necessarily span host and home locations. These global HR strategies, moreover, are influenced directly by both home and host country industrial relations (IR) systems and union strategies, as well as indirectly by the market and socio-political contexts within which MNCs compete globally and which they attempt to influence in their favor (see Frenkel 2005, for example, on this latter point).

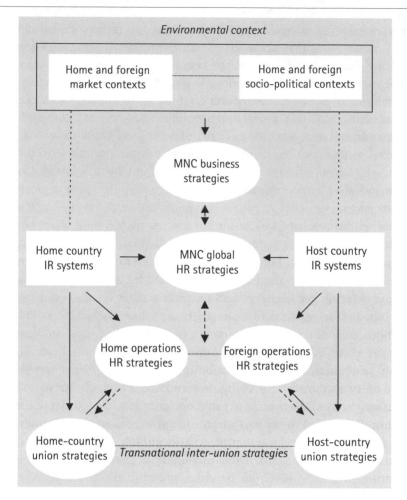

**Fig. 24.1. An analytical framework**

## 24.2.1 The Influence of HR Considerations on FDI Decisions

Key to any analysis of global HR strategies is FDI, investments that include minority, joint, and majority ownership arrangements and vary by whether they are made in 'greenfield' sites or by merger and acquisition. As treated in the economics literature, companies engaging in FDI believe they enjoy some 'ownership' advantage(s) over competitors operating in other countries, advantages they can exploit abroad. In exploiting ownership advantages, decisions about where and how much to invest across alternative locations are a matter of comparative 'location' advantages. Included among these potential location advantages are market size, proximity to customers, infrastructure, investment incentives, taxation, ease of divestment, and labor costs (e.g. Dunning 1993; Casson and Buckley 1998).

Cast within the business strategy literature, 'ownership' advantages can be translated into 'competitive' advantages, which can be exploited by MNCs strategically positioning themselves in their global markets (i.e. via cost leadership vs. differentiation, defensive vs. offensive, and narrower vs. wider scope positioning). Regardless of the primary market-positioning objectives underlying FDI decisions, MNCs seeking to act rationally will take into account the unit labor cost differences across alternative host locations. Several recent studies yield strong and highly consistent evidence that MNCs typically (but not always) invest less than they would otherwise in those countries in which IR systems are characterized by factors viewed by employers as driving up unit labor costs; either directly or indirectly by restricting the freedom of employers to manage human resources (e.g. Cooke and Noble 1998; Cooke 2001a; Bognanno et al. 2005).

More specifically, the evidence generally shows that, all else the same, MNCs invest less in countries with lower average levels of education and higher average hourly compensation costs. This finding is consistent with the expectation that MNCs invest more in countries in which unit labor costs, not just hourly compensation costs, are lower as a result of productivity differences. MNCs also invest less in countries that place more restrictive workplace policies and regulations on management's discretion to direct the workplace (e.g. in regard to lay-offs and the imposition of works councils). Furthermore, MNCs invest less than they would otherwise in countries in which collective bargaining contexts would be perceived as more constraining. Here, we find that countries having higher levels of union penetration and in which contract negotiation structures are centralized beyond the company-wide level (mainly at the industry-wide level) attract less FDI than they would otherwise. Finally, some evidence indicates that FDI is lower in countries with records of greater labor–management conflict, as evidenced by lost days of work due to work stoppages.

In summary, it appears that MNCs generally take into account HR considerations in deciding where and how much to invest across alternative host locations. Although the statistical estimates in these studies indicate that IR system factors have substantial effects on FDI decisions, these studies do not provide much insight into actual challenges faced when MNCs attempt to introduce new HRM policies and practices to their foreign subsidiaries. Yet, to the extent that MNCs find it more or less costly to implement preferred HRM policies and practices in some foreign locations than in others (treated as the 'ease in exploiting' ownership advantages in the economics literature), MNCs seeking to act rationally will invest more in those locations in which the local capacity and receptivity to organizational change are greater.

## 24.2.2 The Diffusion of Preferred HRM Strategies Abroad

To take a closer look at the issues and dynamics that unfold in managing human resources abroad, we can turn to a growing and largely case study literature about the diffusion of preferred HR strategies to foreign locations. At the center of decisions regarding diffusion, the home offices of MNCs can expect to encounter local isomorphic pressures from foreign locations to maintain long-embedded localized workplace policies and practices (Ferner and Quintanilla 1998). As argued by Kostova (1999), the successful diffusion of new HRM policies and practices will be more difficult or costly to achieve, the greater the differences in workplace cultures, norms, customary practices, laws, and institutional arrangements between the country-of-origin and host country locations. The degree of local resistance, therefore, will be a factor of how radical or extensive any change the parent seeks to achieve at the subsidiary level.

It appears from numerous case studies and a few cross-sectional surveys of such efforts that the extent of diffusion varies widely along a continuum. At the one extreme of the continuum, Bird et al. (1998) report that some Japanese MNCs have been insistent on and successful in replicating home-based HRM systems across their foreign subsidiaries. Believing that their HRM systems offer substantial competitive advantage, these MNCs have engaged in intensive efforts to mold foreign workplaces to their satisfaction via extensive recruitment and selection activities coupled with substantial reorientation and training for both managers and employees. By way of further example, McDonald's has been largely successful in diffusing its HR strategy throughout its chain of European fast-food restaurants. According to Royle and Towers (2003), however, to minimize local resistance to the diffusion of its uniform worldwide policies, McDonald's has apparently circumvented long-standing, institutionalized forms of employee representation. In particular, Royle and Towers conclude that it has aggressively deterred employee interest in union representation, has avoided compliance with collective bargaining agreements, and has either evaded creating or maneuvered to dominate local and national works councils.

At the other extreme of the continuum, some MNCs have apparently found that the anticipated benefits do not outweigh the costs of overcoming local resistance to the diffusion of HRM practices from abroad and, thus, have decided against or abandoned efforts to transfer preferred HRM practices. For example, in their study of Japanese television assembly transplants in the USA, Kenney and Tanaka (2003) found that MNCs abandoned their efforts to diffuse their preferred Japanese-style 'learning bureaucracies,' characterized as work environments placing primary focus on creating learning environments in which all employees actively contribute to continuously improving performance. According to the authors, American traditions and cultures manifested in Fordist workplace systems (governed by hierarchical job protection and seniority rights and distinct divisions between management and labor) proved to be too deeply rooted in acquired plants to justify or allow for the diffusion of preferred HR strategies that emphasized extensive training in problem-solving, active suggestion programs, and off-line small group activities such as quality control circles. Similarly, Brewster and Tregaskis (2003) found in their cross-sectional study of MNCs with operations in several European countries that the institutional and cultural antecedents of host locations effectively blocked foreign MNCs from diffusing contingent employment practices (e.g. the hiring of part-time, temporary, and fixed-term contract employees) beyond what was customary in given locales.

In between these extremes on the continuum, MNCs have simply maintained some highly embedded policies and practices in their foreign locales while transferring to them other policies core to the parent's preferred HR strategies. Policies diffused, however, are often modified in practice to varying degrees to accommodate local workplace cultures and institutional arrangements. For example, in their study of a UK–US-owned pharmaceutical MNC, Edwards et al. (2005) describe how the corporate headquarters' efforts to diffuse preferred HRM practices (variable pay tied to job grading and performance) were met with local resistance. They found, however, that locales were marked by sufficient degrees of 'malleability,' which allowed the MNC to structure alternative practices largely in line with its preferred policies. In a similar vein, Gamble (2003) found that even in light of the cultural distance between Chinese and UK workplaces, the efforts of a British-owned retail firm to transfer preferred HRM practices to China were largely successful, but nonetheless, shaped by 'subtle and ineluctable processes of transformation.' A study of US-owned AT&T's effort to diffuse a universal, corporate-wide cultural change program in its Scottish NCR subsidiary demonstrates, furthermore, how critical it is that corporate executives create sufficient incentives and provide convincing justification for change in order to gain the support of local managers and employees (Martin et al. 2003).

It is apparent, furthermore, that unions have played central roles in resisting the diffusion of preferred HRM policies and practices abroad. In the Florida and Kenney (1991) study of automobile manufacturing, US unions were unwilling to accept the individualized pay systems based on merit and seniority sought by Japanese-owned MNCs. In the Kenney and Tanaka (2003) study of television assembly plants, US unions played a role in blocking the transfer of the preferred Japanese HRM system. In their study of German subsidiaries of US- and UK-owned MNCs, Schmitt and Sadowski (2003) found that subsidiaries were more likely to retain existing collective bargaining and co-determination practices than they were to retain existing HRM practices the parents sought to change. One can draw from these and other analyses that unions by the nature of their function as representatives of affected employees and by the countervailing power they enjoy are more inclined and/or better able to resist management initiatives at transforming workplaces than are unrepresented foreign locations.

Based on this literature, it would appear that MNCs should anticipate encountering barriers and at least some resistance across their foreign subsidiaries to any HRM changes sought, especially in the case of unionized sites. It follows that MNCs need to make cost–benefit calculations of the expected net gain derivable from substituting preferred or modified HRM practices for existing practices in their subsidiaries. Only if there were a sufficient net gain achievable after subtracting out the costs of transforming the workplaces of their foreign locales would MNCs rationally pursue the diffusion of preferred HRM policies and practices abroad.

## 24.2.3 Taking Union Representation into Account

As discussed, MNCs generally attempt to limit their exposure to union representation and collective bargaining, believing that the 'efficiency' gains achievable from operating without union representation are greater than the 'voice' gains achievable from operating with union representation. The presumption that unions in general are on net costly appears to carry over into the global HR strategies pursued by MNCs where they have invested abroad. Based on a number of recent studies, it is apparent that many if not most MNCs attempt to avoid union representation across their foreign operations when the costs of avoidance are not viewed as too high. For example, Purcell et al. (1999) found that MNCs did not strongly resist union representation in the manufacturing sector when it appeared that the costs of avoidance outweighed the benefits. In contrast, where the costs of union avoidance in the finance and tourism sectors were not seen as high, Japanese MNCs aggressively avoided union representation of their subsidiaries. In their study of five US-owned MNCs with subsidiaries in the UK, Ferner et al. (2005), likewise, found that decisions to avoid union representation are dependent on a mix of factors influencing the capacity and costs associated with avoidance. Similarly, numerous other studies indicate that MNCs have made concerted efforts to avoid unions, for example, regarding German-owned MNCs with subsidiaries in the UK (Beaumont et al. 1990) and European and Japanese-owned MNCs in the USA (Cooke 2001b). Furthermore, by pitting unionized operations against other unionized and non-union operations as each vies for limited investment and jobs, MNCs have positioned themselves to extract concessions from their unionized operations at home and abroad (see e.g. Marginson and Sisson 2002; Martinez Lucio and Weston 1994).

The crux for unions representing the workforces of given MNC operations is either to compete with each other over scarce capital investment and production or to form transnational inter-union partnerships for the purpose of negotiating directly with MNC headquarters, namely over the central global issues of FDI and movement-of-work decision-making. Under the first scenario, one can surmise that only stronger unions situated in critical links within a MNC's global network of operations will be in a position to resist management's threat of relocating work and consequent demands for concessions. Under the second scenario, unions have engaged in fairly limited cross-border activities to directly confront MNCs over their FDI and transnational movement-of-work decisions. Some global union federations have formed 'world company councils' comprised of unions from different nations representing workers of given MNCs, but these councils appear to have limited themselves to cross-border information-sharing, consultation, and modest support for each other's struggles (see e.g. Gollbach and Schulten 2000; Marginson and Sisson 2002). There have also been cross-border campaigns conducted by sympathetic sister unions in the face of aggressive anti-union efforts by MNCs (see e.g. Juravich and Bronfenbrenner 2003), but these transnational campaigns are uncommon. Even under the exceptional opportunity of the European Works Council Directive, which offers a legally mandated forum for unions representing various locations of a given MNC across European borders, few unions have taken advantage of the opportunity to forge even minimal alliances (see e.g. Beaupain et al. 2003).

These coordinated transnational activities to date are undoubtedly too modest for unions to mount sufficient and sustainable resistance to MNCs seeking to weaken unions and wrest concessions from them. Whether or not unions will eventually forge cross-border partnerships for the purpose of negotiating on a transnational basis with MNCs depends on whether or not they can overcome substantial barriers. Here, we find that differences in union organizations and IR systems across countries make the forging of inter-union partnerships difficult to achieve (see e.g. Gennard and Ramsay 2003; Hyman 1999; and Cooke 2005a). One can surmise that the ability of unions to forge partnerships and engage MNCs in transnational bargaining over FDI and movement-of-work will require that unions first recognize they are essentially in a prisoner's dilemma in which cooperation among them yields the greatest opportunity to influence the HR and investment decisions of MNCs and, in turn, optimize gains for union members. Second, as players in an iterated non-zero sum game, unions will need to develop strategies that satisfy the necessary conditions and incentives of cooperation, which are not easily satisfied but are, nevertheless, not insurmountable (see Cooke 2005a, for elaboration). If unions eventually forge cross-border partnerships, the role of collective bargaining would undoubtedly take on much greater importance in the formulation and carrying out of global HR strategies.

## 24.2.4 The Environmental Context and Issues of Corporate Social Responsibility

As framed herein, global business strategies and, in turn, global HR strategies are influenced and constrained by both the economic and socio-political contexts within which MNCs compete. As discussed earlier, particularly relevant to MNC strategic decisions regarding FDI and the diffusion of preferred HRM policies and practices are differences in the labor markets, workplace cultures, collective bargaining contexts, and related laws across countries. These location differences are all products of IR systems that have evolved uniquely out of the broader environmental contexts of countries.

Beyond being responsive to differences in IR systems and complying with employment laws, looming large over the strategic decision-making of MNCs are increasing demands to act as socially responsible corporate citizens both abroad and at home. At the forefront of widespread public debate about corporate social responsibility, along with environmental concerns, are employment and workplace concerns; namely about improving labor standards and minimizing the loss of good-paying jobs as MNCs from highly industrialized countries increasingly shift investment and outsource work to low-wage developing countries. Although any synthesis of the literature regarding these employment and workplace issues is well beyond the intended scope of this chapter, the issues at hand are surely pertinent to the formulation of global HR strategies. Towards at least sketching out the fundamental strategic decision-making required of MNCs, we can draw on a broader literature about corporate social responsibility (CSR).

The concept or definition of CSR has been treated differently by authors but, in general, we can think of CSR as a company's actions providing some greater social good than a company would provide otherwise were it not to take into account the social interests of key societal stakeholders. As conceptualized by McWilliams and Siegel (2001), for example, companies should make decisions about CSR just as they make any investment decision; that is, with expectations of returns. 'To maximize profit, the firm should offer precisely that level of CSR for which the increased revenue (from increased demand) equals the higher cost (of using resources to provide CSR). By doing so, the firm meets the demands of relevant stakeholders—both those that demand CSR (consumers, employees, community) and those that "own" the firm (shareholders)' (McWilliams and Siegel 2001: 125). In their recent review and meta-analysis of the empirical literature, Orlitzky et al. (2003) add that attention to CSR has generally resulted in positive financial performance for companies that have largely responded to the damage incurred to their reputations by not acting socially responsibly.

With respect to global HR strategies, the question at hand for MNCs is how to address the calls by labor and human rights NGOs, unions, other citizen interests groups, investors, the media, and the public at large to act more socially responsibly in regard to labor standards and the shedding of workers associated with FDI and the movement of work to low-wage countries. Following the logic and evidence in the CSR literature, to the degree that customers, prospective employees, and investors are influenced negatively by a MNC's reputation regarding labor standards and displacement of workers, global HR strategies should be adjusted accordingly. Any adjustment first requires some assessment or estimation of the loss in profits due to forgone sales, productivity, and needed capital attributable to the MNC's poor CSR reputation. Against that loss in profits and seeking to act rationally, MNCs can be expected to take actions to eliminate their losses. Here we find that many MNCs (especially in the clothing manufacturing and retail sector) have attempted to protect or improve their brand reputations, as evidenced by a proliferation of 'company codes of conduct.'

As reviewed in some detail by Tsogas (1999), these codes range considerably in their content. At a minimum, codes of conduct express the value and principles guiding the MNC in its endeavor to act socially responsibly. For those that go beyond these general statements, the types of global HR provisions covered typically include (*a*) prohibitions against various forms of discrimination, child labor, and harsh discipline and (*b*) guidelines laying out minimum workplace conditions and policies. These codes apply not only to how the MNC manages its own operations but often how the MNC expects suppliers to manage their operations. A central criticism levied against these codes of conduct is that MNCs fail to monitor and enforce compliance with them, a criticism or concern that has led some MNCs to either contract with independent organizations or develop their own internal capacity to monitor compliance (see e.g. Frenkel and Scott 2002).

The level at which MNCs set global employment and workplace standards and the degree to which they ensure that their own operations and those of suppliers comply with those standards is bound to vary widely. That variance would appear to hinge on the damage to reputations and consequent loss in profits attributable to the reactions of customers, employees, and investors responding to public media exposure of MNCs' tolerances of socially substandard practices. Thus, the greater the costs incurred for acting socially irresponsibly in regard to labor standards, the higher the standards set and the more stringent the compliance with those standards. In developing global HR strategies, therefore, MNCs that invest in and/or outsource to low-wage countries would rationally take into account assessments of the demand for CSR. In turn, MNCs would set HRM policies and practices governing their own foreign operations and those of foreign suppliers, as well as set policies governing reductions-in-force in their domestic operations, that optimize profitability.

## 24.2.5 Aligning Global HR and Business Strategies

As synthesized by Boxall (this Handbook, Ch. 3), the strategic HRM literature generally has held that to optimize the net gain derivable from HRM, policies and practices underpinning HRM systems need to be well aligned and these HRM systems, in turn, need to be effectively aligned with broader business and organizational strategies. As synthesized by Allen and Wright (this Handbook,

Ch. 5), the 'resource-based' view of the firm has also come to play an increasingly important role in the business and HRM strategy literatures. Drawing on these fundamental notions of business and HRM strategy, any analysis of the alignment of global HR strategies with business strategies will necessarily need to take into account (1) externally focused market-positioning priorities and (2) internally focused resource-based assets. On the first account, Boxall summarizes the strategic HRM research in which researchers, using 'contingency' and 'configuration' models, have shown some linkages between various market-positioning priorities and HRM choices made by companies.

On the second account, Wright et al. (2001: 710) take a resource-based asset perspective to make a strong conceptual case that HRM envelops a set of core competencies 'comprised of human capital, social capital … and organizational capital (i.e., processes, technologies, data bases).' In a similar vein, Boxall and Purcell (2003) make a compelling case to conclude that a resource-based view is essentially a 'knowledge-based' view of the firm. From this vantage point, the management of HR is largely one of creating and exploiting knowledge in ways that organizations are able to learn and adapt more quickly than competitors. Importantly, 'managing knowledge inevitably means managing both the company's proprietary technologies and systems (which *do not* walk out the door at the end of the day) and the people (who *do*). It implies management of the ongoing interaction between these two aspects of a firm's knowledge system' (Boxall and Purcell 2003: 88) Wright et al. and Boxall and Purcell have identified a critical extension of HRM strategy, which is especially applicable to global HR strategies.

As argued by these authors and others, human resource and technological capabilities go hand in hand, an observation fully consistent with both the business strategy and management of technology literatures. As conceptualized by Porter, for example, the management of technology and human resources are discrete but interdependent activities underlying a company's value chain; activities that 'involve human resources, purchased inputs, and a "technology" for performing them, broadly defined to include organizational routines.' (Porter 1991: 102). Achieving and sustaining competitive advantage, in turn, becomes a factor of how well companies integrate various interdependent activities and align these integrated activities with market-positioning decisions. As synthesized by Nagarajan and Mitchell (1998), the management of technology and innovation literature, likewise, emphasizes that technological capabilities are the product of the management of integrated subsystems of resource-based assets, which include physical assets, non-physical knowledge, techniques, and processes. Similarly, Teece et al. (1997) articulate the concept of 'dynamic capabilities' wherein sustainable competitive advantage depends on a coordinative management process of honing integrated technological, organizational, and managerial processes that cannot be easily replicated by competitors.

Drawing on this literature, Cooke (2005*b*) argues that because technological and human resources are in part substitutes, yet are inextricably intertwined, companies invariably choose which capabilities to emphasize and how best to integrate the two. Cooke then hypothesizes that MNCs are more likely than national companies to develop workplace strategies emphasizing technological capabilities over HR capabilities. The basis of his argument is that because of local isomorphic constraints to altering existing workplace cultures, norms, customary practices, and institutional arrangements across borders, the difficulty and costs associated with the transnational diffusion of workplace strategies emphasizing HR capabilities are greater than the difficulty and costs associated with diffusing workplace strategies emphasizing technological capabilities. Consistent with his central hypothesis, he finds in his study of the automotive component supplier industry that after taking into account differences in market-positioning priorities and other factors, MNCs are indeed far more likely than national firms to pursue workplace strategies emphasizing technological capabilities over HR capabilities.

It follows that essential to the successful development and deployment of global HR strategies are strategic decisions about the optimal emphasis on and integration of HR and technological capabilities, taking into account the ease and costs associated with diffusing alternative workplace strategies across borders. As highlighted in my broader analytical framework (Fig. 24.1), also essential to the success of formulating global HR strategies are decisions about how best to align such HR and technological capabilities with strategic decisions regarding market-positioning and where to invest abroad.

# 24.3 SUMMARY AND FUTURE DIRECTIONS

Given the early stage of scholarly enquiry into a complex and widely encompassing subject, there are numerous unanswered questions about various fundamental issues and dynamics underlying the deployment of global HR strategies. An overriding challenge before us is the development and refinement of a general framework that encompasses and integrates the full range of global HR strategy decisions. Without such a framework, neither as HR scholars nor as professionals are we able to engage in comprehensive strategic analyses requisite to the successful deployment of global HR strategies. Towards this end, my primary objective in this chapter has been to articulate a simplified but fairly comprehensive analytical framework, one that at least captures and links the key strategic decisions MNCs face in formulating their global HR strategies. Under an assumption that management *seeks to act* rationally in the pursuit of optimizing profits, I have identified and discussed the strategic decision-making rationale underlying five salient inter-related components of my framework depicted in Fig. 25.1. In this final section I very briefly recap our discussion of each component and suggest future directions of enquiry under each.

The first component of global HR strategic decision-making addressed earlier was about the influence of differences in IR systems on FDI decisions. Surprisingly, there has been almost no attention given to this kind of decision-making in the global HR strategy literature. Yet, where MNCs make greenfield investments, acquire operations, and expand or contract their foreign subsidiaries invariably influences MNCs' global HR strategies; including decisions about the diffusion of HR and technological capabilities abroad, about union representation, and about CSR. Given the robustness of the evidence regarding the effects of differences in IR system factors on FDI patterns, it would be remiss of HR scholars and professionals not to take into account more fully the critical role that differences in IR systems play in overall global configuration decisions and, in turn, in the formulation of global HR strategies.

It is the decision-making regarding the diffusion of preferred HRM practices abroad that was the second component of global HR strategies addressed herein. On this issue we find a rich case study literature about the challenges MNCs face in deciding on what HRM policies and practices should be diffused, if any, and how these get implemented. A fundamental question that goes begging in this literature is whether or not and under what conditions the diffusion of HR strategies (in whole or in part) yields performance gains. Although we can cull from the literature (1) a number of important factors that influence the prospects for success and (2) various types of costs incurred in effectively diffusing any preferred HR strategies abroad, we have not yet assessed the relative importance of either. From a strategic analysis perspective of evaluating alternative global HR strategies, this is a critical assessment MNCs need to make (again, assuming MNCs seek to act rationally).

The third component of global HR strategies addressed focused on the role of union representation and collective bargaining on MNC decisions of where to invest abroad, about union avoidance where they have invested, and on the diffusion of preferred HRM policies and practices across foreign operations. One future direction of enquiry raised in our discussion is the prospect that MNCs will need to formulate transnational collective bargaining strategies given the possible rise of cross-border inter-union alliances or partnerships formed for the purpose of coordinating responses to, if not negotiating over, a MNC's FDI and cross-border movement-of-work decisions. Some HR scholars and professionals might under-standably dismiss this kind of strategic assessment and preparation as unnecessary, believing any such collective bargaining developments are too remote. However, MNCs with organized locations serving as critical links in their global network of operations risk incurring unwanted and unnecessary disruption to their global operations were they not to develop global HR strategies accounting for such developments.

The fourth component addressed in this chapter dealt largely with the issue of corporate social responsibility as it applies to global HR strategies. As the continued expansion and reach of corporate globalization is bound to lead to increasing FDI in and outsourcing to low-wage, developing countries of the world (dare I say China and India?), the issues of labor standards and the shedding of domestic workforces will undoubtedly stay at the forefront of public concern and debate. As discussed, the CSR literature provides useful insight into how MNCs can frame their strategic assessments regarding CSR more broadly. Missing in the literature, however, are any empirical analyses of the costs incurred and benefits derived from MNC efforts to accommodate public demands regarding improvements in labor standards abroad and minimization of the loss of jobs at home. Hence, another important future direction for scholarly enquiry and practical strategic assessment would be the study of how MNCs have responded to calls for greater social responsibility along these lines and evaluations of the effects of alternative global strategies deployed to accommodate these CSR demands on MNC performance and worker outcomes.

The last component of strategic decision-making addressed in this chapter was about the alignment of global HR strategies with business strategies. Although there have been a number of empirical analyses showing some linkage between HR and competitive positioning strategies, the literature is nearly void of any empirical enquiry as to how MNCs go about aligning their global HR and global market-positioning strategies. Additionally, little attention has been paid in the literature until very recently to how MNCs integrate HR capabilities with other resource-based asset capabilities, in particular with regard to technological capabilities. Further study along this line wherein we examine the transnational diffusion of HR policies and practices integrated with technology-driven policies and practices (as well as other resource-based capabilities) would appear to be a promising and needed line of enquiry. Importantly, the literature has yet to offer any empirical analyses of the *effects* of alternative choices of alignment on MNC performance, a limitation in the literature that also warrants our attention.

Finally, in addition to the future directions just identified, there are numerous other issues and challenges that fall just below the strategic decision-making level about the formulation of global HR strategies but that are, nonetheless, critical to the success of any strategies deployed. Stated differently, it is one thing to 'talk a good game' (strategy formulation) and another to 'play a good game' (strategy implementation). With respect to strategy implementation, the first set of issues includes decisions about the actual HRM policies and practices that will be embraced and applied. These are addressed in some detail by the authors of the other chapters in this Handbook, albeit they have not focused on the global dimension of HR strategy and practice. MNC choices about these actual HRM policies and practices would need to take into account the global dimension of HR strategies and be tailored accordingly as companies seek to act rationally in the pursuit of optimizing profits. Analyses of these global HRM choices offer yet another important future direction for enquiry.

The second set of issues germane to the implementation of global HR strategies includes global control, coordination, and integration at the center and related international staffing. At the heart of this challenge is the ability to manage a multinational enterprise that, on one hand, 'thinks globally' but, on the other hand, 'acts locally' (a well-worn mantra but a poignant one, nevertheless). At question here is: how can the corporate center best develop and manage its human resources across multidivisional or transnational organizational structures, allowing for appropriate degrees of variation and autonomy while integrating diverse, interdependent units via the exercise of sufficient control over and coordination of international operations? (See, in particular, Schuler et al. 1993; Bartlett and Ghoshal 1998; and Boxall and Purcell 2003.) Especially challenging to MNCs is the control, coordination, and integration required in managing HR disruptions incurred as a result of joint ventures, mergers, and acquisitions, the latter which have historically accounted for much of FDI (see e.g. Aguilera and Dencker 2004; Boxall and Purcell 2003).

An emerging literature regarding the effective control, coordination, and integration of global HR strategies addresses the central role of building 'social capital' throughout the global operations of MNCs (see e.g. Tsai and Ghoshal 1998; Inkpen and Tsang 2005). Taylor (2005: 8) summarizes the importance of global integration via the building of social capital in the following way: 'in order to be truly effective, IHR [international HR] must become a champion of an integrated HR system, a communicator of the reasons for it, and a booster for the overarching global vision of the firm that underpins the need for interdependence.' She also makes a strong case that MNCs seeking to act socially responsibly in regard to environmental sustainability would enhance their success in doing so by developing social capital throughout their global operations. Applying this same logic to analyses of CSR in regard to labor standards and the shedding of domestic workforces offers another potentially fruitful line of enquiry.

Invariably tied to the success of efforts at control, coordination, and integration are staffing decisions regarding expatriate assignments. Here the literature emphasizes that international work experience can be a vital asset to MNCs if, indeed, a MNC's cadre of expatriates can serve as an effective conduit for developing essential cross-border relationships and social capital throughout global networks, and their unique international experiences and knowledge are fully tapped by corporate headquarters (see e.g. Takeuchi et al. 2005; Suutari and Brewster 2003). Future enquiries that link more closely how the development of social capital and expatriate assignments facilitate the implementation of global HR strategies hold promise of illuminating the role played by the center in controlling, coordinating, and integrating its diverse but interdependent global network of operations.

In closing, it goes without question that the formulation, implementation, and persistent adjustment of global HR strategies is a highly complex, if not daunting challenge to MNCs. It also goes without question that the impact of global HR strategies on the bottom line of MNCs, on millions of employees, and on the wider social good is quite substantial. With that in mind, our plate for further enquiry and strategic analyses is surely full.

# REFERENCES

AGUILERA, R. V., and DENCKER, J. C. (2004). 'The Role of Human Resource Management in Cross-border Mergers and Acquisitions.' *International Journal of Human Resource Management*, 15/8: 1355–70.

BARTLETT, C., and GHOSHAL, S. (1998) *Managing across Boundaries: The Transnational Corporation*. New York: Random House.

BEAUMONT, P., CRESSEY, P., and JAKOBSEN, P. (1990). 'Some Key Industrial Features of West German Subsidiaries in Britain.' *Employee Relations Journal*, 12/6: 3–8.

BEAUPAIN, T., JEFFERYS, S., and ANNAND, R. (2003). 'Early Days: Belgian and U.K. Experiences of European Works Councils.' In W. Cooke (ed.), *Multinational Companies and Global Human Resource Strategies*. Westport, Conn.: Quorum Books.

BIRD, A., TAYLOR, S., and BEECHLER, S. (1998). 'A Typology of International Human Resource Management in Japanese Multinational Corporations: Organizational Implications.' *Human Resource Management*, 37/2: 159–72.

BOGNANNO, M. F., KEANE, M. P., and YANG, D. (2005). 'The Influence of Wages and Industrial Relations Environments on the Production Location Decisions of US Multinational Corporations.' *Industrial and Labor Relations Review*, 58/2: 171–201.

BOXALL, P., and PURCELL, J. (2003). *Strategy and Human Resource Management*. New York: Palgrave Macmillan.

BREWSTER, C., and TREGASKIS, O. (2003). 'Convergence or Divergence of Contingent Employment Practices? Evidence of the Role of MNCs in Europe.' In W. Cooke (ed.), *Multinational Companies and Global Human Resource Strategies*. Westport, Conn.: Quorum Books.

CASSON, M. C., and BUCKLEY, P. J. (1998). 'Models of the Multinational Enterprise.' *Journal of International Business Studies*, 29/1: 21–44.

COOKE, W. N. (2001a). 'The Effects of Labor Costs and Workplace Constraints on Foreign Direct Investment among Highly Industrialised Countries.' *International Journal of Human Resource Management*, 12/5: 697–716.

—— (2001b). 'Union Avoidance and Foreign Direct Investment in the U.S.A.' *Employee Relations Journal*, 23/6: 558–80.

—— (2005a). 'Exercising Power in a Prisoner's Dilemma: Transnational Collective Bargaining in an Era of Corporate Globalisation?' *Industrial Relations Journal*, 36/4: 283–302.

COOKE, W. N. (2005b). 'Integrating Technology and Human Resources: The Influence of Global Business Strategies on Workplace Strategy Choices.' 'Governing the Global Workplace' conference, University of Minnesota (forthcoming in *Industrial Relations*).

—— and NOBLE, D. (1998). 'Industrial Relations Systems and US Foreign Direct Investment Abroad.' *British Journal of Industrial Relations*, 36/4: 581–609.

DUNNING, J. H. (1993). *Multinational Enterprises and the Global Economy*. New York: Addison-Wesley.

EDWARDS, T., COLLIER, X., ORITS, L., REES, C., and WORTMANN, M. (2005). 'How Important are National Industrial Relations Systems in Shaping Restructuring in Multinational Companies?' *European Journal of Industrial Relations*, 12/1 (forth coming).

FERNER, A., and QUINTANILLA, J. (1998). 'Multinationals, National Business Systems and HRM: The Enduring Influence of National Identity or a Process of Anglo-Saxonisation.' *International Journal of Human Resource Management*, 9/4: 710–31.

—— ALMOND, P., COLLING, T., and EDWARDS, T. (2005). 'Policies on Union Representation in US Multinationals in the UK: Between Micro-politics and Macro-Institutions.' *British Journal of Industrial Relations* (forthcoming).

FLORIDA, R., and KENNEY, M. (1991). 'Organisation vs. Culture: Japanese Automotive Transplants in the U.S.' *Industrial Relations Journal*, 22: 181–96.

FRENKEL, S. (2005). 'Towards a Theory of Dominant Interests, Globalization and Work.' In M. Korczynski, P. K. Edwards, and R. Hodson (eds.), *Social Theory at Work*. Oxford: Oxford University Press.

—— and SCOTT, D. (2002). 'Compliance, Collaboration and Codes of Labor Practice: The *Adidas* Connection.' *California Management Review*, 45/1: 29–49.

GAMBLE, J. (2003). 'Transferring Human Resource Practices from the United Kingdom to China: The Limits and Potential for Convergence.' *International Journal of Human Resource Management*, 14/3: 369–87.

GENNARD, J., and RAMSAY, H. (2003). 'Strategic International Laborism: MNCs and Labor in the Graphical Sector.' In W. Cooke (ed.), *Multinational Companies and Global Human Resource Strategies*. Westport, Conn.: Quorum Books.

GOLLBACH, J., and SCHULTEN, T. (2000). 'Cross-border Collective Bargaining Networks in Europe.' *European Journal of Industrial Relations*, 6/2: 161–79.

HYMAN, R. (1999). 'Five Alternative Scenarios for West European Unionism.' In R. Munck and P. Waterman (eds.), *Labour Worldwide in the Era of Globalisation*. New York: St Martin's Press.

INKPEN, A., and TSANG, E. (2005). 'Social Capital, Networks, and Knowledge Transfer.' *Academy of Management Review*, 30/1: 146–65.

JURAVICH, T., and BRONFENBRENNER, K. (2003). 'Out of the Ashes: The Steelworkers' Global Campaign at Bridgestone/Firestone.' In W. Cooke (ed.), *Multinational Companies and Global Human Resource Strategies*. Westport, Conn.: Quorum Books.

KENNEY, M., and TANAKA, S. (2003). 'Transferring the Learning Factory to America? The Japanese Television Assembly Transplants.' In W. Cooke (ed.), *Multinational Companies and Global Human Resource Strategies*. Westport, Conn.: Quorum Books.

KOSTOVA, T. (1999). 'Transnational Transfer of Strategic Organizational Practices: A Contextual Perspective.' *Academy of Management Review*, 24/2: 308–24.

McWILLIAMS, A., and SIEGEL, D. (2001). 'Corporate Social Responsibility: A Theory of the Firm Perspective.' *Academy of Management Review*, 26/1: 117–27.

MARGINSON, P., and SISSON, K. (2002). 'European Dimensions to Collective Bargaining: New Symmetries within an Asymmetric Process?' *Industrial Relations Journal*, 33/4: 332–50.

MARTIN, A., and ROSS, G. (2000). 'European Integration and the Europeanisation of Labor.' In M. Gordon and L. Turner (eds.), *Transnational Cooperation among Labor Unions*. Ithaca, NY: Cornell University Press.

MARTIN, G., BEAUMONT, P., and PATE, J. (2003). 'A Process Model of Strategic HRM/LR Change in MNCs: The Case of AT&T and NCR in the U.K.' In W. Cooke (ed.), *Multinational Companies and Global Human Resource Strategies*. Westport, Conn.: Quorum Books.

MARTINEZ LUCIO, M., and WESTON, S. (1994). 'New Management Practices in a Multinational Corporation: The Restructuring of Worker Representation and Rights?' *Industrial Relations Journal*, 25: 110–21.

NAGARAJAN, A., and MITCHELL, W. (1998). 'Evolutionary Diffusion: Internal and External Methods Used to Acquire Encompassing, Complementary, and Incremental Technological Changes in the Lithotripsy Industry.' *Strategic Management Journal*, 19: 1063–77.

ORLITZKY, M., SCHMIDT, F. L., and RYNES, S. L. (2003). 'Corporate Social and Financial Performance: A Meta-analysis.' *Organization Studies*, 24/3: 402–41.

PORTER, M. E. (1991). 'Towards a Dynamic Theory of Strategy.' *Strategic Management Journal*, 12: 95–117.

PURCELL, W., NICHOLAS, S., MERRETT, D., and WHITWELL, G. (1999). 'The Transfer of Human Resource and Management Practices by Japanese Multinationals to Australia: Do Industry, Size and Experience Matter?' *International Journal of Human Resource Management*, 10/1: 72–88.

ROYLE, T., and TOWERS, B. (2003). 'Regulating Employee Interest Representation: The Case of McDonald's in the European Union.' In W. Cooke (ed.), *Multinational Companies and Global Human Resource Strategies*. Westport, Conn.: Quorum Books.

SCHMITT, M., and SADOWSKI, D. (2003). 'A Cost-Minimization Approach to the nternational Transfer of HRM/IR Practices: Anglo-Saxon Multinationals in the Federal Republic of Germany.' *International Journal of Human Resource Management*, 14/3: 409–30.

SCHULER, R. S., DOWLING, P. J., and DE CIERI, H. (1993). 'An Integrative Framework of Strategic International Human Resource Management.' *Journal of Management*, 19/2: 419–59.

SUUTARI, V., and BREWSTER, C. (2003). 'Repatriation: Empirical Evidence from a Longitudinal Study of Careers and Expectations among Finnish Expatriates.' *International Journal of Human Resource Management*, 14/7: 1132–51.

TAKEUCHI, R., TESLUK, P. E., YUN, S., and LEPAK, D. (2005). 'An Integrative View of International Experience.' *Academy of Management Journal*, 48/1: 85–100.

TAYLOR, S. (2005). 'Emerging Motivations for Global HRM Integration.' Forthcoming in A. Ferner, J. Quintanilla, and J. Bonache (eds.), *HRM Integration and Adaptation*. New York: Palgrave-Macmillan Press.

TEECE, D. J., PISANO, G., and SHUEN. A. (1997). 'Dynamic Capabilities and Strategic Management.' *Strategic Management Journal*, 18/7: 509–33.

TSAI, W., and GHOSHAL, S. (1998). 'Social Capital and Value Creation: The Role of Intrafirm Networks.' *Academy of Management Journal*, 41: 464–76.

TSOGAS, G. (1999). 'Labour Standards in International Trade Agreements.' An Assessment of the Arguments.' *International Journal of Human Resources*, 10/2: 351–75.

UNTCAD (2004). *World Investment Report 2004*. New York: United Nations.

WRIGHT, P. M., DUNFORD, B., and SNELL, S. A. (2001). 'Human Resources and the Resource Based View of the Firm.' *Journal of Management*, 27: 701–21.

CHAPTER 25

# TRANSNATIONAL FIRMS AND CULTURAL DIVERSITY

## HELEN DE CIERI

## 25.1 INTRODUCTION

GLOBALIZATION has impacted significantly on many firms, with substantial implications for human resource management (HRM). Geopolitical, social, economic, and technological changes have created opportunities for managers and employees to interact with culturally diverse populations (Wong-Mingji and Mir 1997). The development of cultural diversity in the workforce presents substantial and complex challenges for HR scholars and managers as they strive to determine the potential implications of cultural diversity for firm effectiveness. This chapter examines cultural diversity issues, which are increasingly viewed as a critical aspect of management in transnational firms.

# 25.2 UNDERSTANDING CULTURE AND CULTURAL DIVERSITY

The concept of *culture* refers to the beliefs, values, and attitudes shared by people within a given group and used to guide their thoughts, reasoning, actions, and interactions (Brown 1963). Following Kroeber and Kluckhohn's (1952) review of more than 160 definitions of culture, Kluckhohn (1954: 73) developed a definition of culture that has become widely accepted:

Culture consists of patterned ways of thinking, feeling and reacting, acquired and transmitted mainly by symbols, constituting the distinctive achievement of human groups, including their embodiment in artefacts; the essential core of culture consists of traditional (i.e., historically derived and selected) ideas and especially their attached values.

A substantial body of research has explored the ways in which, in different cultures, individuals construe themselves and others. Markus and Kitayama (1991) identified that one's construal of self, of others, and the interdependence of the two, has implications for cognition, emotion, and motivation. Understanding the cultural context for self- and other-construal should help to explain individual behavior and the outcomes of that behavior. An individual's self-construal of culture, or cultural identity, is derived from their membership of distinct socio-cultural groups (Cox 1993). As Ely and Thomas (2001: 231) say, cultural identity is 'socially constructed, complex and dynamic.' Cultures evolve as societies adapt to changes in their environment; globalization has brought many opportunities, but also challenges and pressures for change.

Javidan and House (2001) advocate that managers and employees in transnational firms should understand and be aware of *cultural diversity* and its implications, and possess the skills to deal with cultural differences in an appropriate way. Workforce diversity is not a new concept for scholars or practitioners, yet the effective management of diversity is an elusive goal in many firms. Globalization of markets has brought a broadening of mindsets amongst executives and increasing awareness of the need to understand cultural diversity (Leung et al. 2005).

Early research on HRM in transnational firms was principally concerned with expatriate selection and training, usually for expatriate management assignments (Dowling and Welch 2004). Expatriates remain an important aspect of transnational staffing strategies. However, recent research has broadened the focus of research, to recognize the increasing diversity of international work assignments, moving away from long-term expatriation towards more flexible forms of international work, such as transnational project teams, short-term assignments, and virtual assignments. Recent evidence suggests that international assignments, particularly the non-standard types, are increasingly being undertaken by employees outside the senior levels of management (Harris and Brewster 2003). Other individuals are self-initiating international careers, by moving between countries as part of their job search. Recent research also explores issues such as HRM initiatives for host-country nationals (Bartlett et al. 2002) and the extent to which transnational firms may seek to localize their HRM practices (Aycan 2005). Much of the research exploring international HRM issues has focused on Western firms, those headquartered in the USA or Europe. However, there is a growing literature examining organizations operating in non-Western regions, and in emerging and transition economies (Ramamurti 2004). Overall, the field of international HRM is evolving as researchers and practitioners seek to understand factors such as the cultural contexts that influence transnational firms.

## 25.3 LANDMARK STUDIES IN CROSS-CULTURAL RESEARCH

International HRM research has been influenced by research in the field of comparative anthropology, such as Kluckhohn and Strodtbeck's (1961) framework of cultural variation. Kluckhohn and Strodtbeck (1961) developed *values orientation theory*, which has been used in cross-cultural research to examine variation in social interaction styles; they identified six dimensions along which a society can be placed: relationships to nature, beliefs about human nature, relationships among people, nature of human activity, conception of space, and orientation to time.

Within the management field, landmark research by Hofstede (1980) established a stream of research exploring the relationship between national cultural diversity and management practices. Hofstede provided the foundation for a research stream that views national culture as a key factor in organizational processes; organizations are viewed as manifestations or consequences of national culture. Hofstede identified five cultural dimensions: power distance, individualism–collectivism, masculinity–femininity, uncertainty avoidance, and (in later research) short-versus long-term orientation (Hofstede 2001).

Following Hofstede's work, several researchers have sought to identify other cultural dimensions. For example, Schwartz (1994) found seven culture-level dimensions of values, namely affective autonomy, conservatism, egalitarian commitment, harmony, hierarchy, intellectual autonomy, and mastery. More recently, the GLOBE (Global Leadership and Organizational Behavior Effectiveness) project has investigated national cultural diversity. The GLOBE project has involved 160 researchers who have collected data over seven years from 18,000 middle managers in sixty-two countries (House et al. 2004). These managers were compared on nine cultural dimensions: performance orientation, future orientation, assertiveness, uncertainty avoidance, power distance, institutional collectivism, family collectivism, gender egalitarianism, and humane orientation. Adopting an approach somewhat similar to Hofstede's research, and based in theory, House and colleagues sought to provide a comprehensive view of the cultural practices of different countries. The national cultural characteristics identified in the GLOBE research have implications for many areas, such as communication preferences and management style (Javidan and House 2001).

While these landmark cross-cultural studies have made valuable contributions to our understanding of cultural diversity, several researchers have queried the emphasis that has been placed on national culture. Nationality is often used in research as a measure of national cultural diversity. Research has shown that national culture has an impact on a variety of organizational activities, and national cultural diversity continues to be an important issue for transnational firms (see Earley and Gibson 2002). However, it is recognized that cultural diversity may be observed not only at national levels but also at regional or intranational levels. Husted (2003: 428) points out that national cultures 'usually represent the values and practices of the dominant groups in society, and not of the marginalized.' Also, Leung et al. (2005) point out that it is important to be aware of the perils of attribution errors with regard to cultural diversity. As Leung et al. (2001) note, such errors can lead to misunderstandings and problems in the workplace, when applied in areas such as HR practices.

Hofstede's model has been widely applied in international management but substantial debate surrounds the work and several theoretical and methodological criticisms have been directed at it (e.g. Chiang 2005). On theoretical terms, major criticisms of Hofstede's work focus on his conceptualization of culture and labeling of the dimensions. On methodological grounds, major concerns include the generalizability of Hofstede's findings and criticisms of his method of data collection. Gerhart and Fang's (2005: 973) reanalysis of Hofstede's research raises this criticism to a new level by questioning the dominant role of national culture in international management:

While we are certain that national culture differences can be critical and that insensitivity to national culture differences can and does result in business failure (as well as failure and career consequences for individual managers), one can still ask whether national culture, defined in terms of values, is *this* important and whether its effects are *this* pervasive and systematic.

## 25.4 THE CONVERGENCE–DIVERGENCE DEBATE

While recognizing criticisms of Hofstede's work, the importance of national culture is an enduring issue in international business research (Peng 2004). Much of the discussion surrounding the implications of national cultural diversity is related to the convergence–divergence debate, which is widely viewed as an important issue in the management of transnational firms (Myloni et al. 2004). Since Kerr et al. (1960) presented the thesis that the organizational and institutional patterns of industrial societies are converging, or becoming more similar, despite disparate politics, ideology, and cultures, many researchers have explored not only similarities and differences across cultures worldwide, but whether these are dynamic.

The convergence hypothesis suggests that there is increasing similarity in organizations and managerial practices worldwide, based on the argument that the common requirements of management—or a common logic of industrialism—disregard the importance of cultural differences. Additionally, contextual contingencies, such as the growth in worldwide communications and travel and greater interdependence and collaboration between organizations and nations (Doz and Prahalad 1991), are seen to be factors eroding differences between organizations and management practices.

If national cultures are indeed converging, then a universalist approach to management practices would be expected to emerge; this would enhance the transfer of managerial practices between units of a multinational corporation and, therefore, global coordination. However, since the 1970s, the convergence hypothesis has received substantial criticism and is regarded by many leading scholars as overly simplistic and optimistic (Leung et al. 2005).

These criticisms, then, lend support to the divergence hypothesis, whereby organizations maintain their culturally based dissimilarities (Adler et al. 1986). In contrast to the convergence hypothesis, the divergence hypothesis postulates that the *form* and *content* of functional specialization that develops with growth would vary according to culture. According to the divergence hypothesis, any attempt to integrate units of a transnational firm must take into account the differentiation inherent between units. The divergence argument is that differences in approaches to management practices are enduring; these differences are predominantly attributed to a 'country of origin effect,' generally assumed to be produced by the interaction of local culture and institutional factors (Aycan 2005).

A third view, sometimes referred to as 'crossvergence,' suggests that there is convergence in some areas of international business, such as consumer values and lifestyle preferences, although divergence of cultures persists in several significant respects. Further, several factors may simultaneously lead to convergence and divergence. For example, information and communication technology may facilitate global communication for many, but some ethnic groups will reject new technologies and the related lifestyle and cultural values. '[T]hrough the process of globalization, cultures influence each other and change, but whether or not these changes will bring about cultural convergence is yet to be seen' (Leung et al. 2005: 361).

# 25.5 CURRENT RESEARCH ISSUES IN CULTURAL DIVERSITY

Cultural diversity has been studied from a variety of theoretical perspectives and using a variety of research methods. In the last decade or so, a major area of research interest and debate has focused on the relationship between cultural diversity and performance. Other noteworthy research areas include the implications of cultural diversity for knowledge-sharing, transnational teams, and cultural intelligence. Each of these research issues has implications for HR managers in transnational firms.

## 25.5.1 The Relationship between Cultural Diversity and Performance

There has been ongoing debate about the relationship between cultural diversity and performance in firms such as transnational enterprises.

### 25.5.1.1 The 'Dysfunctional Diversity' View

Many researchers have noted problems associated with cultural diversity, such as misunderstandings or confusion when individuals from different cultures fail to understand each other (Miroshnik 2002). Numerous studies have proposed that diversity is related to poorer performance outcomes (Richard et al. 2004). It has been argued that workforce diversity will lead to communication problems and dysfunctional conflict, with negative implications for organizational performance (e.g. Pelled et al. 1999).

Cultural diversity may lead to reduced communication and to reinforcement of existing stereotypes. For transnational firms, problems such as the lack of literacy skills in the local workforce of a developing country, or an expatriate's lack of local language skills, may act to restrict the opportunity for effective communication. Whatever the reason, poor communication may lead minority group members to feel a lack of empathy with organizational or managerial goals, and this in turn may limit their willingness to participate in workplace processes.

At an organizational level, many firms have responded to globalization and increased their diversity by using offshoring or outsourcing strategies. The movement of jobs to locations with comparatively cheap labor, such as the 'offshoring' of jobs in the information technology industry to India and China, has led to substantial debate. While this movement is argued to increase shareholder wealth, there has been considerable concern raised over negative outcomes such as related job losses in countries such as the USA and Australia (Jones 2005).

## 25.5.1.2. *The 'Value-In-Diversity' View*

In contrast, the 'value-in-diversity' approach assumes that diversity in work groups will enhance effectiveness (Cox 1993; Miroshnik 2002). This research stream developed in part as a response to the recognition that workforce diversity was increasing, and managers needed to develop ways to effectively manage the different views and characteristics of the new, diverse workforce (see this Handbook, Ch. 13). This research stream is focused to some extent on adding value by enhancing organizational effectiveness and performance. This perspective suggests that culturally diverse groups, such as multicultural project teams in transnational firms, will generate different opinions, engage in more thorough critical analysis, and thus make better-quality decisions (Shaw and Barrett-Power 1998).

Cox (2001) identified five ways in which diversity could add value to an organization: improved problem-solving; increased creativity and innovation; increased organizational flexibility; improved skill variety in the workforce; and improved marketing (e.g. increased customer base). For example, a diverse workforce is proposed to help organizations to understand the different needs and values of the cultural groups that comprise their client base (Friday and Friday 2003; Wentling 2000).

On the other hand, there are recognized costs associated with managing diversity poorly. When organizations do not manage diversity well, there is increased likelihood of turnover and absenteeism among minority groups. In addition, organizations that do not manage diversity well may be in breach of legislation and may incur associated costs. There are also indirect costs, such as the loss of organizational reputation and inability to attract high-quality employees to the organization.

While there has been considerable research exploring the 'value-in-diversity' approach, many questions remain unanswered. For example, the evaluation of diversity programs remains an area for attention. While many transnational firms have implemented diversity initiatives, it is difficult to measure the relationship between diversity initiatives and organizational performance outcomes. Recent research has begun to explore the factors that moderate the relationship between diversity and performance (Grimes and Richard 2003; Richard 2000). Richard (2000: 174) concluded that cultural diversity does add value to a firm but the effects of diversity 'are likely to be determined by the strategies a firm pursues and by how organization leaders and participants respond to and manage diversity.'

### 25.5.1.3 *Developing an Integrated Approach*

Richard et al. (2004) sought to integrate the opposing views by developing a theoretical framework based on Blau's (1977) theory of heterogeneity and social identity theory (Tajfel and Turner 1985), which posits that, in groups that are culturally homogeneous, members will communicate more frequently and in a greater variety of ways, due to their shared views. This, in turn, increases the group members' satisfaction and cooperation, and decreases intra-group conflict. In contrast, in culturally heterogeneous groups, social categorization processes lead to the formation of divisions (or ingroups and outgroups), in turn leading to greater conflict and creating barriers to communication. However, the relationship between heterogeneity and conflict is not linear. Blau (1977) posited that high levels of cultural heterogeneity could overcome barriers associated with moderate heterogeneity, as group members become more diffused over social categories of diversity and ingroup/outgroup identities are less marked. Therefore, Richard et al. (2004) hypothesized that cultural diversity in management groups has a U-shaped curvilinear relationship to performance; their empirical findings did not fully support this hypothesis yet raised an interesting issue for future exploration. As discussed in section 25.6, the design and implementation of HRM practices need to be integrated with the strategy of the transnational firm, to address the demands of cultural and institutional factors in the global and local context.

## 25.5.2 Knowledge-Sharing

Managers in transnational firms face two important and sometimes conflicting challenges related to knowledge-sharing. First, they need to create and leverage employees' knowledge throughout the global network (Nohria and Ghoshal 1997). Knowledge creation and sharing largely depends on the willingness and commitment of employees to engage in the necessary yet complex tasks of coordination and communication (Minbaeva et al. 2003). Leveraging of knowledge enables a transnational firm to take advantage of worldwide access to information, learning, and creativity, to develop competitive products or services. Further, leveraging knowledge helps the firm to deal with the uncertainty related to operating in a global, volatile environment (Suder 2004).

Second, transnational firms face the challenge of effectively managing employees from diverse cultural and social backgrounds. While successful knowledge creation and transfer depends on effective HR strategies such as the development of transnational teams, this task may be made more difficult by the diversity of the workforce. As noted earlier, cultural diversity may both add value and be dysfunctional. Knowledge-sharing depends to some extent on social cohesion, but cultural diversity can hinder the development of social cohesion between employees (Cramton and Hinds 2005). The geographic distribution of operations in transnational firms may exacerbate the difficulties of knowledge-sharing. For example, geographic distribution makes the task of communicating a unified strategic vision and set of values more difficult (Engle et al. 2001). Hence, challenges for HR managers include the design and implementation of effective communication across the firm and strategies to develop a shared mindset.

## 25.5.3 Transnational Teams

Transnational project teams, which rely on cross-cultural collaboration, are increasingly used in organizations. A study by McDonough et al. (2001) found that 22 percent of participating firms reported that they would use globally distributed teams for new product development in the next few years. Transnational teams encompass members with different nationalities; team members have different national and/or cultural backgrounds and are cooperating to achieve a shared goal (Earley and Gibson 2002). There is considerable variation within such teams; the work patterns and circumstances may be quite varied; while some teams will work at a shared location for the duration of the project, others will be virtual teams or will gather at one location for only part of the project.

Cross-cultural research, such as that building on Hofstede's research, has suggested that national culture should explain between 25 and 50 percent of variation in attitudes (Gannon 1994). However, this has been questioned recently (Gerhart and Fang 2005) and research exploring whether, and how, this diversity might affect the performance of transnational teams is inconclusive. As noted earlier, diversity may have both positive and negative effects on work group performance. Factors that influence the effectiveness of transnational teams include the types and magnitude of cultural diversity, the organizational context, geographic spread and location of team members, different expectations of working practices, in addition to the characteristics of the task itself (James and Ward 2001). Taking such factors into consideration, it is suggested that the performance of transnational teams will depend to some extent on the management processes; global leadership is therefore emerging as an important area of investigation and interest. Challenges for HR managers related to transnational teams include the design and implementation of appropriate recruitment and selection processes, programs for transnational leadership development, and implementation of support structures for transnational team members, to assist when conflicts may arise.

### 25.5.4 Cultural Intelligence

One area of emerging research that may provide useful ways to address the challenges of managing cultural diversity is the research led by Earley (2002; Ng and Earley 2006) exploring the concept of 'cultural intelligence.' This concept refers to 'an outsider's seemingly natural ability to interpret someone's unfamiliar and ambiguous gestures the way that person's compatriots should' (Earley and Mosakowski 2004: 139). Cultural intelligence includes cognitive, behavioral, and motivational elements (Earley 2002): understanding this concept should help individuals to manage cultural diversity in more effective ways.

The concept of cultural intelligence can be usefully applied to transnational teams. For example, team members with higher cultural intelligence should be able to achieve more effective team interactions, such as knowledge-sharing, leading to superior team outcomes (Earley 2002). Cultural intelligence also contributes to the effectiveness of international work. Successful expatriation relies to some extent on the cultural intelligence of the individual expatriate and those around him or her, such as host-country colleagues. An expatriate with high cultural intelligence should be able to adapt effectively to the host culture and to select those features of the local cultural context that will be most likely to help the expatriate spouse and family to adjust to the foreign assignment (Earley 2002). Although research related to cultural intelligence is embryonic, it is suggested that there is potential for HR managers to design and implement employee selection, development, and performance management processes to assess and enhance cultural intelligence (Earley and Mosakowski 2004; Ng and Earley 2006).

# 25.6 PRACTICAL APPLICATIONS: MANAGING CULTURAL DIVERSITY IN TRANSNATIONAL FIRMS

Theoretical and empirical developments regarding cultural diversity have informed and been informed by management in transnational firms. Many transnational firms have recognized that managing cultural diversity is a critical part of strategic management. It is particularly important for managers in transnational firms to balance the often conflicting needs of global efficiencies and coordination (integration) with responsiveness to factors such as political pressures in each local market (differentiation) (Doz and Prahalad 1991). To manage the global/local dilemma, there are several important areas for HR managers' attention, as discussed below. For HRM in transnational firms, alignment between the business and HR strategy, structure, and HR practices, and external factors such as national culture and institutional characteristics, is argued to lead to enhanced outcomes for individuals and organizations (De Cieri and Dowling 2006, in press).

## 25.6.1 HRM Practices

A stream of research has explored the transferability of HR practices from one cultural context to another (e.g. Sparrow et al. 1994). Transnational firms are particularly important vehicles for this transfer of management practices, sometimes leading to hybrid forms of management, such as 'HRM with Chinese characteristics' (Zhu et al. 2005). This transfer may be not only from headquarters to subsidiary within a firm; it may cross organizational boundaries, for example, where indigenous firms adopt, or mimic, the practices of foreign firms.

However, there is ongoing debate about the extent to which HRM strategy and practices are transferable worldwide. According to Myloni et al. (2004), the extent to which culture has an influence on HR practices varies according to the HR practice. Further, Aycan (2005) reiterates the point that culture is not the only influence on HRM practices, providing a framework and series of research propositions to guide analysis of the interaction between cultural and institutional factors and how they influence the design and implementation for HRM practices. This framework is supported by a body of research literature that has explored cross-cultural differences across major areas of HRM such as strategy and planning, job analysis, recruitment and selection, performance appraisal, training and development, and compensation.

To consider recruitment and selection as an example, it is suggested that recruitment and selection criteria are culture bound. In the USA, emphasis is typically placed on selection criteria that are predictive of future job performance; in societies that are collectivist and place emphasis on high power distance, relationships and networks (*guanxi*) are important in selection processes. Recruitment and selection methods are influenced by cultural factors; for example, while interviews are widely used in many cultures, the way in which they are used varies considerably. Institutional factors also influence recruitment and selection; the presence of trade unions and legislation such as equal employment opportunity laws are predicted to lead to more formal, transparent, and bureaucratic recruitment and selection processes (Aycan 2005). Industry characteristics, such as a shortage of skilled labor, and firm characteristics, such as size, will also influence the recruitment and selection practices utilized by a firm. Larger firms tend to use more standardized and formal processes.

Similarly, some aspects of performance appraisal are argued to be strongly influenced by culture. Aycan (2005) suggests that what is considered 'good performance' is culture bound. Individualistic cultures tend to emphasize objective and quantifiable measures that focus more on productivity, quality of work, and efficiency. In contrast, collectivist cultures are more likely to emphasize group harmony and relationships. Culture also affects the type of performance evaluation and the ways in which performance feedback may be given. Moreover, institutional factors such as industry characteristics influence performance appraisal. For example, private sector, manufacturing firms tend to emphasize productivity and work outcomes.

Diversity management initiatives are argued to be an important part of transnational HRM practices, as they enhance appreciation of socio-political and cultural differences *and* similarities (see this Handbook, Chapter 13). Diversity management initiatives are specific activities, programs, policies, and any other formal processes designed to improve management of diversity via communication, education and training, employee involvement, career management, accountability, and cultural change. For example, diversity initiatives may include practices such as training programs to reduce stereotyping and to improve cross-cultural sensitivity and skills (Wentling 2000). Some transnational firms have developed global approaches to diversity initiatives. For example, Thomas (2004) reports that IBM is developing a global strategy to better address diversity issues facing the company around the world. However, researchers have suggested that diversity management initiatives typically require a decentralized approach (Egan and Bendick 2003), because diversity initiatives are required to be responsive to local cultural and institutional factors, such as equal employment opportunity laws. Further, Egan and Bendick's (2003) research shows that differing attitudes to diversity management across national contexts have led some MNCs to emphasize local responsiveness for diversity management initiatives.

## 25.6.2 HRM Structure

In addition to HR practices being influenced by culture and institutional factors, the structure of the HR function itself is an enduring and important concern for transnational firms (De Cieri and Dowling 1997). Research has shown that transnational firms with a variety of modes of operation, including, for example, joint ventures and/or wholly owned subsidiary units, across a diverse range of national contexts, are likely to have network structures. Network structures provide flexibility by giving autonomy to local/country operations that are quite independent, while also facilitating communication between these separate activities to enable global integration of activities (Bartlett and Ghoshal 1992). It might be argued that the HR structure should be aligned with the organizational structure. However, where local conditions require a high level of local responsiveness, as may be the case for diversity initiatives, HR structures are more likely to emphasize decentralized decision-making.

## 25.6.3   HRM Roles

Cultural diversity is an important consideration for transnational firms and there are specific implications for HRM. Researchers have suggested core competencies for managers in transnational firms in order to deal with potential negative aspects of diversity and to emphasize positive aspects of diversity, including empathy, an emphasis on employee engagement, and the ability to incorporate diverse views. Further, the complexity of operating across multiple countries and employing multiple national categories of workers leads to specific role requirements for HR managers in transnational firms (Dowling 1999), as discussed below.

### 25.6.3.1 *More Human Resource Activities*

In a transnational firm, HR managers must engage in a number of activities that would not be necessary in a single-country operation, such as international relocation and support for expatriates, host-government relations, or arranging language translation services. For example, HR managers may be required to play important roles in corporate governance, such as the design, implementation, and maintenance of corporate codes of conduct (Beatty et al. 2003). However, training in and enforcement of codes of conduct may be difficult in some host-country environments (Dowling and Welch 2004).

### 25.6.3.2 *The Need for a Broader Perspective*

HR managers in transnational firms face numerous challenges when designing and implementing programs for culturally diverse groups or more than one national group of employees working in one location (e.g. expatriates and locals working in the Chinese operations of a US-based firm). Complex equity issues arise, particularly with regard to compensation policies, when employees of various nationalities work together. Understanding the perspectives of the various employee groups is an important aspect of developing effective management of cultural diversity.

### 25.6.3.3 *More Involvement in Employees' Personal Lives*

A greater degree of involvement in employees' personal lives is necessary for the management of employees in a transnational firm than would be typical in a single-country operation. As noted earlier, in response to the high costs and other problems associated with expatriation, other forms of international work, such as short-term assignments and transnational project teams, have become more common (Harris and Brewster 2003).

International work, such as transnational project teams, requires cross-cultural interactions and understanding of the variations in norms and expectations between national cultural groups (Earley 2002). The HR manager's roles may include providing an appropriate range of services, such as pre-departure training and on-site support for international workers.

### 25.6.3.4 *Changes in Emphasis as the Workforce Mix of Expatriates and Locals Varies*

As foreign operations mature, the emphases put on various HR activities change. For example, over time, fewer expatriate assignments will be required. HR managers may be involved in activities such as workforce planning, selection, and management development for local staff.

### 25.6.3.5 *Risk Exposure*

Concerns about security and global risks (Suder 2004) have led many transnational firms to rethink their approaches to HR strategies and global mobility of employees (GMAC Global Relocation Services, National Foreign Trade Council, and SHRM Global Forum 2003). Most transnational firms must now consider political risk and terrorism when planning international meetings and assignments (Czinkota et al. 2004). Terrorism has also clearly had an effect on the way in which employees and firms assess potential international assignment locations. For example, in some locations where US expatriates have been the target of violent attacks, firms may remove that group of expatriates, replacing them with other nationalities or locals. In this context, HR managers may be involved in decisions regarding reduction of the use of expatriates, developing emergency evacuation procedures for volatile locations, and/or ceasing operations in a location that has become too difficult.

### 25.6.3.6 *More External Influences*

As a firm's global spread increases, the range and complexity of external influences are likely to increase. Cultural factors to be understood by managers and employees include the generally accepted practices of doing business in each of the various host countries in which the firm operates. As discussed earlier, the transferability or culture-boundedness of HRM practices is an important concern.

## 25.6.4 Managerial Competencies for Cultural Diversity

Recent research and practice in transnational firms has focused on developing global managers with the skills, abilities, and other characteristics (such as the abilities to be geographically mobile and to act on their individual knowledge) to achieve organization and individual-level performance goals. Managers are increasingly realizing that for their organizations to become or remain competitive in global markets, they need to attract, motivate, and retain people who are accepting of diversity, have strong personal networks, and who excel in collaborative work (Tung 1993). There are increasing calls for HRM strategies to develop managers who are flexible, mobile, multi-skilled, and multidisciplinary, and who possess a high degree of cross-cultural sensitivity.

It has been argued that HRM practices that incorporate diversity initiatives in transnational firms lead to improvements in the firm's operational and managerial effectiveness by helping managers and employees to adapt to diverse contexts (Evans et al. 2002). For example, in the case of Japanese firms in China, Chinese employees work with Japanese managers, despite historical rivalry between the two nationalities. Liu et al. (2004: 730) suggest that identifying 'co-operative goals and applying abilities for mutual benefit contribute(s) to effective leadership even when managers and employees have different nationalities.'

## 25.6.5 Employees in Developing Countries

Countries such as China and India provide examples of nations where the 'liberalization of the economy, and the extra competition from overseas firms, has put a lot of pressure on the personnel function of ... domestic companies to prepare and develop their human resources' (Budhwar and Baruch 2003: 701). In such countries, the impact of foreign direct investment is complex and has been the subject of considerable debate (Jones 2005). For transnational firms, and particularly for HRM professionals, there are opportunities to contribute to developing countries via initiatives such as the introduction of vocational training programs and career planning and management, the facilitation of cross-national technology and knowledge transfers, and the provision of advice to governments, trade unions, consumers, and communities, as well as employers in developing countries. However, such initiatives have been criticized for assuming the appropriateness of universal application of Western approaches to HR development.

# 25.7 FUTURE DIRECTIONS FOR THEORY, RESEARCH, AND PRACTICE

Overall, in the past, many Western researchers and managers have assumed that Western approaches to management are universally applicable. Traditional approaches of dealing with cultural diversity have included efforts to conform to 'best-practice' (usually Western management practice), and 'force-fitting stand-ardized practices and techniques in an effort to homogenize people and cultures in offices and factories around the world' (Wong-Mingji and Mir 1997: 359). While this tendency for universality may have been understandable, examination of HR practices and structures in transnational firms has brought issues of cultural diversity to the fore and a reconsideration of the assumption of universality is required. As Wright and Brewster (2003: 1303) point out:

> While one cannot help but recognize some universal values (e.g. people should be com-pensated for their work) or truths with regard to HR practices (e.g. people need training to perform effectively, etc), it is in the diversity of practices where individuals, groups and organizations maximize their outcomes.

Cross-cultural theory and research have provided numerous important contri-butions to knowledge of work attitudes, employee behaviors, and management practices in transnational firms. However, there remain many areas for future investigation. Leung et al. (2005) have identified four themes that they suggest should be addressed in research on culture and international business; these also have implications for the development of theory and practice related to cultural diversity.

First, much of the extant research has utilized a simplistic view of culture that tends to assume stability rather than recognizing the dynamism of culture. Leung et al. (2005: 374) propose instead 'multi-layer, multi-facet, contextual, and systems views of culture.' Similarly, Huang and Van de Vliert (2003) suggest that multilevel modeling will provide a useful theoretical perspective for researchers exploring cross-national diversity of organizational behavior.

Second, it is suggested that there needs to be better understanding of the complex effects of culture (Gerhart and Fang 2005; Leung et al. 2005). While research has shown that national culture is a predictor of numerous individual-level outcomes, such as perceptions and behaviors, it has also been found that culture does not explain a large amount of variance in such outcomes; other variables are also important predictors. Culture alone does not have sufficient power to explain individual behaviors. Leung et al. (2005: 368) suggest that 'it is more useful to address the issues of *how* and *when* [culture] makes a difference.' These authors identify three moderators of cultural impacts, social identification, stage of group development, and technological uncertainty, suggesting that a better understanding of such moderators will help managers to develop more effective HRM practices and management programs. In sum, research is needed that explores how and when culture and cultural diversity make a difference to indi-viduals and to organizational performance.

Third, it is argued that researchers and practitioners need to develop a better understanding of the complex interrelationships between cultural diversity, cultural change, and environmental variables such as social, economic, and political factors that may moderate and/or mediate the effects of culture (Aycan 2005; Leung et al. 2005). HR managers in managing cultural diversity face particular challenges. Related to this, there is a dire need to develop understanding of effective HR strategies for risk management in the twenty-first century.

Fourth, numerous researchers have recommended improvements in research methodologies. Multi-method approaches to research are becoming more prevalent. Further, there are developments in the operationalization and use of constructs with sound psychometric properties, and appropriateness for different cultural contexts (Cheng and Cooper 2003).

Finally, to develop our understanding of cultural diversity and transnational firms, there needs to be greater integration between theory, research, and practice. At present, there is divergence between academics and practitioners with regard to foci and approaches to exploring the implications of cultural diversity. Academics have tended to focus more on individual attitudes and behaviors, while practitioners have sought to understand the links with strategy and firm performance. In some areas, a research–practice gap exists, with research lagging behind the current needs of HR practitioners and managers in transnational firms. The gap may not be easy to fill, as there are complex issues to define, measure, and address. There is also a practice–research gap, with management practice in some aspects lagging behind research (Wasti and Robert 2004).

## 25.8 SUMMARY AND CONCLUSIONS

Overall, the emphasis and direction for the management of cultural diversity places emphasis on the development of organizational cultures that are not only tolerant of diversity but also encourage flexibility and inclusion. There are diverse views about what constitutes effective HRM in transnational firms; and this diversity should be encouraged, not ignored. HR managers in transnational firms face an important challenge in managing the complexities of balancing organizationally consistent policies with responsiveness to local conditions. To do so requires an understanding of both global and local conditions, and the complex relationships between them.

## REFERENCES

ADLER, N. J., DOKTOR, R., and REDDING, S. G. (1986). 'From the Atlantic to the Pacific Century: Cross-cultural Management Reviewed.' *Journal of Management*, 12: 295–318.

AYCAN, Z. (2005). 'The Interplay between Cultural and Institutional/Structural Contingencies in Human Resource Management Practices.' *International Journal of Human Resource Management*, 16: 1083–119.

BARTLETT, C., and GHOSHAL, S. (1992). *Transnational Management: Text, Cases and Readings in Cross Border Management*. Boston: Irwin.

BARTLETT, K. R., LAWLER, J. J., BAE, J., CHEN, S.-J., and WAN, D. (2002). 'Differences in International Human Resource Development among Indigenous Firms and Multinational Affiliates in East and South East Asia.' *Human Resource Development Quarterly*, 13: 383–405.

BEATTY, R. W., EWING, J. R., and THARP, C. G. (2003). 'HR's Role in Corporate Governance: Present and Prospective.' *Human Resource Management*, 42: 257–69.

BLAU, P. M. (1977). 'A Macrosociological Theory of Social Structure.' *American Journal of Sociology*, 83: 26–54.

BROWN, I. C. (1963). *Understanding Other Cultures*. Englewood Cliffs, NJ: Prentice-Hall.

BUDHWAR, P., and BARUCH, Y. (2003). 'Career Management Practices in India: An Empirical Study.' *International Journal of Manpower*, 24/6: 699–721.

CHENG, J. L. C., and COOPER, D. L. (2003). 'A Strategic Context Approach to International Human Resource Management Research.' *Leadership in International Business Education and Research. Research in Global Strategic Management*, 8: 235–50.

CHIANG, F. (2005). 'A Critical Examination of Hofstede's Thesis and its Application to International Reward Management.' *International Journal of Human Resource Management*, 16: 1545–63.

COX T. H. (1993). *Cultural Diversity in Organizations: Theory, Research and Practice*. San Francisco: Berrett-Koehler.

—— (2001). *Creating the Multicultural Organization: A Strategy for Capturing the Power of Diversity*. San Francisco: Jossey-Bass.

CRAMTON, C. D., and HINDS, P. J. (2005). 'Subgroup Dynamics in Internationally Distributed Teams: Ethnocentrism or Cross-national Learning?' *Research in Organizational Behavior*, 26: 231–63.

CZINKOTA, M. R., KNIGHT, G. A., and LIESCH, P. W. (2004). 'Terrorism and International Business: Conceptual Foundations.' In G. G. S. Suder (ed.), *Terrorism and the International Business Environment: The Security–Business Nexus*. Cheltenham: Edward Elgar.

DE CIERI, H., and DOWLING, P. J. (1997). 'Strategic International Human Resource Management: An Asia-Pacific Perspective.' *Management International Review*, 37/1: 21–42.

—— —— (2006, in press). 'Strategic Human Resource Management in Multinational Enterprises: Developments and Directions.' In I. Björkman and G. Stahl (eds.), *Handbook of International HRM Research*. Cheltenham: Edward Elgar.

DOWLING, P. J. (1999). 'Completing the Puzzle: Issues in the Development of the Field of International Human Resource Management.' *Management International Review*, 39 (Special issue 3): 27–43.

—— and WELCH, D. E. (2004). *International Human Resource Management: Managing People in a Multinational Context*, 4th edn. London: Thomson.

Doz, Y., and Prahalad C. K. (1991). 'Managing DMNCs: A Search for a New Paradigm.' *Strategic Management Journal*, 12: 145–64.

Earley, P. C. (2002). 'Redefining Interactions across Cultures and Organizations: Moving Forward with Cultural Intelligence.' *Research in Organizational Behavior*, 24: 271–99.

—— and Gibson, C. (2002). *Multinational Teams: A New Perspective*. Mahwah, NJ: Lawrence Erlbaum and Associates.

—— and Mosakowski, E. (2004). 'Cultural Intelligence.' *Harvard Business Review*, October: 139–46.

Egan, M. L., and Bendick, M., Jr. (2003). 'Workforce Diversity Initiatives of U.S. Multinational Corporations in Europe.' *Thunderbird International Business Review*, 45: 701–27.

Ely, R. J., and Thomas, D. A. (2001). 'Cultural Diversity at Work: The Effects of Diversity Perspectives on Work Group Processes and Outcomes.' *Administrative Science Quarterly*, 46: 229–73.

Engle, A. D., Mendenhall, M. E., Powers, R. L., and Stedham, Y. (2001). 'Conceptualizing the Global Competency Cube: A Transitional Model of Human Resources.' *Journal of European Industrial Training*, 25: 346–53.

Evans, P., Pucik, V., and Barsoux, J.-L. (2002). *The Global Challenge: Frameworks for IHRM*. New York: McGraw-Hill Irwin.

Friday, E., and Friday, S. S. (2003). 'Managing Diversity Using a Strategic Planned Change Approach.' *Journal of Management Development*, 22: 863–80.

Gannon, M. J. (1994). *Understanding Global Cultures: Metaphorical Journeys through 17 Countries*. Thousand Oaks, Calif.: Sage.

Gerhart, B., and Fang, M. (2005). 'National Culture and Human Resource Management: Assumptions and Evidence.' *International Journal of Human Resource Management*, 16: 971–86.

GMAC Global Relocation Services, National Foreign Trade Council, and SHRM Global Forum (2003). *Global Relocation Trends 2002 Survey Report*. Warren, NJ: GMAC Global Relocation Services.

Grimes, D. S., and Richard, O. C. (2003). 'Could Communication Form Impact Organizations' Experience with Diversity?' *Journal of Business Communication*, 40: 7–27.

Harris, H., and Brewster, C. (2003). 'Alternatives to Traditional International Assignments.' In W. Mayrhofer, G. Stahl, and T. Kuhlmann (eds.), *Innovative Anstatze im Internationalen Personalmanagement (Innovating HRM)*. Munich: Hampp Verlag.

Hofstede, G. (1980). *Culture's Consequences: International Differences in Work Related Values*. Beverly Hills, Calif.: Sage.

—— (2001). *Culture's Consequences*, 2nd edn. Thousand Oaks, Calif.: Sage.

House, R. J., Hanges, P. J., Javidan, M., Dorfman, P. W., and Gupta, V. (2004). *Culture, Leadership, and Organizations: The GLOBE Study of 62 Societies*. Thousand Oaks, Calif.: Sage.

Huang, X., and Van de Vliert, E. (2003). 'Comparing Work Behaviors across Cultures: A Cross-level Approach Using Multilevel Modeling.' *International Journal of Cross-cultural Management*, 3: 167–82.

Husted, B. W. (2003). 'Globalization and Cultural Change in International Business Research.' *Journal of International Management*, 9: 427–33.

James, M., and Ward, K. (2001). 'Leading a Multinational Team of Change Agents at Glaxo Wellcome (now Glaxo SmithKine).' *Journal of Change Management*, 2/2: 148–59.

JAVIDAN, M., and HOUSE, R. J. (2001). 'Cultural Acumen for the Global Manager: Lessons from Project GLOBE.' *Organizational Dynamics*, 29: 289–305.

JONES, M. T. (2005). 'The Transnational Corporation, Corporate Social Responsibility and the "Outsourcing" Debate.' *Journal of American Academy of Business*, 6/2: 91–7.

KERR, C., DUNLOP, J. T., HARBISON, F., and MYERS, C. A. (1960). *Industrialism and Industrial Man*. Cambridge, Mass.: Harvard University Press.

KLUCKHOHN, C. (1954). *Culture and Behavior*. New York: Free Press.

—— and STRODTBECK, K. (1961). *Variations in Value Orientations*. Westport, Conn.: Greenwood.

KROEBER, A. L., and KLUCKHOHN, C. (1952). *Culture: A Critical Review of Concepts and Definitions*. Boston: Harvard University Press.

LEUNG, K., SU, S. K., and MORRIS, M. (2001). 'Justice in the Culturally Diverse Workplace: The Problems of Over and Under Emphasis of Culture.' In S. Gilliland, D. Steiner, and D. Skarlicki (eds.), *Theoretical and Cultural Perspectives on Organizational Justice*. Greenwich, Conn.: Information Age Publishing.

—— BHAGAT, R. S., BUCHAN, N. R., EREZ, M., and GIBSON, C. S. (2005). 'Culture and International Business: Recent Advances and their Implications for Future Research.' *Journal of International Business Studies*, 36: 357–78.

LIU, C., TJOSVOLD, D., and WONG, M. (2004). 'Effective Japanese Leadership in China: Co-operative Goals and Applying Abilities for Mutual Benefit.' *International Journal of Human Resource Management*, 15: 730–49.

McDONOUGH, E. F., KAHN, K. B., and BARCZAK, G. (2001). 'An Investigation of the Use of Global, Virtual, and Colocated New Product Development Teams.' *Journal of Product Innovation Management*, 18: 110–20.

MARKUS, H. R., and KITAYAMA, S. (1991). 'Culture and the Self: Implications for Cognition, Emotion and Motivation.' *Psychological Review*, 98: 224–53.

MINBAEVA, D., PEDERSEN, T., BJÖRKMAN, I., FEY, C. F., and PARK, H. J. (2003). 'MNC Knowledge Transfer, Subsidiary Absorptive Capacity and HRM.' *Journal of International Business Studies*, 34: 586–99.

MIROSHNIK, V. (2002). 'Culture and International Management: A Review.' *Journal of Management Development*, 21: 521–44.

MOLLICA, K. A., GRAY, B., and TREVIÑO, L. K. (2003). 'Racial Homophily and its Persistence in Newcomers' Social Networks.' *Organization Science*, 14/2: 123–46.

MYLONI, B., HARZING, A.-W., and MIRZA, H. (2004). 'Human Resource Management in Greece: Have the Colours of Culture Faded Away?' *International Journal of Cross-cultural Management*, 4: 59–76.

NG, K.-Y., and EARLEY, P. C. (2006). 'Culture + Intelligence: Old Constructs, New Frontiers.' *Group & Organization Management*, 31/1: 4–19.

NOHRIA, N., and GHOSHAL, S. (1997). *The Differentiated Network: Organizing Multinational Corporations for Value Creation*. San Francisco: Jossey-Bass.

PELLED, L. H., EISENHARDT, K. M., and XIN, K. R. (1999). 'Exploring the Black Box: An Analysis of Work Group Diversity, Conflict, and Performance.' *Administrative Science Quarterly*, 44: 1–28.

PENG, M. W. (2004). 'Identifying the Big Question in International Business Research.' *Journal of International Business Studies*, 35: 99–108.

RAMAMURTI, R. (2004). 'Developing Countries and MNEs: Extending and Enriching the Research Agenda.' *Journal of International Business Studies*, 35: 277–83.

RICHARD, O. C. (2000). 'Racial Diversity, Business Strategy, and Firm Performance: A Resource-Based View.' *Academy of Management Journal*, 43: 164–77.

—— BARNETT, T., DWYER, S., and CHADWICK, K. (2004). 'Cultural Diversity in Management, Firm Performance, and the Moderating Role of Entrepreneurial Orientation Dimensions.' *Academy of Management Journal*, 47: 255–66.

SCHWARTZ, S. H. (1994). 'Beyond Individualism/Collectivism: New Dimensions of Values.' In U. Kim, H. C. Triandis, C. Kagitcibasi, S. C. Choi, and G. Yoon (eds.), *Individualism and Collectivism: Theory, Method and Applications*. Newbury Park, Calif.: Sage.

SHAW, J. B., and BARRETT-POWER, E. (1998). 'The Effects of Diversity on Small Work Group Processes and Performance.' *Human Relations*, 51: 1307–25.

SPARROW, P., SCHULER R. S., and JACKSON, S. E. (1994). 'Convergence or Divergence: Human Resource Practices and Policies for Competitive Advantage Worldwide.' *International Journal of Human Resource Management*, 5: 267–99.

SUDER, G. G. S. (ed.) (2004). *Terrorism and the International Business Environment: The Security–Business Nexus*. Cheltenham: Edward Elgar.

TAJFEL, H., and TURNER, J. (1985). 'The Social Identity of Intergroup Behavior.' In S. Worchel and W. Austin (eds.), *Psychology and Intergroup Relations*. Chicago: Nelson-Hall.

THOMAS, D. A. (2004). 'Diversity as Strategy.' *Harvard Business Review*, September: 98–108.

TREGASKIS, O., HERATY, N., and MORLEY, M. (2001). 'HRD in Multinationals: The Global/ Local Mix.' *Human Resource Management Journal*, 11/2: 34–56.

TUNG, R. L. (1993). 'Managing Cross-national and Intra-national Diversity.' *Human Resource Management*, 32: 461–77.

WASTI, S. A., and ROBERT, C. (2004). 'Out of Touch? An Evaluation of the Correspondence between Academic and Practitioner Concerns in IHRM.' In J. L. C. Cheng and M. Hitt (eds.), *Managing Multinationals in a Knowledge Economy: Economics, Culture and Human Resources*. London: JAI Press.

WENTLING, R. M. (2000). 'Evaluation of Diversity Initiatives in Multinational Corporations.' *Human Resource Development International*, 3: 435–50.

WONG-MINGJI, D., and MIR, A. H. (1997). 'How International is International Management? Provincialism, Parochialism, and the Problematic of Global Diversity.' In P. Prasad, A. J. Mills, M. Elmes, and A. Prasad (eds.), *Managing the Organizational Melting Pot: Dilemmas of Workplace Diversity*. Thousand Oaks, Calif.: Sage.

WRIGHT, P. M., and BREWSTER, C. V. (2003). 'Editorial: Learning from Diversity: HRM is Not Lycra.' *International Journal of Human Resource Management*, 14: 1299–307.

ZHU, C. J., COOPER, B., DE CIERI, H., and DOWLING, P. J. (2005) 'A Problematic Transition to a Strategic Role: Human Resource Management in Industrial Enterprises in China.' *International Journal of Human Resource Management*, 16: 517–35.

# PART IV

## MEASUREMENT AND OUTCOMES

CHAPTER 26

..................................................................................................................

# HRM AND BUSINESS PERFORMANCE

..................................................................................................................

## JOHN PURCELL

## NICHOLAS KINNIE

## 26.1 INTRODUCTION

..................................................................................................................

THE search for causal links between strategic HRM and business performance has dominated both academic and practitioner debate for over two decades. Boselie et al. (2005) found 104 research papers published in reputable academic journals over a ten-year period up to the end of 2003. A continuing stream has flowed since then. This focus on one issue in HRM has led it to be described as 'the HRM Holy Grail.' If an unambiguous causal connection can be established between HRM practices and organizational performance then it will have significant and positive implications for the subject. The practitioner's search for legitimacy and a place at the board table will be enhanced. In business schools, HRM academics will be on a par with colleagues in finance rather than being the poor relations, as is too often the case.

Unfortunately, this state of nirvana remains a long way off. Numerous review papers (at least eleven have been published since 2000) have found this field of research often wanting in terms of method, theory, and the specification of HR practices to be used when establishing a relationship with performance outcomes. The function of this chapter is not to review all of the methodological and theoretical challenges. This can be found elsewhere, for example in Wright and Gardner (2003) and Wall and Wood (2005), nor to summarize the evidence: Boselie et al. (2005) have done an excellent job here. Rather, we pose more fundamental questions such as what is meant by performance, how an HR system is to be configured, how the causal chain between HR practices and performance outcomes is to be modeled, and what this means for research in the area. Most importantly, it challenges what we mean by Human Resource Management. What should be included and what aspects of organizational life are beyond the scope of the subject? Recent research is reviewed to argue that culture, leadership, line manager behavior, and operational management all need to fall within our area of interest. Before getting into the substance of these points, it is necessary to say something about the type of problems that have bedeviled research in the area.

# 26.2 Problems of Method

Wright and Gardner (2003: 312) summarize these problems:

While evidence mounts that HR practices are at least weakly related to firm performance, significant methodological and theoretical challenges exist ... Methodologically, there is no consensus regarding which practices constitute a theoretically complete set of HR practices; how to conceptually categorize these practices; the relevance of business strategy; the appropriate level of analysis; or how HR performance and firm performance are to be measured ... Theoretically, no consensus exists regarding the mechanism by which HR practices might impact on firm outcomes.

Many, if not most, studies have used postal surveys sent to single responders such as a senior HR manager. They are asked from a predetermined list of HR practices to indicate which are in use and, often but not always, to estimate the proportion of employees covered by each practice. Often the same respondent is asked to estimate the productivity, performance, or profitability of their firm relative to others in their sector. Alternatively, published accounting data is used. Statistical techniques of varying degrees of sophistication are then used to explore the nature of the relationship between the two sets of variables. One of the earliest studies here and the most notable was that of Huselid (1995) and few subsequently have reached his level of sophistication. The general conclusion is that there is a clear observable relationship between the adoption of HR practices and performance outcomes with generally the greater the number of practices in place, the stronger the positive relationship. Gerhart (2005: 175) summarizes some of the evidence:

One standard deviation increase in HR system practices (relative to the mean) designed to enhance workforce ability, motivation and opportunity to contribute was associated with roughly 20% better firm financial performance. Consider that this finding means that firms one standard deviation above the mean are 120% of mean performance, while those one standard deviation below the mean are at 80% of mean performance, making for a 120/80 = 50% advantage of being +1 standard deviation versus −1 standard deviation. This is a large difference.

Gerhart (2005: 177) goes on to rather spoil the story by suggesting that the 'effect size is so large as to perhaps not be credible.' Large-scale databases of multiple numbers of firms or branches of large organizations have been able to establish representative data showing the nature of this relationship. 'Sophisticated' HRM, often referred to as High-Performance Work Systems (HPWSs) or High-Commitment Management (HCM), has been associated with better performance.[1] What, of course, is not at all clear is the direction of the relationship. Cross-sectional research can only reveal associations, not causality, and it is equally plausible that excellent firms will both be able to afford sophisticated HR systems and wish to invest in them.

The methodological downside to this type of research, which some may be fatally flawed (Wall and Wood 2005), can be summarized in three ways. First, respondents may have incomplete knowledge, for example of how many employees are covered by a particular practice, especially if the respondent is located at the corporate office of a firm with numerous business units. There is also the difficulty of assuming that HR practices are translated into actual practices, as discussed later. If multiple respondents are used to try to overcome this problem there is surprisingly little consensus between them (Gerhart et al. 2000). The overall reliability of HR practice measures is 'frighteningly low' (Wright and Gardner 2003: 316). There is also an attribution problem where the HR respondent in a successful firm may assume that a practice exists or how else could the firm be successful? Second, one cannot rely on the same person to estimate HR practices and performance. This 'common method variance' is equally frightening. Third, no account is taken of the lag effect. How long does it take for an HR practice to impact on performance? Measuring HRM and performance in the same time period cannot possibly show that HRM drives performance (or the reverse that good performance drives better HRM). Wright et al. (2005: 412) are even harsher. They note that 'by far the most prevalent design [in the sixty-six studies they reviewed] is what we call "post-predictive" because it measures HR practices after the performance period resulting in actually predicting *past* performance' (their emphasis). Thus, overall, 'the literature on the HRM-performance relationship has (a) universally reported significant relationships between HRM and performance, (b) almost exclusively used designs that do not logically allow one to draw causal conclusions, and (c) very seldom actually tested for a reverse causal order' (Wright et al. 2005: 416).

---

[1] We discuss the limitations of this approach, especially the importance of contextual factors (Guthrie 2001; Arthur 1994; Datta et al. 2005; Capelli and Neumark 2001; Way 2002), in more detail below.

These same authors then argue that three criteria need to be used to establish cause. First, cause requires that the effect be present when the cause is present and be absent when the cause is absent. Second, the proposed cause must exist in time prior to the proposed outcome and, third, all other variables that might cause the outcome are controlled for (Wright et al. 2005: 411). These are tough criteria and, when used as far as possible by Guest et al. (2003) and by themselves, no unambiguous HR-performance effect is uncovered (but by the same token one cannot 'suggest that HR practices *do not* have a positive impact on performance') (Wright et al. 2005: 433, their emphasis).

# 26.3 THE PROBLEM OF PERFORMANCE

Interestingly, Guest et al.'s study used both 'objective' (i.e. published) performance data and their respondents' subjective evaluation of their firms' performance relative to their competitors. Using this subjective test, HRM was associated with 'high comparative performance' (2003: 311). It is premature to write off such subjective evaluations and rely exclusively on objective performance or profit measures. In multisector studies, such as Guest et al. (2003), it is necessary to control for sectoral variances in profitability. Some sectors generate much higher returns than others. Informed respondents may have a better idea of sectoral conditions than revealed by simple published returns. It is also extraordinarily difficult to meet the third criterion for causal studies, that of controlling for all other potential causal influences. As Hitt et al. note in their study in professional service firms, 'firm performance is a function of many variables both inside and outside a firm ... Thus, for one set of variables (human capital in their study) to explain 3.6% of the variance in firm performance may be significant' (2001: 25). Published corporate accounts are problematic since they cover different business units and perhaps countries where different HR systems are likely to be in place in part because of different regulatory or institutional regimes (Paauwe 2004).

There are two much more fundamental problems with the use of financial performance data. First, it is far removed from HRM influence—too distal. Second, it takes for granted that firms seek to structure their HR systems to maximize financial outcomes, often in the short term seen in shareholder value.

The problem with published financial measures is that no convincing explanation can be provided as to why, or indeed how, HR practices have an influence. As such, the research is remarkably uninformative from a practitioner point of view beyond the knowledge that the 'more' HR practices the better (the so-called 'Huselid curve'). This has led many researchers to use, or at least call for, the adoption of more proximal measures of performance which seem more likely to be directly influenced by, or an outcome of, worker behavior. Typical here would be employee turnover and absence, scrap rates, sales per employee, and customer satisfaction. Harter et al. (2002: 273) found that there was a rank ordering in their correlations between overall employee satisfaction/engagement and measures of performance. The highest were with customer satisfaction, loyalty, and employee turnover followed, in rank order, by safety, productivity, and, lastly, profitability. Proximal measures are not without their difficulties. They too need to be adjusted for sectoral variants. Typical measures of labor management performance like turnover and absenteeism are highly variable between sectors with nursing and teaching, for example, exhibiting higher than average sickness rates. Retail firms and call centers have higher than average labor turnover, at least in the UK. Useful work in retail banking involving comparisons between large numbers of branches using identical HR practices has been done by Gelade and Ivery (2003) and Bartel (2004). An increasing number of large firms in sectors where staff are customer related now collect their own data from surveys of employees and customers mixed with operational measures and financial performance to develop sophisticated models of HR and performance for their own purposes. The seminal work undertaken in Sears in the USA in the late 1990s has been a major influence (Rucci et al. 1998).

The assumption that profitability and financial performance is (or should be) the end goal of HRM is a more profound issue. There are a number of reasons for questioning such a belief. First, as Jacoby (2005) had shown in his comparison of US and Japanese firms, there are major differences of emphasis with the former dominated by shareholder value and the latter using more of a stakeholder approach. The work of Paauwe (2004) leads credence to the view that we need to take account of 'varieties of capitalism,' as noted too by Godard (2004). The focus almost exclusively on shareholder value may be a case of 'US exceptionalism.' Even if shareholder value were accepted as the dominant and legitimate end goal for HRM this use of short-term financial indicators may fail to satisfy shareholders in the longer term. Ostroff and Bowen (2000: 216) draw attention to 'the persistent finding that organizational effectiveness is multi-dimensional.' Emphasis on organizational agility and the search for sustained competitive advantage places different requirements on HRM in its contribution to organizational success. Wright and Snell (1998) neatly summarize the need for 'fit and flexibility' and note the tensions between the two. Fit is related to competitive strategy now, and thence to financial performance; flexibility is building adaptability for future purposes. Increasing turbulence in the business environment and seemingly growing frequency of exogenous shocks places a premium on the latter. Boxall and Purcell (2003) add a third fundamental goal for HRM, social legitimacy. This can be seeking to be 'an employee of choice' or meeting social expectations enshrined in law and social practice. While attempts are often made to justify certain HR practices in terms of their bottom line contributions, the ultimate purpose of some, like diversity policies, is the eradication of discrimination. This is not to deny the importance of HRM contributing to performance; merely to note that financial performance is only one dimension of effectiveness.

## 26.4 THE PROBLEM OF THE SCOPE OF HR PRACTICES

Having dealt with problems concerning the dependent variable, performance, we now need to consider the input to the model of HRM: the HR practices used in analyses. Alas, many problems abound here too. There is no agreement on what constitutes 'HR practices' let alone a full set of them. Boselie et al. (2005) identified twenty-six general categories of practices used by researchers. Most researchers construct a list of practices but there is no agreement on what or which practices to include. While core practices associated with recruitment and selection, training and development, and performance management (appraisal and variable pay) are nearly always included, others like job design and involvement are much more sporadic.

There is little debate on where lists of practices come from or what criteria to use in their construction. The lists appear to emerge from sets of practices normally associated with activities undertaken by well-staffed, sophisticated HR departments in large firms often linked to so-called 'transformational' approaches to the management of labor. These predetermine what type of HR practices are hypothesized to lead to outcomes of higher performance as made clear by Pfeffer's list of seven practices 'for building profits by putting people first' (1998). Behind such choices is the long-standing debate of whether HRM requires 'a distinctive approach to employment management' (Storey 1995: 5), sometimes referred to as 'developmental humanism' or 'soft' HR, or a generic term covering all aspects of the management of labor (Boxall and Purcell 2003: 4). The former tends to focus on 'innovative' HR policies while the latter takes a broader perspective to include, for example, collective work relations often excluded from American studies (Deery and Iverson 2005). Godard's (2004) review of the 'high-performance paradigm' (HPP) finds little support for links with performance but notes increases in work stress (an outcome not usually included in studies). He observes that 'it is again possible that practices traditionally considered to yield positive outcomes for workers such as traditional group work or information sharing are as effective or even more effective than practices associated with HPP' (2004: 360). We need to find a list which does not assume positive outcomes and may reveal negative associations with performance, or no links at all.

Attempts to resolve this 'list' problem have led to a focus on 'HR architecture' (Becker and Gerhart 1996; Wright and Gardner 2003). This proposes that 'HR practices ... be classified into four levels, including guiding principles, policy alternatives (different practices), products (competences and behaviors that practice promotes) and practice-process (the effectiveness of execution of the practice)' (Wright and Gardner 2003: 314). Researchers need to choose the level or levels of practice to investigate rather than rely on an undifferentiated list.

The firm's overall approach to HRM is established in guiding principles. Wright and Boswell (2002: 253) suggest that there is now 'a consensus ... emerging around conceptual categories of employee skills, motivation and empowerment.' This allows for a broad conception of HR architecture to cover policies designed to build and retain human capital and to influence employee behavior (motivation and empowerment). This is now usually referred to as 'ability, motivation and opportunity' (AMO) (Boxall and Purcell 2003).

AMO broadens the architecture dimensions to cover 'knowledge, skills, ability' (KSA) (e.g. Delery and Shaw 2001), motivationally based policies implied in intrinsic and extrinsic incentive structures and rewards, and opportunities to contribute and participate on and off the job. Once AMO is used as an analytical structure, the policy alternatives (second level) and 'products' (third level) can be specified. They will vary from firm to firm. No definitive list of 'best practices' suggested by those advocating a universalistic model of HRM can be predicted. Rather, a range of policy alternatives appropriate to the firm in its sector (or country) can be identified (Datta et al. 2005) and different mixes of policies may have the same performance outcome ('equifinality'). This neatly sidesteps the problem of 'horizontal fit' which requires the number, strength, and combination of practices to be identified, which is especially troublesome where the hypothesis is that the effect of combinations of practices is multiplicative (see Ch. 19). Bowen and Ostroff (2004: 206) note that 'different sets of practices may be equally effective so long as they allow a particular type of climate to develop (e.g. climates of innovation or service).' Thus, the use of an analytical structure such as AMO helps us to deal with the problems of deciding which HR practices should be studied. This is especially so since the need is to focus on the combined impact of HR practices rather than the utility of each individual practice.

# 26.5 THE PROBLEM OF THEORY

The use of AMO begs the question of how the choice of appropriate practices influences performance. This is the problem of theory. Even if robust causal correlations are found between the adoption of a certain mix of practices and performance we do not know why this occurs. We have no evidence on the nature of any intermediary processes that need to occur to produce such relationships. Not for nothing is this referred to as the 'HR black box.' Boselie et al. (2005: 77) confirm 'the impression that the "linking mechanism" between HRM and performance and the *mediating* effects of key variables are largely disregarded. Indeed, while we found plenty of acknowledgement of the existence of the "black box" and some speculation on its possible contents, few studies tried to look inside' (emphasis in the original).

Looking inside the black box requires specifying an HR causal chain. At the centre of the chain are employee attitudes and behavior and it is this which raises the most vital question in the HR–performance debate. If 'the distinctive feature of HRM is its assumption that improved performance is achieved through people in the organisation' (Guest 1997: 269), why is it that so few researchers actually study the people: the employees and their attitudes and behavior? While Delery and Shaw (2001: 190) argue that 'HRM practices and job design have the most significant direct influence on the skills, motivation and empowerment of the workforce,' they go on to say that 'measuring the most important aspects of workforce characteristics may, however, be beyond our capabilities.' They do not say why. Only three out of twenty-five studies examined by Wall and Wood (2005) and eleven of the 104 reviewed by Boselie et al. (2005) used employee survey data. Edwards and Wright (2001: 570) correctly assert that 'it remains rare for studies to assess links in the chain, with effects on employee commitment being a particularly rarely studied issue.' This absence is hard to understand, let alone justify, given the tradition of employee-centered research in organizational behavior and industrial relations. It stems, almost certainly, from the use of multiple-firm datasets where single management respondents are only able to indicate the intended practices and their coverage. They cannot reliably report on employee perceptions of these practices as they experience them. Thus, the usual steps in research, of theory determining the research questions and thence the choice of method, have been reversed. Methodological considerations have determined what questions can be asked while factors beyond the reach of the chosen method, however important, have been ignored. As Guest (2001: 1095) candidly put it, 'almost inevitably, both for the sake of brevity and to increase the chances of publication, many published papers tend to play down a number of methodological and analytical concerns.'

Wright and Nishii (2004) address this issue by proposing an elaborated model of the HR causal chain which is divided into five steps, moving from intended, to actual, to perceived HR practices, followed by employee reactions, and then performance. This model provides an excellent basis for understanding the links between HRM and performance, but it needs further development. First, we examine the subsets of the casual chain in more detail. We then go on to look at

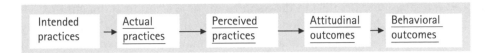

**Fig. 26.1. Revised HR causal chain**

the role of line managers and then place the causal chain within its wider organizational context.

The purpose of Fig. 26.1 is to identify the key causal steps in the chain from intended HR practices to performance outcomes. It does not seek to show all interconnections, nor map in any accurate way the HRM experience of a given firm and its employees. The model allows attention to be focused on critical steps that have to be taken if HRM is to have a performance outcome.

Our principal development of the Wright and Nishii model subdivides employee reactions into employees' attitudinal reactions and their subsequent behavior. Three types of behavior need to be specified, namely the competencies needed to perform the job, discretionary behavior, and turnover and absence (or retention and attendance). These types of employee behavior are highly interelated yet are logically and empirically distinct. These lead to a model which then has the following key features:

- *Intended HR practices* are those designed by senior management to be applied to most or all of the employees and concern employees' ability, motivation, and opportunity to participate. These practices will be influenced by the articulated values of the organization and found in the HR manual or the appropriate web pages. These also include the ways work is structured and organized since this has an impact on employee attitudes and behavior.
- *Actual HR practices* are those which are actually applied, usually by line managers (discussed in more detail below). There may often be a substantial difference between the espousal and the enactment of HR practices in an organization (Hutchinson and Purcell 2004).
- *Perceived HR practices* require that attention is focused on how employees experience and then judge the HR practices that are applied to them. What they perceive may be different from, or the same as, intended and may be judged through a lens of fairness and organizational justice. *Perceived HR practices* can again be classified using the AMO model. This needs, also, to cover perceptions of overall work climate seen, for example, in levels of trust (Whitener 2001) and employees' job experience (pace, effort, autonomy, challenge, stress, etc.).
- *Attitudinal outcomes* include attitudes employees hold toward their job and their employer and/or levels of morale or motivation. This especially includes employees' willingness to cooperate and their overall satisfaction with their job.

- *Behavioral outcomes* flow in the main from these attitudinal dimensions. This can be learning new methods of working, engaging in behavior which is beyond that required, such as organizational citizenship behavior (OCB) (Coyle-Shapiro et al. 2004*a*), or seen in levels of attendance and remaining in the job (or their opposites).
- *Performance outcomes* can be distal or proximal and can be restricted to short-term definitions of performance or can be expanded to include measures of effectiveness.

Relating employee attitudes to behavior and thence to performance is relatively new in HRM but there are a growing number of studies that have done this (for example Ostroff and Bowen 2000 and Judge et al. 2001). 'This line of research,' concludes Gerhart (2005: 179), 'suggests that positive workforce attitudes create value.' In seeking to understand this downstream connection between attitudes and performance, and upstream between HR practices and attitudes, there is much to be gained from social exchange theory (Coyle-Shapiro et al. 2004*b*). In summary, social exchange applied to HRM theory suggests 'HR practices are viewed by employees as a "personalized" commitment to them by the organization which is then reciprocated back to the organization by employees through positive attitudes and behavior' (Hannah and Iverson 2004: 339). Perceived organizational support (POS) may be linked to particular policies of salience to employees but it is the overall effect, or the 'strength' of the HR system (Bowen and Ostroff 2004), and employees' broader conceptions of the employment relationship which are critical. This discussion of social exchange theory reopens the debate of what HRM is.

# 26.6 THE PROBLEM OF WHAT IS HRM

If it is the overall effect of the HR system, or its 'strength', which employees respond to, then the parameters of such a system need to equate as closely as possible to the employees' experience of the world of work and the range of practices the employer uses to structure this. What are the features of organizational life which are likely to influence employee attitudes and behavior? HR practices, as we have traditionally viewed them, will be a necessary, but never a sufficient, component. The role of line managers as agents enacting HR practices, and the transmission of organizational culture (sometimes referred to as 'climate'), will need to be included. Both of these touch on questions of leadership and the nature of the relationship between manager(s) and employee(s). Critical features of the firm's operational system as it affects employees, seen in staffing levels, job design, and the 'social relations of production' (Edwards and Wright 2001: 581), will be relevant since these determine how many employees are required, the interface with technology, skill levels required, and strongly influence what people actually do at work. Beyond these, factors such as organizational values and culture will be influential.

Scholars have only recently begun to apply these features of organizational behavior to HRM and its effects on performance. Wright et al. (2005: 419) give examples of leadership, organizational culture, and line management enactment influencing performance. They argue that 'a "spurious" relationship might exist if there were an actual true co-variation between the measures of HR practice and performance yet, there was no direct causal relationship between the two variables.' HR practice measures may be acting as proxies for these wider variables of leadership, culture, and manager behavior. They conclude that 'studies that do not control for a full set of variables that might cause performance may lack the data necessary for making valid causal inferences' (ibid.: 420). However, to be able to apply controls, the variables must be measured. The justification for collecting such data merely to control for variances, alongside the usual suspects of firm age, sector, size, and certain workforce characteristics, can only be made if there is a clear, unambiguous, agreed definition of what HRM is. This is far from the case. From a practitioner perspective, questions of leadership, culture, and managerial behavior are commonly seen to fall within the HR manager's area of activity with growing roles in the management of change and organizational transformation. Thus, on grounds of theory, and from both employee and HR manager perspectives, it is argued that a wider definition of HRM is necessary. Some use the wider term 'people management' (Paul and Anantharaman 2003; Purcell et al. 2003). This has some merit since it signals a wider research agenda and avoids one of the pitfalls in HR–performance research where respondents erroneously believe the research is about the efficacy or the importance of the HR department. This is a very different question from that considered here.

We need, therefore, to develop our causal chain model further if we are to capture these key additional features discussed in the most recent research. Figure 26.2 pays attention to the experience of HRM by employees, especially to the role of the line manager when implementing HR practices, and sets this within the wider context of the operational system and the culture and climate of the organization. The model does not predict a particular research method. Indeed, as many review papers have noted, there is a need for qualitative and quantitative research at unit level, firm level, sector, and country if we are to understand both the relationship between HR practices and performance outcomes and the dynamics of the interconnections.

## 26.6.1 The Vital Role of Line Managers

The omission of line managers as HRM agents, and more broadly in managing or leading employees, is seen as 'curious' by Delery and Shaw (2001: 136) 'given the

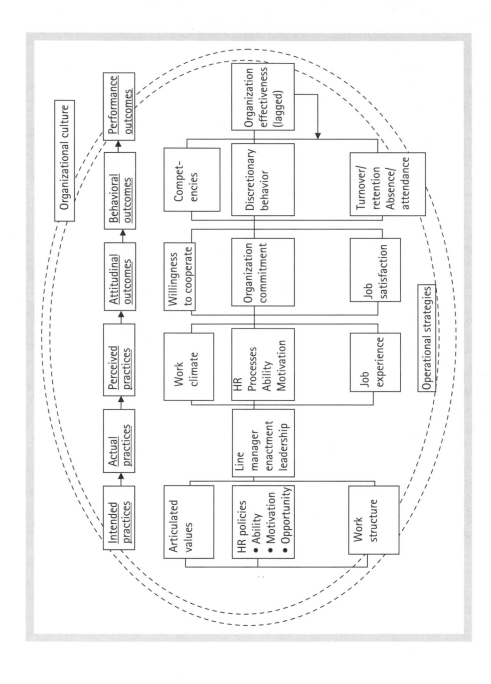

**Fig. 26.2. People management, HRM, and organizational effectiveness**

success of many practices often considered "high performance" hinges on the nature of the inter-personal relations in the organisation.' Truss (2001: 1136) uses the concept of agency and shows qualitatively and quantitatively in Hewlett Packard that 'managers act as a powerful mediator between the individual and HR practices'. Social exchange theory (Whitener et al. 1998) has been used to examine the antecedents of managerial trustworthy behavior and, more recently, uses the term 'leader–member exchange' (LMX) and applies it to the HRM–performance debate. LMX is seen to be critical since 'more effectively developed relationships are beneficial for individual and work unit functioning and have many positive outcomes to firm performance' (Uhl-Bien et al. 2000: 138). Managers as agents can play important roles in the transmission of values and climate. Becker et al. (1996) showed that there is a stronger relationship between commitment to supervisors and performance than found between commitment to the organization and performance. This 'more cognitively proximal focus' exerts greater influence on employee behavior (Redman and Snape 2005: 304). Perceptions of LMX provide evidence of the quality of the relationship, which may then show the extent of 'alignment or congruence between individual and managerial goals' (Bowen and Ostroff 2004: 209) while simultaneously being more direct in their influence over employee attitudes.

In our HRM causal model the distinction between 'intended practices' and 'actual practices' draws attention to the frequently experienced gap between espoused HR practices and their enactment. While some HR practices may impact on employees directly, most rely on line manager action or support. Employee perceptions of HR practices are thus likely to be strongly shaped by how their managers apply these HR practices, and influence the immediate work climate where they work. Indeed, since the line manager is the dominant influence in both, it is likely to be hard for employees to distinguish between them in any meaningful way. There are numerous examples of line managers modifying HR practices and of their difficulty or unwillingness to enact a whole range of HR policies (Whittaker and Marchington 2003). Both Purcell and Hutchinson (2006) and Guest and Conway (2004) observe that there is much greater variance in employee perceptions of their line manager's 'leadership behavior' than in satisfaction with HR practices. Guest and Conway (2004: 19–32) show that supervisory leadership is the strongest factor associated with organizational commitment and work satisfaction as well as with other attitudinal factors such as loyalty to consumers. It is not just the quality of the LMX relationship but also the extent to which line managers are perceived to be the providers of effective HR practices. This dual role leads Bowen and Ostroff (2004: 216) to suggest that 'a strong HRM system coupled with a visible supervisor may foster stronger relationships among HRM, climate and performance than each would individually.'

## 26.6.2 Operational Management Systems

Research which focuses exclusively on HR practices has the effect of isolating HRM from other aspects of organizational life. HPWS research, especially in manufacturing (see Chapter 20), necessarily broadens the research agenda to cover flexible production, work systems, and HPWS practices. 'The argument', writes Wood (1999: 369), 'is that high-performance systems that are integrated with the wider organization will yield stronger results than those that are not.' This is where the concept of 'embeddedness' is important. 'HR creates value when it is embedded in the operational system of an organization that enhances the firm's capabilities' (Becker and Gerhart 1996: 782). These authors use other terms, such as 'operational fabrics' (1996: 788) and 'firm infrastructure' (1996: 794), suggesting that HR practices must be aligned with the firm's unique business problems. At one level, this is a question of fit with operational strategies. At another level, the very choices firms make on operational strategies have a direct impact on workers—their jobs and task variety, staffing levels and thus effort, work time and social relations at work—and strongly influence line management roles in directing workers. Boxall (2003) shows in the service sector how the type of markets served influences the knowledge content of jobs required for service, the type of work design, competitive dynamics, and types of strategic HRM. Batt (2002) provides detailed examples of this in call centers while Appelbaum et al. (2000) show this in manufacturing industry.

It can be argued that operational strategy, in the same way as business strategy, can be seen as a major influence over choices of HR systems but it is unnecessary to include it within research focused upon the impact of HR on performance. However, some features of operational management relating to the organization of work are so influential on employees that they need to be included, as shown in our model. In particular, aspects of perceived job design like effort, autonomy, challenge, and stress need to be included (Ramsay et al. 2000). As does teamwork (Harley 2001). Boselie et al. (2005) found that a minority of studies (forty in the case of teamwork, twenty-five in the case of job design) included some aspects of operational management. These job features are so central to work experience, and are likely to be strongly related to job satisfaction and commitment, that their exclusion will probably be the cause of covariance. This means that they are variables which need to be controlled for or which have to be included within the research, either as part of the HR system or as moderating variables.

## 26.6.3 Organization Culture, Climate, and Values

Guest et al. (2003: 291) adopt a resource-based view of strategy (RBV) in searching for the HR–performance link. They note the importance of 'the management of organisational culture' but do not research it or control for it. Yet culture is usually seen as a critical intangible asset in RBV (Barney and Wright 1998). Culture, often defined as embedded assumptions and shared values (O'Reilly and Chapman 1996), 'function(s) both as [an] antecedent to the HRM system and as a mediator of its linkage to firm performance ... [These] organizational assumptions and values shape HRM practices which, in turn, reinforce cultural norms and routines that can shape individual and firm performance' (Bowen and Ostroff 2004: 205). Gordon and DiTomaso (1992) use consistency of value-sharing as a test of strong cultures. Values are likely to be articulated by senior management in part as a reflection of their own, or the organization's inherited, value system. It is these values which, in part at least, are likely to shape HR architecture and HR practices.

Thus, the starting point is to identify these articulated values and then assess the extent to which they are shared. This is similar, but not identical to, organizational 'climate.' This is defined by Bowen and Ostroff (2004: 205) as being 'a shared perception of what the organization is like in terms of practices, policies, procedures, routines and rewards, what is important and what behaviours are expected.' While Bowen and Ostroff suggest that 'HRM practices and the HRM system will play a critical role in determining climate perceptions' (2004: 205), it is just as likely that culture and climate influence both the choice of HR practices and how these practices are perceived by employees. This is an empirical question which has yet to be answered. We need to measure culture/climate if we are to assess the relative importance of these and HR practices and assess how the one mediates the other in linking to performance. We have therefore placed it as a contextual ring outside the central HRM causal chain, as shown in Fig. 26.2.

# 26.4 CONCLUSIONS

This chapter has focused on the problems experienced in seeking to assess the extent to which HRM impacts on organizational performance. Paradoxically, many researchers report positive associations but are unable to do so in a way which is sufficiently convincing to meet strict tests in the theory of causality or generate sufficiently robust evidence of either HR practices or performance. Four types of substantive problems have been considered. First is the problem of performance measures. These range from distal financial measures to proximal indicators, which are more likely to be directly influenced by employees, and are thus more obvious outcomes of HR practices. It is doubtful whether objective measures of performance are necessarily the only outcomes of interest since longer-term firm viability and, for some, the maintenance of sustained competitive advantage is likely to require flexibility and agility. These requirements may influence the design of HR systems as much as achieving shorter-term performance outcomes. In some cases, they may even be the dominant outcome requirement. A third end goal of HRM is the pursuit of social legitimacy and the requirement to meet societal expectations and regulations which vary from country to country. In practice, all three outcomes—productivity, flexibility, and legitimacy—are likely to be required to a greater or lesser extent. 'A superior performance in HRM ... implies an outstanding mix of outcomes across these three areas' (Boxall and Purcell 2003: 8) (see Chapter 3).

The second cluster of problems concerns the choice of HR practices. There is an extraordinary lack of agreement among researchers on what practices to include and a paucity of explanation on why particular lists are chosen. The use of 'HR architecture' identifying four different levels of HRM provides some logic and order in the choice of practices. The use of generic categories of practice such as KSA and AMO is particularly helpful since different combinations may have the same outcome.

Third, progress in HRM–performance research can only be made if theory is focused on the causal chain between practice and outcome. Employees are at the heart of all casual chains because they are the focal point of HR practices and they deliver performance. Employee responses to HR practices have not been included in most research designs, until recently, and this has impoverished the field. Once employees are put center stage, involving very different research designs and datasets, it becomes possible to advance the theory of HRM and performance. Social exchange theory offers one possible avenue for development within HRM.

The focus on employees' reactions to HR practices—their perceptions of them, not just as practices, but in terms of fairness and justice, motivation and effectiveness in influencing attitudes and behavior—takes us back to the debate on what HRM really is. Other features of organizational life are likely to influence employee attitudes and behavior so much that they cannot be excluded. These are the role line managers play in the delivery of HR practices and in establishing relationships with employees, features of the operational management system which affect job design and job experience, and organizational culture and its sub-area, climate. The covariance problem is so strong that either these factors need to be controlled for or, and this is the route preferred here, they need to be incorporated in our definition of HRM. Once we have a robust, theoretically sound, model of HRM and a clear view of the causal chain, it will be possible, with research focused mainly on employees, their responses to people management, and organizational outcomes, to move to the next step in the search for the HRM Holy Grail.

## REFERENCES

APPELBAUM, E., BAILEY, T., BERG, P., and KALLEBERGH, A. (2000). *Manufacturing Advantage: Why High Performance Systems Pay off.* Ithaca, NY: ILR Press.

ARTHUR, J. (1994). 'Effects of Human Resource Systems on Manufacturing Performance and Turnover.' *Academy of Management Journal*, 37: 670–87.

BARNEY, J., and WRIGHT, P. (1998). 'On Becoming a Strategic Partner: The Roles of Human Resources in Gaining Competitive Advantage.' *Human Resource Management*, 37: 31–46.

BARTEL, A. (2004). 'Human Resource Management and Organizational Performance: Evidence from Retail Banking.' *Industrial and Labor Relations Review*, 57/2: 181–203.

BATT, R. (2002). 'Managing Customer Services: Human Resource Practices, Quit Rates, and Sales Growth.' *Academy of Management Journal*, 45: 587–97.

BECKER, B., and GERHART, B. (1996). 'The Impact of Human Resource Management on Organizational Performance: Progress and Prospects.' *Academy of Management Journal*, 39/4: 779–801.

BECKER, T., BILLINGS, R., EVELETH, D., and GILBERT, N. (1996). 'Foci and Bases of Employee Commitment: Implications for Job Performance.' *Academy of Management Journal*, 39: 464–82.

BOSELIE, P., DIETZ, G., and BOON, C. (2005). 'Commonalities and Contradictions in Research on Human Resource Management and Performance.' *Human Resource Management Journal*, 13/3: 67–94.

BOWEN, D., and OSTROFF, C. (2004). 'Understanding HRM–Firm Performance Linkages: The Role of the "Strength" of the HRM System.' *Academy of Management Review*, 29: 203–21.

BOXALL, P. (2003). 'HR Strategy and Competitive Advantage in the Service Sector.' *Human Resource Management Journal*, 13/3: 5–20.

—— and PURCELL, J. (2003). *Strategy and Human Resource Management*. Basingstoke: Palgrave.

CAPPELLI, P., and NEUMARK, D. (2001). 'Do "High Performance" Work Practices Improve Establishment Level Outcomes?' *Industrial and Labor Relations Review*, 54: 737–75.

COYLE-SHAPIRO, J., KESSLER, I., and PURCELL, J. (2004a). 'Exploring Organizationally Directed Citizenship Behaviour: Reciprocity or "It's my Job" '. *Journal of Management Studies*, 41/1: 85–106.

—— SHORE, L., TAYLOR, S., and TETRICK, L. (eds.) (2004b). *The Employment Relationship: Examining Psychological and Contextual Perspectives*. Oxford: Oxford University Press.

DATTA, D. K., GUTHRIE, J. P., and WRIGHT, P. M. (2005). 'Human Resource Management and Labor Productivity: Does Industry Matter?' *Academy of Management Journal*, 46/1: 135–45.

DEERY, S., and IVERSON, R. (2005). 'Labor–Management Cooperation: Antecedents and Impact on Organizational Performance.' *Industrial and Labor Relations Review*, 58/4: 588–601.

DELERY, J., and SHAW, J. (2001). 'The Strategic Management of People in Work Organizations: Review, Synthesis and Extension.' *Research in Personnel and Human Resources Management*, 20: 165–97.

EDWARDS, P., and WRIGHT, M. (2001). 'High Involvement Work Systems and Performance Outcomes: The Strength of Variable, Contingent and Context Bound Relationships.' *International Journal of Human Resource Management*, 124: 568–85.

GELADE, G., and IVERY, M. (2003). 'The Impact of Human Resource Management and Work Climate on Organizational Performance.' *Personnel Psychology*, 56: 383–404.

GERHART, B. (2005). 'Human Resources and Business Performance: Findings, Unanswered Questions, and an Alternative Approach.' *Management Revue*, 16/2: 174–85.

—— WRIGHT, P., MCMAHAN, G., and SCOTT, S. (2000). 'Measurement Error in Research on Human Resources and Firm Performance: How Much Error is There and does it Influence Effect Size Estimates?' *Personnel Psychology*, 53: 803–34.

GODARD, J. (2004). 'A Critical Assessment of the High Performance Paradigm.' *British Journal of Industrial Relations*, 42/2: 439–78.

GORDON, G., and DiTOMASO, N. (1992). 'Predicting Corporate Performance from Organizational Climate.' *Journal of Management Studies*, 26/6: 783–98.

GUEST, D. (1997). 'Human Resource Management and Performance: A Review and Research Agenda.' *International Journal of Human Resource Management*, 8/3: 263–76.

—— (2001). 'Human Resource Management: When Research Confronts Theory.' *International Journal of Human Resource Management*, 12/7: 1092–106.

—— and CONWAY, N. (2004). *Employee Well-Being and the Psychological Contract: A Report for the CIPD*. London: CIPD.

—— MICHIE, J., CONWAY, N., and SHEEHAN, M. (2003). 'Human Resource Management and Corporate Performance in the UK.' *British Journal of Industrial Relations*, 41/2: 291–314.

GUTHRIE, J. P. (2001). 'High-Involvement Practices, Turnover and Productivity: Evidence from New Zealand.' *Academy of Management Journal*, 44: 180–90.

HANNAH, D., and IVERSON, R. (2004). 'Employment Relationships in Context: Implications for Policy and Practice.' In J. Coyle-Shapiro, L. Shore, S. Taylor, and L. Tetrick (eds.), *The Employment Relationship: Examining Psychological and Contextual Perspectives*. Oxford: Oxford University Press.

HARLEY, B. (2001). 'Team Membership and the Experience of Work in Britain: An Analysis of the WERS98 Data'. *Work, Employment and Society*, 15/4: 721–42.

HARTER, J., SCHMIDT, F., and HAYES, T. (2002). 'Business-Unit-Level Relationship between Employee Satisfaction, Employee Engagement and Business Outcomes: A Meta-analysis.' *Journal of Applied Psychology*, 87: 268–79.

HITT, M., BIERMAN, L., SHIMIZU, K., and KOCHHAR, R. (2001). 'Direct and Moderating Effects of Human Capital on Strategy and Performance in Professional Service Firms: A Resource Based View Perspective'. *Academy of Management Journal*, 44/1: 13–28.

HUSELID, M. (1995). 'The Impact of Human Resource Management Practices on Turnover, Productivity, and Corporate Performance.' *Academy of Management Journal*, 38: 635–72.

HUTCHINSON, S., and PURCELL, J. (2003). *Bringing Policies to Life: The Vital Role of Front Line Managers*. London: CIPD.

JACOBY, S. (2005). *The Embedded Corporation: Corporate Governance and Employment Relations in Japan and the United States*. New York: Princeton University Press.

JUDGE, T., THORESEN, C., BONO, J. and PATTON, G. (2001). 'The Job Satisfaction—Job Performance Relationship: A Qualitative and Quantitative Review'. *Psychological Bulletin*, 127: 376–407.

O'REILLY, C., and CHAPMAN, J. (1996). 'Culture as Social Control: Corporations, Culture and Commitment'. *Research in Organizational Behaviour*, 18: 157–200.

OSTROFF, C., and BOWEN, D. (2000). 'Moving HR to a Higher Level: HR Practices and Organizational Effectiveness.' In K. Klein and S. Kozlowski (eds.), *Multilevel Theory, Research and Methods in Organizations: Foundations, Extensions and New Directions*. San Francisco: Jossey-Bass.

PAAUWE, J. (2004). *HRM and Business Performance: Achieving Long-Term Viability*. Oxford: Oxford University Press.

PAUL, A., and ANANTHARAMAN, R. (2003). 'Impact of People Management on Organizational Performance: Analysis of a Causal Model.' *International Journal of Human Resource Management*, 14/7: 1246–66.

PFEFFER, J. (1998). *The Human Equation: Building Profits by Putting People First*. Boston: Harvard Business School Press.

PURCELL, J., and HUTCHINSON, S. (2006). 'Front-Line Managers as Agents in the HRM–Performance Causal Chain: Theory, Analysis and Evidence'. *Human Resource Management Journal* (forthcoming).

—— KINNIE, N., HUTCHINSON, S., RAYTON, B., and SWART, J. (2003). *Understanding the People and Performance Link: Unlocking the Black Box*. London: CIPD.

RAMSAY, H., SCHOLARIOS, D., and HARLEY, B. (2000). 'Employees and High-Performance Work Systems: Testing inside the Black Box.' *British Journal of Industrial Relations*, 38/4: 501–31.

REDMAN, T., and SNAPE, E. (2005). 'Unpacking Commitment: Multiple Loyalties and Employee Behaviour'. *Journal of Management Studies*, 42/2: 301–28.

RUCCI, A., KIRN, S., and QUINN, R. (1998). 'The Employee–Customer–Profit Chain at Sears'. *Harvard Business Review*, 76/1: 82–97.

STOREY, J. (1995). *Human Resource Management: A Critical Text*. London: Routledge.

TRUSS, K. (2001). 'Complexities and Controversies in Linking HRM with Organisational Outcomes'. *Journal of Management Studies*, 38/8: 1121–49.

UHL-BIEN, M., GRAEN, G., and SCANDURA, L. (2000). 'Indicators of Leader–Member Exchange (LMX) for Strategic Human Resource Management Systems.' *Research in Personnel and Human Resources Management*, 18: 137–85.

WALL, T., and WOOD, S. (2005). 'The Romance of HRM and Business Performance, and the Case for Big Science'. *Human Relations*, 58/4: 429–62.

WAY, S. (2002). 'High Performance Work Systems and Intermediate Indicators of Firm Performance within the US Small Business Sector.' *Journal of Management*, 28/6: 765–85.

WHITENER, E. M. (2001). 'The Impact of Human Resource Activities on Employee Trust.' *Human Resource Management Review*, 7/4: 389–404.

—— BRODT, S. E., KORSGAARD, M. A., and WERNER, J. M. (1998). 'Managers as Initiators of Trust: An Exchange Relationship Framework for Understanding Managerial Trustworthy Behaviour.' *Academy of Management Review*, 23/3: 513–30.

WHITTAKER, S., and MARCHINGTON, M. (2003). 'Devolving HR Responsibility to the Line: Threat, Opportunity or Partnership?' *Employee Relations*, 36/3: 245–61.

WOOD, S. (1999). 'Human Resource Management and Performance.' *International Journal of Management Reviews*, 1/4: 367–413.

WRIGHT, P., and BOSWELL, W. (2002). 'Desegregating HRM: A Review and Synthesis of Micro and Macro Human Resource Management Research.' *Journal of Management*, 28/3: 247–76.

—— and GARDNER, T. (2003). 'The Human Resource–Firm Performance Relationship: Methodological and Theoretical Challenges.' In D. Holman, T. Wall, C. Clegg, P. Sparrow, and A. Howard (eds.), *The New Workplace: A Guide to the Human Impact of Modern Work Practices*. London: John Wiley.

—— and NISHII, L. (2004). 'Strategic HRM and Organizational Behaviour: Integrating Multiple Level Analysis.' Paper presented at the 'What Next for HRM' conference, Rotterdam.

—— and SNELL, S. (1998). 'Towards a Unifying Framework for Exploring Fit and Flexibility in Strategic Human Resource Management.' *Academy of Management Review*, 23/4: 756–72.

—— GARDNER, T., MOJNIHAN, L., and ALLEN, M. (2005). 'The Relationship between HR Practices and Firm Performance: Examining Causal Order.' *Personnel Psychology*, 58: 409–46.

# CHAPTER 27

# MODELING HRM AND PERFORMANCE LINKAGES

## BARRY GERHART

## 27.1 INTRODUCTION

My focus here is on methodology in the literature on human resources (HR) management and performance.[1] Whenever a theoretical model of HR and performance is tested and estimated using empirical data, a binary decision regarding whether the model is supported (yes or no) is typically made. If support is found, it is either because the model is correct or the method is wrong (i.e. a false positive, or Type I, error of inference). If support is not found, it is either because the model is wrong or the method is wrong (i.e. a false negative, or Type II, error of inference).

I thank Ingo Weller for his helpful comments on an earlier version.

[1] 'Performance' often refers to financial or operating performance in the literature. The models discussed here apply equally well to performance as defined by stakeholders other than shareholders (e.g. Brewster 1999; Paauwe 2004). Obviously, different stakeholders' (shareholders, employees, customers, public) interests are not identical, but there is often a substantial shared interest in the ongoing viability of the organization.

Either type of error, of course, causes problems. Research may incorrectly deem an effective HR system as ineffective or an effective HR system as ineffective. Incorrect research inferences may stifle research in a fruitful area or create a cottage industry in an area not worth the bother. If, as we hope, research has some effect on managerial policy and practice, these errors of inference could likewise lead to errors in the adoption or retention of HR systems in organizations.

I have two general goals in this chapter. First, I hope to help readers better evaluate the contribution of published research on HR and performance. Second, I hope to help authors in preparing their work for publication and avoid problems that may otherwise lengthen the review process or adversely affect the publication decision. I begin with a simple model.

# 27.2 A Simple Model of HR and Performance

The typical approach in HRM and performance is to use a model like the following:

$$\text{Perf} = \beta_0 + \beta_{\text{perfhr}} \, hr + \epsilon$$

where population parameters are: $\beta_0$, the intercept, $\beta_{\text{perfhr}}$, an unstandardized regression coefficient representing the performance–HR relationship, and $\epsilon$, the error or disturbance term, which captures all unspecified causes of Perf. This is the classical linear regression model. Estimation using sample data, by ordinary least squares (OLS), for example, yields:

$$\text{Perf} = b_0 + b_{\text{perfhr}} \, hr + e$$

Under standard assumptions, the OLS/classical regression estimator is unbiased and efficient among the class of linear estimators (the Gauss–Markov theorem). Unbiased means that the mean (or expected value) of the distribution of b across repeated samples is equal to the population parameter, $\beta$. Efficient (or best) means that b has minimum variance (relative to other estimators in the class) across the distribution of repeated samples.[2] Adding the assumption that the disturbance term is normally distributed turns the model into the classical normal regression model, which facilitates hypothesis-testing and formation of confidence intervals (e.g. Greene 1993: ch. 10). In empirical work on HR and performance, this basic model can and should, of course, be expanded to include other determinants of performance.

[2] Efficiency is only meaningful in conjunction with bias because any constant (e.g. b =4, the uniform number for hockey players Bobby Orr and Chris Gerhart) will be an efficient estimator, but of course, is likely to be a biased estimator.

# 27.3 ESTIMATING AND INTERPRETING EFFECT SIZES

In the model above, the unstandardized regression coefficient is the primary effect size estimate. However, HR research draws from multiple disciplines, and its methodology reflects this fact. Likewise, the approach to effect size varies across disciplines. For many in HR, the main foundation is in psychology. Psychology-based research has traditionally focused, sometimes exclusively, on statistical significance testing. However, psychologists have increasingly recognized the problems with this approach (Cohen 1994; Schmidt 1995). Statistical significance tests alone tell us whether our statistical estimates meet some minimum level of precision, which is important, but it is only a binary index. Knowing that a relationship is non-zero is, by itself, not terribly interesting. With a sufficiently large sample size, even relationships that are so small as to be trivial with respect to practical relevance can be statistically significant.

In studies of HR–performance, where large sample sizes are difficult to obtain, given the unit or firm level of analysis, the opposite problem, that practically important relationships may be missed because of inadequate statistical power, is more common. Standard practice in statistical significance-testing is to fix the Type I error rate (usually at $p = .05$), thus forcing an increase in Type II error (i.e. a decrease in statistical power) rates as sample size decreases. Rosnow and Rosenthal (1989) show that in the case of a population $r = .10$ (a reasonable estimate for the HR-performance correlation)[3] and using a significance level of $p = .05$, the ratio of Type II to Type I error is 2 with $N = 1000$, 10 with $N = 400$, and 17 with $N = 100$. Likewise, Cohen (1992) shows that with a population $r = .10$ and $p = .05$, to have a .80 probability of detecting the effect (i.e. statistical power) would require $N = 783$, a sample size much larger than typically used in the HR–performance literature.

Thus, statistical significance-testing is not enough. What we really need in an area like HR and performance, which aspires to have practical implications, is (a) a meaningful index of effect size (Becker and Gerhart 1996), typically an unstandardized regression coefficient, if the dependent variable is measured on a ratio scale (e.g. profitability, shareholder return, turnover, uptime), and (b) a confidence interval placed around the effect size that conveys the precision of the estimate. Both are important because investing in an HR system having a mean effect that is smaller, but less variable/uncertain, could, for example, be preferred to investing in an HR system having a larger mean, but also a higher variance, effect. Smaller variance (i.e. the standard error of the regression coefficient) is achieved as

---

[3] Based on Gerhart et al. (2000a: 809), $r = .10$ is a realistic estimate of the HR-performance correlation when examining the Huselid (1995) study.

the sample size and $R^2$ for the performance equation increases and as the collinearity of HR with other independent variables decreases (e.g. Cohen and Cohen 1983: 109).[4]

When effect sizes are expressed in unstandardized regression coefficient terms and the variables are in ratio scale form (e.g. dollars), it changes the discussion of research findings and the discussion of implications from what it is when a binary test of statistical significance is the focus (Becker and Gerhart 1996). Indeed, many of the issues I discuss below may not matter a great deal if the inference goal is to simply make a binary statistical significance decision. In contrast, when one begins to estimate and report policy-relevant effect sizes (for instance, firms using HR system A have 20 percent higher profits than firms using HR system B, e.g. Huselid 1995—see below), one finds that conclusions can change significantly, depending on methodological issues such as the level of reliability (which, in turn, depends on estimating reliability correctly). Therefore, once one interprets point-estimate effects of HR-related variables on natural metric outcomes like profits and total shareholder return, one is forced to a much greater degree to think about whether the effect sizes are plausible or not.

There are other advantages as well to using unstandardized regression coefficients rather than standardized regression coefficients. First, whereas unreliability in the dependent variable biases the standardized regression coefficient, it does not bias the unstandardized regression coefficient. (Unreliability in the independent variable biases both types of regression coefficients and unreliability in either the independent or dependent variable also leads to downward bias in $R^2$.) Second, range restriction in the independent variable (variance in the sample is less than its variance in the population) biases the standardized regression coefficient toward zero, but does not bias the unstandardized regression coefficient (Cain and Watts 1970; Cohen and Cohen 1983; Darlington 1990).[5] This bias in the standardized coefficient is a major drawback, and, as Cain and Watts observe, stems from this effect size estimate being 'dependent upon the particular policies pursued when the data were collected'; and if these policies have restricted variance, using the standardized coefficient 'runs the risk of declaring a policy feeble simply because historically it was not vigorously applied' (199: 236). (Range restriction in the independent variable does lead to downward bias in $R^2$. Range restriction in y biases both standardized and unstandardized regression coefficients. See discussion of sample selection bias.)

---

[4] Sometimes an author claims that when a regression coefficient is not statistically significant, 'if we had used a larger sample size, the coefficient would have reached statistical significance.' This is not necessarily correct because the regression coefficient varies across samples, meaning it could be smaller in a different sample. So, while it is correct that the confidence interval around the coefficient would be smaller in a larger sample, *ceteris paribus*, it is unlikely that the confidence interval would be centered around the same coefficient estimate in that larger sample.

[5] Range enhancement, by contrast, leads to an upward bias in the standardized coefficient.

Not surprisingly then, guidelines for statistical methods (even) in psychology journals now admonish researchers that 'if the units of measurement are meaningful on a practical level ... then we usually prefer an unstandardized measure (regression coefficient or mean difference) to a standardized measure (r or d)' and that 'it helps to add brief comments that place these effect sizes in a practical and theoretical context' (Wilkinson and the Task Force on Statistical Inference 1999: 599). Likewise, a recent article on meta-analysis (Bond et al. 2003) calls for cumulating effect sizes in terms of 'raw mean differences' whenever meaningful, rather than using standard deviation units or other standardized effect sizes (e.g., d, r).

# 27.4 CHALLENGES IN INFERRING CAUSALITY AND POTENTIAL SOLUTIONS

Cook and Campbell, drawing on John Stuart Mill, give three necessary conditions for inferring causality: (*a*) covariance between cause and effect (i.e. a non-zero effect size), (*b*) time precedence (cause occurs in time before the effect), and (*c*) 'rule out alternative interpretations for a possible cause and effect connection' (1979: 31). It is useful to keep in mind, however, the following points. First, effect size estimation and ruling out alternative causal models is often not separable. The wrong causal model (e.g. omitting variables, ignoring reciprocal causation) often results in biased effect size estimates. As another example, a statistically significant and credible causal relationship may be of trivial magnitude. Second, the requirement to 'rule out' alternative models may have the unfortunate effect of leading researchers to believe that they must choose between two models, rather than combining elements of both. This is especially a problem with reciprocal causation, where researchers sometimes seem determined to show that causation runs one way or another, but not in both directions. I return to this point later.

The three specific issues I have chosen to address below arise from the violation of one assumption of the earlier described classical regression/OLS model (Duncan 1975; Wooldridge 2002: 50–1): that the independent variable (HR here) and e are independent, or cov(HR,e) = 0.[6] These three issues are: measurement error ('errors in variables'), specification error (usually referring to omitted variables), and simultaneity (i.e. reciprocal or non-recursive causation).[7] Sample selection bias

---

[6] There are other important assumptions (e.g. homoskedasticity, lack of autocorrelation).

[7] Wooldridge (2002: 50) observes that in applied econometrics, the term 'endogenous' is used to refer to any right-hand side variable that that is correlated with the disturbance term. He also notes, however, that the term endogenous has a more traditional meaning (Alwin and Hauser 1975): any

can be viewed as a form of the omitted variable problem (Heckman) and is therefore discussed in that section.

When the cov(HR,e) = 0 assumption is violated, OLS is no longer unbiased and a search for alternative estimators may be undertaken. While other estimators, in theory, are capable of providing less biased (or in large samples, more consistent) estimates,[8] it is important to remember that these estimators make their own assumptions, which if not sufficiently met, can lead to no better, or even worse estimates than provided by OLS.

## 27.4.1 Measurement Error and Construct Validity

### 27.4.1.1 *Random Measurement Error*

The standard paradigm for studying HR and performance has been to define and measure HR in terms of HR practices, by either asking the percentage of employees covered by a practice or by using a likert-type rating scale that asks the degree to which a practice is used, important, etc. The strength of implementation of practices has not generally received much attention (Bowen and Ostroff 2004), nor have employee descriptions of practices been used. Rather, for better or worse, a single managerial respondent typically provides the HR practice information.

For some reason, the HR and business performance literature has been fixated on internal consistency (e.g. Cronbach's alpha) reliability, which provides an estimate of how much error in responses stems from the sampling of items from the universe of items in a particular construct domain, given the traditional reflective measurement model. Although this aspect of reliability is important, recent evidence indicates that the far more serious source of measurement error in measuring HR is the sampling of raters. This fact has been either (*a*) ignored, or (*b*) mistakenly addressed using an index, $r_{wg}$, that is not a reliability and which gives an overly optimistic view of measurement error (Gerhart 1999). Gerhart, Wright, and colleagues (Gerhart et al. 2000*a*, 2000*b*; Wright et al. 2001) have documented that measurement error due to raters in studies using the *firm* level of analysis is substantial. For example, in their first study, Gerhart et al. reported an interrater reliability of no more than .30 and probably more like .20.

What are the consequences? First, such low interrater reliabilities mean that the HR practice scores a researcher obtains for a particular firm depend more on the

variable that is explained within a set of equations, or in a path model, any variable that has a unidirectional arrow leading into it. Likewise, an exogenous variable is one that is not explained in the system, and in a path diagram, has no unidirectional arrows leading into it. To avoid confusion, I use the terms exogenous and endogenous in the latter sense.

[8] Roughly speaking, consistency means that in large samples, an estimator's probability density function (or distribution) approaches that of the population parameter as the sample size increases.

particular person completing the survey than on what practices are actually used in the firm because the HR practice scores are idiosyncratic, rather than being consistent across different managerial respondents.

Second, the correction for attenuation in an unstandardized regression coefficient, though little discussed, differs from the correction for attenuation in a correlation (Gerhart 1999; Gerhart et al. 2000a). The corrected regression coefficient is equal to the observed regression coefficient divided by the reliability of HR, whereas the corrected correlation is obtained by dividing by the *square root* of HR's reliability *and* performance's reliability. Therefore, unreliability in the independent variable, HR has a larger impact on the unstandardized regression coefficient than on the correlation.[9]

Thus, the 20 percent effect of HR on firm performance (for an increase in 1 SD in HR practices) found by Huselid and others (see Gerhart 1999), once corrected, becomes a 67 percent (.20/.30) effect size using the .30 reliability estimate. That is the effect size compared to the mean. If comparing low ($-1$ SD) and high firms ($+1$ SD), the high firms are 167 percent of the mean and the low firms are at 33 percent of the mean, which implies that the high firms have 167/37 = 4.5 times higher performance. Is this effect size credible? (Keep in mind that other influences on firm performance, e.g. finance, marketing, operations, etc. are typically not included in obtaining such estimates.) If not, it may indicate a need to re-examine the entire approach. With a more positive assessment, it is still clear that methodology (reliability estimation in this example) matters a great deal in quantifying the impact of HR.[10]

In research on HR and performance, there are multiple sources of measurement error (both items and raters in the case here). This is best addressed by estimating a generalizability coefficient (Cronbach et al. 1972), which is equivalent to a reliability that recognizes multiple sources of error. Gerhart et al. (2000a) provide a tutorial and example.[11] One standard econometric approach to correcting for measurement

---

[9] In the case of more than one $x$ variable, the effects of measurement error are more complex. In fact, in the multivariate case, it is mathematically possible for measurement error to result in upward bias in a regression coefficient. We discuss two-predictor scenarios later in this chapter.

[10] When using the plant/facility as the level of analysis, which is the typical unit of analysis in industry-level studies (e.g. Batt 2002; Hunter and Lafkas 2003; MacDuffie 1995), evidence suggests that reliability may be significantly better (Gerhart et al. 2000b). This finding makes sense because plant practices are easier to observe, both because plants are smaller on average than firms, and because there is less likely to be variation in actual HR practices within a plant compared to within a firm with multiple sites (and many employees).

[11] A nicely done study by Wall et al. (2004) that might (incorrectly in my view) be interpreted as showing that reliability is less of an issue than we have suggested. Wall et al.'s approach in measuring HR practices included the following steps: (a) three different people per company were interviewed, (b) 'evidence from each interviewee was *cross checked with that from others* (emphasis added), and with additional information from company documents and a tour of the manufacturing facility' (2004: 101). Finally, (c) 'based on this information, two researchers, unaware of company performance, independently rated the extent of use of each of the practices' (p. 101). This process essentially

error is the use of instrumental variables, usually using two-stage least squares estimation (discussed later). In the multivariate case, LISREL is very useful.

In our own recent work (Fulmer et al. 2003), we have talked about employee relations as a source of competitive advantage, conceptualized and measured in terms of (multiple) employee (not a managerial informant's) views. A methodological advantage of this approach is that multiple responses from each organization are averaged, which, with enough responses, virtually eliminates measurement error due to sampling of raters. What employees perceive, think, and feel about HR and employee relations may also have more theoretical credibility as a cause of business performance than what Purcell (1999) described as 'crude' measures of HR practices.

### 27.4.1.2 *Non-random Measurement Error*

Single-respondent reports of HR practices can cause additional problems, especially if the same respondent also serves as the source of performance data. This design may result in measurement errors in HR and performance being correlated. For example, a respondent may consistently have positive or negative response errors across scales. Or, firms having better performance may over-report levels of HR effectiveness or even use of practices thought to be desirable (Gerhart 1999).

There has been much debate about whether this common method variance makes a difference in management research findings. While method variance may not make much difference in binary tests of statistical significance (Doty and Glick 1998), it does influence effect size. Specifically, Doty and Glick's meta-analysis found that correlations between an array of measures used in organizational behavior were 25 percent higher, on average, when both measures were based on single source self-reports than when they were not. They also found that this difference was larger still when the study design was cross-sectional.

Strategies for control of common methods variance include the use of the multitrait-multimethod matrix (Campbell and Fiske 1959) to assess convergent and discriminant validity, with later approaches applying structural equation modeling (e.g. Alwin 1974). In the absence of multiple methods (and thus the ability to identify and remove method variance this way), a more recent suggestion is to use a marker variable (Lindell and Whitney 2001), which theory says should have no relationship with other constructs in the study. Any observed relationship is thus assumed to be due to common method variance only. This relationship is then partialed from the relationships of substantive interest. As discussed later,

eliminates any measurement error by (apparently) permitting no disagreement and then once any disagreement in interviewee data is eliminated or reduced, giving this homogenized data to two raters. Not surprisingly, their ratings of the same, homogenized information are highly similar. It should also be noted that Study 1 in Wall et al. was at the plant level of analysis (where the second Gerhart et al. 2000b study found that reliabilities were generally higher).

longitudinal data can also be used to remove person-specific, time-invariant omitted variables of this sort. Finally, when conducting aggregate-(e.g. organization-) level analyses, Ostroff et al. (2002) have developed a method where different subsamples are used to measure different constructs, eliminating within-person correlations.

### 27.4.1.3 Construct Validity

The empirical methods discussed above are important in assessing construct validity. However, construct validity cannot be established by empirical methods alone. Rather, they must be interpreted in the context of a careful definition of the construct and its role in a nomological network (Schwab 1980). Indeed, Schwab (p. 34) notes that 'Since the criterion in construct validity is conceptual, direct tests are not possible.' Therefore, one must first decide whether the conceptual definition of the construct is adequate, then consider the empirical evidence. One could argue that early studies of HR and performance did a reasonable job of defining the HR construct, but the correspondence of the chosen measures with the definition was not always what one might have liked. For example, Huselid (1995) essentially conceptualized HR as having an impact on ability, motivation, and opportunity to contribute (see also Appelbaum et al. 2000). (I would add cost as a fourth mediating variable, Gerhart in press.) However, his two HR scales were only indirectly related to these sub-constructs, or perhaps more accurately, mediating variables. Consider, for example, that the two highest-loading items on his first HR scale, 'employee skills and organization structures,' were: 'What is the proportion of the workforce whose job has been subjected to formal job analysis?' and 'What is the proportion of the workforce who are included in a formal information sharing program (e.g. a newsletter)?' The question is whether these items are critical components of the HR domain and are they the major drivers of ability, motivation, opportunity to contribute, and cost.

### 27.4.1.4 Summary

To accurately describe the magnitude of the HR–performance relationship, one must report a practically meaningful effect size estimate, typically an unstandardized regression coefficient, as well as its precision (e.g. the confidence interval). Further, the definition and measurement of 'HR' (and performance, for that matter) can greatly influence observed effect size estimates.

## 27.4.2 Omitted Variable Bias

Many factors presumably influence performance, but most empirical studies include a short set of right-hand-side variables beyond those related to HR. Huselid and Becker (2000) argued that omitted variable bias was likely the major statistical challenge in HR and performance research. They suggest, for example, that 'firms that understand the advantages of high performance HR are also good at other types of management (e.g., marketing, operations)' (p. 851). Another variable that must be included in research on HR and performance is industry, with narrower (three-digit or four-digit SIC code) being preferable to more coarse categories (one-digit or two-digit SIC code). The use of 'industry studies' in automobile assembly plants (MacDuffie 1995), telecommunications (Batt 2002), and financial services (Hunter and Lafkas 2003) uses single industry samples as a way to control omitted variables and to understand the industry-specific institutional workings of HR and performance. Recent evidence provides further support for the idea that this relationship may vary by industry (Datta et al. 2005).

To estimate the magnitude of bias from omitting a relevant variable (e.g. industry, management quality/expertise in non-HR areas), call it 'control,' take the fully (i.e. correctly) specified equation to be (Kmenta 1971: 392–93):

$$\text{perf} = b_0 + b_{\text{perfhr.control}}\text{hr} + b_{\text{perfcontrol.hr}}\text{control} + e,$$

but we omit control and estimate instead:

$$\text{perf} = a_0 + b_{\text{perfhr}}\text{hr} + e*$$

Then the expected value of $b_{\text{perfhr}}$ will equal not $b_{\text{perfhr.control}}$, but rather:

$$b_{\text{perfhr}} = b_{\text{perfhr.control}} + b_{\text{perfcontrol.hr}}d_{\text{controlhr}}$$

where $d_{\text{controlhr}}$ is the regression coefficient from the auxiliary regression of control on the included independent variables (hr only in this example):

$$\text{control} = d_0 + d_{\text{controlhr}}\text{hr} + \text{residual}.$$

The bias in estimating $b_{\text{perfhr.control}}$ grows more severe as $d_{\text{controlhr}}$ and $b_{\text{perfcontrol.hr}}$ become more different from .00. In this two-variable example, $d_{\text{controlhr}}$hr is a direct function of $\rho_{\text{controlhr}}$. However, with more independent variables, it would be mathematically possible for $\rho_{\text{controlhr}}$ to be 'large,' but for $d_{\text{controlhr}}$ to be 'small' due to the inclusion of other independent variables. This then means that it is incorrect to say that omitted variable bias exists when the omitted variable 'is correlated with' the dependent variable and any of the included independent variables. Rather, it is the *partial* relationship of the omitted variable with the included variable that matters.

There are two traditional approaches to reducing omitted variable problems. The first is the randomized experiment, which has the major advantage, in sufficiently large samples, of achieving what Cook and Campbell (1979) refer to as equivalent groups. By definition, cov(hr,e) = 0 under successful random assignment. Moreover, this equivalence can be achieved without any knowledge whatsoever or statistical control of potential omitted variables. Although this is a unique advantage, some evidence indicates that non-experimental designs can produce results quite similar to experimental designs *if* the studies are similar in other design characteristics such as degree of attrition, type of control group, size of pretest differences between groups, and degree of self-selection (Heinsman and Shadish 1996).

A second approach is statistical control using regression analysis, or equivalently when the treatment is a group variable, analysis of covariance (ANCOVA). A problem with ANCOVA, however, is that the researcher must not only be able to identify and include all variables that, if excluded, (significantly) bias the effect estimate, she or he must also measure them reliably because partialing unreliable control variables results in undercorrection for group differences (e.g. Cohen and Cohen 1983). In the multivariate case, the most practical way to correct for measurement error is to use a structural equation model (SEM) such as LISREL. As also noted below in our discussion of matching and propensity scores, even if relevant variables are included and measured without error, conclusions may still be difficult if the groups differ significantly on these control variables. Cochran (1957), in an example cited by Rubin (2001), uses the following example to demonstrate this point:

suppose that we were adjusting for differences in parents' income in comparison of private and public-school children, and that the private-school incomes ranged from $10,000–$12,000, while the public-school incomes ranged from $4,000–$6,000. The covariance [analysis] would adjust results so that they allegedly applied to a mean income of $8,000 in each group, although neither group has any observations in which incomes are at or near that level. (pp. 265–6)

Three other approaches to omitted variable bias may be less familiar to readers of this chapter and are thus covered in somewhat more depth.

### 27.4.2.1 *Propensity Scores*

Fulmer et al. (2003) used matching in their study by comparing the financial performance of companies on the Fortune list of 100 Best Companies to Work For with that of a set of companies matched on industry, size, and previous financial performance. A more sophisticated approach to matching is propensity scores (Rosenbaum and Rubin 1983). In the two-group case (treatment, control), the propensity score is the probability, conditional on a set of covariates, that a subject receives a treatment.[12] It is derived by regressing the binary treatment

---

[12] Estimating the effect of HR on performance really requires knowledge of what would have happened to the same employees or companies had they been covered during the period by a different HR system. This is not a new idea, but it has received much attention in the statistics literature of late, much of it around Rubin's work ('Rubin's causal model' or 'Rubin's model of potential outcomes'). Much of its application has been to experimental designs where intended treatment

variable (e.g. using logistic regression) on a set of covariates. Rosenbaum and Rubin show that, in large samples, the propensity score approach ensures that 'if treatment and control groups have the same distribution of propensity scores, they have the same distribution of all observed covariates, just like in a randomized experiment' (Rubin 2001: 171). (Consistent with Cochran's example, Heinsman and Shadish 1996 found that the size of pretest differences between groups was one of the most important factors in leading to different findings from experiments versus non-experiments.)

The advantage of using propensity scores over matching on multiple covariates is that the latter can become unwieldly as the number of covariates increases. Compared to simply including covariates in a regression model, propensity scores also use fewer degrees of freedom. Also important is that propensity scores, when used as recommended, are used only to compare groups and subgroups with very similar propensity scores, thus addressing the concern raised in the Cochran (1957) quote above.

The limitations of propensity scores are similar to those for the classical regression of ANCOVA model. Although only similar propensity scores are compared, these continue to be based only on known/observable covariates. Any non-response is assumed to be random/ignorable (Rubin 1976) and it is also assumed that the treatment variable is exogenous to the outcome or Y variable. Another assumption is that the responses in one treatment group are not affected by the treatment received by respondents in other groups (e.g. as in the case where the groups compete for resources or access to treatment), referred to as the stable unit-treatment value assumption (SUTVA, Rosenbaum and Rubin 1983). Finally, although they can be used in the case of a continuous treatment variable (for an example, see Hirano and Imbens 2004), propensity scores have been primarily used in cases where the independent variable is categorical (as in an ANOVA design).

The propensity score approach is currently receiving a great deal of attention in econometrics and has been used in medical research as well. Some evidence suggests that propensity scores can produce treatment effect estimates from quasi-experimental designs close to those of randomized experiments (Dehejia and Wahba 1999; Hirano et al. 2003). Not surprisingly, the method works best when characteristics of the non-equivalent groups are similar and when variables are measured in the same way for both groups (Heckman et al. 1997), but there is a debate regarding how typical that situation is and thus how broadly useful propensity score matching is (see point-counterpoint, *Journal of Econometrics*, March/April 2005). To date, there appear to be no applications of propensity scores in the management literature.

---

(e.g. training, no training) may differ from experienced treatment (e.g. some in training condition may not attend, whereas some not in the training condition may gain knowledge of what is taught). An application of this model to the HR–performance literature may be where intended HR policy differs from experienced HR policy.

## 27.4.2.2 Selection Bias Correction

Sample selection bias refers to the case where observations above or below a certain threshold on $y$ are not observed. The result is bias in the regression coefficient. (Similar selection on the independent variable does not ordinarily cause this problem. Rather, it is a range restriction problem, as discussed earlier.) Heckman (1979: 155) shows that sample selection bias is a special case of omitted variable bias. Thus, as noted below, the correction involves creating a new variable to add to the model.

In the HR and performance literature, sample selection bias may arise, for example, because firms or plants having less effective HR strategies may be less likely to survive than those having more effective HR strategies (Gerhart et al. 1996). The consequence of observing only firms/plants that survive might be a downward bias in the estimate of the HR and performance relationship.

The Heckman two-step correction procedure (Heckman 1979) estimates a selection equation and a substantive equation. The selection equation (often using probit or logit) models the probability that observations from a population are included in the sample at hand. Based on the selection equation, the inverse Mills ratio, the probability of being excluded from the sample, is estimated and then added as a variable to the substantive equation, which here would be the relationship between HR and performance. (See Berk 1983 for a primer on selection bias.) Whether this 'correction' produces improved estimates depends, however, on the specific characteristics of the data and the nature of the estimates obtained from the selection equation (Stolzenberg and Relles 1997). Thus, whenever a selection bias correction is used, it is necessary to report the full selection equation results (variables, coefficients, and fit).

## 27.4.2.3 Fixed Effects

A fixed effects model can be considered where there are longitudinal data on both HR and performance, as well as sufficient variance in changes in HR and performance over time. This estimator is also known as the dummy variable, within-subjects, or first difference (in the special case of two time periods only) estimator. To see the potential advantage, specify equations for the relationship between HR and performance for time $t-1$ and time $t$, respectively with $b_{t-1} = b_t$:

$$\text{perf}_t = \text{hr}_t b + e_t$$

$$\text{perf}_{t-1} = \text{hr}_{t-1} b + e_{t-1}$$

Decompose the residuals into a time-varying, $v$, and time-invariant, $u$, parts:

$$\text{perf}_t = \text{hr}_t b + v_t + u$$

$$\text{perf}_{t-1} = \text{hr}_{t-1}b + v_{t-1} + u$$

Subtract the second equation from the first:

$$(\text{perf}_t - \text{perf}_{t-1}) = (\text{hr}_t - \text{hr}_{t-1})b + (v_t - v_{t-1})$$

The key result is that $u$, the omitted, time-invariant (i.e. 'fixed') component, is eliminated. Thus, any bias due to time-invariant omitted variables is also eliminated. With more than two waves of data, it is mathematically equivalent to pool cross-sections and include dummy variables for each firm (in this example).

Huselid and Becker (1996) used a fixed effects model and reasoned that if this estimate for the HR–performance coefficient was similar to the estimate based on cross-sectional data, it would reduce any concern about omitted variable bias in studies that have used cross-sectional data. Recognizing that fixed effects estimates (operationalized as difference scores with two waves of data) are often smaller than the cross-sectional estimates because of more serious measurement error problems in the former,[13] Huselid and Becker (1996) wisely corrected for unreliability in their fixed effects estimates. However, they did not correct their cross-sectional estimates. Gerhart (1999) found that upon additionally correcting the coefficient derived from the cross-sectional data, it was nearly twice as large (.240) as the comparable fixed effects coefficient of .125. This suggests, in contrast to Huselid and Becker's conclusion, that omitted variables may be a problem in cross-sectional studies.

There are (other) costs (beyond measurement error) in using fixed effects. One is that time-invariant variables fall out of the model described. Another is that degrees of freedom are lost from the denominator. This is most easily seen in the dummy variable specification where $n-1$ dummy variables are added to the equation (where $n$ = number of firms). This leads to less efficiency. Thus, it is recommended that a test be conducted to determine whether fixed effects belong in the model before using the estimates from the fixed effects model. If not, the recommended model is the error components model (Hausman 1978) and is estimated using generalized least squares (GLS), which accounts for the dependence of the disturbance terms across time.

### 27.4.2.4 Control Variables: Sometimes 'Too Much of a Good Thing'

Because omitted variable bias arises from using a model that omits relevant variables, the natural inclination may be to add 'control' variables to a model

---

[13] It has long been known that reliability problems are exacerbated by using difference scores (Cronbach and Furby 1970), though these can be corrected for unreliability using structural equation models (e.g. Gerhart 1988). Other studies probably underestimate the magnitude of the HR–performance relationship because they use difference scores without correcting for measurement error (e.g. Cappelli and Neumark 2001).

whenever possible in a regression/ANCOVA approach. However, as Blalock (1961: 871), building on work by Simon (1954), observed, 'the question of when and when not to control for a given variable seems to be more complex than is often recognized.' Duncan (1975: 22) likewise cautions against adding control variables 'not for any clearly defined purpose, but simply because it is a "good idea" to look at partial' relationships.

The problem is that whether to control for a variable depends on the causal model. Consider, for example, two of the causal models that can be used in a three-variable case. Two variables are HR and performance. Let the third variable be a composite of ability, motivation, and opportunity to contribute (AMO). A 'partial mediation' model is:

$$\overline{HR \rightarrow AMO} \xrightarrow{\ \ } performance.$$

Another model ('control') is

Use the hypothetical correlation matrix:

|  | HR | AMO | Performance |
|---|---|---|---|
| HR | 1.00 | | |
| AMO | 0.40 | 1.00 | |
| Performance | 0.20 | 0.40 | 1.0 |

With the partial mediation model, the direct effect of HR on performance is .048 and the indirect effect (via AMO) is .152. Thus, the total effect of HR is .200. In contrast, using the control specification, the total effect of HR is .048 (direct effect = .048, no indirect effect). Thus, using the mediation specification leads to the total effect of HR being estimated as roughly five times larger in magnitude than when using a control specification. (The estimates here can be obtained using LISREL or by using the Alwin and Hauser 1975 approach.)

### 27.4.2.5 *Summary*

There are several approaches that may reduce omitted variable bias. However, some of these approaches (e.g. Heckman's procedure) rest on assumptions that may not always be supported by the data. It was also noted that including more control variables does not always make for better estimates, but rather depends on the theoretical model.

## 27.4.3 Simultaneity

In a recursive model, causation runs in one direction. In a non-recursive model, causation is reciprocal (Duncan 1975). In other words, there is simultaneity. To illustrate, consider the following model and example adapted from Duncan (1975: ch. 5), which has two exogenous variables, $x_1$ and $x_2$, and perf and hr as endogenous variables (variables in standard score form to simplify things):

$$\text{perf} = b_{\text{perf}1}x_1 + b_{\text{perfhr}}\text{hr} + v$$

$$\text{hr} = b_{\text{hr}2}x_2 + b_{\text{hrperf}}\text{perf} + u$$

Thus, in this model, hr → perf and perf → hr.

Ordinary least squares (OLS) estimates of the regression coefficients in this model are biased because the disturbances/residuals are no longer independent of the right-hand-side variables in the model (see Duncan 1975: 77). For example, given that perf → hr, then $v$, the disturbance term in the perf equation, must also be related to hr. Thus, $\text{cov}(\text{hr},v) \neq 0$, which will lead to bias in estimating $b_{\text{perfhr}}$. Specifically, Duncan shows that (as applied here) rather than $b_{\text{perfhr}}$, the OLS estimate will equal:

$$b_{\text{perfhr}} + r_{\text{hrv}}/(1 - r_{\text{hr1}}^2).$$

The second part of this equation is referred to as simultaneity bias.

### 27.4.3.1 *Two-Stage Least Squares (2SLS) and Instrumental Variables (IV)*

One approach to dealing with simultaneity (or endogeneity in a purportedly exogenous variable) is instrumental variables (IV), often estimated using two-stage least squares (2SLS). (As previously noted, IV/2SLS can also be used to address omitted variable and measurement error problems.) Consider again the equations:

$$\text{perf} = b_{\text{perf}1} x_1 + b_{\text{perfhr}}\text{hr} + v$$
$$\text{hr} = b_{\text{hr}2} x_2 + b_{\text{hrperf}}\text{perf} + u$$

The basic idea of instrumental variables is to replace a right-hand-side variable, hr, suspected of being correlated with the error term with a predicted value, hr−hat, which is not correlated with the error term. Using 2SLS, hr−hat is obtained by regressing hr on the full set of exogenous variables, which must include at least one instrument. This is the first stage of 2SLS. The second stage is re-estimating the perf-equation by replacing hr with hr−hat.

An instrument is a variable that is included in the equation for hr, but is excluded from (or fixed to zero in) the equation for perf and thus influences perf only through hr. This zero/exclusion restriction is necessary to identify the equation (i.e. be able to meaningfully estimate its parameters). A necessary condition for identification, the order condition, requires that the number of exogenous variables excluded from an equation must be at least as large as the number of endogenous variables included in the equation (Greene 1993: 592). (A condition sufficient for identification, the rank condition, is beyond the scope of the present discussion, but is defined in most econometrics texts.) In our example, the perf equation is likely identified, even though hr is included, because $x_2$ is excluded and serves as an instrument for hr.

The key is that the IV/2SLS procedure, if successfully implemented, results in hr−hat (unlike hr) being independent of $v$, eliminating the source of the problem. The IV/2SLS estimator is consistent, rather than unbiased. The Hausman (1978) test for endogeneity is often used. The logic is that if endogeneity is a problem, then the IV/2SLS estimator should differ from the OLS estimator. The test involves adding the residual, $u$−hat, from the HR equation to the perf equation (and keeping HR in the perf equation also). If the standard $t$ or $z$ statistic for the coefficient on $u$−hat is significant, there is evidence of endogeneity (Wooldridge 2002: 118−20).

The success of the IV/2SLS procedure depends on the theoretical justification for the instrument (i.e. the credibility of the assumption that $cov(perf/x_2|hr) = 0$) or equivalently that $cov(u, x_2) = 0$, as well as a sufficiently large partial $R^2$ (i.e. partialing the other exogenous variables) between the instrument, $x_2$, and the variable being replaced using the first-stage regression, hr (Bound et al. 1995; Larcker and Rusticus 2005; Staiger and Stock 1997). This has two clear implications for researchers. First, a convincing conceptual rationale must be made for using the instrument. Second, the full results of the equation used to obtain the predicted/instrumental variable values must be reported. Bound et al. (1995: 449) conclude that 'the use of instruments that jointly explain little of the variance in the endogenous variable can do more harm than good' and note that their results 'emphasize the importance of examining characteristics of the first-stage estimates', especially the 'partial $R^2$ and F statistic on the excluded instruments in the first-stage regression.' Both Bound et al. and Staiger and Stock (1997) also note that despite the consistency property (a large-sample or asymptotic property) of IV/2SLS, even large samples cannot compensate for a low $R^2$, as demonstrated by their re-analysis of the Angrist and Krueger (1991) study, which used IV/2SLS in a sample of 300,000 to 500,000 observations.

In the HR and performance literature, a search turned up three studies (Bae and Lawler 2000; Huselid 1995; Huselid et al. 1997) that have taken the possibility of simultaneity between HR (practices) and performance seriously enough (and judged instruments to be available) to use IV/2SLS.[14] The latter two studies

[14] IV/2SLS is rare in the psychological literature. An introduction (James and Singh 1978) and an example (Schmitt and Bedeian 1982) appeared years ago, but as recently as 1996, *Psychological Methods*

reported that they used a Hausman test for endogeneity, but did not report specific results.[15] None of the three studies reported results of the first-stage regression, which as we have seen, are necessary to evaluate the IV/2SLS procedure. Only Bae and Lawler reported what they used (company years in operation, log of number of employees, whether a joint venture firm) as instruments. We should note, however, that this increased emphasis on the first-stage results did not appear in the literature until after some of these studies of HR and performance were already completed.

Another potential use of IV/2SLS would be to examine the relationship between attitudes and performance discussed below. However, in the case of the performance equation, what variable would make sense as an instrument for attitude? Many texts are silent on the question of where one might look for possible instruments. Kennedy (1992) suggests some general candidates for instruments, most relevant here being the lagged value of an independent variable. One possibility would be to use attitude from an earlier time period as an instrument for current attitude. Wooldridge (2002: ch. 5) provides several examples of how IV/2SLS has been used in economics studies (e.g. on education and wages) and the ingenuity required to find a good instrument.

Finally, the 2SLS estimator will have a larger variance across samples than the OLS estimator. For this and other reasons, it is important to test whether this loss of efficiency is offset by an increase in consistency. Wooldridge (2002) provides a helpful discussion of how to proceed in this regard.

### 27.4.3.2 *LISREL*

A SEM approach such as LISREL (Joreskog and Sorbom 2002) can also be used to estimate parameters of simultaneous equation models. LISREL is most useful when there are (*a*) measurement error issues or significant work to be conducted on the dimensionality and validity of constructs, (*b*) simultaneity issues, or (*c*) where a system-wide/full-information estimator (e.g. maximum-likelihood) is useful either to increase efficiency (by recognizing cross-equation error term correlations) or to provide for a goodness of fit test for a system of equations.

If none of these conditions hold, then LISREL may be unnecessary and the American Psychological Association Guidelines on statistical methods (Wilkinson et al 1999) recommendation of 'choosing a minimally sufficient analysis' should be kept in mind. In addition, econometricians have long relied more heavily on limited information/single-equation estimators such as 2SLS to a greater degree

published an article entitled 'An Illustration of the Use of Instrumental Variables' by Foster and McLanahan, implying some novelty of IV/2SLS.

[15] The Hausman test (e.g. Wooldridge 2002: ch. 6) compares the OLS and 2SLS estimates. If the estimates are the same, they should differ only by sampling error. If the estimates are different (not just statistically, but practically), there may be reason for concern with endogeneity.

than full-information/system estimators such as maximum-likelihood because the latter (Bollen 1996; Curran et al. 1996; Kennedy 1992): (*a*) assume multivariate normality, (*b*) while having superior asymptotic/large-sample properties, may not perform as well in finite samples, which empirical research uses, and (*c*) allow a specification error in one equation (e.g. an incorrectly specified zero path) to bias parameter estimates for other equations.

### 27.4.3.3 *Longitudinal Data and Time Precedence*

As noted earlier, Cook and Campbell (1979) identified time precedence of cause and effect as a necessary condition for causal inference. Longitudinal data is necessary to satisfy this condition. Interestingly, a recent review finds that this condition is not only rarely met in the HR and performance literature, but worse, HR is typically measured after performance (Wright et al. 2005). So, there is clearly a great deal of room for improvement on this front.

Wright et al. (2005) also raise the possibility of reciprocal causation, especially when HR is defined in terms of employee attitudes. They do not estimate a model with reciprocal causation, but do present correlations of an HR practice index and an employee attitude measure with performance outcomes collected both before and after the HR/attitude measures in 45 to 62 units of an organization. They then seek to determine whether (*a*) research design (causal ordering of HR and performance) and (*b*) controlling for concurrent performance diminishes the correlation between past HR practices and subsequent performance (i.e. in a design having correct time precedence if interested in the HR → performance path).

For some reason, their results do not seem to show any effect of design (i.e. whether correct time precedence exists) on the correlations. As one might expect, when concurrent performance is controlled, the relationship of HR/attitude with later performance is substantially diminished. The question is why. Wright et al. consider a number of explanations: the relationship is non-recursive, the relationship is spurious, or that it is due to temporal stability in both sets of variables.

The first and third explanations seem quite similar. As Gerhart and Milkovich (1990) noted, if the causal model is something like:

$$\mathrm{hr}_{t-2} \rightarrow \mathrm{perf}_{t-1} \rightarrow \mathrm{hr}_t \rightarrow \mathrm{perf}_{t+1}$$

then, yes, controlling for perf at $t-1$ will reduce the relationship between hr at time $t$ and perf at $t+1$, especially if hr and perf are stable over time and have stable reciprocal effects on one another over time. But, by controlling perf at $t-1$, one is also removing the earlier effect of hr at $t-2$. So, they warned against over-control.

Controlling for the lagged value of performance almost never yields empirical estimates that correspond to the conceptual model. Indeed, it is a mis-specification to control for the lagged value of performance in a model that seeks to explain differences in the level of performance across firms or units. By including a lagged value, the model, in fact, becomes a change model. To see this, begin with the model:

$$\text{perf}_{t+1} = b_1 \text{perf}_t + b_2 \text{hr}_t + e_{t+1}$$

Then, impose the restriction, $b_1 = 1$, and rearrange terms to obtain:

$$\text{perf}_{t+1} - \text{perf}_t = b_2 \text{hr}_t + e_{t+1}$$

Thus, by regressing firm performance at time $t + 1$ on firm performance at time $t$ and HR at time $t$, the model estimates the effect of HR *level* at $t$ on the *change* in firm performance between times $t$ and $t + 1$. This is fine if this empirical specification coincides with the conceptual model. For example, change in performance would be the appropriate dependent variable if during the period between time $t$ and time $t + 1$, some companies changed their HR practices and the researcher was able to measure HR at these two time periods. However, this is almost never the case in HR and performance research. Rather, HR is usually measured at a single point in time. In that case, it is not clear that one would expect an unchanging set of HR practices to lead to a change in performance.

A recent study by Schneider et al. (2003) uses longitudinal data on both firm performance and HR (measured as aggregate employee attitude, specifically job satisfaction). For each facet of job satisfaction and overall job satisfaction, they estimate (*a*) sat → perf, the correlation of job satisfaction measured at time 1 with profitability variables measured at time 2, time 3, and so forth, and (*b*) perf → sat, the correlation of profitability variables measured at time 1 with job satisfaction measured at time 2, time 3, and so forth. They find that the correlations in the (*b*) analyzes are generally larger than those obtained in the (*a*) analysis. They conclude from this that profitability is more likely to cause job satisfaction than job satisfaction is to cause profitability. Likewise, a look at their proposed research model (that follows the empirical portion of their study) portrays job satisfaction almost solely as an outcome variable, not as a key cause of behaviors or firm performance.[16]

In my view, however, there is no need for a contest here. Consistent with the simultaneous equation model discussed earlier, employee attitude can be both a cause and a consequence of financial performance. While financial performance in year $t$ may precede employee attitude for year $t + 1$, it is also true that employee attitude in year $t-1$ precedes financials for year $t$ and so on. (See the above discussion on whether to control for a lagged dependent variable.) To say that causality runs in only one direction may not be accurate.

[16] Their model also shows high-performance work practices influencing production efficiency and, in turn, financial performance with *no* mediating variables (or moderators for that matter). This seems to move us in the wrong direction. We should be focusing on opening the proverbial 'black box' (Becker and Gerhart 1996), not hypothesizing its existence.

Note also that Schneider et al.: (*a*) rely exclusively on bivariate correlations, meaning no control variables are used, (*b*) provide no effect sizes in dollar terms, so it is difficult to interpret the policy relevance of their findings, (*c*) do not explain why the correlation of satisfaction with financial outcomes is sometimes stronger the longer the lag until the financial outcomes are measured, (*d*) use only short-term financial performance, rather than long-term measures, which might better capture employee attitudes/relations as a source of sustained competitive advantage (e.g. Fulmer et al. 2003), and (*e*) few of the sat → perf and perf → sat correlations discussed above actually differed statistically.

### 27.4.3.4 *Summary*

It is unlikely that causation runs in only one direction between HR and performance. Simultaneous equation models offer the prospect of a more accurate and nuanced description of this relationship. However, the challenging assumptions of these models, for example, regarding instrumental variables, may be difficult to satisfy.

## 27.4.4 Causal Inference and Mediators

Becker and Gerhart (1996) emphasized the importance of specifying and testing intervening causal mechanisms as a way to better understand how HR influences performance, as well as its importance in assessing the credibility/causality of the relationship. However, as Purcell (1999: 29) observed, the field has tended to 'take for granted' that 'often very crude' measures of HR practices are mediated by things like 'worker effort, morale, cooperation, attitudes, and behaviour.' More recently, workforce ability, motivation, and opportunity to contribute (AMO) have been hypothesized as key mediators (Appelbaum et al. 2000; Boxall and Purcell 2003). Again, however, this hypothesis is largely untested (Gerhart in press).

The classic approach to testing and estimating mediation, described by Alwin and Hauser (1975), begins with the reduced form of the model, which refers to an equation for each endogenous variable that includes only purely exogenous variables on the right-hand side.[17] This is contrasted with the structural model, which includes all right-hand-side variables, exogenous or otherwise. The total effect is defined as the coefficient on the exogenous variable in the reduced form equation. The direct effect is defined as the coefficient on the exogenous variable in the structural equation. The indirect effect is defined as the total effect minus the direct effect.

A later paper by Baron and Kenny (1986) uses a similar logic in testing for mediation, but with greater emphasis on statistical significance testing. However,

---

[17] Recall that endogenous variables have determinants in the model, whereas exogenous variables have no determinants (i.e. are unexplained) in the model.

they are careful to note that mediation is not an all or nothing phenomenon and thus statistical significance testing is not sufficient for assessing the degree of mediation. Rather, one must focus also on the percentage change in the regression coefficient when the mediator is added to the equation (moving from the reduced form to the structural equation), consistent with Alwin and Hauser. Recent work comparing tests of mediation further demonstrates the drawback of relying exclusively on statistical significance tests, in part, because of their very poor statistical power in most mediation tests (MacKinnon et al. 2002).

## 27.4.5 Testing for Fit or Moderation

Few seem to believe that the 'best practice' or 'universal' model of HR is valid. Most of us find that unlikely and can make plenty of persuasive arguments for why HR practices must display (*a*) internal/horizontal fit among themselves, (*b*) external/vertical fit with strategy, and (*c*) fit with the institutional (including country) environment (Boxall and Purcell 2003; Dowling and Welch 2004; Paauwe and Boselie 2003).

The fact, however, is that there is precious little (formal research) evidence that (*a*), (*b*), or (*c*) make much difference to business performance (Dyer and Reeves 1995; Gerhart in press; Gerhart et al. 1996; Wright and Sherman 1999). This is not to say there is no evidence on any of these three aspects of fit. For example, with respect to (*c*) above, the regulatory environment may preclude or mandate certain HR practices, depending on the country.

In the case of horizontal fit, however, a case can be made that there is evidence, but it has been misinterpreted as supportive evidence (Gerhart in press). For example, an important study by Ichniowski et al. (1997) used monthly observations on thirty steel finishing lines.[18] Their dependent variable was line uptime and their independent variables were HR practices, either alone, or combined via cluster analysis into HR systems. Their key conclusion was that 'Systems of HRM policies determine productivity. Marginal changes in individual policies have little or no effect on productivity. Improving productivity requires substantial changes in a set of HRM policies' (p. 37).

For each HR individual practice, Ichniowski et al. (1997) estimated a separate equation. Each HR practice's coefficient was then compared, with and without HR system dummy variables in the equation. The individual HR practice coefficients were smaller when the HR system dummy variables were in the model. This formed the basis for Ichniowski et al.'s conclusion that changes in sets of HR policies are necessary. However, as Gerhart et al. (1996) noted, the fact that the

---

[18] Note that a working paper version of this article was available in 1993, meaning the influence of the study was felt before 1997.

HR system variables (see 1996: 28) were derived on the basis of the individual HR practices using a clustering algorithm likely means that the HR system variables were collinear with the individual practices. As such, the fact that the coefficients on individual HR practices are diminished when the HR system variables could just show collinearity. It is not clear why such evidence indicates fit or complementarities between individual HR practices.[19]

The Ichniowski et al. (1997) method of testing internal fit continues to be used. For example, like Ichniowski et al., the research reported in Appelbaum et al. (2000) is well done and interesting. However, their approach to testing for fit has similar problems. They conclude that 'The synergies created by bundling these [HR and work] practices together have a stronger effect on performance than do the individual practices' (1997: 142). My re-examination of their results, however, turns up nothing that really supports this claim.[20]

The concern here is that unwarranted claims regarding fit/synergy have unwanted consequences for research and policy. From a policy point of view, we do not want to tell companies that they have to 'buy the whole package' of HR system practices to obtain improvement if, in fact, that is not necessary. This general issue is one that very much needs to be addressed more carefully.[21]

Finally, there are three other areas where researchers sometimes do not follow recommended practice. First, when testing for interactions by entering a cross-product term, it is necessary to have all lower-order effects in the model that involve those variables. For example, to test a three-way interaction between HR, business strategy, and country, one must include not only the three-way cross-product, but also the three main effects and the three two-way cross-product terms. Second, it is recommended that when testing an interaction, one rules out the possibility that an observed interaction is due to a quadratic effect (MacCallum and Mar 1995). Third, when plotting an interaction (always recommended), care must be taken to include only values that actually exist in the dataset. So, for example, it is necessary to first verify that there are firms two standard deviations

---

[19] Ichniowski et al. do not report the $R^2$ for the equations using (a) separate HR practices, and (b) HR practices combined into clusters/systems. Thus, there is no means of comparing the fit of (a) versus (b) based on their article.

[20] When I simply add the linear effects of the individual HR and work practices variables, I obtain predicted values of their uptime dependent variable that are quite similar to those obtained using the system variables (derived using cluster analysis). In addition, the adjusted $R^2$ for the performance equation containing the separate HR practices is larger (.81 in their table 8.7) than the $R^2$ in the corresponding performance equation containing the HR clusters/systems (.75 in their table 8.8). This provides no support for synergy.

[21] A broader issue is whether fit is an overly static concept, which has received too much attention, to the detriment of related issues, such as 'sustainable fit,' which 'can be achieved only by developing a flexible organization' (Wright and Snell 1998: 758). Useful here would be longitudinal data on how firms are able to respond in HR areas (practices, employee skills, employee behaviors, p. 758) over time to changes in their competitive environments.

above the mean on HR practices and two standard deviations below the mean on a differentiation business strategy before including such a point in the figure.

### 27.4.6 MultiLevel Models and Concepts

Sometimes the goal of a paper is to study the effect of HR policy on performance, but it uses a design where there is no organization-level or unit-level variance in HR. The typical approach in such cases seems to be to regress a perceptual measure of effectiveness (e.g. employee attitude) on a perceptual measure of HR (e.g. opportunity to contribute). However, this analysis is a person-level analysis and any relationship between HR and performance in this design is likely due to common method variance if a single unit or organization has a single HR policy. The exception would be if it can be shown that what appears to be a single policy is implemented differently in different parts of the organization, perhaps by supervisors. But, to do this, one must show that at this supervisor/work group level of analysis, there is sufficient between relative to within group variance (using the appropriate ICC index), and then conduct the study at that level of analysis, not at the person level of analysis. Whatever the level of analysis, it must be shown that self-reports are not idiosyncratic to the respondent, but rather reflect a higher level (unit or firm) property. It is very difficult to publish a paper that uses a single source for all measures, but many such papers continue to be submitted to journals.

Hiearchical linear modeling (HLM, Raudenbush and Bryk 2002) is increasingly used for multilevel data and has application to the HR and performance literature where individual data nested within organizations/units is used (Ostroff and Bowen 2000). Typically, data at the person level is nested within units or organizations and thus is not independent, contrary to the assumption made by the classical regression/OLS model. HLM has the advantage of incorporating ICC analyses and of estimating standard errors that are corrected for the dependence of observations nested within units/organizations. However, many statistical packages accomplish the same thing by allowing estimation of robust standard errors.

## 27.5 Conclusion

My goal here has been to identify challenges in estimating effect sizes and drawing causal inferences in research on HR and performance and to consider possible solutions to these problems. In each of the areas discussed, researchers regularly engage in methodological practices that could be improved and that may result in incorrect conclusions regarding theory and practice. Guest et al.'s (2003) summary concluded that:

Despite the positive thrust of most published empirical findings, Wood (1999) among others has noted that the quality of the research base supporting the relationship between HR and performance is relatively weak. ... questions remain about the measurement of both HR and performance, and about the weight and relevance of tests of association and causation. (p. 295)

While there is often a (well-motivated) call for better theory in HR, it is just as important to improve methodology. Some improvements require additional resources (e.g. multiple raters, longitudinal data), but others do not (e.g. presenting meaningful effect size estimates and interpretation, testing for fit correctly, correcting for random measurement error when the relevant reliability information is available, using alternative estimators). If we are to draw policy inferences from our research, we need to be as confident as possible in our findings and conclusions. Keeping a focus on methodology is an important requirement to do so.

# REFERENCES

ALWIN, D. H. (1974). 'Approaches to the Interpretation of Relationships in Multitrait-Multimethod Matrix.' In H. L. Costner (ed.), *Sociological Methodology, 1973–74*. San Francisco: Jossey Bass.

—— HAUSER, R. M. (1975). 'The Decomposition of Effects in Path Analysis.' *American Sociological Review*, 40: 37–47.

ANGRIST, J. D., and KRUEGER, A. B. (1991). 'Does Compulsory School Attendance Affect Schooling?' *Quarterly Journal of Economics*, 106: 979–1014.

APPELBAUM, E., BAILEY, T., BERG, P., and KALLEBERG, A. (2000). *Manufacturing Advantage: Why High-Performance Systems Pay off*. Ithaca, NY: Cornell University Press.

BAE, J., and LAWLER, J. J. (2000). 'Organizational and HRM Strategies in Korea: Impact on Firm Performance in an Emerging Economy.' *Academy of Management Journal*, 43/3: 502–17.

BARON, R. M. and KENNY, D.A. (1986). 'The Moderator Mediator Variable Distinction in Social Psychological Research.' *Journal of Personality and Social Psychology*, 51: 1173–82.

BATT, R. (2002). 'Managing Customer Services: Human Resource Practices, Quit Rates, and Sales Growth.' *Academy of Management Journal*, 45: 587–97.

BECKER, B., and GERHART, B. (1996). 'The Impact of Human Resource Management on Organizational Performance: Progress and Prospects.' *Academy of Management Journal*, 39: 779–801.

BERK, R. (1983). 'An Introduction to Sample Selection Bias in Sociological Data.' *American Sociological Review*, 48: 386–98.

BLALOCK, H. M. (1961). 'Evaluating the Relative Importance of Variables.' *American Sociological Review*, 26: 866–74.

BOLLEN, K. A. (1996). 'An Alternative Two Stage Least Squares (2SLS) Estimator for Latent Variable Equations.' *Psychometrika*, 61: 109–21.

BOND, C. F., WIITALA, W. L., and RICHARD, F. D. (2003). 'Meta-analysis of Raw Mean Differences.' *Psychological Methods*, 8: 406–18.

BOUND, J., JAEGER, D., and BAKER, R. (1995). 'Problems with Instrumental Variables Estimation when the Correlation between the Instruments and the Endogenous Explanatory Variables is Weak.' *Journal of the American Statistical Association*, 90: 443–50.

BOWEN, D. E. and OSTROFF, C. (2004). 'Understanding HRM–Firm Performance Linkages: The Role of the "Strength" of the HRM System.' *Academy of Management Review*, 29: 203–21.

BOXALL, P., and PURCELL, J. (2003). *Strategy and Human Resource Management*. Basingstoke: Palgrave Macmillan.

BREWSTER, C. (1999). 'Different Paradigms in Strategic HRM: Questions Raised by Comparative Research.' In P. Wright et al. (eds.), *Research in Personnel and Human Resources Management*, Supplement 4. Greenwich, Cann.: JAI Press.

CAIN, G. G. and WATTS, H. W. (1970). 'Problems in Making Policy Inferences from the Coleman Report.' *American Sociological Review*, 35/2: 228–42.

CAMPBELL, D. T., and FISKE, D. W. (1959). 'Convergent and Discriminant Validation by the Multitrait-Multimethod Matrix.' *Psychological Bulletin*, 56. 81–105.

CAPPELLI, P., and NEUMARK, D. (2001). 'Do High Performance Work Practices Improve Establishment-Level Outcomes?' *Industrial and Labor Relations Review*, 54: 737–75.

COCHRAN, W. G. (1957). 'Analysis of Covariance: Its Nature and Uses.' *Biometrics*, 13: 261–81.

COHEN, J. (1992). 'A Power Primer.' *Psychological Bulletin*, 112: 155–9.

—— (1994). 'The Earth is Round (p<.05).' *American Psychologist*, 49: 997–1003.

—— and COHEN, P. (1983). *Applied Multiple Regression/Correlation Analysis for the Behavioral Sciences*. Hillsdale, NJ: Erlbaum.

COOK, T. D., and CAMPBELL, D. T. (1979). *Quasi-experimentation*. Chicago: Rand McNally.

CRONBACH, L. J., and FURBY, L. (1970). 'How Should we Measure Change - or Should we?' *Psychological Bulletin*, 74: 68–80.

—— GLESER, G. C., NANDA, H., and RAJARATNAM, N. (1972). *The Dependability of Behavioral Measurements: Theory of Generalizability of Scores and Profiles*. New York: John Wiley.

CURRAN, P. J., WEST, S. G., and FINCH, J. F. (1996). 'The Robustness of Test Statistics to Nonnormality and Specification Error in Confirmatory Factor Analysis.' *Psychological Methods*, 1: 16–29.

DARLINGTON, R. B. (1990). *Regression and Linear Models*. New York: McGraw-Hill.

DATTA, D. K., GUTHRIE, J. P., and WRIGHT, P. M. (2005). 'Human Resource Management and Labor Productivity: Does Industry Matter?' *Academy of Management Journal*, 48/1: 135–45.

DEHEJIA, R., and WAHBA, S. (1999). 'Causal Effects in Non-experimental Studies: Re-evaluating the Evaluation of Training Programs.' *Journal of the American Statistical Association*, 94: 1053–62.

DOTY, D. H. and GLICK, W. H. (1998). 'Does Common Methods Variance Really Bias Results?' *Organizational Research Methods*, 1: 374–406.

DOWLING, P. J., and WELCH, D. E. (2004). *International Human Resource Management*, 4th edn. London: Thomson.

DUNCAN, O. D. (1975). *Introduction to Structural Equation Models*. New York: Academic Press.

DYER, L, and REEVES, T. (1995). 'Human Resource Strategies and Firm Performance: What do we Know and Where do we Need to Go?' *International Journal of Human Resource Management*, 6: 656–70.

FOSTER, E. M., and McLANAHAN, S. (1996). 'An Illustration of the Use of Instrumental Variables: Do Neighborhood Conditions Affect a Young Person's Chance of Finishing School?' *Psychological Methods*, 1: 249–60.

FULMER, I. S., GERHART, B., and SCOTT, K. S. (2003). 'Are the 100 Best Better? An Empirical Investigation of the Relationship between Being a "Great Place to Work" and Firm Performance.' *Personnel Psychology*, 56: 965–93.

GERHART, B. (1988). 'Sources of Variance in Incumbent Perceptions of Job Complexity.' *Journal of Applied Psychology*, 73: 154–62.

—— (1999). 'Human Resource Management and Firm Performance: Measurement Issues and their Effect on Causal and Policy Inferences.' In P. Wright, L. Dyer, J. Boudreau, and G. Milkovich (eds.), *Strategic Human Resources Management in the Twenty-First Century.* Supplement to G. R. Ferris (ed.), *Research in Personnel and Human Resources Management*. Stamford, Conn.: JAI Press.

—— In press. 'Human Resource Systems.' In C. Ostroff and T. Judge (eds.), *Perspectives on Organizational Fit.* Frontiers of Industrial and Organizational Psychology series.

—— and MILKOVICH, G. T. (1990). 'Organizational Differences in Managerial Compensation and Firm Performance.' *Academy of Management Journal*, 33: 663–91.

—— and RYNES, S. L. (2003). *Compensation: Theory, Evidence, and Strategic Implications.* Thousand Oaks, Calif.: Sage.

—— TREVOR, C., and GRAHAM, M. (1996). 'New Directions in Employee Compensation Research.' In G. R. Ferris (ed.), *Research in Personnel and Human Resources Management.* Greenwich, Cann.: JAI Press.

—— WRIGHT, P. M., McMAHAN, G. C., and SNELL S. A. (2000a). 'Measurement Error in Research Human Resources and Firm Performance: How Much Error is There and How Does it Influence Effect Size Estimates?' *Personnel Psychology*, 53: 803–34.

—— —— —— (2000b). 'Measurement Error in Research on the Human Resources and Firm Performance Relationship: Further Evidence and Analysis.' *Personnel Psychology*, 53: 855–72.

GREENE, W. H. (1993). *Econometric Analysis.* London: Macmillan Publishing Company.

GUEST, D., MICHIE, J., SHEEHAN, M., and CONWAY, N. (2003). 'A UK Study of the Relationship between Human Resource Management and Corporate Performance.' *British Journal of Industrial Relations*, 41: 291–314.

HAUSMAN, J. A. (1978). 'Specification Tests in Econometrics.' *Econometrica*, 46: 1251–71.

HECKMAN, J. J. (1979). 'Sample Selection Bias as a Specification Error.' *Econometrica*, 47: 153–61.

—— ICHIMURA, H., and TODD, P. E. (1997). 'Matching as an Econometric Evaluation Estimator: Evidence from Evaluating a Job Training Programme.' *Review of Economic Studies*, 64: 605–54.

HEINSMAN, D. T. and SHADISH, W. R. (1996). 'Assignment Methods in Experimentation: When Do Nonrandomized Experiments Approximate Answers from Randomized Experiments?' *Psychological Methods*, 1: 154–69.

HIRANO, K., and IMBENS, G. W. (2004). 'The Propensity Score with Continuous Treatments.' Working Paper, Economics Department, University of California-Berkeley.

—— —— and RIDDER G., (2003), 'Efficient Estimation of Average Treatment Effects Using the Estimated Propensity Score.' *Econometrica*, 71: 1161–89.

HUNTER, L. W. and LAFKAS, J. J. (2003). 'Opening the Box: Information Technology, Work Practices, and Wages.' *Industrial and Labor Relations Review*, 56: 224–43.

HUSELID, M. A. (1995). 'The Impact of Human Resource Management Practices on Turnover, Productivity, and Corporate Financial Performance.' *Academy of Management Journal*, 38: 635–72.

—— and BECKER, B. E. (1996). 'Methodological Issues in Cross-sectional and Panel Estimates of the Human Resource–Firm Performance Link.' *Industrial Relations*, 35: 400–22.

—— —— (2000). 'Comment.' *Personnel Psychology*, 53: 835–54.

—— JACKSON, S. E., and SCHULER, R. S. (1997). 'Technical and Strategic Human Resource Management Effectiveness as Determinants of Firm Performance.' *Academy of Management Journal*, 40/1: 171–88.

ICHNIOWSKI, C., SHAW, K., and PRENNUSHI, G. (1997). 'The Effects of Human Resource Management Practices on Productivity: A Study of Steel Finishing Lines.' *American Economic Review*, 87/3: 291–313.

JAMES, L. R., and SINGH, B. K. (1978). 'An Introduction to the Logic, Assumptions, and Basic Analytical Procedures of Two-Stage Least Squares.' *Psychological Bulletin*, 85: 1104–22.

JÖRESKOG, K. G., and SÖRBOM, D. (1999). *LISREL 8: Structural Equation Modeling with the SIMPLIS Command Language*. Lincolnwood, Ill.: Scientific Software International.

KENNEDY, P. (1992). *A Guide to Econometrics*, 3rd edn. Cambridge, Mass.: MIT Press.

KMENTA, J. (1971). *Elements of Econometrics*. New York: Macmillan.

LARCKER, D., and RUSTICUS, T. (2005). 'On the Use of Instrumental Variables in Accounting Research.' Working paper, University of Pennsylvania.

LINDELL, M. K. and WHITNEY, D. J. (2001). 'Accounting for Common Method Variance in Cross-sectional Research Designs.' *Journal of Applied Psychology*, 86: 114–21.

MACCALLUM, R. C., and MAR, C. M. (1995). 'Disinguishing between Moderator and Quadratic Effects in Multiple Regression.' *Psychological Bulletin*, 18: 405–21.

MACDUFFIE, J. P. (1995). 'Human Resource Bundles and Manufacturing Performance: Organizational Logic and Flexible Production Systems in the World Auto Industry.' *Industrial and Labor Relations Review*, 48: 197–221.

MACKINNON, D. P., LOCKWOOD, C. M., HOFFMAN, J. M., and WEST, S. G. (2002). 'A Comparison of Methods to Test Mediation and Other Intervening Variable Effects.' *Psychological Methods*, 7: 83–104.

OSTROFF C., and BOWEN, D. E. (2000). 'Moving HR to a Higher Level: HR Practices and Organizational Effectiveness.' In K. Klein and S. Kozlowski (eds.), *Multilevel Theory, Research, and Methods in Organizations*. San Francisco: Jossey-Bass.

—— KINICKI, A. J., and CLARK, M. A. (2002). 'Substantive and Operational Issues of Response Bias across Levels of Analysis: An Example of Climate-Satisfaction Relationships.' *Journal of Applied Psychology*, 87: 355–68.

PAAUWE, J. (2004). *HRM and Performance: Unique Approaches in Order to Achieve Long-Term Viability*. Oxford: Oxford University Press.

—— and BOSELIE, J. P. (2003). 'Challenging "Strategic HRM" and the Relevance of Institutional Setting.' *Human Resource Management Journal*, 13/3: 56–70.

PURCELL, J. (1999). 'Best Practice and Best Fit: Chimera or Cul-de-Sac?' *Human Resource Management Journal*, 9/3: 26–41.

RAUDENBUSH, S. W. and BRYK, A. S. (2002). *Hierarchical Linear Models*. Thousand Oaks, Calif: Sage.

ROSENBAUM, P., and RUBIN, D. (1983). 'The Central Role of the Propensity Score in Observational Studies for Causal Effects.' *Biometrika*, 70: 41–55.

ROSNOW, R. L. and ROSENTHAL, R. (1989). 'Statistical Procedures and the Justification of Knowledge in Psychological Science.' *American Psychologist*, 44: 1276–84.

RUBIN, D. B. (1976). 'Inference and Missing Data.' *Biometrika*, 63: 581–602.

—— (2001). 'Using Propensity Scores to Help Design Observational Studies: Application to the Tobacco Litigation.' *Health Services & Outcomes Research Methodology*, 2: 169–88.

SCHMIDT, F. L. (1995). 'Statistical Significance Testing and Cumulative Knowledge in Psychology: Implications for the Training of Researchers.' *Psychological Methods*, 1/2: 115–29.

SCHMITT, N., and BEDEIAN, A. G. (1982). 'A Comparison of LISREL and Two-Stage Least Squares Analysis of a Hypothesized Life-Job Satisfaction Reciprocal Relationship.' *Journal of Applied Psychology*, 67: 806–17.

SCHNEIDER, B., HANGES, P. J., SMITH, B., and SALVAGGIO, A. N. (2003). 'Which Comes First: Employee Attitudes or Organizational Financial and Market Performance.' *Journal of Applied Psychology*, 88: 836–51.

SCHWAB, D. P. (1980). 'Construct Validity in Organizational Behavior.' *Research in Organizational Behavior*, 2: 3–43.

SIMON, H. A. (1954). 'Spurious Correlation: A Causal Interpretation.' *Journal of the American Statistical Association*, 49: 467–79.

STAIGER, D., and STOCK, J. H. (1997). 'Instrumental Variables Regression with Weak Instruments.' *Econometrica*, 65: 557–86.

STOLZENBERG, R. M., and RELLES, D. A. (1997). 'Tools for Intuition about Sample Selection Bias and its Correction.' *American Sociological Review*, 62: 494–507.

WALL, T. D., MICHIE, J., PATTERSON, M., WOOD, S. J., SHEEHAN, M., CLEGG, C. W., and WEST, M. (2004). 'On the Validity of Subjective Measures of Company Performance.' *Personnel Psychology*, 57: 95–118.

WILKINSON, L., and the Task Force on Statistical Inference (1999). 'Statistical Methods in Psychology Journals.' *American Psychologist*, 54 August: 594–604.

WOOD, S. (1999). 'Human Resource Management and Performance.' *International Journal of Management Reviews*, 1: 397–413.

WOOLDRIDGE, J. M. (2002). *Econometric Analysis of Cross Section and Panel Data*. Princeton: Princeton University Press.

WRIGHT, P. M. and SHERMAN, W. S. (1999). 'Failing to Find Fit in Strategic Human Resource Management: Theoretical and Empirical Problems.' In P. Wright et al. (eds.), *Strategic Human Resources Management in the Twenty-First Century*. Supplement to G. R. Ferris (ed.), *Research in Personnel and Human Resources Management*. Stanford, Conn.: JAI Press.

—— and SNELL, S. A. (1998). 'Toward a Unifying Framework for Exploring Fit and Flexibility in Strategic Human Resource Management.' *Academy of Management Review*, 23: 756–72.

—— GARDNER, T. M., MOYNIHAN, L. M., PARK, H. J., DELERY, J. R., and GERHART, B. (2001). 'Measurement Error in Research on Human Resources and Firm Performance: Additional Data and Suggestions for Future Research.' *Personnel Psychology*, 54: 875–901.

—— —— —— and ALLEN, M. R. (2005). 'The Relationship between HR Practices and Firm Performance: Examining the Causal Order.' *Personnel Psychology*, 52: 409–46.

# CHAPTER 28

# FAMILY-FRIENDLY, EQUAL-OPPORTUNITY, AND HIGH-INVOLVEMENT MANAGEMENT IN BRITAIN

STEPHEN WOOD

LILIAN M. DE MENEZES

## 28.1 INTRODUCTION

FAMILY-friendly, equal-opportunity, and high-involvement initiatives have increasingly been at the forefront of discussions of human resource management since the 1990s. They are widely viewed by academics and policy makers as critical ways of simultaneously improving the well-being of workers and the efficiency of organizations. Moreover, they are often presented as related practices. In this chapter we first discuss how they are perceived to be related and the research thus far on their links to organizational performance. We then report a study designed to test these associations.

## 28.2 Theoretical and Research Background

Family-friendly, equal-opportunity and high-involvement management are perceived to be related for a number of reasons. On the one hand, the work enrichment that is central to Lawler's (1986, 1991) and Walton's (1985) high-involvement management is expected to enhance workers' satisfaction and well-being at work and reduce the spillover of negative emotions from work to family life. On the other hand, it has been argued, on the basis that 'personal time is a legitimate employee need,' that the equality and diversity agendas imply that any effective high-involvement management must be extended from employee involvement to embrace issues of working time (Bailyn 1993: 87). In a similar vein, Guest (2002) argued that many presentations of high-involvement management or related concepts have been employer-centered, and concludes that a truly worker-centered approach will include family-friendly practices. The implication is that models of high-involvement management have so far focused on labor flexibility and skill acquisition in order to create the social system that will support the requirements of modern technical systems rather than addressing workers' concerns as a top priority (Guest 2002: 338). This problem of neglecting worker interests has been accentuated by the increasing marginalization of work enrichment in the literature that tests the link between high-involvement management and performance, as the emphasis has been placed on skill acquisition and motivational methods such as variable pay (Wood and Wall 2007). It is important to restore work enrichment to a central place in human resource management if we are to capture the core of the high-involvement concept and also to pursue family-friendly management and equal opportunities. The pursuit of family-friendly management and the achievement of equal opportunities can in turn help to create the conditions in which people can work in a more highly involved way. Crucially, this may signify to employees that management views the workforce as a major asset and is concerned about its well-being, as well as allow them to work unimpeded by family pressures.

Such arguments are normatively oriented, concerned with what should be. On the one hand, they may be taken to imply that a serious move towards any of the triad of types of management—family-friendly, equal-opportunity, and high-involvement—will involve the other two and in so doing create an authentic high-commitment management. We might then expect, if employers are institutionalizing the practices associated with these forms of management, that they are doing so in an integrated way, as part of an overall approach to human resource management. The extreme of the normative argument implies that the three sets of practices will only have a significant effect on performance when they are used in conjunction with each other. Anything short of this integrated package will not work. Taking a less extreme version, the argument implies that the effect of one type of management will enhance the effect of the others, and their effect, if used in isolation, will be limited.

The link between family-friendly management and equal opportunity is typically made on the basis that the achievement of the latter depends on reducing the constraints on equal access to opportunities and the full utilization of people's talents. Women are particularly disadvantaged, so the argument goes, by their childcare responsibilities, and any attempt to aid these should therefore reduce constraints on their achievement of parity with men. Family-friendly management, we should expect, would focus initially on women and their childcare issues, as opposed, for example, to eldercare.

The association between high-involvement management and family-friendly management is typically made on the grounds that the latter is an important means of gaining the motivation and commitment required to make high-involvement working the norm (Berg et al. 2003: 172; Osterman 1995: 685). Satisfying demanding work should also reduce work-to-family conflict, while family-friendly practices may reduce family-to-work conflict (Batt and Valcour 2003). Equal-opportunity management is linked to high-involvement management because it is seen to ensure the development and utilization of human resources to their maximum potential.

In reality, however, the theoretical associations that underlie the integration thesis may not be shared by managers or tally with their perspectives on human resource management. At the extreme, it is often argued that managers, at least in the Anglo-Saxon world, have tended to select human resource practices on a piecemeal basis. Their reasons for picking one practice are thus different from those that influence their choice of others, and hence their choice of all practices is not guided by an underlying approach. This argument has been made particularly in relation to high-involvement practices by Sisson (1995: 106) and Appelbaum and Batt (1994: 124). It has often been justified by the observation that the use of such practices is low across the whole economy. However, low adoption does not necessarily mean a lack of coordination in the use of practices. It could be that the same organizations are the main users of all or a significant set of practices. Moreover, if there were such a pattern in the use of practices, this could indicate an underlying approach to the management of the workforce.

The emphasis in the literature on any of family-friendly, equal-opportunity, or high-involvement management has not, however, been on examining the empirical relationship between the practices that are associated with them. Rather it has been centered, particularly in the case of high-involvement management, on links to performance. Furthermore, while the attention has been on treating these practices as a system or bundle (see e.g. Huselid 1995; MacDuffie 1995), there has been a lack of appreciation of the different meanings of such terms. Appelbaum et al. (2000: 33–4) interpreted this focus on bundles or clusters of practices as meaning that (*a*) practices are complementary; (*b*) synergies exist between practices that lead to positive interaction effects on performance; and (*c*) the practices form a coherent set or integrated system. They summarize the key studies of the human resource management–performance link as suggesting that 'bundles, systems, or configurations of internally coherent practices can be identified, and that such systems of practices do a better job of explaining establishment performance than the individual practices do.'

However, such an overview conflates three different approaches to the relationship between practices and hence perspectives on the human resource management–performance link. It treats the complementary nature of practices, synergistic relationships, and integrated approache as if they were equivalent, when they are different. First, a complement of practices consists of all those practices that individually have a positive association with performance. As such, a complement of human resource practices would be made up of the practices that are best in the main domains of human resource management (such as recruitment, selection, and training). Each would not detract from the performance of the others. Consequently, negative interactions between practices are not expected. Second, synergistic practices are those that enhance the effect on performance of another. A high-performance synergistic set would be one in which all the practices interact positively with each other, so that the combined use of the practices has 'a greater effect on performance than the sum of effects of the individual practices' (Appelbaum et al. 2000: 134). At the extreme, all the $n$-way interactions between a set of $n$ practices are significantly positively related to performance. Third, an integrated approach implies that the practices reflect an underlying distinctive orientation on the part of management towards human resource management, and that it is this orientation that is positively associated with performance. The individual practices are more than simply complements. Adopting practices in a pre-specified form may not be crucial, but having key practices in some form or another is important. The absence of one or more such practices may undermine the whole approach.

The extreme form of the family–work integration approach implies the third perspective. It is the underlying orientation of management, embedded to such an extent that it is reflected in the organization's culture, that will make for a high-performing organization based on workers having a good balance between work and non-work. However, in the absence of such a holistic approach, it may be that discrete orientations underlie the use of each set of practices: family friendly, equal opportunity, and high involvement. In this case, it may be that the underlying orientations have a synergistic relationship with organizational performance.

Most of the empirical studies of the links between performance and the three types of practices have focused on high-involvement management and have largely tested the complementary perspective. The few studies of family-friendly practices have concentrated largely on individual practices (e.g. Bewley and Fernie 2003; Dex and Smith 2002; exceptions include Perry-Smith and Blum 2000), while equal-opportunity practices have been neglected. Few studies have tested synergistic effects (see Wood 1999a; Wall and Wood 2005 for a summary of the high-involvement management and associated studies) and even fewer have tested the integrated perspective. The studies of both family-friendly and high-involvement practices reveal a mixed picture, as there is diversity across practices, performance measures and samples. There are certainly no strong grounds on the basis of the studies for expecting a universal positive link between any of the three management forms and performance. There are even arguments that suggest we might find some negative relationships. For example, following Hochschild (1997), there is the argument that high-commitment management achieves its performance effects through creating an overcommitted workforce and that family-friendly practices are needed to overcome the negative effects of this on non-work life. If this is the case, family-friendly practices may have a negative effect on performance.

The few exceptions to the focus on performance that have stepped back and examined the use of human resource practices have also produced uneven results. Some suggest that there is no clear pattern to the use of these practices (Osterman 1994; Gittleman et al. 1998); others suggest that there is some coherency to the use of practices and that one or more orientations may well underlie this (Wood and Albanese 1995; Wood and de Menezes 1998; Wood 1999b; Wood et al. 2003; de Menezes and Wood 2006). The difference in results may well reflect different analytical methods, as de Menezes and Wood (2006) show that investigations based on cluster analysis may be less powerful than those based on statistical models.

In the next section, we report our study, which illustrates how the three types of management can be jointly investigated. It particularly focuses on exploring the integration argument, and thus assesses whether there is a tendency towards an integrated worker-and-family-centred on high-involvement management and whether it heralds superior organizational performance.

# 28.3 Our Study

We designed a study to explore whether family-friendly, equal-opportunity, and high-involvement practices are being used in an integrated way or reflect discrete managerial approaches and to assess the nature of their links to organizational performance. We explored these questions using a British dataset that covers all sectors of the economy, private and public.[1]

The data is from the *Workplace Employee Relations Survey* of 1998 (WERS98),[2] which is the fourth in a series of surveys aimed at achieving a 'better understanding of the processes which underlie employment relationships' (foreword to Millward et al. 1992). Questions on family-friendly management and equal-opportunity practices were included in the survey for the first time in 1998, and the range of questions in the 1998 survey on high-involvement practices increased from previous surveys in the series. Our study used data from a structured interview with the senior manager at the site responsible for employee relations. The 1998 survey was of a sample of 2,191 workplaces with ten or more employees across the whole economy. This was achieved through a response rate of 80.3 percent.

## 28.3.1 The Use of Family-Friendly, Equal-Opportunity, and High-Involvement Practices in WERS98

Family-friendly management involves employers having an underlying commitment to help employees obtain a balance between work and family obligations. Equal-opportunity management is oriented towards eliminating any differentiation of opportunities, resources, and rewards based on the membership of a sociological group, for example based on gender, ethnicity, or age. It is thus concerned to ensure that jobs, wages, promotions, and employment benefits in the organization are fairly distributed. High-involvement management is oriented towards work enrichment and flexible working methods and ensuring that employees have the skills and motivation to use their discretion and decision-making powers for the benefit of the organization. These three approaches to aspects of management are expressed in management practices, and if they exist we ought to see a pattern in the use of a range of practices associated with them. For example, if family-friendly management is an identifiable managerial approach in the UK, we would expect practices concerned with childbirth to coexist with those related to child rearing. If this is more than simply a parent-oriented family-friendly policy, these in turn will

---

[1] The United Kingdom's Economic and Social Research Council funded this research (Grant number R000238112).

[2] The 1998 Workplace Employee Relations Survey is a survey that is jointly sponsored by the UK's Department of Trade and Industry, the Advisory, Conciliation, and Arbitration Service, the Economic and Social Research Council, and the Policy Studies Institute. The National Centre for Social Research was commissioned to conduct the survey fieldwork on behalf of the sponsors. WERS98 is deposited at the Data Archive at the University of Essex, UK. Neither the sponsors nor the Data Archive have any responsibility for the analysis or interpretation of the material contained in this chapter.

be accompanied by practices associated with eldercare and other such problems. Similarly, if an integrated orientation towards family-friendly, equal-opportunity, and high-involvement management exists, we would expect that practices, for example related to childbirth, will coexist with work enrichment or equal-opportunity practices.

Two types of family-friendly practices may be identified: (1) those that create flexibility in the timing and location of work so the employee can more readily accommodate family demands, and (2) those that provide a substitute carer for the employee (Bailyn 1993: 67; Bond et al. 1998). Because of our focus on their connection with high-involvement management, we are particularly interested in their provision for non-managerial employees. Of those practices measured in WERS98, the first type concerned with flexible working is most commonly used (Table 28.1). But none of these practices is adopted in the majority of the workplaces across the whole economy. The most frequently available practice is the entitlement to work part-time (46 percent of all workplaces in the economy, 58 percent of the sample); this is followed by parental leave (34 percent, 43 percent) and job-sharing (28 percent, 38 percent). The provision of a workplace nursery and childcare subsidies is very rare, the figures for the whole economy being 3 percent and 4 percent respectively (8 percent and 7 percent in the sample).

The equal-opportunity practices included in WERS98 are: maintenance of workplace records on the ethnic origin of employees; collection of statistics on posts held by men and women; monitoring of promotions by gender, ethnicity, etc.; reviews of selection and other procedures to identify indirect discrimination; reviews of the relative pay of different groups; and adjustments to accommodate disabled employees. The most adopted practices are records on ethnic origin and

Table 28.1 The provision of family–friendly practices for non–managerial employees

| | In WERS98 (unweighted percentage) | In the economy (weighted percentage) |
|---|---|---|
| Parental leave | 43 | 34 |
| Working from home | 18 | 13 |
| Term-only contracts | 20 | 16 |
| Working part-time | 58 | 46 |
| Job-sharing | 38 | 28 |
| Workplace nursery | 8 | 3 |
| Childcare subsidies | 7 | 4 |

Table 28.2 The provision of equal–opportunity practices for non–managerial employees

|  | In WERS98 (unweighted percentage) | In the economy (weighted percentage) |
|---|---|---|
| Records on ethnic origin | 46 | 30 |
| Statistics on posts held by men and women | 44 | 25 |
| Promotions monitored by gender, ethnicity, etc. | 21 | 11 |
| Reviews of selection to identify indirect discrimination | 35 | 21 |
| Reviews of relative pay between groups | 22 | 14 |
| Adjustments to accommodate disability | 47 | 26 |

adjustments to accommodate disability, which are nonetheless only adopted by just over a quarter of the workplace population in Britain (see Table 28.2).

High-involvement practices can be classified according to Bailey's work organi-zation–skills–motivation triad (Appelbaum et al. 2000; Batt 2002; Huselid 1995; de Menezes and Wood 2006), which is centered on the way work is organized and jobs are defined (cf. Parker et al. 1997) with human resource practices acting as supports to the successful implementation of high-involvement work systems. These entail work practices that enrich jobs, enhance the flexibility of workers, and increase the involvement of workers, particularly in idea generation. They are often defined in terms of their opposite, Taylorism, so for example Gittleman et al. (1998: 100) see them as representing 'a movement away from a traditional, hierarch-ical structure in which employees have rigid, narrowly defined roles'. Accordingly, they are associated with practices such as teamworking, self-directed or otherwise; 'on-line' or 'in-work' practices such as functional flexibility, self-inspection, and empowerment; and 'off-line' or 'out-of-work' practices, which are mainly connected with idea-capturing, such as suggestion programmes and quality circles.

The two other dimensions are viewed as supporting human resource practices for this work organization. Skill acquisition practices are the means by which individuals are given training and information that increases their knowledge and capabilities and equips them to engage with flexible work practices. The motivational practices are designed to ensure that the organization recruits and retains people who are motivated to work in a highly involved manner, and are typically taken to include incentive payment systems, job security guarantees, and the use of internal recruitment to fill jobs.

In WERS98, three variables relating to job autonomy and enrichment are included: job variety, method control, and timing control, alongside four other relevant work organization practices: teamworking; functional flexibility; quality circles; and suggestion schemes. The skill acquisition practices included in our study are: induction procedures; team briefing; information disclosure; appraisal; and training oriented towards human relations. In WERS98, the motivational practices are: survey feedback method; motivation as a major selection criterion; internal recruitment; single status between managers and non-managers; job security guarantees; and variable pay. We also analyzed a general training measure, whose distribution is nearly uniform in the sample and thus does not vary enough for tests of its association with other variables. The most adopted practices are team briefing (87 percent in the sample and 82 percent in the economy) and motivation as a selection criterion (87 percent in the sample and 86 percent in the economy). The least adopted practice is job security (15 percent in the sample and 10.6 percent in the economy). All in all, we observe a significant variation in adoption levels but only a few practices are widely used (Table 28.3). The most used practices are concerned with information-sharing.

Table 28.3 The provision of high-involvement practices for non-managerial employees

|  | In WERS98 (unweighted percentage) | In the economy (weighted percentage) |
| --- | --- | --- |
| Job variety | 41 | 47 |
| Method control | 22 | 28 |
| Timing control | 19 | 24 |
| Teamworking | 69 | 59 |
| Functional flexibility | 51 | 46 |
| Quality circles | 55 | 37 |
| Suggestion schemes | 39 | 32 |
| Team briefing | 87 | 82 |
| Induction | 84 | 73 |
| Training for human relations | 49 | 39 |
| Information disclosure | 85 | 86 |
| Appraisal | 56 | 50 |
| Survey feedback | 33 | 22 |
| Internal recruitment | 35 | 25 |
| Motivation as a selection criterion | 87 | 86 |
| Job security | 16 | 11 |
| Single status | 58 | 57 |
| Variable pay | 37 | 26 |

All family-friendly practices are positively associated with each other, but this association varies significantly between pairs of variables (e.g. the correlation between job-sharing and part-time contracts is equal to 0.51, while the correlation between parental leave and childcare subsidies is equal to 0.10). All equal-opportunity practices are positively associated and the correlation is slightly stronger, on average, than that among family-friendly practices. Most of the high-involvement practices are also associated with each other with the exception of the three work-enrichment measures and motivation as a selection criterion. The three variables concerned with work enrichment—job variety, method control, and timing control—are weakly correlated with each other and with most of the other variables in the sample. This pattern of correlations means that no practices are being used as substitutes for each other. Even workplace nursery provision and childcare subsidy are not alternatives.

The associations across types of practices vary significantly, but the majority are statistically significant, though some practices are not associated or negatively associated. For example, the correlation between adjustments to accommodate disability and job-sharing is 0.35, that between statistics on gender composition and parental leave is 0.26, while that between variable pay and workplace nursery is an example of a negative correlation ($r = -0.10$), as is that involving internal recruitment and term-only contracts ($r = -0.11$).[3]

## 28.3.2 An Integrated Employee-Centered Management?

An integrated approach to management implies more than the fact that practices tend to coexist; it means that their association reflects an underlying orientation on the part of management. The correlations that exist between practices are then explained by this underlying orientation. In other words, if this orientation did not exist, all the practices would not be associated with each other. It could, for example, be that an association between appraisal and variable pay simply reflects the fact that appraisal results are fed into a performance-related pay system. Similarly, an association between job security and quality circles or suggestion schemes might exist simply because managements introduced the employment guarantees to aid idea-capturing. We can assess whether an orientation underlies the whole set of family-friendly management, equal-opportunity, and high-involvement practices by using latent variable analysis, the generic name for a family of statistical models used for testing for common factors (of which factor analysis is the best known).[4] (We do, however, exclude from this analysis those practices that we have already seen are unrelated to other practices of a similar type in this study: work enrichment and motivation as a selection criterion.)

---

[3] The non-parametric correlation coefficients and their significance are available at www.shef. ac.uk/iwp/wers.html

[4] For an introduction to the latent variable model used see Wood (1999b: 411–14).

We find that the three types of management are discrete from each other. However, an orientation does underlie the equal-opportunity practices (reliability R = 0.83), and some but not all of the family-friendly and high-involvement practices (Wood et al. 2003: 237–9). In the case of family-friendly management, we find that the subset of practices concerned with flexible working are explained by an underlying orientation, which we call 'family-oriented flexible management' (reliability R = 0.75). Those concerned with childcare—workplace nursery and childcare subsidies—are discrete from this, which may partly reflect the low use of these two practices. Of the high-involvement practices, excluding work-enrichment, work-organization and skill-acquisition practices reflect an underlying orientation, which we can treat as a measure of high-involvement management (reliability R = 0.68). This, it should be stressed, is distinct from work enrichment and the motivational practices.

Although positively correlated, a latent variable model does not fit the motivational practices, and thus these do not reflect an underlying orientation, for example a management orientation towards providing high-quality jobs or creating a strongly motivated workforce through locking employees into internal labor markets and rewarding good performance.

One-dimensional patterns in the use of specific subsets of practices have therefore been found: one type of family-friendly practice that is connected with flexible working arrangements; all equal-opportunity practices; and the work-organization and skill-acquisition high-involvement practices. What we have termed family-oriented flexible management is distinct from the provision of childcare help, and work enrichment is not a part of the dominant model of high-involvement management being practiced in the UK. The selection of motivational methods is not determined in general, if at all, by whether management is pursuing a high-involvement approach. Finally, there is no evidence of an underlying holistic orientation that combines family friendliness, equal opportunity, and high involvement into an integrated employee-centered high-commitment management.

However, the three orientations are correlated to some extent. The correlation coefficient is 0.46 for family-oriented flexible management and equal-opportunity management, 0.40 for equal-opportunity management and high-involvement management; 0.36 for family-oriented flexible management and high-involvement management. When we control for other variables (e.g. the size and nature of the workforce and sector of the economy) using regression analysis,[5] all three are significantly related to each other, but the relationship between family-oriented flexible management and high-involvement management is not particularly strong.

The regression analysis also confirms the distinctiveness of the three concepts as the variables with which they are associated differ. The only variable that is

---

[5] The results of all the regression analyses reported in this chapter are available from the first author, s.j.wood@sheffield.ac.uk

associated with all three is whether management takes a consultative approach to employees, measured by the extent to which it regularly consults through a formal channel on a range of issues (such as health and safety, productivity, training, technology, and work organization). Yet its relationship to family-oriented flexible management is not particularly strong. There are also sectoral differences. Both family-oriented flexible management and equal-opportunity management are significantly more likely to be found in the public sector. In contrast, high-involvement management is less likely in the public sector. Within the private sector itself, high-involvement management is significantly more prevalent in financial services and significantly less likely to be used extensively in manufacturing, construction, hotels and restaurants, transport and communication, other business services, and other community services.

In addition, organizations with human resource departments are more likely to have family-oriented flexible management and equal-opportunity management, but are less likely to have high-involvement management. The size of the workplace, as measured by the number of employees, is positively related only to equal-opportunity management. But the size of the larger organization, of which the workplace is a part, is related to both family-oriented flexible management and high-involvement management. In the case of family-oriented flexible management, organizations with over 5,000 employees are significantly more likely to adopt it, while in the case of high-involvement management, organizations with 100 or more employees are more likely to practice it than organizations with less than 100 employees. The proportion of the workforce that consists of managers is positively associated with both equal-opportunity and high-involvement management, while the proportion of the workforce that consists of women is positively linked to family-friendly management, and weakly related to high-involvement management.

### 28.3.3 The Association Between Family-Friendly, Equal-Opportunity, and High-Involvement Management and Performance in WERS98

We can only test the impact of identifiable phenomena. It is thus not possible to assess whether the integrated approach is associated with superior performance. We therefore tested the associations involving family-oriented flexible management, equal-opportunity management, high-involvement management, and the individual work-enrichment and motivational measures. We assessed these associations on three economic performance measures—financial performance, labor productivity, and change in labor productivity—and two human resource outcome measures—labor turnover and absenteeism.

In the absence of any independently sourced measures, all the economic outcomes considered are based on an assessment made by the managerial respondent according to five-point scales. Wall et al. (2004) have nonetheless shown that such data are consistent with the assumed more 'objective' audited accounting data. The three performance measures are not strongly related to each other (the Spearman correlation coefficient is 0.48 for financial performance and labor productivity, 0.26 for labor productivity and change in labor productivity, and 0.20 for financial performance and change in labor productivity), and certainly cannot be summarized in one overall organizational performance scale.

Using regression analyses, we found that high-involvement management has a significant independent association with financial performance (P-value = 0.042) and labor productivity (P-value = 0.001). Equal opportunity and family-oriented flexible management are not related to either, and none of the orientations is associated with the change in labor productivity. Of the motivational and other practices excluded from the orientation, variable pay is associated with one economic outcome, change in productivity (P = 0.03). Moreover, this association between variable pay and productivity change is strengthened by high-involvement management, which means that high-involvement management only has a significant effect when employees' pay varies with performance.

In addition, equal-opportunity management may have a positive effect on financial performance if high-involvement management is practiced in the workplace. Equal-opportunity management may also have a positive effect on the level of productivity where high-involvement management exists, but this only holds for the private sector.

Labor turnover is measured as the ratio of the number of employees who resigned from the establishment in the twelve months prior to the interview as a proportion of the total employees at the time of the interview; and absenteeism is the percentage of work days lost through employee sickness or absence in the workplace over the last twelve months.

Equal-opportunity (P = 0.034) and high-involvement management (P = 0.049) are associated with lower levels of labor turnover. The presence of both does not strengthen these associations. Family-oriented flexible management is, however, not related to labor turnover. Nor are any of the motivational or work-enrichment practices, including job security guarantees.

Equal-opportunity management is associated with lower levels of absenteeism (P = 0.05). Moreover, its beneficial effects on absence are intensified where high-involvement management is practiced. Family-oriented flexible management is only related to lower levels of absenteeism (P = 0.04) when it is underpinned by top management valuing family–work balance. Without this, it will have no impact. Of the motivational supports, job security is positively associated with absence levels. This implies that people who are more secure in their jobs are less worried about having time off, as they feel that doing so will not jeopardize their career prospects. This conclusion is also supported by the fact that absence is also higher in workplaces where there are hard-to-fill vacancies, which may suggest to employees that they are not readily dispensable, so taking time off is seen as less costly.

Finally, to assess whether the impact of any of the forms of management is contingent on other factors, rather than universal, we tested to see if any associations between the orientations and the outcome variables are moderated by the size of the workplace or a larger organization of which it is a part or by the extent to which the organization faces a turbulent market environment. No such moderated relationships were discovered. We also considered, in the light of the claims that trade-union voice should enhance the effectiveness of high-involvement management (see e.g. Kochan and Osterman 1994: 105–7), whether the presence of a recognized union strengthens any of the associations between the orientations and the outcomes, and again found no evidence of this.

In summary, of our three orientations, high-involvement management is most strongly associated with organizational outcomes. It is related to financial performance, labor productivity, and labor retention, as well as to change in labor productivity when variable pay is used in conjunction with it. In addition, where it is practiced, equal-opportunity management is associated with financial performance and, in the private sector only, the level of productivity. High-involvement management also intensifies the tendency for equal-opportunity management to lower absence. Family-oriented flexible management has little or no effect on outcomes, but where top management values a family–work balance, it can reduce absence.

# 28.4 CONCLUSIONS

The chapter has shown that in Britain there is no evidence yet of an integrated high-commitment management. Nonetheless, there appear to be discrete orientations underlying the use of family-oriented flexible, equal opportunity, and core (work and skill acquisition) high-involvement practices. Moreover, there is a tendency for these orientations to coexist, but this reflects idiosyncratic local factors.

The performance results provide little support for the 'business case' in favor of family-friendly and equal-opportunity initiatives, which is the argument for employee-centered methods on the grounds that they are supportive of key organizational objectives. But, equally, neither set of practices has a negative effect on performance. We have nonetheless found that high-involvement management is positively associated with financial performance, labor productivity, and labor retention. In addition, where high-involvement management is adopted, equal-opportunity management will have a positive effect on financial perform- ance. Equal-opportunity management is associated with lower absence levels, and again this is strengthened when high-involvement management is adopted. When family-oriented flexible management is underpinned by top management valuing employees having a balance between work and family responsibilities, it is also associated with lower absenteeism.

The limited number of associations between organizational performance and family-friendly and equal-opportunity managements may be used to reinforce the arguments for a holistic approach. It could be precisely because the employee involvement, equality, and diversity issues are not integrated that the current approaches are not as successful. Moreover, the lack of recognition that the potential benefits of such an integrated approach may be high may very well explain the relatively low take-up of many of the practices that we have studied.

Alternatively, there are other possible explanations for the results. For example, one is that family-friendly and equal-opportunity policies neither symbolize to employees any wider 'corporate concern' for employees (Grover and Crooker 1995: 274) nor create within employees a 'generalized sense of obligation to the work- place' (Lambert 2000: 811). Or it may be that, while policies are manifest in practices, these practices are not so effectively implemented or operated as to have a telling impact on the lives, commitments, and perceptions of employees.

Taking the results at face value, the first implication is that a high-involvement approach to management should have positive effects on economic performance and labor stability. This is likely to be so regardless of whether it includes a significant element of work enrichment. The second implication is that we should be directing attention to equality, diversity, and family–work conflict, and even work enrichment on equity grounds alone. Yet, our focus has been on short-term economic outcomes and, as Boxall and Purcell (2003: 6–13, 242–5) remind us so forcibly, human resource initiatives, from an employer's perspective, need to be judged by other criteria as well. Salience should also be given to longer-term economic objectives concerned with innovation and adaptation, which Boxall and Purcell call organizational flexibility, and the need for organizations to have social legitimacy.[6]

Certainly, making arguments on the basis of the impact of employee-centered approaches on short-term economic outcomes ignores their potential contribution to other goals. The argument that approaching family friendliness, equal opportunity, and high involvement in a holistic, high-commitment way may help to ensure that

---

[6] The institutional theory argument that organizations need to respond to pressures for both efficiency and legitimacy has been a particularly important consideration in the studies of the use of family-friendly practices (see e.g. Goodstein 1994, 1995; Ingram and Simons 1995; Milliken et al. 1998), but as yet no attempt has been made to test their impact over the long term or on the legitimacy of the organization.

they are tackled successfully and contribute to all three criteria remains intuitively appealing. Moreover, our results do not deny the possibility that even short-term economic effects might be more pronounced were more employers to adopt this holistic approach. But, in the absence of such evidence, we should avoid getting entrenched on the business case terrain as it encourages the mindset that issues of equality, fair treatment, and work–non-work conflict only need to be addressed insofar as they have immediate effects on company profits.

## REFERENCES

APPELBAUM, E., and BATT, R. (1994). *The New American Workplace*. Ithaca, NY: ILR Press, Cornell University Press.

—— BAILEY, T., BERG, P., and KALLEBERG, A. L. (2000). *Manufacturing Advantage: Why High Performance Work Systems Pay off*. Ithaca, NY: Cornell University Press.

BAILYN, L. (1993). *Breaking the Mold*. New York: The Free Press.

BATT, R. (2002). 'Managing Customer Services: Human Resource Practices, Quit Rates, and Sales Growth.' *Academy of Management Journal*, 45/3: 587–97.

—— and VALCOUR, P. M. (2003). 'Human Resources Practices as Predictors of Work–Family Outcomes and Employee Turnover.' *Industrial Relations*, 42/2: 189–220.

BERG, P., KALLEBERG, A. L., and APPELBAUM, E. (2003). 'Balancing Work and Family: The Role of the High-Commitment Environment.' *Industrial Relations*, 42/2: 168–88.

BEWLEY, H., and FERNIE, S. (2003). 'What do Unions do for Women?' In H. Gospel and S. Wood (eds.), *Representing Workers*. London: Routledge.

BOND, J., GALINSKY, E., and SWANBERG, J. (1998). *The 1997 National Study of the Changing Workforce*. New York: Families & Work Institute.

BOXALL, P., and PURCELL, J. (2003). *Strategy and Human Resource Management*. Houndmills: Palgrave Macmillan.

DE MENEZES, L., and WOOD, S. (2006). 'Identifying Human Resource Management in Britain Using the Workplace Employee Relations Survey.' *International Journal of Human Resource Management*, 17/1: 1–33.

DEX, S., and SMITH, C. (2002). *The Nature and Pattern of Family-Friendly Employment Policies in Britain*. Bristol: The Policy Press.

GITTLEMAN, M., HORRIGAN, M., and JOYCE, M. (1998). ' "Flexible" Workplace Practices: Evidence from a Nationally Representative Survey.' *Industrial and Labor Relations Review*, 52/1: 99–113.

GOODSTEIN, J. (1994). 'Institutional Pressures and Strategic Responsiveness: Employer Involvement in Work–family Issues.' *Academy of Management Journal*, 37/2: 350–82.

—— (1995). 'Employer Involvement in Eldercare: An Organizational Adaptation Perspective.' *Academy of Management Journal*, 38/6: 1657–71.

GROVER, S. L., and CROOKER, K. J. (1995). 'Who Appreciates Family-Responsive Human Resource Policies: The Impact of Family-Friendly Policies on the Organizational Attachment of Parents and Non-parents?' *Personnel Psychology*, 48/2: 271–88.

GUEST, D. (2002). 'Human Resource Management, Corporate Performance and Employee Well-Being: Building the Worker into HRM.' *Journal of Industrial Relations*, 44/1: 335–58.

HOCHSCHILD, A. R. (1997). *The Time Bind: When Work Becomes Home and Home Becomes Work.* New York: Metropolitan Books.

HUSELID, M. A. (1995). 'The Impact of Human Resource Management Practices on Turnover, Productivity and Corporate Financial Performance.' *Academy of Management Journal*, 38/3: 635–72.

INGRAM, P., and SIMONS, T. (1995). 'Institutional and Resource Dependence Determinants of Responsiveness to Work Family Issues.' *Academy of Management Journal*, 5: 1466–82.

KOCHAN, T., and OSTERMAN, P. (1994). *The Mutual Gains Enterprise.* Boston: Harvard Business School Press.

LAMBERT, S. J. (2000). 'Added Benefits: The Link between Work–Life Programs on Firms' Productivity.' *Academy of Management Journal*, 43/5: 801–15.

LAWLER, E. (1986). *High-Involvement Management.* San Francisco: Jossey-Bass.

—— (1991). 'Participative Management Strategies.' In J. W. Jones, B. W. Steffy, and D. W. Bray (eds.), *Applying Psychology in Business. The Handbook for Managers and Human Resource Professionals.* Lexington, Mass.: Lexington Books.

MACDUFFIE, J. P. (1995). 'Human Resource Bundles and Manufacturing Performance: Organizational Logic and Flexible Production System in the World Auto Industry.' *Industrial and Labor Relations Review*, 48/2: 197–221.

MILLIKEN, F. J., MARTINS, L., and MORGAN, H. (1998). 'Determinants of an Organization's Responsiveness to Work–Family Issues: An Integration of Competing Theories.' *Academy of Management Journal*, 41/5: 580–92.

MILLWARD, N., STEVENS M., SMART, D., and HAWES, W. R. (1992). *Workplace Industrial Relations in Transition.* Aldershot: Dartmouth.

OSTERMAN, P. (1994). 'How Common is Workplace Transformation and How can we Explain Who Does it?' *Industrial and Labor Relations Review*, 47/2: 173–88.

—— (1995). 'Work/Family Programs and the Employment Relationship.' *Administrative Science Quarterly*, 40/4: 681–700.

PARKER, S., WALL, T., and JACKSON, P. (1997). 'That's not my Job: Developing Flexible Employee Work Orientations.' *Academy of Management Journal*, 40/4: 899–929.

PERRY-SMITH, J. E., and BLUM, T. C. (2000). 'Work–Family Human Resource Bundles and Perceived Organizational Performance.' *Academy of Management Journal*, 43/6: 1107–17.

SISSON, K. (1995). 'Human Resource Management and the Personnel Function.' In J. Storey (ed.), *Human Resource Management.* London: Routledge.

WALL, T., and WOOD, S. (2005). 'The Romance of Human Resource Management and Business Performance and the Case for Big Science.' *Human Relations*, 58/4: 429–62.

—— MICHIE, J., PATTERSON, M., SHEEHAN, M., WOOD, S., CLEGG, C., and WEST, M. (2004). 'On the Validity of Reported Company Financial Performance.' *Personnel Psychology*, 57/1: 95–118.

WALTON, R. (1985). 'From Control to Commitment in the Workplace.' *Harvard Business Review*, 63/2: 77–84.

WOOD, S. (1999a). 'Human Resource Management and Performance.' *International Journal of Management Reviews*, 1/4: 367–413.

—— (1999b). 'Getting the Measure of the Transformed Organization.' British *Journal of Industrial Relations*, 37/3: 391–418.

—— and ALBANESE, M. (1995). 'Can you Speak of a High Commitment Management on the Shop Floor?' *Journal of Management Studies*, 32/2: 215–47.

WOOD, S. and DE MENEZES, L. (1998). 'High Commitment Management in the UK: Evidence from the Workplace Industrial Relations Survey and Employers' Manpower and Skills Practices Survey.' *Human Relations*, 51/4: 485–515.

—— and WALL, T. (2007). 'Work Enrichment and Employee Voice in Human Resource Management-Performance Studies.' *International Journal of Human Resource Management*, forthcoming.

—— DE MENEZES, L., and LASAOSA, A. (2003). 'Family-Friendly Management In Great Britain: Testing Various Perspectives.' *Industrial Relations*, 42/2: 221–50.

CHAPTER 29

SOCIAL
LEGITIMACY
OF THE HRM
PROFESSION
A US PERSPECTIVE

THOMAS A. KOCHAN

## 29.1 INTRODUCTION

THE human resource management profession faces a crisis of trust and a loss of legitimacy in the eyes of its major stakeholders. The two-decade effort to develop a new 'strategic human resource management' (HR)[1] role in organizations has failed to realize its promised potential of greater status, influence, and achievement. This chapter focuses on these developments in the USA by putting the current situation in a longer historical and comparative context and outlines the values, power relationships, and institutional factors that shape the role of HR. I then suggest a

Portions of this chapter build and expand on Kochan 2004.

[1] For the sake of simplicity I will use the term HR in a generic fashion in referring to those responsible for managing employment relations, recognizing the specific terms have changed over the years from personnel, to industrial relations, to human resource management, and perhaps to other terms yet to come.

number of steps that HR professionals might take to redefine their role and professional identity and rebuild their legitimacy. The central task is to achieve a better balance between employer and employee interests at work. The starting point for this task is to undertake an explicit examination of the values and norms that underlie the HR profession and its associations. The chapter argues that HR professionals need to treat business strategy as an endogenous variable, be more externally focused and skilled at building networks and productive alliances with other groups and institutions, become more analytical and able to document the benefits associated with effective HR policies and practices to firms and employees, and be skilled at managing in an increasingly transparent society and information savvy workforce. The changing gender composition of the HR profession may affect its success in making these changes and meeting these challenges. Ironically, however, significant change in the status and legitimacy of the HR profession may require a rebalancing of power in employment relations.

## 29.2 CHALLENGE TO LEGITIMACY: THE BREAKDOWN IN THE SOCIAL CONTRACT

> A regime which provides human beings no deep reason to care about one another cannot long preserve its legitimacy.
>
> (Sennett 1998: 1)

The first sentence of Richard Sennett's critique of contemporary workplace relations should serve as a rallying cry for the human resource management (HR) profession. HR derives its social legitimacy from its ability to serve as an effective steward of a social contract in employment relationships capable of balancing and integrating the interests and needs of employers, employees, and the society in which these relationships are embedded (Boxall and Purcell 2003; Lansbury 2004; McGregor and Cutcher-Gershenfeld 2005).

At no time since the founding of the HR or personnel profession is this challenge more difficult and yet more critical, especially in the USA. There is an unfortunate but broad consensus among American researchers, policy analysts, and business leaders that the social contract that allowed workers and employers to prosper together in the decades that followed the Second World War broke down in the past two decades (Kochan 2001). The visible signs of this breakdown varied from one country and setting to another. In the case of the USA it could be seen in multiple trends:

- increased use of lay-offs, not as a last resort, but as part of organizational restructuring or movement of work to lower-cost locations;
- increased working hours for individuals and family units;

- increased inequality of income and stagnant or declining real wages for a majority of the workforce and a break in the historic relationship between profits, productivity, and real wage growth;
- loss of retirement income and shifts in the pension risk to employees as firms shifted from defined benefit to various forms of defined contribution plans;
- declining health care coverage and shifts of cost increases to employees, and
- loss of employee voice at work and in political and social affairs as labor movement membership and power declined to pre-1930 levels.

These trends were well established before the US stock market's Internet bubble burst and the corporate scandals erupted in the early years of the twenty-first century. Following these latter two developments, trust in American corporations fell precipitously (*USA Today* 2002). Given all of this, it is not surprising that in recent years how to restore trust in management has become a central topic of discussion among corporate executives, leaders of government bodies and international agencies, and management researchers (Bartunek 2002; Lewis 2002; New York Stock Exchange 2002; Kochan and Schmalensee 2003).

The US HR profession faces the same crisis of trust as does management in general, in part because it is (or should be) part of senior management in corporations and even more so because it always has had a special professional responsibility to balance the needs of the firm with the needs, aspirations, and interests of the workforce and the values and standards society expects to be upheld at work. How the HR profession responds to the challenge of rebuilding a viable social contract at work will shape not only its legitimacy but also its future influence in organizations and in society, and for HR researchers, their status in the social science community.

This chapter focuses on HR in the USA While the extent to which the developments discussed here apply to other countries is best left to the judgement of those most knowledgeable about their own settings, brief historical comparisons are made with HR in several other countries to place HR in the USA in a broader global and historical context and to demonstrate that the HR profession is shaped in part by differences in national institutions.

# 29.3 How We Got Here: From Personnel to Strategic HRM

Like other professions, HR is shaped by a mixture of values, pressures, and institutional arrangements. Child (1969) shows how the early stages of HR in

Britain were shaped by the Quaker traditions of its founders. They saw their role as attending to the welfare of the workforce. Their Quaker traditions also led them to take what Fox (1971) labeled a pluralist as opposed to a unitary view of the firm, pre-dating those who would later view the corporation from a multiple stakeholder rather than a shareholder perspective. Those values were reinforced by a strong and growing labor movement in Britain up until 1970 and by the corresponding rise of labor relations considerations and specialists to the top of the HR agenda and function in corporations (CIPD 2005). The effects of the Thatcher government policies and the steady decline of British unionism have eroded these pluralist views among British HR professionals. However, the return of a Labour government and various corporate governance commission reports have kept alive debate over the responsibilities of corporations and HR (CIPD 2005).

In Japan, HR professionals are embedded in corporate governance structures that give greater weight to balancing employee and shareholder interests (Aoki 1988). As a result, HR is viewed as one of the most influential functions within Japanese firms and the top HR executive typically is a member of the board in large corporations. While recent economic pressures have led Japanese firms to adapt some of their employment practices, HR executives continue to have greater influence and status in their firms than do their American counterparts (Jacoby 2005).

In Germany and other countries within the European Community, labor and social policies and corporate governance structures require greater employee consultation and representation, and society expects a higher level of attention to employee and community interests (Wever 1995). These arrangements reflect, in part, pressures exerted on Germany in particular following the Second World War to strengthen its democratic institutions to avoid a return to fascism. In recent years, pressures to increase flexibility in European labor markets led to some changes in labor laws and regulations, but recent European Community rules and regulations reinforce the importance of the 'triple bottom line' (economic, social, and environmental performance) (PriceWaterhouseCoopers 2002) and information and consultation rights of workers (Marginson et al. 2004). These historic and current institutional features make it more necessary for HR professionals in these contexts to be able to achieve a balance of employee and employer and societal expectations and interests at work than is the case in the USA. Whether these institutional features continue to play this role in the future or erode in the face of further changes in labor market and social policies remains a topic of considerable debate and uncertainty.

The origins of the personnel and HR profession in the USA are generally traced back to the rise of Scientific Management in the early years of the twentieth century (Kaufman 1994; Jacoby 2005). These roots gave US HR a stronger focus on efficiency than employee welfare. Business and personnel historians (Bendix 1956; Brown and Myers 1957; Jacoby 1985) also emphasize the strong unitarist and deep-seated anti-union ideology of American management. Moreover, the US model of corporate governance is based on a shareholder maximizing principle leaving no formal role or informal norm for employees as stakeholders. So it is not surprising that the commitment to balancing worker and employer interests has been somewhat weaker in the values of HRM professionals in the USA than in other countries.

Over time, however, the pressures of trade unions, tighter labor markets for professional and technical talent, and expansion of government regulations also affected the views and approaches of HR and other managers in American corporations. As the power of these external forces grew, managers made pragmatic adaptations, took a more multiple stakeholder view of the firm and their role, and developed the skills and organizational practices needed to accommodate the power of these forces (Kochan et al. 1984; Jacoby 1985; Baron et al. 1988; Dobbin and Sutton 1998). As in Britain, labor and industrial relations specialists rose to the top of the HR function in the decades following the Second World War. So by 1970, at what was perhaps the pinnacle of the power of US unions and pressure from newly enacted and enforced government regulations, one HR historian concluded:

A humane and satisfying organization, as well as profitable operations, has become a criterion of successful executive performance [sic]. ... Today most executives are aware the wants and needs of workers extend far beyond wages, and they have accepted that the responsibility of helping workers fulfill the psychological needs requires them to make employment a more rewarding and satisfying experience. .... Sound personnel relations are highly desirable, not merely as a requisite to an efficient and profitable business operation, but as a contribution to society in general, as a fulfillment of moral and ethical demands. (Milton 1970: 1–2)

Since 1970, however, changes in the US and the global economy shifted the dominant view of the firm espoused by corporate executives, labor movement power and commitment to vigorous enforcement of government regulations declined, and the view and approach of HR professionals has been transformed. Recent decades of HR scholarship and professional activity in the USA have been dominated by efforts to shift from a functional, personnel administration approach to a strategic human resource management perspective. The largest professional association in the country changed its name and focus accordingly from the American Society for Personnel Administration (ASPA) to the Society for Human Resource Management (SHRM). This change symbolized a deeper shift in the professional identity and role of HR. As union power and pressure from government enforcement agencies declined and international and domestic competitive pressures intensified, HR professionals slowly lost their ability to challenge their organizations to balance employee and firm interests. Power over employment strategies and practices shifted from labor and industrial relations specialists to HR generalists and increasingly to line managers and executives (Kochan 1980; Freedman 1990).

As a result, HR professionals sought to 'partner' with line managers and senior executives in developing and delivering human resource policies that supported the firm's competitive strategies. The dominant effect of this inward shift in perspective was to more closely align HR professionals with the interests and goals of the firm, at least the goals as articulated by the top executives with whom HR professionals sought to align. Indeed, one of the most respected of America's HR professionals (Doyle 1993) once described this development as HR professionals becoming what he called 'perfect agents' of top management (a not too complementary analogy to the Peter Sellers character who sought to be the alter ego of his boss). By the end of the twentieth century, the transformation in the American HR role was largely complete. As a result, HR professionals lost any semblance of credibility as stewards of the social contract because most HR professionals had lost their ability to seriously challenge or offer an independent perspective on the policies and practices of the firm.

Perhaps the clearest indicator of the inability of HR professionals to challenge their CEOs or other top executives is the fact that in the USA CEO pay relative to the average worker exploded over this time period, moving from a ratio of 40:1 in the 1960s and 1970s to over 400:1 today. Another indicator comes from surveys of HR professionals themselves. Surveys asking HR leaders in the 1990s to rank their profession's most important goals and priorities reported that six of the seven most important priorities reflected the needs of their organizations or their HR unit. The first workforce concern to make it on this list (promoting diversity) came in seventh on their list (Eichinger and Ulrich 1996). A final indicator comes from the harsh critique titled 'Why we Hate HR' (Hammonds 2005) that presents survey data from an HR consultancy firm (the Hay Group) showing a majority of employees feel performance appraisals are unfair and only about half of non-managerial employees believe their firms have interests in their employees' well-being. Based on these data and interviews with HR academics and practitioners, Hammonds (2005: 40) sums up the state of the profession as follows:

After close to 20 years of hopeful rhetoric about becoming 'strategic partners' with a 'seat at the table' where the business decisions that matter are made, most human-resources professionals aren't nearly there. They have no seat, and the table is locked inside a conference room to which they have no key. HR people are, for most practical purposes, neither strategic nor leaders.

Meanwhile, as (and perhaps in part because) the HR profession was turning inward, pressures on the workforce slowly began to mount, one by one. Over the past decade workers and families have endured longer working hours in the face of stagnant or declining wages, lost or had dramatically diminished pensions, rising health insurance costs, and spreading job insecurity. Even in 1999, at the peak of the dot.com boom, a national survey conducted by *Business Week* found that three-fourths of Americans believed the benefits of the 'new economy were unequally distributed, only a third saw it as increasing their own incomes, and only about half saw the boom as making their own lives better' (*Business Week* 1999). By 2003, another business organization, the Conference Board, reported its national surveys showed that fewer than half of workers were satisfied with their jobs. Less than 40 percent were satisfied with their wages, health insurance, or pensions (*Boston Globe* 2003). With the arrival of the Bush administration came a shift to a more pro-business and anti-worker government policy. Overtime coverage was reduced, rules allowing states to fund paid family leave were repealed, briefs opposing affirmative action were filed in key Supreme Court cases, labor–management partnership agreements in the federal sector and on large-scale construction projects were disbanded, and thousands of federal workers' rights to participate in collective bargaining were cancelled by an Executive Order making the Orwellian claim that collective bargaining would be a 'threat to national security.'

The net result of these diverging HR priorities, government policy shifts, and workforce pressures is that we now have perhaps a wider gulf between the perceived needs and interests of firms and their employees than at any time since the Great Depression of the 1930s. Indeed, the cumulative effects of these pressures and the breakdown in trust in corporations suggests the American workplace may be like a pressure cooker about to blow (Kochan 2005).

These pressures and the decline in the ability or willingness of the HR profession to address them are perhaps more acute in the USA than in other countries where cultural norms and institutional arrangements enforce a stronger sense of corporate responsibility and commitment to balancing the interests of multiple stakeholders and where labor power has not declined to as low a level as in the USA. If the US HR profession is to rebuild its status, legitimacy, and trust, it will need to achieve more equitable balance among the different stakeholders at work and to do so it will need to reassess what values underlie it, break out of its internal focus, and rebuild relationships and alliances with the workforce and other external stakeholders.

# 29.4 Meeting the Challenge: What can be Done?

## 29.4.1 Starting Point: Values and Professional Norms

As a card-carrying member of the US-based SHRM and the National Academy of Human Resources (NAHR), I often find myself at odds with the knee-jerk reaction and opposition these organizations and my fellow members take toward any proposals to update and modernize public policies governing work and employ-ment relations. This is the case even though many of us have documented the need to update policies that were enacted to support the industrial and largely domestic economy and male breadwinner workforce of the 1930s to catch up with the changing economy and workforce of today (Osterman et al. 2001; Kochan 2005). The dominant HR policy stance reflects the lack of a clearly articulated set of professional standards for the HR profession. While one must be realistic in recognizing that HR professionals are ultimately employed by and represent management, the absence of such a code or set of standards leaves HR profes-sionals with little basis for challenging or questioning the dominant values and ideologies of the more senior and more powerful corporate executives within the individual firms that employ them. At a very minimum, HR professionals should hold each other accountable for enforcing legal standards and principles embodied in national legislation and the fundamental human rights at work recognized by the International Labor Organization. Even this is problematic in the USA where a large body of empirical evidence has demonstrated that US labor law no longer is effective in protecting one of these basic rights, namely freedom of association (Commission on Worker Management Relations 1994). Yet, for the past quarter-century, HR leaders have steadfastly resisted all efforts to fix these problems and to update and modernize American labor law (Mills 1979; Kochan 1995).

If the strength of a profession in part is judged by the strength of the professional norms enforced and promoted by professional societies, the HR profession, at least in the USA, must rank among the weakest (Jacoby 2005). Accountants, lawyers, physicians, and other health care professionals are all subject to professional certification and/or other standards that embody clear principles for guiding professional behavior regardless of the particular firm or organizational setting in which they work. While there are various certification exams that are available to HR professionals, there is no evidence that they are treated as requirements for entry-level positions or for advancement within the HR function of most firms. In the absence of a collectively developed, shared, and enforced set of professional standards that reflect a clear set of values, no individual HR professional is able to challenge his or her more powerful seniors on sensitive firm or public policy issues. Thus, developing a stronger HR professional set of standards is a necessary condition for restoring its social legitimacy.

## 29.4.2 Reframing the Role of Strategy in Strategic HR

Paralleling the movement from personnel management to strategic HRM has come a debate in the scholarly HR literature over whether there exists a common set of best HRM practices capable of achieving high levels of organizational performance or whether strategic HRM requires a contingent approach (Chadwick and Cappelli

1999). The contingency view argues that firms that want to compete on the basis of innovation, growth, and quality need matching human resources strategies that invest heavily in their human resources and implement state-of-the-art high-performance work organization practices while firms that choose to compete on the basis of low costs need to follow more traditional command and control, high-turnover strategies that require little human resource investment and result in low wages and labor costs (Wright and Sherman 1999). Others have argued that mixed strategies are possible so that even competing on the basis of low costs does not necessarily require the full range of traditional low wage and command and control practices (Boxall and Purcell 2003).

I believe this fully or partially contingent view of strategic HR further reduces the credibility and trust of HR professionals and researchers. It is the wrong way to frame the role HR professionals should play in strategic debates within their firms or in broader social policy debates. In a global or domestic market economy with variability in wages, the only way that firms and employees can prosper *together* is to compete on the basis of high-productivity, high-human resource investment strategies. This in turn requires adoption and successful management of high-performance human resource practices.

Earlier industrial relations researchers implicitly took this view of their role. Slichter et al. (1960) used the term the 'shock effect' to describe in detail how industrial relations professionals helped their organizations adapt to negotiated wage and benefit improvements that reflected the power of unions from the 1940s through the 1960s. That is, union pressures led to higher wages which had to be recouped by higher productivity. The central task of industrial relations and personnel managers was to advise management on how to professionalize their operations and adapt strategies in other aspects of management practice (pricing, marketing, operations, technological change, etc.) to achieve higher productivity. Dobbin and Sutton (1998) documented the same effect for government policies enacted in the 1960s and 1970s.

Thus, rather than take corporate strategies as an exogenous determinant of HR strategies, HR researchers and professionals should be advocating adoption of corporate strategies that can sustain good and improving employment practices and outcomes *and* achieve high levels of organizational performance. That is the view of strategy that is now embedded in most contemporary models of industrial relations (Kochan et al. 1986; Boxall and Purcell 2003).

## 29.4.3 Human Resource Strategies in a Knowledge Economy

Conceptualizing the role of strategy in this way allows one to then consider and take up the challenge of translating the rhetoric about building a 'knowledge economy' and promoting 'lifelong learning' into tangible benefits for the economy and society, for individual firms, and for the workforce. This will not be as easy as some thought it would be.

The twenty-first century burst upon us in an era of seemingly unbounded optimism about the future. This was expected to be the century in which know-ledge and skills, or more technically, human capital, finally found its place as the most critical resource and strategic asset to organizations. Yet five years into the new century, a new worry has arisen. Even knowledge work is now at risk of being outsourced to independent contractors or 'offshored' to lower-cost employees in developing countries. How is the need to invest in and treat knowledge workers as valuable assets to be reconciled with cost pressures that put them at risk of being outsourced? Clearly, some of the more routine knowledge-intensive work will move to lower-cost environments. Blanket opposition is neither feasible nor, in the long run, good for either developing or highly industrialized economies. Instead, the key lies in staying on and pushing out the frontiers of knowledge, invention, and innovation in products and processes. But what can HR profes-sionals do to help their firms overcome the concern that following a strategy of investing in, while others are offshoring, their work will put them at a competitive disadvantage?

The only viable answer to this question is for the HR profession to reach out to external parties and build the *collective* efforts needed to develop the neces-sary skill base. No individual firm has adequate incentives to invest in the general training and education needed to support a knowledge-based economy. This is even more true today as modern communications technologies make it easier to move work to where the talent is most abundant and cheapest and the expected tenure of employees in a single firm (for voluntary and involuntary reasons) is shorter than in the past. This implies that HR professionals need to work together to help schools and universities to graduate people with the capabilities both to invent the next generation of products and services *and* to move quickly and effectively from invention through the innovation process to the market.

While support for schools is important, industry will remain an important source of 'lifelong' education, training, and human capital development. But individual firms will under-invest in education and training if their competitors are not contributing their fair share to the workforce development process. This is another reason why the profession must look outward at rebuilding linkages with professional associations, unions, local colleges and universities, and government agencies to generate support for and deliver the general training needed to fuel a knowledge-based economy.

Another reason why HR professionals need to become more externally focused as knowledge becomes more important is that managing knowledge work and workers increasingly involves multiple organizations, contracting relationships, and informal networks. The move to outsource non-core activities (ironically including a good deal of HR training, record-keeping, and other functional tasks) increases the portion of work done by contractors, suppliers, or in other non-standard employment relationships. As movement of work to offshore contractors increases, so too does the complexity of monitoring and managing these relationships and ensuring that the core knowledge and skills needed to remain competitive are maintained within the organization or available from a network of trusted, proven suppliers. Managing these mixed types of employment arrangements and multi-party networks in which they are embedded will likely be an increasingly important and challenging aspect of HR work.

## 29.4.4 From Knowledge Workers to Knowledge-Based Work Systems

Too often the terms 'knowledge worker' or 'the knowledge economy' are equated with the elite professional, managerial, and technical workforce. Yet we know that front-line workers likewise can, and must, be mobilized to contribute their knowledge and skills for an organization and its employees to prosper in a knowledge economy. A great deal of effort, experience, and evidence has been amassed in the past two decades over how to build knowledge-based work systems that allow front-line workers to develop and utilize their skills. This is the signal achievement of HR scholars and practitioners of the strategic HR era. And the way it was achieved illustrates another feature of what is needed for the next generation of HR professionals to achieve legitimacy and influence in their organizations and society: a deeper analytical focus.

A key study in the automobile industry undertaken in 1982 showed strong relationships between work and labor relations practices and processes and plant performance (Katz et al. 1983). Then, a few years later, a major breakthrough in communicating this potential to executives came when study of the Toyota-GM joint venture known as the New United Motors Manufacturing Inc. (NUMMI) led to a methodology for comparing work hours per car and defects per car at that plant with others in the industry. The differences reported were startling, showing a 2 to 1 differential in productivity and quality between NUMMI and sister plants with old and new technology but traditional labor relations, human resource, and production systems (Krafcik 1988). This data laid the foundation for the best-selling book *The Machine that Changed the World* (Womack et al. 1990). Later would come the international comparisons of assembly plants (MacDuffie 1995; MacDuffie and Pil 1997), documenting the generalizability of these findings and outlining the features of the integrated set of production, human resource, work organization, and labor relations practices that produced these high levels of performance. By the late 1990s, this new paradigm was generally accepted in the industry. Organizations around the world were engaged in efforts to adapt its features to fit their different cultural and institutional settings (Kochan et al. 1995).

Over the course of the 1990s, similar analyses were also carried out in a wide variety of industries including apparel, computers, telecommunications, steel, office equipment, and airlines. While the diffusion of these new practices and knowledge-based systems is not universal, Huselid and Becker (2001) extended this analysis across industries and produced estimates that moving from the mean to one standard deviation in use of high-performance practices was associated with an average 23 percent higher rate of return and 8 percent higher market value. These types of numbers, even if off by a significant fraction, get managers' attention.

This data has a number of well-documented methodological limitations (Purcell 1999; Gerhart et al. 2000) that caution against the view that there is a single best set of HR or work system practices that will produce high performance in all settings. My own view of this evidence and the various methodological critiques is that there are significant potential returns to productivity and quality from implementing knowledge-based work systems that are *well tailored* to the specific technical and organizational settings. However, there are also costs associated with implementing, sustaining, and diffusing these work systems across large organizations and considerable difficulty and likely error in measuring their effects. The lesson from this is the need for HR professionals to be more analytical and skilled in understanding how to design and implement tailor-made systems wherever there is potential for enhancing performance by better drawing in the knowledge of the full workforce. By doing so, more environments where this potential exists will be identified.

Will employees automatically benefit from implementation of these systems? Here the evidence is also mixed. While there is clear evidence that most employees prefer jobs that use their skills and provide them discretion over how to do their jobs, and field studies showing positive correlations between job satisfaction and implementation of knowledge-based work systems (Appelbaum et al. 2000), there are also case studies and critiques documenting that these systems can increase stress and do not necessarily translate into higher pay or greater job security (Godard 2004; Ramsay et al. 2000). On balance, however, the evidence shows that if employee concerns are taken into account in implementing these systems or they, and/or their representatives, are directly involved in their design and oversight, they hold considerable potential for narrowing the gap between the interests of firms and those of employees (Batt and Appelbaum 1995; Black and Lynch 2001; Kochan et al. 2005).

## 29.4.5  Looking Beyond Workplace Performance: The Dual Work–Family Agenda

As much as significant progress has been made in understanding and implementing knowledge-based work systems, the singular focus on workplace outcomes (productivity, quality, etc.) needs to expand to take into account the changing labor force and the increasingly close interdependences between work and personal/family life. As Bailyn and Fletcher (2003) argue, today's work systems and processes have to be held accountable for achieving a dual agenda: high levels of performance at the workplace and the ability to meet personal and family needs. To do so will once again require HR professionals to engage a wider set of stakeholders.

The growing need to better balance or integrate work and family needs has not gone unnoticed in American firms. Indeed, over the past decade or so many firms have implemented 'family friendly' policies. Experience shows, however, that these policies suffer from a fundamental problem: they are underutilized for fear that using them will hurt one's career prospects (Eaton 2003; Drago et al. forthcoming). A study of Boston law firms found that over 90 percent had policies on the books that allowed associates (young lawyers not yet promoted to be partners) to work reduced hour or part-time schedules. Yet only 4 percent of those eligible in fact took up this option (Women's Bar Association of Massachusetts 2000). The same survey explained why so few took the option: one-third of the lawyers surveyed believed that taking this option would seriously damage their careers because they would be stigmatized as less than 'fully committed' professionals. Drago et al. (forthcoming) found a similar effect among college faculty with again one-third engaging in what they call 'bias avoidance' behavior to keep from hurting their career. Thus, both professional norms and organizational cultures need to change along with the formal policies.

Engaging the workforce and their professional societies in rethinking how work and careers are structured is only the first, necessary step in engaging the broader set of stakeholders that will need to be engaged if the challenge of integrating work and family responsibilities is to be met. Debate over these issues will eventually shift to the public policy arena. If the HR profession takes the same knee-jerk oppositional stance to new public policies to provide the flexibility and income supports (i.e. paid family leave modern workers and families need to meet their dual responsibilities), it will perpetuate and extend the long-standing business–labor impasse into this area of social policy. In this case, however, it will not just be organized labor that the HR profession finds itself opposing. It will be the women and family advocates, a group that will be much harder to label as a 'special interest' or some 'outside third party.' The question in my mind, therefore, is whether HR professionals will engage in constructive dialogue, analysis, and negotiations with women and family advocates and policy experts to design a sensible approach to this and other aspects of work–family policy, or hunker down, continue to oppose new policies, and then have to live with whatever new policies are eventually enacted.

## 29.4.6 Restoring Voice at Work

There is an irony associated with the general decline in organized labor experienced around the world in recent decades, and its precipitous decline in the USA. HR professionals have, at least in the USA, been vocal in their support of 'union-free' strategies and policies within their corporations. Yet as union power declines, so too does the power and influence of HR professionals within their firms. Thus, while each party is reluctant to recognize it, HR and labor unions are tied together in a symbiotic relationship in which one's power is a direct function of the other's. This suggests that a return to higher status and legitimacy of HR professionals depends on the success of efforts to revitalize the labor movement and other worker advocacy groups.

More is at stake, however, than considerations of power. No democratic society can prosper (some would say survive) if employee voice is suppressed at work or silent in political discourse. That is why strong institutional roles for labor were implanted in the laws and structures of post-war Germany and Japan by British and American occupational governments. That is also why freedom of association is now accepted as a universal and fundamental right by the international business, labor, and government representatives to the International Labor Organization and is embedded in nearly all codes of conduct negotiated between industry groups, corporations, and non-governmental organizations (NGOs) working together to enforce common labor standards through global supply chains (Mamic 2004).

History suggests that the void in worker representation now present in American society is not likely to remain unfilled in perpetuity. Indeed, a wide variety of increasingly active employee advocacy groups are emerging in attempts to fill this void. These include student and NGO groups advocating global labor standards and accountability for the actions of firms' overseas contractors, religious, immigrant, and ethnic-based community organizations, some of which work in coalition with traditional unions and some of which operate independently, identity groups functioning within organizations to mentor and advocate for their members, and, as mentioned above, women and family advocacy groups (Kochan 2005). Moreover, there are signs of a more militant resurgence within existing labor movements in the USA, Britain, and Australia.

How the HR profession responds to these emergent efforts to restore worker voice will have a profound impact on the future of worker/labor management relations. Because only 8.5 percent of the private sector workforce is now unionized, the vast majority of American HR professionals also have little or no experience in working or negotiating with employee representatives. The evidence is clear that a simple return to traditional arm's-length labor management relations would not well serve the workforce, employers, or the larger economy and society. Thus, the question is whether HR professionals will have the skills and experience base to help build the types of constructive and modern labor management relationships and partnerships that are required in settings where employees are represented. A simple oppositional stance to any forms of independent worker voice or representation will clearly decrease the likelihood that constructive and effective labor management models will emerge. The more likely result of this type of defensive and oppositional stance will be another phase of adversarial relationships that are poorly suited to the needs and desires of the contemporary economy and workforce (Freeman and Rogers 1999; Kochan 2005).

## 29.4.7 Rebuilding Trust with an Information-Hungry and Savvy Workforce

A generation of young people watched as their parents put in long hours of work only to be rewarded with increased insecurity or actual loss of jobs and/or pension savings in the wake of the breakdown of the post-war social contract. The next generation of HR professionals will confront a skeptical workforce that is not ready to simply bestow its trust in top management and is well prepared to use the tools of modern information technology and social networks to move when job conditions do not meet their expectations.

How can trust at work be rebuilt with this type of workforce? It can only be done by providing the transparency and openness and opportunities for development that young people want from their jobs, and over time the fairness and equity they will come to expect with age, tenure, and growing family responsibilities. Employees will be expecting the same rights and access to information as do financial investors. Most young people today are highly skilled in using the Internet to satisfy their information needs. This implies that HR professionals will have to become as skilled as the people employed by their organizations.

The need to modernize HR processes to fit the Internet age will affect all functional areas of HR, including collective bargaining negotiations. Recent experiences in the US airline industry illustrate how the workforce can be out in front of developments in this area. Labor and management negotiators in the airline industry in the USA have experienced a great deal of difficulty in ratifying collective bargaining agreements in recent years with approximately 18 percent of agreements having been rejected by rank and file employees (von Nordenflycht and Kochan 2003). In a number of these cases, rank and file groups have built their own websites to comment on negotiations and critique tentative agreements, sometimes by sending out information even before the officially designated negotiating teams could describe the terms of the agreement. In conversations about this develop-ment, a number of labor and management professionals lamented it, almost in hopes that somehow they could return to the old days where they controlled all communications with the media and to constituents. Instead of lamenting the new phenomena, HR and labor relations professionals will need to figure out ways to use the new technologies in negotiations to keep members informed with accurate and current information.

## 29.5 CHANGING DEMOGRAPHICS OF HR PROFESSIONALS

In the twentieth century, when labor relations was the dominant functional specialty in employment relations departments, the field was largely the province of men. Today, women constitute an increasing proportion of professionals entering and working in our field. For example, in the USA from 1987 to 2002, the number of women in the HR profession increased from 64 to 76 percent. The same trend is visible in the number moving up into higher managerial positions in the HR and labor relations profession; 53 percent in 1987 to 65 percent in 2002 (Keefe 2004). The same trends can be seen in our best university programs that are producing the people most likely to become the next-generation HR leaders. Women account for 56 percent of the 2003 entering Masters' class at Cornell's School of Labor and Industrial Relations, for example. The British CIPD reports that women now account for 53 percent of its membership (CIPD 2005).

What effects will the feminization of the HR function have on the profession? One unfortunate effect, if the American data is an indication, is that the feminiza-tion of the profession may lead to a relative decline in salaries. As more women were entering the profession between 1983 and 2002 in the USA, real wages of HR professionals declined by 8 percent while real wages of other professionals with college degrees grew by approximately 23 percent (Economic Policy Institute 2005). On a more positive note, another possible (but not guaranteed) effect could be a greater sensitivity to the need for flexible policies that support efforts to integrate work and family responsibilities. Perhaps it will take this demographic shift for the HR profession to strike a better balance between the interests of firms and the workforce.

## 29.6 CONCLUSIONS

The key lessons from this overview of the recent history of the US HR profession can be summarized quite simply:

1. The quest for greater acceptance and influence with top management has gone too far and accounts for some of the inability of the HR profession to discipline top management excesses that produced the corporate scandals, runaway CEO compensation, and the overall breakdown in trust in corporations that now prevails.

2. The pressures building in workplaces following the breakdown in the social contract at work call for leadership from the HR profession to help better balance worker and firm needs and interests, rebuild trust, and help shape a new social contract capable of achieving and supporting mutual gains for firms, employees, and society. This will require reframing the approach to strategy and contingency in HR models and practices.

3. The substantive areas with the most potential for contributing to a new social contract that fits the needs and realities of today's economy and workforce include:

   (a) Making knowledge work and work systems pay off for firms and employees;

   (b) Integrating work and family/personal concerns by evaluating all HR policies and practices against the 'dual agenda' of workplace and family outcomes; and

   (c) Supporting efforts to restore voice and transform labor–management relations to serve as an innovative force in society and help improve the performance of organizations, industries, and the overall economy.

4. To address these substantive challenges, the next generation of US. HR professionals will need to be:

   (a) More externally focused and skilled in building and maintaining alliances and productive relationships not only with line managers and senior executives but also with each other, educational institutions, professional associations and networks, labor market intermediaries, unions, and government policy makers;

   (b) More analytical and able to justify support for progressive HR policies based on their demonstrated and documented bottom line results, and:

   (c) More skilled in using information and principles of transparency to deliver and communicate HR polices and the range of information that employees want and need.

These changes can only be achieved if the HR profession redefines its values and holds itself accountable for building an employment system that is judged to be fair by all the stakeholders involved. Whether this shift in professional norms will evolve gradually or will have to await the passing of the torch to a new generation or the resurgence of more militant forms of worker voice and representation remains to be seen.

# REFERENCES

Aoki, M. (1988). 'Toward an Economic Model of the Japanese Firm.' *Journal of Economic Literature*, 28/1: 1–27.

Appelbaum, E., Berg, P., and Kalleberg, A. (2000). *Manufacturing Advantage*. Ithaca, NY: Cornell/ILR Press.

Bailyn, L., and Fletcher, J. K. (2003). 'The Equity Imperative: Reaching Effectiveness through the Dual Agenda.' CGO Insights, Simmons Graduate School of Management. www.simmons.edu/som/cgo.

Baron, J., Dobbin, F., and Jennings, P. D. (1988). 'Mission Control? The Development of Personnel Systems in U.S. Industry?' *American Sociological Review*, 53: 497–514.

Bartunek, J. M. (2002). 'How Can We in the Academy of Management Respond to Corporate Scandals?' *Academy of Management Executive*, 16/3: 138.

Batt, R., and Appelbaum, E. (1995). 'Worker Participation in Diverse Settings: Does the Form Affect the Outcome, and if so, Who Benefits.' *British Journal of Industrial Relations*, 33/3: 353–77.

Bendix, R. (1956). *Work and Authority in Industry*. New York: Wiley.

Black, S. E., and Lynch, L. M. (2001). 'How to Compete: Impact of Workplace Practices and Information Technology on Productivity.' *Review of Economics and Statistics*, 83/3: 434–45.

*Boston Globe* (2003). 'Workers are Dissatisfied with their Jobs.' *Sunday Boston Globe*, 26 October: D1.

Boxall, P., and Purcell, J. (2003). *Strategy and Human Resource Management*. London: Palgrave Macmillan.

Brown, D. V., and Myers, C. A. (1957). 'The Changing Industrial Relations Philosophy of American Management.' In *Proceedings of the Ninth Annual Winter Meetings of the Industrial Relations Research Association*. Madison: Industrial Relations Research Association.

*Business Week* (1999). 'Hey, What about Us?' *Business Week*, 27 December.

Chadwick, C., and Cappelli., P. (1999). 'Alternatives to Generic Strategy Typologies.' In P. M. Wright, D. Dyer, J. W. Boudreau, and G. T. Milkovich (eds.), *Strategic Human Resource Management: Research in Personnel and Human Resources Management*, Supplement 4. Greenwich, Conn.: JAI Press.

Chartered Institute of Personnel and Development (2005). 'Personnel Management: A Short History.' www.cipd.co.uk/subjects/hrpract/hrtrends/pmhist

Child, J. (1969). *British Management Thought*. London: Allen and Unwin.

Commission on the Future of Worker Management Relations (2004). *Fact Finding Report*. Washington: Departments of Commerce and Labor.

DOBBIN, F., and SUTTON, J. (1998). 'The Strength of a Weak State: The Employment Rights Revolution and the Rise of Human Resource Management Divisions.' *American Journal of Sociology*, 104: 441–76.

DOYLE, F. (1993). 'GE's Doyle Urges HR to Embrace a World of Change.' *Work in America Report*, 18/March: 3.

DRAGO, R., COLBECK, C., STAUFFER, D., VARNER, A., BURKUM, K., FAZIOLI, J., GUZMAN, G., and HABASEVICH T. R. (forthcoming). 'The Avoidance of Bias against Caregiving.' *American Behavioral Scientist*.

EATON, S. C. (2003). 'If You Can Use Them: Flexibility Policies, Organizational Commitment, and Perceived Performance.' *Industrial Relations*, 42/2: 145–67.

Economic Policy Institute (2005). 'Datazone.' www.epinet.org/datazone05/wagebyed

EICHINGER, B., and ULRICH, D. (1996). *Human Resource Challenges*. New York: The Human Resource Planning Society.

FOX, A. (1971). *A Sociology of Work and Industry*. London: Collier-Macmillan.

FREEDMAN, A. (1990). *The Changing Human Resource Function*. New York: The Conference Board.

FREEMAN, R. B., and ROGERS, J. (1999). *What do Workers Want*. Ithaca, NY: Cornell University/ILR Press.

GERHART, B., WRIGHT, P. M., McMAHAN, G. C., and SNELL, S. A. (2000). 'Measurement Error in Research on Human Resources and Firm Performance: How Much Error is there and How Does it Influence Effect Size Estimates?' *Personnel Psychology*, 53/4 Winter: 803–34.

GODARD, J. (2004). 'A Critical Assessment of the High-Performance Paradigm.' *British Journal of Industrial Relations*, 42/2 June: 349–78.

HAMMONDS, K. (2005). 'Why we Hate HR.' *Fast Company*, August: 40–2.

HUSELID, M., and BECKER, B. (2001). *The HR Scorecard*. Boston: Harvard Business School Press.

JACOBY, S. M. (1985). *Employing Bureaucracies*. New York: Columbia University Press.

—— (2005). *The Embedded Corporation*. Princeton: Princeton University Press.

KANTER, R. M. (1977). *Men and Women of the Corporation*. New York: Basic Books.

KATZ, H., KOCHAN, T. A., and GOBEILLE, K. (1983). 'Industrial Relations Performance, Economic Performance and the Quality of Working Life.' *Industrial and Labor Relations Review*, 37: 3–17.

KAUFMAN, B. E. (1994). *The Origins and Evolution of the Field of Industrial Relations*. Ithaca, NY: Cornell University ILR Press.

KEEFE, J. (2004). Personal correspondence: Current Population Data on IIR Professionals, 1987–2002.

KOCHAN, T. A. (1980). *Collective Bargaining and Industrial Relations*. Homewood, Ill.: Irwin.

—— (1995). 'Using the Dunlop Report for Mutual Gains.' *Industrial Relations*, 34: 350–66.

—— (2001). 'Rebuilding the Social Contract at Work.' *Perspectives on Work*, 4/1: 1–25.

—— (2004). 'Restoring Trust in the Human Resource Management Profession.' *Asia Pacific Journal of Human Resources*, 42/2: 132–46.

—— (2005). *Restoring the American Dream: A Working Families Agenda for America*. Cambridge, Mass.: MIT Press.

—— and SCHMALENSEE, R. L. (eds.) (2003). *Management: Inventing and Delivering the Future*. Cambridge Mass.: MIT Press.

KOCHAN, T. A., MCKERSIE, R., and CAPPELLI, P. (1984). 'Strategic Choice and Industrial Relations Theory.' *Industrial Relations*, 23/1: 16–39.

—— KATZ, H., and MCKERSIE, R. (1986). *The Transformation of American Industrial Relations*. New York: Basic Books.

—— LANSBURY, R. D., and MACDUFFIE, J. P. (1995). *After Lean Production*. Ithaca, NY: Cornell University/ILR Press.

—— MCKERSIE, R. B., EATON, A., ADLER, P., SEGAL, P., and GERHART, P. (2005). 'The Kaiser Permanente Labor Management Partnership: 2002–2004.' http://mitsloan,mit.edu/iwer.

KRAFCIK, J. F. (1988). 'Triumph of the Lean Production System.' *Sloan Management Review*, 30: 41–52.

LANSBURY, R. D. (2004). 'Work, People, and Globalization: Toward a New Social Contract for Australia.' *Journal of Industrial Relations*, 46/1: 102–9.

LEWIS, R. (2002). 'The CEO's Lot is Not a Happy One.' *Academy of Management Executive*, 16/4: 38–42.

MACDUFFIE, J. P. (1995). 'Human Resource Bundles and Manufacturing Performance: Organizational Logic and Flexible Production Systems in the World Auto Industry.' *Industrial and Labor Relations Review*, 48: 197–221.

—— and PIL, F. (1997). 'Changes in Auto Industry Employment Practices: An International Overview.' In T. A. Kochan, R. D. Lansbury, and J. P. MacDuffie (eds.), *After Lean Production*. Ithaca, NY: Cornell University/ILR Press.

MCGREGOR, D. and CUTCHER-GERSHENSFELD, J. (2005). *The Human Side of the Enterprise*, annotated edn. New York: McGraw Hill.

MAMIC, I. (2004). *Implementing Codes of Conduct*. Geneva: International Labor Office.

MARGINSON, P., HALL, M., HOFFMAN, A., and MULLER, T. (2004). 'The Impact of European Works Councils on Management Decision-Making in UK and US-Based Multinationals: A Case Study Comparison.' *British Journal of Industrial Relations*, 42/2: 209–34.

MILLS, D. Q. (1979). 'Flamed Victory in Labor Law Reform.' *Harvard Business Review*, 53: 99–102.

MILTON, C. R. (1970). *Ethics and Expediency in Personnel Management*. Columbia: University of South Carolina Press.

New York Stock Exchange (2002). 'Corporate Governance Rules and Proposals.' www.nyse.com, 7 October.

OSTERMAN, P., KOCHAN, T., LOCKE, R., and PIORE, M. (2001). *Working in America: A Blueprint for the New Labor Market*. Cambridge, Mass.: MIT Press.

PRICEWATERHOUSECOOPERS (2002). 'PWC Barometer Survey Results on Triple Bottom Line Reporting.' www.srimedia.com/artman/publish/article_169.shtml.

PURCELL, J. (1999). 'The Search for "Best Practice" and "Best Fit": Chimera or Cul-De-Sac?' *Human Resource Management Journal*, 9/3: 26–41.

RAMSAY, H., SCHOLARIOS, D., and HARLEY, B. (2000). 'Employees and High-Performance Work Systems: Testing inside the Black Box.' *British Journal of Industrial Relations*, 38/4 December: 501–31.

SENNETT, R. (1998). *The Corrosion of Character*, New York: W. W. Norton.

SLICHTER, S., HEALY, J. J., and LIVERNASH, E. R. (1960). *The Impact of Collective Bargaining on Management*. Washington: The Brookings Institution.

*USA Today* (2002). 'Poll: Trust in Corporations Waning.' www.usatoday.com/money/2002-07-15-trust-poll_x.htm

VON NORDENFLYCHT, A., and KOCHAN, T. A. (2003). "Labor Contract Negotiations in the Airline Industry." *Monthly Labor Review*, 7: 18–28.

WEVER, K. (1995). *Negotiating Competitiveness*. Boston: Harvard Business School Press.

WOMACK, J. P., JONES, D. T., and ROOS, D. (1990). *The Machine that Changed the World*. New York: Rawson.

WOMEN'S BAR ASSOCIATION OF MASSACHUSETTS (2000). *More than Part-Time*. A report of the Employment Issues Committee of the Women's Bar Association of Massachusetts. Boston.

WRIGHT, P. M., and SHERMAN, W. S. (1999). 'Failing to Find Fit in Strategic Human Resource Management: Theoretical and Empirical Problems.' In P. M. Wright, L. D. Dyer, J. W. Boudreau, and G. T. Milkovich (eds.), *Strategic Human Resources Management in the Twenty-First Century*, Supplement 4. Greenwich, Conn.: JAI Press.

# INDEX

Note: The following abbreviations are used:
HR: Human Resource.
HRM: Human Resource Management